Praise for

Toward Sustainable Communities

Toward Sustainable Communities represents the best kind of resource in this time of rapidly evolving approaches to making our cities and towns resilient, healthy and just. By providing both strong frameworks for understanding community sustainability and pragmatic information on current best practice, this book is a treasure for policymakers, planners, thought leaders and anyone working to shape the future of our communities.

— Tom Osdoba, Chair, Portland Sustainability Institute

In the global era, sustainability as much as ever needs strong community anchoring, to create spaces for local innovation and engender civic engagement. Mark Roseland's powerful and far-reaching work provides both the intellectual arguments and practical guidance to enable sustainable communities to flourish. A must-read for researchers, policy-makers and practitioners alike.

— Professor Simon Joss FRSA, International Eco-Cities Initiative, University of Westminster

This new and revised edition of *Toward Sustainable Communities* demonstrates how local government and communities are leading the transition towards a sustainable future. Complete with numerous creative ideas, practical examples and stories from around the world, it's a must read for anyone working to help communities thrive in these uncertain times. Mark Roseland has also taken his research and work to the next level by creating a new on-line community called "Pando | Sustainable Communities", which will serve as an invaluable source of information and network for researchers, policy makers and community sustainability professionals from around the world.

— John Purkis, Senior Advisor and Senior Manager, Sustainable Communities, The Natural Step Canada

Over successive iterations of this seminal text, Roseland has deepened our understanding by combining theory and practice in increasingly elegant ways. Now we also have a new tool, the Community Capital Scan to assess proposals and plans for their contribution to sustainable development, and *Pando*, an online community for local sustainability-focused researchers and practitioners. The path toward sustainable communities just got much clearer.

— Julian Agyeman, Chair, Department of Urban + Environmental Policy + Planning (UEP), Tufts University

In the absence of global governance institutions that can meet the historic challenge of transitioning the world towards sustainability, the new edition of Mark Roseland's book, *Toward Sustainable Communities*, shines an important light on the impressive accomplishments and transformational potential of local action. Building on his 20 years of scholarship in the field, Roseland deftly situates community sustainability efforts in the broader policy arena and introduces the 'community capital framework' to advance a systems perspective that enhances our understanding of the complexities involved. The book provides a wealth of real-world examples and tools aimed at mobilizing citizens as well as governments. It is an invaluable resource for practitioners and policymakers alike.

— James Goldstein, Director, Sustainable Communities Program, Tellus Institute

This fourth edition is a tour de force, a marvelous up-to-date amalgam of history, theory, and examples reinforced with a comprehensive description of tools that we can use to establish truly sustainable communities. And while Dr. Roseland does not shy from recognizing the scale of the challenge, his sense of optimism runs through the volume like an unbroken thread, right to the final sentence: "Sustainable communities will not… merely 'sustain' the quality of our lives — they will dramatically improve it." Those words cogently capture why every community, arrondissement, county, province, state and national leader — worldwide — should read and absorb this book.

— Thomas F. Pedersen, PhD, FRSC, FAGU,
Executive Director, Pacific Institute for Climate Solutions, Canada

As any sustainability professional knows, the battle for sustainability will be won — or lost — in cities. After all, the way cities are designed and governed determines over 80 percent of its residents' resource demand. There is no better guide than Mark Roseland, for showing us what's possible so we can win this battle. Please give this book to every local official you know.

— Mathis Wackernagel, Ph.D., President, Global Footprint Network

In a world where despair comes too easily, *Toward Sustainable Communities* awakens our collective creativity. Mark Roseland calls on us to imagine our communities as vibrant, healthy places where we connect with our neighbours, work with the natural world and live well. He recognizes the increasingly crucial role for local governments in leading the way to this vision and provides many examples of practical actions to get us there.

— Josha MacNab, Director, Sustainable Communities Group, Pembina Institute

For practitioners and interested members of the public alike, figuring out the true meaning of sustainability remains a challenge. Mark Roseland's book provides many practical insights that will help put the complexities of sustainable development into a meaningful perspective.

— Glenn Miller, Vice President, Education & Research, Canadian Urban Institute

Toward Sustainable Communities is an excellent guide to the ways that cities and towns, both urban and rural, are pursuing strategies for long-term growth and viability that does not impinge on the resources available to future generations. It is very well organized and comprehensive in its coverage. I especially commend the author for including lots of case studies as well as practical information on how to work toward sustainability. This book is an important reference for anyone working to promote community sustainability.

— Andre Shashaty, President, Partnership for Sustainable Communities

4th EDITION

Toward Sustainable Communities

SOLUTIONS for CITIZENS and their GOVERNMENTS

Mark Roseland

new society
PUBLISHERS

Cover design by Diane McIntosh.
Main image: David Flanders, UBC-CALP; insets L to R © iStock (vasiliki);
© iStock (JEwhyte); © iStock (J Bryson); author supplied.

Printed in Canada. First printing May 2012.

New Society Publishers acknowledges the support of the Government of Canada
through the Book Publishing Industry Development Program (BPIDP)
for our publishing activities.

Paperback ISBN: 978-0-86571-711-4
eISBN: 978-1-55092-506-7

Inquiries regarding requests to reprint all or part of *Toward Sustainable Communities* should be
addressed to New Society Publishers at the address below.

To order directly from the publishers, please call toll-free (North America)
1-800-567-6772, or order online at www.newsociety.com

Any other inquiries can be directed by mail to:

New Society Publishers
P.O. Box 189, Gabriola Island, BC V0R 1X0, Canada (250) 247-9737

Library and Archives Canada Cataloguing in Publication

Roseland, Mark

Toward sustainable communities : solutions for citizens and their governments / Mark
Roseland. – 4th ed.

Includes index.

ISBN 978-0-86571-711-4
  1. City planning. 2. City planning--Environmental aspects. 3. Sustainable
development. I. Title.

HT169.C2R67 2012   307.1'216   C2012-901950-X

New Society Publishers' mission is to publish books that contribute in fundamental ways to
building an ecologically sustainable and just society, and to do so with the least possible impact
on the environment, in a manner that models this vision. We are committed to doing this not just
through education, but through action. The interior pages of our bound books are printed on
Forest Stewardship Council®-registered acid-free paper that is **100% post-consumer recycled**
(100% old growth forest-free), processed chlorine free, and printed with vegetable-based, low-
VOC inks, with covers produced using FSC®-registered stock. New Society also works to reduce
its carbon footprint, and purchases carbon offsets based on an annual audit to ensure a carbon
neutral footprint. For further information, or to browse our full list of books and purchase se-
curely, visit our website at: www.newsociety.com

Contents

Acknowledgments

In the years since the first edition of this book appeared, interest in sustainable communities has exploded (due at least in part to the impact of the book). What was a difficult but manageable task for one person to accomplish in 1992 was no longer possible in 1998, even less possible in 2005, and by 2012 was a complex process requiring months of work by dozens of people and organizations. Fortunately, many people helped directly or indirectly in bringing this edition to fruition.

First and foremost, this book came together with the assistance of researchers from the Centre for Sustainable Community Development and the School of Resource and Environmental Management at Simon Fraser University, in particular: Larissa Ardis, senior research co-ordination and developmental editing; core research team Julie Lowry, David Angus, Jenna Bedore, Sandra Warren, Stefanie Jones and Freya Kristensen; volunteer researchers Marcus Peng and Catherine Parsons; and volunteer photo researcher John Hu. I could

not have been more fortunate than to have these talented and capable people working with me. They were instrumental particularly in producing part 2 of this edition, but they also assisted as needed with all aspects of producing the manuscript. While it has been some years since Sean Connelly, David Hendrickson, Chris Lindberg and Michael Lithgow were essential contributors to the third edition of the book (and many other projects since then), and even more years since Maureen Cureton and Heather Wornell were essential contributors to the second, their collective efforts are still appreciated even if not fully reflected in this fourth edition. It is extremely heartening to work with a bright new generation of thinkers and future leaders who will be making important contributions to sustainable communities for many years to come.

This edition benefits from the contributions of several colleagues (see contributor bios), both from Vancouver and around the world, in several ways. Julian Agyeman, Oliver M. Brandes, Jielian Chen, Victor Cumming, John

Dagevos, John Emmeus Davis, Spring Gillard, Todd Litman, Sean Markey, Dale Mikkelsen, Janet Moore, Jennie Moore, Britta Ricker Peters, Coro Strandberg, Ray Tomalty and Jessica Woolliams each contributed specific pieces that appear as boxes in various chapters. All of these contributors also provided thoughtful reviews of specific chapters, as did Gordon Harris, President and CEO of the SFU Community Trust; Josha MacNab, Associate Director of the Pembina Institute's Sustainable Communities Group; Tom Pedersen, Executive Director of the Pacific Institute for Climate Solutions; Helen Spiegelman, President of the Product Policy Institute; Andre Shashaty, President of the California-based Partnership for Sustainable Communities; and Hannah Wittman, SFU professor of Sociology and Latin American Studies, and an Associate with the Centre for Sustainable Community Development.

Several other individuals also deserve specific mention for their contributions. The Community Capital Tool (chapter 17) could not have been developed without the indefatigable guidance and support of John Dagevos and his colleagues from the Telos, Brabant Center for Sustainable Development, Tilburg University, Netherlands. Dale Mikkelson of SFU Community Trust contributed enormously to chapter 14, and particularly to the description of the UniverCity project. My colleague Sean Markey of the SFU Centre for Sustainable Community Development and School of Resource and Environmental Management responded with constructive reviews well above and beyond my requests for his assistance.

I am delighted that Konrad Otto Zimmerman, Secretary General of ICLEI – Local Governments for Sustainability, wrote the foreword. Konrad and his partner Monika Zimmerman, Director of the ICLEI Capacity Centre, have inspired me with their dedication and accomplishment over the years, and I am honored to have Konrad's thoughts on these pages. The forewords for the first and third editions were penned by Jeb Brugmann, Konrad's predecessor as founding ICLEI Secretary-General, so Konrad's foreword to this edition is in keeping with a tradition established over the 20 years since the first edition was published.

I appreciate the support of my colleagues on the board of the SFU Community Trust both for deciding to make the UniverCity project into a model sustainable community and for endorsing the time and effort of Trust staff — particularly Gordon Harris, Dale Mikkelsen and Jesse Galicz — in assisting me with research and graphics for this edition. The photos from UniverCity that appear throughout this edition are a generous contribution.

For many of the other wonderful images and artwork in this edition, I am grateful to Richard Register and to David Rousseau. Thanks as well to Stephen Sheppard and his colleagues at the Collaborative for Advanced Landscape Planning at the University of British Columbia for some of the visualization images in chapter 2 and on the cover. I am also indebted to Timothy and Della Schafer for graphics acquisition and photo editing.

Thanks also to my colleagues in the Centre for Sustainable Community Development and the School of Resource and Environmental Management (REM) at Simon Fraser University, as well as in the Department of Geography, for giving me the freedom to focus my teaching on sustainable communities. My students used the previous editions as a text and provided valuable feedback as well as new material for this edition. Indeed, dozens of student research papers as well as several theses and dissertations over the years have deepened my understanding of the field and influenced the conceptualization and presentation of this edition. Each of the faculty, staff, instructors, program coordinators, participants and students who have been a part of our academic, professional and outreach programs have contributed in some way to this edition. I am thankful as well to the Dean of the SFU Faculty of Environment and to all of the Dean's office staff for their ongoing administrative support of the SFU Centre for Sustainable Community Development, and to the staff of REM for their support of my activities there.

My thanks also to Ingrid Witvoet and the entire team at New Society Publishers for encouraging this completely revised and updated fourth edition; the trust we have established over the years since the 1998 edition has facilitated the production of this manuscript despite some significant life challenges during the process.

Major research support for this edition comes from the Pacific Institute for Climate Solutions, as well as in-kind support from the BC Climate Action Secretariat and the Union of British Columbia Municipalities. These organizations are also supporting creation of *Pando | Sustainable Communities* (see appendix), and their willingness to support both the book and the Network has inspired me. In this respect, I am particularly grateful to Ben Finkelstein, Emanuel Machado and Jared Wright.

Research reflected in parts of this edition has been supported through several other projects, grants and funds. In particular, funding from the Social Sciences and Humanities Research Council (SSHRC) of Canada provided the foundation in chapter 3 for the work on market mechanisms for sustainable community development, and SSHRC funding for the BC-Alberta Social Economy Research Alliance provided a foundation for parts of chapter 12 on the social economy and community economic development. Support for testing the community capital framework (chapter 1) in Mexico, Ukraine and Bolivia has come in part from the Canadian International Development Agency through international projects of the SFU Centre for Sustainable Community Development. Support for development and international deployment of the Community Capital Tool (chapter 17) has come in part from the far-sighted generosity of Jennifer Simons and the Simons Foundation to the SFU Centre for Sustainable Community Development.

Also embedded in these pages is evidence of related research support over the past many years from Canada Mortgage and Housing Corporation, the Simon Fraser University work-study program, the President's Research Fund at Simon Fraser University, the Science Council of British Columbia, the Forum for Planning Action, the University of British Columbia Centre for Human Settlements, the University of British Columbia Task Force on Healthy and Sustainable Communities, Friends of the Earth and from the National Round Table on the Environment and the Economy, which published and distributed the first edition.

I would be remiss if I did not acknowledge the many people whose work is described in this book, as well as the hundreds of people whose work is referenced and cited. All of them have in some way provided support or inspiration along the way, and this book would not be possible without them. There are so many people who have contributed directly or indirectly to this edition that credit for its virtues must be widely shared; however, responsibility for its failings must rest with me.

Last but by no means least, I am beholden to Susan Day, my friend, confidant, advisor and partner, for carrying much of my load during this long and demanding process, and for sustaining our dreams; to my stepson Sean Rigby, and to my children Miranda Roseland and Aaron Roseland, who represent the future we are trying to make sustainable. Miranda and Aaron came into this world between the second and third editions. As I noted in the preface to the third edition, their arrival made my life circumstances surrounding the production of that edition markedly slower but infinitely sweeter. Now that they are a bit older, and I am hopefully a bit wiser, the significance of this book becomes more personal with each passing year. A sustainable future may still be within their generation's grasp, but if so it will require an enormous and sustained effort to achieve. With that in mind, I dedicate this book to all those who are working toward sustainable communities and a sustainable future.

Preface to the Fourth Edition

I have a long-standing interest in social ecology — the relationships between people that effect the relationship of society as a whole with nature. I'd been working in the area of social ecology and appropriate (sometimes called "intermediate") technology for a decade by the time the United Nations World Commission on Environment and Development popularized the term *sustainable development* in 1987. The insight that first resulted in this book came from a fortuitous opportunity in 1990 to help the City of Vancouver think out its role in contributing to the causes of global (as well as local) environmental problems as well as its potential role in contributing to the solutions to these problems. Many of our most critical global environmental issues are rooted in local, day-to-day problems. Atmospheric pollution and climate change, for example, can be altered by local citizens and government officials making enlightened decisions about local traffic congestion and inefficient land-use patterns. Local decisions about such issues benefit all of us globally.

For over two decades now, I have devoted my intellectual energy to documenting, assessing and inspiring municipal and regional decision-making toward sustainable community development. In the absence of effective, coordinated international leadership on these issues, it is clearly evident that most of the action — and traction — has so far been happening at the local level, where there is still a huge untapped potential for effecting national and global system change based on local innovation and commitment.

While global environmental change is accelerating, there is a wealth of important information that can help us set the planet on a sustainable course. Although this information is increasingly becoming accessible through the Internet, little of it is available through mainstream media sources. I have endeavored to make these ideas, tools and resources accessible. Those concerned citizens, elected officials and municipal staff who prompted me to write this book are the people for whom it is written.

Toward Sustainable Communities: A Resource Book for Municipal and Local Governments was originally published in 1992 and distributed by the government of Canada's National Round Table on the Environment and the Economy. Over 12,000 copies were distributed internationally, and the book has also been widely used as a textbook in university courses.

The late Brahm Wiesman, professor emeritus and former Director of the School of Community and Regional Planning at the University of British Columbia, was one of the first people to read a draft of the original manuscript. He told me in 1992 that the book was destined to become a classic. Although I was flattered, at the time I had no idea of what becoming a classic might mean. Twenty years and four editions later, I'm starting to comprehend it.

When the first edition was published, almost no one else was using the term *sustainable communities*. Today, due in part to the influence of this book, universities have programs and professorships in sustainable community development, federal governments have sustainable community offices or initiatives, local governments have sustainability offices and officers, and corporations have VPs with similar titles. I am proud, for example, that my home city of Vancouver, Canada, has committed itself to becoming the greenest city in the world by 2020 — and I hope it has lots of competition!

The book received much critical and popular acclaim. Jeb Brugmann, the founding Secretary General of ICLEI — Local Governments for Sustainability, called it "a rare compendium of tested, practical suggestions, helpful contacts, and essential references to use in setting community planning and development on a sustainable course." Doreen Quirk, President of the Federation of Canadian Municipalities,

said it "will assist your municipality in developing an integrated approach to sustainable development for the 21st century."

The completely revised and updated second edition, published in 1998 by New Society, changed slightly in orientation, as reflected in the new subtitle *Resources for Citizens and Their Governments*. The third edition, published by New Society in 2005, was again completely updated and revised. In particular, the community capital framework in the opening chapters was a conceptual leap forward, and had been shown to resonate with diverse audiences in several different parts of the world, from urban, rural and aboriginal Canada to Mexico, Ukraine and Bolivia.

I thought long and hard about whether to write this fourth edition. After much deliberation, I decided that 2012 would be the perfect time to release a substantially overhauled fourth edition of *Toward Sustainable Communities*. The year 2012 marks the 20th anniversary of the Rio Earth Summit, the 10th anniversary of the Johannesburg World Summit on Sustainable Development and the 20th anniversary of the publication of the first edition of *Toward Sustainable Communities*.

For this fourth edition, I wrestled at length with the question: "What is a resource book in 2012 and beyond?" With the rise of e-books and related digital technology, I questioned whether writing a book was still the best way to communicate both the intellectual message and the practical value of *Toward Sustainable Communities*. Ultimately I decided that the book still has an important role to play in society, but that the best way to publish *this* book in 2012 and beyond was as a book "plus" — with the "plus" being some kind of digital companion piece. That "plus" has now evolved into

Pando | Sustainable Communities, a new project I am leading to link sustainable communities researchers (for example, academics involved in sustainable communities research) with local government practitioners to mobilize collaboration toward sustainable community development.

This fourth edition is now completely revised and updated, and differs from the earlier editions in several important ways:

- The orientation has changed again slightly, as reflected in the new subtitle: *Solutions for Citizens and Their Governments*.
- The conceptual community capital framework in chapter 1 is more advanced and has also evolved in chapter 17 into an online tool, created in collaboration with my colleagues at the Telos Sustainability Institute at Tilburg University in the Netherlands.
- This edition demonstrates changes in the field since the last edition by, for example, devoting more attention to community food systems (in the chapter on greening), and including a new chapter on green buildings and another new chapter on communities integrating sustainability. This last chapter focuses in part on the award-winning UniverCity community at Simon Fraser University near Vancouver, Canada. This is a project I have personally worked on for over a decade, as a charter board member of the Trust overseeing the development. UniverCity was not far enough along to describe in the 2005 edition; now it is a story well worth sharing. Photographs from the UniverCity project are included throughout the book.
- Recognizing that the field of sustainable communities has grown exponentially

since the original edition 20 years ago, this edition includes contributions from several colleagues from Vancouver and around the world, demonstrating the depth of expertise that now exists in this field as well as the community of scholars and practitioners who are coming together to mobilize collaboration for sustainable community development. This reinforces the conceptual approach of the book and also underscores the potential of *Pando | Sustainable Communities*.

- This edition has many more fabulous graphics, and is printed on better quality recycled paper than was available only a few years ago, for a crisper and more pleasing look and feel.
- The book itself no longer includes a resources section at the end of each chapter, since such sections would be dated before the book was released; instead, readers are referred to *Pando | Sustainable Communities* for up-to-date resources and related information, provided by a growing global community of scholars and practitioners.
- This edition of *Toward Sustainable Communities* is available not only on paper, but in many electronic book formats, and is designed to also be a rewarding read on a digital device.
- We anticipate a number of digital tools, apps and the like related to the book to be developed over the coming month and years; these and many others will be more easily discoverable through *Pando | Sustainable Communities*.
- Through *Toward Sustainable Communities* and *Pando | Sustainable Communities*, the foundation, tools, solutions and motivation for mobilizing collaboration for sustainable

community development will be advanced. With my colleagues from *Pando | Sustainable Communities* we will be better able to assist people around the world to mobilize their settlements toward sustainable communities. *The Pando | Sustainable Communities*, referred to throughout the book and described in more detail in the appendix, is intended in part to effectively make this book a living document.

I consider myself fortunate to have had the opportunity to tackle this book for a fourth time. While I am grateful for the critical and popular acclaim received by the previous editions, I believe that this edition is indeed the classic that Brahm Wiesman predicted 20 years ago.

This book is dedicated to the citizens and local government officials around the world who have developed the wide array of initiatives that make it possible. Your efforts to create a sustainable future have sustained me as well.

— Mark Roseland,
Vancouver, British Columbia

Foreword

by Konrad Otto-Zimmermann

Toward Sustainable Communities is an inspiring, hopeful and important contribution. Mark Roseland has not only captured and consolidated the legacy of more than two decades of community sustainability efforts from around the world, he has also formed them into a foundation for a viable and desirable future. This book clearly demonstrates that the progress we are making in addressing key sustainability issues such as climate change is being built largely from cities and towns, in that most resilient and hopeful tradition of social innovation. With its modern accoutrements of digital tools and social networks, *Toward Sustainable Communities* is the single most significant book of its kind. It demonstrates that the future we need can be achieved, and that the future we need can be a future we want. *Toward Sustainable Communities* is essential reading for everyone who wants a sustainable world, now and in the future.

In our communities we seek a better quality of life, whether in the south or north, in poor or affluent conditions. However, to achieve sustained human wellbeing, a healthy and productive environment is required. Communities that are environmentally sustainable, socially equitable, and economically viable are suitably positioned to respond to changes in the natural and built environment, changes which ultimately impact both the health of communities and the planet. An adequate understanding of the dynamics of the community system is essential to ensure that the flow of resources can be made more efficient and in the long term sustainable. In human settlements, whatever form they take, sustainable options in terms of waste, water management, sustainable transport options, green economies, the protection of ecosystems etc. need to be rigorously pursued. Any settlement including urban areas needs to become more resource efficient and promote holistic sustainability initiatives in order to create healthy communities.

A community is a rich source of capital, which can be used as a powerful means to shape local solutions for sustainable development. Communities are characterized by natural, physical, economic, human, social and culture attributes, which if utilized properly can be an effective capital basis for mobilizing community action. Local governments and therefore local communities are increasingly being recognized for their potential role in dealing with environmental issues. Sustainable communities ensures the continuation of this and in doing so pursue a framework under which communities engage in activities that are environmentally sustainable while actively involving local citizens. This provides ample opportunity for local communities to support their national governments in addressing their numerous challenges. Indeed, if sustainable development is ever going to be achieved, it needs to begin with citizens at the grassroots level, whereby local success can be translated into national achievements. A common fundamental aspect of a sustainable community is to ensure that inclusive and participatory decision making is an integral part in achieving an improvement in quality of life, a healthy environment and a viable local economy.

Where and how we live is the basis upon which sustainable community development is assessed. The term community is an overarching umbrella for neighborhoods, villages, rural areas, cities and mega cities (which actually host a multitude of communities), all of which have their own distinctive and definitive community dynamics. However, what is common amongst them is the potential unity of action. Citizens form communities, and vice versa, and this provides an excellent opportunity for comprehensive action. The sphere of the community and the relationships that exist within that sphere is an important avenue to garner

citizen support into cohesive and coherent action to achieve sustainable development. Such action can ensure a higher demand for more environmentally friendly products and services, reduced waste generation etc., all under the overarching objective of improving community quality of life and protecting the local human and natural environment.

The fourth edition of *Towards Sustainable Communities: Solutions for Citizens and Their Governments* is a further enrichment of the discourse on local community-based efforts to achieve sustainable development that the first edition began in 1992. It is the continued recognition of a never more prescient fact — that local action, strongly entrenched in community participation, is fundamental in confronting local, regional and global sustainability challenges. The fourth edition is another diverse and insightful account of local action towards sustainable communities and how such locally-based initiatives continue to form an influential part of municipal and local government sustainability action. It adds to a growing body of knowledge of how national governments can build upon their citizens' local efforts to ensure sustainable development.

From an ICLEI perspective, I am delighted to commend Mark Roseland and his colleagues on this comprehensive analysis of sustainable community action that again provides a useful and illustrative source for cities and their local governments as they aim to green their cities and their urban economies under the overarching objective of sustainable development. In ICLEI, we have actively sought for the recognition of local governments, the most proximate level of governance to citizens, for the potential role they have in complementing their national governments efforts to achieving sustainable development. Sustainable community development is not a homogenous concept but incorporates a myriad of ideals and policy initiatives. It comes from across the entire geographical and political landscape, urban and rural, liberal and conservative, but what is important is that local citizens in their local communities are involved in the process from the inception. This book reinforces this idea and represents a fundamental approach to achieving global sustainable development — sustainable communities.

Through *Toward Sustainable Communities* and other works Mark Roseland has helped ICLEI in its efforts to bring researchers and local authority practitioners together in a common agenda. This edition of *Toward Sustainable Communities* is particularly significant for ICLEI as it is being launched at the ICLEI 2012 World Congress in Belo Horizonte, Brazil (associated with Rio+20) along with *Pando | Sustainable Communities*, the associated social media network Mark has lead development of. *Pando* is designed to mobilize collaboration between sustainable communities researchers and practitioners. *Pando* represents a major step forward in a vision that ICLEI and Mark Roseland have shared for many years. ICLEI has been glad to have Mark involved in our work over the past years, and we very much look forward to expanding that collaboration with him and his growing number of colleagues in the years ahead.

Bonn/Germany, April 2012
Konrad Otto-Zimmermann
Secretary General
ICLEI – Local Governments
for Sustainability

How This Book Is Organized

Toward Sustainable Communities is designed to be both stimulating and useful; in that sense, most of the chapters (particularly those in part 2) can stand alone and be read out of sequence. However, there is a strong storyline running through the book, and readers will get more out of any particular chapter and understand how tools and initiatives are categorized throughout the book if they at least read part 1 before reading any of the chapters in part 2; they will get even more out of any particular chapter if they also read part 3.

Part 1 explores the meaning of sustainable development and its implications for communities, and develops a community capital framework for addressing sustainable community development. It concludes with a chapter on thinking strategically, which examines policy instruments for sustainable community development. These instruments provide the organizational structure for the tools and initiatives in the chapters of part 2.

Part 2 is a set of sustainable community building blocks including greening, energy, transportation, housing, climate and economic development. All the chapters are completely revised from the previous edition, and together demonstrate the maturing of the field (and perhaps of the author). For example, compared to the 2005 edition, the chapter on greening devotes considerably more attention to issues of food security, self-sufficiency and sovereignty. There is also a new chapter on green buildings, and another new chapter on communities integrating sustainability, which focuses in part on the UniverCity community development at Simon Fraser University near Vancouver, Canada. Each chapter in part 2 provides an overview explaining the topic and its relevance to sustainable communities, followed by a set of tools and initiatives. These building blocks are a set of planning tools, practical initiatives and associated resources that have helped citizens and their governments move toward sustainable communities. While not every tool will fit every community, many of them will fit quite well.

Part 3 focuses on mobilizing citizens and their governments toward sustainable communities. It concentrates on governing sustainable communities and tools for managing community sustainability, and includes a new chapter explaining the Community Capital Tool we have developed in association with colleagues at the Telos Sustainability Institute at Tilburg University in the Netherlands. The tool is based on the community capital framework developed in part 1, and underscores the thematic cohesion of the book. The final chapter concludes with some lessons for designing effective sustainable community development policies and thoughts for the challenge ahead. This is followed by an appendix on *Pando | Sustainable Communities*, a new project that I am leading to link sustainable communities researchers (e.g., academics) and practitioners (e.g., local governments) to mobilize collaboration toward sustainable community development.

The book is not intended to be comprehensive; rather, it attempts to identify and document the current range of initiatives toward sustainable communities. Dozens of tools, initiatives and resources are presented in these pages, accompanied by hundreds of references to aid interested readers in their own research. Certain tools and initiatives may be missing because we didn't know about them, but many others were omitted because of space and budget limitations. We have presented those that seemed most readily transferable to other communities. However, as the field is rapidly growing and changing, readers can stay on top of new developments by going to the *Pando | Sustainable Communities*, which is intended, among other things, to effectively make this book a living document.

This volume is part of a larger ongoing (at this point, apparently lifelong) research project. If you are aware of sustainable community initiatives and resources other than those described here, or are involved in developing your own sustainable community initiatives, please send your information and/or documentation to me or share it as appropriate with *Pando | Sustainable Communities* (pando.sc).

Part 1

Sustainable Communities, Sustainable Planet

Part 1 explores the meaning of sustainable development and its implications
for communities, and develops a community capital framework for addressing
sustainable community development. It concludes with a chapter on thinking
strategically, which examines policy instruments for sustainable community
development. These instruments provide the organizational structure
for the tools and initiatives in the chapters of part 2.

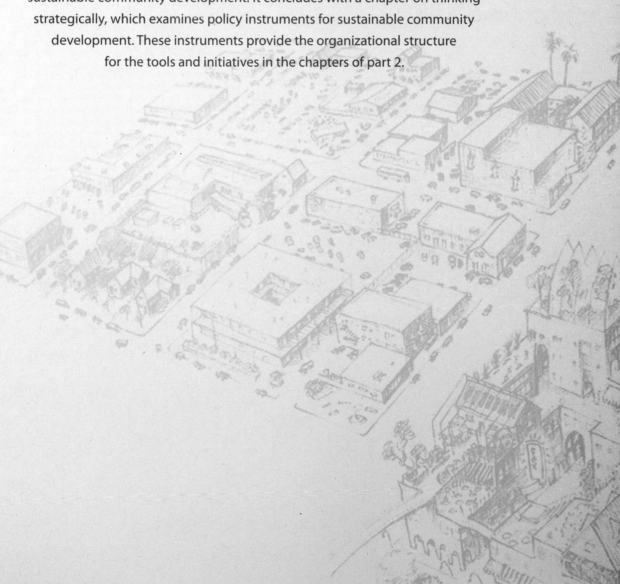

Chapter 1

The Context for Sustainable Communities

In communities in North America and around the world, citizens and their governments are embracing sustainability, not as an afterthought tacked onto official community plans, but as a new way of thinking about their future. Motivations vary, but include a desire to secure the means to survival, improve the quality of community life, protect the environment and make inclusive and participatory decisions. As well, they reflect concern about our fellow citizens' well-being, longing for a sense of satisfaction that money can't buy and pride in the legacy we leave for the future. Together, they have created a movement that is inevitable and unstoppable.

As this book demonstrates, this movement toward sustainability is no guarantee that we will achieve sustainability; several indicators show that we are losing ground and that the outcome is certainly not inevitable. However, sustainability can deliver on these hopes. It promises to help us create communities that are cleaner, healthier and less expensive; enjoy

greater accessibility and cohesion; and be more self-reliant and secure in energy, food and economic resources. Sustainable communities are not merely about "sustaining" the quality of our lives — they are about *improving* it.

This chapter introduces the context for sustainable communities, starting with an examination of the global context, concept and history of sustainable development. From there we explore the concept of community capital as a framework for making sustainable development real in our communities. This community capital framework binds together the many topics presented in this book into a cohesive whole, and underlies all the subsequent chapters. The chapter culminates by explaining that this book is not about stopping development; rather, it is about doing development differently. Finally, it concludes with an outline of the subsequent chapters.

Thinking Globally

On October 31, 2011, the human population

reached 7 billion. The United Nations projects that global population will peak at 9.3 billion in 2050 (UNFPA 2011). Our growing numbers will challenge all nations in terms of food production, the availability of land for human use and the ecological integrity of the land left undeveloped. Scholars have long warned us about the possible implications. Almost 200 years ago, English economist Thomas Malthus argued that all populations will succumb to famine and disease as a result of unabated growth. In their 1972 classic *Limits to Growth*, Meadows et al. pointed out that while populations grew exponentially, the technology to increase the availability of resources only grows linearly. More recently, Diamond (2005) demonstrated that population pressures in combination with fragile ecosystems and myopic political institutions have led many civilizations to collapse.

People around the world are starting to consider that the population problem in the South is less significant a problem than overconsumption and wasted resources in the North. The impact on our environment is affected not only by the population, but by the level of consumption or affluence and the technology available. Resource consumption varies greatly across all countries and income levels: in 2005, 76.6 percent of the world's resources were consumed by the wealthiest 20 percent of the global population, and the poorest 20 percent consumed just 1.5 percent of the resources (World Bank 2008). The effect on the environment of this wealthiest fifth is similarly

One-Planet Living

By Jennie Moore

One-planet living is living within the means of nature. Specifically, it refers to a lifestyle that does not demand more ecological goods and services (i.e., biocapacity or natural capital) than the Earth's ecosystems can sustain on a global annual basis. A more precise term is one-Earth living since there are many planets, but only one Earth that is capable of supporting life as we know it. One-planet or one-Earth living relies on the ecological footprint (footprintnetwork.org) to measure how much global average biocapacity is required to supply the resources and to assimilate the wastes associated with a given population's average lifestyle. The World Wide Fund for Nature (2010) has calculated that for the global population to live sustainably within the ecological carrying capacity of Earth, the share of average biologically productive land and water that could be utilized by each individual is less than two hectares. In reality, however, there is extreme inequity in the distribution of Earth's resources. For example, if everyone lived the way that an average North American does, close to eight global hectares per capita, we would need at least four and half Earth-like planets (WWF et al. 2010). If everyone lived the way that an average African does, at just over one global hectare per capita, we could live sustainably on our one and only Earth (WWF et al. 2010).

Various initiatives are underway to explore what one-planet living entails in different places around the world. Perhaps the most famous example is the Beddington Zero Energy Development (BedZed) that follows the One Planet Living framework developed by BioRegional, a not-for-profit social enterprise (bioregional.com). Situated near London, England, some residents at BedZed are demonstrating that changes in lifestyle, particularly to reduce reliance on fossil fuels, can bring one-planet living within reach.

disproportionate: it contributed 40 percent of the global carbon emissions in 2006 (World Watch Institute 2008). Viewed through the lens of per capita resource consumption, the population question takes on new dimensions: a woman in India would need to have ten children to match the resources consumed by one American child (WWF et al. 2010).

Bringing the developing nations up to North American living standards would require a five- to ten-fold increase in world industrial output (WCED 1987), yet the contingent combination of depleted resource stocks (e.g., fossil fuels, fisheries, forests) with degraded life-support systems (e.g., ozone depletion, global warming, acid rain) demonstrates the impossibility of the entire world consuming and polluting at the rate of North Americans. This challenge may be beyond nature's capacity, and therefore, beyond our capability (World Watch Institute 2011).

Ecological Footprint

One way to consider human impact on natural resources and ecosystems is to consider our ecological footprint: the land area and related natural capital on which we draw to sustain our population and production structure (Wackernagel and Rees 1996; WWF et al. 2010).

Natural capital refers to any stock of natural assets that yields a flow of valuable goods and services into the future. Natural capital includes non-renewable resources such as fossil fuels and minerals, renewable resources that can provide goods and services (such as food, clean water and energy) in perpetuity if managed sustainably, and the capacity of natural systems to continue providing critical goods and services while absorbing our pollutants and emissions (such as the atmosphere's capacity to regulate the planet's climate).

The ecological footprint tool that Wackernagel and Rees developed compares human demand for resources to the renewable resources available on Earth. It estimates the global hectares (gha) required for human demand by adding up all of the area required to provide these renewable resources, the area of built infrastructure, and the area needed to absorb waste. Although the tool cannot measure everything, its most recent iteration measured crops, fish, timber, grass for livestock and carbon dioxide emissions. The Earth's biocapacity, which represents the renewable resources available for consumption, is also measured in global hectares that represent an average of bio-productive capacity for all land types (WWF et al. 2010).

Citizens of the United States and Canada have ecological footprints that are among the world's top ten: while the global average is just 3 gha, they consume about 8 and 7 gha per capita annually (WWF et al. 2010). The United Arab Emirates and Qatar top the list with 10 gha per person.

Scholars also estimate that, in the 1970s, humanity entered a state known as *ecological overshoot* (WWF et al. 2010): that is, we began producing more resources than ecosystems can regenerate. The WWF's *Living Planet Report* (2010) calculated that it would take 1.5 years to regenerate the resources used in 2007 alone. How is this possible? These numbers were calculated looking at the newly regenerated portion of the resource, which is conceived of as *resource interest*. When our use exceeds this interest, we are drawing down our natural capital and entering a state of overshoot; in ecological footprint terms, we are then appropriating carrying capacity from "distant elsewheres" (Wackernagel & Rees 1996).

And there is the reality of climate change. Humans are producing far more greenhouse gases than our ecosystems can absorb. In fact, the increase in carbon emissions alone is one of the largest changes in the composition of our footprint since it was calculated by *Living Planet Report* in 1998. In just one decade, carbon emissions, as a portion of the ecological footprint, have increased by 35 percent. Today they account for more than half of the global ecological footprint (WWF et al. 2010).

Ecological footprint analysis confirms that we need to minimize consumption of essential natural capital. But how do we do this in the face of such daunting challenges while maintaining or improving quality of life? The answer, of course, is in planning for development that is sustainable.

Sustainable Development

In December 1983, in response to a United Nations General Assembly resolution, the UN Secretary-General appointed Gro Harlem Brundtland of Norway to chair the independent World Commission on Environment and Development. In April 1987, the Commission released its much-heralded report, *Our Common Future*. The Brundtland Report (as it is often known) showed that the poorest fifth of the world's population has less than 2 percent of the world's economic product while

There are many ways to define sustainability. The simplest definition is: A sustainable society is one that can persist over generations, one that is farseeing enough, flexible enough, and wise enough not to undermine either its physical or its social systems of support.

— Donella Meadows, Dennis Meadows
and Jorgen Randers, *Beyond the Limits* (1992)

the richest fifth has 75 percent; and that the 26 percent of the world's population living in developed countries consumes between 80 and 86 percent of non-renewable resources and 34 percent to 53 percent of food products (WCED 1987). The report emphasized the principle and imperative of *sustainable development*, which it defined as "meeting the needs of the present without compromising the ability of future generations to meet their own needs," and endowed the concept that had been refined for years with new political credibility.

The term *sustainable development* has been criticized as ambiguous and open to contradictory interpretations. Confusion results when it is conflated with *sustainable growth*, an oxymoron as nothing physical can grow indefinitely. While increases in population, production and size are aptly described as growth, qualitative changes, such as improvements in health care, knowledge, quality of life, walkability, density and efficient resource use, are more accurately described as "development."

Sustainable development has also been used to connote *sustainable use*, which can only relate to use of renewable resources that is within their capacity for renewal (IUCN 1991). As well, the term is sometimes confused with protection of the environment, or even sustained *economic* growth (presumably to pay for, among other things, protection of the environment). But the very concept of environmental protection is based on the separation of humanity from nature. As a society, we point to a few things we think of as nature — some trees here, a pond there — draw a box around them, then try to "protect" what's within the box. In so doing, we risk ignoring the fact that human activity outside that box — housing, economic development, transportation and so on — has a far

National Governments Recognize Sustainable Communities

In a marked shift since the 2005 edition of this book, in 2009 the US Environmental Protection Agency (EPA) joined with the US Department of Housing and Urban Development (HUD) and the US Department of Transportation (DOT) in a "Partnership for Sustainable Communities." The partnership aims to help improve access to affordable housing, more transportation options and lower transportation costs while protecting the environment in communities throughout the US (EPA 2011a). The partnership is managed by the EPA's Office of Sustainable Communities to address the Agency's priorities for water,

air and the cleaning up of communities and substantially furthers the Administration's objectives with respect to environmental justice (EPA 2011b).

The Government of Canada also launched a Sustainable Communities Initiative in 2009, funded through Canada Mortgage and Housing Corporation's housing research fund. The EQuilibrium™ Communities Initiative is intended to provide financial, technical and promotional assistance to six neighborhood development projects across the country chosen through a national competition (CMHC 2009).

greater impact on the environment than do our so-called environmental policies.

Finally, sustainable development is too often misconceived as a trade-off between the environment and the economy. In fact, protecting ecosystems and developing sustainably needn't mean job loss or economic downturn. It's about a new way of thinking about economic development over the long term, and a more accurate valuation of ecosystem components in production (Sachs 2008).

If sustainable development is not sustaining growth, protecting the natural environment or making trade-offs, then what is it? The term *sustainable* implies a constant, or the ability of a system to maintain, uphold or preserve its functions. But when used in the context of sustainable development or sustainability, it cannot simply mean to maintain the system we currently have — because this implies that our current system is functioning well now. Sustainability requires changes and improvements to ensure that future generations will have access to the same environmental

benefits that current generations have enjoyed. Sustainable development, therefore, is about changing communities in qualitative ways to a level that is optimal to sustain our existence on the planet. Thus, sustainable development, as it is understood and defined in this book, is not just about "protecting" the environment or maintaining what we have today.

Sustainable development requires fundamental economic and social change to improve human well-being while reducing the need for environmental protection. In sum, sustainable development must be a different kind of development. It must be a proactive strategy to develop sustainability.

Three Core Elements of Sustainable Development

Sustainability has three critical components: the environment, the economy and society. Social equity demands that we balance the needs of the biosphere with the needs of the vast majority of the human population, the world's poor. This means we can no longer rely on our 200-year tradition of material growth

Towards a More "Just" Sustainability

By Julian Agyeman

In recent years, it has become increasingly apparent that *environmental quality* is inextricably linked to, and inseparable from, *human equality*. From local to global, wherever environmental despoliation and degradation are happening, it is almost always linked to questions of social justice, equity, rights and people's quality of life in its widest sense.

Globally, Wilkinson and Pickett (2009) showed that greater inequality within countries drives up what they call "competitive consumption" as people try to keep up with the Joneses. This increases carbon emissions. Similarly, it has been shown by Torras and Boyce (1998) that countries with a more equal income distribution, greater civil liberties and political rights and higher literacy levels (such as Sweden, Denmark, Norway and Finland) tend to have higher environmental quality (measured in lower concentrations of air and water pollutants, and access to clean water and sanitation) than those with less equal income distributions, fewer rights and civil liberties and lower levels of literacy.

In a survey of the 50 US states, Boyce et al. (1999) found that states (predominantly southern) with greater inequalities in power distribution (measured by voter participation, tax fairness, Medicaid access and educational attainment levels) had less stringent environmental policies, greater levels of environmental stress and higher rates of infant mortality and premature deaths. At an even more local level, a study by Morello-Frosch (1997) of counties in California showed that counties that were highly segregated in terms of income, class and race had higher levels of hazardous air pollutants.

The message seems to be loud and clear: From global to local, human inequality is bad for environmental quality.

The concept of *just sustainability* bridges this environmental quality–human equality divide, which is ignored in much of the current *environmentally focused* sustainability debate. *Just sustainability* is "the need to ensure a better quality of life for all, now and into the future, in a just and equitable manner, whilst living within the limits of supporting ecosystems" (Agyeman et al. 2003, 5).

Just sustainability foregrounds four related focal areas of concern:

- Quality of life,
- Present *and* future generations,
- Justice and equity and
- Living within ecosystem limits.

If sustainability is to become a process with the power to *transform*, as opposed to its current environmental, stewardship or *reform* focus, justice and equity issues need to be incorporated into its very core. Our present "green" or "environmental" orientation of sustainability is basically about tweaking our existing policies. Transformative or *just* sustainability implies a paradigm shift, which in turn requires that sustainability takes on a redistributive function. To do this, justice and equity must move center stage in sustainability discourses, if we are to have any chance of more sustainable communities.

In summary:

Sustainability . . . cannot be simply a "green," or "environmental" concern, important though "environmental" aspects of sustainability are. A truly sustainable society is one where wider questions of social needs and welfare, and economic opportunity are integrally related to environmental limits imposed by supporting ecosystems (Agyeman et al. 2002, 78).

as the primary instrument of social policy. We all agree with the ideal of sustainable development, like other political objectives of its kind (e.g., justice, democracy), and disagree over what it entails. Nevertheless, sustainable development has a core meaning that remains, however it is interpreted. Three core elements of sustainable development are:

- *Environmental considerations must be entrenched in, and constrain, economic policy-making.* Environmental and economic objectives must be placed within a common framework that allows recognition of parallel objectives.
- *Sustainable development requires a commitment to social equity.* This includes not just creation of wealth and the conservation of resources, but also their fair distribution among and within nations, including at least some measure of redistribution between developed and developing nations. Social equity also requires the fair distribution of environmental benefits and costs between generations.
- *"Development" does not simply mean "growth,"* as measured by indicators of economic performance such as gross national product (GNP) that cannot distinguish between positive and negative outcomes resulting from economic transactions. Development implies qualitative as well as quantitative improvement.

Strong or Weak Sustainability?

In the early 1990s, economists such as Herman Daly and David Pearce considered how to conceive of sustainability in economic terms. They asked what it would mean for each generation to leave a stock of assets at least as great as that which they had inherited themselves. There are two possible ways to interpret this: "weak sustainability" and "strong sustainability." Weak sustainability implicitly aggregates all types of assets, reflecting the neoclassical economics assumption that non-natural assets can substitute for natural assets, and would not see it as problematic if natural assets were used up as long as the profits they generate provide an equivalent endowment to the next generation. In contrast, strong sustainability recognizes that, in most cases, non-natural assets cannot be substituted for natural assets, because irreversible processes (such as species extinction or ecosystem destruction) mean that the former cannot be converted back into the latter.

Based on these considerations, Daly, Pearce, Robert Costanza and others began to distinguish between weak and strong sustainability, insisting that we must differentiate between assets that are natural and those that are not (Costanza 2003). Strong sustainability, they argued, recognizes that whatever the level of human-made assets, an adequate stock of natural

Pricing the Planet

A team of 13 ecologists, economists and geographers estimated the present global value of 17 ecosystem "services" is US$16 trillion to $54 trillion a year, with a likely figure of at least $33 trillion. Ecosystem services are services essential to the human economy, including climate regulation, water supply, soil formation, pollination, food production, raw materials, genetic resources, recreation and culture. To come up with the figure, the team estimated the cost of replacing — if that were possible — the ecosystem services of the natural environment. In comparison, the gross national product of the world, which is all the goods and services produced by people each year, was about $18 trillion (Costanza et al. 1997).

assets is critical in securing sustainability (Daly 1989; Ekins et al. 2003). All this suggests that weak sustainability is grossly insufficient; natural capital stock should only be destroyed if the benefits of doing so are very large or if the social costs of conservation are unacceptably large (Neumayer 2010). It also begs a key question: Are we even capable of knowing the full costs and benefits of destroying or conserving natural capital stock?

The debate between strong and weak sustainability heightened awareness of the field of ecological economics. Ecological economics aims to address the interdependence and co-evolution of human economies and natural ecosystems. It differs from environmental economics, the mainstream economic analysis of the environment, by virtue of its treatment of the economy as a subsystem of the ecosystem and its emphasis upon preserving natural capital. Its adherents argue that strong sustainability is the way forward, and that natural capital cannot be simply conceptualized as an input to the economic system (Neumayer 2010).

Many valuation techniques have been devised to put a value on all of the ecosystem services in the world (see Pricing the Planet), and many more ecosystem services have been valued on a smaller scale. But this approach has its critics. They argue that valuing ecosystem services in this way is based on erroneous assumptions that the market is the only system by which to compare welfare and value, that welfare can be accurately represented in monetary terms, that monetary value implies substitutability, and that technology will solve most problems (Chee 2004). Costanza and Folke (1997) also recognized that economic valuation of nature becomes even more difficult when social equity is also a goal of ecosystem

management. Liu et al. (2010) have maintained that affixing a monetary value to ecosystem services is mostly theoretical, and meant to give the world of markets and the world of conservation a common language.

Rees (1991) has argued that, when we consider that the potential benefits of conservation approach infinity, costs become irrelevant. Indeed, the economic benefits of destroying natural capital stock or the social costs of conservation may seem large, but only as a function of our inability to adequately assess such costs and benefits. This suggests that it is time for a different kind of framework for planning and decision-making — one guided by the understanding that natural capital stock should not be destroyed.

Understood in terms of natural capital and natural income, or principal and interest, sustainable development acquires new meaning. The bottom line for sustainability is that we must learn to live on our natural income rather than deplete our natural capital. For example, there are those who cheer the idea that even in the most somber climate change scenarios — which assume runaway population growth, minimal technological advancement and the lowest standard of living — rich countries would grow 1 percent every year and poor countries would grow 2.3 percent. Our great-grandchildren in rich countries would be two-and-a-half times wealthier than we are today; in poor countries, the figure would be a stunning nine times wealthier (Visscher 2011). However, economic growth with an ecological deficit is anti-economic and makes us poorer rather than richer in the long term (Daly & Cobb 1989). Sustainability therefore requires that we minimize our consumption of essential (and especially non-renewable) natural capital while simultaneously finding ways to close the poverty gap (Porritt 2005).

Resilience and Sustainability

A more recent current of sustainability thought refers to concepts of *resilience*. First introduced to the sustainability literature by the renowned natural scientist C.S. Holling (1973), resilience refers to a system whose state of equilibrium is in fact characterized by thresholds, uncertainty and periods of gradual change interspersed with periods of rapid change. According to Walker et al., resilience is "the capacity of a system to absorb disturbance and reorganize while undergoing change so as to still retain essentially the same function, structure, identity, and feedbacks" (2004, 2). The term *resilience* has been applied to communities to describe a method of dealing with crisis and adapting to change (e.g., Campanella 2006; Comfort et al. 2004). Specific tactics include communication systems for crisis response, working with public-private partnerships and other activities that can diversify risk **across institutions and time** (Campanella 2006; Hultman & Bozmoski 2006; Tobin 1999).

Resilience in community planning is a key driving principle behind the "transition initiative" (formerly the "transition town initiative"). In 2005, Hopkins introduced the term during a community process called the "Energy Descent Action Plan" of the town of Kinsale, Northern Ireland. The process outlined steps the community could take to reduce carbon emissions, prepare for an economy post-peak oil and ultimately transition to more sustainable socio-technical systems (Haxeltine & Seyfang 2009). With climate change and peak oil on the horizon, Hopkins (2008) and others (such as Odum & Odum 2001) had argued that we

will inevitably have to live with a smaller energy footprint, that we should be planning for it collectively, and that our communities currently lack the resilience to survive the shock of skyrocketing energy prices. Towns across the UK, Australia and the United States are now using this framework to plan for sustainability. As of June 2011, there were 360 transition initiatives underway in 34 countries (Transition Network 2011).

While both are moving in the same direction, the concepts of sustainability and resilience are vying for the same definitional space. Where Hopkins has argued that "the concept of resilience goes far beyond the better known concept of sustainability" (2008, 54), most other scholars have used sustainability as the broader concept to encompass all types of transitions and changes (Haxeltine & Seyfang 2009). Much early work on resilience focused on "the capacity to absorb shocks and still maintain function," but there is another aspect of resilience that "concerns the capacity for renewal, re-organization and development,

> Resilience, then, embraces change as the natural state of being on earth. It values adaptation over stasis, diffuse systems over centralized ones, loosely interconnected webs over strict hierarchies. It favours diversity (both biological and social) and redundancy, and it works best with a range of interchangeable, modular components. It places paramount value on natural capital (the trees in the forest, the oil in the ground) and social capital (the hearts and minds and passionate actions of the public). It responds best with tight feedback loops, where, for example, the squandering of that capital has immediate, negative consequences. It encourages learning new tricks and following local rules and customs.
>
> —Turner, 2011, 53

which has been less in focus but is essential for the sustainability discourse ... in a resilient social-ecological system, disturbance has the potential to create opportunity for doing new things, for innovation and for development" (Folke 2006). It is in this respect that resilience supports the normative nature of sustainability by recognizing that a sustainable society is one that is actively seeking to become a better society (e.g., Newman, Beatley & Boyer 2009). Indeed, as Kamp (2011) noted, "the quest for sustainability is the modern variant of the Industrial Revolution, and it offers entire generations the opportunity to do meaningful work and redesign societies."

Community Capital
Community Capital Framework

There are myriad ways to understand and conceptualize community. The term *community* refers to a group of people bound by geography and with a shared destiny, such as a municipality or a town. The term *North America* in this book refers primarily to communities in the developed countries of North America, in other words, those in the US and Canada. For sustainable community development, it is useful to think of community in terms of so-called capital, a number or collection of local assets, community resources that can produce other benefits through investment (Flora et al. 2004). The SFU Centre for Sustainable Community Development (e.g., Roseland 1999; 2000) and others (e.g., Emery & Fey 2006) use this notion of community capital as the foundation for sustainable community development. Generally speaking, sustainable community development strategies should favor bottom-up over top-down approaches; redistribution over trickle-down; self-reliance over dependency; a local rather than a regional, national or international focus; and small-scale projects rather than grand-scale or mega-projects. As well, they should be designed with extensive public participation; seek to improve society and the environment as well as the economy; and result in increased equity, equality and empowerment (Brohman 1996).

Originating from the World Commission on Environment and Development's definition of sustainable development (see chapter 1), there have been several efforts to describe sustainable community development in terms of three types of capital: economic, social and ecological capital (e.g., Goodland 2002; Rainey et al. 2003). However, from our perspective, working with the three large types of capital is cumbersome and challenging. Therefore, we use six smaller, more nuanced forms of capital: natural, physical, economic, human, social and cultural capital. These six forms of capital are the backbone of the Community Capital Framework (Figure 1), which seeks *balance* between all the capital. In pursuing balanced development, we ask whether each form of capital benefits from a proposed initiative. For example, does the preservation of a natural ecosystem encourage economic development through tourism or will it hurt industry in the area? Can trails be added to a protected area to promote physical health benefits in the community? And can the same protected area be used for education and cultural events?

It is important to understand that an increase in a single capital can generate multiple benefits across the other forms of capital (Gutierrez-Montez 2005). For example, an increase in economic capital through successful community economic development initiatives will create opportunities for more jobs (human capital) and generate financial resources to maintain and replace aging community infrastructure, such as roads and public buildings (physical capital). If economic development initiatives thoughtfully consider the needs of the community, they will also increase social and cultural capital. This flow of resources across capital has been termed the "upward spiral" of community capital (Emery & Fey 2006; Wheeler 2004). But this same effect can happen as a "downward spiral" too — when one form of capital becomes deeply eroded, then the others will likely decrease.

The Community Capital Framework has been developed to consider the effects of decision-making on each form of community capital. It has been designed with a systems thinking perspective that regards each form of community capital as a sub-system of the larger whole community system. Since the early 2000s, we have used the Community Capital Framework in a variety of community types — big, small, rural, urban, developed, developing — in many areas around the world — North America, Latin America, Eastern Europe — with resounding success. The framework resonates with different communities because it encourages participants to think strategically and holistically with regard to existing capacity, sustainability principles and potential long-term impacts of specific projects, policies and activities.

Six Forms of Community Capital

NATURAL CAPITAL

Although the term *natural capital* has been around for almost a century, it was ecological economists such as Robert Costanza (1989) and Herman Daly (1989) who introduced it into the dialogue around sustainability. Natural capital refers to any stock of natural assets that yields

The fact of the matter is that we depend on ecosystems and the services they provide in order to do what we do: run businesses, build communities, feed our populations and much more. Whether we consider the more obvious, immediately vital examples — the need for soil that can grow food or for clean water to drink — or the less obvious but equally significant things like oxygen production during photosynthesis or waste processing by bacterial decomposers, we cannot avoid the conclusion that we depend on the environment for our existence. If we damage or destroy the capacity of the environment to provide these services we may face consequences for which we are completely unprepared (Strange & Bayley 2008).

a flow of valuable goods and services into the future. Natural capital includes non-renewable resources (such as fossil fuels and minerals), renewable resources that can provide goods and services (such as food, clean water and energy) in perpetuity if managed sustainably and the capacity of natural systems to continue providing critical goods and services while absorbing our pollutants and emissions (such as the atmosphere's capacity to regulate the planet's climate). Because the flow of benefits from ecosystems often requires that they function as intact systems, the structure and biodiversity of ecosystems is another important component of natural capital (Goodland 2002; Wackernagel & Rees 1996). As well, irreplaceable areas of outstanding natural beauty are considered natural capital.

Enhancing our natural capital means living within its ecological limits: using less of it, minimizing our waste, leaving more of it untouched and generally ensuring that our actions do not degrade its functional integrity. The benefits that flow from natural capital can be considered *natural income*.

PHYSICAL CAPITAL

Physical capital is the infrastructure that helps people obtain their basic needs, such as shelter, access to clean water, unspoiled food and a supply of energy. It also creates an opportunity for people to be productive by providing stocks of material resources, such as equipment, buildings, machinery and other infrastructure that can be used to produce goods and a flow of future income.

The origin of physical capital is the process of spending time and other resources constructing tools, plants, facilities and other material resources that can, in turn, be used in producing other products (Ostrom 1993). Physical capital is sometimes referred to as produced capital (NRTEE 2003), manufactured capital (Goodland 2002) or public capital (Rainey et al. 2003).

There is a strong relationship between physical and human capital. Insufficient physical capital can limit human capital by requiring more effort needed to satisfy basic needs and achieve productivity. In rural communities challenged by poor sanitation facilities, the time lost when someone becomes sick limits community members' ability to focus on productive financial gain. This will limit new resources from entering the community.

Improving physical capital includes focusing investment, both financial and non-financial, on community assets such as public facilities (e.g., hospitals and schools); water and sanitation; efficient transportation; safe, quality housing; adequate infrastructure and telecommunications.

ECONOMIC CAPITAL

Economic capital refers to the ways in which we allocate resources and make decisions about our material lives. It is essential for building a stable and viable economy. Economic capital within a community consists of two distinct types of resources, *financial* and *business*. Individuals and organizations use financial resources, such as money and access to affordable loans, to achieve well-being and generate wealth through goods and services production. Business resources, such as locally owned and operated companies, are the suppliers and consumers within a community that generate employment and income. They transform community resources into products and services that encourage the circulation of money within the community.

Economic capital can be maintained and strengthened by supporting economic diversification across sectors and employers, local needs production to reduce economic leakage caused by importing and by supporting local enterprise development through access to loans and credit and technical assistance.

HUMAN CAPITAL

Human capital is the "knowledge, skills, competencies and other attributes embodied in individuals that facilitate the creation of personal, social and economic well-being" (OECD

Understanding Capital

Since the language used to describe community capital is borrowed from the field of economics, economic capital is generally the most easily understood form of capital. Take currency as an example, if the money within a community stays in the bank generating interest, it provides very little benefit for the community. However, if that same money is used to build a community center, it would generate a variety of immediately realized benefits for the community. These benefits can be considered community income (Emery & Fey 2006).

2001). It contributes directly to the labor productivity of a community and is sometimes described as the "livelihood asset," representing a person's ability to pursue and achieve individual livelihood objectives (DFID 2003). Such objectives vary from person to person and have a variety of influences, such as culture, income and personal preferences. Health, education, skills, knowledge, leadership and access to services all constitute human capital (Callaghan & Colton 2008).

Human capital is formed consciously through training and education and unconsciously through experience (Ostrom 1993). It needs continual maintenance by investments throughout one's lifetime (Goodland 2002). It is eroded through the inability of a person to meet basic needs, such as access to food, clothing, shelter and education, as well as failure to achieve expectations in work and productivity (Callaghan & Colton 2008).

Increasing human capital requires a focus on areas such as health, education, nutrition, literacy and family and community cohesion. Increasing it also requires input from other forms of capital — physical (shelter, schools and medical infrastructure), economic (employment and income), social (peace and safety) and cultural (identity and belonging) capital are all needed to enhance human capital (Hancock 2001). It also requires creating opportunities to build pride and freedom through realistic expectations and achievements (Callaghan & Colton 2008).

SOCIAL CAPITAL

Social capital constitutes the "glue" that holds our communities together. It is community cohesion, connectedness, reciprocity, tolerance, compassion, patience, forbearance, fellowship, love, commonly accepted standards of honesty, discipline and ethics and commonly shared rules, laws and information. It has both an informal aspect related to social networks and a more formal aspect related to institutions and social development programs. The Organisation for Economic Co-operation and Development (2001) defines social capital as "the relationships, networks and norms that facilitate collective action." Others describe it as the shared knowledge, understandings and patterns of interactions that groups of people bring to any productive activity (Coleman 1990; Putnam 1993).

Social capital differs from other forms of capital in several significant ways. It is not limited by material scarcity, meaning that its creative capacity is limited only by imagination. Consequently, it suggests a route toward sustainability, by replacing the fundamentally illogical model of unlimited growth within a finite world with one that is less constrained by the availability of material resources (Prigogine & Stengers 1984; Tainter 1995). It has two distinct characteristics that make it unique from the other capital: social capital does not wear out upon being used, and if unused, social capital deteriorates at a relatively rapid rate (Ostrom 1993). Social capital also has limitations that other forms of capital do not. It is non-transferable and cannot be created instantly, and the very fact of trying to consciously create it or direct it can create resistance. People resist being instrumentalized for even the best of reasons (Dale & Newman 2010; Flora & Flora 1993).

Multiplying social capital contributes to stronger community fabric, and establishes bonds of information, trust and inter-personal solidarity (Coleman 1990; Jacobs 1961; Lehtonen 2004), whereas a loss, or deficit, results in high levels of violence and mistrust (Jacobs 1961).

Past sustainable development efforts have focused less on building social capital (and human and cultural capital) than other capital (Lehtonen 2004). Why is that so? A number of studies identify governance structures as the main barrier to social capital development (Dale & Newman 2010). Though social capital is largely neglected in discussions of public policy, Putnam (1993) reasons that social capital substantially enhances returns on investments in physical and human capital. However, unlike conventional capital, social capital is a public good, i.e., it is not the private property of those who benefit from it. Thus, like other public goods, from clean air to safe streets, social capital tends to be under-provided by private agents. The ties, norms and trust that constitute social capital are most often created as a by-product of other social activities and then transferred from one social setting to another (Hayami 2009).

The modern concept of social capital is described as the relations between individuals and groups. It can take several forms, some of which are mutually recognized bonds, channels of information, and norms and sanctions.

In this sense, social capital is related to the concept of social ecology, as developed in the works of the late Murray Bookchin. Social ecology is the study of both human and natural ecosystems, and in particular, of the social relations that effect the relation of society as a whole with nature. Social ecology goes beyond environmentalism, insisting that the issue at hand for humanity is not simply protecting nature but rather creating an ecological society in harmony with nature. The primary social unit of an ecological society is the sustainable community, a human-scale settlement based on ecological balance, community self-reliance and participatory democracy (Bookchin 1987).

Enhancement of social capital requires communication, interaction and networking between community members (Dale & Newman 2010; Onyx et al. 2004). It requires attention to effective and representative local governance, strong organizations, capacity-building, participatory planning, access to information, and collaboration and partnerships.

CULTURAL CAPITAL

Cultural capital is the product of shared experience through traditions, customs, values, heritage, identity and history. Although sometimes subsumed under the heading of social capital, it deserves its own category.

Cultural capital is the cultural and traditional resources of a community (Flora, Flora & Fey 2004). It is many things, both tangible and intangible: singing, dancing, stories, food, rituals, spirituality, ceremonies, celebrations, heritage buildings and art. Cultural capital defines community, influences decision-making and shapes how people communicate with one another. It is something that a community shares both socially and across generations (Callaghan & Colton 2008). French sociologist Pierre Borideau (1986) was the first to describe cultural capital, believing it exists in three different states: embodied (state of the mind/body), objectified (through cultural objects like instruments and costumes) and institutionalized ("rules of the state").

In mainstream Western society, particularly in the US and Canada, cultural capital is often under-valued. However, it is particularly important in aboriginal communities that use local ecological knowledge to guide resource management and decision-making (Cochrane

2006). Cultural capital also plays a strong role in communities with long histories and traditions.

In communities rich with culture and natural resources, cultural capital has influence over management objectives, efficiency of process and demand for natural resources (Cochrane 2006). When embraced, cultural capital can increase human and social capital by improving health and well-being and promotes stewardship and preservation of natural capital (Cochrane 2006). It can be used to increase economic capital through productivity and tourism opportunities (Flora, Flora & Fey, 2004)

Enhancing cultural capital implies attention to traditions and values, heritage and place, the arts, diversity and social history. It is closely linked to social capital, in that the amount of social capital present in the community will either constrain or promote cultural capital (Callaghan & Colton 2008).

The Foundation for Sustainable Community Development

Strengthening these six forms of community capital is the foundation for sustainable community development (SCD). The key to understanding this approach to development is recognizing that it is based largely on appreciation of community assets (as well as realistic acknowledgement of challenges or, in conventional terms, deficits).

For example, a transportation system that is oriented to walking, cycling and public transportation rather than the private automobile contributes to natural capital by saving energy and reducing emissions. It contributes to human capital by reducing health-damaging air pollution and motor vehicle accidents, and by increasing the amount of exercise people get. It may contribute to social capital by increasing the social networking required for car-sharing, carpooling and other more social means of getting around, in addition to the social interaction that may occur in the use of public transport. Finally, it contributes to economic capital by reducing congestion and by reducing the costs of transportation if people do not need to own a car or perhaps are only part owners in a car-sharing or carpooling system. This in turn increases disposable income, which may be spent on more health-enhancing products and services (Hancock 2001).

COMMUNITY MOBILIZATION

The Community Capital Framework (Figure 1) conceives of SCD as a balanced enhancement of all of these capital, with a critical element at its center: community mobilization. Why? Because there is no single sustainability prescription that would fit all communities, because every path forward comes with opportunity costs that need to be carefully considered, and because participatory planning is critical to the sustainable development process — from visioning through to evaluation of results. For people to prosper anywhere they must participate as competent citizens in the decisions and processes that affect their lives (Gran 1987). Sustainable community development is thus about the quantity and quality of empowerment and participation of people.

In summary, applying the concept of sustainable development to communities requires mobilizing citizens and their governments to strengthen all forms of community capital. Elements of this framework include minimizing consumption of essential natural capital and improving physical capital, which in turn require the more efficient use of urban space. This sustainability framework also includes

> There is no endeavour more noble than the attempt to achieve a collective dream. When a city accepts as a mandate its quality of life; when it respects the people who live in it; when it respects the environment; when it prepares for future generations, the people share the responsibility for that mandate, and this shared cause is the only way to achieve that collective dream.
>
> — Jaime Lerner, former Mayor of Curitiba, Brazil

strengthening economic capital, increasing human capital, multiplying social capital and enhancing cultural capital. Community mobilization is necessary to coordinate, balance and catalyse community capital. The significance of these criteria for the future of our communities and our society is elaborated in the following chapters.

Doing Development Differently

Several key arguments inform this book. First, the term *sustainable development* acquires tangible meaning when understood in terms of natural capital and natural income. The bottom line for sustainability is that we must learn to live on our natural income rather than deplete our natural capital. Economic growth is illusory if accompanied by a growing ecological deficit, since over time it makes us poorer rather than richer (Daly & Cobb 1989). Sustainability therefore requires that we minimize our consumption of essential natural capital.

Second, community capital and social equity demand that North Americans, who are among the world's most inefficient and wasteful consumers of materials and energy (e.g., WCED 1987), find ways of living more lightly on the planet. At a minimum, we will have to increase the efficiency of our resource and energy use. More likely, we will also have to reduce our present (not to speak of projected) levels of materials and energy consumption.

Third, reducing our materials and energy consumption need not diminish and, in fact, would likely enhance our quality of life and the public domain — in other words, it could strengthen our community capital. It is important to distinguish here between "quality of life" and "standard of living" (Jacobs 1993). Standard of living generally refers to disposable income for things we purchase individually, whereas quality of life can be considered as the sum of all things which people purchase collectively (e.g., the healthcare system, public education, policing), or those things that are not purchased at all (e.g., air quality). Standard of living refers solely to the private domain, whereas quality of life refers to the public domain, the realm of community capital.

Fourth, the critical resource for strengthening community capital is not money — rather, the critical resources are trust, imagination, courage, commitment, the relations between individuals and groups, and time, the literal currency of life. Many of the issues that people relate to most intimately — family, neighborhood, community, decompression from work, recreation, culture, etc. — depend on these resources at least as much as money. This is not to say that economic security isn't important — it is — but focusing solely on money to provide security is using 19th century thinking to address 21st century challenges.

Taken together, the direction to which these arguments point is clear. We must explicitly aim to nurture and strengthen community capital in order to improve our economic and social well-being. Government and corporate decisions should be reviewed for their effects on all forms of community capital. Programs and policies need to be effected at every level to ensure that community capital is properly considered.

In a nutshell, we need to *do development differently*.

Looking Ahead

In chapter 2 we move from the more global perspective of this chapter to focus on the regional, community and neighborhood level, and illustrate what we mean by sustainable community development. Chapter 3 concludes part 1 by addressing the question of how to achieve sustainable community development through making community policy. Together these three chapters provide a foundation for part 2.

Part 2 includes 11 chapters examining each of the sustainable community building blocks, from food and water and waste, to energy and transportation and land use, to housing, green buildings, community economic development and climate change. Part 2 concludes with a chapter on communities integrating sustainability, which illustrates how many communities and local governments are now broadening their efforts from single-sector initiatives to more comprehensive integration of all of these building blocks.

Part 3 focuses on mobilizing citizens and their governments toward sustainable communities, beginning with a chapter on governing sustainable communities. It proceeds with chapters on tools for community sustainability and the Community Capital Tool we developed based upon the framework described above. Part 3 concludes with a reflection on lessons and challenges.

Fig. 1.1: *Community Capital: A Framework for Sustainable Community Development. Sustainable development requires mobilizing citizens and their governments to strengthen all forms of community capital. Community mobilization is necessary to coordinate, balance and catalyze community capital.*

Community Capital Framework

The Community Capital Framework has been designed from the following principles:

- Communities need all six forms of capital to achieve well-being and sustainability. No single capital is sufficient in creating or supporting sustainability.
- It is important to understand your community's capital, including strengths and weaknesses.
- Capital interact with each other; changes in one form of capital may generate positive or negative changes in other forms of capital.

The appendix describes *Pando | Sustainable Communities*, a new initiative intended, among other things, to effectively make this book a living document.

Chapter 2:

Sustainable Community Development

Sustainable development is a concept that is commonly applied very broadly, and to the planet as a whole. But our planet is made up of a giant network of interconnected communities. What does it mean to develop sustainably in one community? What one community engages in affects all communities — perhaps in minutes in a single region, and over years and generations across borders and continents. Therefore, in order to effect change on a global scale, we must first change our own communities.

To make sense of the sustainability imperative at the community level, we need a new focus on place. As discussed throughout this book, although the sustainability imperative is universal, the particularities of each place are unique. Conventional analysis rarely serves us well in this regard — community gets relatively little attention beyond a narrow and outdated notion that local governments are merely the janitors responsible for removing our garbage and fixing our potholes, while the "important" issues are in the realm of senior governments.

In much of the social sciences, community is seen as irrelevant and shaped by forces beyond its control. Even in ecological science, the focus is often on limiting the impact of our communities, rather than evolving them into more viable ecological forms (Brugmann 2008).

The complexity of the sustainable development challenge, combined with the inability or unwillingness of senior governments to lead on global issues such as climate change, underscores that it is time for a new way to think about communities, their role in contributing to unsustainable development and their enormous, largely untapped potential to demonstrate that sustainable development on a global scale is indeed possible. Communities can be laboratories for policy invention; local initiatives can and do provide the models for national level policies and programs (Otto-Zimmerman 2011).

In chapter 1, we explained a framework for sustainable community development. In this framework, applying the concept of sustainable development to communities requires mobilizing citizens and their governments to strengthen all forms of community capital. Elements of this framework include minimizing consumption of essential natural capital and improving physical capital, which in turn require the more efficient use of urban space. It also includes strengthening economic capital, increasing human capital, multiplying social capital and enhancing cultural capital.

This chapter builds on this framework, recognizing that the challenges for developed and developing country communities will be different. We next examine unsustainable communities — the backdrop for our concern — and then proceed to deepen our understanding of sustainable communities. It concludes with a series of images that help illustrate the notion of sustainable community development.

A sustainable community describes not just one type of neighborhood, town, city or region, but the activities that a community engages in to sustain the environment and empower their citizens. A sustainable community is not a static entity; rather, it is continually adjusting to meet the social and economic needs of its residents while preserving the environment's ability to support it (Bridger and Luloff 2001). There are now hundreds of communities that have defined their vision of a sustainable community. This definition from a Minnesota citizen-legislator

taskforce was advanced in 1995 but is equally relevant today:

> [A sustainable community is] a community that uses its resources to meet current needs while ensuring that adequate resources are available for future generations. A sustainable community seeks a better quality of life for all its residents while maintaining nature's ability to function over time by minimizing waste, preventing pollution, promoting efficiency and developing local resources to revitalize the local economy. Decision-making in a sustainable community stems from a rich civic life and shared information among community members. A sustainable community resembles a living system in which human, natural and economic elements are interdependent and draw strength from each other (Minnesota SEDEPTF 1995, iii).

Challenges for Developed and Developing Communities

We often distinguish between developed and developing (or industrialized and industrializing) nations, but the picture is more complex than that. All developed country cities have within them a "Third World" city; similarly, every developing country city has within it a "First World" city (Perlman & O'Meara Sheehan 2007). In this book, we will use the terms *developed* and *developing* to describe countries and communities.

The communities of the developing world face challenges that are distinctly different than those faced by communities of the developed world. From the perspective of sustainable development, the basic problem with developed

No one fully understands how, or even if, sustainable development can be achieved; however, there is a growing consensus that it must be accomplished at the local level if it is ever to be achieved on a global basis (ICLEI et al. 1996, 1).

cities is that they are unsustainable, whereas the basic problem with developing cities is that they lack essential services. Most developed city dwellers are adequately housed and fed, but they meet their needs by consuming at rates the planet cannot afford and polluting at rates the planet cannot tolerate. Many developing city dwellers cannot meet their basic needs for food, clean water, clean air, fuel, transport and an environment free of disease-causing agents. While this dichotomy is not absolute — because there is poverty in most developed cities, and many developing cities live beyond their means in terms of consumption of natural resources such as firewood and water — it helps illuminate the essential challenge of sustainability in any community: meeting basic needs without depleting or degrading natural capital (Devuyst 2001; Lithgow et al. 2005).

With their inadequate urban policies and technology, the cities in developed countries set the standard to which city managers in developing countries aspire — low-density single-family dwellings, car-dominated transport systems, unchecked waste, omnipresent air conditioning and profligate water use (Newman & Kenworthy 1999). The role of the cities of the industrial world deserves much more scrutiny in the context of human settlements and the environmental crisis, precisely because their impact on the world's ecosystems is so enormous.

The Unsustainable Community

For the first time in history, more than half of the world's people now live in urban areas. The way these urban areas are developed will largely determine our success or failure in overcoming environmental challenges and achieving a sustainable future for our planet.

In North America, most cities were built using technologies that assumed abundant and cheap energy and land would be available forever. It was cheap energy that influenced the construction of our spacious homes and buildings, fostered our addiction to the automobile and increased the separation of our workplaces from our homes. Communities therefore grew inefficiently and became dependent on lengthy distribution systems. Urban sprawl was also the result of car-centered transportation development, mortgage policies that encouraged single detached homes, zoning policies that encouraged the separation of land uses and the failure of our markets to account for the value of open space and the costs of freeway congestion (Blais 2010). Urban sprawl is one legacy of abundant fossil fuel and our perceived right to unrestricted use of the private car whatever the social costs and externalities (Newman, Beatley & Boyer 2009).

The limitations of the old model have become clear. Where once it was cheaper, both in terms of land and fuel, to buy homes in the periphery of a city, this is no longer the case:

> The more sprawling the metropolitan area is, the higher the percentage of family budget devoted to auto use. When these additional costs are factored in, the "affordable" house in a third-ring suburb is not nearly so affordable, a fact made sadly obvious when in 2008 the combination of sky-high gas prices and the mortgage meltdown led to the virtual abandonment of many subdivisions in third-ring suburbs (Condon 2010, 4).

Although many communities continue to build 1950s-style suburbs as if families were

Sustainable Rural Communities

By Sean Markey

As the movement toward sustainable communities gathers solar-generated steam, its application to the rural and small-town setting currently lags behind. There are a variety of reasons for this gap, including a relative lack of research on sustainable rural communities and the extent to which the literature tends to treat rural places as "not urban," rather than as settings with different histories and trajectories of development. The misapplication of urban sustainability planning to rural places generates frustration among rural peoples (that they are not being understood, or are somehow being blamed for their "way of life") and scores of un-implementable community planning reports.

Two core issues of context help to make sustainability relevant to rural communities: 1) looking to sustainable forms of development to address fundamental issues of restructuring and community viability and 2) understanding how sustainable community planning may contribute to economic diversification and overall rural competitive advantage.

First, rural communities in Western industrialized nations have experienced similar impacts associated with both political and economic restructuring over the past 30 years. Politically, the advent of a neoliberal-inspired policy agenda has dramatically reduced levels of government responsibility for and involvement in the delivery of rural development and services. Economically, rural communities have struggled to adjust to the advent of flexible production systems, labor-shedding technologies and a severing of direct industry participation in rural development.

Second, in a case of poor timing, governments and industry have been withdrawing their commitments to rural community development just as the nature of competitiveness in the global economy has changed. Remaining economically relevant and competitive now demands high-quality services and infrastructure amenities. New approaches to competitiveness place an added burden on the capacity of communities and regions to construct a receptive and adaptive infrastructure environment (including physical, social, cultural and human forms of capital). From a rural perspective, the capacity of communities to respond to the demands of the new economy (in terms of attracting and retaining both workers and businesses) is limited.

Sustainable rural community development offers solutions to both of these challenges by focusing on two key issues: viability and livability. First, sustainable planning offers numerous (and now well-tested) solutions for rural communities that are seeking to renew or establish cost-effective, energy-efficient forms of infrastructure. While community planners and politicians may be motivated by wanting to "do the right thing," the long-term cost implications associated with delivering effective services mean that sustainable solutions are a significant asset in terms of maintaining community viability going forward. Rural communities need better access to information (like this book!) and decision-making systems that will allow them to better understand how these practices and systems may directly improve resilience going forward.

Second, when you ask rural people why they live where they do, their answers almost always have to do with … quality of life. This includes the small-town lifestyle, access to nature and sense of community common in rural places. Far from threatening the rural "way of life," sustainable community development, when used correctly and with a rural lens, is completely compatible with preserving rural quality of life and creating a development foundation that protects and enhances a community's sense of place. Rural sustainability is rooted in a commitment to livability that may then become a foundation for future viability.

large and had only one breadwinner, as if jobs were all downtown, as if land and energy were endless and as if another lane on the freeway would end congestion, oil production has arguably peaked, our workplaces have been transformed, and real wages have decreased.

Other local and regional consequences of sprawl, such as congestion, air pollution, jobs-housing location "imbalance" and longer commuting times are now commonly recognized. Yet until recently, few researchers acknowledged that the land-use pattern of North American cities also has serious global ecological ramifications.

Cities and towns demand a high input of resources — water, fossil fuels, land and all the goods and materials that their populations and enterprises require. The more populous the city and the richer its inhabitants, the larger its ecological footprint is likely to be in terms of its demand on resources. Although some of our communities may appear to be sustainable, analysis of the ecological footprint of industrial communities shows that they appropriate carrying capacity not only from their own rural and resource regions, but also from distant elsewhere. Most cities of developed regions of North America, Europe, Japan, Australia and other places only have forests, parks and nature reserves nearby because such land is not being used to meet the demand for food and other natural resources that are instead imported. In other words, they are "importing" sustainability. The flip side of this is exporting ecological degradation, or unsustainability, because excessive extraction of natural resources in distant places often causes serious problems of environmental degradation there.

While ecological footprints have commonly been used on a country scale, they can also be calculated and applied on a local scale. Sonoma County calculated that their residents required 22 acres of land and sea per person to account for the resources consumed by each resident (Sonoma County 2002). The report was an effective communications tool that led to all municipalities in Sonoma to reduce their carbon dioxide emissions by 20 percent (Wackernagel 2006). Other municipalities, such as the City of Petaluma and Carollo's engineering department, used the ecological footprint as a criterion to select the most appropriate sewage treatment option (Sonoma County 2002). The City of Vancouver, BC, also used the ecological footprint to assess options for achieving their Greenest City 2020 goals. Vancouver's Greenest City Action Plan includes a short-term goal to achieve a 33 percent reduction in the City's ecological footprint by 2020 and a longer-term goal to achieve a 75 percent reduction, commensurate with one-planet living, by 2050 (City of Vancouver 2011).

Ecological footprint analysis can be equally illuminating for rural communities. During 2007, the amount of people living in a rural area dropped below 50 percent — but migration of rural residents toward cities does not necessarily reduce the rural community footprint. Rural large-lot development, often viewed as an environmentally friendly form of development and supported in plans and bylaws, should properly be classified as rural sprawl. Impacts and costs such as loss of wildlife habitat, resource consumption and stormwater contamination associated with urban, suburban and rural sprawl are not equal and can be viewed as a continuum, increasing as lot size increases. Rural sprawl may well be the most damaging and costly form of sprawl (Buchan 2004).

What sprawl (both urban and rural) demonstrates is that it is the pattern of growth, rather than the amount of growth, that is the critical determinant of levels and efficiency of resource use and of traffic congestion. They also show that a critical sustainability objective for our communities is more efficient use of urban space. Cities and rural districts have enormous opportunities to solve environmental challenges; they can and must pioneer new approaches to sustainable development and community management. Local governments must assume the responsibility and marshal the resources to address the sustainability problems facing their communities (ICLEI 2002).

Toward Sustainable Communities

It's been a quarter-century since the Brundtland Commission named our problem, two decades since the United Nations Conference on Environment and Development produced the Rio Declaration that spelled out principles for sustainable development and more than 15 years since the Kyoto Protocol set ambitious and internationally endorsed targets for reducing greenhouse gases in the Earth's atmosphere that induce climate change. Although the learning continues, one key insight has become crystal clear: for anything to happen on a global level, change must first come from local communities. In fact, it's only at the community scale that we can actually demonstrate that sustainable development is possible — and thus scale it up. And as it turns out, many of these issues are far more manageable on the community scale. This book reveals the diverse and numerous paths that can lead all of us toward sustainable communities by bringing together a broad range of ideas about urban planning, transportation, public health, housing, energy,

economic development, natural habitats, public participation and social justice.

There are a variety of terms related to *sustainable communities* used by people in this field, including sustainable urban development, eco-cities, resilient cities and urban sustainability. I prefer the terms *sustainable communities* and *sustainable community development* because: 1) they acknowledge the majority of small and mid-sized human settlements that don't see themselves as "cities," 2) they relate to the 25-plus-year discourse of sustainable development (widely understood to have three components: environment, economy, and society) and 3) they are community-focused and solutions-oriented with respect to all three of these dimensions.

As I have written about elsewhere (e.g., see Roseland 2000), there is a long-standing conceptual core foundation for what I call sustainable communities. However, whether we call them ecocities or bioregions or sustainable urban development, the important point is that we can fairly easily distinguish those ideas and practices from the conventional urban development ideas and practices that are dominant throughout most of the world.

Within this still-emerging synthesis lies a vision of a better society, but it continues to be overshadowed by spiraling ecological degradation, economic dysfunction and social inequity. Our challenge is to keep focused on this bigger picture and on advancing together where we can agree.

Sustainable community development is about where and how we live, whether in villages, towns, suburbs or mega-cities. It is about what some people call *human settlements*.

Whenever agricultural or forest land is cleared for other purposes, whenever roads are built or expanded, whenever a new shopping center or subdivision is created, whenever an urban area is "redeveloped" — in short, whenever the natural or built environment is changed through human action, the health of our communities and our planet is affected. Sustainable community development is universal and can be applied at any scale, although its applications must be tailored to each unique situation and respect local conditions and opportunities (Roseland 1997).

So what could sustainable communities actually look like?

Let's revisit that excellent definition penned by those astute Minnesota citizens. A sustainable community is one that:

> uses its resources to meet current needs while ensuring that adequate resources are available for future generations. It seeks a better quality of life for all its residents while maintaining nature's ability to function over time by minimizing waste, preventing pollution, promoting efficiency and developing local resources to revitalize the local economy. Decision-making in a sustainable community stems from a rich civic life and shared information among community members. A sustainable community resembles a living system in which human, natural and economic elements are interdependent and draw strength from each other.

This last phrase hints at an important insight from the field of urban ecology: environmental politics must pay as much, if not more, attention to the qualities of the built environment as it now typically does to a fictitiously separated and imagined "natural" environment. Communities should thus be viewed as ecosystems, nested within larger ecosystems. Like natural systems such as lakes or forests, they transform energy (human labor, capital, fossil fuels) and materials (timber, iron, sand and gravel, information, etc.) into products that are consumed or exported and into by-products. In natural systems, these by-products are recycled, but often in our communities, they go unused as wastes. By analyzing the flow of materials, people, energy, capital and waste in our community ecosystems, we can identify opportunities to reorganize our activities and re-integrate them with natural processes. In doing so, we can use resources more efficiently, minimize or discover new uses for waste, and make energy go further (Newman & Jennings 2008).

At least part of the solution involves reversing what Newman and Kenworthy (1999) refer to as the most unsustainable form of human settlement yet developed: the low-density, automobile-dependent suburb. To address this relatively recent phenomenon, they recommend that we make cities more urban and the countryside more rural.

The former can be accomplished by "re-urbanizing" city centers and sub-centers, re-orienting transport infrastructure away from the automobile, removing subsidies on the automobile, and providing a more public-oriented urban culture, assisted by attractive urban design (townscapes, streetscapes, malls and squares), and by *traffic calming* measures that facilitate bicycle and pedestrian use of residential areas and major roads. Making the countryside more rural can be accomplished by means such as protecting and encouraging sustainable agriculture and forestry in rural areas and moving towards bioregionalism (for example, substituting human-made resource management area boundaries with the actual boundaries of air- and watersheds) as the basis of local government boundaries and responsibilities.

For any given locale, the ideal form of human settlement should take cues from energy supply options: for example, higher densities make most efficient use of district heating and public transport networks, while lower densities may make solar energy more viable. The location, gross density and form of new development should therefore be determined in conjunction with programs for energy supply and conservation technologies (CitiesPlus 2003). Land-use planning becomes synonymous with community energy planning.

This more bioregional approach also suggests a direction for sustainable development of large cities. In contrast to development that favors a highly developed center, the constant incursion of sprawl into undeveloped countryside and ever-lengthening commutes and supply routes, a more "nodal" approach should be employed. This would promote the development of more complete, compact, walkable and transit-friendly communities, concentrated around neighborhood centers that have been selected as a compromise between "ideal" centers — which would be selected according to the natural features of the landscape such as ridge lines and steep slopes — and the existing centers. Surrounded by a greenbelt and connected by a well-designed transit system, cities can grow vertically rather than horizontally — allowing surrounding lands to be reclaimed as open space, forests, agricultural land and wildlife habitat. This pattern of growth benefits people and the environment. As Figure 2.1 shows, Chicago planners have already embraced this concept: compare their projections of unchecked business-as-usual patterns of growth with one that locates community centers along well-serviced transit corridors. (see Fig. 2.1, color page C-1)

Images of Sustainable Communities

To visualize the trajectory of more sustainable community development, it is helpful to contrast its outcome with that of the status quo.

Fig. 2.2: A Nodal Vision of Urban Development: These images by Eco-City Builders Founder Richard Register show Berkeley in its present state (left), and project forward to how it could look in 25 to 90 years (middle), and in 40 to 125 years (right). They suggest a sustainable trajectory of development in which cities choose to check sprawl by concentrating new development into smaller, walkable centers, each sited to best ecological advantage. Over time, this allows rehabilitation of surrounding land for purposes such as production of food and other necessities, enhancement of biodiversity and recreation. This development path can ensure sufficient population density and a healthy mix of services, housing types and jobs that help make low- or no-carbon alternatives to cars, such as walking, cycling and high-quality transit, more socially and economically viable.

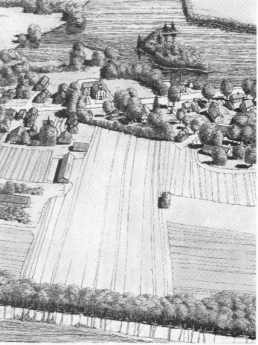

Fig. 2.3:
Preserving Rural Beauty and Function. These images by Dodson and Associates Ltd. illustrate that the same concept can be applied to rural areas. Compare the effects of development on the beauty, character and natural capital of a rural community before development (top left), after conventional development (top right) and following a more creative approach to development (below).
(CREDIT: DODSON & ASSOCIATES LTD.)

In their classic 1988 work, Yaro et al. set out practical planning standards that rural New England towns can adopt to protect their distinctive character, while at the same time accommodate economic growth. Illustrating actual sites in western Massachusetts, their drawings show each site before development, after conventional development and after what the authors call "creative development" (Figure 2.3). In both development schemes, the same number of units has been added. While they have many differences, the most critical is that the conventional approach dramatically alters the land-use pattern (e.g., agricultural lands are lost to suburban sprawl), while the creative approach absorbs growth without destroying future options (e.g., natural capital, in the form of agricultural land, remains intact).

The principle used in Massachusetts is equally applicable today, as is demonstrated

Fig. 2.4: *Five city blocks for the footprint of one. Richard Register considers how the services and housing in five loosely planned city blocks could be provided in one highly walkable, multi-leveled ecovillage, replete with more interesting architecture, greenery and greenhouses, pedestrian overpasses and strategically sited buildings that make best use of natural light, heat and shade.*
(CREDIT: RICHARD REGISTER)

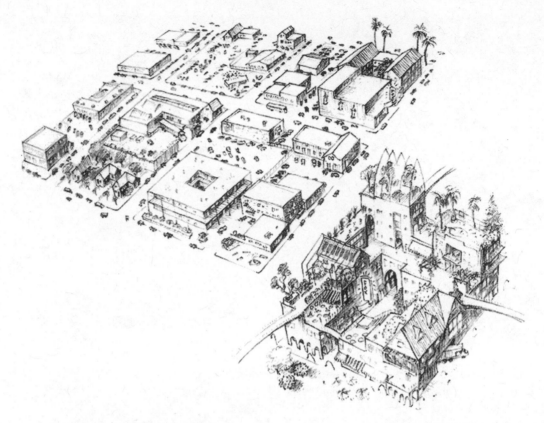

by the visualization (CALP 2010) of alternate futures for the low-lying British Columbia district municipality of Delta. It will likely cope with climate change-induced sea-level rise in the coming century that will threaten the community's agricultural lands. Delta could rezone its agricultural land and populate it with detached, single-family homes. Alternatively, Delta could choose to make its center more dense with a greater variety of housing types, services and transit, thereby preserving precious agricultural land (see Fig. 2.5, color page C-1).

The following two illustrations (CALP 2010) help us visualize greater sustainability at the neighborhood level. Figure 2.6 shows two different visions for Kingsway, a busy traffic artery connecting Vancouver, British Columbia, with the suburb of Burnaby. Note how a sustainable city vision can transform the present incarnation of auto-dominated growth into a more vital and livable realization of many of the concepts discussed in this book: mixed-use zoning; streets devoted to walking, cycling and public transport; heavy reliance on renewable energy sources; rooftop gardens and greenery; and ample public space for social interactions.

As the following visualization shows, the same ideas can be applied to the suburbs. Figure 2.7 reveals how the concepts in this book can enhance the livability and affordability of suburban neighborhoods, through emphasis on more live/work arrangements, local businesses, greener infrastructure, energy efficiency, renewable energy, community gardens and pleasant public spaces, and greater transportation mode choice.

In many communities, forward-thinking people are already applying these concepts at the block level. They're living in new co-housing developments, and discovering how to retrofit co-housing to existing housing stock. For example, some neighbors in single-family detached housing have chosen to remove the fences from their individual backyards and repurpose underutilized garages, attics and basements to create a kind of "village cluster" that boasts greater variety of housing options, dramatically enhanced shared space, opportunities for urban agriculture, some shared tools and equipment and a common house. Such arrangements can easily accommodate small or home-based businesses; they could be designed to "recycle" obsolete corporate/industrial parks, shopping centers and office complexes. As the lifestyle and economic advantages (such as lower housing costs, a greater sense of community and the capacity to accommodate a greater range of ages, abilities and family sizes) become clear, residents choose from many possible forms of ownership, from condominium corporations to a non-profit corporation with resident control, limited-equity cooperatives, community land trusts or mutual housing associations.

Sustainable community development today is as much a matter of "how" as it is of "what." We know what we need to do: greener buildings, cleaner energy and so forth. The challenge is how to actually make progress in each of these areas. Chapter 3 addresses this question by focusing on making community policy, which

Fig. 2.6a, b: *More sustainable urban futures. These visualizations by David Flanders show an unremarkable urban streetscape redesigned for a low-carbon world. In it, we will find: zoning for mixed uses; streets made more amenable to walking, cycling and public transport; heavy reliance on renewable energy sources; rooftop gardens and greenery; and ample public space for social interaction.* (Credit: David Flanders, UBC-CALP)

in turn provides a foundation for examining each of the sustainable community building blocks in part 2.

a

b

Fig. 2.7 a, b: *Suburban neighborhoods come back to life. As Jon Laurenz shows us, more sustainable futures for suburbia include a better mix of housing types and work opportunities, more energy-efficient homes, productive community gardens, markets supplying local foods and infrastructure that supports a greater variety of transit modes.* (CREDIT: JON LAURENZ, UBC-GREENSKINSLAB)

- If we wait for the governments, it'll be too little, too late.
- If we act as individuals, it'll be too little.
- But if we act as communities, it might just be enough, just in time.

— Hopkins 2011 (p. 17)

Chapter 3

Making Community Policy

There are many ways to mobilize citizens and their governments toward sustainable communities, but there are also many barriers and obstacles that hamper our progress in this direction. We cannot realistically expect most people to choose sustainable options if they appear to be more difficult or expensive than unsustainable choices. The question arises, then, how can we change the systems around us, level the playing field and provide ample opportunities for individuals to make behavioral choices that improve their communities? Innovative approaches are required to recalibrate values based on sustainability, as described in chapters 1 and 2, with *policy* levers that balance regulation and market-oriented approaches to renovating existing and creating new forms of sustainable development.

This chapter begins by reviewing the policy process, understanding how policy instruments, strategies and actors function within the policy process: who are the actors involved in making community policy? What kinds of strategies can be used? What kinds of policy instruments are available? And how can we align these actors, strategies and instruments toward sustainable communities? Second, we take a closer look at market mechanisms for sustainable community development in the context of the policy process, an exciting area of policy development for sustainable development. We then examine in more detail four categories of policy instruments, showing how each is and can be used by local governments in North America and beyond. Each of these four categories of instruments — voluntary initiatives, financial incentives, expenditure and regulation — is described and illustrated with examples from various jurisdictions. These categories are used as a way to organize the tools and initiatives presented in each of the chapters on a sustainable community building blocks" that follow in part 2. Next, the chapter provides a specific focus on local governments (critical actors in sustainable community development). We look at an example of how to advance sustainability in the marketplace and at municipal tax-shifting for emissions reduction. Finally, we conclude with a discussion of constraints on implementation and ideas for how to overcome those barriers.

The Policy Process

Like just about everything else in our society, choices about sustainability exist in the context of market forces and, to varying degrees, the regulation of those forces. But who has the power to make such choices? Several *actors* can be identified. These include individuals, firms, government, what is sometimes referred to as a social or third sector based on voluntary initiative, as well as combinations of one or more of these types. Community actors define the community's values and visions and influence and/or participate in its formal (and informal) governance, which is explored further in chapter 15. These in turn shape the identification of issues and the design of policies. Policies themselves create community and market signals that influence actions and shape community outcomes (as measured by changes in human, social, cultural, natural, physical and economic capital). The outcomes in turn influence every aspect of the community, from the creation of new actors to the revision of policies (Hendrickson et al. 2011).

Policy *strategies* that help move all of these actors towards more sustainable behavior can be classified into three broad approaches: *price-based*, *rights-based*, and *market friction reduction*. Price-based approaches adjust the prices of goods and services to reflect environmental costs, while rights-based approaches assign rights and obligations to actors involved. Market friction reduction approaches seek to improve the efficiency of the market (Whitten, Bueren & Collins, 2003).

There are numerous policy *instruments* that local governments can use to set up conditions conducive to more sustainable behavior. Using a framework developed by Jacobs (1993), this book classifies policy instruments into four types: voluntary initiatives, financial incentives, expenditure and regulation. In recent years, there has been increasing interest in the use of specifically market-based approaches, or "economic instruments," in environmental policy. These tools influence the behavior of economic agents by providing financial incentives to environmentally improved behavior,

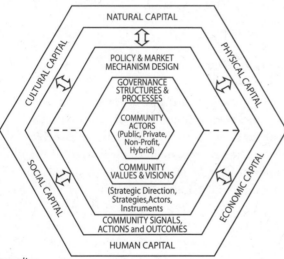

Fig. 3.1:

Making community policy

builds on the community capital framework (Figure 1, in chapter 1) of six capital types coordinated, balanced and catalyzed by community mobilization. Here community mobilization is represented by the nested hexagons that are read from the inside out. Community actors define the community's values and visions that influence and/or participate in its formal (and informal) governance. These in turn shape the identification of issues and the design of policies. Policies themselves create community and market signals that influence actions and shape community outcomes (as measured by changes in natural, physical, economic, human, social and cultural capital). The outcomes in turn influence every aspect of the community, from the creation of new actors to the revision of policies. (CREDIT: HENDRICKSON ET AL., 2011) or disincentives to damaging behavior. Such policy instruments — taxes, charges, subsidies, tradable permits, deposit-refund schemes, performance bonds and so on — have been particularly favored within the discipline of environmental economics, where they originated.

As this book will show, each type of instrument offers opportunities to utilize market mechanisms as a means of allocating resources efficiently and incentivizing more sustainable behavior. Thanks largely to insights from the field of environmental economics, market mechanisms are being fruitfully applied in areas such as transportation, climate change, biodiversity conservation and energy consumption (Engel, Pagiola & Wunder 2008; Eriksson, Nordlund & Garvill 2010; Roseland & Jacobs 1995).

It is important to understand that economic instruments should not be viewed in isolation. In practice, they are inextricably part of a structure and process of community management that in turn reflects wider and holistic objectives — environmental, economic, social and ethical — in society.

Policy and Market Mechanisms

Markets are where goods and services are bought and sold, governed by supply and demand. Market prices influence the nature of a product and service; its supply and demand; individual decisions; and the business climate of market actors (such as governments, businesses, associations and non-profits). Markets can provide feedback, foster innovation and allocate resources.

Market *mechanisms* are interventions in the operation and functioning of the market that help to stimulate sustainable outcomes and discourage unsustainable ones in a number

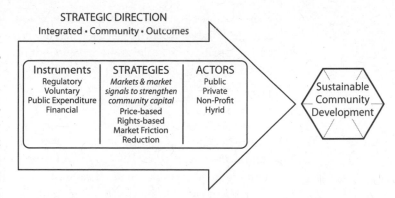

of ways. In theory, market mechanisms can: 1) reduce the economic costs of achieving particular targets (such as environmental protection) to allow actors greater flexibility in how they comply through cost-effective manners, 2) create technological innovation because they stimulate economic incentives (e.g., tax reductions, tradable permits) as cost-effective means of achieving targets, 3) generate revenue because resources are used for related activities or government spending, 4) increase client flexibility by selecting a convenient service and greater user choice (e.g., school vouchers) and 5) increase transparency and accountability of information flows, such as cost permits for reducing greenhouse gas emissions (Hendrickson et al. 2011).

However, many analysts question the reliance on markets as arbiters of the value of social, economic or environmental policy-making. They suggest that conventional market mechanisms are inadequate to preserve biophysical resources, reduce greenhouse gas emissions and align economic drivers with sustainable development principles.

The market approach can be contrasted by or used in combination with an ecological economics perspective that prioritizes the scale of the economy to the relative size of the

Fig. 3.2:
Making community policy for sustainable community development means focusing on integrating and aligning strategic direction, using markets and market signals to strengthen community capital. This process involves actors (private, public, non-profit, hybrid), strategies (price-based, rights-based, market-friction-reduction) and instruments (voluntary, regulatory, financial, public expenditure), aligned together toward sustainable community development.
(CREDIT: HENDRICKSON ET AL. 2011)

ecosystem. Conventional market mechanisms assume a weak sustainability perspective because distribution, scale and access to public goods are not directly addressed in pursuit of profit. As discussed in chapter 1, weak sustainability implies that natural capital, or the Earth's natural resources and ecological systems that provide life-support services for communities, can be exchanged or substituted with manufactured, non-natural capital.

Sustainable community development, on the other hand, assumes a strong sustainability perspective. Strong sustainability implies maintaining and, in many cases, regenerating life-support services, such as clean water and air, biological and genetic diversity and soil fertility. These forms of natural capital have no substitutes because they are essential to human survival.

In the current financial climate of doing more with less, decision-makers are seeking to employ market mechanisms in ways that embrace sustainable community development principles. Market mechanisms for sustainable community development are tools, policies and practices expressly designed to influence market decisions, consumer behavior, market structures and access to resources that advance sustainable community development principles. Examples include a local government procurement strategy that favors a local supplier to support the local economy, or an incentive to support a specific product or environmentally friendly purchase (e.g., a hybrid car instead of a sports utility vehicle).

Market mechanisms do not act in isolation of policy formation but are implemented, assessed and linked to targets, metrics and action plans. Examples include green development bonuses, corporate social responsibility programs,

energy pricing structures, green procurement programs, affordable housing, employer subsidized transit passes and cap-and-trade emission credits. Market mechanisms for sustainable community development can foster greater accountability, transparency, strategic direction and outcomes to complement conventional economic doctrine because they are designed to: 1) acknowledge that all policies impact the market, 2) challenge popular notions that certain mechanisms, such as incentives are always market-friendly, while environmental regulations always impede market efficiencies (for example, that a carbon tax will unduly impede the economy rather than drive innovation), 3) optimize environmental, social, and economic benefits rather than assume short-term economic benefits are always in a community's best interest and 4) question whether economies can grow indefinitely when physical and resource constraints are directly linked to finite ecosystems (Hendrickson et al. 2011).

POLICY INSTRUMENTS

This book provides numerous examples of how policy instruments are employed to achieve community objectives like these through chapters that focus on topics such as water, waste, energy, climate, transportation, land use, housing, community economic development, green building and climate change. Of course, not every example is applicable to every community: local circumstances will determine the most appropriate policy option.

Two target populations for policy instruments can be identified: the general public and individual firms or industries. The use of instruments to influence the behavior of the public can be called *demand management* (see chapters on energy, water, transportation and community economic development). Since supply of resources can only be augmented to a certain point, this inherently requires that demand for resources be managed.

Policy instruments that try to move firms and industries toward sustainability are not generally considered to be demand management, but they too serve the purpose of reducing aggregate resource consumption. They represent a notable departure from traditional engineering approaches that tend toward expansion of infrastructure and augmentation of supply.

For communities to move effectively toward sustainability, citizens and their governments should understand the range of policy instruments available to them and the wider context of how community policy is made.

As discussed above, this book uses a framework developed by Jacobs (1993) to classify policy instruments available to local government into four types: voluntary initiatives, financial incentives, expenditure and regulation. The Jacobs framework is summarized below:

- Voluntary Initiatives
  - Volunteers, volunteer associations, and non-governmental organizations
  - Information dissemination
  - Technical assistance
- Financial Incentives
  - Pricing
  - Taxes and charges
  - Subsidies and tax incentives
  - Grants and loans
  - Vouchers
  - Surety bonds
- Expenditure
  - Monitoring
  - Contracting and procurement
  - State enterprise
  - Public-private partnerships
- Regulation
  - Laws and standards
  - Licenses and permits
  - Tradable permits
  - Quid pro quos

Generally speaking, *voluntary initiatives* describe actions taken by individuals and firms of their own accord, and to which government offers supports such as information and technical assistance. *Financial incentives* include measures that change the cost/benefit equation in order to make sustainable activities more attractive, and many make smart use of market mechanisms. *Expenditure* more directly involves government operations and budgets, and includes elements such as fiscal policy. *Regulation* proscribes the legal requirements and boundaries for action by individuals, business and the social sector (Hendrickson et al. 2011).

Each type of instrument is explained in greater detail below and illustrated by real-life examples, most of which are elaborated on in the following chapters. As you will see, many of these examples could reasonably be classified as more than one type. Almost any government activity (even policy-making), for example, involves some expenditure of public funds; similarly, many forms of regulation serve to support volunteer initiatives or serve as a financial incentive. The point is not to draw hard-and-fast distinctions between policy instrument types, but to suggest the overall range and types of available instruments and explain how they work.

Voluntary Initiatives

Many actors take voluntary actions towards sustainability, and there are many ways that local governments can support and encourage such efforts. In addition to fostering a sense of community, volunteer effort can accomplish great changes, while reducing costs to government and regulatory burdens. An example is the European Union Eco-label, a voluntary labeling scheme that provides manufacturers with an incentive to produce environmentally friendly products and services, while enabling consumers to differentiate their purchases on the basis of environmental criteria (European Commission 2011). A similar initiative called

Advancing Sustainability in the Marketplace
By Coro Strandberg

The business case for sustainability has been made. Today, "corporate social responsibility" (CSR) is considered a business imperative — a route to game-changing innovation and shareholder value. CSR is mainstreaming.

Leading CSR companies generate improved benefits for communities and the environment. They reduce product and operational waste, energy use and greenhouse gas emissions, material and water consumption and emissions to air, land and water. They design products that take life-cycle impacts into account and source from green and socially responsible companies. Sustainability leaders provide living wages, improve the health and safety of their workplaces and train and hire people with employment barriers, such as low-skilled youth or new immigrants. Businesses committed to sustainability are community contributors, enhancing local social and environmental conditions through volunteering, in-kind assistance, partnerships and sponsorships.

The opportunity for local governments is to consider how to create an enabling environment to encourage more companies — large and small — to become CSR champions. First, walk the talk. Municipalities which expect businesses to improve their social and environmental impacts need to be leaders themselves, within their own operations. Municipalities can adopt sustainability commitments for how they do business day to day and incorporate these commitments into their purchasing, hiring and workplace practices. They can have a CSR lens on decisions, whether these relate to capital projects, land-use plans, budgets or business plans. By measuring, improving and reporting their social and environmental performance, local governments can showcase how they expect organizations in their jurisdiction to operate. And, as CSR role models, they can share their experience with others to encourage replication.

In addition to internalizing a sustainability ethic in their management practices, local governments can support businesses to follow suit by providing a suite of how-to tools such as metrics, case studies, online calculators and best practice tips. Compiling a directory of green and socially responsible vendors, products and services can help promote a sustainable supply chain in the region. Catalyzing reuse markets can advance a green economy. Some local governments provide sustainability awards to businesses, while others go further and support efforts to certify businesses that satisfy sustainability criteria to improve their success in the marketplace.

Local governments have many tools at their disposal beyond command-and-control regulation. Creating an enabling environment for business which incentivizes sustainable practices through the marketplace is a certain route to more sustainable communities locally and globally.

Eco-Logo has been launched in Canada (Environment Canada 2011).

VOLUNTEERS, VOLUNTEER ASSOCIATIONS AND NON-GOVERNMENTAL ORGANIZATIONS

Individuals and firms may carry out these activities by themselves, convene ad hoc associations or contribute through non-governmental organizations. They range from independent initiatives at the scale of one's own home, to more ambitious large-scale groups with government involvement.

An example of this is found in St. Paul, Minnesota, where some 23,000 volunteers have planted close to 60,000 native trees and shrubs and restored more than 2,000 acres of land in the Mississippi, Minnesota and St. Croix river valleys. A volunteer design team comprised of a landscape architect, a community representative and an ecologist drafted a plan for each parcel of land and cleared it with individual landowners (Great River Greening 2011).

Similarly, the City of Kelowna, British Columbia, enlists the assistance of volunteers to help the City maintain and monitor sections of nearby creeks and streams to protect water quality and habitat for wildlife (City of Kelowna 2011).

INFORMATION

Government disseminates information to the public by means of public education or social marketing to encourage voluntary action towards more sustainable behavior; as well, it can serve as a repository of useful information. These can constitute effective forms of demand management.

The Power Smart energy conservation program of BC Hydro, British Columbia's energy utility, does exactly that (BC Hydro 2011).

Corporate Social Responsibility

Ceres is a broad coalition of environmental organizations and socially responsible investment groups, formed to promote environmental responsibility among businesses and local governments. In September 1989, Ceres set forth the Valdez Principles — named after the Exxon Valdez oil tanker spill in Alaska — as broad standards for evaluating corporate activities that directly or indirectly affect the biosphere. The principles were adopted in the hope of working with companies to create a voluntary mechanism of self-governance, and to help investors make informed decisions. The Valdez Principles call for elimination or minimization of pollution, sustainable use of natural resources, reduction and safe disposal of waste, energy conservation, environmental risk reduction, marketing of safe products and services, damage compensation, hazard disclosure, selection of environmental directors and managers and annual environmental audits.

Several governments and over 70 major corporations have signed the Valdez Principles or use environmental investment guidelines based on them. For example, corporate signatories include American Airlines, Coca Cola, Ben & Jerry's, Nike, The Body Shop, Interface and VanCity Savings.

Ceres provides information and assistance in relation to the Valdez Principles, corporate shareholder campaigns and community efforts to encourage local governments to adopt environmental investment policies (Ceres 2011).

Another example is found in Orange County, California, where the Municipal Water District offers a water management and irrigation certification course free of charge for landscapers called "Protector del Agua," originating from the Irrigation Training and Research Center at California Polytechnic University in San Luis Obispo (ConserVision Consulting 2009).

Government and community leaders can also encourage more sustainable behavior by issuing public statements. Official declarations and public recognition by local government of local sustainability champions can also provide powerful reinforcement.

TECHNICAL ASSISTANCE

Government may also provide expertise for individuals and firms in support of their voluntary initiatives. The Government of British Columbia has "business energy advisors" to advise participating firms on reducing energy consumption (Government of British Columbia 2011).

Financial Incentives

Financial incentives can utilize market forces for behavior change. Some may require regulatory support. Pricing, taxation, charges, subsidies, tax incentives, grants, loans, vouchers and surety bonds all fall under this category.

PRICING

As products of supply and demand, market-determined prices don't always reflect their true costs to people (in terms of social and health impacts, for example) or the environment (in terms of pollution, ecosystem degradation, species depletion or contribution to climate change). Compounding this problem are government policies that serve to artificially suppress input prices, and which amount to "perverse subsidies." They result when the positive effects of a subsidy are outweighed by its negative effects (van Beers & van den Bergh 2009). Examples include massive government subsidies to fossil fuel production, which lowers energy prices; provision of free or low-cost water, resulting in wasteful water use; "support" to fisheries resulting in over-exploitation, and government-financed road construction leading to overcutting of forests and habitat destruction (Brown 2010).

Perverse subsidies are often related to pressure by profit-seeking interests to subsidize unsustainable behavior and promote unlimited expansion and growth. Local governments should seek to identify and remove them, and seek more effective approaches to valuation of resources and monetization of pollution and ecological services. Examples can include ending the widespread practice of offering free or heavily subsidized parking, and moving from "blocky" lump-sum pricing on public services to graduated per-use pricing.

TAXES AND CHARGES

Taxes and charges can be applied to activities that generate negative impacts to help account for their costs, or simply to discourage unsustainable behaviors. For example, congestion charges and road pricing can help local governments recover some of the social costs of private automobile use. The Central London congestion-charging system has reduced car congestion by 30 percent and increased drivers' use of public transit (Transport for London 2004). System revenues support bicycle infrastructure improvements, transportation planning, infrastructure maintenance and development (Transport for London 2011).

In British Columbia, the provincial government introduced a revenue-neutral carbon tax that utilizes market mechanisms to reduce carbon emissions. What this means is that aggregate taxation remains the same, but income taxes have been reduced and partially replaced by a carbon tax on activities that contribute to the province's emissions (Province of British Columbia 2011).

Minneapolis, Minnesota, adopted a stormwater runoff charge for owners of residential, commercial and vacant properties. The charge is based on property type and the area of impervious surface on the property, which serves to incentivize property owners to incorporate stormwater management techniques that reduce the quantity or significantly improve the quality of stormwater runoff from their property (United States Environmental Protection Agency 2008).

SUBSIDIES AND TAX INCENTIVES

Subsidies and tax incentives are popular policy options for governments, as they enhance visibility and perception of active management of issues while encouraging more sustainable activities. Variations include rebates, rewards and vouchers.

New York State offers tax deductions for green roofs. New York City building owners who install vegetation on at least half their available roof space can offset $4.50 in property taxes for each square foot of green roof they install for one year, up to a maximum of $100,000 (New York City 2009).

Toronto, Ontario, offers a 28 percent discount from general water rates to firms that submit water conservation plans to the City's water conservation office. Plans must include details of a water-use audit and when and how the facility will implement audit recommendations (City of Toronto 2011).

Seattle, Washington, uses graduated disposal fees to encourage recycling: for example, recyclables can be dropped off free of charge, and the per-ton fee to dispose of a load of clean yard waste is 33 percent lower than for an equivalent amount of regular trash (City of Seattle 2011).

GRANTS AND LOANS

Local government can offer grants and loans to individuals and firms to support actions it would like to encourage, sustainability initiatives or development of green business or industry. When loans are offered at favorable rates or to actors who would have not been able to obtain a loan independently, they are in effect subsidies.

The New York Department of Environmental Protection distributed $3 million in grants through a green infrastructure grant program that encouraged individuals and firms to submit applications for projects that use green infrastructure to reduce the quantity of stormwater entering the system and reduce impervious surfaces in the city (New York Department of Environmental Protection 2011).

In the Netherlands, a *green fund* has been developed as a major source of private funding for ecological projects and investments. Financial institutions operate the fund, with investments certified and guaranteed by the government and interest made tax-free. Participating institutions must invest at least 70 percent of these funds into certified green projects. Funds have also supported projects in district heating, organic farming, ecological landscape restoration and sustainable buildings (Dagevos 2011).

VOUCHERS

Vouchers are a form of subsidy that can support sustainable choices, while allowing individuals and firms to choose what goods or services to subsidize. For example, an energy utility can provide its customers with coupons for the purchase of energy-efficient compact fluorescent light bulbs. Research suggests that people perceive discounts on regular prices as more of a benefit than an equivalent reduction in the regular price; purchase satisfaction is also increased (Darke 2003).

SURETY BONDS

Local governments can require surety bonds from actors as a condition of permit to undertake a given activity. These are cash deposits made by individuals or firms at the outset of an activity, which are refunded if the activity is successful. If not refunded, they can be spent by government on similar purposes. For example, the United States Surface Coal Mining and Reclamation Act of 1977 established cleanup performance requirements for abandoned mines and required surety bonds. In lieu of enforcing compliance, government may use posted funds to perform similar functions (Kysar 2010).

Expenditure

Expenditures involve use of public funds to support government policy goals. It can include procurement and spending activities as part of its own operations as well as those in the market. Monitoring, contracting, procurement, state enterprise and public-private partnerships also fall under this category.

The City of Vancouver, British Columbia, established a sewage waste-heat district heating system in the Olympic Village, the Southeast False Creek sustainable development built prior the Vancouver 2010 Winter Olympics. It is expected to reduce building-related greenhouse gas emissions as part of the City's efforts toward having all new developments be carbon-neutral by 2020 (City of Vancouver 2011).

MONITORING

Local government can promote sustainability by monitoring performance and compliance of individuals, firms and its own operations. For example, New York's Leak Detection Unit identified opportunities to save the City 225 million liters (60 million gallons) of water per day from leakage (NYCDEP 2003).

CONTRACTING AND PROCUREMENT

Government can make more environmentally sound choices in its own procurement practices for its operations, such as choosing hybrid and electric cars instead of sport-utility vehicles (Rahm & Coggburn 2007).

Portland, Oregon, is such an example. Its Sustainable Procurement Policy prioritizes public expenditure on goods and services that minimize negative environmental impacts, are fair and socially just and are fiscally responsible (City of Portland 2008).

Bellingham, Washington, began a green-power purchasing program by committing to purchase enough third-party certified renewable energy credits to offset 100 percent of the electricity used for the City's municipal operations (American Council on Renewable Energy 2010).

STATE ENTERPRISE

Government itself can undertake commercial activities that bring about more sustainable outcomes. These can include non-profit or community development corporations that finance and support particular interests. State enterprises should be differentiated from government agencies that operate purely toward policy goals, as well as conventional firms that are primarily profit-seeking.

British Columbia's Pacific Carbon Trust is an example of a state-owned corporation (*Crown corporation* in Canada) that facilitates the provincial government's efforts in carbon emissions trading within British Columbia. The Government of British Columbia is its sole shareholder (Pacific Carbon Trust 2011).

Aoimori Railway in Aoimori Prefecture, Japan, is an example of state enterprise in transportation. After private operators of the region's rail system upgraded their operations by introducing high-speed rail, the old tracks — which run parallel to the new system — were basically abandoned in places where the amount of local railway traffic made it uneconomic for them to operate. The government of Aoimori Prefecture became the majority shareholder of a new enterprise that operates these sections of the system, with local municipalities and a consortium of other investors holding minority stakes (Aoimori Prefectural Government 2011).

Public-Private Partnerships

Public-private partnerships are collaborations between government and firms to provide services and/or infrastructure. To the extent that firms can offer expertise and efficiencies in construction, operation and financing that publicly owned facilities can't, these collaborations can reduce costs for taxpayers.

One such partnership in Olds, Alberta, saw the town upgrade its old and at-capacity wastewater treatment plant through a system in which a bacterial treatment is injected into the wastewater pipes before wastewater reaches the treatment plant. This project increased the plant's capacity at no additional cost to the municipality (Federation of Canadian Municipalities 2011).

Regulation

Regulations are specific statutory requirements set by government that individuals and firms must comply with. Carbon emissions legislation specifying annual reductions in British Columbia and California are examples of regulation. Laws, standards, licenses, permits and quid pro quos all fall under this category. For example, government can limit water contamination from industrial activities by requiring wastewater treatment. Building code and zoning laws can be used to encourage particular types of community development. Governments can also support sustainability by changing or eliminating laws (deregulation), such as those which artificially suppress energy prices.

Laws and Standards

A simple law can have significant effects. A law requiring water meters on residential properties, for example, can curtail wasteful water usage by making property owners accountable for associated costs (City of Calgary 2010).

Westchester County, New York, bans disposal of all cell phones and their batteries in regular trash; all handsets and batteries must be collected at county-certified facilities (Rechargeable Battery Recycling Corporation 2011).

Santa Monica has set standards for recycling space in new buildings. Residential buildings with 10 units must allocate 9 square meters (100 square feet) to recycling, and additional area for additional units. The standard is similar for commercial buildings (City of Santa Monica 2011).

LICENSES AND PERMITS

Licenses and permits regulate specific behaviors and activities, such as building construction, industrial pollution and automobile use. A nominal fee may be charged for such items.

Boulder, Colorado, experienced extreme growth pressures of around 6 percent per year between 1960 and 1970. As a result, the City defined limits to growth in the city with a cap on new residential developments. Residential building permits were limited to 450 building permits per year (Fodor 1999).

TRADABLE PERMITS

Tradable permits provide additional flexibility for firms to comply with regulation. While the aggregate environmental impact is reduced, individual firms have the option to pay a premium to continue activities that government seeks to curtail. An example is emissions trading, which allows firms to exceed statutory emissions limits by purchasing quotas from other firms within limits. With regulatory support, this approach can function as a market mechanism. Emissions trading was successful in controlling sulfur dioxide emissions, nitrogen dioxide emissions and the associated acid rain in the United States (Rubin 2009).

QUID PRO QUOS

Governments may negotiate with firms to take certain actions in exchange for allowing them to engage in certain activities. For example, Sacramento, California, grants developers a 5 percent reduction in the amount of parking space they must provide in return for providing bicycle facilities, a 15 percent reduction for providing marked van- and carpool spaces, and a 60 percent reduction for purchasing transit passes for tenants of new offices. A variation on this theme may see government provide property to developers in exchange for particular types of development.

Local Government and Community Policy

Although the precise characteristics of sustainable community development in any particular place will be unique, movement toward sustainable communities can happen anywhere. Sustainable community development requires action to create viable local economies that are just, peaceful, resilient and eco-efficient.

Local government has an important role in meeting these objectives. Areas of local government involvement include ecologically efficient use of resources and their waste residues; energy-efficient transportation and land-use patterns; reduction of social and economic polarization; and the integration of marginalized people into efforts towards sustainable community development. Given these general concerns for local governments, some broad policy goals might include the following: reducing per capita car use; reducing per capita water consumption; increasing the percentage of local land in parks; and improving cycling and pedestrian infrastructure.

Local governments are ideally situated to enact some of these policies due to their role in providing goods and services that significantly influence local resource use. Examples include setting development patterns and charges, utilities standards, building codes, infrastructure, eco-industrial planning, local

Municipal Tax Shifting for Emissions Reduction

Like many communities in the province of British Columbia, West Vancouver has followed the provincial government's lead by aiming for substantive reductions in carbon emissions: targets include a 33 percent reduction from 2007 levels by 2020, and an 80 percent reduction by 2050. West Vancouver is a mid-sized community with an unusually high percentage of residential buildings; these produce the majority of the municipality's emissions. Because the municipality is constrained by jurisdictional limitations from addressing the other major source of emissions in the district — transportation — a significant portion of homeowners will need to retrofit their buildings to reduce emissions from energy consumption in order to help the community meet its targets and thereby avoid the cost of carbon offsets to cover its emissions. How can this be accomplished in a manner that effectively rewards homeowners who retrofit, and without increasing the overall tax burden?

One approach could see the municipal government restructure its property tax calculation, shifting the municipal portion of property tax away from the current property value-based regime and onto an emissions-based regime. Emissions generation could be measured by energy use. By allocating the municipal portion of property tax on tons of carbon emissions assessed by government inventory rather than on aggregate real estate value, the municipal government could derive a per-ton charge for emissions. This could be applied in a revenue-neutral fashion, with no net change in taxation.

Let's look at how this would play out with five residential properties (numbered 1 to 5 below) with nearly identical property values but very different patterns of energy use. Under the current property tax regime, all five property owners pay the same rate of tax. But if taxes were assessed based on energy use, homes 2 and 3 would have a strong incentive to reduce consumption

and/or retrofit their properties to increase energy efficiency, and their unsustainable lifestyles would no longer be subsidized by owners of homes 1, 4 and 5. These more conservative users of energy would thereby reap the financial rewards of their more sustainable behaviors.

Under an emissions-based regime like this, all property owners would be accountable for their own emissions, with the heaviest emitters paying more and conservative users less. No one would be forced to change their behavior, but when held financially accountable for their own behavior, they may well consider the opportunity to do so. As well, they can determine how they will reduce energy use. The most incentivized to reduce their emissions would be the heaviest emitters, which would produce the most significant impact on municipal emissions as a whole.

The model predicts that as property owners find ways to reduce their emissions, municipal tax revenue could decrease. But this need not reduce the total of municipal tax revenue: as in a conventional tax regime based on property values, the municipality has the ☞

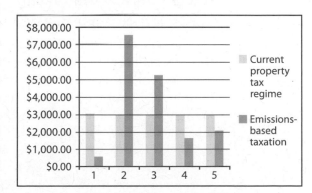

Fig. 3.3. *Comparison of property taxes for five houses with different energy use patterns, as calculated under a conventional tax regime and an emissions-based tax regime.*

option to readjust the per-ton emissions charge annually to reflect the demands of municipal expenditures. Under this regime, which assesses property owners' emissions relative to those of other property owners, there would be continuous competition to become more efficient. The system would be self-reinforcing, in that it continues to reward those who are at the head of the pack in terms of sustainability choices.

economic investment, regional competitiveness and workforce education. Municipalities remain pivotal in the allocation and provision of services such as water, sewage, waste collection, public transit, land-use planning, libraries, public safety, animal control and economic development (Madsen 2004).

Local jurisdictions can apply market mechanisms for sustainable community development. Market mechanisms oriented to sustainable development offer municipal officials a toolkit of market and regulatory approaches to target inherently unsustainable community development and respond to complex realities such as air pollution, homelessness and greenhouse gas emissions (Boli & Emtairah 2001).

Recognizing and Overcoming Constraints on Implementation

As previously noted, many of these policy instruments could be classified as more than one type. The critical challenge, however, is not in sorting the instruments by category, but in determining which instrument best suits the unique needs of a given community.

Governments facing declining revenues and increasing demand for services have tough decisions to make. In the past, regulation was the instrument of choice, but in many jurisdictions, associated enforcement and compliance costs make it the instrument of last resort. Increasingly attractive to local government are policy options that promote voluntary initiatives, as well as those that eliminate perverse subsidies and utilize market mechanisms to better account for true costs. They have the obvious advantages of imposing comparatively little financial and regulatory burden to government, holding individuals and firms more accountable for their decisions while leaving them with options, and rewarding those who make sustainable choices by releasing them from price structures that would otherwise force them to subsidize the unsustainable activities of others. In either case, local governments weighing the merits of regulation versus market mechanisms need to bear in mind that regulation is not necessarily unfriendly to business and markets — on the contrary, most industries welcome and benefit from some level of regulation. Conversely, the use of market mechanisms is not necessarily more likely to produce outcomes comparable to those of laissez faire markets (Hendrickson et al. 2011; Jacobs 1993).

Jurisdictional issues must also be considered. Local government jurisdiction also varies widely across regional and international boundaries. Jurisdictional authority of Canadian municipalities, for example, is more limited than among their American counterparts, which also vary by considerably by state. Some instruments may be more appropriately implemented at a regional or national level,

while others may be more suitable for local municipalities.

This book embraces the principle of subsidiarity, which suggests that policy decisions should be made at the most local level possible, while balancing the recognition that local areas are parts of larger systems and do not exist in isolation (Marshall 2008). Although lacking the broad jurisdiction and power of more senior governments, local governments are better positioned to formulate policy that is suited to the unique environmental, economic and social circumstances of their own communities. Indeed, where senior governments are unwilling or unable to show leadership in meeting the sustainability challenge, the following chapters demonstrate that local communities can develop the innovative policies to advance the sustainability agenda.

Fig. 3.4: *Eco-City Builders founder Richard Register has spent most of his adult life considering how cities can be designed and rebuilt to be ecologically healthy, beautiful and enjoyable places to live. His drawings illustrate many creative ideas. Here, he visualizes San Francisco's Union Square (left) as a car-free zone with creative architectural enhancements, multiple levels and walkways for pedestrians and cyclists, re-opened waterways, resplendent greenery and plenty of productive greenhouses nearby.*

(Credit left: ruthbruin2002 ("Ruth L") on Flickr, Creative Commons; Credit right: Richard Register)

Opportunities in Sustainability

The Natural Step is a Swedish not-for-profit organization that responded to the Brundtland Report (World Commission on Environment and Development 1987) by developing a comprehensive framework that helps organizations develop practical approaches to sustainability while realizing new opportunities, reduced costs and dramatically reduced ecological and social impacts. Specifically, its focus is on applying outcome-oriented planning to sustainability principles and planning methodology (The Natural Step 2011).

Many firms have gone on to show that, through more intelligent designs that mimic natural biological systems, it is indeed possible to develop manufacturing processes and products that are more efficient and less wasteful. By adopting a business model that recognizes that accumulated goodwill serves to differentiate themselves from the competition, firms prove that they can become more sustainable *and* more competitive (Hawken 1999).

The example of Interface, a carpet manufacturer, shows how firms can operationalize the *Natural Capitalism* approach described by Hawken (1999). In its Shanghai manufacturing operations, the firm redesigned processes to reduce energy requirements by 92 percent, thereby reducing construction costs in the process and increasing efficiency, all while requiring no technological changes. Innovations in materials produced a product of superior strength, lower resource input and higher recyclability. Offering flexible new business models that removed the "lumpy" nature of carpet ownership, the firm went from a seller of carpets to a floor-covering service. Their new approach significantly reduced the amount of carpet waste (Lovins, Lovins & Hawken 1999).

In *Climate Capitalism: Capitalism in the Age of Climate Change*, Lovins and Cohen (2011) argue that business has a central role to play in meeting the challenges of climate change. Currently, energy prices reflect government interventions in fossil fuels and renewable energies that amount to "perverse subsidies," with consequently harmful environmental impacts. By recognizing the reality of climate change, firms will be well positioned to identify new opportunities and solutions that highlight efficiency, innovation and market solutions.

Part 2

Sustainable Community Building Blocks

The framework introduced in part 1 proposes that applying the concept of sustainable development to North American communities requires mobilizing citizens and their governments to strengthen all forms of community capital. Community mobilization is necessary to coordinate, balance and catalyse community capital. This section of the book, part 2, is a set of sustainable community building blocks. Each chapter provides an overview explaining the topic and its relevance to sustainable communities, followed by a set of planning tools, practical initiatives and associated resources that have helped citizens and their governments move toward sustainable communities. While not every tool will "fit" every community, many of them will fit quite well.

Since the powers of municipal and local governments vary considerably, proponents of sustainable community initiatives must research their issues and fashion an approach that works within the specific legal framework of their jurisdiction. For example, a creative municipal solid waste management bylaw will have to fit the specific municipal situation, as well as the legislative framework of the province or state.

Chapter 4

Cultivating Greener, Food-secure Communities

Imagine your community made greener and more abundant in locally grown, readily available food. What might it include? Streets lined with fruit and nut trees, creeks meandering through urban neighborhoods, window boxes bursting with geraniums and fragrant basil, rooftops that host grasses and food production, wildflowers blooming amid rows of houses and vibrant, busy community gardens. Such integration of nature and communities can create healthy, civilizing and enriching places to live (Maller et al. 2005).

As important as envisioning what makes communities more green and abundant is identifying what does not. It is clear that many urban areas lack green space, especially in lower-income neighborhoods, but simply incorporating more flowers and grass is not a sustainable answer. For example, sod strips along boulevards and poorly designed playing fields and parks may soften concrete expanses and offer some recreational value, but demand costly amounts of water, fertilizer, herbicides and maintenance while contributing little in terms of wildlife habitat and food self-sufficiency.

North American communities of all sizes are waking up to the idea that we can do better. They have absorbed some fundamental insights of *urban ecology*, which studies the relationships between organisms in urban environments and views urbanized environments as part of living ecosystems. These include the recognition that nature, even in urban environments, provides extremely valuable environmental services — like cooling, water filtration, pest control, cleaning of our polluted air and absorption of carbon dioxide to help mitigate climate change. Unlike "conventional" greening, more sustainable approaches to greening take more realistic account of such services.

Moreover, reintegrating nature into our communities promises so much more. We can transcend the alienation between humans and the natural world that is a product of conventional community design, and which lulls many people into thinking that food comes from supermarkets, water comes from faucets, and wastes are simply taken "away." Reconsidering our communities as living ecosystems also expands our awareness of environmental issues, which we often associate with comparatively remote regions (such as species extinction and oil spills), to include those in our own backyards.

By adopting strategies and techniques that protect and restore ecology, we can reconnect with nature while we green and feed our communities. This chapter explores how communities are significantly enhancing these services through better land-use choices. These include preserving and restoring aquatic areas and open green space sustainably; incorporating site-appropriate plantings and green infrastructure into built environments; and cultivating places to support multiple functions such as food production, wildlife habitat,

recreation and beautification. As citizens and local governments have discovered, getting involved in community gardens, planting trees or participating in stream stewardship projects can improve our health, protect our ecosystem, foster local self-reliance, build community and even provide some of our food needs. Afterall, who doesn't enjoy a fresh home-grown tomato?

The Case for Greening

Although green spaces and greener infrastructure can certainly make our communities easier on the eyes, they also deliver the following benefits.

Save Money: The economic argument for green space and greener infrastructure is strong. Simply planting trees and using alternative ground cover to sod yields lower water, energy and maintenance. By providing shade, windbreaks and evapotranspiration (lowering

Bioregionalism

The term *bioregionalism* is the idea of being connected to the place we call home. It's about living within the ecological limits of our surrounding environment, thereby ensuring the region's ability to provide services (such as food or clear air and water) in the future (Gray 2007). The term comes from *bio*, the Greek word for "life," and *regio*, Latin for "territory to be ruled." Together they mean "a life-territory, a place defined by its life forms, its topography and its biota, rather than by human dictates; a region governed by nature, not legislature" (Sale 1985). It's a place where humans are part of the natural environment and strive to protect and restore it.

Bioregionalism's long-term goal of self-reliance, where most of the basic necessities of life are produced within the bioregion, is a fundamental concept that

will help us move toward creating sustainable communities (Carr 2004). Having "place-based knowledge" of the surrounding environment (such as cultural history and ecological knowledge), growing your own food or buying locally grown food, participating in political decision-making, as well as investing in the local economy through locally owned banks are all manifestations of bioregionalism. An example of bioregionalism can been observed in New Zealand, where local governments have observed the benefits of ecosystem services and redrawn boundaries based on watersheds (Gray 2007). By doing so, human society can be organized based on the ecological constraints of the watershed and live in a manner that protects and enhances the surrounding environment.

ambient temperatures), properly positioned trees cut about 25 percent of average annual residential energy costs (approximately $500) over a comparable house in an unsheltered area (USDOE 2005, as cited in Pimentel 2006). Green roofs (discussed later in this chapter) help insulate buildings and lower energy costs.

Regulate Temperatures: Urban areas are significantly hotter than surrounding rural areas. Dark heat-absorbing materials such as concrete and brick, the absence of tree or vegetative cover and waste heat from buildings, industry and automobiles all raise city temperatures. Highrises create an "urban canyon," trapping heat and restricting it from being released into the atmosphere (Alexandri & Jones 2008). In addition to exacerbating the effects of heat waves on public health, this *urban heat island effect* increases demand for air conditioning (Ihara et al. 2008). Scientists estimate the total electricity costs for offsetting the effects of heat islands in the US at more than $1 billion per year on energy bills (Akbari et al. 2008). Cities can counteract the heat island effect by planting more trees, increasing vegetated land within the city and using light-colored paints and building materials to reduce absorption of solar radiation. A 2006 study conducted in Tokyo suggests that strategic use of vegetation along building walls could reduce air temperature by 1.2 degrees Celsius and energy demands for cooling by 40 percent (Kikegawa et al. 2006).

Conserve Water: Sustainable landscaping, which emphasizes planting of indigenous species or native plants adapted to local climates and leaves some naturally vegetated areas untouched, requires less irrigation than non-native species. It can help communities achieve water conservation goals. Green roofs can also

Fig. 4.1: *Living walls or green walls are vertical gardens attached to the exterior or interior of a building. They do more than just beautify — they actually help improve air quality. This "Apartment therapy" by Green over Grey in a West End Vancouver loft incorporated 892 plants from 85 species into an 8'-by-16' wall.*
(Credit: Mike Weinmaster, Green over Grey, Living Walls and Design Inc.)

help communities reach water conservation goals by capturing and filtering rainwater, which can then be used for non-potable uses such as toilet flushing or irrigation.

Absorb Pollutants: Plants absorb carbon dioxide and other climate change-inducing

Fig. 4.2:
Community-supported agriculture programs, like this one at the South Coast Farms in San Juan Capistrano, not only delivers bins of fresh, local produce to subscribers, it also helps support the regional economy, secures the livelihood of local farmers and promotes a greater connection to food.
(CREDIT:
JODI LAOGSDON)

pollutants. It is estimated that one tree with a 50 m³ crown sequesters 11 kilograms of carbon a year (Leung et al. 2011).

Host Wildlife and Plants: Wild plant and animal populations have more than intrinsic value; they also serve as important proxy measures of the health and life-supporting capacity of entire ecosystems. But urbanization has radically impacted ecological processes and decimated wildlife habitat by disrupting migratory pathways and fragmenting forests and other ecosystems. Well-designed green space that incorporates the natural features of the area and maintains vegetation biodiversity can provide suitable habitat for breeding, protection from predators and food.

Manage Water Resources: Much of the rain that falls on impervious paved surfaces enters stormwater drains or nearby creeks or streams. Green infrastructure such as green roofs, vegetated swales and rainwater gardens can capture this stormwater runoff, filter out pollutants and recharge groundwater supplies.

Support Public Health: Community green spaces provide places to play, meditate, gather, rest and rejuvenate. Controlled studies have found that exposure to green space can improve well-being and health through the reduction of stress and mental fatigue (Groenewegen et al. 2006).

Create More Livable Cities and Connect with Nature: Getting involved in ecological restoration brings us closer to the natural environment, enhances our connection with ecological processes and strengthens social capital by creating opportunities to know our neighbors.

Produce Food and Enhance Well-being: Functional green space landscaped with community gardens and food plants enhances food security in our communities, promotes social capital among neighbors and increases the health and well-being of gardeners and their families who benefit from locally grown food. Research by Gorham et al. (2009) showed that residents living close to community gardens felt they contributed to neighborhood revitalization and feelings of safety.

Opportunities for Greening

Where can citizens and local governments get started? Our public green spaces, aquatic systems and community infrastructure, as well our own home and business spaces, offer fertile territory to cultivate these services.

Greening Parks and Open Spaces

While many neighborhoods need more green space, period, other communities are struggling to overcome the "parks as ornaments, something to look at but not to use" problem.

In either situation, parks and other open spaces are a great place to start rethinking our approaches to green space. They can host numerous activities and features that preserve and build community capital; in particular, its human, social, cultural and natural forms.

Traditionally, parks have been designed and managed by people who lack experience in ecological landscaping or appreciation of the range of opportunities that parks can offer — for recreation, education, naturalist activities, wildlife habitat, farming, community gardens, indigenous species planting and more. Management practices are now changing to deliver multiple services. One of these is Queen's Park in Toronto, Ontario. Its xeriscape garden features 140 drought-resistant plants that are well-suited to the regional climate; its ecological landscaping reduces maintenance, operating and watering costs by about 70 percent (City of Toronto 2011). Local university students and faculty use the garden to conduct projects and experiments, and plants and clippings are available for purchase. Similarly, Loulet Park, an underutilized public park space in North Vancouver, British Columbia, was transformed into an urban farm that provides food for the community, educational opportunities and a place for social capital to grow (Linzey 2011).

In many communities, citizens and non-government organizations are also discovering creative ways to meet local recreational and ecological needs. They're developing and maintaining new green spaces on vacant lots, traffic islands, rooftops and abandoned industrial lands. These open spaces, created by community members, reflect local values because their own sweat and labor are the impetus for implementation.

Fig. 4.3: *Traffic circles work to slow traffic in residential neighborhoods. This Vancouver traffic circle was built by the city and planted by local residents.*

Fig. 4.4: *Creek "daylighting" projects restoring formerly culverted, paved-over streams back to a more natural state to improve aesthetics, increase wildlife habitat, improve water quality and help stormwater surges in urban areas.*
(Credit: Richard Register)

Restoring Urban Aquatic Systems

In urban areas, naturally occurring streams, ponds, beaches and marshes have often been filled in, neglected or manipulated beyond recognition. Protecting and restoring them can revitalize neighborhoods and commercial areas, and give us a place to connect. Healthy aquatic systems are full of life and offer communities a place for art, science and celebration of nature. Conceived in this way, restoration projects can infuse community activism with a creative and inspirational dimension that has profound implications for grassroots efforts to revitalize our cities.

Stream corridors, creeks and marshes are also vehicles for education about local history and ecology, and places for rest, recreation and neighborhood beautification. Preservation and restoration projects of aquatic systems in urban areas also have numerous ecological benefits: they can increase biodiversity, provide habitat for fish and wildlife, restore native vegetation, act as natural filtration systems for greywater and accommodate stormwater runoff.

Creek daylighting is a powerful restoration strategy. It involves returning creek beds to the surface from their current underground, culverted state. Although up-front costs can be high, the long-term benefits are many. Stream corridors are among the most varied ecosystems, and streams effectively store and absorb stormwater runoff over their vegetated and riparian surfaces. Once stream restoration projects are complete, there are many more activities to be done. Volunteer community groups can organize clean-up and education programs or partner with local governments and others to fund monitoring programs. Citizens can lobby for ordinances that protect riparian zones (through Official Community Plan policies, zoning and environmental protection bylaws, development permit areas, comprehensive development and density bonusing, conservation covenants and so forth). Such measures help us move from private to participatory citizenship, taking responsibility for the local ecosystem in our urban areas. (see Fig. 4.5, color page C-2)

Fig. 4.6:
Renowned landscape architect Cornelia Hahn Oberlander designed this semi-intensive green roof for the Vancouver Public Library in Vancouver, Canada.
(Credit:
Sarah Rankin)

Greening Local Infrastructure

Local governments are increasingly grasping the strategic value of "greening" municipal infrastructure to support and enhance ecological functions of the natural environment. Green infrastructure is lighter, cheaper and smarter than conventional urban infrastructure; roads, sidewalks, parks and stormwater management systems can all be greened (Condon 2010). By maximizing natural ecosystem functions, green infrastructure can reduce the environmental impact of development and significantly reduce construction, maintenance and refurbishment costs.

A potent example is found in green roofs, rooftops that are either fully or partially covered in growing medium and plants. A green roof can be as simple as a two-inch (5 cm) covering of hardy, low-lying succulents, generally termed an "extensive" system, or as complex as a fully accessible park complete with trees, called an "intensive" system. Extensive systems are usually less accessible, non-recreational spaces that provide less variety in vegetation but require less growth medium, less maintenance and less water. Intensive green roofs require more water and maintenance and are generally more expensive than extensive systems, but provide substantial recreational, agricultural and energy-saving benefits (USEPA 2008). Green roofs can also help beautify our communities, providing calm and natural places to relax and socialize, as well as reduce heating and cooling needs (thus reducing our greenhouse gas emissions), mitigate the urban heat island effect, improve air quality indoors and out, filter pollutants, create habitat for small critters and birds, offer places to socialize and host food gardens.

The world leader in green roofs is Germany, where an estimated 10 percent of flat roofs in

Fig. 4.7: *The Green Alley project in the midtown area of Detroit revitalizes neglected back alleys into vibrant greenways for pedestrians and bicyclists. Detroit.* (Credit: Peggy Brennan\Green Garage)

the country incorporate roof-top gardens; however, they are becoming more popular in North America (USEPA 2008). Chicago has emerged as a leader in this respect by promoting green roof development through incentive programs, such as expedited building permit processes and service-fee waivers for developers installing green roofs (EPA 2008).

Greening our infrastructure can also help us create pleasant new green spaces. In Chicago's eastside, one developer converted a dreary alley adjacent to its urban redevelopment project into a permeable space with courtyards with gardens, park benches and places for people to gather. The City noticed the benefits the alley

Standing on the View

Step out through a hatch onto the roof of the Vancouver Public Library at Library Square — nine stories above downtown — and you'll find yourself in a prairie, not an asphalt wasteland. Sinuous bands of fescues stream across the roof, planted not in flats or containers but into a special mix of soil on the roof. It's a grassland in the sky. At ground level, this 20,000-square-foot garden . . . would be striking enough. High above Vancouver, the effect is almost disorienting. When we go to the rooftops in cities, it's usually to look out at the view. On top of the library, however, I can't help feeling that I'm standing on the view — this unexpected thicket of green, blue and brown grasses in the midst of so much glass and steel and concrete.

Living roofs aren't new. They were common among sod houses on the American prairie, and roofs of turf can still be found on log houses and sheds in northern Europe. But in recent decades, architects, builders and city planners all across the planet have begun turning to green roofs not for their beauty — almost an afterthought — but for their practicality, their ability to mitigate the environmental extremes common on conventional roofs.

To stand on a green roof in Vancouver — or Chicago or Stuttgart or Singapore or Tokyo — is to glimpse how different the roofscapes of our cities might look and to wonder, Why haven't we always built this way?

— Klinkenborg, 2009

brought to the neighborhoods and started a citywide Green Alley pilot program in 2006. By 2008, the program had converted over 3,500 acres of pavement to permeable surfaces, and by 2010, more than 100 green alleys had been created (Buranecn 2008; City of Chicago 2011). As we shall see in the extensive discussion on water management in the following chapter, projects like these can also help us manage water resources better, through infiltration of rainwater through rain gardens, permeable surfaces and other modified conveyances that eliminate the need for complex sewer systems to handle large storm events.

Greening Private Spaces

Urban ecology principles can be fruitfully applied to backyards, corporate parks and private gardens. Organizations, such as the Toronto-based non-profit Evergreen, work with businesses on many projects that transform corporate spaces into green space. Similarly, voluntary programs, such as British Columbia's Naturescape BC, offer pointers on inexpensive ways to restore, preserve and enhance wildlife habitat on private properties. Naturescape's public education materials show how to get squirrels, birds and butterflies to frequent balconies and backyards. Local governments can also promote change through education, incentives and regulations that require alternatives to turf and pesticides.

A growing number of developers, planners and landscape architects are also going green in a meaningful way. Forward-thinking developers are moving to protect existing vegetation in residential housing projects by incorporating trails and nature preserves. They are also using ecological function, such as wetlands and bioswales, to provide surface-water management and other services (See chapter 5). Many businesses are rethinking the concept of corporate office parks. Patagonia's distribution center in Reno incorporates xeriscaping and green stormwater runoff management into its award-winning design. AT&T converted the manicured lawns at two of its corporate campuses in Illinois into prairie wildflowers, saving about $75,000 in maintenance, fertilizer and irrigation costs. Similarly, UPS protected creeks and woodlands at its headquarters in Atlanta, Georgia (Rocky Mountain Institute 1997).

Even golf courses — a notoriously unsustainable land use — can be and are being greened. Conventional golf courses carve fairways out of forests and deserts; guzzle massive amounts of fertilizers, pesticides and water to irrigate miles of Kentucky blue grass; and require endless labor to manicure greens and fairways to perfection. Audubon International and other agencies now have programs to assist golf course designers and maintenance staff to create ecologically responsible golf courses. Boardwalks at Squaw Creek Golf Course in Squaw Valley, California, have carried golfers over marsh and meadow areas since its opening in 1992. The owners restored acres of native grasses and enhanced natural filtration ponds that feed Squaw Creek. Audubon certified Squaw Creek as a "cooperative sanctuary," and apart from using small amounts of nitrogen, the golf course is maintained organically to protect the aquifer it sits upon.

Tools and Initiatives

Voluntary

WATER-EFFICIENT LANDSCAPING

There are numerous communities promoting water efficient landscaping. One study comparing conventional and water-efficient landscapes in Northern California found that

> **Integrated pest management** includes a suite of techniques that, used in combination, seek to minimize or eliminate the use of pesticides and herbicides. Some strategies include: planting pest-resistant species, encouraging beneficial critters like toads and ladybugs, and planting species, such as marigolds, garlic, onion and pansies, which naturally deter insects.

the latter accounted for savings of 54 percent for water, 25 percent for labor, 61 percent for fertilizer, 44 percent for fuel and 22 percent for herbicides (Rocky Mountain Institute 1998). The City of Austin, Texas, has a "Go Green" campaign, which encourages residents to use water-efficient and chemical-free landscaping practices at their homes (City of Austin 2011). It distributes fact sheets identifying good practices for water-efficient landscaping and xeriscaping, and partners with nurseries to train retail staff to advise customers on water-efficient plant selection.

TREES FOR TUCSON

This Tucson, Arizona, program is affiliated with the American Forests' Global ReLeaf Program. It provides information to homeowners, neighborhood groups and schools on low-water plants and trees appropriate to the local environment. In its first decade of operation (1993-2003), the program provided community members with over 30,000 trees. Organizers calculated that each tree would save more than $20 in air-conditioning costs by providing shading and evapotranspiration, for a total of $236.5 million over the next 40 years. Officials also estimated that planting 500,000 trees will save the city $600,000 in storm drainage management in 40 years. Programs include Trees for Shade, Trees for the Community, Trees for Schools, Trees for Neighborhoods (Street Trees), Trees for Commemoration, Tree Tours and Tree Care Workshops (TCBI 2011).

GREEN STREET STANDARD PLANS

Green Street Standard Plans were recently completed by the City of Los Angeles (2010) and posted on the Web so that any developer can incorporate them into their designs, get a regular permit and start work. The City-approved plans incorporate best management practices for elements that increase green space and permeable areas with a view to stormwater management and beautification and utilization of neglected space.

GREEN ROOF RESOURCES GUIDE

The City of Los Angeles has also developed a resource guide for individuals and groups interested in developing green roofs in the city. It includes information on how to plan, design and maintain a green roof (City of Los Angeles 2006).

GREEN GUERRILLAS

This organization began in 1973 with a group of neighbors on the lower east side of Manhattan in New York City who were tired of the destruction of their community. In an effort to use community gardening as a tool to reclaim urban land and have people work together, the Green Guerrillas cleaned and greened a vacant lot in an area known as Bum's Row. Today that lot boasts meandering paths, a grape arbor, a pond, flowers, fruits and vegetables. Green Guerillas now helps over 300 community organizations green lots and install public art in New York City, through education, organization, advocacy and youth engagement (Green Guerillas 2011).

GREENING THE GREAT RIVER PARK

Since 1995 in St. Paul Minnesota, over 23,519 volunteers have planted 59,448 native trees and shrubs and restored more than 2,000 acres of land in the Mississippi, Minnesota and St. Croix river valleys. The initial work focused on a mostly privately owned 4.8-kilometer (3-mile) industrial stretch of the Mississippi River. A volunteer design team comprised of a landscape architect, a community representative and an ecologist drafted a plan for each parcel of land and reviewed it with the owner. The success of the initial project led to the creation of the non-profit organization, Great River Greening, in 1999. The program is funded by charitable donations and the state's Environment and Natural Resources Trust Fund (GRG 2011).

CREATIVE COMMUNITY GREEN PROJECT

East Vancouver, BC, has fewer parks per capita than any other neighborhood in the city. Modest funding from local grants and city support helped a group of citizens, including an architect and a landscape architect, come together and convert a vacant lot into a playground and park. With no vegetation or streams on the barren lot, the group found another way to create some connection with nature. A meandering stream was designed and built with mosaic tiles, assisted by a local artist who taught school children and community groups how to create ceramic tile mosaics. Large boulders (free by-products of excavation work) and logs were brought in for children to climb on, and locals planted trees. Over 500 people volunteering more than 4,000 hours made Mosaic Creek Park the pride of the community. It is truly the pride of the community that built it (City of Vancouver 2011).

CITY GREENING PROJECT

Toronto's Evergreen Brick Works, previously known as the Don Valley Brick Works industrial site, has been transformed into a community gathering center and urban park. The site was developed by the non-profit organization Evergreen in collaboration with the City of Toronto, local schools, businesses and other NGOs to strengthen the relationship between nature, culture and community through experiential learning, collaboration and fun. Nominated in 2010 by National Geographic as a geotourism hotspot, the Brick Works comprises 16 rehabilitated buildings that house a local farmers' market, native plant nursery, office space, event rental space, café and pavilions for outdoor events. The site hosts children's summer camps, workshops and community events; it also includes a 1,858-square-meter native plant demonstration garden as well as 16.5 hectares of ecologically restored parkland (Evergreen 2011).

UPGRADING FROM GRASS

Turenscape, an architecture and landscape design firm based in Beijing, China, demonstrated how agriculture can be integrated into the urban environment to provide food and other ecological services. At the Shengyang Architectural University, rice fields and other native crops are planted on university grounds instead of sod or grass. Rice paddies are irrigated with collected stormwater, which helps manage stormwater runoff, especially during the wet season. Sheep "cut" the grass instead of electric lawn mowers, frogs help control insects, and fish increase the rice fields' productivity. The site

annually hosts planting and harvesting festivals, where students help plant and harvest the rice that is sold as "Golden Rice" in the university canteen and as souvenirs to visitors (Yu 2009).

EDUCATION AND INFORMATION

The City of Portland, Oregon, offers information regarding green roofs and buildings via workshops, ecotours, hotlines and other types of technical assistance as part of their ecoroofs program (City of Portland 2011a).

LAND TRUSTS AND CONSERVATION TRUSTS

Typically funded by government, citizens and/or non-government organizations, community land trusts are effective tools for preserving land. They acquire, hold and/or lease land for social purposes, including affordable housing, parks, preserves, community gardens and farming. (For more information about land trusts, see chapter 10.) In British Columbia, a unique land trust agreement between the District of Saanich and the Capital Regional District saved an abandoned parcel of farmland from being converted into a residential development. The land was bought by the District of Saanich, which created a new zoning legislation it called a Renewal Demonstration Farm Zone. The land was then leased to the Haliburton Community Organic Farm Society to practice and promote sustainable farming, engage community members in sustainable food production, restore and enhance the biodiversity on the farmland, demonstrate the viability of small-scale farming and provide opportunities for education about agro-ecology (Haliburton Farm 2011). Land trusts also exist in the United States, with California having the most — a total of 198 (Land Trust Alliance 2005). In 2009, the Sonoma Land Trust acquired 5,630 acres at the Jenner Headlands, with the support of ten public and private funding partners. As a result, 3,100 acres of redwood and Douglas fir forest, 1,500 acres of rare coastal prairie and eight watersheds of Jenner Headlands will be protected (Land Trust Alliance 2009).

Financial Incentives
REWARDS FOR ECO-FRIENDLY LANDSCAPING

State governments and municipalities are incentivizing greener landscape design. For example, the City of Albuquerque, New Mexico, offers financial incentives to property owners who xeriscape: the city credits water bills 75 cents for every square foot of lawn xeriscaped, to a maximum of 2,000 square feet (Albuquerque Bernalillo County Water Use Authority 2011).

INCENTIVIZING GREEN ROOFS

As part of its Grey to Green initiative, the City of Portland offers property owners and developers that meet its floor-to-area ratio (FAR) bonus policy for central city buildings an incentive to add more ecoroofs. It funds up to $5 per square foot (which typically amounts to 25 to 100 percent of installation costs) of ecoroof projects (City of Portland 2011a). As of June 2008, New York state law allows New York City building owners who install vegetation on at least half their buildings' available rooftop space to offset, for one year, $4.50 in property taxes for each square foot of green roof installed. The credit covers about a quarter of the cost of installation and is capped at $100,000 (New York City 2009). Toronto's Eco-Roof Incentive Program offers grants of $50 per square meter of greened roof for eligible projects, to a maximum of $10,000 for single-family homes and $100,000 for all other buildings (City of Toronto 2011). At UniverCity,

the model sustainable community adjacent to Simon Fraser University in British Columbia, developers are awarded a density bonus of up to 10 percent that use green roof technology to help manage stormwater (UniverCity 2011; read more about UniverCity in chapter 14).

Expenditure
CREEK DAYLIGHTING PROJECT

In El Cerrito, California, the non-profit Urban Creeks Council spearheaded a project to daylight a strip of long-culverted creek as part of a citywide storm drain renovation program. Labor was provided by the East Bay Conservation Corps. The restoration project created gentle meanders, pools and riffles to diversify flow, increase water quality and halt erosion. Banks were stabilized with native plant species. To date, the City of El Cerrito has restored and/or daylighted portions of Baxter Creek at Poinsett, Baxter Creek Gateway Parks and Cerrito Creek at the city's southern boundary (City of El Cerrito 2011).

WATERSHED RESTORATION

The Wheaton Branch restoration is one phase of a larger ongoing watershed restoration of Sligo Creek in Montgomery County, Maryland, by an interdisciplinary team of staff from several public agencies including the Maryland National Capital Park and Planning Commission. Located in a highly urbanized area, 55 percent of Wheaton Branch's watershed is covered by impervious surfaces. The project is addressing everything from control of runoff at the stream headwaters to bank stabilization and fish restocking. Ongoing monitoring confirms that, in addition to improving water quality, the project has reestablished native fish species (from 3 in 1988 to 11 in 2011) in the Upper Sligo Creek main stem (Montgomery County 2011).

GREEN ROOF DEMONSTRATION PROJECT

Outside the fifth-floor cafeteria of Atlanta, Georgia's City Hall is the first City-owned green roof in the southeast United States. This 3,000-square-foot green roof is a model for downtown businesses and offers a place for employees to eat, relax and socialize. The city is monitoring the green roof performance in terms of energy efficiency, rainwater retention and plant survival. It is also comparing plant growth in different soil depths (City of Atlanta 2011).

WATER STEWARDSHIP GRANTS

The Community Watershed Stewardship Program is a partnership between Portland's Bureau of Environmental Services and Portland State University. The program engages Portlanders in enhancing the health of local watersheds through property consultations, while promoting public awareness of our connection to these natural systems. Since 1995, it has granted $885,000 to 192 projects (City of Portland 2011b).

Regulation

Municipal governments play a critical role in the sustainable management of green spaces, and citizens can influence their local officials to act. Efforts can take the form of government policy, bylaws or regulations and/or be driven by NGOs, citizens or private initiatives. Conservation commissions and environmental advisory boards can partner with local organizations and other municipal governments to support local greening. With political will, the options multiply.

ENVIRONMENTALLY SENSITIVE AREAS STRATEGY

Municipal governments can conduct environmentally sensitive area (ESA) studies and inventories to determine where substantial leave-strips, setbacks and protection of green space and watercourses are needed most. In 1994, the City of Burnaby, British Columbia, adopted an ESA strategy that continues to serve as its comprehensive policy framework for environmental sustainability. The strategy applies environmentally sensitive planning and management principles to protect public green lands. Principles include creating a linked ESA network, maintaining larger contiguous public open spaces, preserving ecological continuity, encouraging protective zoning of parklands, achieving zero net-increase of runoff, controlling construction damage, planting native species, protecting micro-habitats and preserving ecological function (City of Burnaby 2011). The city also engages in annual State of the Environment Reporting and partners with local NGOs and other levels of government on initiatives from stream-keeping to land-use planning, and has enacted a watercourse protection bylaw (City of Burnaby 2004).

NATURAL LANDSCAPE PROTECTION BYLAW

Communities can amend existing landscape ordinances to encourage planting native plants. Native planting ordinances can reduce water use and maintenance costs, create wildlife habitat and preserve property values. The City of Toronto, Ontario, has a Ravine and Natural Feature Protection Bylaw that is designed to protect the city's sensitive ravine and wooded ecosystems. The bylaw prohibits planting of identified invasive species on properties near ravines and natural areas, and prohibits any change or interference with trees or natural land topography (City of Toronto 2011). To support this bylaw, the city encourages property owners to landscape with native plants by offering free consultation services and native plant guides.

XERISCAPE BYLAW

In 1991, Florida passed the first state xeriscape bylaw in the US. It required xeriscaping to be applied to all newly developed and existing public properties over a period of five years. In 2000, the South Florida Water Management District passed a Xeriscape Incentive Rule that provides technical assistance to local governments that submit draft xeriscape ordinances. All local governments that operate water supply

systems in Florida have adopted water conservation ordinances, and even citizens are affected. Anyone who buys an automatic lawn sprinkler must also install a rain sensor to ensure the system shuts off when it begins to rain.

GREEN ROOF BYLAW

In 2009, Toronto became the first city in North America to pass a green roof bylaw. It applies to new commercial, institutional and residential development applications with a minimum gross floor area of 2,000 square meters, and to all new industrial development regardless of size. The bylaw includes a graduated roof coverage requirement ranging from 20 to 60 percent (City of Toronto 2009). Similar laws already exist in Japan, Switzerland, Germany and France. The City of Toronto is also being creative and proactive in greening its own structures: for example, the Eglinton West subway station's tar roof is being transformed into a 9,000-square-foot garden (ICLEI 2011). Leading by example is an excellent way for local governments to promote green infrastructure initiatives.

Strengthening Our Community Food Systems

Most people pay little attention to where their food comes from, but moving toward sustainability requires we do that and more. We need to think about our food as coming from a *food system* that includes everything from tabletop to ground and back again: what we eat; how it's grown, produced, processed, packaged, transported and sold; and what we do with what's left over (Gillard 2011).

As with any system, we should examine where inefficiencies lie with a view to making it more sustainable. According to de la Salle and Holland (2010), North Americans use

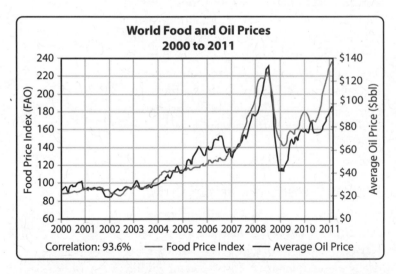

Fig. 4.8: *This graph plots world Food Price Index data from the UN Food and Agriculture Organization (FAO) and the monthly average oil price from the US Energy Information Agency (EIA). The strong correlation between the two offers evidence that our food system is heavily dependent on petroleum products. By supporting products and practices that require less energy and produce less waste, we can increase our food security.*

(CREDIT: PAUL CHEFURKA PAULCHEFURKA.CA/OIL_FOOD.HTML)

approximately nine times more energy on food production and transportation than the energy they receive from ingesting the food. That means that 90 percent of the energy used to get the food to our dinner tables is lost through energy-intensive farming practices, processing and long-distance transport. This is largely because the food system we have created is heavily dependent on the use of petroleum products to cultivate, process, transport, store and sell our food.

We also need to look at our food system's hidden costs. Weber and Matthews (2008) compared the life-cycle greenhouse gas (GHG) emissions associated with food production against long-distance distribution (aka food-miles) in the US and found that the average US household emits 8.1 tons of food-consumption-related CO_2 emissions annually. Food production practices account for 83 percent of these emissions, while about 15 percent are caused by transportation. However, since different food groups exhibit a large range in GHG-intensity (on average, red meat is around 150 percent more GHG-intensive than chicken or fish), they suggest that "dietary shift can be a more effective means of lowering an average household's food-related climate footprint than 'buying local.' Shifting less than one day per week's worth of calories from red meat and dairy products to chicken, fish, eggs, or a vegetable-based diet achieves more GHG reduction than buying all locally sourced food."

On average in the US, fresh produce in supermarkets travels about 1,500 miles between its points of production and consumption (Hill 2008). Our food system also pollutes the environment with toxic pesticides, threatens biodiversity with genetically modified and non-native food crops and continues to deplete the world's fish stocks. Because our food system is so globalized, it exploits natural resources and physical labor of other regions, shifting our food security burdens elsewhere.

What would a just, sustainable community food system look like? The University of California's Sustainable Agriculture Research and Education Program defines a sustainable community, or local, food system as a "collaborative network that integrates sustainable food production, processing, distribution, consumption and waste management in order to enhance the environmental, economic and social health of a particular place" (UC SAREP 2011).

Food systems that prioritize sustainable local production of food are inherently tied not only to the health of individuals, but to the short- and long-term economic, social and environmental health of communities. They protect the land that produces the food; support the local economy through local production; empower community well-being through increased health and decreased illness; increase our sense of community; and increase environmental health through reduced production

How Food-secure Are We?

With one of the most abundant food systems in the world, North Americans may believe that food security is mostly a challenge of developing nations. But in 2008, about 43 million US residents per month received federal food stamps; more than 75 percent of these were families with young children, and about 30 percent were elderly or disabled people (CBPP 2010). In March 2010, Canada recorded its highest level of food bank use ever: 867,948 people, a 19 percent increase over 2000 levels (Food Banks Canada 2011).

Reflections on Food Sovereignty

By Spring Gillard

My grandparents were the epitome of food self-reliance. Grandma always had a large food garden; she pickled and canned everything, not just fruits and vegetables, but whole chickens from their flock and trout from their pond. She made noodles from scratch for her sublime soups. Grandpa contributed too: he made cheese and sausages, which he smoked in a backyard smokehouse, and grew the grapes for his potent wine. They could put on a banquet at a moment's notice.

My memories of their home sum up food security for me: being completely self-sufficient in terms of your own food supply. The UN definition of food security emphasizes that everyone in a community should have consistent and adequate access to healthy, nutritious, culturally appropriate food. To that I would add: without ever having to ask, "Is this safe to eat?" For me, the term *food security* conjures up visions of lysteriosis or terrorists sabotaging the food supply with anthrax, so I prefer to talk about *food sovereignty* and *food self-reliance*, which requires a resilient food system.

My research and work with the Vancouver Food Policy Council and a community group (the Westside Food Security Collaborative) taught me how vulnerable a food system can be. I learned that, at any one time in British Columbia, there are roughly three days of food on grocery store shelves. I wondered: If food shipments were cut off for reasons like natural disasters or fuel shortages, how would we manage? Although 50 percent of our food is grown in this province, we are still vulnerable. Our government estimates that to produce our food in the next couple of decades, we will need 49 percent more irrigable land under agricultural production. We must protect our farmland, and yet we continue to promote unconscious growth and development.

I decided to take a closer look at my own community's food system, and invited others to join me. Partnering with the Westside Food Security Collaborative, I developed a series of tours called Exploring the Food System on the West Side. We started with a general exploration of the neighborhood food system and toured several urban farms. Next we visited a working market farm at the University of BC, where, in addition to visiting with the cows and the chickens, we were taught about indigenous food systems by members of the Mayan and Aboriginal gardens. We examined the role of grocery stores in a healthy community and looked at waste. We investigated composting set-ups, from backyard to multi-family (co-ops, apartment buildings) and commercial (restaurants and grocery stores). Finally, we visited our social service agencies to learn more about our emergency and charity food programs. Throughout, we identified our food system's assets and the gaps. We found out that Vancouver's West Side fared pretty well in some areas; for example, we had a lot of food gardeners, and many people were composting. But unless you count chocolateries, bakeries and breweries, we came up short on the processing side.

So what can ordinary citizens do? My tour findings informed a presentation I developed, called Feeding Ourselves: How Do We Fare? In it, I suggest ways to get out and explore your own neighborhoods as I did — and highlight five ways to help strengthen your community's food system:

1. Start, find and get involved with a local group working on food issues. Find out if there is a food policy council in your area, attend a meeting and join in their work. Many North American food policy councils are listed at foodsecurity.org.
2. Explore the food system in your neighborhood or region. What are its assets and gaps? How does your community fare in terms of food security? ☛

If you are working with a community group, try mapping your foodshed: define the geographical and ecological boundaries of the region that grows your food and take stock of its strengths, weaknesses and opportunities to enhance food self-reliance. Learn about indigenous food systems at indigenousfoodsystems.org.

3. Eat local, buy local. Support markets, shops and restaurants that feature local, sustainable foods. Join a community kitchen, food co-op or buying club, or subscribe to a weekly produce box. For local foods near you in the US, check out localharvest.org and sustainabletable.org; in Canada, eatwellguide.org or cog.ca.

4. Grow your own food. Learn how to can, pickle, preserve, bake bread or make cheese. Take a foraging workshop so you can harvest local mushrooms, berries and other wild foods safely.

5. Read *The 100-Mile Diet* (Vintage Canada 2007; published in 2007 by Harmony Books in the US as *Plenty*) if you haven't already. Host a 100-Mile Diet dinner or challenge your family and friends to eat within a designated geographical area or foodshed for a week — or a month. For more dinner ideas, visit eatgrub.org.

of emissions and lower use of fertilizer and pesticides.

The Three Ss: Security, Self-Sufficiency and Sovereignty

When talking about local food systems, one often hears references to the concepts of food security, food self-sufficiency and food sovereignty. According to the United Nations Food and Agriculture Organization, "food security exists when all people, at all times, have physical, social and economic access to sufficient, safe and nutritious food to meet their dietary needs and food preferences for an active and healthy life" (FAO 1996). This concept, based on improving access to food for households and communities, is not concerned with where food comes from or how it is produced.

The question of food self-sufficiency and food sovereignty often arises when thinking about sustainable development. Food self-sufficiency refers to a community's capacity to meet its food needs using locally available resources. Food sovereignty goes one step further to address how food is produced. According to Wittman et al. (2010), food sovereignty is the right of peoples to control their own food systems, including markets, ecological resources and food cultures. Proponents of food sovereignty advocate the democratization of access to and control over land and other resources (i.e., water, seeds, agricultural knowledge), and also promote agro-ecological production practices that involve a blend of traditional and local knowledge and modern agricultural science to increase food production, preserve genetic and cultural diversity and conserve soil fertility and biodiversity.

Sustainable Food Policy

Community food systems are affected by food policies adopted at levels that range from local

to global. Well-designed food policies can help
to encourage sustainability by increasing green
spaces and reducing food packaging. They can
contribute to the economy by supporting local
food producers, processors, distributors and
retailers. As well, they can foster social sustainability through community kitchens and
nutritional outreach programs.

Some of the aspects of city life that might
be touched by food policies include urban
agriculture: where food can be grown (in community gardens, on rooftops, on boulevards)
and whether or not that food can be sold com-
mercially; farmers' markets: where they can be
situated and what bylaws, zoning and permitting might govern them; the allowable size and
location of grocery stores; availability of free
and low-cost meals; whether or not you can
have chickens in your backyard or keep bees;
what kind of street food your city offers; the
extent of recovery and redistribution of surplus food from grocery stores, restaurants and
caterers; the composting of food waste; and institutional food purchasing (Gillard 2011).

Communities are finding creative ways to
help their citizens grow and cultivate their
own food — plants and proteins alike. Urban
bylaws are being adjusted to allow residents to
raise chickens and goats, and permit backyard
aquaculture. Food policies can support and
complement these strategies to increase food
security, sovereignty and self-reliance. Measures
include protecting existing agricultural parcels
through land-use planning, zoning and bylaws;
organizing food production, storage, processing and distribution into central locations,
such as markets or food hubs that may include
restaurants and retail and make food production and consumption the focus of celebration,
education and sharing; and developing systems

that repurpose food waste or divert excess to
community members in need through low-
cost grocers and food banks (de la Salle &
Holland 2010; Gillard 2011).

As many communities are discovering, re-
localizing food supply chains to enhance local
food production and consumption can also
stimulate community economic development
(DeWeerdt 2009; Graham, Healy et al. 2002;
Little, Maye et al. 2010; Seyfang 2006; Swenson
2007). For example, in Portland, Oregon,
local farmers were missing out on Oregon's
$70-million school lunch market because mass-
produced lunch fare could be provided more
cheaply. A grant that provided a 7-cents-per-
meal subsidy for local produce changed that,
ultimately generating an additional 84 cents of
in-state economic activity (in wages, upgrades
or investments in food production facilities
and consumer purchasing) per dollar invested,
as compared with the 50 to 60 cents per dollar
in incremental economic activity that is usually
generated by each dollar spent on a product or
service. Children reported that they liked the
food better too! (Richardson 2007).

A Bounty of Benefits

Citizens are enhancing their communities' access to locally and sustainably produced food
by growing food in every location imaginable
— in parks, vacant lots, abandoned industrial
lands, rooftops and on vertical surfaces — but
they don't always enjoy official support. In
some communities, health bylaws still prevent
farmers' markets within city limits; other bylaws restrict the use of parks for growing food;
codes and covenants favor lawns and parking
lots; and real estate development competes
with agriculture for land tenure. But many
local governments change their tune when

they understand the benefits of stronger community food systems:

Food security: Sustainable community food systems make us all less vulnerable to perils (such as shortages and price increases) of international food systems. Although climate, agriculture limitations and consumer preferences make it unlikely that North American communities will become completely food self-sufficient, it is very possible for communities to increase residents' access to fresh, nutritious and affordable food. Local, community-grown food can help also feed the poor. On the east side of Vancouver, BC, many local gardeners share the fruits of their labor with homeless people, and low-income residents rely on the seasonal bounty of the Strathcona community garden for much of their food supply (Gillard 2011).

Pollution reduction: Sustainable food production lowers food miles, which lowers greenhouse gas emissions, and promotes organic growing methods, which reduces groundwater pollution from chemical pesticides and fertilizers. Home-grown food reduces packaging waste and energy consumption. Organic food waste, which typically accounts for about 30 percent of household waste, can be composted for use in local farms and gardens and thereby reduce the burden on local landfills.

Ecological services: Appropriately sited small-scale agriculture can reduce soil erosion, decrease surface runoff and preserve or increase wildlife habitat.

Economic development: Local food production creates local jobs in food production, processing, delivery, retail, recovery and waste management. It brings entrepreneurial opportunities and keeps money circulating within the community.

Agricultural Urbanism

While community groups and food activists have been working for decades to strengthen the food system, food has been largely missing from official community planning and design processes. *Agricultural urbanism* has emerged as a planning, policy and design framework that promises to help put food back into city-building (de la Salle & Holland 2010). Agricultural urbanism emphasizes ten principles that should inform community food system projects and initiatives: 1) Take an integrated food and agriculture systems perspective; 2) Create a rich experience of food and agriculture; 3) Build on the food and agriculture economy; 4) Increase access to food; 5) Educate about food; 6) Manage to support sustainable food systems; 7) Provide food and habitat for other species; 8) Organize for food; 9) Construct sustainable infrastructure for food and agriculture; and 10) Bring food and agriculture into the full suite of climate change solutions (de la Salle & Holland 2010).

Fig. 4.9: *Cascade Community Gardens (Pea Patch) in Seattle's South Lake Union District overflows with produce and flowers.* (CREDIT: DAVID ROUSSEAU)

Setting Community Food Projects up for Success

According to Gillard (2011), the most successful community food programs are often multi-layered. For example, they link chefs directly with growers, match a farm with a school lunch program, encourage grocers and caterers to donate their surplus quality food to neighborhood social service agencies for their meal programs or employ and feed the people they serve.

Pothukuchi (2007) observed that successful community food initiatives tend to:

- Show progress in meeting particular community food needs.
- Gain community buy-in and support of activities.
- Adapt effectively to changing and unforeseen conditions.
- Be able to build and strengthen effective community-based networks.
- Develop innovative, multi-sector approaches.
- Build community food leadership.
- Sustain selected activities after start-up funding ends.
- Be able to hit the ground running.

Fig. 4.10: *In May 2011, community members began the new Cornerstone community garden space provided by the Chautauqua County Rural Ministry (CCRM), a grassroots organization that helps the homeless, working poor and disenfranchised in Chautauqua County, NY. The CCRM also runs the Chautauqua County Gleaning Project in which volunteers recover unharvested fruits and vegetables from local farm fields for redistribution to food pantries, soup kitchens and community members throughout the county. The Gleaning Project aims to make a healthy impact in the community and the greater movement of alleviating hunger, reducing waste and teaching gardening skills.* (Credit: Sarah Sorci)

Education: Sustainable community food systems paired with food-related curriculum can encourage healthy eating habits among youth (Hand et al. 2010). Community gardens, farmers' markets and other community food places and events can host workshops and training to citizens for growing, processing, storing and cooking food.

Health and well-being: Successful community food systems reduce food contamination risks of large-scale agriculture processes (APA 2007). They also strengthen community connections to food sources, building trust between food producers and community members through face-to-face interactions at markets and other retail locations. By increasing access to healthy and nutritious food, they help reduce the risk of diet-related chronic diseases. Edible planting and permaculture can enhance our green spaces and promote more environmentally sound landscaping alternatives.

Enhance cultural capital: Strong community food systems support cultural diversity.

Many immigrants are unable to find traditional produce at local grocery stores, or find it at affordable prices. Urban agriculture provides an inexpensive way for people to cultivate traditional foods at home.

Tools and Initiatives

Voluntary

COMMUNITY-SUPPORTED AGRICULTURE

Many urban dwellers are benefiting from community-supported agriculture (CSA), which allows both growers and consumers to share responsibilities of cultivating a vibrant local food system. Typically, local farmers on the urban fringe grow food for a group of city-resident subscribers, who agree to buy it before the growing season begins. By keeping money in the community, this form of agriculture secures the livelihood of local family farmers, supports the local economy, fosters greater self-reliance for food supplies and helps people remain connected with the food they consume. Orti Solidali (or Solidarity Gardens) is a CSA project in Rome, Italy, that works to create more sustainable food systems through agricultural practices and social support. It supports four gardeners who are refugees, and socially disadvantaged youth that have received training in organic agricultural practices. For 300 Euros per year, 60 subscribers receive weekly boxes of fresh produce from its 60 garden plots. Each subscriber is assigned to a specific garden plot and enjoys input into the garden design and cultivation, thereby personalizing their CSA box (Pinto et al. 2010).

EDIBLE SCHOOLYARD

The schoolyard of Martin Luther King Jr. Middle School in Berkeley, California, is not your typical concrete playground; it's been transformed by students into a garden that produces organically grown fruits and vegetables. These are eventually used in the cafeteria, which is served by a classroom kitchen. Every year, the school introduces over 900 students to the finer points of organic gardening and healthy eating (ESY 2011).

REDISCOVERING INDIGENOUS FOODS

The T'sou-ke First Nation on Vancouver Island, British Columbia, has created a food security program that includes a greenhouse and garden used to grow indigenous food plants. Community members run workshops to teach traditional methods of processing, preparing and preserving traditional foods (CIER & T'sou-ke Nation 2010).

VERTICAL GARDENING

In the United States, Will Allen of the national non-profit organization Growing Power has worked with Kubala Washatko Architects to design a five-story vertical farm. The building, to be sited in Milwaukee's inner city, will grow vegetables, house aquaculture and hydroponic capabilities, capture rainwater for irrigation and provide classrooms for agricultural education. As of this writing, the building is waiting for approval from the Milwaukee Plan Commission (Supan 2011).

BACKYARD AQUACULTURE DEMONSTRATION PROJECT

In Maui County, the University of Hawai'i has partnered with a local high school to create a backyard aquaculture demonstration that trains local residents to grow fresh fish and produce in their backyards. The project enhances food security while helping people rediscover nutritious and affordable traditional foods and install low-cost, small-scale aquaculture and agriculture systems on their properties. As of 2011, the project had helped ten families install working systems and had secured funding for five more (University of Hawai'i 2011).

HEALTHY COMMUNITY STORES

Community groups are working to improve access to fresh foods, particularly in food "deserts" — areas underserved by quality grocery stores and often home to low-income citizens. In San Francisco, a group of university students collaborated with a corner-store owner to bring fresh fruit and vegetables to a food desert; the store became a pick-up spot for members of a Community Shared Agriculture program (more details below). Today, many stores like this across the US comprise the Healthy Community Stores network (The Food Trust 2011).

FARMERS' MARKET ALTERNATIVES

Some community groups are setting up smaller *pocket markets*: temporary fresh produce markets that can be offered in food deserts and other key locations like seniors' centers, neighborhood houses, hospitals and churches. Such groups include FoodRoots from Victoria, BC, and Farm to Family of Richmond, BC.

MARRYING SOCIAL AND FOOD SERVICES

In Smithers, BC, a non-profit association of parents (the Grendel Group) lamented the lack of organized opportunities for developmentally delayed kids in their small, remote community. To address this, they developed a catering company called Grendelivery and launched it with funding help from local and regional foundations. Since 2005, Grendelivery

has offered developmentally delayed kids stimulating, supervised social interaction and work experience while providing community members with a simple but tasty rotating menu of order-out lunches and customized menus for catered events. This highly successful program prioritizes produce sourced from local farmers.

CONTRIBUTION AND REHABILITATION

Some inmates at the Leavenworth penitentiary in Kansas maintain a garden where they grow fruits and vegetables for community members in need. The food is given away, and the experience has helped some inmates get jobs after they are released. In 2010, over 80,000 pounds of produce was distributed to feed those in need in the greater Kansas City area. Organizers aim to increase the farm's capacity and produce 200,000 pounds in 2011 (Fussel 2011).

FOOD POLICY ADVOCACY

Food policy organizations are community or regional groups that aim to strengthen local food security. These groups are similar to food policy councils described below, but do not necessarily have a formal liaison to city council. They are essentially vehicles for food activists to advance sustainable food policy projects and programs and connect them with policy-making. Holistic in approach, these organizations address both the causes and effects of hunger and work for short- and long-term change in food production, processing, distribution and access, public education and research and waste reduction. They vary from informal volunteer groups, such as Peterborough's Food Policy Action Coalition, to more established non-profits, such as Toronto's Food Share, which has an executive director, paid staff, a volunteer board and over 2,800 volunteers (Food Share 2009).

Financial Incentives
LOW-COST GROCERY STORES AND CAFÉS

Some regional health authorities are funding initiatives that make healthy food available at subsidized prices. One of these is the Potluck Café, a social enterprise that operates in a low-income neighborhood of Vancouver, BC. It operates a successful catering and event-planning business, hires and trains many local residents with multiple barriers to employment and serves healthy, affordable meals.

TAX INCENTIVES FOR CONVERSION TO URBAN FARMLAND

Faced with a shrinking population, unemployment and poverty, Detroit is using urban farming as a tool for revitalization. The city is capitalizing on some of its 200,000 tax-delinquent parcels of land (approximately 30,000 acres) by providing tax incentives to transform them into profitable urban agricultural farmland. One local initiative, Hantz Farms, has partnered with Michigan State University and the W.K. Kellogg Foundation for added expertise in community food systems, agriculture and soil science. Although still in its infancy, the initiative is expected to bring employment, food security, economic diversification, pollution reduction and tourism to Detroit (Hantz Farms 2011).

Expenditure
FOOD POLICY COUNCILS

Food policy councils are springing up across North America. Some are run by grassroots organizations; others are created by municipal, regional or state governments. The councils are made up of volunteer experts and stakeholders drawn from food-related sectors. Often a paid city staff person or food policy coordinator serves as liaison (and sometimes referee!) between the council and local government. Councils advise government on food issues, recommend policies, set goals and strategies for achieving them and advocate for communities on food-related issues. Many food policy councils develop food charters that serve as blueprints for just, sustainable community food systems (Gillard 2011). Baltimore is an example of a city with a Food Policy Task Force that aims to create a sustainable community food system (Baltimore 2009).

COMMUNITY GARDEN SPACE

In partnership with the non-profit P-Patch Advisory Council, this City of Seattle program provides more than 23 acres of strictly organic community garden space to 4,400 gardeners in 35 neighborhoods. Special programs serve refugees, low-income, disabled and youth gardeners, and its Lettuce Link project delivers 8 to 10 tons of fresh produce to food banks every year. Since its inception, several community gardens have been started throughout Seattle, along with a community-supported agriculture program (City of Seattle 2011).

Regulatory
FOOD SECURITY BYLAW

Belo Horizonte, Brazil has declared food a human right. It dedicates one percent of its budget to innovative programs like urban farm stands, protein-rich school meals and community restaurants, ensuring that every one of its citizens is fed (Gillard 2011). Its commitment to food sovereignty and to allowing citizens to define their own food and agricultural policies is enshrined in municipal law. Since the bylaw was enacted in 1993, this city of 2.5 million has seen a 75 percent decrease in children hospitalized for malnutrition and 25 percent decrease of people living in poverty (World Future Council 2009).

URBAN AGRICULTURE BYLAWS

Vancouver, BC, has updated its animal control and zoning bylaws to permit residents to keep beehives and chickens in backyards (City of Vancouver 2011). Other cities with similar bylaws include New York, Chicago, Portland and Seattle, as well as BC cities including Victoria, Surrey and New Westminster. In 2009, the City of Parksville, BC, amended its zoning bylaw to permit urban property owners to cover up to 20 percent of their land with market gardens (Islands Trust 2011).

Chapter 5

Water and Sewage

North America is abundant in lakes and rivers, but in many regions, water resources are in critical supply. Thanks to climate change, pollution, urbanization, population growth and intensification of oil and gas development, resource extraction and increasing manufacturing, the pressure on this precious resource is only increasing. Yet, notwithstanding great advances in water conservation in places like California and other arid regions, North Americans continue to use far more water per capita than citizens of other OECD nations. Both Canada and the United States are among the world's heaviest per capita users of water. On average, United States water consumption is more than double the average for all OECD countries; Canada trails close behind (OECD 2005, 136-139). In their homes alone, Canadians and Americans use over 300 liters per day per person (Environment Canada 2010; United States Environmental Protection Agency 2008a).

Our wasteful expenditure of this precious form of natural capital is catching up to us.

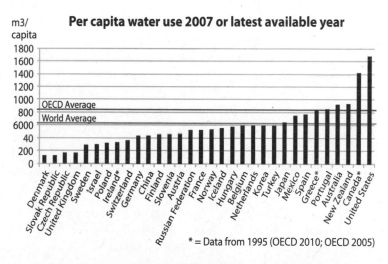

Per capita water use 2007 or latest available year

m3/capita

* = Data from 1995 (OECD 2010; OECD 2005)

Fig. 5.1: *According to the latest available data, Canada and the United States have the highest water use (quantified in cubic meters per capita) among OECD countries, China and the Russian federation. Residents of the US and Canada use more than double the world average of water on a per capita annual basis.* (CREDIT: OECD FACTBOOK 2010: ECONOMIC, ENVIRONMENTAL AND SOCIAL STATISTICS)

Even in areas that receive significant amounts of rain, such as the Pacific Northwest, increasingly drier summer seasons, retreating glaciers and urban growth challenge water supplies and threaten to overwhelm existing infrastructure. Rapid water extraction and pollution is damaging fish stocks and degrading the health of streams and rivers, many of which we rely on for drinking water. Water consumption and treatment for residential, commercial and industrial purposes inflates our demand for energy, which in turn contributes to the production of greenhouse gases. Maintenance and expansion of physical capital such as infrastructure to supply, deliver and treat water exacts a heavy tax burden on citizens and governments.

Both urban and rural communities, especially those that depend on groundwater for their water supply, are seeking solutions that satisfy their water needs, while reducing or minimizing environmental and financial costs associated with supply, sewage treatment and infrastructure expansion. Local governments, especially those in communities where water infrastructure is nearing the end of its useful life, can also see this as the opportunity it is — to move beyond conservation, reconsider their philosophy of water management and enact real change. This chapter will explore some of the most significant and successful strategies for doing just that: demand-side management, Soft Path principles for water management, alternative sewage treatment, wastewater reclamation and integrated resource recovery and planning.

Promoting Water Conservation

In North America, we waste water because it's cheap, but is it? In most regions, a portion of our water supply and sewage treatment costs are paid annually through general tax revenue or property taxes. The rest is paid through regular water bills. The price we pay for water does not accurately reflect the true costs required to pump, distribute and treat water. Compared to other OECD nations, Canada and the United States have the highest water consumption rates and the lowest water prices. Low water prices also mean that infrastructure is not being maintained or repaired and that necessary system upgrades are not being implemented.

Studies indicate that charging users based on the volume of water consumed at prices high enough to cover all service costs will not only encourage conservation but provide funds to maintain infrastructure and support additional water conservation programs (Brandes, Renzetti & Stinchcombe 2010). For example, volumetric water pricing used by the San Antonio Water System in Texas provided enough funds to offer customers two free high-efficiency toilets per household (Brandes et al.). While some Canadian water providers have also introduced water metering and pay-per-volume rates, one quarter of Canadian homes and one fifth of

Why Should Communities "Rich" With Natural Water Resources Conserve Water?

Although the value of water conservation and stewardship is not always obvious to residents of "water-rich" communities, reducing demand for water saves local governments money on water treatment and distribution in the short term and on water infrastructure maintenance and replacement in the long term. Because delivering, treating and heating water requires energy, reducing water demand also saves energy and reduces greenhouse gas emissions. A study by Griffiths-Sattenspiel and Wilson (2009) reported that 38.3 million tonnes of carbon dioxide emissions could be avoided if every US household installed water-efficient fixtures and appliances.

Canadian businesses are still charged a flat rate (Environment Canada 2010).

Although true-cost pricing for water may be the simplest solution, many communities facing population growth and soaring demand continue to seek physical and financial ways to expand water supply. But building deeper wells and bigger dams is not ecologically or financially sustainable in the long term. By encouraging and even requiring more efficient use of existing resources instead (known as demand-side management), communities can satisfy their needs, while saving money and conserving existing water supplies. From simple faucet aerators and low-flush toilets to sonar leak detection units, volumetric pricing and the Soft Path approach to planning (discussed below), there are a host of solutions for reducing waste, conserving water and inspiring behavioral change. Some of these demand-side approaches can be employed by individual homeowners, tenants, building owners or occupants; others can be implemented by builders or developers; and still others require participation of local or regional governments, water service departments or public works.

Financial benefits of demand-side management strategies include direct savings from lower water usage and reduced sewage costs resulting from less wasted water. Additionally, the city and its taxpayers avoid the cost of treatment and supply for each unit of water conserved. While consumers may not realize it when they leave a tap dripping, or a lawn sprinkler running, more efficient use of water may also avoid the huge capital cost of constructing additional reservoirs and expanding treatment plants.

Although the business and environmental case for such strategies is clear, municipal governments may also need to introduce incentives or policies to encourage water conservation, as well as restrictions or penalties to reduce wasteful water behavior (See chapter 7 for more discussion of demand-side management).

The Water–Energy Connection

Water and energy are inextricably linked. Energy is used to provide water-related services, and water is used to generate energy — for example, to cool thermal or nuclear plants, power turbines in hydroelectric facilities, or to extract oil from tar sands. While much of the water is returned to the source and available for reuse, it is often returned in a degraded state that pollutes our streams and rivers. Although "greener" energy, such as hydropower or run-of-the-river hydroelectricity, is generally viewed as more viable sources, these too can severely impact ecosystem health.

Large amounts of energy are required to pump, treat and deliver water to homes and businesses. In Ontario, municipalities, which are largely responsible for the provision of water, report that a third to half of their energy consumption — double that of street lighting — is due to providing water and wastewater services (PAGI 2008). In the United States, a national survey suggests that 13 per cent of the total amount of electricity produced in the entire country is used to pump, treat and heat water (Griffiths-Sattenspiel & Wilson 2009). By creating policies for water conservation and efficiency, then, municipalities can reduce energy consumption, greenhouse gas emissions *and* save costs associated with water treatment and distribution.

Soft Path

While demand-side management will always be a critical component of more sustainable water systems, a more holistic approach is now taking water management to the next level. Drawing from experiences in energy conservation, the Soft Path for water is a planning approach that, similar to demand-side management, strives for efficiency in water use — but goes beyond this by scrutinizing our current water-use habits and patterns (Brandes & Brooks 2007). This planning approach addresses not only *how* we use water, but also *why* we are using water in the first place. It seeks to make lasting changes in habits and practices of water users by thinking well into the future and creating the institutional and management changes today to move us on a more sustainable path. Four principles distinguish the Soft Path from conventional planning and management of water resources:

Treat Water as a Service Rather Than an End in Itself

Except for a few human uses (drinking and washing), water is a means of accomplishing a task and not the end product. This change of perspective allows planners, water managers, engineers and decision-makers to focus on innovative alternatives to water-based services, rather than just on how to supply enough water for an ever-increasing demand.

Make Ecological Sustainability a Fundamental Criterion

Soft Path recognizes ecosystems as legitimate users of water. As such, environmental constraints are built into the planning system from the start, in order to ensure sufficient water quantity and quality is returned back to nature. (see Fig. 5.2, color page C-2)

Match the Quality of Water Delivered to the Quality Needed at End Use

High-quality water is critical to human health. However, not all water we use needs to be of drinking water quality. By matching the quality to the end use, we save time and money in treatment. For example, wastewater from laundry, dishwashing and bathing in the home, also known as greywater, can be recycled for outdoor irrigation, toilet flushing or hot water reuse rather than immediately released into our sewer systems. Fresh water is simply too precious to only be used once. Fully operational Soft Path systems ensure water cascades through multiple uses — with water from one use becoming an input for another.

Plan from the Future Back to the Present

Traditionally, planning involves starting in the present and projecting into the future. Soft Path planning does the exact opposite. It first identifies a desirable future state for society (in terms of water sources and uses) and then works backwards to identify policies and programs to achieve that desired state (Brandes & Brooks 2007).

Role of Senior Government

In Canada and the United States, governments at the federal and provincial/state levels play a role in water management and provision. Although the federal authority is less directly involved with urban water services, it supports conservation by promoting national standards and guidelines, providing valuable data and research on water use and providing infrastructure grants. The provinces and states promote conservation at the municipal level by educating municipal councillors and utilities, mandating efficiency through plumbing and building codes, and providing grants for water-efficient fixtures and appliances. For example, the Ontario government's Water Opportunities Act 2010 requires each municipality and water service provider to prepare a municipal water sustainability plan to promote water efficiency. Under the Act, municipalities serving less than 5,000 people are offered financial assistance for projects such as fixing leaking pipes and installing water meters.

Tools and Initiatives

There are many ways for communities to achieve water efficiency. The most common solutions are voluntary and mandatory curtailment programs implemented by local governments, requesting or requiring customers to water their gardens only at certain times or on certain days. These programs work best when accompanied with education and promotional programs that help customers understand the financial savings and environmental benefits, as well as the local supply issues associated with water consumption. Incentive programs and education about efficient hardware and techniques can also promote customer participation in water conservation, as can bylaws and ordinances that require plumbing and irrigation products and techniques.

Voluntary

WATER EFFICIENT DEMONSTRATION GARDEN

The West Basin Municipal Water District, located in Southern California, sponsors a water-efficient demonstration garden to educate the public about water-efficient irrigation systems. The garden demonstrates how the use of drip irrigation, weather-based irrigation systems, rain and runoff capture systems, permeable surfaces, drought-tolerant landscaping and mulch

Demand-side Management in California

Gleick et al. (2005) found that total urban water use in California could be reduced by almost 30 per cent from 2000 levels by 2030 using existing tools and technologies to reduce demand. More importantly, the majority of the water could be saved at a lower cost and without the many social, environmental and economic consequences of constructing any new sources of supply. If these technologies were employed, California would not need to find and operate a new water supply project for several decades.

Soft Path in Oliver, British Columbia

The Soft Path approach was applied to the Town of Oliver, British Columbia (Brandes et al. 2007). Oliver is facing water shortages due to population growth and changes in regional climate. Using the Soft Path approach, analysts found that Oliver could reduce projected water demands for 2050 by 50 per cent as compared to projected demands under the status quo. This could be achieved through demand-side management techniques (e.g., high-efficiency dishwashers, xeriscaping, outdoor water-use bylaws, system-leakage audits) as well as Soft Path approaches (like composting toilets, alternative sources of water such as rainwater and reclaimed water, and programs that promote more water-savvy behaviors). By doing so, the town would not need to find new water sources.

can save water and reduce runoff. Each year, the District holds a free Smart Landscape Expo where the public is invited to tour the garden, participate in workshops related to water conservation and purchase native plants, water efficient sprinklers, rain barrels and other water-conserving devices (West Basin Municipal Water District 2011).

EDUCATION PROGRAM FOR LANDSCAPE CONTRACTORS AND HOMEOWNERS

Originally called Protector del Agua, the California Friendly Landscape Training Program is sponsored by the Metropolitan Water District of Southern California and is offered free through the Municipal Water District of Orange County. The District offers two courses (one for homeowners and one for landscape contractors) designed to teach students about the relationships between plants, soil and water. Students learn how to evaluate the moisture needs of a landscape, measure the efficiency of the existing irrigation system and adjust or replace irrigation systems to avoid water wastage. (Municipal Water District of Orange County 2011).

WATER AUDIT SOFTWARE

In 2010, the American Water Works Association released free water audit software designed for municipal water utility providers. The software, which is applicable in American and Canadian contexts, allows water utilities to conduct a preliminary water audit to help determine how much water is being lost and from where (American Water Works Association 2011).

Financial Incentives
SMART WASH CLOTHES REBATE PROJECT

The City of Guelph, Ontario, in partnership with Guelph Hydro, offers multi-residential units or residents of single-family dwellings a $100 rebate for purchasing an Energy Star-rated front-load washing machine. The program also offers commercial, industrial and institutional facilities a $200 rebate for such purchases. The program, which began as a pilot project in 2008, was so successful that it has been fully implemented as part of Guelph's initiative to conserve water (City of Guelph 2011).

SAVE MONEY BY CONDUCTING A WATER AUDIT

As part of the Regional Municipality of York's Water for Tomorrow program, this Ontario municipality is offering free water-use audits to industrial, commercial and institutional business owners, as well as building owners and property managers. If the recommendations of the water audit are implemented (e.g., retrofit of current appliances), applicants are eligible to receive a one-time incentive of $0.30 per liter of water saved on an average day, or 50 per cent of the total capital cost of the retrofit up to a maximum of $50,000 (Water for Tomorrow 2011).

DECLINING BLOCK RATE

Starting in 2008, the City of Toronto has used a declining block rate to charge industrial facilities that use high volumes of water for operation. Industrial facilities are eligible for a 28 percent discount on the general water rate, provided they conduct water-use audits and submit water conservation plans to the City's Water Conservation Office. Plans must include details of the audit, as well as when and how audit recommendations (for example, to conserve water) will be implemented. If a plan is accepted by the city, the first 6000 cubic meters of water consumed for industrial operations will be charged the general rate; any additional water used will be charged at the reduced rate. Facilities must also submit an annual water reductions progress report to continue receiving the reduced rate (City of Toronto 2011).

INCLINING BLOCK RATE

The tourist town of Tofino, British Columbia, has a winter population of less than 2,000 and a summer population of over 20,000. Over the past five years, the District has introduced pricing reforms to address water shortages and generate funds for infrastructure maintenance. New rate structures include a fixed levy and five different consumption tiers on an inclining block scale. A seasonal surcharge doubles rates during the summer months when water consumption is at its highest. Residential developments and businesses are charged different rates.

Expenditure

WATER AND ENERGY-EFFICIENT DEMONSTRATION COMMUNITY

The Region of Durham, Ontario, in conjunction with Tribute Communities, Natural Resources Canada and the Federation of Canadian Municipalities, developed a water-and-energy-efficient demonstration community of 175 new homes. Half the homes received the standard fixtures and appliances, while the other half received water-and energy-efficient fixtures and appliances such as clothes washers, dishwasher, toilets, showerheads, fridges and drought-tolerant landscaping. The study demonstrated that per day each household that received the efficient appliances/fixtures saved 132 L of water (a 22 percent reduction), 2.6 kWh of electricity (a 13 percent reduction) and 0.59 m3 of natural gas (a 9 percent reduction) as compared to homes that were built with standard appliances. The savings resulted in a 1.19 tonne reduction in CO_2 emissions per household per year. The study also compared the costs of such upgrades to the amount of money saved and calculated a payback of approximately 3.4 years (Veritec Consulting Inc. 2008).

SECONDARY WATER METER PROJECT

The Weber Basin Water Conservancy District, in partnership with the Bureau of Reclamation, State of Utah and the Utah State University, is conducting a project to determine the water savings associated with secondary water metering. Beginning March 2011, 1,000 water meters on secondary residential water systems (which provide untreated water for irrigation purposes) will be installed, generating a monthly water report that will enable residents to monitor their secondary water usage. The project is part of a larger effort to meter all secondary water connections (Weber Basin Water Conservancy District 2011).

LEAK DETECTION AND REPAIR PROGRAM

The City of Mount Pearl, Newfoundland, with a population of over 25,500 residents, scrutinized its extremely high consumption rates by conducting a leak detection analysis of its water distribution pipes. Without interrupting water supply, the analysis revealed over 60 leaks. Once the leaks were located and repaired, monthly water consumption rates dropped considerably, resulting in a yearly savings of $150,000 (Fricke & Manuel 2005).

ULTRA-LOW-FLUSH TOILET DISTRIBUTION PROGRAM

The Metropolitan Water District and the Los Angeles Department of Water & Power jointly sponsored a free ultra-low-flow toilet distribution project to its customers in the Los Angeles area. From 1990 to 2006, 1.3 million water-wasting toilets were replaced with water efficient toilets. Community-based organizations handled the actual distribution of the toilets in the inner city of Los Angeles. The program successfully replaced 90 percent of all single-family residential toilets (Mono Lake Committee 2011).

Regulatory
WATER METERING AND EFFICIENT FIXTURES

The City of Calgary passed a bylaw in 2006 requiring all residential customers to install water meters by 2014. The bylaw also requires all new homes and commercial construction, including any renovations that need a plumbing permit, to install low-water-use fixtures for toilets, urinals and faucets. This bylaw also prohibits the installation of once-through cooling systems, such as refrigerators or air-conditioning systems that cycle water only once through their systems before discarding it (City of Calgary 2010a).

OUTDOOR WATER-USE BYLAW

Quebec City passed a bylaw in 2008 that makes it illegal to allow water to run off a private or public property and to break or allow hoses and spray nozzels to deteriorate such that water is lost or wasted. The bylaw also regulates the use of potable water for lawn-watering, washing of driveways or parking lots or filling pools and ponds. Penalties for breaking the law range from $150 to $4,000 (Ville de Quebec 2008).

Water Quality And Sewage Treatment

The quality of water affects the quality of the life it touches. In many communities, both groundwater and surface water systems have deteriorated in quality. Water pollution in combination with high rates of water extraction can seriously harm hydrological systems. Wastewater treatment is of particular concern.

Conventional sewage treatment systems produce an often-toxic by-product called sludge, which is difficult to dispose of, and use hazardous compounds in the treatment process, which end up in the environment. Without massive federal subsidies, most communities cannot afford to build and operate advanced wastewater treatment facilities that reduce these harmful environmental impacts.

Wastewater treatment plants can also contribute to social injustice. The burden of accommodating these aesthetically displeasing, often malodorous, plants often falls on people living in low-income areas, which are rarely home to those making the decisions about the location of plants. Fortunately, the rise of the environmental justice movement has had real victories. For example, the environmental justice organization WE ACT was a key player in improving the operation and management of the North River Sewage Treatment Plant in Harlem (New York), which was releasing large amounts of noxious emissions that led to foul odors and respiratory problems for local residents (WE ACT 2011).

In many North American cities, stormwater and sewage is collected and transferred to the water treatment plant using the same sewer system. Although these combined systems are primarily located in older parts of the city, they are still a major water pollution concern for approximately 772 American cities (United States Environmental Protection Agency 2008b). During heavy rains or snow melt, these systems are often unable to process the large amount of incoming water, resulting in overflow and release of raw sewage directly into rivers and streams. In New York alone, 30 billion gallons per year of wastewater is discharged into streams and rivers as a result of combined sewer overflows (New York Department of Environmental Protection 2011).

More conservative water use can reduce the amount of stormwater and waste entering the sewer system, and therefore improve water quality by helping reduce loads on sewage treatment plants and avoiding overflow. Treatment plants also work better with reduced flows because detention time can be increased if plants aren't overburdened.

Groundwater quality can also benefit from reduced water use. By avoiding large draws on groundwater supplies, saltwater intrusion is prevented, and soil contaminants from agricultural pesticides or fertilizers, landfills, toxic-waste sites or sewage lines are not drawn up to the surface to contaminate drinking water supplies.

Water quality is also affected by pollution from agriculture, industry, households, automobiles and sedimentation from cleared land. For example, elevated concentrations of nitrate due to fertilization practices have been documented since the early 1970s in the Abbotsford-Sumas aquifer that serves drinking water to nearly 10,000 people in Washington State and 10,000 people in southwestern British Columbia (Chesnaux, Allen & Graham 2007). Reducing pollution and preventing degradation to the quality of our water is the most sustainable way to preserve this precious resource, which requires changes in our patterns of land use, auto dependency and economic activities. While this book's chapters on land use, transportation and greening illustrate many efforts in this direction, this section will primarily discuss "end of the pipe" strategies for wastewater treatment.

Sewage treatment plants themselves are major contributors to water pollution, as many cities only have primary treatment (settling tanks that remove two-thirds of suspended solids and one-third of the biological oxygen demand) of waste. Contaminants that degrade aquatic systems and fish habitat are thus discharged into local waterways. Other urban treatment plants provide secondary treatment that removes most of the biological oxygen demand and suspended solids; however, very few plants conduct tertiary treatment to purify wastewater before discharge. The high monetary cost of treatment precludes these efforts, yet the true cost of degradation to the ecosystem and deteriorating water quality and fish stocks may be greater to communities. Sustainable water management aims to treat

Land Use and Water Resources

Land-use decisions have significant impacts on water quality and quantity. Commercial, industrial and urban centers tend to have higher levels of impervious surfaces, such as roads, parking lots, sidewalks and rooftops. These surfaces prevent water from percolating through the soil and recharging groundwater supplies. This is especially a problem for communities that rely on wells for their water. Impervious surfaces also increase stormwater runoff, leading to higher levels of water pollution and physical degradation of natural streambeds, directly impacting fish and watershed health. Farmland and open spaces such as golf courses release pesticides and fertilizers into the aquatic ecosystem, adding to degradation of water quality. The use of fertilizers and the production of waste from residential areas also contribute to water pollution and can affect critical drinking water supplies (Planning with Power 2009).

effluent at its pollution *source*, thus holding the polluter responsible for avoiding or eliminating water contamination. The goal is also to treat wastewater so that it is as high or higher quality than water coming into urban water systems.

Reclaiming and reusing treated wastewater (instead of discharging it to waterways) can significantly reduce the amount of water sent for treatment, improve water quality and delay expansion of potable water supplies and distribution systems. Reclaimed water can be used for non-potable purposes, such as irrigating golf courses, flushing toilets, creating water features to serve as meeting places or cooling

Fig. 5.3: *Solar aquatics systems (SAS) mimic the natural purifying process of a wetland. In this SAS designed by JTED and engineered by Natural Systems International for the Omega Institute, wastewater is directed through a greenhouse with clear-sided tanks that the right balance of organisms and plants cleanse the water.* (Credit: Andy Milford Creative Commons license)

for industrial purposes. Seawater can also be used for industrial cooling to reduce demand on potable water.

Because treated wastewater is nutrient-rich, it is often applied directly to the land where it is used as fertilizer and applied to forests, agricultural crops, parks or golf courses. The water is filtered as it is stored in the vegetated soils and woodlands, and percolates through the ground to recharge water tables. In Florida alone, over 7 million cubic meters (567,000 acre-feet) of water is reused each year for irrigation, industrial cooling and processing, commercial purposes (e.g., toilet flushing), restoring wetlands and for groundwater recharge (Bryck et al. 2008). For a discussion about how wastewater and sewage can be used to produce various types of energy, see chapter 7.

If treated to a potable water standard, wastewater can also be returned to a city's potable water reservoir or be injected into aquifers or groundwater supplies to augment drinking water.

Nature and natural processes can be used to effectively treat wastewater in both rural and urban communities. Aquatic plants, marshes or wetlands can filter wastewater and absorb nitrates, phosphates and even heavy metals and other toxins through their roots. Some developers and communities are using existing marshes to treat wastewater, while others are constructing artificial wetlands or *solar aquatic systems* (SAS). Although the SAS is not yet considered a mainstream technology, it is currently in use throughout the world. Within North America for example, the Audubon Society's park at Corkscrew Swamp near Naples, Florida, has successfully used SAS technology since 1994 to treat wastewater and sewage from its visitors' center.

Green Infrastructure

In addition to the afore mentioned strategies, green infrastructure offers communities ecological and economical options to manage stormwater runoff, maintain or restore natural hydrology and protect surface and groundwater quality. Rural communities, which typically have higher levels of permeable surfaces than do most cities, are in a particularly good position to develop green infrastructure.

In areas with significant amounts of paved surfaces, such as parking lots or streets, large volumes of water that falls during rain events runs straight off the surface, entering stormwater drains or nearby creeks or streams. Most often, water entering stormwater drains is diverted straight into a stream or creek without being treated.

To reduce the load on stormwater infrastructure and protect stream water quality, some communities are managing runoff using permeable surfaces and overland flow into rain gardens, planter boxes and vegetated swales. These structures capture stormwater and filter it through soil and/or vegetation, thereby removing pollutants and improving water quality before it reaches the water table or is discharged into nearby water bodies.

Other stormwater management strategies such as green roofs, rain barrels and rainwater gardens can be used to capture rainwater, thereby reducing the volume and discharge rate of water into the stormwater system. Vegetation planted alongside a stream or river bank can improve stream health and water quality. A strip of vegetation can act as a buffer by filtering and slowing polluted runoff, preventing soil erosion, absorbing flood waters and providing riparian habitat for wildlife. Detention ponds offer another way of controlling and purifying

Solar Aquatic Systems (SAS)

SAS is a biologically integrated technology that treats sludge, sewage and industrial process wastewater to high-quality specifications at low cost. It can use a combination of plants, micro-organisms (bacteria, algae), snails and fish in greenhouses to filter and consume contaminants. An SAS mimics wetlands in processing waste, but is typically more compact so that more waste can be processed in a smaller area. A well-designed SAS can produce water that is pure enough for drinking, but in North America, fear of system failure precludes this practice, so the clean water is typically discharged or used for non-potable uses such as irrigation. In addition to providing ecologically responsible ways of processing sewage without toxic chemicals, wetlands and SAS can serve as recreational amenities, bird sanctuaries and tourist attractions.

Fig. 5.4: *Detention ponds in the community of UniverCity Burnaby, BC, are used to manage peak flows of stormwater and mitigate the effect of large volumes of water on ecosystems downstream from the development.*
(Credit: SFU Community Trust / UniverCity)

stormwater run-off. These are built to collect and detain stormwater from nearby communities, thereby retarding outflow to streams or the stormwater system during heavy rainfall events or snowmelts. Detention ponds can also purify wastewater by detaining and allowing

---

Using Green Infrastructure for Stormwater Management

Vegetated swales: Also known as "grassed channels," swales are gently sloping depressions that naturally collect and drain water but which are enhanced with dense vegetation to capture and treat runoff from rooftops, streets or parking lots. Plants and check dams slow down the water, allowing sediments and pollutants to settle out. Some water infiltrates the soil while other water is transported elsewhere, such as into a stream, creek or stormwater system. Swales can reduce the number and cost of storm drains and piping when developing an area.

Rainwater gardens: Similar to vegetated swales, rainwater gardens use soil and a variety of flood or drought-tolerant plants to capture and filter out pollutants from stormwater runoff. Gardens are typically located in a shallow depression and are an aesthetically pleasing way to manage stormwater.

Planter boxes: These are small contained and vegetated areas designed to collect and treat stormwater. Treated water is either infiltrated into the ground as groundwater or discharged back into the stormwater drainage system. Planter boxes do not require much space and can add aesthetic appeal and wildlife habitat to city streets, parking lots and commercial/residential areas.

Green roofs: These are roofs that are partially or completely covered with a waterproof membrane, a growing medium (such as soil) and planted vegetation. Green roofs absorb rainwater (thereby reducing stormwater runoff), mitigate the heat island effect (see chapter 9), reduce heat loss and energy consumption of the building, provide habitat for birds and filter air and water pollutants.

Rain barrels and cisterns: These containers collect and temporarily hold rainwater from rooftops. Rain barrels can be connected directly to a building's downspout to collect and store water for later use in the garden or domestically for laundry or toilet flushing.

Detention ponds: Ponds can be designed and constructed to manage stormwater during peak flow events such as flooding, spring melt and heavy rainfall.

Fig. 5.5: *Rain gardens beautify while using soil and drought- or flood- resistant plants to filter out pollutants from stormwater run-off.* (CREDIT: SFU COMMUNITY TRUST / UNIVERCITY)

pollutants to settle out or by incorporating aquatic plants that filter and remove pollutants. This filtered water can then be used to irrigate nearby golf courses or other landscapes. In addition to managing stormwater, ponds can become places for outdoor recreation (Wang, Cossitt & Dormuth 2008).

Tools and Initiatives

Voluntary

ADOPT-A-STREAM PROGRAMS

Adopt-a-Stream programs provide the opportunity for organizations, families, individuals and clubs to help the City of Kelowna, BC, maintain and monitor a section of a creek/ stream, thereby protecting local water quality and wildlife habitat. Volunteers participate in the program for a minimum of two years, during which they are responsible for picking up litter and debris along the stream bank, removing invasive weeds and painting yellow fish symbols on storm drains to remind residents to avoid dumping harmful substances down these drains (City of Kelowna 2009).

GREEN ALLEYWAYS

The Chicago Department of Transportation's Green Alley Program began as a pilot project in 2006 and has since been widely adopted with the installation of more than 100 green alleys. Alleys are retrofitted using permeable pavement that is light in color, reflective and made of recycled materials. The project aims to create alleys that minimize heat radiation and reduce flooding and stormwater runoff through increased infiltration. The retrofit also aims to reduce light pollution by outfitting alleys with streetlights that direct light downwards (The Civic Federation 2007).

Fig. 5.6: *Permeable pavements allow rainwater to percolate through to the soil below, avoiding the sewer system and recharging groundwater supplies. Many people would have a hard time telling permeable pavements apart from regular pavement, but as this project in Detroit Michigan shows, choice permeable paving materials can be really distinctive.* (CREDIT: PEGGY BRENNAN FROM GREEN GARAGE DETROIT)

Expenditure

RAIN GARDEN TO MANAGE STORMWATER

As part of an ongoing effort to protect the water quality of Crystal Lake, the City of Burnsville, Minnesota, along with the Metropolitan Council and the Dakota County Soil and Water Conservation District, funded a prototypical rainwater garden system. The project involved retrofitting 17 residential properties within a 5.3-acre neighborhood with individual rain gardens. The gardens, which were designed to capture street runoff through the installation of curb cuts at each garden, reduced runoff volumes by 90 percent. Each garden was maintained by the individual homeowner (Barr Engineering Company 2006).

WASTEWATER RECLAMATION PLANT

The City of San Diego, California, is funding an Advanced Water Purification Demonstration Project at its North City Water Reclamation Plant. The city currently imports over 80 percent of its water from sources that are steadily dwindling. The project, which is scheduled to run until 2013, would augment water reservoirs and offer residents a local and sustainable water supply. If it proves viable, the purification facility will collect and treat wastewater to a potable standard, directing the treated water to the city's drinking water reservoirs (Holding 2010).

REUSE OF WASTEWATER FOR INDUSTRIAL COOLING

Starting in 2002, the Hampton Roads Sanitation District, located in Virginia, has delivered 500,000 gallons of treated wastewater per day to Giant Industries, Inc., where it is used for cooling and other industrial purposes at the company's nearby refinery. Instead of using potable drinking water, this partnership allows for the reuse of wastewater for industrial purposes, which provides a cost-effective alternative and helps protect water resources (Hampton Roads Sanitation District 2011).

SOLUTION FOR AGING SEPTIC TANK SYSTEM

The rural fishing village of Victoria, Prince Edward Island, with a population of approximately 77 year-round residents, is a popular tourist destination in the summer. It needed a low-cost solution to its aging septic system that frequently failed and discharged sewage into the adjacent bay and groundwater. In partnership with Engineering Technologies Canada, the village of Victoria retrofitted 57 residential and 6 commercial properties with a new wastewater system designed to adjust to increases in waste flow during the tourism season. On each property, sewage is first collected in a septic tank where primary treatment occurs. The wastewater is then transported to treatment pods where pollutants are removed. The remaining waste (effluent) is collected and sent to a land-based site for disposal. The new system, which requires only one part-time operator, successfully eliminated all phosphorus and fecal coliform discharges into the bay, reduced suspended solids by 90 percent and nitrogen by 29 percent in discharged water, cut CO_2 emissions related to pumping out holding and septic tanks by 54 percent and has rid the village of occasional bad smells (Federation of Canadian Municipalities 2011; Orenco System Ltd. 2011).

PRE-TREATMENT USING BACTERIA

The Town of Olds, Alberta (population: approximately 7000), upgraded its 30-year-old at-capacity wastewater treatment plant without expanding any infrastructure. In partnership with Waste Not Ltd., the town installed a system that injects a bacterial treatment into the wastewater pipes before the wastewater reaches the treatment plant. Injection of the bacterial treatment allows breakdown of solids and pollutants to occur in locations throughout the entire sewer collection system, thereby optimizing the entire infrastructure. This project has resulted in an increase in the plant's capacity by 45 percent without incurring any new infrastructure costs and has reduced the volume of generated effluent requiring disposal by 25 percent (Federation of Canadian Municipalities 2011).

WATER RECYCLING PROGRAM

California's Orange County Water District began its Green Acres Project in 1991. The project has the capacity to reclaim 7.5 million gallons of water per day for irrigation at parks, schools and golf courses, as well as for industrial purposes. The project currently provides reclaimed water for five cities in the surrounding area (Orange County Water District 2008).

APPLYING EFFLUENT TO AGRICULTURAL LAND

Calgary's Calgro Program began in 1983 as a joint partnership between the Province of Alberta and the City of Calgary. Every year, 20 million kilograms of effluent (biosolids) produced during the wastewater treatment process is used as fertilizer on local farms. In some municipalities, it is applied on golf courses or forestland. Receiving biosolids through the program is free for participating farmers approved by the Alberta Environment Office (City of Calgary 2010b).

GROUNDWATER RECHARGE SYSTEM

In response to dwindling water supplies, the Orange County Water District in Southern California in partnership with the Orange County Sanitation District funded a new groundwater replenishment system. It recycles treated wastewater that would have otherwise been discharged into the Pacific Ocean into purified drinking water through a two-stage treatment process. The highly purified water is then discharged back into the river, where it filters through the ground and replenishes groundwater supplies used for drinking water.

Every day, the system recycles 70 million gallons of wastewater into drinking water (Orange County 2011).

Financial Incentives

DISCOUNT FOR DISCONNECTING

The City of Portland's Downspout Disconnection Program offers private property owners a one-time discount of up to $53 on their stormwater charges for each downspout disconnected from the combined sewer system. The program has successfully disconnected 50,000 downspouts from the sewer system, allowing more than 1.2 billion gallons of stormwater per year to infiltrate lawns and gardens rather than stormwater systems (City of Portland 2011).

GREEN INFRASTRUCTURE GRANT

To better manage stormwater, the New York Department of Environmental Protection established its green infrastructure grant program. Private property owners, businesses and organizations are encouraged to submit applications for projects that use green infrastructure to reduce the quantity of stormwater entering the system and reduce impervious surfaces in the city (e.g., bioretention swales, constructed wetlands, porous concrete, rain barrels and cisterns). Up to $3 million will be provided for green infrastructure projects that will be chosen based on quality of proposal, grant requirements, community involvement and sustainability (New York Department of Environmental Protection 2011).

Regulatory

STORMWATER CHARGE

In 2005, the City of Minneapolis, Minnesota, adopted a stormwater charge for owners of residential, commercial and vacant properties.

The charge, which is based on the type of dwelling and amount of impervious service, is collected by the city and transferred to a Stormwater Fund which is used to pay for the operation, maintenance and improvement of the stormwater system. The charge is determined according to the type of property (e.g., single-family residential versus non-residential) and its amount of impervious surface area. It can be reduced if property owners incorporate structural or non-structural stormwater management techniques that reduce the quantity or significantly improve the quality of stormwater runoff. Other cities such as Philadelphia, Pennsylvania, Lenexa, Kansas and Portland, Oregon, also charge a stormwater fee (United States Environmental Protection Agency 2008c).

INTEGRATED WATER CHARGE

In 2007, Halifax Water, Nova Scotia, became the first utility in Canada that regulates water, wastewater and stormwater use. On top of a fixed charge, customers pay three variable charges based on their water consumption: a water consumption charge that reflects the costs associated with pumping, treating and distributing water; a wastewater and stormwater charge that covers sewer and sanitary sewer system operating costs; and an "environmental protection charge" that reflects infrastructure, operating and capital upgrade costs for the municipal wastewater collection system. Having all aspects of the urban water cycle charged and reflected in separate bills ensures all service costs are recovered and that customers are aware of the linkages between these subsystems and how they can save on both their water and wastewater bills (Brandes, Renzetti & Stinchcombe 2010).

BYLAW FERTILIZER APPLICATION

In 2009, a bylaw in West Chester County, New York State, was passed that severely limits the sale and use of lawn fertilizers containing phosphorus. (County of Westchester 2009).

GREYWATER SYSTEM FOR NEW RESIDENTIAL UNITS

In 2008, the City of Tucson, Arizona, began requiring all new residential buildings to install a separate outlet for discharge of greywater for direct irrigation of landscape. New units must also have a separate drainage system and plumbing for lavatories (including hand sinks), showers and bathtubs to allow for future installation of a distributed greywater system (City of Tucson 2008).

Integrated Resource Planning

Water efficiency and ecologically responsible ways of managing water quality and wastewater are key features of sustainable community development, but a number of barriers inhibit progress. One of the greatest is the compartmentalization of municipal or regional water and wastewater services. In many communities, water and wastewater treatment departments are totally separate, which makes it difficult to jointly address water issues. Similarly, a planning department may issue building permits while the water and sewage departments grapple with the impacts of new buildings on water supply infrastructure, water quality and capacity for sewage treatment. If their staff, boards, billing, budgets and goals were coordinated, mutual goals could be achieved while minimizing costs and ecosystem impacts.

Integrated resource planning or *integrated water resources management* (IWRM) is a planning and management process for long-range water resource issues that considers all water, land and related resources, within whatever political, administrative, economic or functional boundaries they are defined. IWRM is often applied at the scale of watersheds (Cervoni, Biro & Beazley 2008). It has been advocated as the most viable approach to achieving sustainable freshwater management, and requires coordination among and between various levels of government and departments. IWRM strives for multiple-purpose and multiple-means projects including: use of zoning and other land-use management strategies, regulations, incentive programs, taxation and whatever else works to achieve multiple goals for provision of water and sewage services and other objectives (such as energy efficiency, recreation, flood control, wildlife preservation, irrigation and even economic development). In Ontario for example, 36 Conservation Authorities (CA) currently act as watershed-based-non-profit management agencies. These are financially supported partnerships between the provincial government and municipalities located within the watersheds, and are genuinely collaborative efforts. Guided by an integrated management approach, each one manages the water, land and natural habitats within its watershed through programs that benefit social, economic and environmental needs (Conservation Ontario 2009).

One type of integrated resource planning approach is *integrated resource recovery*. This strategy involves coordination among sectors that have traditionally operated as separate waste management systems, such as local governments, water utilities, agriculture, forestry and transportation. It uses outputs of one waste system, such as nutrients in wastewater, as inputs for another, such as fertilizer for agriculture. By no means is this approach limited to wastewater and water management — it can also be applied to energy management (for example, creating fuel from biosolids produced during wastewater treatment: for a more thorough discussion, see chapter 7).

Integrated resource planning can open the door for community economic development and job creation. For example, while reducing operating and infrastructure costs for communities, water-efficiency programs can create jobs and stimulate markets for water-conserving products and technologies. Use of alternative technologies such as SAS can spawn other benefits, such as jobs, tourism, educational programs and production of flowers, plants and herbs. For further discussion on green economies, see chapter 12.

Tools and Initiatives
INTEGRATED MANAGEMENT OF THE UPPER THAMES RIVER

The Upper Thames River Conservation Authority in southwestern Ontario consists of 17 individual municipalities working together to manage the upper portion of the Thames River. Informed by an integrated management approach, the conservation authority provides programs and services including land-use planning and regulations, flood/water control and dams, watershed research, environmental monitoring, soil conservation, forestry, parks and recreation and community partnerships (Cervoni, Biro & Beazley 2008).

INTEGRATED WATER PROTECTION PLAN

Recognizing the need to protect water supplies and ecosystem health within the Moose Jaw River Watershed, Saskatchewan, over 50 individuals from local municipalities, conservation area authorities, irrigation associations and recreational interest groups engaged in a collaborative planning process. The process identified the threats to surface and groundwater supplies within the 9,360-square-kilometer Moose Jaw River Watershed and suggested key actions to address these threats. Further input and feedback from local residents was also sought through a series of open houses. As a result of the process, the MooseJaw River Stewards Inc. was formed to help implement the recommendations of the plan. These included agriculture water quality monitoring, watershed education and awareness for local residents and protecting fish habitat (Saskatchewan Water Authority and Moose Jaw River Watershed Advisory Committee 2006).

Thinking Like a Watershed: Watershed Governance, *the* Future for Water Sustainability

By Oliver M. Brandes

In North America, as in much of the world, the belief in an era of "unlimited water" is ending and water supply issues are beginning to generate genuine concern. An appetite for sustainable solutions and demands for increased attention to water security is mounting. At the core of any new approach to getting water "right" is an emerging focus on improving the institutions and decision-making structures — and a major innovation in the water field is a clear understanding of the potential and possibilities associated with watershed governance.

In light of population and economic growth, continued aquatic ecosystem degradation, a changing climate, regional water scarcity and increasing water demands for urban growth, economic development and energy and resource production only increases the urgency of new approaches to manage and, importantly, govern fresh water.

Senior governments are grappling with often-outdated institutional and legal mechanisms to address a new, increasingly uncertain and challenging paradigm of water management. The new models that are developed to respond to this challenge must be sensitive to a financially and capacity-limited role for government of all types. This is a real and lasting change for the role of government going forward.

In some progressive jurisdictions, such as Australia, the European Union and even South Africa, new approaches also focus less on managing ecosystems and promoting endless supply expansion and instead emphasize designing with nature, recovering resources from waste, managing demand and engaging community and broader societal participation in making decisions at the watershed scale.

Early evidence of this paradigm shift exists even across North America. In Canada, efforts to modernize water management and policy are evident at the community and provincial level; for example, Alberta's Water for Life Strategy, British Columbia's Living Water Smart plan and Ontario's new *Water Opportunities Act* and water source protection regime. In the United States, the venerable Tennessee Valley Authority represents one of the first serious experiments in a watershed approach dating back to the 1930s. More recently, the so-called western watersheds movement has emphasized collaboration and new forms of participation, including successful initiatives in California, Oregon and Washington State. Together these developments suggest a real and lasting trend toward a more distributed or shared form of water governance where government, First Nations, civil society, community ☞

and economic interests collectively play a significant role in decision-making.

At the forefront of these efforts to address the water challenges of the 21st century is attention to the concept of watershed governance. Watershed governance deals with issues of institutional and legal reform and, specifically, seeks to reinvigorate the role of public institutions by transforming governments from top-down managers to facilitators of local solutions and action in the context of a broader public trust. Watershed governance recognizes the critical importance of civil society as a key facilitator of change and innovation. It fundamentally embraces the idea of the watershed as the starting point for sustainable water management and the serious challenge of integration and holistic resource management at a watershed or basin scale.

Although the concept of a watershed approach is certainly not new — it dates back decades in many pockets of water resource management practice — it has been formally recognized internationally at the 1992 International Conference on Water and the Environment in Dublin, Ireland, which formed Dublin Principles that explicitly include a watershed focus. In the same year, the United Nations Conference on Environment and Development and the resulting Agenda 21 recommended the adoption of watershed-based approaches.

Watershed governance builds on this foundation but goes further by recognizing the crucial link between decision-making and on-the-ground practice and priorities. The overarching goal of watershed governance is to provide opportunities and alternative solutions to traditional approaches to supply-oriented water management and top-down centralized decision-making. As an applied form of ecological governance, it creates an institutional and legal shift toward ecologically based water allocations, integrated land- and water-use decisions and comprehensive demand management and Soft Path approaches. As an applied concept, it helps guide senior governments in their efforts to develop water sustainability through institutional, legal and governance reform. More importantly, however, watershed governance offers an opportunity to catalyze a new system in which society is urged — and even required — to *think like a watershed*. As both a philosophy and practical concept, it means a clear focus on integration, collaboration and taking sustainability, watershed function and community prosperity seriously. Simply put: it requires society to prioritize water as a core consideration in all decisions up and down the watershed, now and into the future.

Chapter 6

Waste Reduction and Recycling

Over the past decade, a growing commitment to sustainability has produced a fundamental shift in the way we think about waste (Lehmann 2011). We've previously focused on the 3Rs: reducing, reusing and recycling. While an important part of the solution, it is now clear that the 3Rs are not enough. Rethinking (the 4thR) solid and hazardous waste brings a startling insight: waste shouldn't and doesn't have to be a part of the consumption cycle.

This new management paradigm would prefer to eliminate the word *waste* from the vocabulary of generations to come, by ensuring that no waste is created in the first place. As in nature, all by-products of production processes would be used for something else; any scraps or materials not going into the final product would be rebuilt or reused in another product. *Cradle-to-cradle*, *zero waste* and *systems planning* embody this perspective, rethinking all aspects of a product — from its design to reuse and recycling.

In Canada and the United States especially, we have a long way to go to reach any kind of future with less waste. The US alone generated 243 million tons of municipal solid waste from residential, commercial and institutional sources in 2009; this amounts to 4.34 pounds per person per day of consumer discards, such as durable and non-durable goods, packaging, food scraps, yard trimmings and miscellaneous organic and non-organic items (EPA 2010a). From 1960 to 2009, per capita waste has increased by 62 percent, while the annual amount of municipal solid waste (MSW) in the US has increased by 275 percent (EPA 2010a). With the increasing global population and the constant challenge of finding appropriate landfill sites, striving towards zero waste is more important now than it ever has been. Mobilizing the community to protect our natural capital will require changes to our cultural practices and economic incentives.

Change, however, is possible and is happening. Per capita waste and the total municipal solid waste in the United States stopped climbing in 2000 and 2007 respectively (see Figure 6.1). Diversion rates in the United States are steadily on the increase, growing almost exponentially in the early 1990s. While it may be too soon to call this a trend, it does suggest that this 4thR rethinking is becoming more widely understood.

This chapter will explore the hierarchy of options for waste management, from rethinking, reducing, reusing, recycling and recovery to disposal, with a focus on systems thinking and striving towards a future without waste.

Waste Hierarchy

The waste hierarchy (see Figure 6.2) not only outlines the most to least desirable waste management strategies, but it can also be viewed as the historical evolution of waste management, beginning with disposal. In the past, waste was "managed" by simply being disposed of in a landfill located on the fringe of a community. In the late 1960s, higher regulatory standards and public resistance to facility siting began to limit access to affordable landfill space (Young 1991). Waste managers responded to these issues with solutions that didn't address any of the root causes of the waste: mega landfills and waste export. These types of solutions are referred to as *end-of-the-pipe*, as they don't consider where the waste came from or how the product that produced it was used.

Recognition that landfill sites were finite led to the addition of another R: "recovery," which refers to the recovery of energy from waste, commonly through incineration. Technologies such as waste-to-energy plants were conceived to recover the energy released when waste is burned.

Moving up the hierarchy, managers conceived of another R option for waste diversion efforts: recycling. But it has become increasingly clear that, while recycling solves the problem of finite landfill space, it moves the mess while doing little to preventing it in the first place.

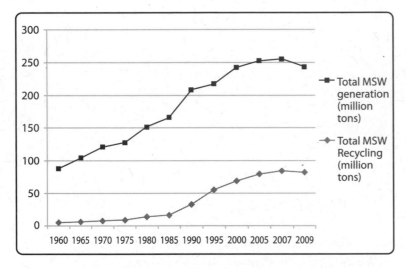

Fig. 6.1: *Municipal solid waste (MSW) generation and recycling in the United States (EPA 2010a). Recycling, composting and waste diversion rates are steadily representing more of the total waste stream, but there is a long way to go to close the gap.*

Fig. 6.2:
A hierarchy of waste.

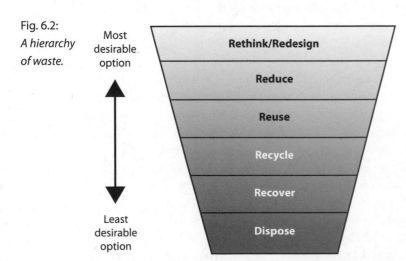

The next two Rs in the hierarchy, reduce and reuse, were heavily promoted beginning in the 1990s through education campaigns, and encourage behaviors which address the root causes of the problem. The top and most evolved strategy, and the one that should be used most frequently, is rethink/redesign, which demands frameworks for not creating waste in the first place.

Types of Waste

What exactly are we talking about when we say "waste"? Analysts tend to organize it into five major categories:

- Municipal solid waste (and industrial solid waste): includes food waste, paper, plastic, textiles, metals and glass. This category encompasses anything that can be recycled; industrial solid waste is typically the same as municipal except on a larger scale.
- Liquid waste: includes sewage from all plumbing systems.
- E-waste: includes all types of electronics.
- Hazardous waste: includes batteries, light bulbs, medicines, chemicals, paint, solvents, pesticides and medical waste.
- Radioactive waste: includes nuclear by-products. (Bournay 2006; Official Journal of the European Communities 2001)

In the past, the upper portions of the waste hierarchy have not been given as much attention as the lower portions. Energy recovery and recycling programs have blossomed across the continent while much less has been done to promote rethinking, reducing or reuse. Reuse and reduction offer the greatest opportunities for eliminating pollution and depletion of natural resources, yet they are often given less consideration than the immediate needs of recycling and disposal.

Let's explore the strategies of the waste management hierarchy, starting with the ones that promise the biggest payback: rethinking and reducing.

Rethinking and Reducing

There are two main players in the rethink and reduce waste strategy: industry/institutions and residents. In 2009, 55 to 65 percent of waste was generated by residences, while the remainder was generated by institutions and industry (EPA 2010a). The EPA Office of Solid Waste and Emergency Response found that 42 percent of US 2006 greenhouse gas emissions were associated with the manufacturing, use and disposal of materials and products (EPA 2009). How should we address these two major groups? The best way to reduce waste and the emissions it produces is by not creating waste in the first place.

Frameworks for Rethinking Waste Management

Many local governments are promoting the vision of a *zero waste* society. The zero waste approach recognizes that waste is avoidable, something that is not a given in the design process, and seeks to eliminate it altogether (Lehmann 2011). Zero waste closes the loop through source reduction; savvy product design; and reuse, repair and recycling back into nature or the marketplace. While it is clear that achieving zero waste will ultimately require fundamental shifts in manufacturing and consumption, communities are finding that striving for zero waste now helps them reduce their ecological footprint (Regional District of Nanaimo 2011).

Subaru is an example of a corporation that is striving to incorporate zero waste principles into its production process. Since May 2004, the company's manufacturing plant in Illinois has managed to divert 99.9 percent of its waste away from landfills, with the remainder being hazardous waste. It has redesigned its processes and looked for creative ways to sell its by-products. The company has used a combination of reduction strategies such as returning packaging to suppliers, reusing materials internally and changing processes like welding to create less waste; and diversion strategies such as sending waste to a waste-to-energy facility and shipping its solvents to a treatment facility. While the latter are still considered waste, Subaru is striving to reduce this component of its zero-landfill strategy (Robinson & Schroeder 2009).

Product life-cycle analysis and *cradle-to-cradle management* are two systems-level approaches to encourage source reduction (Braungart, McDonough & Bollinger 2007). Both start from the recognition that conventional waste management has proceeded as if solid and hazardous wastes emerge out of nowhere, with no connection to previous actions and decisions other than those who consume products. In fact, every product has a life cycle that remains generally unknown to the consumer, and unaccounted for by our economy. That cycle begins on the product designer's drawing board and continues through resource extraction, manufacturing, retailing, purchase or consumption and disposal.

Life-cycle analysis reveals the true costs of products, as well as opportunities to reduce waste at all of these stages. It also reveals the source-reduction benefits of designing for durability. Longer-lasting products aren't thrown out and replaced as quickly. By selecting products based on their entire life cycles, we support the design and manufacture of products that are durable, reusable, repairable, re-manufacturable or recyclable. Product life-cycle analysis therefore offers a strong rationale for change not only in our consumption habits but in design and manufacturing processes (Ayres 1995).

Let's look at an example of a life-cycle analysis with an office chair: one chair is made with a glass-filled nylon base, the other with aluminum. Looking at the impacts from the materials extraction, construction, use and disposal phases, the aluminum chair had much more of an impact when the high-intensity extraction phase was accounted for. Thinking about this impact can encourage the use of recycled aluminum or the use of another material all together (Gamage et al. 2008).

Cradle-to-cradle management refers to managing a product from its "cradle," where it was designed and created, to its use and its ultimate return to the "cradle," where it becomes something else. Building on previous concepts of cradle-to-grave management, in which products were considered in terms of their impact on the environment when disposed of, cradle-to-cradle seeks to create designs that do not assume that waste has to be a part of the cycle (Braungart, McDonough & Bollinger 2007). Cradle-to-cradle is about producers assuming extended responsibility for their products, by making decisions about the product's material composition, durability, toxicity and potential for reuse and recycling to minimize environmental impact (Ayres 1995).

Cradle-to-cradle management is really gaining ground in North America with the adoption of "take-back" laws that place the onus on industry for end-of-life management of products and their packaging. For example, in 2008, New

York City adopted the *Electronic Equipment Collection Recycling and Reuse Act* that requires electronics manufacturers that sell products in the city to accept them back for recycling at no cost to the consumer. Electronics covered by the law are banned from disposal (NYC 2008). The city has also adopted take-back laws for other products, many of which have been superseded by statewide laws of the same vein. Communities can also use regulatory measures, education programs or technical assistance programs to help industry reduce wastes.

Waste as a Behavior

Industry and institutions are not the only ones with a large role to play in rethinking. Consumer demand drives the economic market; if people are buying, someone will be selling.

In the United States, per capita solid waste was 4.34 pounds per day in 2009 (EPA 2010a). Compared to the 0.44 to 1.32 pounds of solid waste per person per day in India, it is clear that consumption patterns play into the amount of waste generated (DEA 2009). Furthermore, most people consider waste collection as free service they are entitled to, the cost of which should be absorbed by government. This can serve as a perverse subsidy which actually encourages more waste.

As well, many people's measure of success can be summed up in the bumper sticker: "The one who dies with the most toys wins." But a large body of empirical research on happiness shows that there is a vast difference between standard of living and quality of life (Torras 2008). More thoughtful indicators, such as how much time we spend with our friends and families and how many walks we take per week, seem to correlate more closely with quality of life. People who rethink their priorities

and habits often realize they just don't need so much stuff! For most of us, this is likely the most effective means of not only waste reduction but higher personal satisfaction.

Reduction Strategies

For industry, source reduction refers to reducing the amount that enters the waste stream before the product is even created. Strategies include modifying processes and procedures to reduce the amount of waste associated with product manufacture, reducing the amount of packaging associated with the product and creating systems that use any by-products from the manufacturing process.

Source reduction is the most cost-effective means of waste management. For cities and towns, source reduction translates into lower costs for municipal waste management services and less burden on landfills. For organizations, businesses and governments, it promises huge savings on disposal costs and greater value from resources. For consumers, source reduction can bring focus to a society that is too often inundated with an abundance of product choices that adds little to our real happiness.

Source reduction complemented by re-thinking of product design and resource use and waste behaviors as well as reuse can lead us to a system with altogether less waste.

REUSE

Reuse is an underutilized component of the waste hierarchy. The potential savings — both financial and environmental — from reuse are truly astounding. When individuals and businesses reuse ink cartridges, batteries, paper, shipping materials, clothing and plastics or buy used items like furniture, they reduce the costs of both waste disposal and new materials.

Identifying new opportunities for reuse and repair not only reduces waste destined for the landfill; it creates business opportunities. Second-hand shops sell everything from clothes to furniture to books and electronic equipment. In the United States, several second-hand markets are billion-dollar industries (Thomas 2004). In Canada, used car sales alone topped $5 billion in 2010 (Statistics Canada 2011). Reuse can also create new service-sector jobs — and with them, opportunities to link job training with reuse and repair businesses. Local governments can provide special zoning, financial incentives and information to encourage reuse, lease and rental businesses.

Legislation can provide a powerful stimulus for reuse and recycling. Bills requiring refillable bottles for certain types of beverage containers emerged in the early 1970s. On average, a beer bottle was reused 15 to 20 times before being reprocessed into a new bottle. The resulting energy savings are enormous. To be effective, however, it is critical that such legislation keep pace with industry trends. For example, despite the environmental benefits of glass bottle reuse, industry has promoted disposable glass or plastic bottles, rendering refillables out of style. As a result, many bottle-deposit systems simply recover materials for recycling as opposed to reuse.

Reuse initiatives can also promote social equity. In the US, Habitat for Humanity supports local building projects that provide families with safe affordable housing in part through profits generated from more than 200 ReStores. These outlets sell quality new and used building materials to the public at significant discounts. In doing so, they also provide affordable building supplies and link people who have quality materials they no longer need with those who use them for home renovation and upkeep (Habitat for Humanity 2011).

While reuse of consumer goods is an important waste management strategy, industrial reuse is an equally potent means of reducing pollution and other by-products from manufacturing processes. Several industries have sought to capitalize on their symbiotic relationships, redirecting wastes for internal reuse or as raw materials for other industries. For example, metal industries transform scrap materials in the production process, and the growth of rubber, plastics, paper and glass recycling industries has generated demand for these previously discarded goods. The goal is cost-savings and ecological responsibility through reuse to eliminate waste. Such *industrial ecology* strategies seek to model industrial systems after natural ecological systems, in natural systems, in which there is no waste. Industrial waste exchanges are already well-established. Some communities in North America are consciously fostering industrial ecology relationships (also known as *industrial symbioses*) by planning *eco-industrial parks* (for more on this, see chapter 12). These host complementary businesses that seek to share by-products and close the loop on industrial waste (O'Riordan et al. 2008).

Level of Local Government Control

The dilemma for local governments is that the most desirable options in the waste management hierarchy (rethinking/redesigning, reducing and reusing) are behavioral choices that are largely outside of its realm — although governments can certainly model these behaviors in their own operations. This lack of control over the most critical elements of the waste hierarchy tends to frustrate waste management planning, as education programs are disconnected from the actual engineering of collection and recovery. Compounding this is that success rates of education programs can be difficult and costly to measure.

But governments do enjoy great influence over recycling, recovery and disposal through waste collection systems and infrastructure investments. To maximize success, it is important to select strategies that position residents, businesses, institutions and the local government as partners in waste management, as each has a significant effect on the system.

Tools and Initiatives: Rethinking, Reducing and Reuse

Voluntary

Waste Reduction Awards Program

The California Waste Reduction Awards Program provides an opportunity for California businesses and not-for-profit organizations to gain public recognition for their outstanding efforts to reduce waste. The program's logo is used on products, in advertising and on public educational materials to recognize waste-reduction efforts (CalRecycle 2011a).

Precycle Program

The regional municipality of Halifax, Nova Scotia, has a public education program called Precycle. It promotes waste reduction by considering the life cycle of a product before buying it (Halifax Regional Municipality 2011).

Electronics Reuse

Non-profit organizations like Free Geek reduce the environmental impact of waste electronics by reusing and recycling donated technology. Through community engagement, Free Geek also provides education, job skills training,

Fig. 6.3: *Free Geek is a non-profit organization that recycles computer technology and provides access to computers, the internet, education and job skills in exchange for community service. Here at its Portland outlet, Free Geek volunteers are reducing e-waste and empowering people with computer use and repair skills and training in free and open-source software. Some outlets host "Windows-less Wednesdays," weekly events in which volunteers orient community members in the basics of free and open-source GNU/Linux software while earning themselves a refurbished computer.* (Credit: Jeff Kubina, Creative Commons.)

Internet access and free or low-cost computers to the public. Free Geek has locations in many cities, including Vancouver, Minneapolis and Providence (Free Geek 2011).

Eco-labeling

Eco-labels are used by producers to communicate their environmental commitments to potential customers. The EcoLogo was developed in Canada in 1988; by 2011, it had certified thousands of products across North America. The program awards certifications by applying relevant criteria to all the life-cycle steps, comparing products to others in the same category and awarding certification only if the company uses an independent third party to verify the data. While not an indicator of the degree to which a product is environmentally friendly or reduces packaging, the EcoLogo can give customers more information to help them potentially reduce their overall waste (Ecologo 2011).

Financial Incentives

The most useful financial instruments, applied by national, provincial/state or local authorities, are arguably those that target the production, manufacturing and design stage of products. Disposal charges (tipping fees) on producers help account for the true costs of disposal and recycling, and serve as financial incentives by eliminating what amount to subsidies of wasteful practice.

TAX CREDITS

These can encourage businesses to base their production on secondary (used or recycled) materials. California's Recycling Market Development Zones program offers tax breaks, free marketing and attractive loans to recycling-based businesses that are established within the more than 88,000 square miles of these prescribed zones (CalRecycle 2011).

DEPOSITS/REFUNDS

Deposits and refunds have been successfully used for beverage bottles for decades; however, the concept can be applied to other materials and products. Arizona recently legislated an increase in the existing deposit amount for automotive batteries. Consumers pay a $5 to $15 deposit, refundable when they return the battery, and retailers must deliver used batteries to an authorized disposal facility. The deposit

reduces illegal dumping of used batteries (Battery Council International 2011).

WEIGHT CHARGES

Charges can be levied to manufacturers to internalize recycling and disposal costs, or discourage use of certain products. Most landfill sites charge by the ton for companies to dump at any given landfill. The City of Seattle charges $145 per ton for self-hauled waste, while charges also apply for residents and businesses (City of Seattle 2011).

PAY AS YOU THROW

Under a Pay As You Throw (PAYT) system, residents that generate less garbage reap savings on garbage collection. Zurich, Switzerland is home to one of the most innovative PAYT systems in the world. It introduced the Zuri-sack, which is the only type trash bag accepted for pick up, and has a fee payable by the originator of waste sent for incineration. Combined with strict penalties for garbage-related offenses and an extensive recycling and organics program, the system successfully reduced waste production from 140,000 to 100,000 tons per year from 1992 to 2005 (Sustainable Cities 2011b). Once limited to a few progressive communities, Pay As You Throw programs have spread to over 7,000 American communities (EPA 2011b). In the United States, PAYT programs divert between 4.6 and 8.3 million tons of municipal solid waste from landfills annually (Skumatz & Freeman 2006).

Regulatory
DISPOSAL BANS

In combination with recycling and organics programs, disposal bans can help reduce municipal and toxic waste entering our landfills. In 2006,

Westchester County, New York, enacted Local Law 702 that bans disposal of all cell phones and their batteries in the regular county waste stream. Phones can be collected at a facility or by an entity certified by the Westchester County Department of Environmental Facilities, including businesses, schools, non-profit organizations, private programs and public sites that already accept household chemical waste (RBRC 2011).

POST-CONSUMER PAINT STEWARDSHIP PROGRAM

North America's first completely industry-funded collection program for paint began in British Columbia in 1994. A provincial product stewardship law requires any company that sells paint to provide return depots for old and unused paint (Environment Canada 2011b).

GERMANY'S GREEN DOT SYSTEM

Implemented in 1993, this system requires manufacturers, users and distributors of packaging to take back used packaging from consumers for recycling. In order to sell in Germany, manufacturers must reduce the amount, weight and dimensions of packaging to make less do more, reuse where possible and make packaging easier to recycle. Since its inception, the program has grown to more than 130,000 participating companies, and some 14.7 million tons of used packaging waste have been recovered and recycled (Packaging Recovery Organization Europe 2011).

WASTE STREAM LICENSING BYLAW

The Regional District of Nanaimo's award-winning zero waste management program combines education, disposal bans and an innovative waste stream management licensing bylaw. Under the bylaw, the district can license all private-sector and non-governmental municipal solid waste management and recycling facilities within the area. Once a licensed facility is established to manage or recycle specific materials, those materials can then be banned from disposal. Overall waste diversion has increased by 65 percent since 2002, and the district has saved about $16 million in capital costs by extending the life of its landfill (FCM 2011).

Expenditure
TAKE-BACK PROGRAM

Smith Falls, Ontario, regularly has take-back events and swap days, where residents can bring in not only their hazardous products like batteries and paint, but also any used item to swap for others (Town of Smith Falls 2011).

ECO-INDUSTRIAL PARK

Kalundborg, Denmark, is home of the world's first eco-industrial park. Several businesses, including a power station, pharmaceutical manufacturer, plasterboard factory, fish farm and oil refinery, are linked through an innovative symbiotic relationship. By-products such as water, steam, surplus gas and other waste materials are redistributed as fuel or resources for other businesses in the park. The waste exchange provides mutual commercial benefits. Kawasaki, Japan, is a successful eco-industrial town that promotes symbiotic industrial relationships as a way to reduce waste in a country already constrained by space (Bahn-Walkowiak & Bleischwitz 2007). Zoning amendments and incorporation into official community plans may be necessary for the success of such initiatives. Governments can foster industrial symbiosis, as the British government has since 2005 through its National Industrial Symbiosis Programme.

Recycling and Composting

Recycling and composting are also known as diversion strategies, in that they divert waste from landfills. Recycling reduces the need for new materials extracted from natural capital and requires less energy to produce the product than the first time. For example, it takes 95 percent less energy to recycle aluminum, 70 percent less energy to recycle plastic, 60 percent less energy to recycle steel and 40 percent less energy to recycle both paper and glass than creating any of these products new (MassRecycle 2004).

Deposit programs are also effective in diverting waste from landfills and recycling used materials. In the US, almost 10 million tons of beverage containers were landfilled or incinerated in 2006. It is estimated that if a ten-cent container deposit was adopted across the United States, the overall recycling rate would be likely to increase from 34 percent to about 85 percent, resulting in the additional recycling of about 8 million tons of bottles and cans. This would reduce greenhouse gas emissions by about 3.7 million tons annually, which would have the same impact as taking about 2.5 million average passenger vehicles off the road (Container Recycling Institute 2008). A program in Vancouver, BC, uses bottle recycling as a way to engage people with barriers to other forms of employment. United We Can is a social enterprise/bottle recovery charity that employs local people to collect bottles from businesses, residences and apartment complexes to be recycled at the United We Can complex (United We Can 2011).

Creating a strong market for recycled products is key to closing the loop between production and consumption. Consumers help do this by purchasing products made from recycled materials, manufacturers by using recycled materials in their products and governments by buying recycled products through their own procurement programs and guidelines (EPA 2011a). For example, the Brazilian State of Minas Gerais has a sustainable procurement policy that emphasizes recycled materials and provides both economic and environmental benefits. Purchase criteria depend on the product or service: for paper, the standard is 25 percent recycled material; for road-paving products, the policy requires use of post-consumer or recycled raw materials that include at least 15 percent rubber. In addition to environmental benefits, the government of Minas Gerais estimates that its procurement policy saved US $61.19 million on purchases made between July 2007 and September 2008 (ICLEI 2009).

Arguments against recycling need to be debunked. One argument, often supported by corporate interests, suggests that, as more technologies become available for waste disposal, we will not need to spend time or money on source separation and collection. This fails to recognize the benefits of recycling such as reduced extraction of virgin raw materials, new industries and jobs in local communities and cost-savings. A more apt argument is that recycling is by no means the only or best solution to waste management; rather, it must complement strategies that address the fundamental issue of waste management: sources of waste. Sustainable waste management promotes cost-effective and environmentally sound recycling as a responsible alternative to landfilling, and in support of the main goals of reduction and reuse.

Composting

Food residuals make up to 60 percent of most residences' garbage. In 1995, the EPA urged us to revisit our conception of food residuals:

It is important to view compost feed-stock as a usable product, not as waste requiring disposal. When developing and promoting a composting program and when marketing the resulting compost, program planners and managers should stress that the composting process is an environmentally sound and beneficial means of recycling organic materials, not a means of waste disposal (7-1).

Properly composted, food and other organic matter can be repurposed as a fertilizer and soil amendment. Whether or not food residuals are framed as potentially useful resources or a component of waste, they too should be scrutinized through the lens of the waste hierarchy. Local governments have discovered composting as a recycling technology that significantly reduces waste management costs and volumes.

Composting can be done at different scales, which entails different methods.

Backyard Composting: There are two general types of backyard composting: continuous and batch. Continuous composting produces compost all year round, but is a little slower than other methods. You can have one or two bins in this method (two bins simply speeds things up). Batch composting can produce great compost in eight weeks, but requires all the compost materials at once and aerating the compost once a day. At their simplest, the bins can be wooden crates, but many composters prefer hard plastic varieties that are designed to keep stray animals out. Tumbler compost systems save space in small backyards and make turning the compost easy, thereby speeding up the composting process.

Speedy, Small-scale Composting: Vermiculture, or worm composting, is a great, smell-free and very quick way to turn a small

Thinking Outside the Blue Box

Blue Box programs are a great success in that they have increased the rate of diversion from local landfills. However, we should also ask: what have they done to promote source reduction or address over-consumption? We must also consider the distance that Blue Box-collected materials must travel to be processed (and associated impacts). By repositioning recycling as a *complement* to waste reduction, rather than as its main focus, we can see the Blue Box as a component of sustainable waste management rather than a convenient means to avoid grappling with how much waste we generate.

Who pays for curbside programs is also an important issue. Currently, most municipal recycling programs are funded by taxpayers, not industry. Does this amount to a hidden subsidy to industry? As long as local governments are forced to pay for recycling programs, manufacturers with wasteful production processes can continue making products without concern for the costs of disposal.

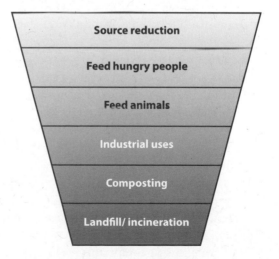

Fig. 6.4: *Similar to the waste hierarchy, this hierarchy of food uses shows the most desirable uses for food residuals, beginning with buying less to ensure there is less waste (source reduction), and ending with the least desirable: throwing it away in a landfill.* (CREDIT: HIERARCHY OF FOOD USES, EPA, 1999)

amount of vegetable peelings into great soil for the garden. It can be undertaken in containers small enough to store in a garage or apartment balcony. Microbe composters or Bokashi composters also process compost very quickly and can accommodate all table scraps.

Industrial-scale Composting: Many technologies now create compost on a much larger scale. There are three general types of large-scale composting systems: in-vessel composting, aerated static pile composting and anaerobic digestion (composting without air), which can be a cold system, much like the at-home versions, or heated up to speed up the process. These industrial processes are known as mechanical biological sorting.

While some communities are offering curbside pickup of yard wastes and food scraps, others are recognizing more cost-effective measures by providing low- or no-cost bins for onsite composting. In addition to providing nutrient-rich fertilizer, composting programs like Half Garbage Waste in Frankston, Australia, can significantly reduce the amount of food waste sent to landfill. Starting in 2006, 1,000 citizens from Frankston took part in a 12-month pilot program that offered citizens a financial incentive to halve the volume of their kitchen waste. Participants were given either a free composting bin or a subsidized worm-compost bin, and within the first three months of the program, citizens had cut their waste from 5 kg to 2.9 kg a week. As a result, waste is now picked up every two weeks rather than weekly, and participants who have halved their waste receive a $20 per year rebate on their garbage collection fee. The program was incorporated into a more comprehensive sustainability initiative called Greenhomes (Sustainable Cities 2011a).

Mid-scale in situ composting technologies are offering options that were not previously available or affordable for restaurants or food manufacturers. Studies show that composting uses significantly fewer resources per gram of waste as compared to land filling and incineration, and is also more efficient in recovering energy from refuse (Marchetini et al. 2007).

Composting also provides local business opportunities. For example, Community Composting is a locally owned, private composting program that has been available in the Greater Victoria Region since 2005. By purchasing a membership, its 1500 subscribers receive a refundable cart and organic waste pickup service every four weeks. On pickup day, each subscriber receives a 20-liter bag of composted soil in exchange for their organic waste. Pickup service is open to single- and multi-dwelling units, businesses, schools and coffee houses (Community Composting 2011).

Tools and Initiatives: Recycling and Composting

Voluntary

eCYCLING

eCycling is the reusing or recycling of consumer electronics. Local governments can promote the development and use of these types of services by banning the disposal of e-waste in landfill sites. The City of Los Angeles instituted such a ban in 2006. They offer free drop-off centers around the city as well as specific events for older electronics, which are then sold to private industry for meltdown and reconstruction (LA Public Works 2011).

RECYCLING FOR KIDS

Denver, Colorado, is targeting the next generation of recyclers with a website just for kids. On the site, Marv the Recyclable Milk Jug guides children through a variety of educational games, quizzes, information and fun homework assignments. The city also has set up recycling programs with several schools (City of Denver 2011).

SOCIAL MEDIA

King County, Washington, promotes recycling and composting via its EcoConsumer public education program. Through the use of social media such as Facebook, Twitter and blogs, residents are informed about recycling and composting pickups, as well as new articles, products and issues regarding waste management. Participants can even track their ecological impact via the waste calculator. Recycling and waste reduction initiatives have resulted in high rates of waste reduction in the county, including a 60 percent reduction from 1997 levels in the City of Bellevue (King County 2011).

SOCIAL MARKETING STRATEGIES

The City of Hamilton, Ontario, achieved a 44 percent waste diversion rate in 2008, up from 16 percent in 2001. Most was attributed to active outreach promotion and education programs. The city uses social marketing strategies, such as student Green Teams to educate the public about organic waste, and recognizes households who have exceeded 65 percent waste diversion with a waste-reduction award (Federation of Canadian Municipalities 2009).

Financial Incentives
VARIABLE TIPPING FEES AND TAX INCENTIVES

Seattle uses reduced tipping fees and tax incentives to encourage commercial recycling. The City waives tip fees for loads of recyclables delivered to transfer stations. The per-ton tip fee for a load of yard debris delivered to these facilities is 33 percent lower than the tip fee charged for trash (City of Seattle 2011b).

SUBSIDIZED BINS

The city of Owen Sound, Ontario, has achieved a high organic waste diversion rate without a curbside food waste collection program. The City promotes organic waste diversion and compensates for its lack of collection services with subsidies for backyard composters and kitchen food waste containers (Federation of Canadian Municipalities 2009).

Expenditure
CREATIVE COMPOST USES

In Big Spring, Texas, a successful roadside compost system has allowed for the creative use of the compost by the city. The road shoulders in the area were susceptible to erosion and were causing significant road damage over the decades. Using compost and other natural materials, the city was able to successfully plant stable, wind-resistant grass (TxDOT 2003).

A ZERO-WASTE SOCIETY

In 2007, Metro Vancouver, composed of 22 British Columbian municipalities and one First Nations group, adopted its Zero Waste Challenge to minimize waste generation and maximize reuse, recycling and recovery of materials deemed for landfills. The initiative aims to reduce each person's waste by 10 percent by 2020 and to divert 70 percent of materials (e.g., food scraps, wood) from landfills by 2015 and 80 percent by 2020. In response to this challenge, the Home Depot partnered with Metro Vancouver to create a depot where customers, residents, small contractors and do-it-yourselfers can deposit used wood. Within two months, the wood waste depot had served over 1,200 individuals and recycled over 255,000 kilograms of wood. The collected wood is processed at a local wood recycling facility and reused as hog fuel and mulch for landscaping/composting (MetroVancouver 2011).

SPLIT-PACKER TRUCKS

The Regional District of Nanaimo diverts more than 4,000 tons of organic waste from landfills annually through a curbside collection project funded by the Federation of Canadian Municipalities' Green Municipal fund. The district has switched to split-packer trucks that combine curbside collection of organics, recyclables and garbage to save gas and reduce emissions. The combination of recycling and waste reduction initiatives have resulted in a 64 percent increase in waste diversion since 2002 (FCM 2011).

PUBLIC-PRIVATE PARTNERSHIPS

Public consultation, education and public-private partnerships have helped create a sustainable waste management system in Edmonton, Alberta. Since 2000, Edmonton's residential food waste has been composted along with bio-solids from a wastewater treatment plant. The Edmonton Waste Management Centre is North America's largest co-composter — a technology that mixes food waste with wastewater biosolids to produce high-nutrient compost. Representing over $565 million in public and private capital investment, the facility is being developed into a waste management center for applied research, demonstration and training, and has resulted in more than a 56 percent diversion of waste from landfill (City of Edmonton 2011; ICLEI 2011).

Regulatory
RECYCLED CONTENT LAWS

Minimum recycled content requirements can be stipulated in local government procurement policies, creating new market opportunities for recyclables. In 2005, New York City passed a number of Environmentally Preferable Purchase Laws related to a number of issues including green cleaning products and recycled content of office supplies (NYC Department of Sanitation 2005).

LANDFILL MATERIAL BANS

Municipal governments can ban certain materials from local landfills to encourage recycling or avoid contamination of landfills by toxic wastes. The Greater Vancouver Regional District, BC, banned Gyprock (wallboard) from local landfills because under wet, oxygen-starved conditions it generates the toxic gas hydrogen sulfide. Because extra charges are levied for disposal of this toxic waste, local businesses have capitalized on this extra fee as they recycle Gyprock into new wallboard (GVRD 2011).

COMPREHENSIVE RECYCLING PROGRAMS

The City of Owen Sound, Ontario, increased recycling tonnage by 55 percent from 2000 to 2005, with 94 percent of the residents participating in the program. This was accomplished through a combination of a comprehensive recycling program that accepts over 30 items at the curb and a regulatory approach to management. The city has implemented limited disposal amounts, landfill bans for recyclable materials and a mandatory recycling policy that results in garbage being left behind if it contains recyclable materials (Federation of Canadian Municipalities 2009).

Recovery and Disposal

As a last resort to extract usefulness from materials, recovery is the process of extracting energy from waste materials. Popular recovery options include waste-to-energy facilities that burn wastes for fuel to produce heat, electricity or other forms of power; these are typically directed into manufacturing processes. It is important to note that, while such facilities may reduce the use of fossil fuels, they also produce significant amounts of carbon emissions — and as many critics have pointed out, risks "locking in" waste production as it becomes a source of energy.

As communities find new ways to recover resource energy, they are also looking for ways to better integrate these efforts in order to derive economies-of-scale benefits. For example, in one study of Vancouver, BC, one company found that all scenarios where liquid waste treatment was combined with municipal solid waste treatment were financially superior to wastewater treatment on its own (Fidelis 2011).

While waste management strategies should strive to divert 100 percent of waste from landfills, we cannot ignore the fact that we are still producing waste. Additionally, there are decades, if not centuries, of waste that has been dumped and buried in our terrestrial and aquatic ecosystems. Existing landfills pose significant risks to our health via the release of toxic gases such as methane and via leachate that can enter our groundwater and aquifers. Long-term waste strategies should not include any new landfills, but in the short to medium term, what do we do with our current landfills? The three main strategies for dealing with the waste we have already landfilled are monitoring leachate, recovering the gas or incinerating the waste for energy.

Leachate Monitoring and Remediation

Leachate is produced as water percolates through landfill sites. Factors affecting leachate formation include the quality of the water entering the landfill, the composition of the waste, temperature and degree of decomposition. Leachate is acidic and often contains metal ions that can contaminate our groundwater. Geosynthetic clay liners, leachate drainage systems and sumps are potential methods of leachate management. In many communities, bioremediation through the uptake of leachate by willow and poplar trees is showing promising results. Monitoring is necessary to gauge the severity of the problem and the effectiveness of remediation measures.

LANDFILL GAS RECOVERY

When food scraps, yard trimmings, paper and wood are landfilled, anaerobic bacteria degrade the materials which produces methane and carbon dioxide. A landfill starts producing these potent greenhouse gases in the first year of operation, and it continues to produce them for decades. Because methane in this concentration is toxic and dangerous, technologies have been developed to capture and use the gas. This can be done by drilling into the landfill and pumping it out via a network of pipes. In the past, such gas was simply flared, thereby losing all of the potential energy, but many landfilling operations are now using the gas as fuel for heating nearby buildings or electricity generation. Methane oxidation, a process that reduces landfill gas emissions using a layer of compost, is another method that may reduce methane without flaring.

WASTE-TO-ENERGY FACILITIES

In 2001, 14.7 percent (33.6 million tons) of municipal solid waste was incinerated in the United States (EPA 2010c). Historically, incineration plants have been heavy polluters that released fly ash and noxious gases that affect human and ecosystem health. But over the past decade, incineration technologies have improved through strict monitoring of burning temperature and the use of pollution control devices such as scrubbers and fly ash collectors. Fly ash produced by these facilities can now be used in the production of concrete, as opposed to simply landfilling it. These facilities reduce the volume of waste in the landfill and produce energy that can be used to heat nearby buildings. Although these technological advances are significant, they still do not negate the fact that these plants are dependent on a constant supply of waste to operate. Most of these plants are not built in light of the long-term goal of phasing out waste altogether, and may truck in waste from other regions to keep operations running. (See chapter 7 for information on district energy.)

Challenges for the Next Generation of Waste Managers

At present, the 3R framework continues to be being promoted by local governments, whose effectiveness at waste management remains constrained by the fact that the most critical elements of the waste hierarchy — reducing, reusing and rethinking — are beyond their immediate control. This suggests that local governments' biggest waste management challenge will be in the forging and management of partnerships. Residents, institutions, contracted collection corporations and infrastructure operators need arrive at a shared vision of a future with less or no waste.

At least as important is overcoming the departmental divides that often exists within local governments, between the policy-makers, planners and engineers implementing the recycling, recovery and disposal programs. Here, too, a shared vision will be critical to changing current practices.

Once internal and external partnerships have been successfully achieved, a set of criteria such as one based on the Global Reporting Initiative (GRI) should be selected to ensure that citizens, government and the private sector are actually implementing the selected waste management program. The frameworks mentioned here — zero waste, cradle-to-cradle and life-cycle analysis — all have the capacity to change our thinking about waste and cultivate a society that is much more protective of its natural capital.

Tools and Initiatives: Recovery and Disposal

Public-private partnerships and other expenditures by local governments are needed to ensure that our existing landfills are not sources of toxic emissions now or in the future.

MONITORING AND LEACHATE REMEDIATION

Since 1997, the City of Kingston, Ontario, has spent over $5 million building and operating a number of remediation-control projects at

Methane Gas and Landfills

- In terms of its global warming potential, methane is 21 times more potent than carbon dioxide.
- Emissions from Canadian landfills account for 20 percent of national methane emissions.
- Approximately 7 megatons (Mt) of carbon dioxide equivalent (CO_2e) of the 27 Mt CO_2e generated annually are captured and combusted. In terms of greenhouse gas emissions reduction, this equates to removing about 5.5 million cars from the road.

— (Environment Canada 2011a)

the former Belle Park landfill site. Current programs include monitoring systems and bioremediation to treat landfill leachate. Tree species that have high levels of water uptake and fast growth, such as black willows, balsam and hybrid poplar, are used in combination with traditional groundwater pumps to extract and treat water that would otherwise carry toxins from the landfill into the groundwater. The landfill is the focus of several education and research projects by surrounding universities (City of Kingston 2011).

Landfill Gas Methane Oxidation

With support from Canada's Green Municipalities Fund, the City of Leduc, Alberta, undertook a pilot methane oxidation treatment of natural gas from their landfill. Methane oxidation includes covering the waste with a synthetic membrane, and then treating the gas using a double-layered biofilter made of compost. The process was shown to remove an average of 63 percent of landfill gases and is a good option for small to medium sized landfills (Federation of Canadian Municipalities 2007).

Waste-to-energy

Copenhagen, Denmark, has dramatically changed its waste management system over the past decade with waste-to-energy plants. Instead of landfills, the city is focusing on reducing waste and using that which is produced as a resource that can be recycled or incinerated for energy. Copenhagen currently recycles 56 percent of its waste and incinerates another 39 percent in its three waste-to-energy plants; only 3 percent goes to the landfill. In 2004, Copenhagen's waste generated 210,000 megawatt-hours of electrical energy and 720,000 megawatt-hours of heat — enough for 70,000 households (Sustainable Cities 2011).

Landfill Gas Capture and Use

In partnership with the US Environmental Protection Agency's Landfill Methane Outreach Program, the town of Dillsboro, North Carolina, established the Jackson County Green Energy Park. The park uses landfill gas captured from the town's closed landfill as fuel for greenhouses, blacksmithing, glass-blowing studios, pottery and other types of artistry. Future phases for the energy park include waste-heat recovery and anaerobic digesters for food waste. The project encourages the success of new artisans and, upon full completion, is expected to create 15 to 20 new jobs. With ongoing support for artisans and increased eco and heritage crafts tourism, the project is expected to have a positive impact on the local economy, in addition to using landfill methane gas for energy production. The project prevents 222 tons of methane from entering the atmosphere annually (EPA 2010b).

Chapter 7

Energy Efficiency and Renewables

Energy production is big business, and it powers our economy just as surely as it fuels our cars and supplies our heating, cooling and lighting. Americans and Canadians should know that, in addition to being among the wealthiest nations on Earth, we are among the world's heaviest per capita users of energy (Gunton & Calbick 2010).

But what costs does our energy-rich way of life exact from our communities, our ecosystem and the world around us? Our excessive energy consumption depletes our natural capital and contributes to climate change, ozone layer depletion, smog, acid rain, oil spills and other forms of pollution. Our extravagant use of non-renewable energy also manifests itself in unnecessary expenditure on heating, cooling, lighting and ventilation; costly inefficiencies in commercial and industrial equipment; tax dollars spent on heavily subsidized resource-extraction industries; and chronic collective vulnerability to fluctuations in international energy markets.

Citizens and their governments hold tremendous power to change this picture. As research and experience repeatedly demonstrate, the most cost-effective alternative to expanding energy supply through massive capital investments in power plant capacity is to reduce our consumption. Equally important are investments that help us make better use of the same amount of energy. By retrofitting existing buildings and designing more energy-efficient buildings, communities can recoup huge savings that could be reinvested in the things that directly support our quality of life and productivity: education and health, community economic development and energy independence.

Many of our incremental energy needs can be viably served by renewable energy sources such as wind, photovoltaic (solar) and cogeneration. And as many communities have discovered, technologies such as ground-source heat pumps and district energy now offer efficient, economic and environmentally responsible alternatives to conventional heating systems. This is not

Fig. 7.1: *The Verdant affordable housing development at UniverCity uses a variety of renewable energy sources, including geo-exchange.* (Credit: SFU Community Trust/ UniverCity)

Energy Efficiency

One method to reduce energy demand is to become energy efficient. *Energy efficiency* simply means "more bang for your buck." It implies use of products (such as refrigerators, light bulbs, washing machines, computers, printers, copiers, industrial motor systems, air conditioners, space heaters and ventilation systems) that deliver the same service as other units, but with a fraction of the energy required. Energy-efficient buildings use strategies and technologies, such as passive solar design, light shelves, light tubes and highly insulated windows to minimize or even eliminate needs for heating, cooling, ventilation systems and daytime lighting.

To homeowners, investments in energy efficiency can mean hundreds, even thousands, of dollars in savings on annual utility bills (Natural Resources Canada 2009a). For large commercial buildings or industrial operations, this can translate into millions of dollars in energy savings. By being more energy efficient, homeowners and businesses also insulate themselves from the uncertainties of escalating energy costs. To utility companies, reductions in energy consumption can reduce revenues — but need not mean reductions in profits.

science fiction — these are off-the-shelf technologies and techniques that are available today. All that is required is public and political will.

In the face of population growth, increasing pressure on energy-supply infrastructure and the need for planning flexibility, some utility companies are reconsidering multi-billion-dollar plant expansions that risk long-term debt, higher operating expenditures and the ever-present risk that economic slumps will slow demand. They have found a profitable alternative: *demand-side management*, which focuses on reducing or managing customer demand rather than increasing producer supply.

Investment in demand-side management has proven to be a smart business strategy in a wide variety of contexts — from publicly owned for-profit companies (Canada's Crown corporations), regionally owned electric generators and independent power producers that provide much of Canada's power, to the United States Department of Energy-owned and -operated power generators, larger shareholder-owned utilities and many municipally owned power generators.

Energy and Local Economies

In many communities, 75 to 90 cents of every dollar spent on energy (electricity and fuel) leaves the local economy to pay generators, refiners and large electric or gas utility companies (Kinsley 2007). But saved energy dollars could be reinvested back into the local economy and circulate several times over, thereby bolstering their effect as a local economic multiplier (see chapter 12 for examples and discussion). Investment in locally sited and owned renewable systems that supply energy to the surrounding community (rather than back to the grid to be distributed elsewhere) helps "plug the leaks" in community energy expenditure, saving money for residents and businesses alike. Local economies become more resilient and less vulnerable to the influence of the global economy (Kinsley 2007).

Demand-side management techniques such as government energy-efficiency programs and energy standards not only save energy but also create jobs. In 2010, implementation of energy standards helped create 340,000 jobs. Job creation occurs by shifting consumer spending away from energy sectors that create relatively few jobs per dollar of revenue (such as energy utilities) toward those that create more (such as the sale, installation and maintenance of energy-efficient appliances, equipment and structural components) (Gold et al. 2011).

Well-designed demand-side management also promises to address social inequities. People with lower incomes tend to live in the least energy-efficient homes, often characterized by drafty rooms, inefficient heating systems and old energy-guzzling appliances. Demand-side programs can provide funding to improve the comfort of their homes and reduce utility bills, thereby helping those who need it most.

Tools and Initiatives: Energy Efficiency

Voluntary

PUBLIC EDUCATION AND INFORMATION PROGRAMS

Conference and Trade Show: The Community Office for Resource Efficiency (CORE) is a non-profit organization that promotes renewable energy and energy efficiency in Roaring Fork Valley and the rest of western Colorado. CORE provides community energy education through forums, presentations and newspaper and magazine articles. CORE also offers a comprehensive Energy Smart for Home program that offers free consultations with a home energy advisor to connect homeowners with information, skilled workers, financing programs, an energy resource library and demonstration equipment. Additional programs include a solar production incentive, a renewable energy mitigation fund and an efficient building program (CORE 2011).

Interfaith Coalition on Energy: Since 1980, the Interfaith Coalition on Energy has helped congregations in Philadelphia trim their energy use. The Coalition sponsors workshops to help congregations of all faiths make their buildings more energy efficient, and they publish a newsletter providing tips on energy efficiency. The newsletter also offers information on where to buy products and services and how to finance building retrofits and efficiency upgrades. Building on its work in Philadelphia, the Coalition also assists in the formation of local energy coalitions throughout the nation (ICE 2011).

Leadership in Energy and Environmental Design (LEED): The LEED Green Building Rating System is a voluntary-participation national standard for assessing building performance and meeting sustainability goals. Developed by the United States Green Building Council (USGBC), LEED accredits professionals and certifies buildings in four levels of awards. For more information, see chapter 11.

Financial Incentives

POWER SMART REBATES

British Columbia's provincial energy utility, BC Hydro, launched its Power Smart program in 1989 to assist customers in conserving electricity and help offset the province's growing demand for electricity. The utility's Power Smart Excellence Awards and Power Smart Certification program recognize residents and businesses that have reduced their power consumption. LiveSmartBC rebates provide homeowners with almost $9,000 worth of incentives for increasing their homes' energy efficiency, and its Energy Conservation Assistance Program provides home-energy evaluation, advice and energy-saving products such as energy-efficient appliances and low-flow showerheads to renters and low-income residents (BC Hydro 2011).

CONSERVATION POWER PLANT

Rather than spend $500 million on a new coal-powered plant, the City of Austin, Texas, built a "conservation power plant" to generate millions of kilowatt-hours of energy savings. The city's energy utility, Austin Energy, offers cash incentives, rebate programs and access to energy auditors for residential and commercial weatherization, retrofit and conservation efforts. The conservation power plant produces an estimated 700 megawatts of energy savings daily — more energy than would have been produced by a coal-powered plant (Barrie 2008).

ZERO-INTEREST LOANS

The City of Toronto's Energy Efficiency Department is offering interest-free loans for energy conservation and green energy projects through its Better Buildings Partnership office. Loans are available to municipal, academic, social service and healthcare-related institutional buildings, not-for-profit organizations and private multi-family buildings. In addition to interest-free loans, multi-family building owners are eligible for the Multi-Family Buildings Rebate which includes financial incentives for energy-efficiency improvements to heating, ventilation and air conditioning systems; lighting; appliance replacements; building envelope upgrades, controls; water heating; and motors, pumps and fans. Energy audits and resident education subsidies are also available (The Low Income Energy Network 2011).

MUNICIPAL BONDS

Many local governments in the United States issue bonds (time-limited, government-backed securities that pay the purchaser a dividend at the end of the bond period) to raise money to construct public buildings and bridges or to repair roads. In April 2009, Boulder County, Colorado, and partner municipalities launched the ClimateSmart Loan Program that allows commercial and residential property owners to obtain financing for renewable energy and/or energy-efficiency improvements. Also known as Property-Assessed Clean Energy (PACE) financing, these loans range from a minimum of $3,000 to a maximum of 20 percent of the property's value or $50,000 (whichever is less). Lower interest rates are offered to residents making less than 115 percent of the area's median income. The loans are financed by a $40 million bonding program that allocates $28 million to residential properties and the remaining $12 million for loan to commercial properties. The majority of the bonds are taxable, but a portion of them are tax-exempt (Institute for Local Self-Reliance 2011a).

Although hundreds of cities are investigating or designing PACE financing programs, most were on hold in late 2010 due to concerns raised by federal mortgage lenders Fannie Mae and Freddie Mac and the Federal Housing

Financing Agency. The concerns surround the PACE lien seniority and the risks that PACE may have on federally backed mortgages. Once this problem is resolved, PACE financing programs are expected to sweep across the United States (Institute for Local Self-Reliance 2011b).

FINANCING HOME ENERGY IMPROVEMENTS

In 2008, the Town of Babylon, New York, created the Long Island Green Homes Program to finance energy-efficiency improvements to any of its 65,000 single-family homes, the cost of which will be repaid by the energy savings accrued from the improvements. The town pays the upfront costs for up to $12,000 per home, while the homeowner pays a monthly fee (a "benefit assessment") structured to be less than the monthly savings on the homeowner's energy bill resulting from the improvements. The program's administration costs are covered by the 3 percent interest rate. The benefit assessment remains with the home if a homeowner sells the property, and failure to pay the monthly benefit assessment results in the charge being added to property taxes associated with the home. The program has saved residents an average of $1,085 per year on oil, gas and electric bills, and a achieved a 20 to 40 percent reduction in greenhouse gas emissions (ICLEI 2011; LIGH 2011).

ENERGY-EFFICIENT MORTGAGES

An energy-efficient mortgage credits a home's energy efficiency in the mortgage itself. Such mortgages give borrowers the opportunity to finance cost-effective, energy-saving measures as part of a single mortgage, and stretch debt-to-income qualifying ratios on loans — thereby allowing borrowers to qualify for a larger loan amount and a better, more

energy-efficient home. While energy-efficient mortgages normally apply to new construction, energy-improvement mortgages allow borrowers to include the cost of energy-efficiency improvements to an existing home in the mortgage without increasing the down payment. Energy-efficient mortgages and energy-improvement mortgages may be supported directly by a financial institute, or backed by local governments, Community Development Corporations, or state, provincial or federal energy-conservation programs. In the United States, the Federal Housing Administration and the Veterans' Administration offer energy-efficient mortgages (Energy Star 2011).

Expenditure

COMMUNITY ENERGY SERVICES CORPORATION

The City of Berkeley, California, established a Community Energy Services Corporation. It offers energy services, such as audits and project management, to commercial, residential and public building projects. The non-profit corporation also helps people find financing for energy-efficiency initiatives (Community Energy Services Corporation 2011).

SETTING EXAMPLES WITH PUBLIC BUILDINGS

What better way to demonstrate the benefits of resource conservation than through building and retrofitting more energy-efficient schools, libraries, hospitals and civic buildings? Here are some examples of local governments that are leading by example.

ENERGY SMART SCHOOL

The school board of Truckee, California, has increased energy efficiency, decreased energy costs and created a healthy sustainable learning environment for students of Alder Creek

Middle School with its Energy Smart school demonstration project. With help from state and industry grants, they invested in high-performance energy-saving design strategies at the school, including a ground-source heat pump, passive solar building design and energy-efficient windows and roof. This has produced energy savings of more than 58 percent, the majority of which are attributed to the ground-source heat boiler (USDOE 2009).

ENERGY CONSERVATION AND SAVINGS PLAN

The City of Phoenix, Arizona, has saved over $75 million since it began auditing and retrofitting civic buildings in the late 1970s. As an incentive for participating in the energy-efficiency program, departments and city agencies get to keep all (or a predetermined percentage) of the money they save from using energy more efficiently, and a professional energy manager monitors and documents all savings. In 1984, city council established the Energy Conservation Savings Reinvestment Plan. Under this plan, the city reinvests 50 percent of all documented energy savings (up to $750,000 annually) to finance energy-efficiency capital projects. These funds were critical in financing a district cooling system and a thermal storage system for the new Phoenix city hall, as well as small-scale cogeneration, solar, air volume and wastewater systems. The reinvestment funds also pay for civic retrofits, the difference of upgrades to energy-efficient office equipment and research for energy-efficient technologies (ICLEI 2008).

The City of Edmonton, Alberta, has a similar program. In 1995, it created a revolving fund aimed at energy retrofits of city facilities. Initially started at $1 million, it was increased in 1999 to $5 million. In 2002, city council

approved an increase in the fund limit of up to $30 million, to be financed by the Alberta Municipal Finance Corporation. Amounts borrowed against the fund are repaid over periods of up to eight years (up to ten years by exception) out of the utility savings, which makes this money available for other energy projects (City of Edmonton 2011).

Regulations

As with other sustainable community sectors, local governments' ability to regulate with regard to energy efficiency and renewable energy often requires legislative or regulatory changes at more senior government levels. Municipal policy-makers therefore need to consider a wider range of policy instruments (see chapter 3). The following examples show energy-efficiency regulatory mechanisms enacted by both senior and local level governments.

ENERGY-EFFICIENCY RESOURCE STANDARDS (EERS)

Passed at the provincial or state level, EERS require utilities to adopt energy efficiency as a clean, cost-effective energy resource by establishing an explicit numerical target for incorporating energy efficiency into the power source mix. This target is established relative to a baseline and can be achieved by implementing energy-efficiency programs that reduce customers' energy use, reducing energy waste in a utility's distribution systems or purchasing energy savings from other utilities or third-party efficiency service providers. Twenty-three states, including Washington, Michigan and Connecticut, have established EERS programs. Connecticut's EERS have resulted in 368 million kilowatt-hours in annual savings and 2.4 million tons of carbon dioxide emissions avoided (ACORE 2010). Similarly, the Province of British Columbia passed the BC Energy Plan that requires the province's energy utility (BC Hydro) to acquire 50 percent of all incremental energy needs through energy efficiency by 2020 (Province of British Columbia 2010).

BUILDING CODES FOR ENERGY EFFICIENCY

In 2010, the City of Burnaby approved a municipal zoning bylaw for the UniverCity community development that makes its building standards the greenest in North America. It is the first bylaw in North America that mandates specific green building practices as part of the development process. The outcome will be buildings that are at least 30 percent more efficient than traditional buildings (UniverCity 2011). The bylaw promotes innovative building practices through a results-based approach that requires a specific increase in efficiency rather than a specific type of energy certification (See chapter 14 for more information.).

SOLAR ACCESS ORDINANCE

Ashland, Oregon, was one of the first cities to implement a regulatory mechanism that prohibits new development from shading existing buildings by ensuring that shadows at the north property line do not exceed a certain height. In essence, it creates solar setbacks. The ordinance is designed to preserve the economic value of solar radiation on structures, to maintain the option for the future use of solar energy, and to support investments in solar energy systems (Sustainable Cities Institute 2011).

ENERGY EFFICIENCY FOR EXISTING BUILDINGS

The City of Berkeley, California, passed a residential and commercial energy conservation ordinance that requires owners of residential and commercial buildings who are looking to transfer, sell or renovate the property to install energy- and water-efficient fixtures. The seller or buyer may assume responsibility for compliance, and the cost of the upgrades may be incorporated into the mortgage financing. The ordinance is part of Berkeley's Climate Action goal of reducing total greenhouse gas emissions by 80 percent by 2050 (City of Berkeley 2011).

Environmentally Responsible Energy Supply

Energy efficiency is about cost-effective techniques that reduce energy consumption. To be truly energy efficient, however, we must shift our reliance from conventional sources that harm our natural environment to renewable sources that are cleaner, reliable and widely available. What are the options? Ecological impacts of large-scale hydro-electric dams are often met with public outrage and protests, and many utility companies and communities in Canada and the United States recognize that nuclear power generation is simply too expensive and short-sighted (where do we put the radioactive waste kept in "short-term" storage at nuclear facilities across North America?). Rising concerns about pollution and climate change are spurring reviews of fuel choices and operating efficiencies of oil, coal and gas-fired conventional power plants (Cooper and Sussman 2011). Pollution-abatement technologies and combustion efficiencies are improving some plants, but renewable energies offer greater opportunities for local self-reliance in energy production for electricity needs. Community-scale projects that use efficient technologies such as cogeneration or district heating are other options to minimize consumption and reduce dependency on fossil fuels.

Renewable Energy Supply

Renewable energy sources are often regarded as new or exotic, but in fact they are neither. Until quite recently, in historical terms, the world drew most of its energy from the sun, either directly from sunlight or indirectly through natural processes associated with winds, rivers and plants. The advantages of renewable energy sources — particularly wind, solar and biomass (plant) energy — are, if anything, more compelling today than ever before.

Renewable energy offers opportunities to reinvest control over energy production into communities, which helps to stabilize energy prices and increase the security of our energy supply. This is because project viability is almost entirely related to its capacity to generate returns on investment rather than on international market volatility around international energy resources such as oil or uranium. Furthermore, as renewables typically have low health impacts, future financial liabilities are also reduced or eliminated. Renewable energy also reduces environmental impacts such as air and water pollution, land disruption and biodiversity loss associated with the extraction and use of conventional energy sources (Pembina 2011a).

Fig. 7.2:
The Verdant affordable housing development at UniverCity uses solar panels to heat hot water tanks and reduce energy costs.
(CREDIT:
SFU COMMUNITY TRUST/
UNIVERCITY)

Additionally, renewable energy projects, in particular those that are community based, can be more socially and environmentally equitable than non-renewable systems. As easily accessible deposits of non-renewable energy resources are depleted, resource extraction will extend to areas (such as the Arctic) where environments and communities are more sensitive and susceptible to the damaging effects of resource extraction. Renewable energy uses local energy sources, thereby avoiding these potential impacts. Localized use of renewable energy can create jobs in all areas of a country — jobs related to renewable energy manufacturing and operations are not necessarily restricted to areas where the energy reserves are found or generated. More importantly, well-managed and operated renewable energy projects can create jobs and stimulate economies in remote locations, including First Nations communities that otherwise rely on diesel-fueled generators (Pembina 2011a), and in rural communities. For example, it is estimated that lease payments for wind turbines in the United States will generate well over $600 million for landowners in rural areas and generate additional local tax revenues exceeding $1.5 billion annually by 2030 (USDOE 2011a).

While renewable energies have not enjoyed the massive subsidies of the fossil fuel and nuclear power sectors, great strides in technological improvements, operating efficiencies and equipment costs, as well as implementation of policies and programs such as feed-in tariffs and net metering, have made renewable energy an ever more viable option. In many parts of the United States, wind technology is now directly cost-competitive with new supply costs for conventional power plants (USDOE 2011b). Thousands of Canadians and Americans use solar hot water panels or photovoltaic (solar-electric) panels to provide domestic hot water and electricity for their homes, and utility companies and communities are increasingly capitalizing on community energy projects (Pembina 2011b). Rooftops all over North America are ideal for installation of solar panels. For example, Toronto's Renewable Energy Co-op (a non-profit community energy organization) offers Ontarians renewable

Renewable Energy Options

Geothermal: Uses heat naturally occurring in the Earth's crust to generate electricity. Recent innovations have led to enhanced systems that can tap into heat resources without the need for hydrothermal convection techniques. (see Fig 7.3, color page C-2)

Geo-exchange (Ground-source Heat Pump): Extracts heat from the Earth to heat buildings, swimming pools or domestic hot water supply using a series of closed-loop pipes containing fluid that absorbs heat from the surrounding earth.

Tidal: Turbines harness the power of ocean currents to produce electricity. Differences in temperature between the deep and shallow ocean can also be used to power heat engines. Tidal power has yet to be widely adopted in North America.

Wave: The energy from the ocean's surface waves or from pressure changes below the surface caused by waves is harnessed and converted into electricity. Harnessing power from wave energy is somewhat further along than tidal power generation.

Micro-hydro: If planned and managed properly, micro-hydro projects exert fewer disturbances on waterways compared to large-scale hydro projects. Small turbines typically use springs, creeks or municipal water-supply lines to generate enough electricity for a single building or an entire town.

Photovoltaic (Solar-electric) Power: Photovoltaic panels produce electricity for independent systems with batteries for storing energy, or supply electricity to the power grid.

Solar Thermal: Solar hot water systems typically provide hot water for showers and baths, swimming pools, hot tubs or radiant heating (space heating). Some solar thermal projects convert heated water into electricity.

Solar Air: Solar air systems absorb energy from the sun to heat air. Air is drawn through holes or channels of the collecting device, picking up heat before it is ventilated through the building.

Nanotechnology and Solar Cells: Cells that create circuits out of single silicon molecules is an emerging technology that has the potential to be both energy efficient and more economical than solar power.

Wind: Stand-alone turbines supply electricity for homes, farms and small communities. Wind farms are clusters of wind turbines generating power for the electrical grid.

Biomass: Plants or organic wastes are burned as fuel. Provided that biomass is produced sustainably, with only as much used as is grown, biomass itself can be sustainable. In general, there are two main approaches to using plants for energy production: growing plants specifically for energy use, and using the residues from plants that are used for other things.

Biofuels: Fuels such as methanol or ethanol can be used as an alternative for most oil or gas needs. Bioethanol is an alcohol made from the fermentation of food crops such as sugar. Because the use of food crops for fuel raises several food security and social issues, new technologies, such as cellulosic ethanol technology, use native grasses or feed stock waste residues as fuel.

energy investment and ownership opportunities through their Solar Share program. It offers securities in the form of bonds and equity shares to large solar systems mounted on industrial buildings and smaller rural, ground-mounted installations. These smaller installations are often mounted in farmers' fields, providing additional revenue and diversification for these small businesses (TREC 2011). In addition, net metering programs and feed-in tariffs have encouraged investment in renewable energy by providing incentives for customers to install onsite systems and establishing a guaranteed pricing structure for energy generated from renewable sources.

District Energy

Currently, most developed nations satisfy their energy needs through large nuclear, hydro-electric or fossil-fuel-powered plants. While these plants benefit from economies of scale, they have a deleterious impact on the environment and must transmit energy over long distances. District energy, in which local, publically owned facilities supply energy to entire streets, neighborhoods or communities, promises great sustainability dividends. In district energy systems, a central plant creates steam, hot water or chilled water and distributes it to each building through a system of underground pipes. The plant may be fueled by biofuels (such as wood chips or sewage sludge), natural gas or other sources. District energy reduces the amount of energy lost in transmitting electricity because the electricity is generated very near where it is used — perhaps even in the same building. This also reduces the size and number of power lines that must be constructed. District energy also eliminates the need for each building to be individually heated or cooled by conventional means such as oil furnaces, baseboard electric heaters or air conditioners.

The central power plant that produces energy for heating or cooling buildings can take a variety of forms, from waste-to-energy facilities to cogeneration plants to ground-source heat pumps. Waste-to-energy plants use fuels such as wood chips or sewage sludge to generate heat (for more information on waste-to-energy, see chapter 6). Some wastes are better suited than others for fuel. While burning wastes is not without environmental impact, it may be more advantageous to burn than dump.

Many district energy systems are based on cogeneration facilities on large sites such as hospitals, universities, factories or hotels. Cogeneration systems, also known as combined heat and power, use a power station to simultaneously generate electricity and useful heat to power and heat buildings, with one-third less fuel than is needed to produce each on its own. While most power plants emit heat during electricity production, which is then released into the natural environment, cogeneration facilities capture this "waste" heat and use it to heat surrounding buildings. Excess heat produced during industrial processes (such as pulp and paper production) can also be used to heat surrounding buildings.

Ground-source heat pumps (also known as geo-exchange) can also serve as district energy systems. They extract heat from the earth to heat buildings, swimming pools or domestic hot water supply. Similarly, water-source heat pumps use water sources, such as ponds, as the source of heat. Ground-source heat pumps use a series of closed-loop pipes containing fluid that absorbs heat from the surrounding earth. The technology can also work in reverse to cool buildings in the summer or keep ice rinks frozen. A related but different technology is geothermal, which extracts heat from hot springs or hot rock areas in the earth. Although geothermal systems are very effective, they require settings with very specific geological characteristics. This tends to preclude their widespread use. Ground-source heat pumps or geo-exchange systems have a long history of residential use in North America, and have seen a rapid growth in commercial and public use as well. The non-profit Geothermal Heat Pump Consortium, Inc. reports that there are over 1,000,000 geo-exchange systems in the United States, resulting in annual savings of nearly 8 billion kilowatt-hours (GHPC 2006).

Sewage waste heat recovery is another innovative district heating source that has proven viable for many communities. These systems recover heat from untreated urban wastewater and transfer it to a hot water distribution system. This process is similar to other geo-exchange applications, but outperforms most geo-exchange systems because it uses a warmer heat source and has lower installation costs (City of Vancouver 2008).

Tools and Initiatives: Renewable Energy and District Energy
Voluntary
GREEN POWER

The Emerald People's Utility District in Eugene, Oregon, offers renewable green power options to their clients: 50 or 100 percent renewable for residential users and 10, 25, 50 or 100 percent

Rural and Remote Energy

Although all communities can benefit from demand-side management and renewable energy, rural and remote communities face unique challenges as they work towards a sustainable future. These relate primarily to transportation, energy supply, capacity, climate and public perception.

In many rural communities, low population densities and remote locations require longer-distance commuting on a daily basis, as well as greater expenditure of energy to transport goods to and from these communities. Smaller local governments, especially in remote communities, often lack the tax base, public support and capacity to research and implement renewable energy programs. As well, smaller remote communities are sometimes able to finance the initial installation of energy projects but lack the resources for monitoring performance or implementing timely repairs.

But innovative solutions to these issues do exist. For communities coping with similar issues on the path towards sustainable energy management, knowledge-sharing is the key. *Pando | Sustainable Communities* is an innovative initiative that provides an online forum for communities of all sizes to learn from each other's successes and failures and remain up to date on research and initiatives that relate to them (see appendix).

One small community that surely has lessons to share is the T'Sou-ke First Nation on Vancouver Island, British Columbia. In 2009, it became the largest community-level solar project in British Columbia by installing a $1.5 million dollar solar project that provides power for its administrative center, fishing building, 25 homes on the reservation and 50 hot water tanks in a neighboring town (T'Sou-ke Nation 2011).

renewable for businesses. Switching to renewable energy costs clients an average of 0.8 cents per kWh, about $5 to $15 per month in addition to the normal monthly bill. Renewable power comes from wind and fish-friendly micro-hydro installations. In addition to educating residents about the option to purchase renewable energy, the Utility also provides subsidies for green power projects (EPUD 2011).

GeoExchange BC

This is an industry association promoting the use of geo-exchange systems, and includes contractors, consultants, engineers, manufacturers and suppliers. GeoExchange BC provides consumer education, promotion, responsible design and proper installation of low-temperature ground-source energy systems. In addition, it provides education, professional development, training and resources for growing the geo-exchange and heat pump industry in BC (British Columbia Ministry of Energy 2010).

Financial Incentives
Cooperative Wind Farms

The government of Denmark is aiming to source 50 percent of Danish electricity con-

sumption from offshore wind power by 2030. In 2000, the city of Copenhagen took part in Middelgrunden, a large offshore wind farm project two kilometers off the city's coast. This public-private cooperative is 50 percent financed by 10,000 stockholders in Middelgrunden Vindmøllelaug and 50 percent financed by Copenhagen Energy, the municipal energy supplier. The Danish government has established tax deductions for families interested in joining such cooperatives (Sustainable Cities 2011a).

Direct Cash Subsidies and Rebates

Direct cash subsidies promote the installation of renewable energy systems by facilitating technology market penetration, cost reductions, consumer education and better tracking of use and sales. Subsidies are typically paid as rebates after the installation of the system. The award-winning Hat Smart Renewable Energy and Conservation Program in Medicine Hat, Alberta, provides sizable subsidies for conservation and renewable power projects in both residential and commercial settings, as well as education campaigns and installation assistance. Subsidies range from 10 percent of the cost of residential energy-efficiency upgrades to 50 percent for residential and commercial renewable energy installations. To date, the program has provided over $900,000 in subsidies on a variety of solar hot water, solar electricity, geothermal and wind projects (City of Medicine Hat 2011; FCM 2011a).

Feed-in Tariffs (FITs)

FITs are one of the most widely used renewable energy policies in the world, and are beginning to be adopted by several levels of government in North America. FITs are regulated incentives

Fig. 7.4: *The city of Copenhagen took part in Middelgrunden, a large offshore wind farm project two kilometers off the coast of Denmark. This public-private cooperative is 50 percent financed by 10,000 stockholders in Middelgrunden Vindmøllelaug and 50 percent financed by Copenhagen Energy, the municipal energy supplier.* (Credit: Siemens Windpower)

that require utilities to pay a fixed premium rate for renewable energy generation, guaranteed for a set period of time — usually 20 years. In Florida, the Gainesville Regional Utilities FIT is the first US FIT modeled after successful European models. Introduced in February 2009, the program offers a fixed 20-year rate to owners of solar photovoltaic systems, ensuring competitive returns on investment of around 5 percent for smaller developers. The program includes rate differentiation (higher rates for smaller projects) to help projects of all sizes develop profitably. In its first year, the utility more than doubled the solar capacity installed in the city (ACORE 2010).

Public Benefit Fund

Benefit funds are used to provide a cohesive strategy and long-term funding for state- and city-run energy programs. They are most commonly supported by a Systems Benefit Charge (SBC), a small fixed fee added to customers' electricity bills each month. Funds are used for energy efficiency and renewable energy research and development, business development, renewable energy projects, industry development and public education programs. For example, the New Jersey Clean Energy Program, supported by an SBC, aims to achieve the following three goals by 2020: reduce energy consumption by at least 20 percent, reduce peak demand by 5,700 megawatts and generate 30 percent of the state's electricity needs from renewable sources (ACORE 2010).

Expenditure
Leading by Example

By committing to purchase renewable energy as a percentage of their total power needs, local governments can reduce their impact on the environment, set an example for residents and promote local energy security and local jobs. In 2006, the City of Bellingham, Washington, began a green power purchasing program by committing to purchase enough third-party-certified renewable energy credits to offset 100 percent of the electricity used for the city's municipal operations (24 million kilowatt-hours). The project goal was to increase green power purchasing in the entire community by 2 percent; however, results have far exceeded projections, with 13 percent (91 million kilowatt hours) of green power now being purchased annually (ACORE 2010).

Cogeneration

Helsinki, Finland, has been operating a district heating system through a public-private partnership for over 50 years. In 2010, it provided heat to over 13,000 customers. District heating covers approximately 93 percent of Helsinki's heating energy requirement (Helsinki Energy Board 2011).

Sewage Waste Heat Recovery

The City of Vancouver, British Columbia, has established a sewage waste heat district heating system in the Southeast False Creek sustainable development (part of its 2010 Olympic Village development). As the City's first district energy project, it will help reduce building-related greenhouse gas emissions that comprise 54 percent of Vancouver's emissions profile, and it is expected to help the city reach its ambitious goal of having all new developments be carbon-neutral by 2020 (City of Vancouver 2011).

Micro-hydro Turbine

The Hupacasath First Nation, in partnership with the Ucluelet First Nation, Synex Energy

Resourced Ltd. and the City of Port Alberni, is running a 6.5 megawatt micro-hydroelectric power project (also known as run-of-river) on China Creek. During peak operation, the plant produces enough energy to power 6,000 homes. The project not only provides the community with an additional energy supply in the form of renewable energy, it also provides local jobs and a new source of revenue (Hupacasath First Nation 2009).

BIOMASS DISTRICT HEATING

Dockside Green, a mixed-use sustainable community in Victoria, BC, houses residential, commercial and light-industrial occupants, and utilizes heat and hot water generated onsite by a renewable energy district heating system. The centralized biomass-gasification heating plant burns synthetic gas produced by the gaseous decomposition of locally sourced waste wood. Dockside Green is the first residential project in North America to use this technology, which is helping the entire development achieve greenhouse gas emission-neutral status from a building-energy perspective (Dockside Green 2011).

GEO-EXCHANGE DISTRICT ENERGY

Waterstone Pier, a residential development in Richmond, BC, uses a geothermal system to heat and cool 140 units. According to the complex's developer, using a geothermal system lowers the monthly energy costs of owning and managing a large complex (Terasen 2011).

Regulations
RENEWABLE PORTFOLIO STANDARDS (RPS)

RPS require retail electricity suppliers to procure a minimum quantity of eligible renewable energy by a specific date, in percentage,

megawatt-hour or megawatt-term. This is often achieved by trading renewable energy credits, which are tradable non-tangible energy commodities that represent proof that one megawatt-hour of electricity was generated from an eligible renewable energy resource. These mechanisms can be implemented at the federal, state/provincial or local scale but are most common at the state scale. As of 2010, RPS requirements or goals have been established in 29 American states. Texas is the leader in RPS, having added 5.5 gigawatts of new renewable capacity since it began in 2002. This initiative has helped create hundreds of jobs and increased the tax base in the rural west due to almost $1 billion of new wind development (ACORE 2010).

SOLAR SURPLUS ACT

Established in 1997, the Million Solar Roofs Initiative (MSRI) is a partnership between states and local communities administered by the United States Department of Energy. In California, MSRI and its partners are working towards the goal of installing 1,000,000 new solar energy systems by 2016. To achieve this goal, the state is helping local governments and individuals remove all barriers for investment in solar energy. For example, the *California Solar Surplus Act* passed in 2009 provides solar system owners fair compensation for the surplus electricity they generate above and beyond their own onsite electricity needs, by either allowing the meters to turn backwards when excess electricity is generated, or by requiring the utility companies to pay for it (Environment California 2011). This type of compensatory program is known as net metering and exists in several regions of Canada as well.

SOLAR ARRAY ORDINANCE

In 2000, Barcelona, Spain, passed a law requiring installation of solar panels on all new large buildings. The objective was to have all new buildings, especially those that consume a lot of water, heat at least 60 percent of their own water using the solar panels. Since 2000, 20 more municipalities in Spain have adopted similar regulations. Barcelona has committed itself to establishing 100,000 square meters of solar arrays, which will reduce the city's carbon emissions by 15,000 tons per year (Sustainable Cities 2011b).

THE MERTON RULE

To reduce carbon dioxide emissions, the Greater London, England, borough of Merton passed the Merton Rule requiring all new developments (including residential, commercial and institutional) to generate at least 10 percent of their energy needs from on-site renewable energy systems. The rule reduced greenhouse gas emissions by 26 per cent and was so successful that it was implemented by several other municipal councils. It has now become part of the nation's planning guidance. Merton has also received several awards for its work on the Merton Rule (Merton Council 2011).

Community Planning and Management Issues

While energy efficiency and greener power supply offer many options for communities, greater benefits are possible if local governments integrate energy considerations into other planning decisions. Energy use and supply are very much linked to strategies and policies for land use, urban development, building sizes, architectural design and standards, transportation planning, environmental protection, air quality and economic development. By integrating these issues into planning, communities can address multiple goals while maximizing cost efficiencies. This requires cooperation among various governmental departments and nongovernmental entities and businesses, and may require changes to conventional ways of planning and costing projects.

Least-cost Utility Planning

A number of communities, governments and utilities in Canada and the United States have implemented least-cost utility planning. Such planning for electricity supplies places investments for energy efficiency and demand-side (as opposed to supply-focused) management on an equal footing with investments for new generating capacity. Energy efficiency is treated as an alternative energy source, and substitution of non-conventional, decentralized, smaller generators for large central generating plants is supported — a perfect application for renewable energy systems and cogeneration. Applications of this concept require close coordination among utility regulators, individual utilities and local governments. To ensure effectiveness, these programs commonly combine technical support and financial incentives for energy efficiency improvements targeted to residential, commercial and industrial consumers (Rocky Mountain Institute 2011).

Tools and Initiatives: Community Energy Management Projects

Comprehensive Energy Planning Model Project

A comprehensive ten-year energy plan and public support helped the island community of Samsoe, Denmark, to slash its CO_2 emissions and become more than 100 percent self-sufficient in renewable energy by 2008. Through the use of 11 wind turbines, four district heating systems and several smaller renewable energy projects, the community of 4,000 was able to convert the island's energy source from coal and oil to renewable energy in just eight years. Currently the island community produces 10 percent more energy than it uses; it sells the rest to the mainland. Samsoe is an internationally renowned demonstration project with an Energy Academy to provide education about renewable energy potential, a forum for conferences regarding new energy technology and a research facility for scientists from around the world (Sustainable Cities 2011c).

LAND PLANNING TO PROMOTE ENERGY CONSERVATION

Portland, Oregon, provides an example of a larger city-region that established a statewide program for land-use planning based on 19 goals related to issues such as land use, energy, housing and natural resource use. As part of the program, local municipalities are required to create comprehensive plans and apply zoning and land division ordinances to help accomplish the 19 goals. One of the goals, related to energy use, states that land and land uses shall be managed and controlled so as to maximize the conservation of all forms of energy. This includes allocating land uses to conserve renewable energy sources, establishing high-density zoning along transportation corridors to reduce personal vehicle use and consumption of non-renewable energy sources and reusing existing or vacant land for development to reduce

urban sprawl (Oregon Department of Land Conservation and Development 2010).

INTEGRATED COMMUNITY ENERGY PLAN

The City of Guelph, Ontario, is experiencing significant commercial, industrial and population growth. Despite this, it has set a goal to reduce the overall energy requirement from the current level of 8,475 gigawatt-hours electrical energy to 6,135 gigawatt-hours electrical energy by 2031 through the use of a Community Energy Plan. This will reduce greenhouse gas emissions per capita from the current 16 tons to 7 tons. The proposed plan incorporates best practices in many areas of community planning, including transportation, energy efficiency, land-use, public and private buildings and renewable energy, in addition to setting aggressive targets for greenhouse gas emissions reduction. As a result, Guelph's Community Energy Plan is gaining national recognition and is being used as an example for other communities (Natural Resources Canada 2009b).

COMMUNITY ENERGY MAPPING

Modeling software and energy planning computer programs have helped communities such as Prince George, British Columbia, and Hamilton, Ontario, include energy decisions in building design and urban planning. The programs quantitatively measure integrated actions to evaluate energy, environmental and economic benefits of decisions about energy supply options, building design, orientation and lay-out, as well as neighborhood density and lay-out, transportation decisions and other urban planning issues (FCM 2011b).

Chapter 8

Transportation Planning and Traffic Management

For most North Americans, *transportation-* and *traffic management* evoke images of cars and freeways. You don't have to be a transportation planner to know why. We have a lot of cars: in 2008, there were over 255 million registered automobiles in the United States alone, almost one for every man, woman and child (PRB 2008; RITA 2008). We spend a lot on our cars: the average driver in America driving 20,000 miles annually spends $12,241 in operating and ownership expenses alone. We spend a lot of time in our cars: according to a study by the Texas Transportation Institute (2010), the average American driver in a large urban area spent 50 hours stuck in traffic in 2009, up 31 hours from 1982. The numbers suggest that we love our cars; however, many people are beginning to realize our relationship with our cars is out of balance.

The term *automobile dependency* was coined in the 1980s by Australian researchers Peter Newman and Jeffrey Kenworthy (1999) to help define our transportation challenges.

This deeply institutionalized dependency was reflected for decades in American Association of State Highway and Transportation's widely used civil engineering manual for road design. It stated that the purpose of efficient street design is to provide "operational efficiency, comfort, safety, and convenience for the motorist" (AASHTO as cited in Burwell, 2009, p 127). Transportation management was about managing *traffic*, which was mainly conceived of as cars. The primary objective of traffic management was to move vehicles in and around communities as rapidly and efficiently as

> "If we build a freeway system or an extended airport system to meet some prediction of future demand, then we should not be surprised to discover that these investments hasten our progress in that direction. Our plans and analyses boomerang so that our efforts are rewarded by the return of the problem, usually with some force and destructive impact."
>
> — Whitelegg 1996

Traffic, Mobility and Accessibility

By Todd Litman

How transportation is defined and measured can affect which solutions are considered best. A particular policy or project may appear worthwhile when transportation system performance is measured in one way, but undesirable when it is measured another way. The table below summarizes and compares three approaches to transportation planning: traffic, mobility and accessibility.

Conventional transportation often reflects the assumption that transportation means *motor vehicle traffic*. From this perspective, anything that increases ☞

	Traffic	Mobility	Accessibility
Definition of Transportation	Vehicle travel.	Person and goods movement.	Ability to obtain goods, services and activities.
Unit of measure	Vehicle miles.	Person-miles and ton-miles.	Trips, generalized costs.
Modes considered	Automobile and truck.	Automobile, truck and transit.	Automobile, truck, transit, cycling and walking.
Common Indicators	Vehicle traffic volumes and speeds, roadway level of service, costs per vehicle-mile, parking convenience.	Person travel volumes and speeds, road and transit, cost per person-mile, travel convenience.	Quality of available transportation choices. Distribution of destinations. Cost per trip.
Assumptions concerning what benefits consumers	Maximum motor vehicle travel and speed.	Maximum personal travel and goods movement	Maximum transport choice and cost efficiency.
Consideration of land use	Treats land-use as an input, unaffected by transportation decisions.	Recognizes that land-use can affect travel choice.	Recognizes that land-use has major impacts on transportation.
Favored transportation improvement strategies	Roadway and parking facility improvements to increase capacity, speed and safety.	Transportation system improvements that increase capacity, speed and safety.	Management strategies and improvements that increase transport system efficiency and safety.
Implications for TDM	Generally considers vehicle travel reductions undesirable, except if congestion is extreme.	Supports TDM strategies that improve personal and freight mobility.	Supports TDM whenever it is cost effective.

motor vehicle traffic speed and volume improves transportation, and anything that reduces motor vehicle traffic speed and volume must be harmful.

A more comprehensive approach reflects the assumption that transportation means *personal mobility,* measured in terms of person-trips and person-kilometers. From this perspective, strategies such as better transit services and rideshare programs may improve transportation without increasing total vehicle-kilometers. However, this approach still assumes that movement is an end in itself, rather than a means to an end, and increased personal movement is always desirable.

Transportation systems have typically been assessed using traffic-based or mobility-based approaches. However, a paradigm shift is occurring, and transport planning is beginning to focus on accessibility — the most comprehensive definition of transportation. It assesses how well a system allows people to reach desired goods, services and activities. Since accessibility is the ultimate goal of most transportation, it is the best definition to use in transportation planning. It recognizes the value of more accessible land-use patterns and mobility substitutes, such as telecommuting and delivery services, as ways to improve transportation while reducing total physical travel.

Many transport projects improve accessibility by some modes, but degrade it for others. For example, increasing roadway capacity and traffic speeds tends to improve access by automobile but reduces it by other modes, such as walking, cycling and transit. Only by defining transportation in terms of accessibility can these trade-offs be considered in the planning process.

Vehicle traffic is relatively easy to measure, so transportation system quality tends to be evaluated based largely on automobile travel conditions (e.g., average traffic speeds, roadway level-of-service, vehicle congestion delay, vehicle operating costs, parking supply), while ignoring other accessibility impacts, including impacts on transit service quality, non-motorized transport and land use accessibility. This tends to favor automobile-oriented solutions and undervalues alternative solutions to transportation problems.

possible using strategies such as one-way streets, synchronization of traffic signals, road widening and construction of left-hand turn bays.

However, research has repeatedly shown that catering to the car through continual expansion of road networks and freeways inevitably leads to increasing congestion, longer commuting times, reduced worker productivity and higher prices due to the inflationary powers of ever-dearer oil (Bartle & Devan 2006). Many transportation professionals and citizens now understand that continuous expansion of our roads and infrastructure to meet motorist demands is a zero-sum game.

Research also shows that maintenance costs of auto-centric development have spiraled beyond our ability to pay. In 2008, the US National Surface Transportation Policy and Revenue Study Commission calculated that America needed at least $255 billion per year in transport spending over the next 50 years just to keep the system in good repair and make the needed upgrades; current spending falls 60 percent short of that amount (*The Economist* 2011).

Today, more sustainable transportation approaches are being adopted by North American planners and the communities they serve. They make better use of the assets we already have and focus on equally important modes of transport such as walking, cycling and innovative public transit designs. With better transport planning, we can create more livable communities where residents can reduce their transportation costs, and lead a healthier, happier lifestyle.

This chapter provides an overview of more sustainable approaches to transportation planning, through which citizens, businesses and local governments may forge transportation systems that increase citizens' mobility and access to opportunities, while making better use of our physical, natural and economic capital. It starts with a clear definition of how communities can define and measure their transportation solutions, followed by a closer look at the legacy of auto-centric planning. It then provides suggestions as to how to best design and manage a sustainable transportation planning system to increase accessibility, promote alternative modes of transport and increase community livability.

America's Most Congested Cities

As cities sprawl farther into distant suburbs, an hour per day in the car has become the national norm. Chicago and Washington lead the list of most congested cities, with drivers spending 70 hours stuck in traffic annually, followed by Los Angeles (68 hours), and Houston (58 hours) (TTI 2010). Similarly, Canadian drivers in 2005 spent nearly 12 full days a year, or close to 275 hours, commuting to work and returning home, and each day the average driver spent an average of 63 minutes commuting (Turcotte 2006).

Auto-centric Communities: The True Costs

Driving a car incurs more costs than gas, insurance, depreciation, maintenance and parking. While these individually borne costs are obvious, others are harder to measure. Single-occupant trips in particular incur significant negative social, economic, environmental and health costs that are usually borne by society:

Table 8.1: The true costs of automobile dependence.		
Type of Imapct	**Costs**	**Description**
Economic (Direct personal notwithstanding)	*Road and Parking Provision*	Municipal and state highway construction and maintenance costs take monies away from other public spending initiatives such as healthcare, education and public transit.
	Traffic Accidents	Road accidents incur substantial costs to local governments due to clean-up and lost economic activity due to road delays and congestion (Mohan 2008).
	Low Fuel Taxes (USA)	America's large subsidies in the form of low fuel taxes increase vehicle miles travelled and encourage rapid growth of motor vehicle use while leaving externalities, like pollution and accidents, to be borne by society (Bartle & Devan 2006).
	External Resource Extraction and Consumption Costs	Fuel production and consumption imposes a variety of external costs typically borne by society (pollution from extraction activities and transportation of oil and fuel by ship, pipelines and freight). As well, ensuring access to foreign oil incurs significant costs to national security budgets (Rubin 2009). ☛

	Table 8.1: The true costs of automobile dependence cont.	
Type of Imapct	**Costs**	**Description**
Economic cont.	*Road noise*	Road noise has a negative effect on housing prices and neighborhood desirability, as well as incurring costs through noise abatement (Nelson 2008).
	Land use impact costs	Land-use decisions influence firm location, household location, real estate development, land prices and density. Regional auto-centric transportation plans routinely ignore these effects and, as a result, exaggerate their mobility benefits while undervaluing more integrated land-use policies such as Smart Growth (Waddell et al. 2007).
	Decreasing land values and housing prices	Research shows that large transportation infrastructure such as elevated expressways and freeways produce significant downward pressure on surrounding land values and housing prices. When expressways are replaced with greenways, tremendous economic benefits result for the surrounding area (Kang & Cervero 2009).
	Congestion, wasted time and money	In Los Angeles alone, congestion costs more than $10.3 billion in wasted time and excess fuel being burned in traffic. This works out to 53 gallons per traveller of wasted fuel and 70 hours of annual delay per traveller (Texas Transportation Institute 2010).
Social	*Reduced access to key services*	Auto-dependent communities reduce access to key services such as health-care, shopping and social activities for the car-less (Farrington et al. 2004).
	Marginalization of vulnerable groups	Bartle and Deven (2006) implicitly link the ideas of *just sustainability* and transportation planning by showing how auto-dominated communities marginalize those without cars by restricting their access to resources and amenities. The groups most commonly affected are the elderly, disadvantaged, disabled, youth and two-parent families with only one car, which represent between 40 to 60 percent of the population in North American cities.
	Transportation diversity and equity	As the number of older people in North America increases, so too will their mobility needs and dependence on alternative methods of transportation.
		In many communities — particularly those that are small, rural and/or remote — alternatives to driving are few. The United States is currently ill-prepared to provide adequate transportation choices for its rapidly aging population (Neal et al. 2006).
	Barriers for pedestrians and bicycles	Profligate road-building for cars makes travel by foot or bike increasingly dangerous and inconvenient for citizens who wish to pursue active transportation alternatives (Frank et al.2010).
Environmental	*Air pollution*	Emissions from vehicle tailpipes such as carbon monoxide, particulate matter, nitrogen oxides, methane and benzene damage our health, damage infrastructure and enhance the greenhouse effect resulting in climate change (Poudenx 2008).
	Water pollution	Runoff from streets pollutes drinking water and reduces recharge rates for our water tables; fuel spills and burning of fossil fuels degrade fish habitat and impact the hydrological cycle. ☞

Table 8.1: The true costs of automobile dependence cont.

Type of Imapct	Costs	Description
Environmental cont.	*Habitat fragmentation*	North America's highways are the major cause of habitat fragmentation. Highways open areas to further human settlement and economic development of resources (Eigenbrod, Hecnar & Fahrig 2007).
	Waste disposal	At the end of their life, automobiles create waste difficult to dispose of. Waste products such as used tires, batteries, junked car bodies, oil and other hazardous materials are expensive to dispose of properly, and are more often just dumped into landfills where they release harmful chemicals into groundwater (Konz 2009).
Health	*Air pollution*	Emissions result in poor air quality, acid rain, smog and poor health. Nearly half of all Americans live in areas with unhealthy levels of air pollution (Bartle & Devan 2006). The American Lung Association (2011) has linked air pollution to increased levels of asthma, cancer, heart disease, heart attack, stroke, high blood pressure, birth defects and brain damage.
	Traffic accidents	Increasing traffic volumes lead to increased traffic fatalities and serious injury as well as significant property damage. Worldwide traffic accidents are among the second leading cause of death for young adults 15 to 44 years old (Mohan 2008).
	Healthcare costs	Vehicle miles travelled per person is positively correlated with obesity, cardiac and pulmonary diseases and other health risks due to increased sedentary lifestyles (Frank el al. 2010).

Saving Through Mode Diversity

There may be more costs involved in driving than most of us realize, but at least we get efficient mobility for our pains ... or do we? One study (Bernstein et al. 2005) found that American households in more automobile-dependent communities devoted more than $8,500 annually, or 20 percent of household expenditures, to surface transportation. Their counterparts in communities with more diverse modes of transportation spent less than $5,500 annually, or 17 percent.

what economists call "externalities." Obvious examples include emissions, noise, land use and pollution-related sickness. As well, indirect subsidization — such as the provision of roads, lowered corporate taxes on oil production and seemingly innocuous programs such as free parking by governments and industry — takes money from other potential uses and thereby obscures the true costs of driving (Shoup 2005). Table 8.1 summarizes the various costs of driving and shows that auto-centric planning serves to erode many forms of community capital (Litman 2009).

Current business-as-usual transportation designs directly impact our natural environment through pollution, profligate land use for roads and highways and segmentation of wildlife habitat. Indirect costs, associated with fossil fuel extraction, production and consumption, are numerous, and are discussed in more detail in chapter 13 on climate change.

In an ideal world, an efficient economic system would prevent market failures such as transportation externalities and achieve the highest return on all forms of capital (financial, human, social, physical, natural and cultural). However, recognizing that all driving-related externalities will never completely disappear, we can significantly reduce their impact through progressive sustainable transportation policies that reflect the true costs of driving. A more efficient transport system improves affordable modes (walking, cycling and public transit), which can provide significant consumer savings and benefits.

Technical Transportation Fixes … or Paradigm Shift?

Motor efficiency and fuel types can be improved to tackle the greenhouse gas emissions and smog they create. Although car manufacturers and lawmakers have been slow to respond, well-established fuel-saving and fuel-switching technologies can improve the cars we use. From hydrogen fuel cells to biodiesel, hybrid vehicles to electric, drivers now enjoy many alternatives to fossil-fuel burning vehicles with more renewable fuel sources predicted to emerge.

Undoubtedly, reducing emissions by switching to renewable fuels will help mitigate and adapt to climate change. But while alternative fuels can do much to address emissions, merely waiting for the arrival of reduced-emissions vehicles does little for the problems discussed above. For example, do these technologies address common transport problems such as road and parking congestion or crash risks to motorists, cyclists and pedestrians on local streets? Do they provide adequate travel options for non-drivers? Communities that devote excessive resources to these individualized modes would be ignoring more fundamental systemic transportation problems.

The Road Home

America's civil engineers routinely give its transport structures poor marks, rating roads, rails and bridges as deficient or functionally obsolete. And according to the 2010 World Economic Forum (WEF as cited in *The Economist* 2011) study on global competitiveness, over the past decade America's infrastructure has gotten worse compared to other OECD countries. The study ranked America 23rd for overall infrastructure quality, between Spain and Chile, citing its roads, railways, ports and air-transport infrastructure as mediocre against networks in Northern Europe. American traffic congestion was also ranked worse than in Western Europe, as average delays in America's largest cities exceeded those of cities like Berlin and Copenhagen. More time on lower-quality roads also makes for a deadlier transport network. With some 15 deaths a year for every 100,000 people, 33,000 Americans were killed on roads in 2010 — a road fatality rate 60 percent above the OECD average (*The Economist* 2011).

In 1964, American historian, philosopher of technology and science, and urban architecture critic Lewis Mumford observed: "Perhaps our age will be known to the future historian as the age of the bulldozer and the exterminator; and in many parts of the country the building of a highway has about the same results upon vegetation and human structures as the passage of a tornado or the blast of an atom bomb. Nowhere is this bulldozing habit of mind so disastrous as in the approach to the city. Since the engineer regards his own work as more important than the human functions it serves, he does not hesitate to lay waste to woods, streams, parks, and human neighborhoods in order to carry his roads straight to their supposed destinations" (Mumford 1963, 179).

Perhaps the next trend in transportation is not a new mode or service but a paradigm shift in how to think about transportation problems and solutions. That shift may well be realized by incremental management innovations that achieve more efficient use of existing

Is Telecommuting a Panacea?

Many large employers are implementing or considering telecommuting options for workers. Telecommuting could lead to a reduction in vehicle trips, but it could also increase them. People working from home may need to make more trips than if all their working requirements existed in one place. Working from the "electronic cottage" can also encourage flight from urban centers, thereby exacerbating urban sprawl and its attendant problems. Telecommuting should therefore be considered as one component of a comprehensive commuter-trip reduction program (Choo, Mokhtarian & Salomon 2005).

Fig. 8.1: *In Stockholm, wide sidewalks, segregated bike lanes and dedicated transit lanes promote co-existence of all transportation modes and contribute to a more vital street environment while improving mobility* and *accessibility for everyone.* (CREDIT: EURIST E.V. (EURIST EUROPEAN INSTITUTE FOR SUSTAINABLE TRANSPORT) CREATIVE COMMONS LICENSE)

transportation systems. This is not as radical as it may sound: many important revolutions result from more effective use of existing infrastructure, technologies and resources, rather than new technology.

This suggests that the best solutions to transport problems are those that encourage efficiency and improve basic mobility and access services (for example, walking and cycling conditions, road system management and public transit services), rather than a new mode or breakthrough technology (Frank et al. 2010; Poudenx 2008; Shore 2006). The first step will be reducing our dependency on the automobile and the vehicle miles travelled in them.

Retooling Our Transportation System

To achieve truly effective solutions to auto-dependency, we would do well to consider how mobility differs from accessibility. Litman (2011a) defines *mobility* as "the movement of people or goods [and] ... assumes that any increase in travel mileage or speed benefits society"; and *accessibility* refers to the "ability to reach desired goods, services, activities, and destinations (collectively called opportunities)." The critical difference between the two perspectives is that mobility frames transportation problems from the viewpoint that movement is an end in itself, rather than a means to an end. It thereby downplays non-motorized modes or land-use factors affecting accessibility. Recognizing the entire spectrum of means by which people access opportunities, the more holistic accessibility perspective provides that there are many ways to improve that access. Solutions, therefore, include improved mobility as well as improved land use to reduce the distance between destinations and improved mobility substitutes such as telecommunications or delivery services. Accessibility can be enhanced by multi-modal transportation and more compact, mixed-use walkable communities, which reduces the amount of travel required to reach destinations (Gray, Shaw & Farrington 2006).

What is needed are win-win transportation solutions: cost-effective, technically feasible reforms that increase travelers' options while removing the perverse incentives of auto-centric transportation planning (Litman 2011a). Win-win strategies reduce total vehicle travel while imparting other benefits such as increased user convenience, reduced congestion, reduced capital expenditures on roadways and parking, reduced traffic accidents, energy conservation, pollution reduction and improved physical fitness and health (Litman 2011a). In short, they improve our quality of life. Similar to the effective climate change solutions outlined in chapter 13, win-win transportation solutions are "no regrets" policies that are justified regardless of the uncertainties about climate change, or other social and environmental impacts.

A critical first step in retooling our transportation system is to look at how our transport systems relate to our uses of land (Waddell et al. 2007). Newman & Kenworthy (2006) revealed significant statistical relationships between key transport and land-use variables, showing that urban density is an important determinant of auto and transit use, as well as the relative role of transit (auto use increases and transit decreases with decreasing density). Road provision, parking and use of non-motorized modes of transportation are all also strongly associated with the pattern of auto-dependence across cities. Reducing automobile dependence requires communities to pursue the following objectives for:

- Land-use: more transit-oriented, higher density and mixed land use to help halt the growth in auto-based development;
- Private transport: stabilized or lower car use and less emphasis on infrastructure for cars;
- Public transport: higher-quality transit systems, especially rail, which are more competitive with cars; and
- Non-motorized transport: greater safety and amenity for walking and cycling and increased use of these modes (Newman and Kenworthy 2006).

Local initiatives can encourage transit over personal automobile use by reducing subsidies to private vehicles; managing transportation demand (discussed below), especially of commuters; and emphasizing bicycle and pedestrian networks as valid components of a regional transportation strategy.

Newman and Kenworthy (2006) also show that, when sufficient urban densities are reached, communities can achieve significant reductions in vehicle miles travelled. To achieve these reduction goals, transportation planners should utilize the concept of "ped sheds:"

According to a study by the Federal Highway Administration, the United States has four million miles of roads. When combined with parking lots, this is approximately 61,000 square miles of paved area — an area slightly smaller than Wisconsin. In *The High Costs of Free Parking*, urban planner Donald Shoup (2005) writes: "Parking requirements create great harm: They subsidize cars, distort transportation choices, warp urban form, increase housing costs, burden low-income households, debase urban design, damage the economy, and degrade the environment."

highly walkable areas of about 300 hectares (1.15 square miles) around local centers and public transit nodes, and transit sheds of about 3,000 hectares (11.5 square miles) around urban villages. Regular transit should connect these urban villages to local centers. Additional strategies for building more complete, accessible, equitable, transit-orientated communities will be covered in chapter 9.

Diversifying our portfolio of public investment in infrastructure is also important to achieving sustainable transportation systems. As discussed above, auto ownership is heavily subsidized through freeway construction, free parking and low fuel taxes (Bartle & Devan 2006). Ending or reducing these could provide local governments greater means to pay for auto-competitive transit systems, especially the preferred forms of public transit for the general public: light rail and streetcars. The following strategies illuminate many paths to win-win transportation solutions.

Table 8.2:
TDM densities as *described in the Victoria Transportation Policy Institute's online encyclopedia.*
(CREDIT: LITMAN, 2011B)

Transportation Management Strategies

Transportation Demand Management

Transportation demand management (TDM) refers to the use of policies, programs, services and products that influence whether, why, when, where and how people travel. Many transport problems are virtually unsolvable without some form of TDM strategy. This is because conventional solutions that ultimately increase total vehicle travel, such as increasing roadway capacity or improving vehicle design, often reduce one problem but exacerbate others, such as pollution and collisions. TDM measures, on the other hand, can motivate people to shift their travel modes, make fewer trips and, when necessary, drive more efficiently. Integrated TDM programs with an appropriate set of complementary strategies are often the most cost-effective way to improve transportation.

Table 8.2			
Transport Options Improvement	**Incentives**	**Land-use Management**	**Implementation Programs**
Transit improvements	Congestion pricing	Smart Growth	Commute trip reduction programs
Walking and cycling improvements	Distance-based fees	Transit-oriented development	School and campus transport management
Rideshare programs	Commuter financial incentives	Location-efficient development	Freight transport management
HOV priority	Parking pricing	Parking management	Tourist transport management
Flextime	Fuel tax increases	Car-free planning	Mobility management marketing programs
Car-sharing	Transit encouragement	Traffic calming	Transport planning reforms
Telework	Parking regulations		
Taxi service improvements			
Guaranteed ride home			

The Victoria Transportation Policy Institute's online encyclopedia offers this list of TDM strategies:

Adopting transportation demand management strategies promises benefits for:

Communities: a greater return on investment in transit, walking, cycling and carpooling facilities; cleaner air; less traffic congestion; and lower health-care costs.

Employers: improved employee recruitment and retention; lowered parking costs.

Individuals: greater choice and convenience; time and cost savings; better health and fitness (FCM 2008).

Some transportation professionals are skeptical that TDM is effective because it requires us to change our travel behavior. Arguing that North Americans are in love with cars and will not voluntarily drive less, they recommend technological fixes or supply increases (for example, wider roads, increased parking capacity, vehicle design improvements) instead. But experience shows that with appropriate education, travel options and incentives, people are often amenable to change. Metro Vancouver, British Columbia, used individualized marketing campaigns to promote active transportation, which resulted in a 9 percent increase in walking, 12 percent increase in transit trips and a 33 percent increase in cycling trips (FCM 2008). The City of Portland promoted the benefits of public transit in a community near a soon-to-be-completed light rail transit line. Residents of the targeted community increased their transit use by 44 percent — almost double that of neighboring communities

without municipal promotions — and reduced their car use by 14 percent (FCM 2008).

Transportation System Management (TSM)

TSM aims to enhance the supply of transportation services by increasing the person-carrying capacity of the road system without building additional road capacity — or by simply allowing congestion to worsen in parts of the system that favor single-occupant vehicles, thereby discouraging such trips. Commonly used measures include high-occupancy vehicle (HOV) and transit-only lanes, preferred parking for HOV vehicles and toll-free privileges for HOVs. In congested urban centers, transit-only lanes are even more effective than HOV lanes as they have the capacity to carry far more people. At freeway speeds, for example, a full bus or rail car can carry as many people as a lane of carpool traffic up to a kilometer long.

Aligning Travel Priorities

An efficient transportation system prioritizes use of scarce resources, such as road and parking space, to favor higher-value trips and more-efficient modes over lower-value and less-efficient travel. It designs first for walking, followed by cycling, transit, transportation of goods and, lastly, vehicles. Cities such as Portland, San Francisco, New York and Vancouver, British Columbia, have reprioritized their surface transportation plans this way and have realized

> "The demand for traffic control . . . was recognized at least as early as the first century AD, when congestion caused Julius Caesar to ban wheeled traffic from Rome in the daytime" (Rajan 1996, 21).

significant gains in community health and reductions in overall GHG emissions (Frank et al. 2006).

Prioritize Walkability

Most trips begin and end with walking, so it's a natural place to start when designing efficient urban transportation. Walkability, arguably the most important element of the transportation system, is affordable to achieve, promote and maintain. Walkable communities put urban environments back on a scale that promotes sustainable use of resources (both natural and economic capital) and leads to increased social interaction and physical fitness, while diminishing crime (Frank et al. 2006).

In fact, community scale is a key determinant of walkability. The Center for Livable Communities, a national initiative of the California-based non-profit Local Government Commission, suggests that for people to take up walking, most services, including elementary

Fig. 8.2: *Bike-sharing programs like Bixi have spread from Europe to North American cities, like Montreal.* (Credit: Shawn Carpenter (spcbrass on Flickr), Creative Commons)

schools, should be reachable by walking within a quarter-mile, while public transit should be reachable within a quarter- to a half-mile (Walkable Communities 2011).

Walkways and other pedestrian improvements are important elements of all public areas. They should not be limited to small pedestrian-zone islands but included as part of the area-wide road network. Communities in Europe, South America and Asia have implemented walking-only shopping districts, and contrary to what detractors in North America claim, property values, rents and vibrancy have increased in these zones (Kang & Cervero 2009)!

Make Cycling Safer, Faster and More Pleasant

Non-polluting and fossil-fuel-free, bicycles are ideal for use in highly congested urban centers and thus have an important role in sustainable transportation strategies. Bikes also help reduce congestion since they demand far less space than motor vehicles. Experience in Davis, California, Boulder, Colorado, and Eugene, Oregon, suggests that areas where bike facilities, such as secure bike storage, showers and bike maintenance facilities, are improved, the number and frequency of cycling trips dramatically increases (Xing, Handy & Buehler 2008).

Many communities are challenged to find the space or finances to build separate bicycle paths. But as many more have found, the answer is in large networks of quiet residential side streets running parallel to main arteries. These residential streets can provide the basis for a network of safe, pleasant bicycle routes — leading to a significant increase in cycling.

Businesses can also encourage healthy living through employee cycling programs. Best practices for employee cycling program development include the following: creating a clear, consistent and positive message about the benefits of non-motorized travel; identifying and overcoming barriers to non-motorized transport; finding opportunities for cooperation with other organizations; working with local planners, employers and employees who cycle to design and improve cycling facilities and services; utilizing cycling, walking and recreational organizations to enlist volunteers; and emphasizing cycling skills and safety education (Gärling & Steg 2007).

Make Public Transit a Viable Option for More People

Improved transportation efficiency hinges on improved public transit service quality, including more routes, service frequency, speed, reliability, plus nicer stops and stations, more comfortable vehicles (clean, uncrowded, effective heating and cooling), convenient user information and payment systems and amenities such as on-board worktables and Internet service. High-quality transit service can attract a substantial portion of discretionary travelers (people who would otherwise drive), providing significant savings and benefits, including benefits to travelers who drive (Litman 2011c).

To increase transit ridership in our communities, transit needs to be accessible. Translink, the transportation authority of Metro Vancouver in British Columbia, embraces a demand-side management strategy that emphasizes the six Ds of transit-orientated communities (Translink 2010):

- Focus **destinations** along frequent transit corridors and restrict growth elsewhere. Destinations should be on the way!

- Create grid-pattern streets with **distances** that are pedestrian and bicycle friendly. Be within a 5- to 10-minute walk of frequent transit service.
- **Design** a clearly defined public realm that promotes active integration of activities.
- **Densify** residential and commercial land uses close to transit hubs.
- Promote **diversity** through accessible pedestrian-friendly developments that have a good jobs-housing mix so that residents

Fig. 8.3: *Hammarby Sjöstad is a new transit-oriented community of 11,000 homes under development on a former industrial site in suburban Stockholm, Sweden. The masterplan included some ambitious environmental targets, including average car ownership of only 0.5 cars per unit. Residents enjoy easy access to two new bus routes (inner-city buses are fuelled by biogas), a new tram line that will link directly to the city centre, a car-sharing scheme (with 25 cars placed around the neighbourhood) and a free ferry service.*
(Credit: La-Citta-Vita on Flickr, Creative Commons)

are never far from work, shopping or other destinations.

- Introduce **demand-management** strategies that make transit use more attractive than driving.

Demand-side approaches like these must be supported by supply-side strategies that ensure regular and frequent service — a minimum of every 15 minutes all day, all week.

It is important to note that higher efficiency and use of public transit need not necessarily demand high-tech. The transportation system in Curitiba, Brazil, serves as a model for cities around the world wanting to implement eco-efficient transportation with environmental benefits, and certainly offers planning lessons for wealthier nations. The city pioneered the idea of an all-bus transit network with special bus-only avenues that were also used to channel the city's growth. Its transit system is rapid and cheap, which encourages people to leave their cars at home — not by restricting cars, but by making transit the best choice. Since 1974, when the city had just one bus line, the city has grown past 1.5 million. While car ownership levels in Curitiba are similar to cities of comparable size (Toronto, for instance), with 49 blocks closed to traffic, Curitiba has made public transit much more convenient than driving (Leahy 2002). In addition, an inexpensive "social fare" promotes equality, benefiting poorer residents settled on the city's periphery. A standard fare is charged for all trips, meaning shorter rides subsidize longer ones. One fare can

take a passenger 70 kilometers. It now boasts the world's highest usage of public transit: 75 percent of all city travel is by transit (Leahy 2002). Curitiba registers Brazil's lowest levels of ambient pollution and per capita gasoline consumption (MacLeod 2004). Cities around the world continue to look to Curitiba as an example of successful urban transit system with 83 cities replicating the Curitiba bus system.

Develop Sustainable Freight Management

Although freight vehicles only represent 10 to 20 percent of total vehicle mileage, their heavy weight and slow acceleration can produce large impacts on road networks and the surrounding community in the form of air and noise pollution. By improving freight transport efficiency and shifting reliance to alternatives modes, communities can reduce traffic congestion and fuel consumption, save on road maintenance costs, reduce air and noise pollution and improve community livability. Improving efficiency can also provide financial savings to shippers.

Improving rail, marine and bicycle transportation infrastructure can make these efficient modes more competitive with other modes such as trucking. In urban areas, distributing goods via human-powered transport such as bicycles can reduce congestion, noise and air pollution and save shippers fuel. For example, Pedal Express operates a fleet of cargo bicycles capable of carrying up to 700 pounds in watertight containers to deliver meals, baked goods, books and post office mail to the San Francisco Bay Area. Other strategies, such as situating manufacturing and assembly sites near markets or coordination among shippers, can improve distribution efficiency and reduce the amount of travel required. For example, rail carloads

"They say everyone has a BMW in Curitiba. You know, BMW: Bus, Metro, Walking" (Lerner 2004).

of grain arriving at the Port of Vancouver are pooled together to reduce congestion and travel distance, regardless of the originating railways and grain company terminal. Encouraging businesses to minimize excessive packaging and increase reliance on local products can reduce the volume and number of goods needed to be shipped elsewhere and boost the local economy. Implementing policies such as weight-distance charges and fuel pricing can also encourage more efficient freight transport (VTPI 2011a).

Create Grid-connected Transport Networks

Sky rocketing oil prices, as a result of declining stocks and increased worldwide demand, have already had profound effects on the way in which we transport goods and people. A shift to electric vehicles, trolley buses and rail is considered to be among the major changes needed in transportation patterns and is already well under way in China. Gilbert and Perl (2010) argue that communities who cling to fossil fuels and diffuse land-use practices will eventually be forced to choose between fuelling their vehicles and feeding their family. They suggest that an electrified grid for transportation of passengers and freight is the most sustainable and salient response to the challenges of peak oil. To facilitate the movement away from fossil fuels and towards an electrified system will require large investments on a national scale. Communities can contribute by preparing transportation plans that make provisions for the necessary infrastructure and changes to the transportation landscape (Gilbert & Perl 2010).

Encourage More Efficient Use of Cars

When all the costs of single-occupant vehicle trips are tallied, it is truly difficult to justify

Are Cars Faster Than Transit?

A 2005 Statistics Canada study found the average one-way commuting time by car was 59 minutes, but for public transit users, the average was 106. For many of us, it is faster to use a car to get to work than public transit, if only marginally so (Neal et al. 2006). Litman (2011c) argues that *average* commuting times are irrelevant to discussions of how to improve urban transportation systems: far more important, from a management point of view, are travel speeds along congested corridors. To the extent that averages include infrequent transit service in many rural settings, they serve to obscure transportation improvements in many urban areas. In areas where public transit has dedicated tracks or a right of way, transit trips are often faster than driving (Litman 2011c).

systems that promote them at the expense of alternatives. Governments and citizen groups have many avenues before them to make car use more efficient through car-sharing, carpooling programs and innovative insurance policies.

Car-sharing (also known as car co-ops or car clubs) refers to sharing the ownership of a car between many members. Over the past decade, the concept has soared in popularity in many North American cities. One of its largest effects on transportation is reduced vehicle ownership. Car-sharing programs remove 4.6 to 20 cars per shared vehicle from the transportation network and increase participants' use of public transit and walking (Shaheen, Cohen & Chung 2009).

Carpooling (also known as ride-sharing) refers to using the empty seats available in commuters' cars to decrease the total number of vehicles on the road. Carpooling programs are appropriate where commuters are headed to the same place at the same set time, and present a lower-cost option than public transit as drivers are not hired (VTPI 2010). Carpooling is easily applicable in all areas, especially rural settings where public transit is infrequent or unavailable.

Car-sharing and carpooling programs enjoy greater success when supported by financial incentives, such as parking fee reductions for the car-share vehicles. York and Fabricatore (2001) showed that subsidies, such as the transit authority paying for empty seats in the carpool vehicle or making comfortable vans available for rent at the same price as cars, would attract 10 to 30 percent of commuter trips as opposed to only 5 to 15 percent, if marketing information were simply given to the potential carpooler.

Another way to encourage efficient use of cars is pay-as-you-drive (PAYD) vehicle insurance, which bases vehicle insurance premiums on how much a car is driven during the term of the insurance policy. In a PAYD system, vehicle premiums are calculated based on vehicle use (measured in minutes or distance); people who drive less are rewarded with lower insurance premiums. Existing higher-risk motorists continue to pay a premium over lower-risk drivers. PAYD insurance pricing can help achieve several public policy goals at once: affordability, consumer savings and choice, fairness, reduced congestion, lower emissions and increased road safety.

"Streets have become dangerous, unlivable environments, yet most people live on them. Streets need to be redefined as sanctuaries; as livable places; as communities; as resident territory; as places for play, greenery, and local history" Donald Appleyard (1980, 34).

Tools and Initiatives
Voluntary
PROMOTING SUSTAINABLE TRANSPORTATION

TransLink's TravelSmart program helps businesses and residents of Metro Vancouver, British Columbia, make smart travel choices and reduce single-occupant car trips. It includes an employer pass program, ride-sharing, car-share (including corporate car-share), active transportation, parking management, guaranteed rides home and telework, all supported by strong promotion (TravelSmart 2011).

PROMOTING CYCLING

Since 1988, progressive residents of Thurston County, Washington, have discovered powerful ways to promote cycling. The Thurston County Bicycle Commuter Contest encourages individuals to bicycle to work, to school and to run errands throughout the month of May. Participants keep track of how often and how far they commute by bicycle and win prizes in a variety of categories. In 2009, the contest had 1,633 participants, while in 2010, the 24th year of the contest saw the greatest number of log books returned at 953 (Thurston County 2011).

CARPOOLING

High-occupancy Vehicles (HOV) lanes promote carpooling. A California study found that during peak hours the HOV lane cars were on average at two-thirds of their capacity, but the lane moved substantially more people than a typical mixed-flow lane operating at congested maximum capacity. Other studies indicate that HOV lanes produce mode shifts to ridesharing (VTPI 2010).

High-occupancy Toll (HOT) lanes are a variation of HOV lanes. Priority for these lanes is given to carpools and buses, as they are not charged toll fees. Single-occupant vehicles can choose to pay the toll, which is adjusted on a sliding scale according to lane congestion. HOT lanes provide commuters with more options without removing lanes as with HOV; maintain the benefits of transit and carpools; are self-financing unlike HOV; and are a good entry point for other road pricing mechanisms in a region (Halvorson & Buckeye 2006).

Websites such as Craigslist, Facebook and Kijiji have created a whole new communication channel for coordinating carpooling. The Craigslist page for every city offers a specific area to match people offering and seeking rides. One Canadian venture, Car-pool Zone, has gone a step further with a website that takes into consideration many more factors than a simple "seeking ride" post. Two local New York smart phone app developers created Weeels, which enables users to locate and organize rides through their phones.

CAR-SHARING

The Web has also enhanced the viability of traditional car-sharing modes of auto-cooperatives, such as ZipCar, the largest provider in the United States. In Canada, Autoshare operates in Ontario, Communauto in Quebec and Modo in BC. The organization CarSharing.org was created to promote best practices in car-sharing and encourage environmentally and socially conscious behavior.

In Bremen, Germany, the car-sharing program Cambio has taken the concept to another level by collaborating with the city's transit authority. Cambio offers members smart cards programmed for entry to the transit system as well as to Cambio cars. It also plans to expand its network so that its smart cards also allow pre-paid access to taxis (Cambio.com 2011).

TRANSPORTATION MANAGEMENT ASSOCIATIONS

Transportation management associations (TMAs) are public-private partnerships whose main focus is to provide commute-trip reduction services to a well-defined area. TMAs help solve transportation problems through stakeholder engagement in a positive environment. The solutions address local transport-related issues by increasing mobility choices to users at low cost while improving transportation infrastructure.

One example of a TMA is the Cambie Corridor Consortium. This Vancouver, British Columbia-based alliance of Cambie Street area businesses, government and citizen groups is committed to reducing single-occupancy traffic by 20 percent, restoring livability to the area and improving air quality by pooling their resources and expertise. From 1994 to 1998, the number of single-occupancy vehicles dropped by 1.6 percent, transit use increased by 25 percent, cycling increased by 5.5 percent, while walking was significantly increased (Tools of Change 2011).

COMMUTER CHALLENGES

The Calgary Commuter Challenge is an annual week-long event designed to encourage commuters to use cleaner, healthier forms of transportation. Participating organizations compete with each other for the highest rates of employee participation. The City of Calgary also competes against other Canadian cities in the nation-wide Commuter Challenge.

The region of Greater Cincinnati implemented the campaign Do Your Share For Cleaner Air to deal with the problem of smog and air quality. When the smog levels are particularly high, citizens are notified and encouraged to change their behaviors to less polluting ones. The focus is primarily on commuting but includes other polluting activities as well.

SHOW BIKE LANES SOME RESPECT

In Vilnius, Lithuania, Mayor Arturas Zuokas appeared in a short video clip that shows him riding atop a military armoured vehicle to flatten a Mercedes parked illegally in a bicycle lane in central Vilnius. "What should the city do about drivers who think they're above the law?" asks the Mayor. After flattening the (stunt) car, Zuokas lectures the driver (an actor), "Next time, park your car legally," as he swings himself onto an electric bicycle and rides off. Within three days, over 2 million people had viewed the YouTube video (YouTube 2011).

Expenditure

WELLNESS WALKWAYS

The City of Vancouver constructed a Wellness Walkway that incorporates ideas for enhancing accessibility in the public realm for people with physical challenges related to sight and mobility. Features of the walkway include sidewalk tinted "sandstone" to reduce glare and aligned curb ramps with directional grooves. Corner bulges have been installed on all corners to shorten street-crossing distances, accessible benches enable easier transitions for people with walking disabilities, and a variety of street trees, fragrant flowering plants and shrubs enhance sensory stimulation.

PEDESTRIAN-ONLY AREAS

Some cities have closed off streets to cars or designed pedestrian malls that offer no access to vehicles. The advantages of creating these car-free areas are many: they increase shopping access for residents, they preserve central city functions, they reduce noise and air pollution, they promote social interaction, and they improve streetscape appearance (Amin 2009). In the United States, Minneapolis, Minnesota, has

4 miles of enclosed overhead passageways in the commercial/retail heart of the city. Stanford University in California has designated 16 blocks on campus as car-free during the day, with only pedestrians, bikes and some buses allowed (People Over Cars 2004).

MUNICIPAL FLEET PROCUREMENT

The purchase of alternative fuel fleets by municipal governments and private companies imparts a powerful sustainability message and significantly reduces area GHG emissions (Woodcock et al. 2009). Despite higher capital costs than fossil fuel vehicles, green fleet procurement can result in significant operational savings over the life of the vehicles, is a valuable marketing tool and is generally popular among consumers and workers alike.

In Boston, new diesel-electric hybrid and compressed natural gas buses are coming to Logan International Airport. The program was approved by the Massachusetts Port Authority board, and buses will be running by 2013 at a cost of nearly $35 million. The board has applied for a federal grant to cover 75 percent of the cost. The Massachusetts Port Authority CEO Thomas Kinton Jr. said of the project: "Not only will the new unified bus system improve air quality through alternative fuels, it will reduce emissions by cutting congestion and dwell times at the terminal curbs" (Care2 2011).

The Montreal 2000 Electric Vehicle Project has shown that adding electric vehicles (EVs) to commercial and institutional fleets is viable in Canada. The project, which integrated EVs into the fleets of ten organizations, brought together government and the private sector to support the introduction of EVs, and to test whether or not the vehicles could help reduce urban smog and greenhouse gas emissions in the Greater Montreal region.

BIKE STATIONS

Installed in Europe for over two decades, a bike station is a 24-hour, secure indoor bike parking facility. They are usually found at the largest transportation hubs, and offer services like showers, lockers, bicycle repair stations and a bicycle sales office. Bike stations are typically registered non-profits that seek to improve the quality of life in urban communities through the development and operation of bike-transit centers and related infrastructure. The first facility to open in the US was the Bikestation in Long Beach, California, in 1996. It was followed by stations in California, Oregon and Washington. The Bikestation at Covina, California, opened in February 2010 and helped complete the first end-to-end systemic transit line in the United States.

BIKE-SHARING PROGRAMS

Bike-sharing programs differ from a simple bike rental service — bikes can be rented at one location and returned at another, unique technology is used for payment (smart cards, mobile apps) and the bike-sharing is designed to be a part of the transit system (Demaio 2010). In 2009, 78 cities in 16 countries had a bike-sharing program with about 70,000 bikes (Midgley 2009). That same year, only two systems existed in the United States and Canada: the Montreal Bixi and the Nice Ride system in Minneapolis. By August 2009, 8,419 Bixi members around the world had travelled more than 3.6 million kilometers, or 87 times around the world, and reduced of greenhouse gases by 909,053 kg. Today, the Bixi technology has spawned bike-sharing programs in London,

England; Washington, DC; Minneapolis, Minnesota; Ottawa and Toronto, Ontario (Bixi 2011).

While bike-sharing is a rapidly growing sector of transit, these programs are most suited to communities with particular characteristics. Midgley's (2009) study of European bike-sharing programs concluded that these programs are best suited for cities of more than 200,000 residents. He also noted that the average implementation time was two years, that many stakeholders need to be involved, and a significant effort for public education on sharing the road was necessary.

TRAFFIC-CALMING

Used widely in Europe and Australia and increasingly in North America, traffic-calming measures include installation of stop signs, traffic circles, speed bumps and chicanes to slow traffic, allowing roads to better accommodate a wider range of users and activities. These measures are used in tandem with traffic demand management to ensure that traffic is diverted to the most appropriate corridors.

Germany's traffic-calming schemes have multiplied into thousands since they were started in the 1970s. Originally intended for residential areas, the technique is now spreading over whole cities. Traffic-calming greatly improves the quality of life in neighborhoods where implemented, and is gathering popularity in many countries. In Denmark, such measures are so well-received that local residents are often willing to pay for them. In West Palm Beach, Florida, traffic-calming measures are integrated into street design when the street is built or reconstructed (rather than adding the feature after the street has been constructed). This approach has proven to be more cost-effective

Fig. 8.4: *Chicanes like this on Rue de la Republique in Sens, France (very popular in residential neighborhoods) serves to slow and direct vehicle traffic while making it safer for walkers and cyclists.*

and equitable, further improving community walkability.

COLLISION DECREASE

Residents in neighborhoods with suitable street environments tend to walk, cycle and take transit more, and drive less. Traffic roundabouts that replace conventional intersections, landscaping in raised center medians and speed reduction strategies can reduce total crashes by 39 percent, injury crashes by 76 percent and fatal crashes by 90 percent (VTPI 2011b).

Examples include Dutch cities like Delft, Groningen and Maastricht. For more than two decades, they have calmed traffic by changing the layout of the residential street, transforming it into a *woonerf*, or "living yard." In the woonerf, cars must navigate slowly around carefully placed trees and other landscaping. Because motor traffic cannot monopolize the entire breadth of the street, much of the space becomes more open to walking, cycling and children's play. Automobiles are free to enter the woonerf, but only as guests, while non-motorized traffic has priority.

Financial Incentives

TRANSIT MARKETING

Discounted transit passes can encourage occasional riders to use transit more frequently and, if implemented when fares are increasing, may avoid ridership losses. Across Canada, the Retire Your Ride program is offering public transit incentives such as transit passes, bicycle discounts and carpool credits to encourage residents to take their old cars off the road (Retire Your Ride 2011).

Tax-exempt transit benefits are provided through Commuter Check USA, a private transit fare savings program that operates through employers. Commuter Checks are purchased by employers, as either a company-paid benefit or by using pre-tax employee-paid contributions. For example, employers are allowed to save 10 percent on their payroll taxes by subsidizing employee commuting costs. The maximum tax-free discount that can be provided to each employee for transit is $230 per month. In 1999, over 35,000 employees and 2,000 employers participated; by 2011, over 300,000 employees were participating (Commuter Check 2011).

The U-Pass program has supplied Washington State University students with a discounted monthly transit pass since 1991, providing campus communities with an array of flexible, low-cost transportation choices. Despite 12 years of population growth, university-related peak traffic levels at the university remain below 1990 levels. Over three-quarters of the campus population commute using an alternative to driving alone. Because the U-Pass program reduces vehicle trips, the university has saved over $100 million in avoided construction costs of new parking spaces. The U-Pass program prevents roughly 8.2 million vehicle miles traveled and 3,300 tons of carbon dioxide from being emitted annually. It has inspired other regional pass programs and has been adopted by campuses in British Columbia, Oregon and Alberta among others (University of Washington 2007).

Employer-transit authority partnerships: Every May in Ada County, Idaho, there is a competition called May in Motion wherein employers can receive free bus passes for employees by meeting a minimum number of requirements on a sustainability checklist. The required activities promote sustainable transportation in employee commutes. Example

requirements include: distributing information on alternative modes of transportation, decorating their place of business to creatively promote May in Motion, offering alternative work hours and telecommuting or setting up a pre-tax account for employees to use to purchase their bus pass. The Ada County Highway District (ACHD) Commuteride team supplies promotional materials to participating employers. The program has drastically increased transit ridership (Commuteride 2011).

FREE OR INEXPENSIVE TRANSIT

In November 2000, residents of the Forest Glen neighborhood of Boulder, Colorado, voted to form a General Improvement District to provide Regional Transit District (RTD) transit passes for all neighborhood residents. All Forest Glen residents are eligible to receive an RTD Eco-Pass, including homeowners and renters. These passes are paid for by residents in Forest Glen as part of their annual property tax. The pass allows unlimited riding on all RTD buses, light rail service to Denver International Airport and Eldora Mountain Resort buses.

Building on the program's success, the City of Boulder uses several synergistic approaches to promote sustainable transportation. It offers transit passes to entire workplaces, schools and neighborhoods, with guaranteed rides home for workplace pass-holders needing to stay late at work or in emergencies. The city has continually improved its physical system to be more supportive of alternative transportation methods, with high-profile monthly reminders and opportunities to try these alternatives.

CONGESTION CHARGES AND ROAD PRICING

Charging a fee for road use can reduce total vehicle travel and road maintenance costs, increase road safety, protect the environment and encourage more efficient land use. The central London congestion charging scheme, implemented in February 2007, reduced car congestion by 30 percent, traffic volume within the zone by 15 percent and crashes by 28 percent. Direct impact of congestion charging on business activity has been small, emissions and fossil fuel consumption have declined and city revenues have received a modest boost (Transport for London 2004). In just the 2009-10 fiscal year, the city raised 148 million pounds from their fees; this was invested directly back into transportation planning and infrastructure maintenance and development (Transport for London 2011).

Express Toll Lanes

State Route 91 in Orange County, California, has ten miles of express toll lanes privately constructed and funded by variable electronic tolls on State Route 91. The Express Lane uses FasTrak electronic transponders to collect tolls that varied from $0.60 to $3.20 per trip in 1998, depending on the level of congestion. In 2008, fees were as high as $9.50 to guarantee a 25-minute savings for single-occupancy vehicles. Carpools with three or more people are given free access. In recent years, the highway maintained more than 30,000 trips per day with 1,400 to 1,600 per hour per lane, and the demand is growing (Richardson et al. 2008).

Innovative Parking Measures

Ending the widespread practice of providing free or heavily subsidized parking promises to relieve both congestion and air pollution. Free or underpriced parking leads to increases in traffic congestion, housing costs, sprawl and pollution (Shoup 2005). Some studies suggest that free parking induces more car travel than free gasoline would. As well, parking subsidies are regressive in that benefits tend to accrue to wealthier people as automobile ownership and use tends to increase with income (Shoup 2005).

Preferential parking for carpools: Portland, Oregon, and Seattle, Washington, are leaders in on-street preferential parking programs for carpools. Poolers are allowed to park downtown all day at specific metered locations, exempted from hourly parking limits and meter fees, and enjoy spaces closest to building entrances.

Increased parking rates: The Canadian federal government increased its parking rates for its employees in Ottawa, resulting in a 23 percent reduction in employees driving to work, a 16 percent increase in their transit ridership and an increase in average vehicle occupancy from 1.33 to 1.41 passengers (Lewyn 2010).

Cash-out plans to compensate for free parking: In the late 90s the State of California required all employers to offer their employees a cash bonus instead of a free parking space. In the eight firms studied, the number of single occupancy vehicle rides dropped by 17 percent, people using carpools increased by 64 percent, transit riders increased by 50 percent and people who walked or biked to work increased by 39 percent (Litman 2010).

Regulations

Automobile Restrictions

The Vauban development: This development of 280 new homes on a former military base is Germany's biggest experiment in "auto-free living." Once dismissed as an "eco-freak" fantasy, the concept is moving off the drawing board and winning real-world converts, even in the land of high-speed autobahns and the Volkswagen "people's car." The nearby city of Freiberg, a city of over 200,000, has built upon car-free successes such as Vauban and made some clear commitments toward increasing active transportation in its 2008 land-use plans. The city has banned car-dependent big-box retailers that draw residents away from the central city shopping districts and neighborhood retailers, designated additional car-free neighborhoods and significantly upgraded its cycling, pedestrian and transit infrastructure (Buehler & Pucher 2009).

Promoting Alternative Fuels

The US Department of Transportation Center for Climate Change and Environmental Forecasting has predicted that most gas substitutes will produce a modest reduction in GHG emissions. But with oil prices reaching new records almost daily, alternative fuels will soon become economically viable. The City of Vancouver, British Columbia, is preparing by developing electric vehicle plans and bylaws that require all new single-family homes to have dedicated electric plug-in outlets; charging infrastructure in 20 percent of all parking stalls in new condos; signing non-exclusive agreements with car manufacturers, provincial and federal governments; and actively promoting zero-emission vehicles through private-public partnerships (City of Vancouver 2011).

Reduction in Required Parking

Several cities have found that parking programs pay. Sacramento, California, grants developers a 5 percent reduction in required parking for providing bicycle facilities, 15 percent reduction for providing marked car/van-pool spaces and 60 percent reduction for purchasing transit passes for tenants of new offices.

Chapter 9

Land Use, Urban Form and Community Design

Strategic land-use decisions permeate every aspect of planning for community sustainability. Many of the building blocks discussed in previous chapters depend in large measure upon how we organize our use of land and the form (for example, streets, shopping areas, parks and civic infrastructure) that use takes.

Since the end of World War II, typical planning paradigms in the United States and Canada have forced development to the fringes of our cities, pushing the suburbs to the countryside. These entrenched land-use practices spread our destinations, increase our need for space and travel and create what is commonly referred to as *urban and rural sprawl*.

Sprawl results from a complex web of technological, social and economic factors such as: the public subsidization of auto-centric transportation and civic infrastructure that enables this type of subdivision; the failures of markets to account for the social value of open space, the social costs of freeway congestion and the capital costs of freeway development; federal

mortgage policies that encourage development of single detached homes; zoning policies that ensure the strict separation of land uses; and parking requirements that ensure large swaths of land will be paved over (Blais 2010). Traditional municipal approaches to development contribute to sprawl through tax codes that encourage construction of single detached houses, provision of extensive sewerage systems and subsidization of road-building. The resulting infrastructure far exceeds that which would have emerged in a user-pay system (Blais 2010). The same market failures that induce urban sprawl also cause *inner city blight*, which results in an exodus from the downtown compact cores of cities to the diffuse suburban fringes (Brueckner & Helsley 2011).

Ewing (2008) identifies two defining dynamics of urban sprawl. First, sprawling communities reduce accessibility between related land uses, forcing residents to travel long distances, often through vacant lots from one developed use to another. Second, sprawling developments are dominated by private land holdings that provide quaint private yards but decimate functional open public space. These dynamics, which can apply equally to land use in rural communities, serve to erode citizens' involvement in civic activities, which reduces social, cultural and overall community capital (Frumkin, Frank & Jackson 2004).

The social, environmental and economic costs of sprawl are well-documented and have become the impetus for civic design and land-use practices that are more sustainable. In North America, the sustainable community planning paradigms of New Urbanism, Smart Growth and the emerging field of Landscape Urbanism seek to establish more sustainable communities through progressive land-use policies that will help to invigorate communities and redevelop and reuse existing buildings and land that can revitalize economies and communities that are falling into decay. Sustainable community planning can recognize and respond to the diversity of our communities by encouraging land uses that accommodate a range of incomes, ages, physical abilities and cultural backgrounds.

As this chapter will show, these sustainable land-use policies and planning frameworks help reinforce the capital that contributes to community mobilization. By creating smaller, compact, transit-friendly and walkable communities, they relieve pressure on our natural capital, reduce expenditure on physical capital, improve conditions for developing economic capital, attract human capital, strengthen our social capital and enhance our cultural capital.

The Costs of Sprawl

It has long been assumed that conventional development enhances the local tax base. However, extensive research now suggests that the costs of sprawl may exceed the benefits of low-density development. The Real Estate Research Corporation (1974) conducted a comprehensive study for the US government, The Costs of Sprawl, and its findings still hold today. Three community types were analyzed: the "low-density sprawl" community (entirely single-family homes, 75 percent in traditional grid pattern, typical of suburban development); the "combination mix" community (20 percent of each of five types of dwellings, half in planned unit developments, half in traditional subdivisions); and the "high-density planned" community (40 percent high-rises, 30 percent walk-ups, 20 percent townhouses and 10 percent clustered single-family homes, all in contiguous neighborhoods). A major conclusion was that sprawl is "the most expensive form of residential development in terms of economic costs, environmental costs, natural resource consumption and many types of personal costs . . . This cost difference is particularly significant for that proportion of total costs which is likely to be borne by local governments" (RERC 1974, 7).

The costs of sprawl were also confirmed in a study by Carruthers and Ulfarsson (2003) of 283 metropolitan counties in the US; they found that the per capita cost of public service provision decreased with higher density and increased with the spatial extent of the urbanized

In its path, sprawl consumes thousands of acres of forests and farmland, woodlands and wetlands. It requires government to spend millions to build new schools, streets, and water and sewer lines. In its wake, sprawl leaves boarded up houses, vacant storefronts, closed businesses, abandoned and often contaminated industrial sites, and traffic congestion stretching miles from urban centers.

— Maryland Governor Parris N. Glendenning (Soule 2006, 9)

land area. Carruthers and Ulfarsson (2007) later updated their study to include per capita spending of all 3,075 counties in the United States, and found that, if the nation's land use had developed to be 50 percent more compact, public services would cost $7.25 billion less annually.

The business case for compact communities would be even more obvious if governments addressed factors that promote sprawl, such as artificially low gasoline prices. For example, in the United States, tax credits and deductions to the oil industry cost the American government billions of dollars annually in lost revenue and help gasoline producers reap record profits. Removing these various exemptions would raise government revenues by $30.6 billion from 2010 to 2019 (US Treasury 2009). Transportation demand management tools discussed in chapter 8, such as removing these perverse subsidies, could provide an enormous increase to investment in public transit, while reflecting the true cost of automobile use.

> According to Ian Parry, senior fellow at Resources for the Future, accounting for the military costs of ensuring oil supplies, public funding for road construction and maintenance and the true environmental, health and social costs of private automobile use would add $1.88 to a gallon costing $2.72 (Parry, Walls & Harrington 2007). According to columnist Ezra Klein, that's almost certainly an underestimation. There are plenty of costs we don't know how to price. How much of our military policy is dictated by our need for secure oil resources? How much instability is created by our need to treat oil-producing monarchies with kid gloves? How much

is the environment worth in a poor country that prefers oil investment to air quality? (Klein 2010)

Even in the absence of supportive national policy frameworks, communities can do a great deal to create more energy-efficient communities by concentrating activities in specific areas and developing a mix of land uses in those areas. We should strive to create communities that can be effectively served by more energy-efficient travel modes, such as public transit, bicycling and walking; and to reduce the average length of daily automobile trips where other modes are not feasible.

Urban Sprawl and Public Health

The over-consumption of nutrient-poor food is often thought to be the root of the obesity epidemic in the Western world. However, a 2007 study conducted by the Institute for European Environmental Policy showed that, although rates of energy and fat intake had declined in Britain since the mid-70s, the obesity rate had steadily climbed (Davis et al. 2007). The study shows that it is a decline in active transportation, namely walking, that is most culpable for the country's increased obesity rates. As it turns out, sloth trumps gluttony when it comes to obesity.

Frumkin, Frank and Jackson (2004) show that when given the opportunity and the amenities to exercise, people do. Neighborhoods that incorporate walkability, higher densities and more green spaces had residents with lower hypertension levels and body weights, and a lower probability of being obese. Key characteristics of neighborhoods that promote an active lifestyle include:

- **Neighborhood density**: Research from the transportation field consistently shows that neighborhoods with higher densities have more pedestrians.

- **Land-use mix**: Mixed-use neighborhoods enable people to walk or bike more readily to work and to accomplish errands.
- **Nearby sidewalks and footpaths:** Communities that have continuous uninterrupted routes, multiple route choices, easily navigable topography and crossing lights facilitate walking.
- **Enjoyable scenery**: Attractive, well-landscaped streets are inviting and promise greater benefits from walking.
- **Other people who are physically active**: Physical activity appears to be contagious, as observing people exercising tends to make the observers want to do the same.
- **Safety**: People are most apt to exercise in areas where they feel physically safe. (Frumkin, Frank & Jackson 2004)

Our expanding waistlines are correlated to our expanding suburbs and increasing reliance on the car. It's no surprise that principles of healthy urban and rural design converge naturally with those of sustainable land use and urban form. When residents feel safe, encounter one another and are given something nice to look at, an amazing thing happens: they begin to walk, run and play toward a more sustainable community.

Land Use and Transportation

Land use, transportation and energy use are intimately related. Better land-use policies can both reduce our needs for transportation and help us get places more energy-efficiently.

Per capita gasoline consumption in North America is now more than 6 times that of Europe and over 30 times greater than Asia, excluding the Middle East (Parry, Walls & Harrington 2007). Research shows that the biggest factor accounting for these differences in energy use appears to be not car size or gas prices, but the efficiency and compactness of land-use patterns (Brownstone & Golob 2009). Communities with lower *automobile dependence* are more centralized, have more intense land use (more people and jobs per unit area), are more favorable to non-auto modes (public transit, foot traffic and bicycle usage), place more restraints on high-speed traffic and offer better public transit (Newman & Kenworthy 2006).

Equally true is that neighborhood urban design is a powerful determinant of whether we choose to own a car and how much we drive — as much or more than common socioeconomic indicators such as income and family size. In a study that compared similar California households from neighborhoods of different densities, Brownstone and Golob (2009) found similar relationships between urban density and automobile ownership rates and mileage per car. The study showed that North Americans who live in less dense communities drive further (and paradoxically, choose less fuel-efficient vehicles) than people in higher-density neighborhoods. The results suggest that automobile dependence can, in part, be addressed through municipal-level policies that increase residential density, improve transit access and favor walking and bicycle use.

Through zoning and other practices, land-use patterns and densities also dictate travel volume, direction and mode. In the US and Canada, our dispersed land-use patterns are typified by the low-density suburb. In addition to automobile dependence, low-density land use creates a complementary set of problems:

- high per capita levels of ground-level ozone (Stone 2008)
- high per capita auto emissions as a result of increased travel and vehicle congestion (Compact development can reduce fuel consumption and CO_2 emissions by 20 to 40 percent) (Ewing, Bartholomew & Nelson 2011)
- high per capita water use (Mitchell et al. 2008)
- loss of important agricultural lands for local food production (Bengston, Fletcher & Nelson 2003)
- increased levels of stormwater runoff (15 percent of rainfall is lost as runoff on suburban land compared with 4 percent on grassland) (Ewing, Bartholomew & Nelson 2011)
- high land requirements in both the block size and the road system required to service it (Ewing 2008)
- high domestic energy use from heating and cooling due to the lack of a shared insulating effect when buildings are grouped (Marshall 2008)
- elevated costs of urban services (utilities, pipes, poles, roads, etc.) by increasing the distances between new developments and existing ones (Stone 2008)
- increased rates of obesity in children and adults (Lopez 2004)
- high levels of social isolation as cars become necessary to participate in social life (Boyce 2010)

This last point deserves special attention, as car ownership is not available to everyone. When our communities require it to participate in social life, who is marginalized and excluded? Clearly, it is the non-drivers — and who are they? They are our children, our senior

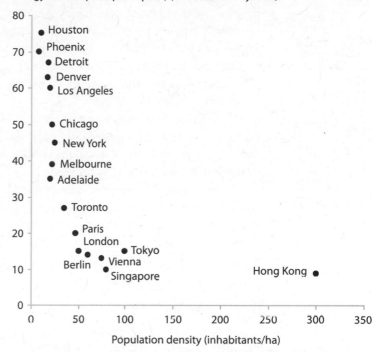

Fig. 9.1: *There is a strong relationship between density and transport-related energy use. Cities that, through legislation, historical development and geography, have chosen dense over dispersed development consume significantly less energy. Source: Peter Newman and Jeff Kenworthy, 1989.* Cities and Automobile Dependence: An International Sourcebook. *Gower, England.* Atlas Environnement du Monde Diplomatique 2007.

(Credit: UNEP/GRID-Arendal. maps.grida.no/go/graphic/urban-density-and-transport-related-energy-consumption1)

citizens, our physically challenged and our very poor (Cass, Shove & Urry 2005).

There is evidence that the sprawl-promoting land use depletes communities' human capital. Today's highly educated, mobile young professionals often prefer vibrant mixed-use developments with stimulating, walkable streetscapes that are well-serviced by transit. As the partner of a successful patent law firm in Troy, Michigan, lamented, "soul-crushing sprawl" explains why his company's premium salaries are insufficient to attract quality employees to the area: "There's a simple reason why many people don't want to live here: it's an unpleasant place because most of it is visually unattractive and because it is lacking in quality living options other than tract suburbia."

All of this underscores the need for a better approach to transportation and land-use planning. In its absence, auto-oriented transportation has, almost by default, guided land use. Instead, land-use planning should guide transportation, and transportation should be designed to accommodate and support planned growth, inducing the needed changes in urban form (Waddell et al. 2007).

Enhancing Connectivity Through Street Layout

Street systems can maximize connectivity by minimizing the distance required to arrive at a destination. Cities generally design their street systems using one of two approaches: *dendritic* or *interconnected* (grid-like) street layouts.

Dendritic (branch-like) layouts are typical of many post-World War II neighborhoods. They consist of quiet cul-de-sac developments built around dendritic street nodules that feed traffic into freeways. This tends to separate transportation corridors and (unlike grids) often provides only one path from home to surrounding arterial roads. For those lucky enough to be at the end of cul-de-sacs, the dendritic system reduces vehicle noise and increases perceptions of safety and security (Johnson & Bowers 2009). But for the approximately 75 percent of residents located on feeder routes and major arterial roadways, dendritic street systems mean many more cars passing by their homes than would be the case in an interconnected grid system (Condon & Yaro 2007).

With dendritic street systems, eventually all trips collect to a single point and congestion is inevitable. Complaints from slow-moving motorists force municipalities to build ever-expanding intersections to handle the ever-expanding traffic, creating a vicious cycle that ultimately erodes livability and leads to declining happiness of residents (Song et al. 2007).

In interconnected systems, city blocks are predominantly connected by narrow residential streets, which are interspersed with wider arterial roadways. There are four types of interconnected systems:

- **Grid pattern**: Most common in Canadian and American neighborhoods that were built between 1840 and 1950. Typically, these are rectangular blocks demarcated by straight, narrow residential streets that intersect and tend to align with cardinal axes. They are easy to navigate and provide the most efficient flow of people.
- Radial pattern: Similar to a grid pattern, although civic centers are connected by radial

The Jevons Paradox

In 1865, when it was supposed that improving coal-burning efficiency in the United Kingdom would save coal, British economist William Stanley Jevons correctly predicted that the efficiencies would lead to more economic uses for coal, and thus greater coal use. The same principle seems to apply to automobile transportation fuel use today. Price mechanisms and urban sprawl ensure that for every increase in technological efficiency there is a rapid increase in the use of vehicles (Rubin 2009).

streets that may not align with the cardinal axes. This helps create a dramatic pattern to the city; however, intersections between the major streets can be complex.

- **Informal web pattern**: Developed out of an absence of planned subdivisions in some American cities prior to around 1840. Major streets in this system were the direct routes that connected old city squares. As cities grew, spaces between the squares were filled in with a gridiron pattern.
- **Warped grid**: Designed to follow the contours of the landscape. These systems can highlight dramatic features of an area and

result in a varied block size. No complete warped-grid cities exist, but many neighborhoods in America have examples.

The disadvantages of interconnected grid systems are that no homes are cut off from the noise of traffic and they use more linear feet of street than do the dendritic systems found in many sprawling suburbs. However, interconnected systems offer major advantages: they make all trips as short as possible, are transit-friendly, provide safe travel for pedestrians and bikes along the residential streets and relieve congestion by providing many alternative routes to the same

Fig. 9.2a, b: **LAND USE ZONING**

NOT *this: Isolation of home from work and services by exclusive zoning*

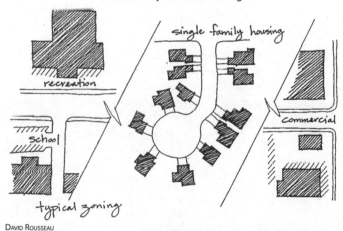

DAVID ROUSSEAU

WHY NOT:

- Excessive commuting requirements; increases automobile dependency.
- Empty residential areas in daytime and commercial areas at night; encourages crime.
- Decreases contact among people; does not build community or support services.
- High commuting costs and traffic congestion.

"All that is not specifically required is strictly forbidden."

THIS: *Proximity of home to work and services by mixed use zoning.*

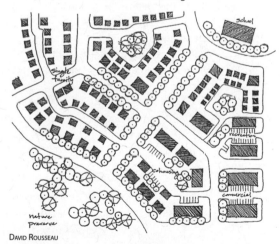

DAVID ROUSSEAU

HOW:

- Design neighborhood centers within walking distance.
- Flexible, mixed use zoning encourages participation in the community.
- Designed for local and in home employment.

"All that is not considered grossly objectionable is permitted."

Fig. 9.2c, d: **SUBDIVISION**

NOT *This: Subdivision of entire parcels into individual lots.*   **THIS:** Cluster designs with commons.

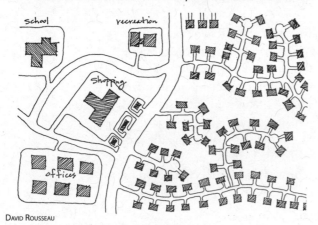

David Rousseau

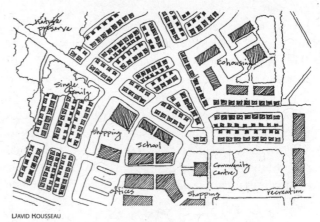

David Rousseau

WHY NOT:

- Lack of common space impairs community self-image.
- Residents isolated behind fences and in automobiles do not meet or watch out for their neighbors.
- Heavy emphasis on the private domain does not encourage participation.
- Utilities are widely extended and services dispersed. Dendritic street layout impedes walking, biking and transit and increases traffic at choke points.

"All residential land is either private or dedicated to the automobile."

HOW:

- Thoughtful public and semi-public space integrated with private lots.
- Design for meeting places and good visual supervision.
- Provide small neighborhood parks, community gardens and playgrounds.
- Cluster designs allow compact utility networks and concentrated services.
- Grid street layout is more conducive to walking, cycling and transit and provides alternative driving routes in the event of an accident.

"A community must have commons."

destination (Condon & Yaro 2010). Given that interconnected street systems facilitate walking, cycling and transit and thus reduce the amount of vehicle miles traveled, they are the preferred layout when designing a sustainable community (Condon & Yaro 2010).

Dense Livable Communities

Higher-density land use could help solve many of the environmental, social, economic and aesthetic problems of sprawl, yet misconceptions about increased density — even moderate density — often prevent communities from adopting compact land-use strategies.

Higher-density development need not mean harsh physical environments; nor does low density land use guarantee more green space and easier living. Compare low-density cities, such as Phoenix (5 people per acre), which are often dominated by unwelcoming, car-oriented commercial strips and vast expanses of concrete and asphalt, to moderate-density Copenhagen. At 19 people per acre, Copenhagen enjoys worldwide renown for its urban charm and livability.

Only 27 percent of its residents use a car to go to work. As chapter 4 shows, appropriately designed dense urban areas can be more vital, host more inviting spaces and boast even more trees and other plants (Newman and Jennings 2008).

Although municipal officials will attest that the numbers of household units per building or per unit of land area can be the subject of intense debate, these are relatively unimportant in terms of human well-being. The most significant indicator that links overcrowding to human stress is the number of people per room (Schwartz 2010). Higher density need not mean overcrowding: there is a world of difference between life in high-rise residential blocks with low numbers of people per room (such as New York City) and life in low-rise shantytown developments with high numbers of people per room (such as parts of Rio de Janiero or parts of Mexico City).

Similarly, higher density cannot be blamed for social ills. Compare, for example, areas of high-density populations with low levels of social disorder (such as most parts of Tokyo) to areas of low-density population with high levels of social disorder (such as parts of Los Angeles). The problems are more likely related to a combination of factors such as low income, poor education and social isolation. Such complicating factors should make us wary of falling for the implicit environmental determinism that is sometimes found in arguments for and against high-density living (Ewing, Bartholomew & Nelson 2011).

Higher-density living also promises to benefit one of the most frustrated population groups in low-density communities: adolescents. When young people begin seeking more and more independence from their parents, they find themselves in an environment where

Greenhouse Gas and Street Patterns

An interconnected street pattern inherently reduces trip length and the concomitant amount of greenhouse gas emissions released into the atmosphere. When combined with sufficient housing densities, close proximity of transit and mixed commercial and residential land uses, interconnected street systems can reduce per capita emissions by at least 40 percent (Condon & Yaro 2010).

Traffic and Health

A study conducted in Los Angeles showed that perceived traffic stress was associated with poorer health and higher rates of depression. The researchers concluded that more parkland in the neighborhood would alleviate the traffic stress on an individual's wellbeing (Song et al. 2007).

Complete Streets

Complete streets are streets where pedestrian, cyclists and cars can co-exist. The elements of a great street include: buildings at similar heights, interesting facades, vegetation and landscaping, window shopping, intersections, defined starting and end points, street furniture and other stopping points.

getting together with friends is made difficult by distance, paucity of public transport, separation of housing from shopping centers and so on. Research shows that American suburban teenagers are more often bored and engage in vandalism more than their counterparts in Sweden living at higher density with easy access to shops, clubs, public transport and so on (Garland 2009). Teenagers in clustered housing are more likely to find peers within walking distance and may have access to shared facilities where they can spend time together, out of sight of home, yet not far away.

Dimensions of Density

Density is a way of measuring land users, land uses or housing intensity on a specified unit of land. Several indicators are commonly used in regard to residential development. **Gross density** includes all land uses within a given area and can be expressed as persons-per-hectare or -acre, or housing units-per-hectare or -acre. **Net density** refers to the number of dwellings located on residential building sites and excludes roads, parks and other non-residential land uses. Net density can also be used as an indicator of density for a given form of housing. **Floor space ratio** compares the area of floor space in buildings to the area of the property or lot. For example, a one-story building that covers the entire site on which it sits has a floor space ratio of 1.0, as does a two-story building on half its lot, or a four-story building on one quarter of its lot.

If real estate prices, rents, health and lifestyle satisfaction are any indication, higher-density living done right can be more desirable than low-density, dispersed, separated land-use developments (Vemuri et al. 2011). Clustered, pedestrian-friendly, transit-oriented communities with ample green space are the key. New approaches to sustainable community design focus on changing priorities in physical planning to promote walkability, biking and transit use; changing land-use patterns to minimize the need for travel; and reconnecting to community values rather than private or isolated values (Newman & Kenworthy 2006).

Rewarding Efficient Use of Land

Land-use planning that doesn't address long-term or life-cycle costs of development infrastructure, such as roads and sewage, leaves taxpayers paying their hidden costs. Citizens in many communities recognize the inequities of this phenomenon, but the solutions commonly proposed rarely speak to the underlying issues.

Land-use Terms

Urban containment: the physical and functional separation of urban and rural areas, and planning processes that aim for efficient forms of towns and cities with minimal impact on surrounding areas.

Densification: increasing the numbers of housing units or commercial facilities built per acre of land, to increase the efficiency of land use and reduce the overall impact of growth.

Urbanization: creation of urban landscapes in formerly rural areas.

Urban areas: characterized by human residential, commercial and industrial structures and activities; can include low-density suburban areas as well as urban cores where human activity is intense.

Compact cities: urban areas that efficiently use land for all purposes through densification and mixing of land uses. Compact cities contrast with sprawl.

Sprawl: an inefficient, expansive use of land for urban activities. The term *suburban* is often used to describe sprawling urban development.

Rural sprawl: an inefficient, expansive use of rural land for hobby farms, acreages and other small-scale low-productivity properties.

Future growth can be viewed as an opportunity to preserve farmland and natural areas and reduce rising car dependency and traffic congestion. By promoting policies that encourage residential intensification and by creating more compact urban areas through infill development, adaptive reuse and brownfield development, communities can reduce infrastructure costs, revitalize urban areas in decline and create more transportation choice (Boarnet et al. 2011).

Growing communities sustainably requires that we go beyond the notion that land is a mere commodity. However, even in conventional economic terms, land is a peculiar commodity in that its supply cannot increase, no matter how high the price. As demand for land grows, the wealth of landowners tends to grow regardless of how well or badly they use the land. In his 1879 classic *Progress and Poverty*, Henry George proposed a solution to this dilemma: taxing away the portion of land value that is produced by anything other than private effort (for example, its natural endowment of resources, proximity to publicly financed assets or other benefits bestowed by non-owners of the land/society). Such a land-value tax would keep private landowners from unfairly capturing the benefits of natural resources, urban locations and public services. George believed that this tax would also encourage landowners either to put their land to its "highest and best" use themselves, or make it accessible to someone who would (Freyfogle 2007).

Several economists have since called for differentiated treatment of land and buildings in property taxation (Bird and Slack 2004). Whereas a higher tax on buildings encourages holding land unused or allowing buildings to deteriorate, a higher tax on land often encourages more efficient use of the property. Since land is not produced, a tax on land is a cost of ownership, not a cost of production. By making land ownership more costly (less desirable), a tax on land actually lowers land prices. Taxing land values helps make many infrastructure investments, like roads and subways, self-financing (Zhao, Das & Larson 2010).

Local governments typically assess vacant properties at far less than their market value, effectively rewarding property owners for keeping their land idle. Property owners may respond better to tax-based financial inducements such as land value taxes to intensify land use and encourage the redevelopment of vacant land, and as a result reduce the incentive for urban sprawl. However, such tax strategies need to be combined with clearly defined growth boundaries to prevent spurts of sprawled growth (Cho, Kim & Roberts 2009).

Because higher land taxes cannot be avoided or passed down entirely to renters, landowners are motivated to generate income from which to pay the tax (Foldvary 2005). The greatest economic imperative to develop land will exist where land values are highest: adjacent to existing infrastructure and amenities. At the same time, reducing taxes applied to buildings makes that development more profitable. Away from infrastructure where land values are low, taxes will be low and there will be less economic motivation for development. The result is more compact development that can be served by existing infrastructure, at lower costs to taxpayers and the environment (Daly & Farley 2010).

Zoning in on Sustainability

One of the main obstacles to creating sustainable communities is the conventional development standards that underlie most zoning codes. Historically, zoning codes were developed to improve public health and create certainty for developers, and were adopted when land costs were low and environmental awareness was less developed (Hodge & Gordon 2007). Kunstler (1996), a proponent of New Urbanism, clarified problematic dynamics associated with these zoning codes:

> What zoning produces is suburban sprawl, which must be understood as the product of a particular set of instructions. Its chief characteristics are the strict separation of human activities, mandatory driving to get from one activity to another, and huge supplies of free parking. After all, the basic idea of zoning is that every activity demands a separate zone of its own. For people to live around shopping would be harmful and indecent. Better not even to allow them within walking distance of it. They'll need their cars to haul all that stuff home anyway. While we're at it, let's separate the homes by income gradients. Don't let the $75,000-a-year families live near the $200,000-a-year families — they'll bring down property values — and for God's sake don't let a $25,000-a-year recent college graduate or a $19,000-a-year widowed grandmother on Social Security live near any of them. There goes the neighborhood! Now put all the workplaces in separate office "parks" or industrial "parks," and make sure nobody can walk to them either. As for public squares, parks and the like — forget it. We can't afford them, because we spent all our money paving the four-lane highways and collector roads and parking lots, and laying sewer and water lines out to the housing subdivisions, and hiring traffic cops to regulate the movement of people in their cars going back and forth among these segregated activities.

Like most tools, zoning can be used for different purposes. New sets of zoning bylaws have emerged to address the downside of current zoning practices. These more flexible approaches to community design can encourage more compact growth patterns and developments that support goals of integrating land uses, intensification and housing diversity, and pedestrian-oriented streetscapes (ACT 2009). Some of the effective tools for efficient zoning include:

- **Planned unit development** gives developers incentives to meet pre-determined land-use goals;
- **Floating zoning** permits special uses within a jurisdiction in accordance with development criteria;
- **Bonus or incentive zoning** provides developers with bonuses and incentives to achieve increased development density;
- **Mixed-use zoning** requires a wide array of types of development aimed at reducing distances between houses and jobs;
- **Land banking** allows outright purchase of land by the public sector well in advance of any development to ensure appropriate land use and;
- **Transit zoning** districts target development in areas with transit systems already in place (Congress for New Urbanism 2004).

Related tools include:

- **Transfer of development rights** allow landowners to get development value on other areas if current holdings are placed in conservation or trust;

- **Conservation land trusts** consist of local, regional or state/provincial organizations directly involved in protecting important land resources for the public benefit;
- **Location-efficient mortgages** aid urban housing affordability;
- **Growth management ordinances** control one or more of the familiar components of land-use planning: the rate, location, type, density, amount, timing and quality of development and;
- **Building permit allocation** allocates housing permits on a merit system that awards points for recreational amenities, landscaping and open space, design quality, impact on the local infrastructure and energy efficiency.

When development plans have passed the rezoning process and the subdivision process begins, our antiquated engineering standards often magnify sprawl through the imposition of gratuitous parking requirements, excessive road widths and other practices (ACT 2009). New engineering standards, dubbed *Alternative Development Standards* (ADS), are helping many communities address environmental and social concerns while reducing the spiraling costs of new infrastructure. Features of the standards, commonly referred to as "traditional neighborhood design," include grid road systems with narrower road widths, smaller lots, use of curbs and sidewalks and car access to houses from rear lanes (ACT 2009). ADS can be implemented at two levels of municipal control:

- **Planning policies and regulations**: Official plans and zoning bylaws set targets for densities, the configuration of lots, parking requirements and acceptable home and building sizes. This helps municipalities achieve goals for housing affordability and diversity.
- **Engineering standards**: Municipalities draft the rules that determine the shape, location and dimensions of rights-of-way,

Greenfields, Brownfields and Greyfields

Pristine undeveloped areas are called *greenfield* sites, while *brownfield* sites are typically urban sites left abandoned, idle or underutilized from previous commercial or industrial activities, and where past actions have caused known or suspected environmental contamination. Abandoned brownfields adversely impact a neighborhood's image and quality of life and may pose risks to human health and the environment. With proper support and partnerships between developers and all levels of government, prioritization of brownfield redevelopment over greenfield developments on the periphery can result in significant environmental improvements to contaminated areas as well as desirable communities to live in (Hula & Bromley-Trujillo 2010).

The growing number of failed or failing suburban strip malls and their associated parking lots present promising opportunities for intensifying and revitalizing communities. These "greyfield" sites are now coming full circle as their owners look for new ways to develop their investments and municipalities are looking for ways to intensify land uses in their communities.

roads, curbs, sidewalks, boulevards, street trees, street lighting, stormwater and sanitary sewer drains, water pipes and linear utilities (electricity, telecommunications and natural gas). They may also determine what are acceptable construction materials and techniques. By reducing the dimensions and resource requirements of physical infrastructure, municipalities can take great strides toward sustainability. (ACT 2009)

Approaches to Sustainable Community Design

There are many approaches to sustainable community design, varying widely in scale and emphasis while contributing to the goal of sustainable communities. However, most seek to invigorate and rejuvenate our communities through more appropriate density, diversity, mixed land use, compactness, sustainable

transport and greening our landscape (Jabareen 2006). The prominent schools of thought on sustainable community design are New Urbanism and Smart Growth.

New Urbanism

The term *New Urbanism* describes a set of planning principles designed to reinvigorate communities and provide a meaningful alternative to suburban sprawl. Variations on New Urbanism include *neo-traditional town planning, pedestrian pockets, transit-oriented developments, complete communities* and *LASTING communities* — Livable, Affordable, Safe, Transit-oriented, Inclusive, Neighborly, Growing.

Although New Urbanism is often characterized as a model for new suburban development, retrofitting existing urban areas is one of its principal tenets. Indeed, most New Urbanist principles have been deduced from successful cities that comprise several independent neighborhoods, or what New Urbanists call "urban villages."

Urban villages provide a lifestyle with minimal car dependence and the kind of densities that make rail highly viable. Evidence suggests that cities that have tried to build or re-establish areas as urban villages, such as Clarendon in Washington DC, Fruitvale in Oakland and Emerson Park in St. Louis, found them to be an extremely attractive lifestyle option (Jacobson & Forsyth 2008).

New Urbanism was perhaps most succinctly described by the Congress for the New Urbanism, a group formed in 1992 comprising architects, urban designers, planners and landscape architects from across North America. Their 1996 charter emphasized that neighborhoods should be diverse in use and population; communities should be designed

Fig. 9-3: *Walkable streets, proximity to public transit and a variety of housing types to suit a range of incomes characterize HOPE VI, a New Urbanist development at North Beach Place, San Fransisco.* (CREDIT: BOB CANFEILD, BRIDGE HOUSING. WWW.MITOD.ORG/HOME.PHP)

NOT *this: Limited housing types: single family detached.*

THIS: *Many housing types.*

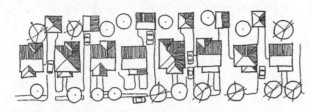

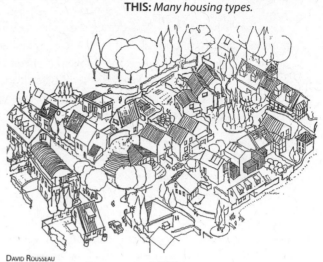

DAVID ROUSSEAU

DAVID ROUSSEAU

WHY NOT:

- Poor range of affordability.
- Leads to limited social and economic mix among residents; ghettoization.
- Inappropriate to aging residents and community-minded people.
- Has highest individual land requirements.
- Financially unstable due to dependence on only one market sector.
  "Everyone wants to live in a suburban home and can afford it."

HOW:

- Provide apartment and townhouses as a more affordable option.
- Design mixed single-family and multi-family neighborhoods for diversity and social enrichment; healthier communities.
- Provide supported seniors housing, co-housing and other options.
- Better financial stability by serving several market sectors.
  "Many people prefer townhouses, apartments and collective housing, particularly at some stage of their life."

for the pedestrian and transit as well as the car; cities and towns should be shaped by physically defined and universally accessible public spaces and community institutions; and urban places should be framed by architecture and landscape design that celebrate local history, climate, ecology and building traditions.

In practice, New Urbanism means:

- designing communities with a connected and permeable public framework of streets and open spaces as the main structuring element of the community

- facilitating easy movement through all parts of the community by foot, bicycle, public transit and automobile, without favoring any particular mode
- fostering community activity by ensuring that buildings enhance pedestrian comfort in the way that they relate to the public streets, and thereby providing an attractive, safe and inviting public realm.
- accommodating and integrating a diverse and wide range of land uses, densities and building types within each neighborhood to include the full range of activities found

Does New Urbanism Make a Difference?

By Ray Tomalty

According to New Urbanist advocates, designing neighborhoods that have pedestrian-friendly streets, higher densities, mixed housing types and local commercial services within walking distance will alter the travel and social behavior of residents. In particular, advocates of New Urbanism claim that residents will:

- use their cars less
- walk and bike more
- interact more with neighbors
- have a greater sense of neighborhood attachment.

To test these claims, we chose four New Urbanist Developments (NUDs) and compared the travel and social behaviors of residents to those found in four comparable Conventional Suburban Developments (CSDs), using a quantitative survey of over 2000 households in the eight neighborhoods.

The data collected showed that:

- NUD residents have a lower auto mode share (as a driver or passenger) than their CSD counterparts (78% versus 85% respectively).
- CSD households travelled 24% further in their vehicles than did those of the NUDs (46 km versus 37.1 km respectively).

- 51% of NUD households reported walking and biking to local services and stores several times a week, compared to only 19% for the CSD households.
- NUD respondents had more interaction with their neighbors than did their CSD counterparts: 35% of NUD residents said they greeted a neighbor almost every time they were out for a walk, compared to 27% for CSD households, and 40% say they socialized face-to-face with their neighbors compared to 34% of CSD households.
- 50% of the NUD respondents compared to 36% from the CSDs reported a high degree of attachment to their neighborhoods.

Our overall conclusion from the study was that New Urbanist claims are largely supported by the evidence: New Urbanist neighborhoods are more socially connected, walkable and less car dependent than their conventional counterparts. These findings are consistent with those from US studies and suggest that building more neighborhoods with these design characteristics will help move our communities towards sustainability.

The full report, entitled "Comparing Canadian New Urbanist and Conventional Suburban Neighbourhoods" by Ray Tomalty and Murtaza Haider, can be downloaded from the CMHC website.

Cities in New Urbanism study		
New Urbanist Development	**Conventional Suburban Development**	**City**
McKenzie Towne	McKenzie Lake	Calgary
Garrison Woods	North Signal Hill	Calgary
Cornell	Woodbine North	Markham
Bois-Franc	Nouveau Saint-Laurent	Montreal

in any healthy community, and to facilitate the provision of public transit

- integrating the natural environment into the new community
- creating universally accessible public open spaces and community institutions that provide a sense of place and act as landmarks of community identity. (Russell 2004)

In the 30 years since its emergence, New Urbanism has learned important lessons practitioners should take note of. For example, some developments identified as "new urbanist" have been built on greenfield sites without ecological design techniques (such as passive solar) or infrastructure (for example, greywater recycling). Critics have called them "sprawl with porches" (Harrison 2009). The "neo-traditional" new town of Celebration in Florida, created by the Disney Corporation, is an example of how early New Urbanism failed to recognize that a community's form and function is primarily shaped by its transportation system, which in that case was the suburban highway and freeways of South Florida (Njoh 2009). As well, such developments may be "designed" to encourage a mix of housing types and a diversity of income levels but offer no mechanism to ensure any stock — never mind an adequate, permanent stock — of affordable housing. For example, it is now difficult for the schoolteachers, babysitters and service workers required by the Celebration community to find affordable residences there (Njoh 2009).

For New Urbanism to be sustainable, it must incorporate the lessons learned above and plan for energy-efficient land use. Communities can promote this through policies that:

- encourage greater density through multiple unit residential developments

- integrate work, residence and shopping in mixed-use development
- zone higher-density development along established transit routes
- decentralize commercial and community services to reduce travel distances, creating self-contained communities with a better balance between employment and population
- place controls on outlying shopping centers, strip development and urban sprawl
- encourage the infilling (development) of existing vacant land in built-up areas
- ensure that major public facilities have provision for walking and bicycling access to transit and
- encourage the development of high-quality walking and bicycling facilities, including development design guidelines to support transportation alternatives to private automobile use, such as provision of onsite lunchrooms, daycare facilities, automated bank teller machines (Farr 2008)

Smart Growth

In the United States in the early 1970s, the social, environmental and economic toll of auto-centric development on cities (long commuting times, costly infrastructure and declining quality of life) became clear. In response, transportation planners, land-use planners and architects developed the foundations of *Smart Growth* (a planning paradigm that shares many of the same qualities as New Urbanism). Smart Growth aimed to address six goals: neighborhood livability; better access to daily destinations and less traffic; thriving cities, suburbs and towns through infill development; sharing the benefits of regional prosperity with all residents; lower costs for infrastructure and lower taxes; and keeping open space open. Smart Growth principles have since evolved to include the following tools for developers:

- promote mixed land uses
- take advantage of compact building designs
- create a range of housing opportunities and choices
- create walkable neighborhoods
- foster distinctive, attractive communities with a strong sense of place
- preserve open space, farmland, natural beauty and critical environmental areas
- strengthen and direct development to existing communities
- provide a variety of transportation choices
- make development decisions predictable, fair and cost-effective
- encourage community and stakeholder collaboration

Communities that employ Smart Growth strategies can create or maintain existing neighborhoods that are safe, healthy, attractive and sustainable. As well, Smart Growth neighborhoods enhance social, civic and physical activities that contribute to community capital, by broadening residents' choices in how they live, get around and interact with others. Plans based on Smart Growth principles help preserve the best features of our past while creating an inclusive, just and sustainable future for the generations to come.

Other Sustainable Community Design Approaches:

- Landscape Urbanism: This approach to community design organizes city structure based on landscapes scales such as a watershed, upon which a city's buildings stand.

Practitioners envision weaving nature and city together into a new hybrid that functions like a living ecosystem (Waldheim 2006). Detractors to this paradigm criticize its "impenetrable language" as being intellectually pretentious rather than conveying ideas clearly. The precepts of Landscape Urbanism have also been accused of defending sprawl in an effort to be contrarian to New Urbanism (Neyfakh 2011).

- Transit Oriented Development: These developments concentrate growth in centers and corridors that are well-served by frequent transit. TOD is discussed in more detail in chapter 8.
- Cluster Development: This looks to preserve large areas of shared outdoor space by increasing housing density on portions of the area to be developed (Kearney 2006).
- Low Impact Development: This approach attempts to reduce stormwater runoff from developments through the use of bioretention technologies such as greenroofs, pervious pavements and grassed swales (Dietz 2007).

Retrofit Our Built Environments

Moving towards sustainability requires that we place at least as much emphasis on how we can make better use of our existing built environment as we do on designing new projects. Retrofitting, upgrading, densification and intensification of existing urban and suburban developments, particularly those built in the post-World War II era when areas were zoned for housing only, is critical (Riddell 2004). Retrofitting comprises three endeavors:

- **Intensifying the inner city** can be achieved through infill of existing central city sites, such as the adaptive reuse of commercial office space into apartments and lofts. As residential spaces increase, shops, schools and clinics will follow. The challenge is to provide access to open space for recreation. Work by Jim (2008) shows that Asian cities increasingly use building rooftops for this purpose.

- **Redeveloping brownfields** offers culturally diverse and service-diverse regeneration opportunities within cities and larger towns, by developing abandoned manufacturing and warehouse districts. Planned with pedestrians and public transit in mind, this type of development will attract residential, as well as light industrial, commercial and office space (Boarnet et al. 2011). Brownfield developments are particularly amenable to mixed use; however, remediation of contaminated land can be costly.

- **Retrofitting suburbia** presents the greatest challenge to the goal of infilling and compaction, primarily due to constraints of existing infrastructure (Boarnet et al. 2011). Municipalities that seek to densify may experience problems of insufficient utilities, poor roads for transit, increased pressure on street parking and resistance from some residents who are unfamiliar with the benefits of compact living. Redevelopment of commercial strip corridors such as old strip malls and parking lots, known as greyfield development, provides excellent opportunities to retrofit suburbia.

Climate Change and the Built Environment

According to the United Nations, urban areas are responsible for 75 percent of global energy consumption and 80 percent of global emissions, and as cities continue to grow, they will be crucial to global climate change mitigation efforts (Kirby 2008). By 2050, the world's urban population is predicted to double from 3.4 billion to 6.3 billion, representing the majority of the world's total population growth over that time. Cities are the centers of financial wealth and scientific innovation, providing the tools and resources to adapt to a changing climate.

Cities are often located in areas prone to climate change impacts, such as coastlines and flood plains, and therefore will face serious threats to their infrastructure and disaster management capabilities. Sea level rise and increased storm surges will jeopardize civic infrastructure. Increased and more intense floods and droughts will stress the ability of cities to provide clean water supplies. Climate change will accelerate rapid urban population growth, sprawl, poverty and pollution as citizens struggle to adapt (Rosenzweig et al. 2010).

The *urban heat island* (UHI) effect is the most glaring example of anthropogenic climate modification as a result of urban sprawl. Cities trap and retain heat more readily than their rural surroundings. UHI effect is directly correlated to: land-use patterns, coverage of impervious substrates like roads and buildings, low albedo (reflective capacity of material), high-heat capacity materials such as roads and traditional roofs, reduced vegetated areas and increased heat retention in canyon-like high-rise building areas (Grimm et al. 2008).

UHI affects not only the local and regional climate but the air quality, water resources, urban biodiversity, human health and ecosystem functioning within and outside the city. UHI contributes to poor air quality through the formation of photochemical smog, resulting in

Unsustainable Home Ownership

The foreclosure epidemic in America devastated communities in many parts of the country between 2008 and 2011. The sub-prime loans that enabled low- and middle-income Americans to purchase houses in the suburbs helped fuel one of the largest housing expansions in US history (Immergluck 2009). Consumer preferences for ever-expanding house sizes in gated communities led to a decline in affordability, racial segregation and economic inequality (Dwyer 2007). As a result of the foreclosures, communities lost revenue due to unpaid property taxes, housing conditions deteriorated, and residents experienced increased social and personal losses (Immergluck 2009).

increased respiratory illness (Endlicher et al. 2008). UHI stresses all organisms living in the city, including people. Warmer cities require more energy to cool them down, thus resulting in a positive feedback loop that serves to exacerbate the need for more energy through more cooling resulting in more GHGs (Grimm et al. 2008).

Urban areas can reduce GHG emissions, improve their resiliency to climate change and create more inclusive livable communities through the sustainable management of their land and constituents. Land-use planning, emissions licensing, building codes, zoning, transit and transportation plans all fall under the jurisdiction of municipal and regional governments. Through the thoughtful application of these tools, municipal councils can increase density, improve connectivity and, most importantly, mitigate the impacts of climate change while helping their citizens adapt to a changing world.

A more extensive discussion on the predicted impacts of climate change for communities can be found in chapter 13. For information on preventing and mitigating the UHI effect, see chapter 4.

Tools and Initiatives
Voluntary
LAND STEWARDSHIP

The Texas Wildlife Association, through its mission to encourage the state's landowners to have an "ethical relationship" to their lands, actively promotes voluntary land stewardship programs statewide. Using high-profile award events, the Texas Wildlife Association publicly acknowledges their members, the professional conservation community and other TWA volunteers for their efforts to conserve the state's water and natural resources.

INCREASING COMMUNITY CONNECTIVITY

Residents of a neighborhood in Christchurch, New Zealand, developed a simple and effective solution to two community problems: overgrown unsightly backyards and a dearth of functional green space. Neighbors within the same block entered a joint venture with city council to combine their underused separate backyards into a public open space (Ignatieva & Faggi 2009).

HOUSING/JOBS BALANCE

When jobs and housing are not in balance, transportation problems are the likely result. Land-use planners can look at the range of incomes and housing costs to determine how far people have to move away from their jobs to find housing they can afford. The imbalance between the location of jobs and housing is the most important determinant for longer commuting and suggests that higher-quality and affordable housing growth close to job-rich communities reduces traffic congestion and air pollution (Cervero & Duncan 2006).

Financial Incentives

HOUSING/RETAIL BALANCE

Establishing a balanced housing/retail ratio is a useful goal for creating livable communities, and research by Turner (2007) shows that achieving equilibrium between housing/retail at high densities is achieved only when local retailers are present. Low densities are likely to occur when no local retailers are present. In order to encourage high densities, the author recommends the application of taxes on large lots or incentives for residents to occupy small lots (Turner 2007).

REDIRECTING DEVELOPMENT

Urban Enterprise Zones (UEZ) provide incentives to increase economic activity on vacant land and structures, using such things as business tax deductions for hiring zone residents, unemployment insurance rebates and sales tax exemptions for the sale of goods and services that will be used within the zone. By encouraging job creation on vacant land that is already connected to nearby residential neighborhoods, the jobs/housing balance can be improved.

In the United States, UEZ programs have shown mixed results. UEZ programs in New Jersey are credited with generating 58,000 jobs and more than $12.5 billion in private investments (Leigh 2003), while UEZ programs in California did not achieve significant increases in employment or private investment (Neumark & Kolko 2010). Turner and Cassell (2007) show that, while UEZ programs can improve economic prospects for their most disadvantaged communities as intended, over time states tend to use them to attract firms

regardless of the economic condition of the zone.

PROXIMITY PLANNING

Striking a balance between jobs and housing, as discussed above, is not enough unless the people who work in a given area have the option of also living in that same area. This requires policies to encourage access by proximity. The State of New Jersey's Housing and Mortgage Financing Agency developed the Live Where You Work homebuyer program to strengthen communities and increase active transportation in the area. Those eligible benefit from attractive mortgage rates, more-flexible loan applications, flexible loan underwriting criteria and reduced commute times. To qualify, the homebuyer must select an eligible property from the state-identified urban target areas.

ACCELERATED PLANNING APPROVALS

According to a study commissioned by the National Housing Supply Council of Australia (2010), the greatest opportunity to encourage infill development of brownfields and greyfields is by increasing the supply of these sites through planning legislation that facilitates these developments. Accelerated planning approvals can accomplish this by reducing the development time frame, thereby reducing costs to the developer.

DEVELOPMENT CHARGE BREAKS

When used, development charges are often applied uniformly across municipalities without regard to the location of the development in question. By applying them more strategically, municipalities can structure these charges to reflect the true costs of infrastructure provision and to encourage infill and redevelopment of existing sites (C.D. Howe Institute 2002).

DENSITY BONUSES

Density bonuses offer developments a level of density that surpasses the allowable floor area ratio (FAR) in exchange for amenities or housing needed by the community. These amenities typically include parks, heritage preservation and affordable housing, but offering increased density in exchange for greener development can also be seen as an amenity to the community (Fraser Basin Council 2007).

Expenditure

RECLAIMING ABANDONED LAND

Boston's Dudley Street Neighborhood is a small neighborhood near downtown that has suffered severe inner-city disinvestment. In response, the community mobilized and created the Dudley Street Neighborhood Initiative that, through negotiation with the city, was granted eminent domain authority over all abandoned land in the neighborhood. So far, it has transformed more than 600 of 1,300 vacant land parcels into affordable rental and leased housing facilities with playgrounds, gardens and community facilities. The vision is to create an "urban village" with mixed-rate housing, jobs and tight community control over land through a community land trust that maintains affordability through 99-year land leases and by restricting resale prices (Pomeroy 2006).

Regulations

NEW FORMS OF LAND OWNERSHIP

In recent years, land trusts and limited-equity cooperatives have experimented with distributing the costs and benefits of land development in much the same way that Henry George proposed, but through new forms of landownership rather than taxation.

Common Property: Boston's Dudley Street Neighborhood Initiative made the land in an inner-city redevelopment area the common property of a non-profit group, while allowing private ownership of homes and other buildings. To date, the project has helped rehabilitate over 1,300 vacant lots for homes, gardens, parks, orchards, playgrounds, schools, community centers and a Town Common (Dudley Street Neighborhood Initiative 2010).

Land Leases: The UniverCity Verdant project in Burnaby, BC, uses innovative pricing strategies and land-leasing agreements between Simon Fraser University and Vancity Enterprises to allow owners to purchase their residences at 20 percent below market value. Owners can realize benefits of price appreciation by selling their units at the 20 percent discount rate of its future market value.

SPLIT-RATE LAND TAXES

A study of fifteen cities in Pennsylvannia found that a tax shift, which placed higher taxes on land than buildings, spurred the regeneration of their blighted land. The new tax regime increased the number of vacant lot sales, new building permits and new dwellings, while at the same time, demolitions declined, according to the authors Banzhaf and Lavery (2010). They concluded: "The primary effect is in more housing units, rather than bigger units, suggesting the split-rate tax is potentially a powerful anti-sprawl tool."

URBAN GROWTH BOUNDARIES

Urban growth boundaries are often set by councils, for a predetermined time period or permanently, to encourage efficient use of land and help protect valuable farmland. They serve to stop urban sprawl, protect open space and improve existing neighborhoods. They are used extensively in Denmark, Australia, Indonesia, as well as many parts of the United States, and are considered one of the most economically efficient anti-sprawl policies (Bento, Franco & Kaffine 2006).

AUTO-FREE DEVELOPMENT

In Scotland, Edinburgh Council established a 120-unit housing development called Slateford Green that incorporated a complete car-free neighborhood with integrated public mobility policies. Trees replaced pavement, the use of recycled materials was encouraged, low-technology processes such as passive ventilation were adopted, and the use of nontoxic materials was promoted (Morris 2005).

Amsterdam's GWL-Terrain is another development that actively discourages car use by providing only limited parking spaces on the perimeter of the development and explicitly incorporating car-sharing services.

The Hollerand development in Bremen, Germany, was one of the first of the car-reduced developments; it led to the widely successful Bremen car-sharing club that has since been successfully replicated throughout Europe and North America (Buehler & Pucher 2009).

The Toronto Islands just off the lakeshore from Toronto's city center is the largest urban car-free community in North America. Used primarily as a recreation area for nearby Torontonians, the islands boast a permanent settlement of 262 homes, one school, two daycares and one church. All motorized traffic is banned from the islands, with access provided by a ferry service from downtown Toronto.

ENERGY-EFFICIENT LAND-USE PLANNING

Partly as a result of Portland's energy-efficient land-use planning, the number of jobs in the downtown has increased by 30,000 since the 1970s, with only a scant increase in traffic; in addition, 40 percent of commuters to the downtown area use public transportation (Song 2004). By encouraging high-density development along transit routes and reducing car use where possible, Portland is showing that limiting urban sprawl is possible (Song 2004).

BUILDING PERMIT ALLOCATION

The Growth Management Ordinance in Boulder, Colorado: This city experienced extreme growth pressures of around 6 percent per year between 1960 and 1970. In 1967, the city implemented one of the first greenbelt systems in the US to serve as a natural growth boundary by defining the limits to the city with open space and parkland. When the annual growth rate was reduced to 1 percent per year in 1995, the city council acted to create a larger share of affordable housing. New housing developments are now allocated according to a formula of 25 percent market housing, 55 percent affordable housing (based on size and other criteria) and 20 percent permanently affordable housing maintained through deed restrictions. The allocation of affordable housing is combined with a housing trust fund that uses an excise tax on new construction to subsidize affordable housing. Despite the significant growth pressure experienced in Boulder, the city has managed and controlled growth by recognizing its financial and ecological limits and adopting policies consistent with those limits (Jackson 2005).

RESIDENTIAL INTENSIFICATION PROGRAMS

These programs create new residential units or accommodation in existing buildings or on previously developed, serviced land. They generally include creation of rooming, boarding and lodging houses; creation of secondary apartments; conversion of non-residential structures to residential use; infill and redevelopment.

Accessory Apartments Policy: The City of Guelph implemented official plan and zoning bylaw changes to permit secondary units as a right in all low-density areas of the city. The registration process was made simple and free. An average of 75 new apartments were built and registered per year, for a total of 600 units since 1995. The new units serve as a major source of affordable rental stock and represent approximately one-third of the residential intensification in the city (Tomalty 2003).

Exemption from Planning and Development Fees: All residential developments in the downtown Ottawa core are exempt from development charges, building permit fees, planning application fees and the requirement to pay for parkland. This has resulted in 64 new housing projects, accounting for 4,300 units either built, under construction or in the approval process (Tomalty 2003).

Chapter 10:

Housing and Community Development

Whether you live in a metropolis that never pauses or a town where everyone knows your name, you'd probably agree that community means so much more than a place to live. It's a place whose identity reflects its unique history and the diverse ages, backgrounds and talents of your town's human and cultural capital. It's a place where shared interests and burdens help people forge solid social networks, and from which all residents derive opportunities for friendship, education, cultural expression, employment, healthcare, security, recreation and adequate housing.

Previous chapters have explored many of the easily measurable "hard" aspects of sustainability, such as infrastructure and energy sources. Housing is arguably one of these, as it is essentially built environments that constitute physical capital and investments of economic capital. But housing is also so intricately tied up with the "softer," less tangible issues of community development that it makes sense to discuss these issues together. A safe, welcoming

and affordable place to call home is vital to one's emotional and economic investment in a community. It plays a starring role in determining our capacity to participate in community activities and decision-making — and thus to mobilize for sustainability.

There are numerous ways that citizens, businesses, organizations and local governments can help ensure that housing not only meets personal needs in an affordable and resource-efficient manner, but also does so in way that fosters connection, neighborliness and social equity. This chapter will explore the relationship of housing to community development, and survey several strategies that communities are using now to advance sustainability in both — often simultaneously.

More Than a Roof Over Our Heads

Housing is a key factor influencing the environmental, economic and social aspects of community development. The Wellesley Institute (2010, 15) succinctly summed up its

177

importance: "Safe, affordable, and healthy housing is not only a basic necessity for human health and human life but also a means to reducing systemic health inequities and lowering associated long-term healthcare costs. A good home is critical to allow people to fully participate in the economic, social and cultural lives of their community and their country."

Many people in North America live without adequate housing, or worse, lack any form of permanent and secure shelter. While homelessness is merely the most extreme symptom of a housing system inadequate to the needs of an urban or rural population, many people who are *not* homeless still occupy housing that is inadequate, unaffordable and insecure — or live in neighborhoods that lack resources and services essential to sustaining a rich and vibrant community life. Assuring decent housing in decent neighborhoods is a complex issue that requires a coordinated approach among multiple sectors and among multiple levels of government.

Affording a Home

Generally speaking, housing (whether rental or ownership) is considered affordable if it does not exceed 30 percent of household gross income. In addition to the 30 percent benchmark, some American states also tie housing affordability to local economic conditions and incomes, adjusting the definition further for those earning 20 percent less than the local average income.

As real estate prices escalate and the cost of living continues to increase, market-rate housing is becoming out of reach for more people — especially larger households. In January 2007, one in four Canadian households were paying more than they could afford for housing

(Wellesley Institute 2010). In Sacramento, 91 percent of low-income renters spend greater than 30 percent of their income on housing (SMHA 2011). While subsidized programs provide assistance to some, others are forced to leave the city to find lower-cost housing in suburbs and small towns. But affordable housing is not just a concern for urban centers; rural communities are challenged to provide low-cost homes for their citizens too. Nor is it only a problem for the unemployed or underemployed; in many communities, the majority of affordable housing is used by working people who are simply caught in the squeeze between rising housing costs and eroding wages.

Compounding the problem is that many affordable market-rate homes that lower-income households purchased or rented using public assistance have been lost to changing market conditions (Davis 2010a). This has especially been a problem in communities where policies and incentives (such as inclusionary zoning and rebates for developers) have created thousands of affordable housing units without any long-term controls over their resale or rerent. In a hot market, occupiers of affordable units are often unable to resist selling their homes or rental units for the highest price possible, thereby pocketing 100 percent of the appreciation, reaping all benefits of the public's investment and eliminating the opportunity for resale or rerent to another low-income individual or family. For homeowners with adjustable-rate mortgages, a rising market can cause financial burden since mortgage payments rise with the market. Similarly, rising real estate values can push up property and insurance costs, causing additional burdens to renters and homeowners. At the other extreme, poor market conditions, such as those experienced during the 2006 collapse of the US housing bubble, can force affordable unit homeowners into foreclosure, thereby losing all public investments and years of progress helping low-income families gain access to real property (Davis 2010a). Strategies such as resale restrictions or linking up with non-market developers such as community land trusts can help preserve the existing stock of affordable housing units.

Many of the publicly subsidized, lower-cost units built in the last few decades have failed to provide healthy, safe and nurturing environments for residents. They have often been concentrated in large buildings that are poorly placed in the community, leading to segregation, difficult commutes to work and limited options for groceries, schools and social programs (Malloy 2009). Single mothers, the aged and infirmed are groups whose needs are often neglected in housing design and planning. By contrast, when designing "housing as if people mattered" (Marcus 1986, 1), architects, planners and developers honor the needs of all people and seek to provide places where all can thrive. Well-designed buildings and complexes can ameliorate crime, encourage learning, promote physical and mental health and encourage social interactions (Cubbin et al. 2008; Mallach 2009).

Non-market Tenure

Not only do market conditions and poor design affect families seeking affordable and healthy housing, market-rate tenures, whether rental or homeownership, can expose individuals to risks and responsibilities they often cannot bear on their own. Risks associated with managing and financing a home or rental unit and the responsibilities of home repair and unit resale can be overwhelming. More often, communities

are turning to non-market developers such as community land trusts (CLT) and limited equity cooperatives (LEC) to assist individuals and families by sharing the responsibilities and risks of homeownership. Increasingly referred to as *shared equity housing*, these non-market forms of tenure prevent the loss of affordably priced units and preserve housing quality and homeownership security. CLTs or LECs ensure that housing affordability is maintained and that units are continuously resold or rented at an affordable price. They ensure units are well-maintained by helping homeowners pay for costly repairs such as roofs and furnaces. Homeowner security is increased by minimizing risks associated with financing through education of prospective buyers/renters regarding their new responsibilities; creation of screens to prevent adoption of predatory or high cost mortgages; and sometimes insistence on being a party to every mortgage to ensure payments are made and foreclosure is avoided. Since these alternative forms of tenure are more resilient to changes in market conditions than market-rate tenures, they have not only survived but spread across the United States and into other countries as well (Davis 2006).

Public Policies Promoting Affordable Housing

Communities can use a variety of policies and incentives to support and encourage affordable housing development such as: as-of-right zoning for affordable housing, supportive housing and higher density housing. In many cities, affordable housing requires exemptions from current zoning regulations; however, by designating these types of housing "as-of-right," the approval process will be smoother as proposals will not require special exceptions. Municipal

Fig. 10.1:
Communities can promote the densification of suburban areas by encouraging construction of secondary suites and laneway houses in unused garages.

governments can also use zoning regulation to negotiate commitments from developers to donate land to community land trusts to build affordable housing. Providing incentives such as rebates or grants for affordable housing or selling municipally owned land at low cost to developers or non-profit organizations can also encourage affordable housing development (FCM 2009; Slaunwhite 2009).

To support affordable housing and community development, communities can also develop linkage programs. These programs collect a portion of the value created by commercial investment in neighborhoods or Central Business Districts undergoing substantial development and direct the value to build affordable housing, provide job training and fund social services in low-income neighborhoods. They can also provide a means for financing investment in environmental protection and restoration (SDHC 2009). Communities can further affirm their commitment to affordable housing development by generating a municipal housing strategy that addresses the need for below-market housing, by directly incorporating affordable housing into the official community plan or by enshrining the right to adequate housing for citizens in law.

Rural communities face unique challenges in providing affordable housing. Rental options are typically limited, and development tends to focus on single-family detached dwellings that are expensive to own and maintain. As well, as a result of small and declining populations, rural communities are often unable to receive government funding to support affordable housing projects (Slaunwhite 2009). To improve housing for low-income households, rural municipalities can create stronger regulations to encourage conversions of existing institutional or industrial properties to rental units, permit secondary suites and garden suites on existing residential properties and encourage the use of community land trusts to secure property for affordable housing units.

Private Strategies Promoting Affordable Housing

Alternative housing development strategies, such as non-profit rentals, limited-equity cooperatives, cohousing, resident-owned communities and non-profit organizations such as community land trusts, can maximize both inclusiveness and housing affordability.

Limited-equity (or zero-equity) housing co-operatives provide a community of not-for-profit homes for individuals of all levels of income (but primarily mid- to low-income). Co-operative housing projects are collectively owned by their members, all of whom live there. Should a member move, the member's shares are repurchased by the cooperative for a fixed price and then resold to another income-eligible individual or family, who then occupies the vacant unit. Residents are expected to participate in the management of the co-op by attending meetings, joining committees or boards or helping with general building maintenance or social events. Co-ops provide residents with a safe and affordable house in a community that shares decision-making, participates in social events together and supports each other. Registered co-ops in Canada and the United States receive money from the government, subsidizing units so that low-income households can afford both the initial cost of purchasing a share in the co-operative and the continuing cost of the monthly occupancy fee to live there.

Cohousing has been rapidly gaining popularity throughout North America as a result of dissatisfaction with the design of conventional residential developments. This housing alternative provides tangibles, such as shared facilities, help with childcare and meal preparation, as well as intangibles, such as a sense of community, support and a feeling of security. With cohousing, residents typically own their individuals homes but share common areas. Residents participate in the planning, management and maintenance of the complex, but individuals are able to decide their degree of participation in community activities. While cohousing creates a sense of community and builds social capital, it is not always inclusive or designed to meet the needs of lower-income households — in the United States, most cohousing developments are now occupied by more-affluent households.

Community Land Trusts (**CLT**) are locally controlled non-profit organizations that acquire, hold and lease out land for the

Resident-owned Communities

Most affordable housing in rural US are located in manufactured housing communities, commonly referred to as mobile home parks. Here, residents own their homes but pay a monthly fee for the land underneath it. While majority of communities are owned and managed by a private investor, Resident-owned Communities USA (ROC USA), a non-profit organization, is leading a national effort to support homeowners who wish to form cooperatives to jointly purchase their communities. ROC USA offers low-interest loans to help finance the purchase, as well as provide co-op training, leadership development, on-going management and technical assistance for infrastructure projects. Resident-owned, as oppose to privately owned communities, benefit from increased security (the land cannot suddenly be sold), lower monthly fees, shared management and a sense of cohesion and community. As of May 2009, 92 manufactured housing communities have been acquired by the 5,000 people who live in them (ROC USA 2009).

Fig. 10.2: *It takes a village: Members of Sunward Cohousing in Ann Arbor, Michigan, take pride in having created a supportive, safe environment for children. Kids enjoy extensive outdoor play areas, car-free pedestrian pathways and kids' space in a common House. Children are encouraged to take part in community-building activities.* (Credit: Sunward Cohousing)

development of permanently affordable housing, the preservation of heritage buildings, the creation of jobs and community facilities and the promotion of other community uses like urban agriculture, neighborhood parks and transit-oriented development. Trusts also manage publicly owned lands, such as bike paths, conservation areas and community gardens. Traditionally, CLTs sell off any housing or any buildings but maintain ownership of the underlying land. This allows the CLT to control the use and resale of the structures, while preserving their affordability, promoting sound maintenance and intervening (if necessary) to prevent foreclosure. The first CLT, established in 1969 near Albany, Georgia, was an outgrowth of the civil rights movement in the American South (Davis 2010b). There are now over 240 CLTs in the United States, supported by the National Community Land Trust Network. There are also fledgling CLT movements underway in Canada, England, Australia and Belgium.

Financing/Subsidizing Affordable Housing

Citizens, non-profit organizations and local governments have developed a variety of strategies to finance affordable housing development and to support people seeking ways to lower housing costs. Non-profit and citizen-run organizations can raise awareness of affordable housing needs within the community and can support individuals or families seeking to lower

Affordable Housing and NIMBYism

Proposed affordable housing projects often meet resistance from people who already live in the neighborhood, fearing such development will decrease property values and bring crime, drug use, violence and poverty to the neighborhood. But these not-in-my-backyard (NIMBY) fears are often unfounded. For example, research (Nguyen 2005) shows that well-maintained, managed and aesthetically pleasing affordable housing dispersed throughout a healthy and vibrant neighborhood has no effect on property values. Furthermore, rehabilitation of abandoned, neglected or physically deteriorated houses into affordable units can actually raise neighboring property values.

The Affordability and Choice Today (ACT) Initiative, a federal program that promotes affordable housing development in local communities, suggests useful strategies to address NIMBYism. Not surprisingly, the best way to gain community support for affordable housing projects is to engage community members at the planning stage. The most successful engagement strategies have clear messages; employ a variety of communication techniques, forums and formats (e.g.,

town hall meetings, websites, flyers, webinars); emphasize project benefits to the community and link projects to community-defined goals (e.g., affordable housing legislation). Local developers, planners, architects and artists should be engaged in the creation of educational materials, and such materials should be provided to community members and the media well in advance of community meetings or open houses. Technical experts and relevant professionals (e.g., biologist, lawyers, heritage preservationists, engineers) should also be engaged in communication.

By no means should community engagement end after projects have been implemented and people have taken up residence. At this point, it is important to gain insight into how the project has affected the community: Have any of the initial concerns expressed by community materialized now that the project has been built? Have the new residents brought benefits to the neighborhood? Information collected from implemented projects can be used to improve projects and quell concerns about future proposed affordable housing projects (FCM 2009).

housing costs. These organizations can also fund construction and provide volunteers to help build the actual units. Affordable housing can also be funded by local governments through grants, municipal bonds or low-interest loans.

Tools And Initiatives: Housing

Voluntary

AFFORDABLE HOUSING PROGRAMS

Housing Scholarship Program: Abode Services, a non-profit organization, manages the Housing Scholarship Program in the Tri-Valley region of California. The program provides housing support to low-income individuals and families while they are enrolled in job training programs. The Allied Housing Linkages Program also provides rent subsidies and employment services to individuals coming out of homeless shelters by working with area housing authorities and private sector landlords to obtain transition housing as people move towards self-sufficiency (Abode Services 2011).

    Habitat for Humanity: This non-profit secular organization with chapters across North America (and across the world) raises funds and in-kind contributions to construct low-cost homes. Habitat then does its own mortgage financing, offering no-interest loans to its homebuyers. Echoing the Amish tradition of community barn raising, volunteers work together to construct houses. Some Habitat chapters are building energy-efficient homes to lower utility costs for tenants; others are experimenting with green building materials such as straw bale and adobe. Although Habitat historically refused to impose any type of affordability controls over the resale of its homes, many chapters are now ensuring houses remain affordable by either teaming up with

Converting Heritage Buildings to Affordable Housing

Adaptive reuse of heritage buildings into affordable homes allows communities to meet heritage conservation goals and increase affordable housing supply. Using existing buildings that are already serviced can reduce costs by 15 percent or more, compared to constructing new affordable units, and can help preserve cultural capital. Conversion often meets less resistance from existing neighborhood residents because the structure already exists. Residents also view the conversion as an upgrade to their neighborhood bringing positive change and enhancing neighborhood vitality and cultural diversity (Parks Canada 2011).

Fig. 10.3: *Volunteers and Habitat for Humanity staff help homeowner Chris Van Buren work on his Bay St. Louis, MS, home. Since its founding in 1976, Habitat has built more than 350,000 houses worldwide, providing a place to call home for more than 1.75 million people.*
(CREDIT: DAVE WALKER, HFH BAY-WAVELAND AREA)

non-profit organizations to provide post-pur-chase stewardship or imposing resale controls of their own.

Community development corporations: Community development corporations (CDC) are a type of non-profit housing organization that guarantees long-term affordable housing options by securing land at low or no cost, obtaining grants and low-interest loans to finance housing projects, securing subsidies for low-income renters and providing a variety of services (e.g., job training and creation) to help residents increase their financial security. Along with other large non-profit housing organizations, CDCs have provided approximately 1.5 million affordable housing units in the United States (Bratt 2009).

SERVICE-ENRICHED HOUSING

Beyond Shelter: Beyond Shelter, a non-profit affordable housing and services provider in Los Angeles, establishes, owns and operates a number of service-enriched affordable housing projects and develops family support and childcare centers. Beyond Shelter's mission is to develop systematic approaches to combat poverty and homelessness among families with children (Beyond Shelter 2011). At each project, an onsite services coordinator helps residents access community resources and services such as childcare, medical care and community activities for children and youth. Tenants participate in resident management committees that manage the building and common areas and plan program development and activities for tenants of all ages (Beyond Shelter 2011).

SELF-HELP HOUSING

Urban Homesteading: The Urban Home-steading Assistance Board began in New York City in 1973 by training tenants to own, rehabilitate and manage their own buildings. Originally started as an advocacy and training center, it has now evolved into one of New York City's leading developers in affordable housing. The board promotes the conversion of city-owned buildings into resident-owned, limited-equity co-operatives. The buildings, acquired by the city through tax foreclosures, are sold back to former tenants. The experience helps build skills, empower people and reduce crime rates in and around these buildings (UHAB 2011).

MUTUAL HOUSING ASSOCIATIONS

Mutual Housing Associations are private non-profit corporations created to develop, own and manage affordable housing. All residents are stockholders and therefore participate in decision-making. Housing Associations unite groups of buildings, such as limited-equity co-ops and low- and middle-income dwellings, into larger associations on the assumption that economies of scale will improve the development, maintenance and operation of housing. Other benefits are providing resident training and professional property resources. The Sacramento Mutual Housing Association operates with the mission to "develop and operate permanently affordable housing that builds strong and stable communities through resident participation and leadership development" (SMHA 2011). The Capitol Hill Housing Improvement Program in Seattle is a community-based non-profit with the aim to provide affordable housing for low-income earners. It has been in operation since 1976 and owns and operates 42 buildings with the mission to provide affordable housing options while preserving Seattle's community character (CHH 2011).

SHARED-LIVING COMMUNITIES

Retrofit Cohousing: Established in 1992, the Doyle Street cohousing complex in Emeryville, California, currently houses 28 residents. With a total of 12 loft-style units and a common house, the complex is an adaptive reuse of an old building that helped to revitalize an economically disadvantaged area. Other features in the complex, such as a community garden, children's play area and facilities for dining outside in warm weather, help create community and a sense of place for the residents (Cohousing Association of the United States 2011).

Inclusive Cohousing: Quayside Village is a 19-unit cohousing community in North Vancouver, British Columbia, with units designed for singles, couples and families. Five units are designated as affordable housing for lower-income families and have resale controls to ensure that long-term affordability is maintained. The community has a common area with shared kitchen and dining facilities, a lounge, shared laundry, craft area, playroom and an office and guest suite. The common house was built using recycled building materials and based on rigorous energy-efficiency standards. With support from the Canadian Mortgage Housing Corporation, the community also has the first multi-family greywater recycling system in Canada (Canadian Mortgage and Housing Corporation 2011a).

Cooperative Housing: Recognizing the need for safe, affordable housing options for single mothers, the non-profit Entre Nous Femmes Housing Society is helping build cooperative housing units in Vancouver, BC. Primarily occupied by single-parent families, the townhouse complexes provide both a home and a community to many previously isolated people. Empowerment of the co-op's members is key.

As of July 2010, the Society owns and manages 409 units in 11 different building complexes (Entre Nous Femmes Housing Society 2011).

COMMUNITY REVITALIZATION PROGRAMS

Women's Community Revitalization Project: The Women's Community Revitalization Project (WCRP) was created in Philadelphia, PA, in 1993, as a way to promote social and economic justice for low-income women and their families by providing affordable housing and supportive services and leadership, advocacy and training opportunities. WCRP has built and managed five affordable housing developments throughout the community, totaling 130 units. Residents have access to employment and housing counseling, leadership building workshops and job training opportunities. The project also has a community greening program that converts abandoned lots into gardens, neighborhood parks and playgrounds, thereby improving public safety, building community and raising property values. In addition, WCRP offers training and technical assistance to other organizations helping low-income families so they can better serve the community (WCRP 2011). Since 2009, WCRP has been spearheading an effort to convince the city government to transfer a portion of the city's poorly managed inventory of 10,000 parcels of land, much of it gained through tax foreclosures, into community ownership. A locally controlled community land trust, administered by WCRP, would receive these parcels from the city and oversee their reuse and redevelopment for affordable housing, commercial space and community gardens.

COMMUNITY LAND TRUSTS

Chicago Community Land Trust: Created in 2006 to ensure the long-term affordability of owner-occupied homes subsidized by the city, the Chicago Community Land Trust (CCLT) has employed a variation of the usual CLT approach. Rather than owning the land under multiple housing projects and using a ground lease to preserve the affordability, condition and security of publicly subsidized, privately owned housing, the CCLT uses a deed of covenant to achieve its subsidy-retention and stewardship goals (Towey 2009).

Champlain Housing Trust: Created in 2006 as the result of a merger between the Burlington Community Land Trust and the Lake Champlain Housing Development Corporation, the Champlain Housing Trust (CHT) provides affordable housing and community facilities in the three counties surrounding Burlington, Vermont. CHT acquires land through purchase, donation or bargain sale. It has also received land and buildings as part of negotiated deals with private developers who must comply with local inclusionary zoning or housing replacement ordinances. If there is not already an existing residential or commercial building on the land, CHT constructs one using government grants and private donations. In the case of CHT's owner-occupied housing, an income-eligible homebuyer purchases the building and leases the underlying land from CHT for a nominal fee (for example, $35 per month for 99 years). Since the cost of the land is not included in the price of the home, the cost of the home is kept low and the homebuyer saves on mortgage costs. By leveraging government grants and subsidies and by restricting the re-sale price of every house and condominium in its portfolio, CHT is able to keep the cost of owning a home up to 30 percent lower than a comparable market-rate home (Fireside 2008). CHT is currently the manager and steward for 1,500 units of rental housing, several shelters and single-room occupancies for persons who were formerly homeless and 8 non-residential buildings containing neighborhood businesses or community services.

Financial Incentives

Municipal Bonds: Municipal bonds have been used to finance the construction and rehabilitation of affordable housing or other community facilities. In many communities, these bonds provide a low-cost financing alternative that reduces risk of loss of loan (Apgar & Narasimhan 2007). For example, the District of Columbia offers tax-exempt municipal bonds to owners financing their own affordable housing. These bonds have below-market interest rates and can decrease the overall average interest rate of an equity portfolio (Diamond 2009).

Block Grants: A block grant is generally a grant provided by national or regional governments with broad or general provisions for using the money on experimental or progressive projects. The US Department of Housing and Urban Development has a Community Block Grant Program that gives annual funding to provide affordable housing services (HUD 2011).

Location Efficient Mortgages: The location efficient mortgage program is designed to reduce urban sprawl, car dependence and greenhouse gas emissions by encouraging homebuyers to settle in communities where public transit, work, shops and other services are close by. Individuals who purchase homes in these types of neighborhoods are offered larger mortgages, based on the idea that they save on transportation costs compared to their suburban counterparts, meaning they have more disposable income and therefore qualify for larger loans. For many, this may mean the difference in qualifying for a home in a high-density area instead of a car-dependent suburb (Natural Resources Defense Council 2009).

Expenditure

Affordable Housing with Childcare Center: In response to rising rents and a lack of affordable housing, the City of Watsonville, California, leased land from the Santa Cruz Metropolitan Transit District for $1 and partnered with the Mid-Peninsula Housing Coalition to build the Via del Mar complex. It is a 40-unit affordable housing development adjacent to a major bus depot. With such a large youth population, the city approved a special-use permit to construct a childcare center as part of the development. It is used by downtown workers and Via del Mar residents, although the latter have priority. The development is adjacent to a major public transit hub and within easy walking distance of shopping, social services, libraries, schools and other educational facilities and cultural venues. Since Watsonville is primarily dominated by agriculture, eight units are reserved for farmworker families (Mid-Peninsula Housing Coalition 2011).

Affordable Housing Replacement Program: The City of Vancouver, in partnership with the Province of British Columbia, has implemented a program to replace low-income rental units (mostly single-resident-occupancy units (SROs) lost to expensive residential developments. To ensure units are replaced, the program enforces three strategies: any developer who converts, demolishes or closes any SROs is responsible for replacing each unit; for each unit demolished, the developer must pay a fee of $1,000; and for each new development, a development cost levy is collected and earmarked for replacement housing. A portion of the money collected from the cost levy is used to support social housing projects developed under BC's social housing program, to buy SRO hotels and upgrade them, to buy land for future social housing and to subsidize the construction of affordable rental housing (Canadian Mortgage and Housing Corporation 2011b).

Community Church Renovated into Affordable Housing: The City of Middleton, Wisconsin, renovated an existing church into affordable senior rental housing. The old Middleton Community Church now offers one- or two-bedroom apartments for rent to qualified seniors (Active Living Options 2011).

Regulation

Commitment to Housing Rights: In 2009, the City of Toronto created the Toronto Housing Charter — Opportunity for All that commits to supporting the housing rights for all citizens. The charter states that all residents should have a safe, secure, affordable and well-maintained home from which to realize their potential, be able to live in their neighborhood of choice without discrimination, enjoy equal treatment in housing without discrimination as provided by the Ontario Human Rights Code and be protected from discriminatory practices that limit their housing opportunities (City of Toronto 2009).

Linkage Program: Linkage programs collect a portion of the value created by investment in neighborhoods undergoing substantial development and direct that value to build affordable housing, to provide job training, and to fund social services in less fortunate neighborhoods. While linkage programs have operated for several years in US cities such as Boston and San Francisco, they are also becoming more popular in other communities. The Linkage Task Force of the San Diego Housing Commission supports the Housing Trust Fund, which is used as seed money and to match affordable housing funding from state and federal governments. The San Diego Linkage fee is $1.06 per square foot of office space, $0.80 per square foot of research and development space, $0.64 per square foot of hotels, retail and manufacturing and $0.27 per square foot of warehouse (SDHC 2009).

Affordable Housing Ordinance: The City of Chicago's Affordable Requirement Ordinance was first passed in 2003 and updated in 2007 to require developers to create affordable units. Any development of ten or more units where the developers purchased land from the city or required a zoning change are required to have 10 percent affordable units, while those receiving financial assistance supplied by the city are required to have 20 percent affordable units. Developers may also choose to pay an in lieu fee of approximately $100, 000 per unit, based on the Consumer Price Index, to the city's Affordable Housing Opportunity Fund (Centre for Housing Policy 2010).

Creating Community

To create a "sense of place" and foster connection among people, the physical placement of buildings must draw people together and encourage an atmosphere of peace, security and pride among residents of a community. In addition to thoughtful building design, clean streets, gardens and trees, places to gather can create a village-like atmosphere even in inner-city neighborhoods. Ideally, closeness to other people is mirrored in closeness to nature and integration of ecology into community living.

However, the physical design of housing and neighborhoods alone cannot create communities. Government policies and the actions and initiatives of local citizens are critical. Churches have often been the center of community, but in more recent times, people have

---

Small Steps to Creating Good Neighborhoods

- **Learn the names of your neighbors**. Develop meaningful relationships and social bonds. Hosting a block party is a good way to meet other residents who don't live in your direct vicinity. Include all residents of the neighborhood regardless of cultural, religious, age or mobility differences.
- **Welcome people who are less mobile or who have disabilities.** These individuals often feel vulnerable and perhaps untrusting of others. Check in with people who have special needs after electricity outages or other problems to make sure they are ok.
- **Develop partnerships with local merchants.** Residents and local businesses often share similar interests and can work together to improve the neighborhood.
- Develop a group email for your block to share news about block events or projects. Neighbors can also share a list of kids who are willing to do small jobs such as babysitting, shoveling snow or mowing lawns.
- **Establish a block safety or neighborhood watch system** to keep kids safe as they play in the neighborhood.
- **Be prepared for emergencies** by having the contact information for your neighbors.
- **Work together with your neighbors to deal with issues like crime, vandalism, speeding cars or problem houses.** Deal with problems while they are still small. Develop good relationships with the local police and work with them to solve problems (Neighborhood Resource Center of Colorado 2011).

also sought connection through involvement in neighborhood groups and activities, and participation in other non-government organizations such as environmental groups.

While responsible participation in governance is important, getting to know your neighbors is a simple first step. Getting involved and creating opportunities for inclusiveness are even bigger steps. True and rich community is a mix of people of many ages, socioeconomic backgrounds, ethnicity and abilities sharing their lives.

Promoting Healthy Communities

A healthy community reflects the health of its citizens. A century ago, municipalities were instrumental in improving public health by preventing the spread of disease through slum clearance, community planning, water treatment and the provision of certain health services. These initiatives were based on the view of health as the absence of disease, and disease prevention as the main challenge for local government. But health is influenced more by the physical and social environments in which

---

Looking Beyond Housing to Community Development
By John Emmeus Davis

Housing has long been a bellwether of neighborhood well-being or, conversely, of neighborhood decline. Many public and private interventions aimed at stabilizing or revitalizing residential neighborhoods have been focused primarily (sometimes exclusively) on improving the local housing stock. This once meant bulldozing entire blocks of "blighted" buildings and replacing them with newly constructed publicly subsidized rentals. Subsequent interventions were aimed at rehabilitating a built environment that already provided affordable housing, or deconcentrating poverty by making it easier for low-income people to "move to opportunity" outside of inner-city neighborhoods or promoting a wider range of incomes by increasing the incidence of owner-occupied housing in neighborhoods dominated by rental housing. The supposition, in every case, was that "good housing," whether defined in terms of condition, affordability or tenure, was sufficient for a "good neighborhood." Secure the one, you secured the other.

The centrality of housing has been challenged in more recent years by a new generation of city planners, non-profit developers and community organizers who have advanced a more comprehensive vision of community development. Without denying that housing can play a large role in determining a neighborhood's fate, they point out that jobs, schools, parks, gardens, stores, safety and services do so as well. Good housing is not enough.

Such criticism has been a useful corrective, generating neighborhood plans and redevelopment strategies that go *beyond housing* in seeking to create communities that are healthy, safe, equitable and sustainable. There is sometimes a risk, however, of pushing the pendulum too far the other way, where housing is removed from the mix of strategies for rebuilding community; where public dollars for affordable housing are diverted to other uses; where too much reliance is placed on market forces to generate housing that persons of modest means can afford. If the non-housing aspects of community development have been slighted in the past, the solution lies not in ignoring housing, but in enhancing the *linkages* between housing and services, housing and transportation, housing and jobs and the like. This, in fact, is what the best of a new generation of planners and developers is endeavoring to do.

we live and work than by interventions of the healthcare system.

Since the mid-1980s, municipal governments in Europe and North America have adopted a broader conception of public health. Although the name *healthy communities* implies a focus on medical care, the World Health Organization (1986) recognized that the fundamental conditions and resources (social determinants) for health are peace, adequate shelter, education, food, income, a stable ecosystem, sustainable resources, social justice and equity. Thus, a healthy community not only provides adequate housing that is affordable, secure and fosters a sense of pride and place — it goes beyond housing to improve citizen health. Healthy communities promote equality amongst all residents and provide access to clean air and water, healthy housing that is affordable and safe, equal access to health services, healthy food options, secure jobs and education. A healthy community promotes mental and physical health and provides equal access to green space and community facilities (Mikkonen & Raphael 2010). Local governments play a big role in all these areas through their impact on public hygiene (waste disposal and water systems), food access and handling, zoning to separate industrial from residential land uses, other public health regulations, recreational facilities, education, transportation, economic development and land-use planning.

The healthy communities approach is based on a worldwide healthy cities movement, which emerged from the World Health Organization and more specifically, the Ottawa Charter in 1986 (World Health Organization 1986). The movement subsequently gained sanction as World Health Organization Europe's healthy cities program. Aspects of the program have been implemented in countries around the world, including Australia, Asia, the United States and Canada (Smith et al. 2008). While Canada's version of the healthy cities program expired in the 1990s due to a lack of funding, many Canadian communities are still establishing programs that address aspects of health such as community safety, youth programs and recreational opportunities.

Tools and Initiatives
Voluntary

Volunteer Park Patrollers: In Vancouver, volunteer park patrollers rollerblade or bicycle around the 15-kilometer (9.3-mile) seawall path in Stanley Park. In addition to enjoying comradery, the wheeling park patrollers ensure that the many cyclists, joggers and rollerbladers are safely enjoying the spectacular public park.

Moorhead Youth Partnership: In 1995, community members in Moorhead, Minnesota, started the neighborhood Healthy Community Initiative, now known as the Metro Youth Partnership. The initiative focuses on improving the well-being of youth through three goals: to engage, empower and equip youth for bright futures. Today the initiative runs three core programs: Asset Champions which builds assets in youth homes, neighborhoods, schools and workplaces; Metrolink mentoring programs; and community scholarships for children aged K-12 to empower youth to participate in enrichment activities (Metro Youth Partnership 2011).

Community Walks: Jane's Walk offers residents the opportunity to meet while walking through the streets of their community; sharing stories and history of the neighborhood. Jane's Walk fosters a sense of belonging and helps overcome geographic, economic and cultural barriers. The walk, inspired by the legendary urban thinker, writer and activist Jane Jacobs, is free and organized by volunteers. Since its inception in 2007, Jane's Walk has been organized in 68 North American cities including Toronto, New York, Ottawa, Washington and Boston. In 2010, over 10,000 people took part in 424 different walks (Jane's Walk 2010).

Greater University Circle Initiative: Since 2005, a coalition led by the Cleveland Foundation (a community-based foundation supported by local donors) has created the Greater University Circle initiative. This initiative focuses on revitalizing and connecting the Greater University Circle area (Cleveland's world-class district of cultural, educational and medical institutions) and its four surrounding neighborhoods. Projects focus on improving housing conditions and offering mortgage and home-repair assistance to low- and moderate-income families, enhancing local school options, providing job training and preferred access to jobs for qualified residents, identifying and promoting opportunities for purchasing products and services locally and enhancing neighborhood safety and security (Cleveland Foundation 2011).

Dudley Street Neighborhood Initiative: The Dudley Street Neighborhood Initiative was formed in 1984 by Boston residents concerned with the grim future of the Roxbury/ North Dorchester neighborhoods which were plagued by arson, disinvestment and neglect. In 1987, the residents jointly created a comprehensive revitalization plan focusing on community development without gentrification, to enhance the physical, economic and human development of the community to create a vibrant and diverse neighborhood. Through a collaborative effort of over 3,000 individuals, businesses, non-profits and religious institutions, vacant lots that previously attracted crime have been transformed into over 400 new affordable housing units, as well as community centers, new schools, parks, playgrounds, gardens and other public spaces. The initiative has also created programs to empower neighborhood youth and support resident participation in community development (Dudley Street Neighborhood Initiative 2008).

Financial Incentives

VanCity Award: VanCity Credit Union in Vancouver, British Columbia, helps to support and publicly recognize citizens and organizations active in the community. Between 2001 and 2009, VanCity offered the $1 million VanCity Award to six projects designed to enhance the social, environmental or economic well-being of the community. For example, the Phoenix Centre Project, run by the Phoenix Drug and Alcohol Recovery and Education Society, was awarded one of the million dollar awards. The project offers addiction services, transitional housing and employment and education services to recovering addicts. Since its completion in 2007, over 100 recovering addicts have been served every year (Vancouver City Savings Credit Union 2011).

Strengthening Sense of Community: Through the Neighborhood Improvement Matching Fund, the City of Raleigh, North Carolina, is offering neighborhood-based organizations funding for projects that help improve neighborhoods and sense of community. Organizations can receive up to $1,000 or 75 percent of the project's cost (Official City of Raleigh Website 2011).

Environmental Fund: Established in 1994, the New York City Environmental Fund provides grants for environmental education, public access and stewardship projects that benefit New York City communities and their citizens. Grants range from $5,000 to $25,000. Past projects include beach cleanups, educational programs for kids and teenagers, environmental awareness campaigns and environmentally based internships. Since 1997, over $9 million has been granted to over 300 organizations in every borough of New York City. The fund also supports larger environmental initiatives working to revitalize neglected natural areas around the city (Hudson River Foundation 2011).

Expenditure

Healthy Communities Coalition: The Ontario Healthy Community Coalition (OHCC) emerged as an informal group from the Healthy Toronto 2000 workshop. It was established formally as the provincial secretariat to provide a broad range of services and resources to help local Healthy Community coalitions become established and flourish province-wide. Their mission seeks to achieve social, environmental and economic health and well-being for individuals, communities and local governments. OHCC provides support through regional community animators who work closely with community groups and coalitions to identify and provide for their training and development requirements. OHCC also produces educational resources, maintains an educational resource library, produces a biannual newsletter and organizes an annual Healthy Communities Conference (OHCC 2011).

Identifying Opportunities for At-risk Youth: A collaboration between the City of Champaign, Illinois, the local school and park district, Don Moyer Boys and Girls Club and the United Way of Champaign established the CommUnity Matters program in 2007. The program provides activities for at-risk youth in three neighborhoods within the city. Activities include summer day camps, sports and arts programs, job and computer training, career counseling and college visits. City officials say that since the program's inception, arrest rates have declined and participants of the program are pursuing college, something they may not have done prior to the program (Wade 2011).

Safety Audits: In Toronto, the Metropolitan Action Committee conducts safety audits of neighborhoods, apartment complexes, shopping centers, parks and other public spaces to evaluate lighting, access to emergency phones, overgrown shrubbery near bus shelters and so on. The safety audits are conducted by community members who live, work and play in the neighborhood and are considered to be safety experts. Government authorities use the information to guide decisions about safety improvements within their jurisdiction. The organization has since produced a guide for auditing women's safety. It has been translated into numerous languages and adapted for use in European and African cities (Metro Action Committee 2011).

Community Police and Patrol: In downtown Vancouver, British Columbia, community police centers are opening up in small storefronts to help bring police closer to citizens. As they walk or bike throughout the neighborhood, police officers get to know local residents and inform community members about opportunities for assistance.

Safe Streets for Seniors: New York City's Senior Pedestrian Safety Program aims to improve road infrastructure to make streets more pedestrian friendly for seniors. Areas with high concentrations of car accidents involving seniors were identified for all New York City boroughs. Initiatives such as calibrating time signals to a walking speed of three feet per second, repairing curbs and pedestrian ramps and installing new crosswalks, pedestrian fencing, ramps and neckdowns or pedestrian refuge islands were conducted in each identified area (New York City DOT 2011).

Regulation

Community well-being and participation can't be regulated into being. However, monitoring and visualizing what a community can be like are integral to ensuring community development. See chapter 15 on governance for more on indicators of community development.

Junk Food Ban in Schools: While trying to target childhood obesity, the World Health Organization called for a ban of junk food, including candy, potato chips and soda, in all elementary schools. As of 2011, the Ontario provincial government has set minimum nutritional standards for food sold in schools and banned the sale of junk food from school vending machines in an effort to improve the eating habits of students. The nutrition standards are designed to ensure that food obtained at school promotes "healthy growth and development" of students (OMOE 2010).

Let's Move Campaign: Launched in the United States by First Lady Michelle Obama, the Let's Move Campaign aims to reduce childhood obesity by educating and motivating citizens to be physically active and eat healthy, motivating leaders from all sectors impacting children's health to make commitments to the movement, passing legislation to support the initiative and working alongside a task force to combat obesity. As part of the campaign, the Healthy, Hunger-Free Kids Act of 2010 was passed. This act authorizes funding for federal school meal and child nutrition programs and increases access to healthy food for low-income children (White House 2010).

Chapter 11

Green Building

The spaces we live, work and play in are very important to our quality of life. On average, North Americans spend approximately 90 percent of their lives indoors (Black & Straube 2007). Buildings also account for 39 percent of energy use in the United States, and worldwide use 13.6 percent of global potable water and 40 percent of raw materials (USGBC 2009a). But all buildings — homes, commercial retail buildings, institutions or industrial buildings — can be built to sustainable standards that reduce these environmental impacts and improve human health and well-being.

Buildings are also manifestations of communities' physical capital and certainly impact our natural capital. Their many functions facilitate the development of social and cultural capital, enhance our human capital through work and education and build economic capital for businesses and organizations. Well-designed buildings can facilitate community mobilization.

This chapter will look closely at buildings as a key component of communities' physical capital, define green building and review the various certification systems, explore the convergence of green building and affordable housing and discuss how green buildings are undergoing a reconceptualization as living buildings.

Redefining Building

Buildings have a life cycle that spans design, construction, operation and demolition. At all of these stages, they can have profound impacts on human health, social interactions and our ecosystems. Conventional methods of building contribute to ecological, social and economic degradation of our communities. In the United States, for example, buildings account for approximately 38 percent of carbon dioxide emissions and 13 percent of water consumption (EIA 2008). In more than 30 percent of US buildings, the indoor air quality of a building is considered "sick," in that it could lead to absenteeism or health problems (Black & Straube 2007).

In design and practice, green building considers location, construction, maintenance and decommissioning to minimize environmental impacts of building and create spaces

Fig. 11.1: *Hammarby Sjöstad, a new community in suburban Stockholm, is transforming a polluted ex-industrial site into a neighborhood for young families with 11,000 apartments. Many green building principles have been incorporated, including passive solar, solar voltaic panels, a sewage collection system that collects waste heat and generates biogas, and linkage of apartments to Stockholm's district heating system.*

(Credit: La-Citta-Vita on Flickr, Creative Commons)

Sick Building Syndrome

Exposure to indoor air pollution can lead to sick building syndrome (SBS), a physiological response to exposure to toxins in residences or workplaces. SBS is known to cause respiratory ailments, skin irritation, hypersensitivity and other general health concerns (EPA 2010b). SBS causes include exposure to mold and mildew, volatile organic compounds (VOC) and other toxic building materials; buildup of potentially hazardous gases; contamination of heating, ventilating and air-conditioning systems; and poor lighting and acoustics (EPA 2010a).

that are conducive to health, quality of life and productivity (CEC 2008; Pyke, McMahon & Dietsche 2010). Green buildings are designed to maximize natural sources of light, heat and ventilation to minimize waste production and conserve energy and water over their life cycles.

The benefits of green building are widespread and well understood. Green buildings are healthier to live and work in. Occupants of green buildings express 27 percent higher satisfaction than their counterparts in non-green buildings, and the buildings' average maintenance costs are 13 percent lower (USGBC 2009a). It is estimated that green buildings are 30 percent more energy-efficient, 30 to 50 percent more water-efficient, emit 35 percent less carbon emissions and produce 50 to 90 percent less waste from construction and operation than conventional North American buildings (CEC 2008; Yudelson 2008). Buildings that incorporate a net-zero energy goal, which means that their energy requirements are offset by energy generated by the site, use less than 50 percent of the energy required in standard construction (NSTC 2008).

To achieve this, green buildings can include sophisticated technologies, such as alternative energy sources (solar or geothermal, for example), greywater recycling systems and energy-efficient appliances. However, much of green building is simply good time-tested design practices — some of which go back to antiquity. More traditional green building practices, such as building orientation and design, maximizing natural light and ventilation, improved insulation and sourcing of recycled and sustainable construction materials, are also key.

Green building often uses what is known as a *whole-building-systems approach*, in which key stakeholders, such as architects, engineers and contractors, collaborate from the beginning of the design process through to the building's operation and maintenance. This has widened the range of skills required beyond architecture and engineering to include a variety of other professions (Pyke, McMahon & Dietsche 2010).

Green Building Certifications

How do we determine how "green" a building is? For example, is a building made with reclaimed timber greener than one made with all locally sourced materials? Certification systems have tackled the difficult task of comparing green buildings by developing objective criteria to evaluate construction designs and practices.

There are several widely recognized certification systems; the standards of each one reflects many years of research and industry knowledge in their creation. Collectively, they evaluate the effects of building practices and describe methods that minimize the social and environmental impact of construction. Although the certifications differ somewhat in focus, they tend to share the following components:

- industry-vetted standards for green building
- transparent checklists and auditing processes
- third-party verification of standards compliance
- a rating system that is easily understandable by industry and consumers

BUILDING RESEARCH ESTABLISHMENT ENVIRONMENTAL ASSESSMENT METHOD (BREEAM): UK AND WORLDWIDE

BREEAM was the first environmental assessment method for new and existing buildings. It uses standards to measure the performance of a building, and rates the building according to a scale of *pass, good, very good, excellent* or *outstanding*. These standards are tailored to the type of building (for example, school, office use or industrial). To date, the program has certified over 200,000 buildings, and over a million buildings are currently in the certification process. As the first green building certification system, BREEAM has arguably influenced all other rating systems (BREEAM 2011).

LEADERSHIP IN ENERGY AND ENVIRONMENTAL DESIGN (LEED): US AND WORLDWIDE

The LEED certification system was designed by the US Green Building Council (USGBC) in the late 1990s to be a transparent and third-party-verified process to certify new green buildings. In 2008, the Green Building Certification Institute (GBCI) was created to administer the certifications. In recent years, the LEED standards have evolved to include not only new buildings but also commercial interiors, existing buildings, school and healthcare facilities and the core and shell of buildings.

The LEED system works on a 100-point scale, awarding point values to categories of

Fig. 11.2: *Dockside Green in Victoria, BC is LEED-certified, incorporating solar and wind power, green roofs, a centralized biomass gasification plant, and a greywater reclamation system.* (CREDIT: JAYSCRATCH, FLICKR. COM, CREATIVE COMMONS)

impacts. The maximum score in each category differs according to the type of projects (for example, *new construction* has a maximum of 26 points for the site choice, while *commercial interiors* has a maximum of 21). Categories include sustainable sites, water efficiency, energy and atmosphere, materials and resources and indoor environmental quality. As well, two bonus categories recognize innovation in design and regional priority, adding up to an additional 10 points. To achieve basic certification, a project must earn 40 to 49 points; 50 to 59 points merits silver, gold projects have achieved 60 to 79 points, and platinum projects must have earned 80 or more points. This certification system is one of the world's most popular, and is used in 41 countries (GBCI 2011; USGBC 2011a).

BUILDING OWNERS AND MANAGERS ASSOCIATION: BUILDING ENVIRONMENTAL STANDARDS (BOMA BESt), CANADA

In 2005, LEED focused solely on new buildings, which created a gap in the certification field. In response, a Canadian organization, the Building Owners and Managers Association (BOMA), launched BOMA BESt: a national certification program based on energy and environmental performance of existing buildings. The program evolved from a Canadian version of the BREEAM method, as well as the Green Globe assessment system, an independent online tool that was purchased and incorporated into a new online BOMA BESt tool. BOMA BESt also incorporated BOMA's previous Go Green Best Practices and Go Green Plus Assessment programs.

BOMA BESt's is a four-level performance certification program. A Level-4 certified building has met over 90 percent of the Go Green Plus Assessment standards and all of the BOMA Go Green Best Practices. Unlike the LEED program, the BOMA BESt has a greater focus on creation of environmental management plans, policies and programs for currently occupied buildings (BOMA 2011).

GREEN BUILDING INITIATIVE: GREEN GLOBES, US

While the Canadian version of Green Globes became BOMA BESt, the Green Building Initiative (GBI) in the United States bought the rights and continued the online certification program under the name Green Globes. This program assesses the environmental performance and sustainability of new and existing commercial buildings. Ratings are completed by a third-party assessor using the online assessment tool. Buildings earn 1-Globe to 4-Globe ratings (GBI 2011).

LIVING BUILDING CHALLENGE, US AND WORLDWIDE

Living buildings are the next wave in green building thinking. The basic concept of a living building is that it goes beyond using green materials and reducing environmental impacts. Living buildings have either a net-zero impact, restore the ecological functions or generate more energy than they consume. In essence, living buildings give back more than they take. The Living Building Challenge was launched by Jason F. McLennan, prior to joining Cascadia Green Building Council as CEO in 2009; the International Living Building Institute was created to administer the challenge. Although living building certification is currently more of a conceptual challenge than a rigorous checklist, three completed projects in 2011 have been recognized as living buildings (ILBI 2011).

Force for Good

By Jessica Woolliams

For the first time in history — or at least since the Industrial Revolution — the building and development industry is poised to be a significant force for environmental good in the next few decades. Yes, good. And yes, I mean the overall building and development industry, not just the small slice of "green" buildings that now makes up perhaps 5 to 10 percent of new building starts in Canada but in the US is expected to reach upwards of 25 percent of the new and retrofit market by just 2013.

The 2030 Challenge — adopted by the US Conference of Mayors, many Canadian cities, the US federal government and many regulatory and industry bodies — requires buildings be built to zero fossil fuel use by 2030. California will require new homes be built to net-zero energy by 2020 and new commercial buildings by 2030; the European Parliament will require all member states to ensure all new buildings are nearly zero-energy buildings by 2021 and all publicly owned new buildings are built to this near-zero energy standard by 2018. Plans and programs are afoot ensuring existing buildings will be brought up to these standards in the years following.

These laws are signs that the building industry is learning. They are learning from the tens of thousands of buildings in Europe built to passive-house standards, that it is possible to affordably reduce energy use to 90 percent below standard construction. They are learning, from tens of thousands of LEED certified buildings around the world, that the increased livability of many green buildings creates greater value than even the energy savings (in increased productivity, better test scores, faster healing rates). They are learning from the first Living Buildings that we can aim not just for zero energy, water and toxins, but to heal our ecosystems and communities.

Communities like Solarsiedlung, in Freiburg, Germany, which generates many times more energy than it uses;

University of California, Davis's West Village, aiming to be one of the largest net-zero energy communities in the US; and Alberta's Drake Landing solar community begin to show what is possible when we start to take energy seriously. The first Living Buildings certified were the Hawaii Preparatory Academy Energy Lab, the Omega Center for Sustainable Living and the Tyson Living Learning Center (at the Living Building level), and Eco-Sense (at the Petal level). They begin to show what is possible when we start to take sustainability seriously. Today's Living Buildings could be tomorrow's Living Communities. If policymakers, industry and consumers line up to support the current momentum, there is a historic opportunity to change humanity's relationship with its home.

Fig 11.3: *Beddington Zero Energy Development (BedZED) is an environmentally-friendly housing development in Hackbridge, London, England. The highly energy-efficient buildings were constructed from renewable or recycled sources within 35 miles of the site and have been designed to use only energy from renewable sources generated onsite, incorporating passive solar, solar panels, a cogeneration plant for heating and electricity, and a greywater reclamation system.* (CREDIT: TOM CHANCE)

Fig. 11.4:
*UniverCity's Child
Care Centre has been
designed to meet
the Cascadia Region
Green Building
Council's Living
Building Challenge.*
(Credit: Courtesy
of Hughes Condon
Marler Architects/
SFU Community Trust,
Burnaby, BC, UniverCity
Childcare Project)

Other Certification Programs

Green Star: Australia

Green Star certification program for homes, commercial buildings, institutions and public buildings scores a building in two assessments and awards points for green practices. A score of 45 or more earns a Green Star certified rating. The program was created in 2003; to date, there is more than 4 million square meters of Green Star certified space in Australia, and another 8 million registered to undergo certification (GBCA 2011).

BuiltGreen: Canada

Taking a slightly different angle, Natural Resources Canada's BuiltGreen program offers certified training programs for construction companies or individuals. Levels of certification include bronze, silver, gold and platinum; all applicants' work is certified by an outside third party (BuiltGreen 2011).

Passivhaus: Germany

A passive house is a building where the inside temperature can be maintained without additional heating and cooling systems. Using techniques such as insulation, double-pane windows, airtight construction and specific designs, these homes use the least amount of energy possible. While there is no third-party certification for a passive house, tools are available for architects to undertake their own self-assessments (Passivhaus Institut 2011).

Marketing Power of Green Building Certifications

The well-researched, industry-vetted and transparent criteria of these certification systems are only half of the certification story. As seen in the examples above, a significant value of green building certification schemes is in building public awareness of what green building is and why we should do it. Certificates offer a ready way to communicate with consumers at all levels.

There is much evidence that green building certification systems have great marketing power. For example, one study of green certified homes in Seattle and Portland found that certified homes in Seattle sold for a premium of 9.6 percent, and from 3 to 5 percent in Portland. Additionally, certified homes were on the market for 18 fewer days than homes that were not certified (Griffin, Kaufman & Hamilton 2009).

Certifications at the Neighborhood Scale

Green building is about much more than the design of buildings in isolation; it also considers the position of buildings among others and in relation to the natural environment in order to promote efficient, healthy places with minimal environmental impacts. Building to a green standard considers the placement of buildings to limit users' transportation requirements, encourage walking and cycling, support social capital, reduce and recycle waste as well as curb wasteful resource use. As well, project designs consider the composition of buildings in a given setting in terms of uses (commercial, office, institutional and housing), housing types and price ranges, as well as access and orientation to recreational facilities, natural areas and parks (USGBC 2011b). LEED Neighborhood Design (LEED-ND) is a certification process for sustainable neighborhood design that integrates green building principles with those of Smart Growth and New Urbanism.

LEED–ND

Developed by the US Green Building Council, LEED-ND grades individual project development plans using objective measurable criteria in three credit categories: smart location and linkage; neighborhood pattern and design; and green infrastructure and buildings. Projects can earn credits in each category and certification when their overall credit total meets established thresholds. This program suits all sizes of projects, from large master-planned communities to small infill projects (USGBC 2011b).

It is important to note that LEED-ND is not intended to substitute for comprehensive municipal plans; nor is it intended to evaluate components of sustainability at the city or regional level. The STAR Community Index for sustainability, developed jointly by ICLEI and the USGBC, is more appropriate when evaluating components of sustainability at the city or county level (ICLEI 2007). As well, LEED-ND works best when evaluating projects whose building square footage consists of at least 50 percent new buildings or buildings undergoing major renovations.

Fig. 11.5: *Passive solar building includes five distinct design elements: an aperture or collector; an absorber; a thermal mass; a distribution method; and a control mechanism. To capture the heat of the sun in the winter, but block the sun in the summer, this passive solar design uses an overhang to control the amount of light entering the house.* (CREDIT: JEREMY LEVINE DESIGN, CREATIVE COMMONS)

Retrofitting Existing Buildings

Although green building is surely the way forward in construction, we cannot hope to address the problem of building-related emissions and energy use simply by constructing *new* green buildings. It's critical that we look at our existing buildings. In the United States, 83 percent of homes were built before 1990, and in the American northwest a whopping 92 percent of homes were built in 1990 or earlier (US Census Bureau 2000; William 2004). Consequently, the importance of retrofitting existing buildings for sustainability cannot be understated.

Retrofitting refers to replacement of older technology with newer technology, without completely changing the entire system. Many things can be retrofitted — such as cars, an IT system or buildings. Applied to green buildings, the term generally refers to implementation of resource-saving technologies in existing buildings. Retrofitting can help reduce carbon dioxide emissions, water consumption and energy use (Birkeland 2009). Similarly, it can reduce utility and maintenance costs, reduce the risk of costly repairs and generate more local jobs (FCM n.d.). Retrofitting can also be applied to neighborhoods. For more information, see chapter 9.

Most of the green certification systems described above have recognized the value of retrofitting and developed standards for existing buildings. But certification isn't the primary reason for most retrofitting: motivating factors are usually energy cost savings, property resale value and ecological concerns.

Green Leases

Retrofitting can be seen as problematic to tenants and landlords in multi-unit homes as lease agreements discourage transparency and gives energy management rights to only one party. This is also known as the *"split-incentive"* problem: for example, the landlord has chosen a monthly averaging plan where the tenant has little influence on monthly rates, or the tenant is paying the energy bills and the landlord has no control on how the tenant uses energy. A *green lease* could solve this problem. A green lease is simply a lease with a section that outlines energy use and shared goals for reduction. It might include shared payment responsibilities and agreed-upon targets for environmental performance by both the landlord and the tenant; it could also include rent increases or decreases contingent on performance on the goals and dispute resolution mechanisms to effectively govern the goals. This type of thinking could also be used for indoor air quality, materials used in the building, recycling or any other environmental initiative (Winton 2008).

Energy Retrofits

In buildings, the main systems that consume energy are space heating, water heating, refrigeration, lighting, cooking and air conditioning (Abrahamse et al. 2005). It's more critical than ever that we examine these systems. Despite the awareness that greenhouse gas (GHG) emissions are accelerating climate change, GHG emissions related to energy use in the United States were 15.8 percent more in 2008 compared to 1990 levels (US DOE 2009).

Retrofitting energy systems in buildings refers to replacing appliances such as fuel- and energy-guzzling furnaces, hot water heaters and refrigerators, and preventing heat loss through proper insulation and air sealing. Financial incentives to do this in residential homes are increasingly offered by governments (see, for example, Natural Resources Canada 2011).

Maximizing the value of retrofits requires that that we collect baseline information and measure our progress. Energy audits offer a way to do this: they can measure current energy use and compare how that use could be decreased through changing technologies, behaviors or both. In Canada, people can earn rebates for energy audit costs through the ecoEnergy program when subsequent audits shows significant decreases in energy use (Natural Resources Canada 2011). More energy-saving ideas are explored in chapter 7.

Water Retrofits

Water conservation programs can encourage the sustainable use of municipal water systems, and postpone or avoid large-scale upgrades. Two common types of water retrofits are toilets and faucets. High-efficiency toilets reduce the amount of water flushed from 20 to 60 percent, depending on the age of the previous toilet (BC Ministry of Housing 2011). Such toilets are now required by law in many regions in North America. Low-flow showerheads and faucets also reduce the amount of water used in daily activities.

One up-and-coming retrofit technology for water conservation is smart meters. Currently used for some electricity programs, smart meters can be installed in homes and commercial buildings to monitor exact water usage per building. Unlike systems in which users are billed based on estimates of their water use, systems that utilize such meters would encourage conservation through tailored rates (Jenkins 2010). Chapter 5 offers more discussion of water retrofits.

Retrofitting our current buildings can significantly reduce emissions and conserve water, but ultimately, the highest gains will require multiple participants working together. Truly changing our built environment will require homebuyers to understand the added value in green homes, municipalities and developers to invest in new technologies and higher-level governments to coordinate national strategies to support resource-saving retrofits (Hendricks et al. 2009).

Green Building Materials

The systems that provide heating, cooling, electricity and water are only part of the green building equation. At least as important are the materials used in construction and the actual construction practices.

By sourcing recycled and local materials and incorporating these into the design, green building can significantly decrease the carbon footprint of the construction process and help certain projects achieve certification. For example, LEED awards points for recycled or reclaimed materials, as well as materials that

have been sourced from within 500 miles of the construction site (USGBC 2009b).

As a building material, reclaimed wood is becoming increasingly popular. Some argue that the reclaimed wood beams found in barns or older homes are larger and stronger than the new materials on the market, due to the fact that they were taken from larger and older trees. Reclaimed wood is also being sourced from forests damaged by forest pests, such as the pine beetle epidemic in British Columbia. In the mid-2000s, countless hectares of trees were harvested early to slow the spread of the devastating beetle and to ensure that the trees could still be used for wood products. While they are not of the same grade as mature, beetle-free trees, there is an abundance of this wood that is sturdy enough for many uses.

Another building material that is much discussed as a sustainable alternative to new materials is concrete aggregate. An alternative to newly created concrete, this aggregate is made up of recycled concrete and, depending on the intended use of the material, other recycled materials such as glass, sand or rock.

Creative Reuse for Affordable Housing

In Victoria, BC, architect and designer Keith Dewey built his home out of eight decommissioned shipping containers. Using shipping containers can be more cost effective than wood or concrete because of the long steel beams in the containers.

By using the containers, Dewey saved the equivalent of five years of electricity and 70 trees, and reduced the construction cost of the home by about 28 percent (Paulsen 2010). Shipping containers have been used for housing around the world. The Container City in London, England, and Keetwonen in Amsterdam, Netherlands, are both examples of using containers to achieve a small footprint and recycled materials design.

While recycled materials reduce costs, they also reduce environmental impacts. One study of two homes, one built with all-recycled materials, the other with all-new materials, concluded that the recycled-material home impacted the environment 45 percent less over the building life cycle, and can decrease the amount of energy needed to operate the building by 17 percent (Thormark 2000; 2006).

Business Case for Green Buildings

The business case for green buildings gets stronger with every new or retrofitted green building. Perceptions that the costs of green buildings are greater than the benefits have proven to be untrue. Furthermore, green buildings also offer a variety of economic, productivity and risk management benefits (Yudelson 2009).

The economic benefits of green buildings are obvious: reduced operating costs, increased building valuation, eligibility for government funding grants and access to capital from responsible property investment funds. As well, green buildings have been shown to increase rent and occupancy rates, creating a win-win

situation in which tenants enjoy healthier homes that are recognized as socially responsible homes with lower monthly energy and water bills. One study compared LEED and US Energy Star-rated properties to non-green and found that green buildings had 4.1 percent greater occupancy and approximately 30 percent higher rental rates. Green buildings sold during the study period fetched on average $171 more per square foot (Dermisi 2009).

Green buildings require a slightly higher initial capital investment, but not that much: In Bradshaw et al.'s 2005 analysis, the average additional expenditure for a green building was just 2.42 percent of development costs. In the context of a life-cycle analysis, this additional upfront cost was negligible compared to the operating savings. Also of note was that 2.42 percent was the average; the actual costs of green building ranged from 18 percent below that of conventional housing costs to 9 percent above, showing that, with careful planning and experience, cost savings are possible (Bradshaw et al. 2005).

Undoubtedly, green buildings cost less to operate over the long term. In most analyses, like the one by Kats (2003) shown in table 11.1, long-term benefits far outweigh higher initial costs: green buildings cost about $3 to $5 more per square foot, but over 20 years, the extra investment yields a benefit of $50 to $65 per square foot.

Productivity benefits of green buildings are related to healthier work environments. One study of green buildings in the US found that maximizing natural light, providing good ventilation and eliminating toxic substances pays off with a decreasing absenteeism and tardiness and longer hours worked. Other benefits included reduced safety violations and

Table 11.1 Financial benefits of green buildings	
Summary of Findings (per square foot)	
Category	*20-Year Net Present Value*
Energy savings	$5.80
Emissions savings	$1.20
Water savings	$0.50
Operations & maintenance savings	$8.50
Health & productivity benefits	$36.90 to $55.30
Subtotal	**$52.90 to $71.30**
Average extra cost of building green	(-$3.00 to -$5.00)
Total 20-year net benefit	**($50.00 to $65.00)**

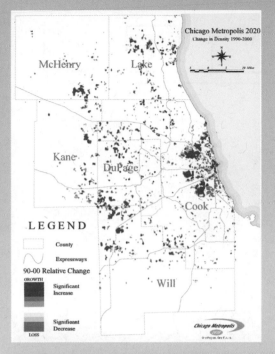

Fig. 2.1: *Chicago's business-as-usual growth (left) is compared to a nodal development plan (right). The nodal development plan indicates where housing development will be intensified. These centers were selected as a compromise between the "ideal" centers — according to the natural features of the landscape such as ridge lines and steep slopes — and the existing centers.*
(CREDIT: CHICAGO METROPOLIS)

Fig. 2.5: *Alternatives to sprawling suburbia. These images show development alternatives for the district municipality of Delta, British Columbia, as seen today (top), or by allowing its fertile agricultural land to be overtaken by sprawling development of single-family detached homes (middle), or by strengthening its economy by densifying its centre with a greater variety of housing, thereby retaining the use of precious agricultural land and protecting future homeowners from climate-change induced rise in sea levels (bottom).*
(SOURCE: CALP (COLLABORATIVE FOR ADVANCED LANDSCAPE PLANNING), 2010. LOCAL CLIMATE CHANGE VISIONING AND LANDSCAPE VISUALIZATIONS: GUIDANCE MANUAL, VERSION 1.1. UNIVERSITY OF BRITISH COLUMBIA. CREDIT: DAVID FLANDERS, UBC-CALP)

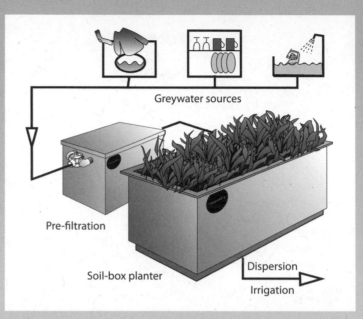

Fig. 4.5: Top left. *Eco-City Builders founder Richard Register shows how, over time, aging built structures (shown in pink) can be removed from around creeks, which can be daylighted and restored to their natural states.*
(CREDIT: RICHARD REGISTER)

Fig. 5.2: Top right. *Greywater systems reclaim, filter and minimally treat water from dishwashing, laundry, showers and bathtubs, allowing it to be reused for irrigation or other purposes.*
(CREDIT: WWW.GREYWATER.COM)

Fig. 7.3: Bottom right. *Geo-exchange systems use the temperature of the Earth to heat and cool buildings.*
(CREDIT: TERRY MURRAY, COURTESY OF MOHONK PRESERVE)

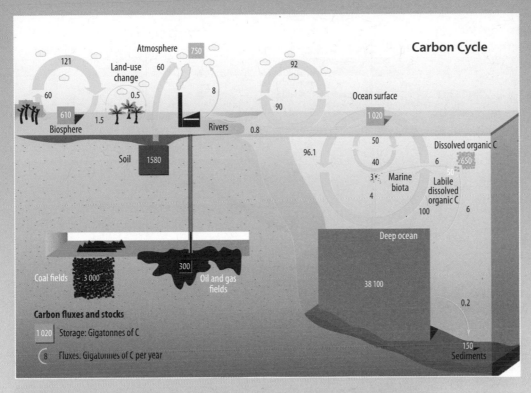

Fig. 13.1: *The carbon cycle: Carbon is the basis of all organic substances, from fossil fuels to human cells. Carbon moves constantly through living things, the land, ocean, atmosphere. When human activity starts driving this very complex cycle, the outcomes can be serious.*

(SOURCES: CENTER FOR CLIMATIC RESEARCH, INSTITUTE FOR ENVIRONMENTAL STUDIES, UNIVERSITY OF WISCONSIN AT MADISON; OKANAGAN UNIVERSITY COLLEGE, BC, DEPARTMENT OF GEOGRAPHY; WORLD WATCH, NOVEMBER-DECEMBER 1998; NATURE. UNEP/GRID-ARENDAL MAPS.GRIDA.NO/LIBRARY/FILES/STORAGE/BLUE-GREEN-CARBON-PROCESS_003.EPS)

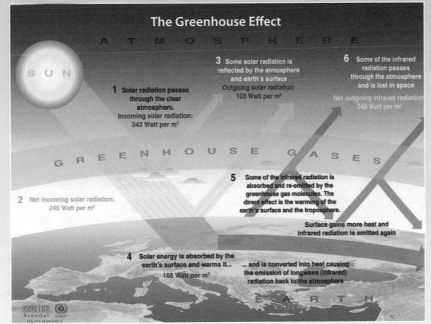

Fig. 13.2

(SOURCES: DESIGNED BY PHILIPPE REKACEWICZ, UNEP/GRID-ARENDAL. SOURCES: OKANAGAN UNIVERSITY COLLEGE, BC, DEPARTMENT OF GEOGRAPHY; UNIVERSITY OF OXFORD, SCHOOL OF GEOGRAPHY; UNITED STATES ENVIRONMENTAL PROTECTION AGENCY (EPA), WASHINGTON; CLIMATE CHANGE 1995, THE SCIENCE OF CLIMATE CHANGE, CONTRIBUTION OF WORKING GROUP I TO THE SECOND ASSESSMENT REPORT OF THE INTERGOVERNMENTAL PANEL ON CLIMATE CHANGE (IPCC), UNEP AND WMO (WORLD METEOROLOGICAL ORGANIZATION, CAMBRIDGE UNIVERSITY PRESS, 1996). MAPS.GRIDA.NO/GO/GRAPHIC/GREENHOUSE-EFFECT)

Fig. 13.3: *Solid lines are multi-model global averages of surface warming (relative to 1980–1999) for the scenarios A2, A1B and B1, shown as continuations of the 20th century simulations. Shading denotes the ±1 standard deviation range of individual model annual averages. The orange line is for the experiment where concentrations were held constant at year 2000 values. The grey bars at right indicate the best estimate (solid line within each bar) and the likely range assessed for the six SRES marker scenarios. The assessment of the best estimate and likely ranges in the grey bars includes the AOGCMs in the left part of the figure, as well as results from a hierarchy of independent models and observational constraints.*

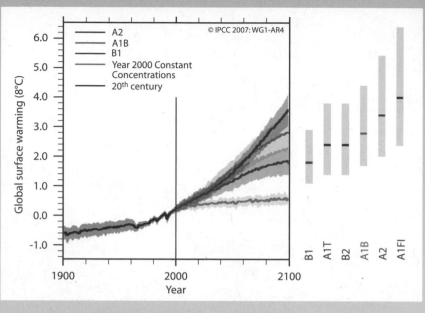

(SOURCES: CONTRIBUTION OF WORKING GROUP I TO THE FOURTH ASSESSMENT REPORT OF THE INTERGOVERNMENTAL PANEL ON CLIMATE CHANGE, 2007. S. SOLOMON, ET AL., EDS., CAMBRIDGE UNIVERSITY PRESS, UNITED KINGDOM AND NEW YORK. WWW.IPCC.CH/GRAPHICS/AR4-WG1/JPG/SPM5.JPG)

Fig. 13.4: *Many people associate climate change with rising sea levels and sudden calamitous weather events like hurricanes (left), but climate change also causes slow creeping changes that can be equally devastating to local economies, such as the biggest forest insect blight this continent has ever seen: the mountain pine beetle epidemic. Damaged timber is evident in the presence of reddish trees.*

(SOURCES: NASA/GSFC/JEFF SCHMALTZ/MODIS (LEFT) AND LUCIA GROSNER (RIGHT))

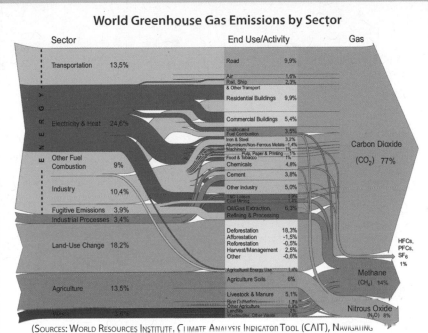

World Greenhouse Gas Emissions by Sector

Fig. 13.6: *World Greenhouse gas emissions by sector. All data is for 2000. All calculations are based on CO_2 equivalents, using 100-year global warming potentials from the IPCC (1996), based on a total global estimate of 41 755 MtCO2 equivalent. Land-use change includes both emissions and absorptions. Dotted lines represent flows of less than 0.1 percent of total GHG emissions.* (Cartographer/designer: UNEP/GRID-Arendal)

(Sources: World Resources Institute, Climate Analysis Indicator Tool (CAIT), Navigating the Numbers: Greenhouse Gas Data and International Climate Policy, December 2005; Intergovernmental Panel on Climate Change, 1996 (data for 2000). maps.grida.no/library/files/storage/world_greenhouse_gas_bysector.jpg)

Fig. 16.1: *Geovisualization tool: Green Maps like this one of Craik, Saskatchewan, recognize and promote local initiatives for environmental sustainability. This map shows features of the Craik Sustainable Living Project (CSLP), a community-endorsed plan to create Saskatchewan's first eco-village and revitalize this rural community in a sustainable way.* (Map courtesy of Craik Sustainable Living Project)

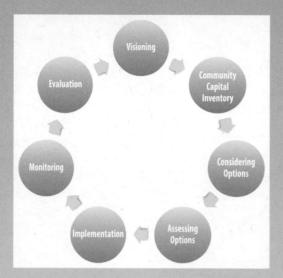

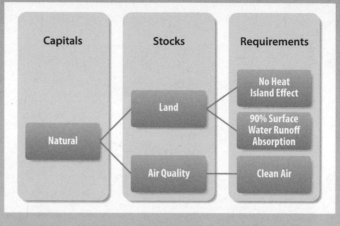

Fig. 17.2: *The analytical framework for the Community Sustainability Balance Sheet and the Community Capital Scan.*

Fig. 17.1: Top left.
Community Capital Framework Steps. The seven steps of the Community Capital Tool are similar to other seven-step strategic planning processes (e.g., Markey et al., 2005, 123). The added value of the Community Capital Tool, however, is the framework itself; it provides well-defined activities and instruments to permit clear and rational decision-making.

Fig. 17.4: *Bottom right. The Community Sustainability Balance Sheet Framework: An overview of the relationships between capitals, stocks, requirements, indicators and norms is shown for a subset of natural capital.*

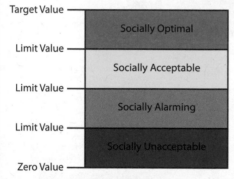

Fig. 17.3: *Indicator Measuring Scale: A unique measuring scale is developed for each indicator.*

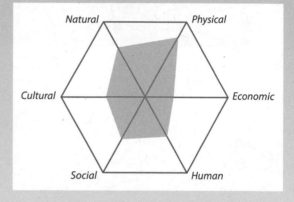

Fig. 17.5: *This figure represents the original state of capital in Centerville.*

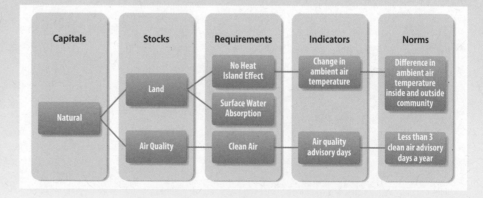

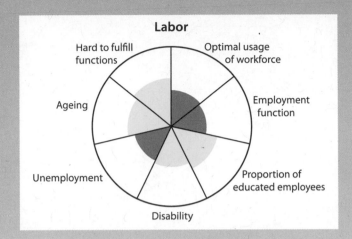

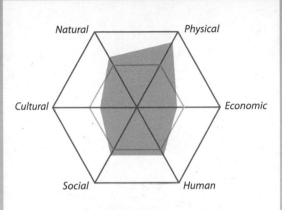

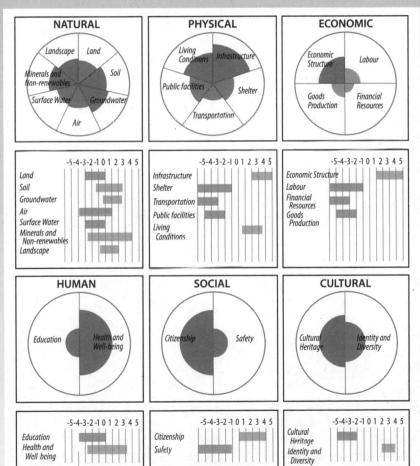

Fig. 17.6: Top left. *The output for the Labor Stock visually displays the capacity for each indicator. The colors of the pie slices represent where the indicator measures on the scale of socially optimal to socially unacceptable (see Figure 17.3). Yellow is socially acceptable, and orange is socially alarming. Green (socially optimal) and red (socially unacceptable) are not shown.*

Fig. 17.7: Bottom left. *The solid bars show the variance in answers among the group. The green bar represents a positive mean value across all respondents, whereas red represents a negative value.*

Fig. 17.8: Top right. *The results of the Scan show that the proposed mixed-use development in Centerville will increase natural, physical, social and human capitals, and decrease economic and cultural capitals. The inner hexagon represents the baseline situation where there is no influence of the proposed project on the capitals.*

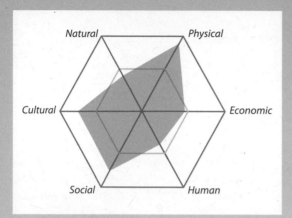

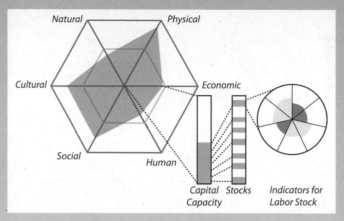

Fig. 17.9: Top left. *The impact of the development on Centerville over time shows an increase in physical, social and cultural capitals and a decrease in natural, economic and human capitals.*

Fig. 17.10: Top right. *This image shows a decrease in Centerville's natural, economic and human capitals and an increase in physical, social and cultural capitals after implementation. The diagram also shows a more detailed image of the changes in economic capital. The bar graph to the left displays the cumulative capacity of the capital, while the bar to the right shows the same capacity broken down by stocks. The circle to the far right displays the results of each indicator (See Figure 17.6 for the individual title for each indicator).*

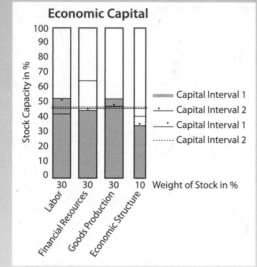

Fig. 17.11: *The four bar graphs depict the change in economic capital stocks over the course of the two time intervals. The X-axis represents each stock and the Y-axis represents their capacity. The width of the bar represents each stock's weight (determined in Step 2: Community Capital Inventory). The black line marks previously measured levels, and the arrows indicate the direction of change (increase or decrease) between the time intervals. The red lines, both dotted (earlier time interval) and solid (current), show the total average capital capacity.*

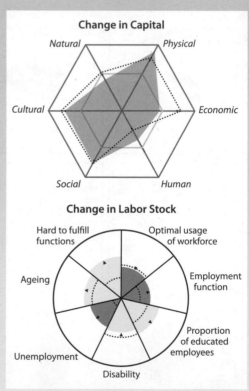

Fig. 17.12: *The monitoring program found an increase in economic, social and cultural capital over time (as shown by the dotted line and arrows). The circle shows more specific detail of the changes in the indicators for the Labor Stock.*

grievances and increased employee recruitment and retention (Miller et al. 2009). In other words, employees enjoyed their work environments more and likely felt more appreciated, which translated into better performance.

Economic, financial, market, legal and political risks can be also minimized through green building. As awareness of the benefits of green building grows, the bar is being raised: people are coming to expect buildings to be developed as ethically as possible. These expectations are growing among the public, financial institutions, government and insurance companies. Many developers and property owners have been turning toward green building to avoid adversity. In doing so, they find that green building practices help earn them a "social license" to operate, with enhanced public support and social capital.

Building Codes and Green Buildings

Although the benefits of green building are well-established, efforts to build green (or even just greener) are too often hindered by building codes developed for a previous age. In many communities, existing regulations pose significant barriers to creativity and innovation with sustainable design, and to green building technologies and methods. Green developers are often required to seek variance from existing codes, which can impose costly delays. Some codes require installation of conventional systems alongside green systems, which creates redundancies and increases development costs. Other codes unintentionally inhibit the use of green technology: For example, communities with groundwater codes that prohibit new wells may unintentionally inhibit the permitting process for geothermal heat pumps (EPA 2010c).

The green building community is making an effort to correct this and support communities who are promoting green building. The US Environmental Protection Agency has created the Sustainable Design and Green Building Toolkit for Local Governments, and the Cascadia Green Building Council has conducted thorough reviews of building codes to identify barriers and highlight alternative solutions.

The City of Burnaby, British Columbia, found a way to avoid code barriers for the UniverCity development, a sustainable urban community for 10,000 people within walking distance of Simon Fraser University. It implemented zoning bylaws that require sustainable design and building in all *new* developments. Specifically, Burnaby required a 30 percent minimum energy-efficiency improvement over existing traditionally designed buildings. This is the first bylaw in North America to mandate specific green building practices as part of the development process. (UniverCity is profiled in chapter 14.)

In some municipalities, procedural obstacles to green building are being addressed by new staff positions and processes. Both Chicago and Los Angeles have created a new green project administrator position with the sole responsibility to expedite green projects through the permitting process. The City of Chicago also waives permitting fees for independent code consultants for large projects above minimum requirements and promises a 15-day permit review for green projects above a certain size and standard (Yudelson 2009).

Green Affordable Housing

Although certified green buildings initially took the form of upscale, architecturally distinct status symbols, the next wave recognized that green building and affordable housing are a natural fit. Energy efficiency and water efficiency makes green buildings more affordable to heat and operate. As well, recycled materials and smarter design can make green homes that are healthier and cheaper to build.

What Is Affordable Green Building?

Habitat [for Humanity] defines sustainable building or green building as providing housing for people with methods, products and processes that create healthy homes and communities that are less expensive to operate, more durable and that conserve resources throughout construction and after. Sustainable building supports the development of families and communities while respecting our natural environment (Habitat for Humanity 2011, 5).

Green Affordable Housing: Quick Tips for Making Housing Development Green

- Reuse building materials from other projects, and ensure on-site recycling during construction.
- Build using recycled material such as engineered lumber, fly ash concrete, steel, recycled tile or cotton insulation.
- Landscape using shrubs and plants native to the area to provide shading, wind protection and noise reduction.
- Install EnergyStar-labeled products such as light bulbs, refrigerators, dishwashers, fans and air conditioners.
- Use compact florescent lights, motion sensors, daylight sensors and dimmers whenever possible.
- Install hard surface flooring wherever possible to improve air quality.
- Install metal roofs to save energy and aid rainwater collection; these may qualify for reduced homeowners' insurance.

(National League of Cities Municipal Action Guide 2009)

In New Orleans, where post-Katrina rebuilding continues, over 50 homes have been built to the LEED Platinum standard at an average cost of only $150,000 each (Paulsen 2011). The Make It Right Foundation has been working with the City of New Orleans to create affordable homes that cost less to operate, provide improved indoor air quality and stand a better chance of surviving hurricanes.

Many communities are starting to embrace green affordable housing. The City of Austin, Texas, runs the Green Builder Program that provides green building construction and operation guidelines, rating system information and marketing plans to successfully develop green affordable housing. In the San Francisco Bay Area, the Green Affordable Housing Coalition promotes green affordable building through information dissemination, support and government lobbying. It also supports the development of projects through case studies that highlight the success and challenges of green affordable development.

One such project is Northgate Apartments in Oakland, California. This development exemplifies a successful mixed-use, multi-family affordable apartment complex. The building was designed using Smart Growth principles. It boasts energy- and water-efficient design and appliances, recycled construction materials, low volatile organic compound construction material, close proximity to public transit, car-sharing and electric car charging station, among other things (Green Affordable Housing Coalition 2004).

Tools and Initiatives
Voluntary

Green Affordable Housing Coalition: This coalition of public and private sector San

Francisco Bay Area professionals is committed to incorporating green building practices into the design, construction and operation of affordable housing. They provide education and outreach to the community (Green Affordable Housing Coalition 2011).

Green Building Challenge: In late 2008, Light House Sustainable Building Centre in Vancouver, BC, proposed a challenge to homeowners, small-business owners and strata councils to green their homes and workplaces in time for the Vancouver 2010 Winter Olympics. The challenge outlined a set of energy, water and waste reduction targets and strategies (Light House Sustainable Building Centre 2010).

Environmental Protection Agency Toolkits: This agency developed a toolkit for residents, building owners and local governments, and provides excellent ideas for sustainable building (EPA 2010c).

Freecycle: With users from over 4,800 communities in 110 countries, the Freecycle.com website connects those with usable free items with others who can use them. A significant portion of the items are recycled building materials, which continues the cycle of giving and receiving and creates less waste.

Planet Reuse: Building on LEED's commitment to local and recycled materials, the US-based website PlanetReuse.com connects construction companies and all types of home and building owners. Users can upload an offer for recycled material, often for free, and others can then pick up and use that material at their own site.

ReStore: Habitat for Humanity has created retail outlets offering surplus building and home supplies to contractors and the public. ReStore encourages materials recycling and keep materials out of the wastestream. All of the proceeds from ReStore go back to the local Habitat for Humanity chapter (Habitat for Humanity 2011b).

Expenditure

New LEED buildings: The City of Portland decided in 2009 that all new city buildings will be made to the LEED Gold standard. Joining Vancouver, British Columbia, and Scottsdale, Arizona, this additional investment made by the cities show a commitment to the health and well-being of its citizens (City of Portland 2011).

Funding Design Costs: Many local governments have funded greener or certified green schools through regulation and expenditure programs, but one US state has created a program — which could be replicable on a municipal level — to fund the "soft" costs of such endeavors. The State of Pennsylvania has allocated a budget to cover necessary administrative and design costs, which individual public schools can apply for to cover these types of costs. The High Performance Green School Planning Grant supports schools with LEED silver certification or two Green Globes or higher (GGGC 2011).

Financial Incentives

Canadian Mortgage and Housing Corporation Loan Insurance Refund: Canadians purchasing an energy-efficient home are eligible to receive a 10 percent premium refund on mortgage loan insurance premiums, as well as extended amortizations without regular premium surcharges from CMHC.

Vancouver Solar Homes Pilot: The City of Vancouver, BC, in partnership with Terasen Gas, Solar BC and Offsetters, offers $3,000 toward the cost of a solar hot water system for residents building new homes. The money covers roughly half the cost of the solar system and is expected to cover 60 percent of a home's hot water heating costs.

Green Retrofit Program for Multi-family Housing: Housing and Urban Development, a department of the US government, provides grants and loans to eligible property owners through the Office of Affordable Housing Preservation (OAHP) to complete green retrofit projects (USDHUD 2009).

Enterprise Green Communities: This is a fund supported by Enterprise Community Partners, Inc. to support green low-income housing development in the United States. Funding is provided to developers building new homes or retrofitting existing infrastructure. All projects supported meet the Green Communities Criteria, which include integrative design; location and neighborhood fabric; site improvements; water conservation; energy efficiency; materials beneficial to the environment; healthy living environment; and operations and maintenance (Enterprise Community Partners Inc. 2011).

Regulations

Minimum Green Building Standards for New Development: In 2001, the City of Seattle, WA, became the first local government in the US to mandate minimum green building requirements. The city requires that all new public buildings greater than 5,000 square feet be built to LEED Silver standard. The City of Vancouver, BC, has a similar regulation that requires all new public buildings to be built to a minimum LEED Gold standard (City of Seattle Department of Planning & Development 2010).

Green Building Development Permit Priority: Green buildings often use new techniques and technology that challenge traditional building practices. This can come with a cost: green building practices can often take longer to review and approve, slowing the projects to a halt. Prioritizing and expediting green building permit applications, over traditional building applications, through the approval process, can overcome this challenge. The City of Bellingham, WA, has such a program, reducing permitting from 28 days to 7 with its Green Project Review Team (City of Bellingham 2011).

Building Technical Assistance Programs: The City of Portland has created the Alternative Technology Advisory Committee to review sustainable technologies against building code requirements and to help building permit applicants utilize green building products and construction practices. The committee supports education and outreach for green development and helps developers overcome code barriers (City of Portland, Bureau of Development Services 2011).

Density Bonus for Green Buildings: Incentivizing developers to build to a green standard in exchange for a greater density is a strategy employed by many communities. The City of Arlington, Virginia, has created a program that uses the LEED certification earned by the new development as a way to reward the developers with additional density (City of Arlington 2011).

Chapter 12

Community Economic Development

In recent years, the inadequacies of conventional economic development have been manifested in increasing economic disparity, under-employment and downsizing. But what is the alternative?

Done well, community economic development can enhance all six forms of community capital. Ecological services can be valued in a manner that preserves or enhances their economic value; social enterprises can help us transcend the limitations of conventional economic development through social solidarity and cultural heritage; and greater emphasis on circulating money within local economies can enhance human, physical, social and cultural capital.

Economic Development Redefined

Sustainable community economic development (CED) is a feasible community-based alternative approach to the economy we are familiar with — an economy focused on growth rather than development, on global trade and currency rather than people and ecosystems. By prioritizing sustainable CED, citizens and their governments choose economic development that provides opportunities for people of different incomes and skills, promotes a better quality of life and protects the environment.

Simon Fraser University's Centre for Sustainable Community Development uses a definition of CED that is decidedly more expansive than traditional definitions of the term. The centre views CED not as an end in itself but as a fundamental component of sustainable community development that integrates economic, social and environmental objectives by considering the relationship between economic factors and other community elements. These include affordable housing, education, natural environment, health, accessibility and arts and culture (CSCD 2011).

From this perspective, community economic development is not just about business creation; it's about creating self-sustaining communities. Communities that protect their natural resource base and preserve the health of their environments contribute to more sustainable economies. Growing public awareness of the limitations of conventional business and industrial growth has prompted many communities to reconsider their models. Many communities (and businesses within them) are recognizing that it is not only possible but advantageous to support a thriving economy while preserving or augmenting natural and other forms of community capital.

Social Economy

In North America and around the world, disparity between rich and poor is growing (World Economic Forum 2011). Our economic systems are exacerbating this problem by failing to put social and human concerns at the center of economic development (Restakis 2006; 2010). So how can community economic development address this? One way is by strengthening what is known as the social economy.

Definitions of *social economy* have evolved in recent years. The term was first used in 18th-century Europe to describe the intellectual foundations of the cooperative movement (Restakis 2010). Today, social economy is defined in a variety of ways, but they share similar themes. Most definitions build from the fundamental concept of the simultaneous pursuit of economic and social objectives through citizen-owned enterprises, cooperatives, credit unions, non-profit organizations, service associations and charities (BALTA 2011; Neamtan & Anderson 2010).

The social economy is often differentiated from public- and private-sector economies by its integration of social goals, reciprocity and solidarity into economic decisions (BALTA 2011). It can also be conceived of as the "third system" of the economy, as described in Figure 12.1 by Pearce (2003): the first system represents the private sector and is primarily profit-driven, while the second system is the domain of the public sector and is focused on redistribution and planning. The third system is about "citizens taking action to meet and satisfy needs themselves and working together in some collaborative way to do this . . . and is based upon the principles of self-help and mutuality, of caring for others and of meeting social needs rather than the maximization of profit".

SOCIAL ENTERPRISE

A social enterprise operates like a traditional business but specifically manages its operations and revenue to achieve social, cultural, community or environmental goals. They are typically set up by citizens in communities and owned by their members. They have democratic decision-making processes that involve clients and workers, give priority to people and work and are based on principles of participation, empowerment and individual and collective responsibility. Promoting social enterprises in a community will help create training and job opportunities for under-skilled or under-employed residents. The most common formats are non-governmental organizations (NGOs) and cooperatives. A concentration of social enterprises not matched elsewhere in North America is found within the province of Quebec. There are more than 7,000 social enterprises in Quebec, employing more than 125,000 people and representing sales of $17 billion annually (Chantier de l'économie sociale 2009). As compared to other provinces, co-ops are leaders in multiple sectors including banking and investments; more than 40 percent of the province's workers are unionized; and a union-driven investment fund (Fonds de solidarité [FTQ]) has regulations for a minimum of 60 percent local investments (Mendell, 2010; Mendell and Neamtam 2009; Neamtan and Anderson 2010; Pearce 2003). Social enterprises in Quebec have a much higher survival rate, 65 percent, as opposed to small to medium enterprises 35 percent, which has been attributed to closer

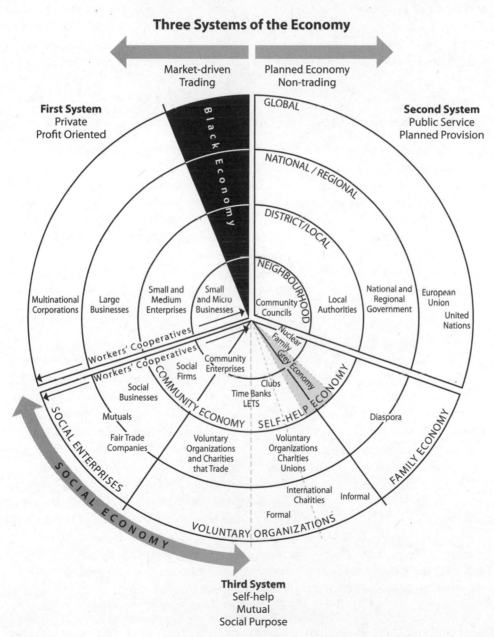

Three Systems of the Economy

Fig. 12.1 *The Third System: As conceived by John Pearce (Social Enterprise in Anytown, Calouste Gulbenkian Foundation, 2003), the first two sub-systems of the economy are activities in the private and public sectors. The "third system" refers to the social economy, including social enterprises, voluntary organizations and family economies.*

community ties, longer-term outlooks, participatory democracy and integrating volunteer work (Chantier de l'économie sociale 2009).

The Emilia Romagna region of Italy is a potent example of a vibrant, well-developed social economy. Located at the foot of the Italian Alps, the region is home to almost four million. Cooperatives are foundational to region's economy; more than 15,000 in the commercial and civil sectors contribute over one-third of the region's gross domestic product. Sectors with the strongest cooperative presence include retail, agricultural production, social services, housing manufacture and construction. Building co-ops carry out most public works, including large-scale engineering, construction

Revelstoke CED: From the Kitchen Table to Long-term Success   By Victor Cumming

Community economic development (CED) requires three types of local long-term activity: community economic planning and decision making, organizational capacity building and implementation of actual enterprises or economic enhancement projects. Revelstoke, a boom (and bust) resource town in the Canadian Rockies, offers a good example (Perry et al. 2000). In the early 1980s, its economy plunged after the completion of two large hydro dams and a railroad tunnel, and a steep decline in the forest industry.

After the creation of a kitchen-table-sized economic development committee (1982) and the hiring of a first-class CED practitioner, a strategy for the community's economic development was rapidly compiled (1985). Over the next 25 years, Revelstoke was able consistently to involve the community in identifying critical economic activities and in building organizations to carry out these activities. To grow the vision and the capacity to seize the initiative when opportunities arose, it was understood that many community leaders were essential. Success depended on "us," not "them."

Economic projects involved:

• Social enterprises: Revelstoke Community Forest Corporation (1993); the Revelstoke Railroad Museum (1995); the community-owned Mt. Mackenzie Ski Hill (1998).

• Institutions with critical roles in the development process: Community Futures Development Corporation (1987); Enterprise Development Centre (1988) with entrepreneur training and a higher-risk commercial loan fund; Revelstoke Credit Union's expansion into commercial loans (1990s); Skills Centre (1996); Community Foundation (1999).

• Public infrastructure: downtown revitalization (1986-88); river walkways; signage (1990s); and now housing, ski hill support infrastructure redevelopment and recreation trails.

These three elements in combination have spawned and enhanced many private businesses locally.

Revelstoke is no ordinary small town. Located in the Canadian Rockies on the Trans-Canada Highway and the Columbia River, it is a major transportation hub and the world's center of heli-skiing. In addition to large hydro developments, it is favored with valuable forest resources and committed people. It has also enjoyed relative political and staff stability. Nevertheless, what sets apart the town's practice of CED is the combination of major community-building economic and social planning initiatives (1985, 1995, 2007), the systematic development of broad-based community leadership, the establishment of successful community institutions and consistent "business risk" taking.

and heritage restoration projects. Forty years ago, Emilia Romagna was ranked at the bottom of Italy's 20 regions in terms of economic performance — today it ranks first. In recent decades, it has re-emerged as one of the most livable regions in Italy. Emilia Romagna has ranked 10th out of 122 economic regions in the European Union (EU) and boasts a per capita income 30 percent higher than the national average and 27.6 percent higher than that of the EU. Its success is particularly noteworthy as it results from ideas and practices considered antithetical to conventional prescriptions for economic development (Roseland & Soots 2007).

An example of the social economy can be seen in the province of Saskatchewan, where it helped the Lac La Ronge First Nation become a key business owner in its region through the creation of the Kitsaki Development Corporation. Community development corporations (CDCs) are non-profit organizations that support CED by offering financial services, educational programs, affordable housing, investing directly in starting and operating enterprises and/or providing other services. In the Kitsaki case, the CDC helped create a socially positive economic base from which to improve the livelihood of the Lac La Ronge people. For decades before the establishment of Kitsaki in 1981, many of the jobs in this north-central region of the province were controlled by businesses in southern Saskatchewan. Many jobs did not benefit locals, and most of the profits were spent outside of the region. To bolster economic development in the region, Kitsaki fostered *social enterprise* through a joint venture strategy that combines community ownership with private-sector partners. Examples of enterprises include wild rice processing, smoked meats,

insurance, and trucking. Through Kitsaki, over 500 jobs have been created (70 percent held by aboriginal people); annual revenues average $50 million (Lewis 2006).

Community development corporations such as Kitsaki offer a range of financial, managerial and other supportive services for CED, but they are only one source of financing. Other community financing institutions or financing programs provide a variety of means to access capital for CED, often referred to as development finance (see the financing community economic development section of this chapter). This is especially critical in areas experiencing disinvestment or shortages of conventional sources of investment capital for business and economic development.

Green Business, Jobs and Economies

Environmental stewardship, pollution control and resource efficiency need not be seen as an economic burden; in fact, they offer significant economic opportunities. For businesses, environmental responsibility can mean lower zenergy-efficiency, water conservation, assured regulatory compliance, enhanced public image and new market opportunities (Epstein 2008). For communities that attract and support environmentally responsible business, the rewards include lighter burdens on local infrastructure (waste disposal, sewage, electric and water utilities, for example), protection of the ecosystem and jobs and tax revenue sources that do not compromise the quality of life for local citizens.

The term *green business* refers to economic activities that avoid harm to the environment or that help protect or improve the ecosystem in some way. By merging the goals and principles of sustainable CED and green business, communities move closer to sustainability.

Some businesses also identify financial savings or benefits associated with environmental improvements to their operations. With a growing market of environmentally aware customers, many companies recognize the bounty of opportunities to sell greener products and services and display a more ecologically responsible image.

Key CED Concepts

Growth vs. Development: In North America, there is prevalent myth that, in order to foster economic development, a community must accept growth. The truth is that growth and development do not necessarily go hand-in-hand. *Growth* is a quantitative change; when talking about communities, it could refer to increases in population size, infrastructure, traffic and so on. *Development* describes qualitative change, such as the opening up of new areas in the community, a change in land use or the emergence of new ways of building. Development without growth can be encouraged by supporting existing businesses and increasing the number of times each dollar circulates within the community (i.e., enhancing the economic multiplier effect). Local purchasing is the primary means of achieving both; it results in more-efficient, self-reliant and economically resilient communities. Citizens have the power to help build such communities by influencing the type of business, industry and employment opportunities in their own backyards (Roseland and Soots 2007).

Economic base model: The economy of a community can be represented by income flows. These income flows can be classified as *basic* or *non-basic*, depending on where the money comes from. Basic income is defined as income that flows into the community from the outside world, in the form of either *employment* income or *non-employment* income.

Basic employment income flows into a community in the form of wages and salaries or self-employed income, from the following three sources:

- From jobs that produce goods and services that are exported elsewhere;
- From jobs that produce goods and services for the tourist sector (outsiders who spend money in the community that was earned elsewhere) or
- From jobs in the public sector, for example, healthcare workers, teachers and government employees, who receive their employment income from senior governments, and not directly from the local residents.

Basic non-employment income is all income that flows into the community that is not employment income. In the model it is aggregated into two groups:

- Transfer payments from senior governments, such as welfare payments, Old Age Security pensions, Guaranteed Income Supplements, Canada Pension Plan, Employment Insurance benefits, Federal Child Tax benefits and other income from government sources.
- Other non-employment income that includes investment income, such as dividends and interest; retirement pensions, superannuation, annuities and alimony.

Non-basic income is employment income generated from jobs in the community that provide goods and services to individuals who live in the community. These jobs are often referred to as non-basic jobs or induced employment. Examples of these include much of retail trade, local transportation services, local financial services and personal services — local dry cleaners, barbershops and hairdressers (Horne 2004).

Local governments, citizens, banks and other financial institutions can help promote green business. Local governments can support, encourage or legislate policies to improve the environmental performance of existing businesses within their communities or attract new ecologically responsible businesses and economic activities. Citizens can lobby governments to pass legislation that promotes ecologically sound economic development. Both citizens and governments can encourage environmentally responsible corporate behavior by choosing to purchase greener products or services from more responsible companies. Banks and other financial intermediaries can support green business development by offering preferred interest rates and applying environmental standards as criteria for loans.

Green business benefits communities by creating green jobs. A job is commonly defined as green if it "works directly with information, technologies, or materials that minimize environmental impact, and also requires specialized skills, knowledge, training, or experience related to these areas" (ECO Canada 2010, 4).

Together, green jobs and business comprise the *green economy*. Considered a subset of the broader economy, the green economy is the "aggregate of all activity operating with the primary intention of reducing conventional levels of resource consumption, harmful emissions, and minimizing all forms of environmental impact. [It] includes the inputs, activities, outputs and outcomes as they relate to the production of green products and services" (Eco Canada 2010, 3). Top areas of opportunity in the green economy include renewable energy and energy-efficiency, building retrofitting and construction, transportation and alternative transportation, and waste recycling and waste

Is Your Business Green?

Businesses that are considered green strive to improve their environmental performance by doing some or all of the following:

- Employ "front of the pipe" strategies that reduce waste, pollution and use of environmentally harmful materials during the production process.
- Employ "end of the pipe" strategies that remove, recover or treat waste at the end of a production process.
- Conserve water, optimize energy efficiency and/or replace some or all energy sources with renewable ones.
- Employ strategies to protect or enhance the environment, preserve biodiversity and protect the ecosystem.
- Target environmental issues for business activities (for example, soil remediation firms).

Fig. 12.2: *"Green collar" workers install a solar water heater on the roof of Pinmore Ceramics Gallery, at Pinmore in Ayrshire, Scotland.*
(Credit: Andrew Aitchison/Ashden Awards)

management (Eco Canada 2010; Renner et al. 2008).

A related term is *green collar economy*, which was first coined by American attorney, environmental advocate and civil rights activist Anthony K. "Van" Jones. He envisioned a national-level alternative to traditional economic development, in which *green collar jobs* comprise the green economy's vocational or trades sub-sector. Not surprisingly, green collar jobs support environmentally friendly technology and skills, such as contractors trained in retrofitting buildings or electricians specializing in solar panel installation systems. They offer wages sufficient to support families and opportunity for long-term careers and provide quality of life. They are most likely to be filled by middle-skilled technicians and trades people who require education beyond high school but not a university degree. As Jones emphasized, creating a green collar economy is not about re-inventing the wheel; rather, it is about retooling existing skills to create environmentally supportive skills. For example, a mechanic who traditionally works on gas combustion engines can learn the skills needed to repair hybrid vehicles (Jones 2008).

Greening the Economy through Economic Demand Management

In the past, and unfortunately still in many communities today, CED was pursued by focusing on social and economic goals at the expense of natural capital. Today, most CED initiatives focus on augmenting individual and community self-reliance through collaborative action, capacity-building and returning control of business enterprises, capital, labor and other resources from the global marketplace to communities. CED initiatives consider communities' natural capital while targeting local job creation and poverty alleviation, and use economic activity as a means to improve the quality of life for citizens.

Development of job training programs, provision of affordable housing and access to alternative debt and equity finance are integral components of CED, as is the social, economic and environmental value of non-monetary transactions (such as bartering) and services (such as child- or elder-care offered by friends and neighbors).

Just as sustainability has prompted a shift in the focus of our transportation and energy planning away from increasing supply to managing demand, sustainable CED can shift from growth (increase in supply of products and services) to *economic demand management*. This approach seeks to satisfy our economic needs without requiring endless growth; it questions the view that growth is synonymous with success and that gross income is a sufficient measure of success. At the same time, economic demand management acknowledges contributions that enhance the community and indirectly help strengthen the economy, such as unpaid work.

By rethinking how we value our time and contributions, we can better evaluate the true costs and benefits of our actions. For example, while unemployment and job insecurity plague many Canadians and Americans, those who are employed work longer hours than people in past decades — which is taking its toll on individuals and families. With the average working person in the United States putting in 180 more hours of work a year in 2006 than their counterpart did in 1979 (Schor 2010), many households are spending a large part of their income on transportation costs to

Building the Conservation Economy

Ecotrust is an enterprising non-profit organization that works with communities and stakeholders to develop alternative approaches to economic challenges. It seeks to promote what it calls the *conservation economy*, wherein community economic development intersects with conservation. The conservation economy "provides meaningful work and good livelihoods, supports vibrant communities and the recognition of Aboriginal rights and title, and conserves and restores the environment" (Ecotrust Canada 2011). Operating under these values, in the US Ecotrust works in Portland to connect foresters who harvest their wood responsibly with the burgeoning green building industry. Through its Forestry Market Connections Program, Ecotrust is building an inventory of woodlots certified by the Forest Stewardship Council; building the supply chain and recruiting distributors; increasing certified land by documenting demand and reducing barriers to certification, financing and forming forest cooperatives; providing bridge financing for purchases of standing inventory, equipment upgrades and certifications through a short-term, highly leveraged revolving fund; and monitoring product flow, building communication and promoting success (Ecotrust 2011).

and from work, childcare services and take-out meals because parents are too tired to cook. What is the financial cost to support this work-oriented lifestyle, and what is the cost to our quality of life? New cars, big houses and the latest computer games can obscure the real costs of economic growth.

In a commodity-intensive economy, people often feel compelled to seek full-time employment and an increasing income. But change is afoot: by re-evaluating our needs and wants and realizing that our true demands are for comfort, security, health and happiness, many of us are finding alternative ways to satisfy them.

Local Self-reliance

One way communities can cater to the needs of their residents and promote their own economic development is by increasing their self-reliance. Local self-reliance is not about isolation; rather, it is about diversification of local economies — to meet local needs, encourage cohesiveness, reduce waste, and enable more sustainable trade practices with other communities.

Local self-reliance is about strengthening connections between consumers and diverse local producers, such as farmers, clothing manufacturers, furniture builders or travel agents. One way to enhance the self-reliance of a community is to identify its imports and, where possible, invest in the local economy by substituting locally made products. As communities organize to find substitutes for imports, people become more aware of the social and environmental impacts of economic activities as well as the benefits of making wise investments in local goods and services. Local self-reliance fosters greater responsibility because the costs and benefits of decisions accrue to the community in which they are made.

Communities seeking to become more self-reliant must look for opportunities to enhance local wealth by developing the community's existing resource base. Every community has some resources — physical, human, social —

Fair Trade Programs

While community economic development emphasizes local self-reliance, it also recognizes interdependency with other towns and regions. Fair trade is a social movement that seeks better trading conditions and secures the rights of marginalized producers and workers (WTFO 2011). Fair trade products represent one of the fastest growing areas of the global food market, with total sales reaching US$1.6 billion in 2004-2005 (Murray & Reynolds 2007).

that can be harnessed for this purpose. The New Rules project, an initiative by the Institute for Local Self-Reliance, was created as a response to crumbling local economies and weakened social communities. Their rules to ensure economic self-reliant communities include:

- Comprehensive plans
- Development moratoria
- Economic impact review
- Financing local businesses
- Formula business restrictions
- Local purchasing preferences
- Neighborhood-serving zones
- Preventing vacant big-box sites
- Set-asides for local retail
- Store size caps

ECONOMIC LEAKAGE

Economic leakage occurs when community members travel outside the community to spend their locally generated income on non-local purchases, or when residents make purchases within the community on products that were originally purchased or manufactured elsewhere. The money spent outside the community represents a loss to the local economy.

Economic development rooted in local ownership and import-substitution serve to minimize economic leakage (Markey et al. 2005).

SUSTAINABILITY AND THE BIG-BOX MODEL

One of the most noticeable and debated impacts of globalization on local communities is the proliferation and increasing dominance of multinational big-box superstores. Are they good or bad for local economies?

Consider the world's largest retailer, Walmart, whose operations — if considered in terms of national economies — would make it the 20th-largest country (Hassett 2009). The often-maligned company has made admirable strides towards sustainability.

In 2004, Walmart launched a long-term sustainability initiative involving leaders and executives from virtually every branch of the company. Environmental consultants and non-profit organizations helped Walmart look at the sustainability of its practices in real estate; use of energy, packaging and raw materials; and electronics waste (Scott 2005). Walmart subsequently announced three new goals: to rely 100 percent on renewable energy, to create zero waste and to sell products that "sustain people and the environment" (Lovins 2010).

By April 2006, Walmart was one of a handful of major retailers and energy companies urging the US Congress to impose mandatory carbon caps on their businesses. In 2007, Walmart sold more than 137 million compact-fluorescent light bulbs in the US, exceeding their previous year's goal by 37 million. Walmart also set measurable goals for fleet efficiency, plastic bag waste reduction, use of only concentrated detergents and opening of GHG-reduced stores; most of these have been met (Walmart 2011). In 2009, Walmart measured each of its suppliers against a sustainability checklist, telling the 60,000 firms that failing audits after 2012 would remove them from Walmart's supplier list (Lovins 2010).

More recently, Walmart committed to doubling its sales of locally grown produce. In 2010, the company committed to selling $1 billion in food sourced from one million small and medium farmers; training one million farmers and farm workers in sustainable farming and increasing the income of the small and medium farms it sources from, by 10 to 15 percent — all by 2015 (Walmart 2010). Furthermore, its Heritage Agriculture program was created to support local US farmers, encourage women- and minority-owned suppliers and buy more ethnic items (McCormack & Pinkston 2010).

But critics of Walmart's sustainability efforts continue to highlight its problematic definition of sustainability (Stack 2010). For example, the Natural Step, a not-for-profit organization dedicated to education, advisory work and research in sustainable development, has argued that Walmart's separation of social and environmental sustainability has obscured issues that clearly relate to both — such as toxic chemicals and heavy metals in products sold at Walmart. Similarly, the Natural Step questions the company's mission of "saving people money so they can live better": When prices can't get any lower and all low-hanging fruit initiatives have been implemented, "will Walmart be willing to save more than just money? That question, helping people lead more fulfilling lives with less stuff, and how we move to more sustainable consumption patterns, faces everyone" (Stack 2010).

Others point to Walmart's disregard for public input and industry experience in its self-regulation programs (Cernansky 2011). For example, the US Food & Drug Administration was in the process of developing nationwide standards for front-of-package labeling when Walmart began to enforce its own rules in 2011. Walmart had also established its own process for screening chemical formulations of products, as opposed to the voluntary process managed by the EPA and FDA (Cernansky 2011). Still others question Walmart's claims. Although Walmart began tracking its suppliers through their 15-question sustainability report card in 2009, critics claim that Walmart — upon finding that a supplier commits, in Walmart's own terms, "egregious violations" — will not keep its promise to stop buying from such firms (Cernansky 2011).

Even considering these criticisms, Walmart deserves full marks for demonstrating that cleaner, greener and less wasteful can be very profitable — even for big business. But does this exonerate the multinational big-box model? Not exactly.

In several respects, big-box stores like Walmart can't compete with locally owned businesses. The latter are more likely to be stable generators of wealth for many years, even generations. When reasonable labor and environmental standards are introduced, locally owned businesses are more likely to adapt to these changes rather than flee. During business downturns, they are less likely to relocate production to lower-cost regions; similarly, they are less likely to move for a slight increase in the rate of return on investment during boom times. This anchoring of locally owned businesses within the community creates stability and minimizes the incidence of sudden and costly departures that are often followed by massive unemployment, lower tax revenues, shrinking property values and deep cuts in schools, police and other services (Shuman 2006).

Although big-box stores like Walmart expand commercial choice and offer low prices, Roseland and Soots (2007) concluded that they contribute little to local economies and instead facilitate economic leakage by siphoning profits out of communities. Big-box retail can also trigger a decline in total economic activity despite increasing overall sales. Given global market fluctuations and propensity to relocate to lower-cost regions, big-box stores like Walmart are less stable than locally owned businesses in the long term; contribute to unemployment and lowered income by displacing local businesses; siphon profits out of communities and facilitate economic leakage; and decrease the number of social capital generating establishments and civic participation (Goetz & Rupasaingha 2006; Roseland & Soots 2007; Shuman 2006).

Financing Community Economic Development

Financing and support for community and new business development projects can come from government agencies, foundations, corporations, venture capital, educational institutes (providing research or training), religious investors and other financing sources organized specifically to support community-based projects. Examples include:

> **Local Development Corporations:** investment companies certified by the Small Business Administration provide funds for job creation and retention in small and medium-sized businesses.
> **Community Development Corporations:** may provide loans, function as real estate developers or invest in local

businesses or community development organizations.

Downtown Development Authorities: levy-based collectives created by local governments to support downtown businesses organize special events, marketing campaigns and finance downtown improvements.

Credit Unions: cooperative, non-profit corporations created by and for people affiliated by a common bond, for the purpose of promoting thrift among members and loaning funds to members at reasonable interest rates.

Community Development Credit Unions: a specific type of credit union, serving low- to moderate-income communities and individuals. The union's goal is community economic empowerment, and they typically provide financial services (such as loans) to people who need them but cannot get them readily from fully commercial banks.

Community Loan Funds: an organization or a program within an organization that obtains money from individuals and institutions and uses it to make loans for community development projects. They usually target community-based organizations that are unable to get loans from conventional sources, offering financial and technical assistance to develop sound financial plans.

Revolving Loan Funds: funds created specifically to provide alternative financing to small businesses and non-profit organizations. Often administered by community development corporations or other non-profits, funding may be in the form of loans provided at lower rates for the level of risk than those offered by conventional lenders and may support business start-up or expansion, job creation or affordable housing.

Micro-enterprise Loan Programs (micro-credit): a few financial intermediaries are serving clients who require very small loans for entrepreneurial initiatives. The programs are a way to help low-income people get access to capital for entrepreneurial initiatives. Borrowers are typically those who are considered high risk because they lack collateral or require amounts too small, therefore too expensive to administrate, to be acceptable for conventional loan programs. Programs are usually organized as lending circles wherein borrowers receive guidance and support from others who have successfully repaid a micro-loan in the past and cannot get additional loans until other members' loans are repaid.

Community Land Trusts and Housing Trusts: strategies to finance affordable housing. (See chapter 10.)

Trust Funds: permanent endowments, dedicated to invest the interest from the capital assets in housing or other community economic development activities. Endowments may be capitalized by one-time contributions, or by annually renewable revenue sources.

Linkage Programs: provide funds for affordable housing, job development and daycare. Linkage works by local governments taking a portion of the value created by investment in areas undergoing substantial development, and directing that value to build affordable housing, provide job training and fund social services in less fortunate neighborhoods.

Reinvestment Policies: The Community Reinvestment Act requires that US depository institutions, such as banks and many insurance companies which extract capital from communities in the form of deposits, reinvest significant portions of their assets in to those communities (Seidman 2005).

SOCIAL ENTERPRISES IN RESOURCE DEPENDENT COMMUNITIES

Community-based natural resource management (CBNRM) is an academic term for managing a common natural resource collectively and democratically within a community (Gruber 2008). Rural communities dependent on one resource have increasingly turned to a CBNRM model to govern their resource, and ultimately their own livelihood. Community forestry is a North American example of CBNRM. In 2011, 58 communities were involved in planning or operating a community forest in the province of British Columbia, representing 1.5 percent of the provincial annual harvest (BC CFA 2011). Community forests can ensure longevity of local jobs, improve quality of life, enforce environmental protection, create value through tourism and provide education and training opportunities for local inhabitants. The Burns Lake Community Forest has enabled the community to: channel funds into much-needed projects such as seniors housing, parks and emergency services; solidify the partnership with the Wet'suwet'en First Nations and employ 50 percent First Nations people in the organization; implement better than regulation level buffers for streams; and donate over

$1 million to the creation of parks and trails within the forest boundaries (BC CFA 2011).

Tools and Initiatives

Voluntary

Voluntary Simplicity: Movements such as Voluntary Simplicity, popularized by Duane Elgin's 1993 book of the same name, encourage people to return to the simple life — to make choices that reduce their costs and give them time to enjoy their families, friends and the world around them. Voluntary Simplicity calls for living in a way that is "outwardly more simple and inwardly more rich" (Elgin 1993). Through a more conserving lifestyle, people are moving toward sustainability and reducing dependence on financial and material affluence for their quality of life (Schor 2010).

Good Neighbor Agreements: The citizens of Stillwater and Sweet Grass Counties (Montana), the Northern Plains Research Council, the Cottonwood Research Council and the Stillwater Protective Association (all non-profit, citizen-driven organizations) successfully negotiated a legally binding agreement with the Stillwater Mining Company. This Good Neighbor Agreement promotes socially and environmentally responsible mining practices and enables citizens to regularly meet with company representatives to avoid and address any problems related to mining operations. It allows mining to occur within the two counties while protecting the surrounding environment. Through the agreement, the mining company has donated the community land for conservation, created a plan to reduce traffic congestion near mine sites and provided for independent environmental audits to protect the communities' water quality (Northern Plains Research Council 2011).

Green Maps: Eco-designer, public educator and consultant Wendy E. Brawer created the first Green Apple Map of New York City in 1992 as a tool for residents and visitors in search of green businesses and environmentally sound tourist opportunities. Today, the New York-based non-profit Green Map System produces green maps in over 700 cities in 55 countries. In addition to identifying eco-friendly ways to spend money, the maps often educate by defining terms like *organic* or *biodynamic* (Green Map 2011).

Casa Verde Builders: Established in 1994, Casa Verde Builders of Austin, Texas, helps high-school dropouts (aged 17 to 25) learn carpentry and construction skills while completing course work to earn a high-school diploma and certificate of mastery. Participants earn a salary for spending 40 hours per week doing studies and working in crews building environmentally responsible housing. They learn sustainable construction techniques by building affordable homes that are sold to low-income families. A private lender and federal funding provide financing for home purchases and mortgages, and proceeds from the sale of these houses are returned to Casa Verde to build more houses. Within the 2008-2009 year, over 80 energy-efficient affordable homes were built (American Youth Works 2011).

Community-supported Agriculture: In hundreds of North American towns and cities, Community-supported Agriculture is gaining popularity as a way for urbanites to supply themselves with fresh vegetables while supporting small local organic farms. Urban families or individuals pay yearly fees for shares that entitle them to weekly shipments of locally grown fruits and vegetables. Purchasers share the risks of farming with farmers — they may receive less of one vegetable than expected, but more of another. In addition to supporting sustainable agriculture, city dwellers strengthen connections with local farmers and the bioregion. (See chapter 4 for more discussion.)

Community-supported Fishery: Inspired by Community-supported Agriculture, several North American communities have established Community-supported Fisheries (CSFs) where small-scale and often family-run fishing operations provide freshly caught local seafood to local markets. CSF helps support independent small-scale fishing in an industry that is dominated by big businesses and aquaculture. Port Clyde, Maine, offers one such example (Jenkins 2009). At the beginning of the fishing season, members of the CSF pay a fee that entitles them to a share of the season's catch and enables fishing businesses to operate their seasonal businesses and cover off-season costs. Purchasers share the risks of fishing with the fishermen, as members are not guaranteed how much of each species they will receive each week. By receiving a flat rate per season, fishers are encouraged to diversify their catches and fish according to demands of the ecosystem. CSFs currently exist in approximately 20 North American communities.

Iisaak Forest Resources: Iisaak is a First Nations-led forest service company operating in Clayoquot Sound, British Columbia. The company is animated by a forestry model that connects forestry practices with the cultural and spiritual values and beliefs of the Nuu-chah-nulth.

Green Business Program: Established by local San Francisco Bay Area governments and regional agencies in 1996, the green business program helps small and medium-sized businesses comply with local, regional and national environmental regulations and offers a framework to further improve environmental performance beyond such regulations. The program certifies small businesses as "green" if they meet a set of regional standards related to water and energy conservation, pollution control and waste reduction. The program has been implemented in nine San Francisco Bay counties. Since 1996, over 2,000 businesses in more than 20 different industries have been certified (City and County of San Francisco 2011).

Greenmarkets: New York City's Council on the Environment, a citizens' organization based in the Mayor's office, initiated a system

Fig. 12.3:
Inspired by community-supported agriculture programs, community-supported fisheries link subscribers to family fishing businesses like that of Otto Strobel in Vancouver, BC.
(Credit:
Shaun Strobel)

Fig. 12.4:

On Salt Spring Island (population approx. 11,000) off the British Columbia coast, Salt Spring Dollars are a successful and widely accepted alternative currency that encourages local spending.

(CREDIT:

SALT SPRING ISLAND

MONETARY FOUNDATION)

of Greenmarkets in 1976. The markets offer many New Yorkers their only chance to get local produce without journeying to the suburbs. Operating 54 sites throughout the city and involving more than 230 farms and fishermen, Greenmarkets also donates about one million pounds of fresh produce to hunger relief organizations annually (GrowNYC 2010).

Bartering and Local Currencies: Bartering provides cash-free access to goods and services for people who may not otherwise have cash available for transactions, thereby strengthening local economies. The "barter" sections on Craigslist websites in many cities are experiencing rapid growth in transactions; it is just one of many websites that facilitate these types of transactions. Local currencies encourage investment and re-investment in local

business and discourage leakage of dollars outside the community. "In Ithaca We Trust" is the community-minded phrase printed on the local currency used in Ithaca, New York. More than 900 local businesses and entrepreneurs there accept "Ithaca Hours" that entitle the bearer to goods or services at participating businesses (Ithaca Hours Inc. 2005). According to founder Paul Glover, a key to its continued success is having a hired networker to promote, facilitate and troubleshoot currency circulation (Glover n.d.). Other local currencies include BerkShares in the Berkshire region of Massachusetts, Salt Spring Dollars on Salt Spring Island, BC, and the Toronto Dollar in Toronto, Ontario. The LETSystem is a local exchange trading system that originated in Courtenay, BC, in 1983. Adopted by hundreds of communities around the world, it uses a computerized accounting system to record transactions instead of paper currency. Each account holder purchases goods and services by transferring credits from their account to a seller. A negative balance does not indicate debt, but a commitment to do work or exchange goods within the community. The LETSystem uses a dollar as the unit of exchange, so accounting is easy and taxes can be paid accordingly.

Financial Incentives

Urban Partnership Bank: A bank with a social mission, the Urban Partnership Bank (UPB) was historically created to write loans to minority neighborhood residents who had previously been denied loans by larger banks. Operating in Chicago, Detroit and Cleveland, the bank offers regular banking services and targeted lending with the mission to "build vibrant urban neighborhoods and to promote economic and environmental sustainability"

(UPB 2011). Although its socially minded predecessor, Shore Trust, a partnership between Shore Bank and Ecotrust, succumbed to the financial crisis of 2008, Urban Partnership has emerged with new management and fewer real estate investments. In 2011, UPB moved to counter the arguably predatory practices of services like payday lending and check-cashing companies by creating less-intimidating micro branches to attract the younger market away from them.

Revolving Loan Fund: The campus sustainability movement has been using revolving loan funds to finance sustainability initiatives. Harvard University has a $12 million fund that provides capital to reduce the college's environmental impact (Harvard 2011). In 2006, Minnesota's Macalester College created the Clean Energy Revolving Fund to finance renewable energy, energy-efficiency and energy conservation programs. The fund finances projects based on financing need and quantifiable savings and/or returns (either on fuel, electricity, water, stormwater fees, etc.). The fund operates by having the cost-saving recipient of the project pay a portion of the returns back to the fund (the recipient keeps the rest for immediate financial relief). This process is repeated over subsequent years until 125 percent of the initial project cost has accrued to the fund — this money can then be used to support more projects. Any future savings are kept by the project's recipients (Diebolt & Herder-Thomas 2007).

Micro-credit or Micro-loans: Muhammad Yunus was awarded the 2006 Nobel Peace Prize, along with the Grameen Bank, for their efforts to support and empower poor in the developing world (mostly women) by offering micro-credit (small loans to individuals possessing no collateral or credit history for self-employment or income-generating activities). Borrowers must belong to a five-member group that oversees borrower behavior and supports each other. Loans are paid back in weekly or bi-weekly installments. A similar program is offered by British Columbia's VanCity Credit Union through its circle-lending or peer-lending program. Small loans are given to emerging home-based business owners who may lack collateral, assets or credit history needed for approval of traditional loans. Borrowers belong to a group of three to six business owners who meet on a regular basis and are responsible for assessing and approving each other's loan interests based on confidence and ability to repay. Group members are collectively responsible for ensuring timely repayment of each group members' loans — all members must be in good standing on their current loans before any group member can receive a new loan (Vancouver City Savings Credit Union 2011).

Expenditure

Eco-industrial Parks: Eco-industrial parks exist to strengthen connections between businesses with complementary production processes. In these parks, the by-product or waste of one business becomes the feedstock or energy source for other businesses. Collaboration in redesigning the industrial "food chain" enables industries to achieve higher standards of environmental performance while improving operating efficiencies and profit margins. Although many emergent eco-industrial parks continue to grapple with challenges of implementing eco-industrial principles, Kalunborg Park in Denmark has shown considerable success: it has forged a system of waste and energy exchange between the local city administration, a power plant, a refinery, a fish farm, a pharmaceutical plant and a wallboard manufacturer (Gibbs & Deutz 2007).

Micro-entrepreneurial and Entrepreneurial Training: Training programs for entrepreneurs, and start-ups especially, can spur job creation within the community and significantly contribute to creating new (and green) jobs. In 2009, the Ewing Marion Kauffman Foundation offered $1 million of training programs to entrepreneurs in communities hard hit by layoffs and the recession in the US. Its FastTrac program encourages local hiring and coaches small local businesses through the start-up challenges (PND 2009). Micro-entrepreneurial training simply refers to business activities on a smaller scale. Commonly pursued in developing countries, organizations like Kiva give small loans and provide the training necessary for the entrepreneurs to succeed (See Micro-credit for more information).

Environmental Business Cluster: Founded in 1994 by the City of San Jose and the San Jose State University Research Foundation, the San Jose Environmental Business Cluster caters specifically to start-up companies offering products, technologies or services related to renewable energy generation, energy storage or efficiency, biofuels, water purification and management, waste and wastewater treatment, recycling and pollution reduction. This incubator offers emerging businesses a variety of services such as access to building space, office supplies, expert coaching and training, advisory services and access to investors. Financial support is provided by over a dozen organizations and has helped over 150 emerging companies (Environmental Business Cluster 2010).

New Dawn Enterprises: Founded in 1976, New Dawn Enterprises in Cape Breton, Nova Scotia, is Canada's oldest community development corporation. From modest beginnings, it has grown to encompass ten companies engaged in a range of activities related to real estate, training and healthcare. Today New Dawn employs upwards of 175 people and serves over 600 Cape Bretons daily (New Dawn 2011). In its pursuit of viable economic activities, it operates much like a business, but its focus is not return on investment but benefits to the community. New Dawn creates jobs, affordable housing and care for the elderly, to name a few social benefits.

Greyston Foundation: For 30 years, Greyston Foundation in Yonkers, New York, has worked to create jobs and housing opportunities for a community with the largest concentration of poverty in the otherwise-affluent Westchester County. Greyston Bakery employs 65 workers

who were formerly homeless or incarcerated. The foundation has also helped to establish local HIV/AIDS programs, family service programs, job training and life skills programs, housing, a Healing Centre, childcare facilities, community gardens and a Technology Education Centre (Greyston Foundation, 2011).

Van Buren County Hospital: The board of directors and staff of Van Buren County Hospital in Iowa began an extensive community planning process in 1990. The goal was to find diverse and creative ways to provide quality medical care and contribute to community health. Instead of buying expensive medical technologies, they set out to improve community health by creating economic opportunities for the county's high number of single mothers, unemployed and low-income residents. With local and state funding, they started a daycare center, computer training program and job linkage services using hospital facilities and computer equipment. In a vocational training program, they used the hospital kitchen to start up a bakery, which now operates at an outside location. By using hospital facilities, the costs of these programs and business start-ups were lower. The hospital generated revenues, local people gained career training and job opportunities, and Van Buren county gained much needed community services (Van Buren County Hospital 2011).

Examining Purchasing Policy: While many state or provincial governments have buy-local programs, local governments have adopted successful smaller-scale policies. In Hamilton, Montana, the City's policy requires local buying for any item or service valued up to $10,000, where the local bid wasn't in excess of 5 percent more than the non-local bids (Schmerker 2010).

Regulation

Greening Improves Bottom Line: Iowa's Fox River Sock Company took advantage of free energy audits offered by Iowa's Osage Municipal Utility Demand-side Management Program and identified opportunities to reduce energy costs per unit output by 30 percent. Since implementing the audit recommendations, the previously struggling Fox River company not only is thriving but has expanded production by about 300 percent and almost tripled its workforce (Fox River 2011). Fox River is not the only beneficiary of the municipality's program: the 3,600 residents of Osage use 25 percent less electricity than the state average, and the city estimates energy savings of more than $1 million per year for residents, local government and local businesses. The savings, which amount to more than $200 per year for homeowners (and more for most businesses), also translates into enhanced economic activity as energy conservation (and associated low utility rates) has drawn new businesses, mostly in manufacturing, to the community, thereby generating over 100 jobs (Russo 2008).

Municipal Bonds: In the US, many local governments have created bonds to raise money for projects in the public interest. Examples include waste treatment facilities, schools, bridges and road upgrades. While the return on investment is low, the financial advantage lies in the fact that the interest is exempt from federal and state taxes when bonds are purchased by residents of the state in which the bonds are issued (MSRB 2011).

Preserving Culture and Developing for Tourism: The City of St. John's, Newfoundland, is well-known for its unique city center, but it has taken significant efforts by local owners and the city to maintain this unique culture and character. From 1986 to 2001, property owners invested over $72 million in renovations, while the city contributed $10 million. Renovation versus rebuilding was encouraged so waste was reduced, developing housing in the city center was encouraged and the result is one of the most vibrant city centers for a city of its size. Tourism visits increased steadily over 2003 to 2008, as did the expenditures of these tourists (For more case study examples, see the Municipal Planning and Financial Tools for Economic Development Handbook).

Chapter 13

Climate Change

Climate change is a thorny and seemingly intractable problem, and it's not hard to see why. In the media, climate change is usually linked to images of forces beyond our control: hurricanes, floods, droughts, fires, migrating disease vectors and drowning polar bears to name a few. Our use of land, energy, water and materials in the modern era is resulting in temperature increases that threaten the capacity of our ecosystems to provide the environmental services we rely on for survival; these in turn prompt more haunting media stories. This vicious cycle can make us feel powerless and apathetic about our future and that of generations to come.

Compounding the problem is that greenhouse gas (GHG) emissions are produced by sources that are as numerous as they are diffuse. Unlike the problem of ozone-layer depletion, which could be substantially addressed through relatively painless phase-outs of ozone-degrading substances, climate change demands fundamental and sweeping long-term changes in how we organize our lives and our communities. To do this, we must mobilize our community capital, recognize our collective vulnerability and address weaknesses in governance.

Meanwhile, national and international efforts like those of climate change conferences in Copenhagen (2009) and Cancun (2010) have shown little success at controlling, let alone reducing, emissions. They are chronically hamstrung by controversy over differentiated responsibilities, the level of financial support of developing countries, technology transfer and trade subsidies and sanctions (Giddens 2009; Hufbauer and Kim 2010). President Obama's scientific advisor John Holdren likened this uncoordinated global effort to "being in a car with bad brakes, driving toward a cliff in the fog" (Weiss 2008). While politics undoubtedly play a role, others see it primarily as an economic problem. Nicholas Stern, former chief economist at the World Bank, called climate change the largest market failure in history:

costs associated with the burning of fossil fuels and changes in land use are externalized by consumers to billions of people around the world who suffer rising sea levels, droughts, floods, devastating storms and depleted water resources (Stern 2007). (see Fig. 13.5: GHG per capita, page 237)

While politicians hedge and economists theorize, there is definite agreement among scientists that average temperatures on the Earth will increase by 2 to 6 degrees Celsius (3.6 to 7.2 degrees Fahrenheit) by the year 2100 (Pachauri & IPCC 2007). Although the precise nature of the impacts will be studied for years to come, the temperature gains are now expected to be irreversible. The current stock of *anthropogenic* (that is, originating from human activity) GHGs in the atmosphere will continue to increase Earth's temperature for at least 1,000 years (Solomon et al. 2009).

In the face of all this, it's no wonder that some people want to throw up their hands and do nothing. But there is good news in this picture.

We need not wait for the federal governments and international bodies that tend to lag rather than lead. When it comes to environmental standards and regulations that can mitigate against and adapt to climate change and other issues, some of the most effective have been developed by sub-national governments. By banning leaded gasoline, reducing dioxin emissions and dealing with acid rain, state/provincial legislatures and municipal councils have shown praiseworthy leadership. They can wield powerful tools to promote adaption to climate change, such as changes to building and tax codes, green procurement policies, incentive programs and a wide variety of voluntary or mandated initiatives. Communities also use tools such as zoning, property tax and transit to reduce emissions effectively. This chapter will offer a broad overview of the cutting-edge adaptation and mitigation strategies being currently implemented in communities like yours — but first, a brief review of the science of climate change and its implications for communities.

The Anthropocene

Climate change has heralded a new epoch. The scientific community has begun to call the period since the invention of the steam engine the Anthropocene, due to humanity's impact on the ecological and geological processes on Earth (Crutzen 2006).

The Stern Report

Former World Bank chief economist Nicolas Stern calculated the cost of keeping CO_2 concentrations below 550 parts per million at around 1 percent of global GDP by 2050. If nothing is done, however, the overall costs and risks of climate change are equivalent to losing at least 5 percent of global GDP each year, for many years to come. The cost of acting is indeed significant, but compared to the world's annual military spending of around 2.5 per cent of global GDP, it is far from prohibitive (Stern 2007).

A Climate Science Primer

Atmospheric carbon primarily originated from volcanic activity and the exchange of carbon between the atmosphere and the oceans (US EPA Office of Atmospheric Programs 2006b). Over the past 10,000 years, carbon, which naturally cycles between the various ecosystems, has been at relatively stable concentrations in the atmosphere. This stability has allowed human civilization to flourish.

The carbon cycle is the biogeochemical cycle by which carbon is exchanged between the hydrosphere, biosphere and atmosphere of the Earth. The movement of carbon through the various spheres occurs because of chemical, physical, geological and biological processes. While some spheres act as sources of carbon (they release more carbon than they absorb), others act as carbon sinks (they absorb more carbon than they emit). Oceans are the largest reservoir of carbon on the planet and act as carbon sinks. An examination of the global carbon budget shows the distribution of carbon between the various spheres and highlights where carbon sources and sinks arise. (see Fig. 13.1, color page C-3)

Carbon dioxide and other GHGs (with the exception of chlorofluorocarbons, or CFCs) are naturally occurring compounds in our atmosphere. These gases, including water vapor, temporarily absorb and re-emit heat radiating outwards from the Earth's surface towards space. Some of this outgoing heat is re-emitted back down towards the Earth; thus, greenhouse gases trap a fraction of outgoing heat, thereby keeping the planet warm enough to sustain life as we know it. The problem that scientists have identified is the exponential rise of GHG emissions from human activities. Such emissions enhance heat retention and cause further warming of the planet. This phenomenon is known as the "greenhouse effect." (see Fig. 13.2, color page C-2)

Many gases can trap and retain heat, but only a few are sufficiently abundant in the atmosphere to have a significant effect on the global climate. In order of abundance, these specific GHGs are:

- Water vapor
- Carbon dioxide (CO_2)
- Methane
- Nitrous oxide
- Ground-level ozone, a component of smog
- Halocarbons such as chlorofluorocarbons (CFCs) and other synthetic gases (Kirby et al. 2008)

Water vapor concentrations in the atmosphere are influenced by average temperatures and are not directly influenced by human activity. The other five GHGs are increasing in concentration as a direct result of human activity, and it is these that create the greatest concern among climate scientists. These "big five" GHGs primarily result from the burning of fossil fuels, deforestation, agriculture and the use of CFCs in manufacturing and refrigeration (US EPA Office of Atmospheric Programs 2006a).

The concentration of CFC-12 is now slowly declining in the atmosphere, thanks to the Montreal Protocol. Some of the other "new" halocarbon gases, synthesized to have a lower ozone-depleting impact, have very high global-warming potentials; these are to be phased out too by the Montreal Protocol, but in the meantime, they are contributing to global warming.

Abundance however is only half the story. Some gases are far more effective at trapping heat (in other words, they have a higher rate of absorption) than others. For example, the

Table 13.1:
Changes in atmospheric concentration of five greenhouse gases, before and after industrialization.
(Credit: Table adapted from Blasing, 2011.

Table 13.1: Changes in GHG since Industrial		
Greenhouse Gas	**Pre-1750 concentration**	**Concentrations in 2005**
Carbon dioxide	280 ppm	388.5 ppm
Methane	700 ppb	1870 ppb
Nitrous oxide	270 ppb	323 ppb
Ground-level ozone	25 ppb	34 ppb
CFC-12[a]	zero	535 ppt

absorption rates of methane and nitrous oxide are much higher than that of CO_2. Methane is 25 times better at absorbing heat and warming the atmosphere than CO_2, while nitrous oxide is 298 times better. As well, some gases reside in the atmosphere much longer than others: CFCs, for example, have a residence time of about 100 years, compared to about a decade for methane. Differences in absorption rates and residence time coupled with different levels of relative abundance in the atmosphere make it difficult to determine the relative contribution of the various gases to climate warming. As a matter of convenience, when speaking of CO_2 levels in the atmosphere, scientists usually assume that the other gases are being considered too (Karl, Melillo & Peterson 2009).

Climate change may well be the defining issue of our time: it is up to us to limit its effects and, in the long term, adapt to the changes that are sure to come. Climate change is already having impacts on the world's communities by putting our food and water in jeopardy, threatening our health and well-being and increasing competition between nations over access to resources. The changes are not just a result of burning fossil fuels. In many parts of the world, forests are being felled for timber, paper and pasture land, releasing more CO_2 and removing valuable carbon sinks (Kirby et al. 2008).

What's a Couple of Degrees to Your Community?

The Intergovernmental Panel on Climate Change (IPCC) has developed a widely used set of emissions scenarios that present possible trajectories for the Earth's temperature over the next 100 years. From these, climate scientists predict the likely impacts to our ecosystems and the global climate system, and extrapolate these to concerns about human health, water resources, rising sea-level and impacts on agriculture (Pachauri & IPCC 2007). (see Fig. 13.3, color page C-4)

Assuming their projections of global temperature increases of 4°C are true, this is how climate change will look when it comes to a neighborhood near you:

- **Ecosystems:** Deserts and dry lands are likely to become hotter, resulting in decreased soil moisture and increased fire, erosion and invasion by non-native plants (Karl, Melillo & Peterson 2009). Traditional ranges of plants and animals have already shifted poleward. Species of North American birds, for example, have shifted their breeding colonies further north as traditional grounds become increasingly inhospitable (Peterson & Martínez-Meyer 2009).
- **Human Health:** Climate change may have profound impacts on human health, as these relate to more extreme heat events, extreme weather events such as hurricanes, migrating disease vectors, increased pollen production and worsening air quality (Costello et al. 2009).
- **Water Resources:** Climate change has altered and will continue to alter the water cycle, affecting where, when and how much precipitation falls and what quantity will be available for human use and consumption. Floods are projected to become more common and severe, as are droughts — primarily in locations already facing serious water shortages. Areas that depend on glaciers and snowpack for water will see runoff times shifting earlier into the spring and flows lowering in the summer (Karl et al. 2009).

- **Sea-level Rise:** Thermal expansion of the world's oceans, coupled with increased melting rates of glaciers and icecaps around the world, suggest that global sea levels could rise by over a meter per century (Rahmstorf 2010). Despite being an upper limit relative to most current projections, a one-meter sea-level rise would mean that some low-lying islands of the world would be underwater by 2100. Low-lying river deltas would either be submerged or flooded more frequently by storm surges and increased precipitation levels. (see Fig. 13.4, color page C-4)

- **Changing Weather Patterns:** Hurricanes and typhoons appear to be increasing in intensity as a result of increasing average ocean temperatures. Coupled with rising sea levels, this means that the storm surges that accompany such massive events will be greater. Civic infrastructure including dykes, dams and roads designed to handle 100-year storm events may be vulnerable (Anthes et al. 2006).

- **Food and Agricultural Production:** Although increased levels of CO_2 in the atmosphere have improved yields for some crops, the predicted temperature rise will have detrimental effects on agricultural production over the long haul. Extreme weather events are likely to reduce crop yields as excesses or deficits of water reduce plant growth rates. Weeds, plant diseases and pests will benefit from increased temperatures, increasing the need for pesticides and herbicides in agriculture (Howden et al. 2007). Livestock grazing pastures are likely to decline in quality as grasslands and rangelands are impacted by GHGs, resulting in lower nitrogen and protein content

Climate Change Impacts Human Health

"Climate change is the biggest health threat of the 21st Century" (Costello et al. 2009, 1693). This statement opened Costello and others' (2009) report *Managing the Health Effects of Climate Change,* a joint publication by the British medical journal *The Lancet* and the University College London Institute for Global Health Commission. In it, the authors outline the major threats and key challenges for global health from climate change. They call for a public health movement that frames the threat of climate change for humanity as a health issue and urge governments, international agencies, non-governmental organizations, communities and academics to work together to better plan for, adapt to and mitigate against climate change.

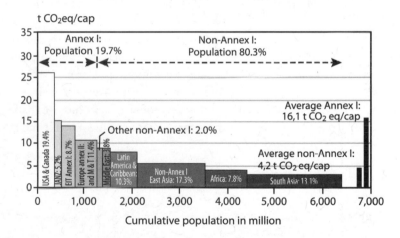

Fig. 13.5: *Distribution of regional per capita GHG emissions (all Kyoto gases including those from land use) over the population of different country groupings in 2004. The percentages in the bars indicate a region's share in global GHG emissions. It is important to note that per capita emissions like these conceal great disparities within national populations.* (CREDIT: ADAPTED FROM BOLIN AND KHESGI, 2001 USING IEA AND EDGAR 3.2 DATABASE INFORMATION (OLIVIER ET AL. 2005, 2006).)

of plants. As well, livestock will face the same heat extremes as humans, resulting in reduced milk production, slower growth and declining fecundity (Smit & Skinner 2002).

The Opportunity for Action

There is nothing given about it; there is nothing set in stone .... We have to make a decision. Do we want to live sustainably and have a better future for everyone, or are we happy to throw four billion years of evolutionary history away, and our futures away, just because we can't think about life without fossil fuels at the moment?

Tim Flannery, head of Australia's Climate Commission and of the Copenhagen Climate Council (As quoted in Smith 2011).

Despite high carbon dioxide emissions levels — levels that rose even throughout the 2008-2009 global economic recession — there is still some good news: we need not wait for industry and government to act on our behalf to combat climate change. Citizens and their communities can and should take the lead — and as the tools and initiatives section of this chapter will show, many are. In fact, the community is arguably the most important level on which we should be taking action — and judging by the pace of international negotiations, it is certainly the easiest place to start. Indeed, unless communities and their governments make a move, national governments won't get the message that we are serious. And we know that municipalities *can* push national and international bodies into action, because they have before. One of the most successful international agreements ever started as a municipal initiative on a pressing international climate issue: the depletion of our ozone layer.

Solutions? Right Here

Unlike CFCs, which were limited to a relatively small number of products, CO_2 and the other GHGs are by-products of critical systems such as transportation, manufacturing, agriculture and construction. To keep climate change to a manageable level while maintaining our

CFCs and the Montreal Protocol

International agreements in the battle to control CFCs offers hope and a way forward for future emissions negotiations. Scientists' discovery of the hole in the ozone layer over Antarctica compelled the world to tackle the threat it posed to human health and well-being. Developed and developing nations met under the auspices of the UN and drafted a resolution to phase out and eventually ban CFC production and consumption. In early 1989, the final document was ratified in Montreal, which gave the protocol its name and the world its first internationally binding protocol on harmful emissions. Under the Montreal Protocol on Substances that Deplete the Ozone Layer and the Vienna Convention on the Protection of the Ozone Layer, production of CFCs was to have ceased by January 1, 1996. Developing countries were given a ten-year grace period to phase out production. The Montreal Protocol has been successful at reducing production and consumption of ozone depleting substances. After reaching a peak in 1990, concentrations of these substances in the atmosphere have been steadily decreasing (UNEP 2010).

quality of life, we need a fundamental rethink about all of these systems. That's why almost all of the principles, tools and community initiatives offered in this book are as linked to the issue of climate change as they are to the more general goal of sustainability. For example:

- Composting our kitchen waste not only makes a great free soil fertilizer and relieves pressure on municipal facilities, it also reduces landfill emissions of one of the most potent greenhouse gases: methane.
- Retrofitting our buildings not only promises to save us money on energy costs and improve our productivity, it can also reduce the carbon emissions that come from heating, cooling and lighting of buildings.
- Making public transit viable for more people not only moves everyone faster and reduces congestion, it also reduces our overall emissions that come from private vehicle use.
- Water conservation not only reduces our water bills and infrastructure costs, it also helps mitigate the effects of climate change-induced drought.
- Grid layouts for our streets create more livable, transit-friendly communities; it also reduces the overall emissions profile of our communities.

The remainder of this chapter will focus on some of the climate change initiatives that don't readily fit under any one chapter heading (such as transportation, land use, water, energy or waste) of this book. The fact that they don't is instructive: it illustrates the multi-faceted nature of the climate change problem and suggests a way to think about the challenges and tailor responses to them. The key lies in holistic thinking.

Holistic thinking seeks to illuminate interactions, interconnections, interrelationships and patterns of change rather than static snapshots of space and time. Through holistic approaches, we can expand our vision to include multiple viewpoints and engage multiple stakeholders. Holistic thinking suggests that, in order to create change, one must recognize the interrelationships between behavioral, social, physical and natural systems at play (Danko 2010). Holistic thinking speaks to different interests, takes stock of the bigger picture and enables a larger variety of stakeholders to speak as well as be heard (Senge 1997). Holistic approaches will ensure that our investments in climate change adaptation and mitigation strategies are diverse and effective, as nobody wins if we make gains on one front while ignoring debits on another.

Combining Approaches to Adaptation and Mitigation

Early responses to predicted climate change impacts have focused on mitigating further emissions and attempting to reverse the trends in atmospheric GHG levels. However, it has become apparent that even the most stringent mitigation efforts will not avoid further impacts of climate change in the next few decades, which makes adaptation essential (Klein et al. 2007). Of course, mitigation will still play an important role because, without it, adaptation for many regions will be impossible (Anderson & Bows 2008). The IPCC (2007) found that by consciously creating synergies between adaptation and mitigation strategies, communities can create effective policies that are more cost-effective and more attractive to more stakeholders, including potential funding agencies (Klein et al. 2007). In its 2007 report, the IPCC concluded that sectors with the greatest opportunities for such synergies are agriculture, forestry, building and urban infrastructure. (see Fig. 13.6, color page C-5)

Mitigation strategies are those that seek to reduce the sources or enhance the sinks of greenhouse gases, while adaptive strategies respond to actual or expected climatic changes to reduce negative impacts or benefit from new opportunities. For example, switching to renewable energy sources or planting more trees to increase carbon uptake are mitigative strategies that reduce greenhouse gases. Planting trees or other vegetation along streets can also be an adaptive strategy for managing predicted increases in stormwater runoff.

While communities have primarily sought to address climate change via mitigation, adaptation has become an equally important tool to manage climate risk and reduce a community's overall vulnerability. A study by Bulkeley et al. (2009) identified a new wave of municipal programs that seek to adapt *and* mitigate through changes to the built environment, transportation and public services. Their study investigated efforts at mitigation and adaptation in ten cities (Beijing, Hong Kong, Delhi, Mumbai, Yogyyakarta, Seoul, Melbourne, Cape Town, Sao Paulo and Mexico City) pursuing climate change policies. Bulkeley et al. (2009) concluded that municipal authorities should:

- Mainstream climate change across different policy domains in order to develop effective policy and action;
- Identify where municipalities can save money by taking action (for example, energy efficiency) to gain the finance and support necessary for action and;
- Engage with stakeholders on a city-wide basis.

Decisions on adaptation and mitigation are taken at differing levels of government with differing degrees of influence between those levels. Effective mitigation requires the participation of major GHG emitters on a global scale, whereas adaptation efforts are more likely to occur at local and regional levels. The climate benefits of mitigation are experienced at a global scale, while the associated costs accrue at a local level; adaptation, on the other hand, accrues benefits and costs at both the local and national levels. Consequently, mitigation is most often pursued through international agreements and national public policies that may be complemented by unilateral or voluntary actions. For example, the United Nations Framework Convention on Climate Change is an international agreement signed and ratified in 1992 by 186 nations, including Canada and the United States, that calls for stabilization of greenhouse gas concentrations in the atmosphere. Adaptation by comparison usually involves private actions of affected parties or communities through local policies and initiatives.

Holistic approaches that adapt and mitigate against climate change require that we look for new and multiple ways to engage people from within and outside of our organizations. An obvious place to start is to visualize the points where issues of climate change naturally intersect with people's other pressing concerns. By locating our initiatives at these intersections, we increase buy-in for climate change initiatives from diverse actors in business, government and civil society, as the following examples illustrate.

Air Quality

Cleaner air is a cause everyone can buy into, and actions to address it easily converge with actions to mitigate climate change.

Air quality problems, such as smog and acid rain, vary according to local conditions, but largely result from the same chemicals that contribute to climate change. For example, ground-level ozone, a component of smog, can inhibit photosynthesis in plants, exacerbate human health problems and contribute significantly to climate change (Garthwaite et al. 2009). Sulphur dioxide, emitted primarily from industrial processes, is a primary cause of acid rain and contributes to plant, forest and crop damage and the deterioration of structures and materials (Mehta 2010). Sulphur dioxide can also provoke or exacerbate health problems (Shea et al. 2008). Nitrogen oxides (a greenhouse gas produced through denitrification, biomass burning and fossil fuel combustion) can increase susceptibility to viral infections such as influenza, irritate the lungs and cause bronchitis and pneumonia. Low-level exposure to carbon monoxide from motor vehicles may exacerbate heart disease and compromise brain function (Shea et al. 2008).

Not surprisingly, solutions designed to address air quality and related health issues can also mitigate climate change. Local governments can and do take significant corrective actions. One example is the Los Angeles South Coast Air Quality Management District (AQMD) plan, the most well-resourced and comprehensive effort to improve air quality ever drawn up locally in the US. While some of the city's proposed actions to improve local air quality were arguably outside their jurisdiction, they were supported by court decisions that highlighted the region's non-compliance with federal air quality standards.

In 2010, the Greater Los Angeles Area had 109 days when the regional air quality did not meet the minimum requirement under federal law. In response, the AQMD developed the "Challenge of 100 Days" with the goal of improving daily air quality in the region. Programs designed to remove pollution sources included a broad base of initiatives such as: funding a portion of the replacement costs in lawnmower exchanges, developing smart-phone apps that report on local air quality, sponsoring international conferences on improving air quality, investing in research and development of electric vehicles, developing green ports that reduce the need for ships to burn diesel fuel while docked, promoting the use of safer solvents that reduce the formation of smog, funding large-scale reforestation programs and promoting responsible personal transportation choices (AQMD 2011).

Disaster Preparedness

Damage due to natural disasters such as floods, hurricanes and droughts have been increasing in intensity and frequency at a greater rate than damage related to earthquakes. Citizens and their governments can use these newsworthy events to deliver timely messages about

Cleaning the Air in Mexico City

In 1990, Mexico City recorded 333 days when ground-level ozone quantities were considered hazardous to human health. Since then, the government has taken action to reduce smog and air pollution in the city by: implementing city-wide monitoring of air quality, replacing oil-burning power plants with natural gas plants, renovating taxi fleets, expanding the metro, launching hybrid buses, licensing private cars to drive only on select days of the week, sponsoring car-free days on city streets to encourage biking and walking and greening the city through rooftop gardens. By 2004, the number of days of dangerous ozone levels had been reduced to 180 (McKinley et al. 2005).

climate change and the importance of disaster preparedness.

The 2003 heat wave in Europe resulted in the "excess" death of 52,000 Europeans and is considered the deadliest climate-related event in Western history (Larson 2006). Meehl and Tebaldi (2004) showed that the heat waves that occurred over Europe and North America coincided with a specific atmospheric circulation pattern that was intensified by ongoing increases in greenhouse gases, which the researchers predicted would lead to more severe heat waves in those regions in the future. Subsequent heat waves in 2006 and 2007 appeared to support their findings, but effective disaster planning and management initiatives helped significantly lower the death toll (Fouillet et al. 2008).

The specter of increased hurricanes, tornados, inundation due to heavy precipitation and heat waves behooves us to enhance our building codes, place boundaries on where we build and improve infrastructure to cope with these events.

Sea-level rise in the United Kingdom is predicted to have serious impacts on coastal cities and towns, with certain consequences for people and economies. The UK government now requires coastal communities to monitor sea-level rises and rates of erosion and to upgrade existing infrastructure. In addition, construction codes are being overhauled to incorporate predicted impacts of sea-level rise (Tol, Klein & Nichols 2008). Similarly, the Australian state of New South Wales has developed guidelines considering sea-level rise in land-use planning and development assessments in their coastal areas. Their aim is to promote sustainable land-use planning guided by the precautionary principle. Coastal regions are developing coordinated strategic regional plans to identify high-risk areas, locate urban development safely and ensure that local plans specify appropriate setbacks (Nelleman & Corcoran 2010).

Disaster preparedness must also consider the nature of the predicted climate change impacts. Not all climate-related disasters take the form of sudden isolated events. Many will develop slowly, impacting large regions and producing *environmental refugees*, people displaced by profound changes to habitat and ecology. Coordinated disaster responses therefore require us to anticipate these slower but equally devastating processes, such as climate-related famines, that may result in large shifts of marginalized people.

Biodiversity

People from many walks of life identify strongly with the state of animals, plants and ecosystems in their own regions. For example, ecotourists and animal-lovers seek to protect charismatic mega fauna such as bears and whales; agriculturalists are vigilant about invasive species; and many indigenous cultures still rely heavily on their immediate natural surroundings for sustenance and survival.

As a result of increasing average temperatures, large-scale poleward shifts in the

Climate Disasters Take Many Forms

Temperate regions are by no means isolated from climate change fallout. For example, steadily warmer winters played a role in the massive pine beetle infestation in British Columbia forests, dramatically impacting one of the province's most important industries and devastating the economies of its many forest-dependent communities. Its economic damage was likened by many analysts to that of a national natural disaster.

traditional ranges of many plants are underway and many arctic and sub-arctic species are in crisis. The polar bear, an iconic denizen of the North, has become the cause célèbre of climate change action. The World Wildlife Fund, Nature Canada, The Center for Biological Diversity and Greenpeace are using its image for education and fundraising campaigns to combat climate change. Thus, rallying support for species conservation and protection of the environment can also been seen as an opportunity to take action against climate change.

Community forests are another site where the interests of numerous groups converge with action on climate change. As many communities have discovered, community-managed forests can provide sustainable forest products, stable employment and recreation opportunities; reduce the ecological impacts of harvesting; and limit the severity of forest fires — all while serving as important carbon sinks (Charnley & Poe 2007).

Just Sustainability

Like sustainability, responding to climate change at its core is a question of equity, for people today and for future generations. Most people readily embrace the idea that everyone should have access to a reasonable share of critical life-giving resources like clean water and air, safe food and adequate shelter; however, research shows that climate change and inaction on it will disproportionately affect poor countries and poor people in rich countries (Costello et al. 2009; Goffman & Steinbeck 2006; Kirby et al. 2008; Pachauri & IPCC 2007). Changing weather patterns, declining agricultural output in developing nations and costs of mitigation

Payment for Environmental Services

The Millennium Ecosystem Assessment (2005) calculated the consequences of ecosystem change for human well-being. It concluded that, in the past 50 years, the world population has doubled and economic output increased six-fold by running down our natural capital assets (MEA 2005). While conversion of natural capital is not necessarily a bad thing, many activities that pollute and degrade the environment rarely pay the true costs of resource exploitation. For example, farmers have market incentives to cut forests in order to create new fields, but aren't required to compensate the public for loss of environmental services those forests provide (such as mitigating climate change by removing air pollutants). The failure of market mechanisms to factor in all costs and benefits of a particular action (such as cutting down a forest) is what economists call a *market failure;* the unaccounted factors (costs and/or benefits) are termed *externalities.* Negative externalities as well as the rate and levels of natural capital conversion by the private and public sectors are higher than they would be if the true costs of land conversion and pollution were actually borne by developers (Engel, Pagiola & Wunder 2008). A Payment for Environmental Services (PES) is a way to remove market incentives for land managers to exploit the natural capital on their lands, most commonly by paying them to preserve the forest. The beneficiaries of the forest's air cleaning services, in this case the public, would pay for its preservation. The amount paid to the land manager is most commonly calculated as the opportunity cost (equivalent to the benefits the land managers would have received had they converted the land).

Energy and Food Security

Rising transportation costs, as a result of increasing oil scarcity and world oil demand, could make today's agro-industrial food distribution model too dear for the average consumer. The effects of floods, droughts and the cumulative stresses of intensive large-scale agriculture coupled with rising transportation costs lead many to believe that tomorrow's food production will occur closer to our dinner tables (Rubin 2009).

and adaptation wreak greatest havoc for those with the least disposable income. Awareness is growing that climate change adaptation strategies must be *just* as well as *sustainable*. "Just sustainability" (see chapter 1) demands that we consider how these resources, and the power to decide how they are allocated, are distributed — from local to international scales. For example, we might ask: What is a fair per capita share of water? Who are the most vulnerable among us during extreme weather events, why is this so, and what can we do to address that? How can our planning processes be made more democratic?

Any course of action that is informed by a just-sustainability ethic requires that we consider elements such as who is most responsible for climate change, what level of burden-sharing is appropriate for assistance to vulnerable communities, how should such assistance be distributed and what form should equitable participation in adaptation planning take. Paavola and Adger (2006) suggest that countries should focus on policies that avoid dangerous climate change, promote forward-looking responsibility, put the most vulnerable first and provide for equal participation of all. Community-level responses should consider residential energy

efficiency, the affordability of essential energy services and the price changes that occur as a result of emissions trading and other responses to climate change (Westmore 2008).

Just sustainability therefore offers one more way that that holistic thinking and synergistic action on climate change can offer opportunities to pose better questions, develop better plans and engage more people.

Energy Security

Peak oil; the environmental threats posed by oil exploration, extraction and transportation; and the ever-increasing human and military costs of securing future oil supplies resonate among people across the political spectrum. Even climate change skeptics are likely already equipped with motives (spiraling dependence on foreign oil supplies) to adopt energy security measures that also help lower carbon emissions. Many tools and initiatives for one do double duty on the other. For example, some energy utilities are reducing demand on existing supplies and infrastructure by offering to purchase excess energy generated by small wind or solar systems installed by homeowners and businesses.

Green Procurement

Local governments can apply holistic thinking by scrutinizing all aspects of their operations for opportunities to be conscious consumers — and apply collective buying power as a force for change. Green procurement is the selection of products and services that minimize environmental impacts. Well-established in some departments of federal government, it offers lessons for local governments. For example, the US Environmental Protection Agency (EPA) developed the Environmentally Preferable

Purchasing (EPP) program to help the federal government "buy green"; in so doing, it stimulates demand for green products and services. The EPA EPP website is an excellent place for purchasers, vendors and consumers to find the latest in green products and procurement policies.

Tapping the Power of the Collective

Holistic thinking also requires thinking beyond the boundaries of our communities. That's why communities who are active on climate change are building and joining coalitions and networks. Critical connections among local, provincial and state governments are being forged through state- and provincial-level initiatives such as the Partners for Climate Protection (PCP) program in Canada.

Municipal governments that have committed to reducing greenhouse gases and acting on climate change have formed a network through the PCP program, funded by the Federation of Canadian Municipalities (FCM) Green Municipalities Fund. Thirty-seven municipalities contributed data on 182 measures for its 2010 PCP National Measures report. Collectively, their municipal initiatives resulted in annual GHG reductions of 350,000 tons and represent more than $145 million in green investments (Federation of Canadian Municipalities 2010). Examples of GHG-reducing initiatives include: lighting efficiency improvements, waste heat recovery systems, bans on idling, district heating, fleet improvements and landfill gas recovery systems. Best practices in community sustainability are celebrated each year with the FCM Sustainable Community awards in the areas of brownfields, buildings, energy, planning, residential development and integrated neighborhood development.

Communities are reaching beyond their borders for support as well. Over 500 municipalities around the world, which collectively represent about 8 percent of the world's GHG emissions, have joined forces with the International Council for Local Environmental Initiatives (ICLEI) Cities for Climate Protection campaign to develop strategies to reduce energy consumption and CO_2 emissions (ICLEI 2004). Each city has pledged to develop a local emissions-reducing action plan.

Communities are also combating climate change by sharing information and successes with each other via online networks. Networks have the capacity to stimulate social innovation and policy diffusion and serve as a source of inspiration for network members. For example, LiveSmartBC, hosted by the Climate Action Secretariat (CAS 2011), provides an online space where municipal and provincial government officials, along with private and public sector practitioners share and discuss ideas on how to mitigate against or adapt to climate change, disseminate "best practices" policy solutions, provide support and stimulate change. A similar network, *Pando | Sustainable Communities* (see appendix) focuses not only on climate change solutions but also on planning for sustainable community development. In addition to local government and practitioners, this network seeks to engage researchers from local universities to harness knowledge and work collectively to move towards sustainability.

By tapping into the collective knowledge and addressing climate change in a holistic and collaborative fashion, communities can make decisions that reduce dependence on greenhouse gases, adapt to changes in climate and promote sustainable development.

Transitioning to a Green Economy: Can We Afford Not to?

In chapter 12, we focused on sustainable community economic development (CED) as a way to integrate economic, social and environmental objectives. Here we look more closely at greening the economy as a whole. Many economists still claim that economic growth is fundamental to human development and that a transition to a green economy could jeopardize world economic recovery after the recession of 2008 (BBC News 2011). However, a 2011 report by the United Nations Environment Program (UNEP 2011) demonstrates that by investing 2 percent of global GDP per year (approximately US $1.3 trillion, which amounts to less than half of the world's defense spending, it is possible to transition to a green economy based on sustainable growth. As defined by UNEP, a green economy is:

> one that results in improved human well-being and social equity, while significantly reducing environmental risks and ecological scarcities. In its simplest expression, a green economy can be thought of as one which is low carbon, resource efficient and socially inclusive. In a green economy, growth in income and employment should be driven by public and private investments that reduce carbon emissions and pollution, enhance energy and resource efficiency, and prevent the loss of biodiversity and ecosystem services. These investments need to be catalyzed and supported by targeted public expenditure, policy reforms and regulation changes. The development path should maintain, enhance and, where necessary, rebuild

natural capital as a critical economic asset and as a source of public benefits, especially for poor people whose livelihoods and security depend on nature (UNEP 2011).

To spur green investments, national and international policies must promote green technology and green jobs. The report's key findings state that a green economy can produce higher growth in GDP and GDP per capita and generate as much or more growth and employment than the best business as usual scenario, while yielding significant social and environmental benefits such as job creation and poverty alleviation (UNEP 2011). Significant government reform on investment and spending is crucial to make the transition to a green economy. A significant amount of financing is also required; this amount however is an order of magnitude smaller than annual global investment.

Switching to a green economy can also produce a number of economic benefits, such as: lower energy costs that come from conservation and energy efficiency; growth of businesses that sell energy-efficient technologies; growth of renewable energy businesses; more disposable income from increasing taxes on the inefficient use of energy and using that money to reduce taxes on income and capital; and reduced repair costs for damage to the environment and human health caused by climate change and other pollutants.

Tools and Initiatives

Voluntary

CLIMATE CHANGE PREPARATION IN LONDON, UK

In 2001, the Greater London Authority set up the London Climate Change Partnership (LCCP), with representatives from a wide range of governments and agencies. The LCCP prepared several guides and strategies for areas of expected impact including transportation, buildings and the financial sector. The official London Plan was revised to incorporate climate change mitigation and adaptation policies; a senior policy officer was appointed to develop a preparedness strategy using a process of extensive stakeholder engagement. The partnership has also published Adapting to Climate Change: Creating Natural Reslience, a comprehensive report on climate change impacts and adaptation measures for the London urban region (LCCP 2009).

EPA CLIMATE LEADERS

Businesses of all sizes — from small to Fortune 500 — in many states have entered formal partnerships with the Environmental Protection Agency (EPA) to develop comprehensive climate change strategies. Partner companies commit to reducing their impact on the global environment by setting aggressive GHG reduction goals. Through program participation, companies create a credible record of their accomplishments and receive EPA recognition as corporate environmental leaders. Climate Leaders Partners range from Fortune 100 corporations to small businesses and represent many industries and sectors, from manufacturers and utilities to financial institutions and retailers, with operations in all 50 states (US EPA 2006).

CLIMATE REGISTRY

The climate registry is an online space where local and provincial/state/territorial governments, as well as businesses and non-governmental organizations within Canada, the United States and

Carbon Pricing

Carbon pricing refers to policy measures that make it more expensive to burn fossil fuels or to purchase goods and services that have large emissions of carbon in their production (Lee 2011). Two ways to price carbon are carbon taxes and *cap-and-trade*. North America's first carbon tax was implemented in 2008 in British Columbia. The modest tax of $20 per tonne of carbon (scheduled increase to $30 by 2012) was designed to be revenue-neutral with personal and corporate tax cuts as well as credits for low-income households (Lee 2011). Cap-and-trade systems differ in that government sets an overall limit on emissions, creates permits equivalent in number to this limit and allocates permits to emitters via auction or grandfathering rules. It is then up to the emitters (such as power producers) to figure out the most cost-effective way to stay under the limit. Since permits are tradable between emitters, companies whose emission levels fall under the cap can sell their surplus permits to those that don't; this creates a powerful incentive for emissions reductions. Originally introduced in the US to control sulphur dioxide and nitrogen dioxide emissions that cause acid rain, cap-and-trade proved effective in bringing about absolute reductions of these gases (Rubin 2009).

A different but much less effective way to reduce GHG emissions is through *carbon offsets*. A carbon offset is a credit for GHG reductions achieved by one party that can be purchased and used to compensate for (offset) the emissions of another. Carbon offsets are typically measured in tonnes of CO_2-equivalents (or CO_2e). They're bought and sold through international brokers and online retailers and trading platforms (Wara & Victor 2008).

Mexico voluntarily report their greenhouse gas emissions based on specific standards for calculation and reporting. Reported emissions are verified by a qualified company. By providing a standardized method, the registry hopes to create a common language for politically and geographically diverse regions to help support actions against climate change. The registry is financed through annual membership fees that range from $450 to $10,000. As of May 13 2011, the registry had 421 members (Climate Registry 2009).

Renewable Energy Commitment

The City of Calgary completed a green power contract in May of 2010 with ENMAX Corporation to provide at least 75 percent of its municipal electricity needs from renewable sources with a plan to increase that share to 90 percent by 2012. Greenhouse gas emission reductions at city-owned facilities are estimated to be 170,000 tonnes by 2012 — a 63 percent reduction from 1990 levels (Partners for Climate Protection 2010).

Incentives
Live Smart BC

In partnership with BC Hydro and FortisBC, the government of British Columbia developed the LiveSmart BC: Efficiency Incentive Program, where homeowners can receive more than $7,000 in rebates for energy-saving improvements and equipment. The program aims to help more than 40,000 BC families improve their homes' energy profiles and take action on climate change.

Energy Buy-back

New Mexico's El Paso Electric Company is offering to buy excess power generated by small (up to 10 kilowatt capacity) and medium (10 kilowatt to 100 kilowatt capacity) solar and wind energy systems installed by homeowners and businesses. All systems must be connected to the utility's grid. Energy is bought at a rate of $0.12 per kilowatt hour for small solar systems and $0.155 for medium systems. For wind systems, the company will purchase excess energy at $0.08 per kilowatt hour for small systems and $0.028 for medium systems. This program is designed to reduce demand on the existing grid and provide incentives for installation of renewable energy systems (El Paso Electric 2011).

Expenditure
Green Procurement

In 2008, the City of Portland, Oregon, adopted a Sustainable Procurement Policy, to direct public spending to goods and services that minimize negative environmental impacts, are fair and socially just and make economic sense now and in the long-term. The Sustainable Procurement Policy complements and builds on many other environmental and social programs in the city.

Climate Parks

Onsevig Climate Park, located in the village of Onsevig, Denmark, has employed a variety of adaptive and mitigative strategies to protect itself against the effects of climate change. The village has constructed a series of dykes to adapt to potential sea-level rises, increased storm frequencies and sudden storm surges. The dykes also collect stormwater runoff for reuse. The village has also experimented with growing algae as a source of biofuel and animal food, as well as using waves and wind to produce energy for the community.

URBAN HEAT ISLAND EFFECT

Toronto Public Health is developing a mapping tool that indicates areas of vulnerability to extreme heat. The maps will incorporate indicators on surface temperatures, green space coverage, housing and social characteristics of at-risk populations, access to air conditioning and locations of cool places. The heat-mapping tool will be used for delivering resources during extreme heat events (Richardson 2010).

ENVIRONMENTAL BUDGETING

The city of Heidelberg, Germany, uses environmental budgeting to promote sustainability. The inclusive and collaborative planning process applies financial budgeting to the management of natural resources, setting targets for energy efficiency, emissions, drinking water and waste. As former mayor Beate Weber explained: "With environmental budgeting, we have a reliable basis for decisions and can check if our aims are being met" (Girardet 2008).

PLANNING FOR CLIMATE CHANGE

Toronto was the first in Canada to establish a city-wide process to respond to its vulnerability to climate change. The steps included the creation of an Adaptation Steering Committee and the development of a framework document. The strategy was underpinned by existing programs that protect against weather extremes and included short-term actions as well as long-term processes for developing a comprehensive strategy (ICLEI 2010).

PLANNING FOR SEA-LEVEL RISE

The City of Halifax has developed one of the most comprehensive analyses of sea-level rise in North America. Through analysis of historical sea-level data and the latest in climate model predications, the city will be able to make sweeping changes to its master plan. Future activities include assessment of property vulnerabilities and measures such as minimum ground elevation for new development, engineered solutions such as raised seawall heights and land-use and development regulations for flood-prone areas (Richardson 2010).

URBAN FOREST MANAGEMENT PLAN

Boasting one of the largest contiguous civic green spaces in the world, Edmonton, Alberta, is taking dramatic steps to protect its urban forest, which helps keep neighborhoods cool, improves air quality, provides wildlife habitat, sequesters carbon, moderates storm runoff and prevents erosion. The city's integrated forest management seeks to address the effects on urban forests of drought, insect infestations, disease and storms. The comprehensive plan includes an inventory of the urban forest, replacement strategies for dead and dying plant material and city-wide outreach and education. The plan is integrated with existing fire, disaster and disease management plans (Richardson 2010).

WILDFIRE PROTECTION PLAN

Texas Forest Service has developed the Community Wildfire Protection Plan (CWPP), a user-friendly set of guides and tools for communities that wish to reduce the risk wildfires pose to the homes, businesses and natural resources. The plan empowers communities to share responsibility in determining the best strategies for protecting against forest fire threats. It includes an innovative online tool to help stakeholders develop their plan, monitor fuel and weather conditions and coordinate responses to wildfires (Texas Forest Service 2007).

Regulation
REDUCING EMISSIONS

Since 2004, California has taken many measures to control GHG emissions. This led in 2006 to a state law that requires overall GHG emissions in California be reduced to their 1990 levels by 2020, prohibits California utilities from signing new long-term base-load power contracts with emissions higher than those from combined-cycle natural gas and requires 20 percent of California's electricity to come from renewables by 2010 (Hanemann 2008).

In 2007, the US Conference of Mayors launched the Mayors Climate Protection Center to monitor the progress toward the goals of the Kyoto Protocol for the 710 municipalities who, independent of federal authorities, agreed to pursue Kyoto goals. The participating cities are committed to innovative land-use policies, forest restoration, changes to the building code and public information campaigns. As well, they have committed to pressuring state and federal authorities to enact policies that meet or exceed Kyoto targets and lobbying Congress to establish a national emissions trading scheme.

GOING CARBON-NEUTRAL

One hundred and seventy-nine of British Columbia's 188 municipalities signed the *BC Climate Action Charter* with the Province and the Union of BC Municipalities, committing to a goal of becoming carbon-neutral by 2012. Each signatory is committed to measuring and reporting their community profile of greenhouse gas emissions. They will also work to create compact, more energy-efficient communities. Achieving carbon neutrality will require BC's local governments to reduce their emissions from buildings and vehicle fleets, purchase carbon offsets and/or develop projects that offset their emissions. Many of the municipalities have shown significant reductions in their GHG emissions, while at the same time enjoying robust economic and social environments.

ECOSYSTEM RESTORATION

In order to slow and adapt to climate change, it is critical to restore nature's capacity to provide environmental services. Restoration programs implemented around the world have shown positive results in biodiversity conservation, water supply regulation, health and wastewater management, food security, climate change mitigation and disaster prevention, while providing economic benefits to the communities that initiated them (Nellemann & Corcoran 2010).

BANNING HARMFUL EMISSIONS

The cities of Irvine, California, and Newark, New Jersey, passed comprehensive bans on ozone-depleting compounds in 1989 and 1990, when international agreements would have allowed their use for another decade. Their leadership helped ensure that ozone depletion was put high on the agenda of senior governments.

ADAPTING TO DECLINING WATER LEVELS

In 2004, the City of Cape Town outlined a 10-point plan for achieving greater water conservation and for aligning civic water policy with national water policy. The initiatives included water restrictions, water tariffs, reducing leaks, pressure management and awareness campaigns. Other initiatives on the table but not yet adopted include to reuse effluent, harvest water from roofs, modify catchment vegetation and use seawater for sewerage.

Chapter 14

Communities Integrating Sustainability

Since *Toward Sustainable Communities* was first published in 1992, a remarkable shift has occurred. Many communities have moved beyond thinking about how specific sectors can be made more sustainable toward thinking about how sustainability can be realized in a very integrated way. Whether building communities from the ground up (greenfield developments) or transforming communities that already exist (brownfield developments), many communities and local governments really are pulling it all together.

This movement is being propelled by multiple forces. In Europe, the cost of energy and lack of landfill sites stimulate innovations based on synergies between generation of energy and waste treatment. In North America, green building principles and rating systems raise standards and awareness among government, industry and citizens alike. On both continents, change is being driven by a growing cadre of consumers, stakeholders, politicians, local government employees, designers, architects and planners that is increasingly well-versed in the "green" aspects of their own sectors and embraces collaboration across cultural, occupational and disciplinary boundaries.

By no means are these phenomena limited to the West. They are increasingly present in the great emerging urban powerhouses of India, China and the Middle East, where motivators also include spiraling population growth and urbanization. Joss (2010; 2011) has identified 79 sustainable or ecocity initiatives around the world. Of these, 34 are in Europe, particularly Scandinavia, the UK and Germany; 27 in Asia/ Australasia, 9 in North America, 4 in Africa, 3 in Latin America and 2 in the Middle East. Some of the most innovative developments are taking place in rapidly urbanizing parts of the world: China, for example, is reported (Wong 2009) to have embarked on an ambitious program to build some 40 new ecocities (including Changxing, Dongtan, MenTouGou, Tangshan Caofeidian, Tianjin Binhai and Wanzhuang).

Ongoing international dialogue and debate on disaster preparedness and response, economic crisis and the need for some measure of self-reliance now encompasses nations where, only two decades ago, sustainability had barely registered. In such regions — where rapid adoption of innovative technologies is not just an option but a necessity — great leaps forward are inspiring thinking around the world. They are poised to become leaders of massive technological, and possibly social, transformations.

Several communities have explicit CO_2 reduction targets as their key aim and focus: for example, Freiburg, in southern Germany, claims to have achieved a 25 percent CO_2 reduction by 2010 (compared with 1992 levels)

Fig. 14.1: *Designed to be the most environmentally advanced development in the United Kingdom, One Brighton in Brighton & Hove, England comprises 172 apartments plus office and community space. Its design integrates roof-top gardening opportunities, creates energy from biomass and solar technologies, provides ready access to local rapid transit and utilizes leading-edge green building technology, all in accordance with the One Planet Living principles.* (Credit: Crest Nicholson BioRegional Quintain LLP)

and aims to go further still; while Destiny, Florida, has signed on to a target of 80 percent reduction by 2050 (compared with 1990 levels of a similarly sized US city). Some go even further by planning for carbon-neutral footprints, such as Logrono Montecorvo, Spain; Masdar in the United Arab Emirates, "the world's first fully carbon-neutral city"; Malmö, Sweden, aiming to be carbon-neutral by 2020 and Black Sea Gardens, Bulgaria, "the world's first carbon-neutral luxury resort" (Joss 2011).

Other low-carbon communities of note include Beddington Zero Energy Development (BedZED), an environmentally friendly housing development in the outer London suburb of Hackbridge; Hammarby Sjöstad, a new community being developed in suburban Stockholm; Kronsberg, Germany, built for the 2000 World Exposition on a 1,200 hectare site located in the southeast city limits of Hannover; and Dockside Green, a 1,300,000 square-foot (121,000 m²) mixed-use community in Victoria, British Columbia, owned by VanCity Credit Union and notable for its developers' insistence on adhering to the strictest possible tenets of sustainable architecture or green building.

What follows is a collection of short profiles that introduce communities around the world that express these broader shifts. While none of them can be considered truly sustainable in the purest sense of the term, all of them exemplify rapid, comprehensive and inspiring movement toward sustainability that all communities can learn from.

The chapter concludes with a detailed case study of the model sustainable community closest to my own home: UniverCity, the community at Simon Fraser University. I have served on the board of the development trust overseeing the UniverCity project since its inception in 1999. I did not include it in the 2005 edition of this book because relatively few of the plans we had made had been implemented at that time. Now, however, UniverCity is a thriving community with thousands of residents, and it is a story worth sharing. Images from

Nanning, China

By Jielian Chen

Nanning has been named one of China's top-10 eco-friendly cities and has won environmental awards, including the UN Habitat Scroll of Honor Award and the Dubai International Award for Best Practices to Improve the Living Environment (Zhaohua 2011).

Nanning, in southern China, is the capital city of Guangxi province and the political, economic and cultural center of Guangxi Zhuang Autonomous Region. Nanning has six city districts and six counties under its administrative jurisdiction. In 2010, the total registered population of the whole city was 7.07 million, of which 2.71 million are from the urban area. The regional total value of production in Nanning is 180 billion yuan (Nanning 2011).

For Nanning to modernize its economy, it must further industrialize and urbanize. These two processes are inevitable, but neither can occur without a commensurate increase in energy consumption. Nanning is highly dependent on coal as its primary energy source.

To address this challenge, Nanning is making great advances in saving energy, reducing costs and utilizing biomass energy, including a "Green lighting and saving electricity project" started in 2008 that saves 200 million kilowatt-hours in electricity per year. It also saves 110 million Chinese yuan (US$17M) every year, as well as reducing 73.2 thousand tons of standard coal consumption (Chaoguang, Weiguang & Zhong 2008).

In 2010, Nanning was selected as one of 17 national demonstration cities for the application of renewable energy in buildings (Nanning 2010). Nanning is also going to pool its resources to increase the share of non-grain fuel ethanol and biodiesel, with an objective that at least 60 percent of the city's taxis and buses will be fueled by biogas (Miaomiao & Shiyan 2011).

Fig. 14.2: *Nanning, capital of the Guangxi province in China, is changing from its reliance on coal to more sustainable energy sources. Nanning has been selected as a demonstration city for renewable energy use in buildings and its electricity savings program has reduced coal usage by 7.3 million tons per year.* (CREDIT: JIJU HUANG)

UniverCity appear in this chapter and throughout the book.

Malmö, Sweden

Located in the southernmost province of Sweden and traditionally supported by marine activities and the shipping industry, Malmö has emerged as one of the country's four major urban centers. With high levels of immigration and a very culturally diverse population of about 310,000, Malmö is perhaps better positioned than many communities to consider change and draw on a wealth of cultural capital in community planning. Effective governance and high engagement of citizens and stakeholders receptive to change makes fertile ground for initiatives that support sustainability and bolster the local economy. In 2000, Malmö became connected to Copenhagen, Denmark, via Europe's longest road and rail bridge: the Øresund Bridge. Since then, Malmö has aggressively diversified, promoting liberal taxation policies and cross-border flows of resources, employment and business opportunities. Malmö is shooting to have local government operations climate-neutral by 2020, and to have the whole municipality running on 100 percent renewable energy by 2030.

Geothermal, wind, solar and biomass/biowaste are well-used energy sources in Malmö, and a number of its new greenfield developments that are considered at the leading edge in terms of green building technologies. Western Harbour, a new community that is rising from a former industrial area, is considered a world-class example of sustainability in architecture and community design. It reflects a strong focus on high energy-efficiency, low-carbon and zero-energy principles; use of healthy building materials; innovative mixed-income housing solutions; connectivity to the landscape through integration of waterways and habitat restoration; and celebration of the region's cultural capital through conscious integration of historical architectural styles. Malmö further seeks to integrate sustainability into daily life through encouragement of local agriculture, garden markets, green roofs, accessible and innovative stormwater features and park/greenspace connectivity. The city's sustainability initiatives not only enhance the lifestyle available to residents; they also serve to attract tourism, university students and new sustainable businesses (Peter 2006, 2008).

Belo Horizonte, Brazil

With 2.4 million people in its metropolitan core and 5.4 million in the surrounding region, the Brazilian city of Belo Horizonte shows that sustainability is not just about investing in energy efficiency and green infrastructure: food security and human and social capital play starring roles.

Responding to the great disparities that exist between rich and poor in Belo Horizonte, the city's government and citizens have undertaken an internationally recognized endeavor to "humanize" the local *favelas* (shantytowns) through measures meant to increase safety, access to services and food security. Initiatives guided by its municipally endorsed food-security program aim to meet three priorities: food security and healthy food using local-sourced food reserves for groups most at risk of malnutrition; solutions within the local economy, such as community-based opportunities to purchase low-priced pre-made meals at subsidized community restaurants and the availability of local "food baskets" to ensure healthy at-home options; and city-wide support and subsidy for increased local production of fruits and vegetables over more lucrative export crops. Government-operated "popular restaurants" take advantage of economies of scale to provide more than 5,000 nutritious meals a day at subsidized prices. The government has also taken steps to support local agriculture, by establishing a huge central farmers market, more than 45 general stores and at least one organic market to sell local farmers' produce. As well, the city buys local produce for the popular restaurants and schools.

Changes in Belo Horizonte were partly enabled by its "Participating Budget" process, which engages the local community annually and allows the citizenry to assist in making critical investments. It has enabled the ongoing support of local food subsidy and the creation of nearly 2,500 low-cost homes. By connecting right-to-food initiatives to the local economy and local land rights, government has won widespread buy-in to many initiatives that further increase the city's livability, such as land conservation and establishment of new parks (Roberts & Rocha 2008; World Mayors 2005).

Southeast False Creek, Vancouver, British Columbia

Southeast False Creek (SEFC) is a waterfront community situated adjacent to the downtown core of Vancouver, British Columbia. For more than 20 years, the district had been designated as a future model sustainable community. After being selected as the host city for the 2010 Winter Olympic Games, the City of Vancouver acted to realize this vision through development of a LEED-ND-Gold-certified, highly walkable mixed-use urban community that would initially house Olympic athletes in Vancouver for the games and later offer sustainable housing

to suit a range of incomes for up to 16,000 residents. Up to one-third of the housing units will be made available at below-market prices for lower-income households, both for purchase and rent. Planners of Southeast False Creek have consciously sought to utilize the region's cultural capital in the form of conservation of heritage buildings that served industrial waterfront purposes, integrating these as themes and focal points in the community plan. Amenities will include a community center, parks, an elementary school, pedestrian seawall, ready access to retail and services and an ecologically restored waterfront.

To date, about 1,800 units (each aiming for LEED-Gold certification) have been built on the site, making Southeast False Creek Canada's largest concentration of LEED-certified buildings and North America's best attempt yet at a sustainable, urban, high-density brownfield redevelopment. In addition to a district energy system that provides space heating and domestic hot water to buildings in the area (partly through recovery of waste heat from the city's central sewer trunk line), the development's buildings include ceiling-radiant technology for space heating and cooling, advanced solar thermal applications and sophisticated measures of indoor air quality (City of Vancouver 2010a; 2010b).

Sonoma Mountain Village, California

Sonoma Mountain Village is a mixed-use community that has been master-planned for a former industrial park 40 miles north of San Francisco, California. Construction is expected to begin in 2012. As the first full One Planet Living-endorsed community in North America and a LEED-ND platinum-certified community, the development is intended to be the

Fig. 14.3: *The Sonoma Mountain Village, outside of San Francisco, has been designed to be a built-green, transit-oriented mixed-use community that achieves a balance of jobs and accommodation. Planners expect it will generate 82 percent fewer emissions than comparable communities in the region.*
(CREDIT: SONOMA MOUNTAIN VILLAGE)

Municipal Sustainability Branding

Cities worldwide are branding themselves as the world's greenest city. Since 2000, Japanese cities have competed for the top spot in the national eco-city contest; in the US, a list of top sustainable cities is published annually (with Portland, Oregon, and San Francisco currently occupying the top spots). Masdar is a prime example of an initiative driven by the ambition to become "the world's first carbon-neutral, zero-waste city." In Germany, both Freiburg and Hamm have been known as "capital" (the latter winning a same-named national award in 1998), while Hamburg has more recently joined the competition by styling its regeneration project as Germany's first "entirely sustainable creative-industrial corporate development." Other cities include Vaxjo and Freiburg which both frequently trade on the label as Europe's "greenest city." Malmö promotes itself variably as climate/solar/ecocity, while Gothenburg aims to become a "super-sustainable city." Hanham Hall refers to itself as England's first zero-carbon development, competing with St. Davids, which claims to be the UK's first carbon-neutral city (Joss 2011).

first zero-carbon community on the continent — promising to set a new standard for comprehensive brownfield development in the United States.

The town's construction reflects a strong commitment to recycling of local materials: for example, its sidewalks will be constructed from concrete salvaged from the former industrial site's parking lots, and every 2,000 square feet of housing will contain six SUVs' worth of recycled local junkyard steel. Solar power will be widely employed in the community's public, retail, industrial, commercial and office buildings and in its nearly 1,700 individual residences, which will range from apartments to luxury homes. In keeping with its One Planet Living-endorsed design, Sonoma is expected to generate 82 percent lower transport emissions. Car- and bike-sharing programs, electric car fast-recharging centers and convenient rail connections promise to reduce auto-dependency. The community will be able produce 65 percent of its own food and use 65 percent less potable water. Social aspects have also been considered: the town's charter will require many local businesses to offer hiring preference to workers from Sonoma, and housing opportunities for low-income households will be double those required by local municipalities (eSolar Energy News 2011; Kraemer 2008; Peters 2009).

Masdar, United Arab Emirates

Masdar is a master-planned community under development about 17 kilometers from the United Arab Emirates (UAE) capital of Abu Dhabi, overseen by a development arm of the local government. It will support a population of about 40,000, serve as an incubator and commercialization agent for green-tech industries and host a university whose core focus will be research and design of (largely building- and energy-related) sustainable technologies. Although consideration of social and cultural capital — particularly as these relate to citizen participation, equity and governance — are notably absent from the Masdar plan, the city and its institutions will surely yield important sustainability insights that can be applied around the world, while helping diversify the UAE economy from its 60 percent dependence on oil-derived wealth. Planners expect Masdar to be the largest "living laboratory" for green building and renewable energy technologies in the world (Gunther 2011; Schwartz 2010).

UniverCity, near Vancouver, British Columbia

Established in 1965, Simon Fraser University is relatively young as a post-secondary institution but is consistently ranked as one of Canada's top comprehensive universities. Its spectacular setting — atop Burnaby Mountain in a Vancouver suburb — is typically regarded by students and faculty alike as an asset: combined with its award winning architecture, the coastal forest surroundings, commanding views of ocean and mountains and readily accessible network of mountain trails that offer a peaceful repose from city distractions. But from a sustainability viewpoint, the campus's comparatively remote location poses a serious challenge. Many casual cyclist-commuters were intimidated by the long ascent to campus. Limited onsite amenities or late-night transit service made the already quiet campus into something of a ghost town come nightfall as staff, faculty and most students left campus by car — often in single-occupant trips — even for basics like groceries.

This began to change in 1996, when SFU won approval from the City of Burnaby to develop a 65-hectare parcel next to the university as a compact, mixed-use and transit-oriented community in return for transferring 320 hectares of SFU's endowed land into the Burnaby Mountain Conservation Area. To facilitate this development, SFU created the Burnaby Mountain Community Corporation (a precursor to what is now known as the SFU Community Trust) and charged it with two purposes. First, it was to develop that 65-hectare parcel into "UniverCity": a model sustainable "complete community" with a diverse range of housing choices, shops, services and amenities. Second, it was to make SFU itself more sustainable, both by creating a supportive enclave for students, faculty, staff and others who wanted to live in a quiet, beautiful and ecologically responsible community, and by directing net revenue from the UniverCity project into an SFU Endowment Fund to that would support teaching and research in perpetuity.

Today, UniverCity is home to more than 3,000, 40 percent of whom are associated with

Fig. 14.4:

Multiple award-winning UniverCity is located atop Burnaby Mountain in Burnaby, British Columbia, adjoining the campus of Simon Fraser University. Once complete, it will house about 10,000 people.

(CREDIT: SFU COMMUNITY TRUST / UNIVERCITY)

Fig. 14.5: *UniverCity's Cornerstone and Hub buildings house 60,000 square feet of retail space, occupied by independent businesses, restaurants and a community grocery store.*
(CREDIT: SFU COMMUNITY TRUST/UNIVERCITY)

SFU as faculty, staff or students who have happily traded long commutes for short walks to work or study. Amenities and services now include a community market, shops, cafés and restaurants, a dentist, a church, a bank, a hairdresser, a travel agent, a real estate office and a LEED Gold-certified elementary school serving 180 kids. When complete, UniverCity will house up to 10,000 people.

From the outset, UniverCity designers have been guided by four key principles that converge neatly with the components of the community capital framework: Environment (natural and physical capital), Economic (economic capital), Equity (social and cultural capital) and Education (human capital). UniverCity's commitment to enhancing these forms of community capital is expressed in the following ways:

Preserve and improve natural capital: The UniverCity development has left most of Burnaby Mountain's nature trails and stunning vistas undisturbed. As part of the UniverCity plan, some 320 hectares were newly set aside for conservation, bringing the mountain's protected area to 600 hectares. The community's award-winning stormwater management system returns nearly 100 percent of stormwater to the ground. This has maintained pre-development stormwater runoff quality and quantity to such an extent that salmon in creeks at the base of Burnaby Mountain are unaffected. As well, UniverCity helps preserve natural capital by encouraging alternatives to single-occupant vehicle use through a wide range of transportation choices. To that end, UniverCity partnered with SFU Community Trust, Vancity Financial Services, and regional transit authority Translink to launch the first Community Transit Pass in North America. It allowed all UniverCity residents unlimited travel throughout the entire regional transit network for less than $30 per month, about 20 percent of the price of a regular comparable transit pass. In addition, the Trust has partnered with Vancouver's Cooperative Auto Network to provide residents low-cost access to community automobiles on an hourly or daily basis.

Consider the site's built capital: UniverCity's LEED-certified buildings and public spaces, including its High Street, are resource-efficient, designed to complement the local context and include essential shopping and services for community members, pedestrian-friendly thoroughfares, a network of bike paths and a town square.

Enhance the community's social capital: To foster a diverse and vibrant community, a mix of housing sizes and tenure options (including strata ownership, rental and shared-equity ownership) will accommodate a wide range of household types; at least one-third will be considered affordable housing. Home prices are kept 20 percent below market value, thanks to a partnership between developer, financier,

VanCity Enterprises, and SFU Community Trust. Young families are an increasing part of UniverCity's demographic profile.

Support the development of human capital: LEED-certified buildings ensure that all occupants enjoy healthy, non-toxic living and working environments. Proximity to the rich educational resources of SFU plus a package of resident benefits that includes access to campus amenities, such as its library, special events, recreation facilities and extensive network of nature trails, supports the personal and intellectual development of all UniverCity residents. UniverCity's elementary school enjoys close ties to SFU's Faculty of Education for purposes of research and teaching assistance, as will a childcare center that is in the works now. As the focus of numerous research projects by SFU faculty and students as well as researchers from around the world, the community itself inspires and contributes to academic inquiry.

Build the community's economic capital: Unique housing options also aid affordability and flexibility for residents: for example, customized zoning allows for legal secondary or "flex suites" in up to 50 percent of the units. These "mortgage helper" suites are equipped with their own bathroom and cooking facilities and can be legally rented out — in many cases, to SFU students. Their success has inspired other municipalities in the region to follow suit with similar bylaws. SFU Community Trust has also created opportunities for community economic development by creating 60,000 square feet of commercial space in its Cornerstone and Hub buildings, much of which is leased by independent businesses, including many SFU alumni. UniverCity will help maximize the value of the SFU Endowment Fund: to date, UniverCity has generated $25 million for the university; ultimately it is expected to generate between $155 million and $170 million (in today's dollars) to the SFU Endowment.

Striving for Better

Several new initiatives position UniverCity to reap even greater sustainability dividends in the future.

In 2010, the City of Burnaby approved a municipal zoning bylaw for UniverCity that makes its building standards the greenest in North America. This is the first bylaw in North America that mandates specific green building practices as part of the development process. All new buildings must be at least 30 percent more energy-efficient and 40 percent more water-efficient than what is specified by federal building codes. SFU Community Trust now offers an incentive to exceed these minimums by offering a 10 percent density bonus to projects that achieve advanced energy goals (reaching an efficiency level that is 45 percent higher than code) or that include upgraded

Fig. 14.6: *Residents of UniverCity enjoy easy access to an extensive network of nature trails on Burnaby Mountain.* (Credit: SFU Community Trust/UniverCity)

Fig. 14.7: *Stormwater management was a priority for designers of UniverCity. The objective of maintaining pre-development stormwater run-off quality and quantity was met by implementing detentions ponds, open watercourses and bioswales. This off-grid windmill serves to aerate a detention pond.*
(Credit: SFU Community Trust/UniverCity)

stormwater management through features such as intensive green roofs.

Also in the works is a neighborhood energy system that will link all new buildings, and possibly to an existing SFU system. In the near term, it will heat and cool buildings using energy from construction wood waste that would otherwise be landfill-bound; in the longer term, it will likely capture waste heat from the university's data center. The system will be installed by a regulated utility provider at no expense to the Trust. Once operating, the system is expected to generate modest revenue for the university and cut the community's emissions by 65 percent.

A third initiative undergoing evaluation now is a transportation innovation that could save users time, save the transit authority money and, at current population and load rates, reduce greenhouse gas emissions by 1,870 tonnes annually: a gondola that would carry residents and other campus users up and down the mountain. Early analyses indicate that a gondola could replace 22,000 transit trips a day (freeing up buses for use in other parts of the Vancouver region) and move 3,000 people an hour — halving the times it currently takes to move that number up and down the mountain.

A fourth initiative is UniverCity's new Child Care Centre, designed to meet this continent's highest green building standard: the Cascadia Region Green Building Council's Living Building Challenge. To do this, the centre is free of toxic materials, obtained the majority of its materials from within a 400-kilometer radius, cost 15% less per square foot to construct than a conventional childcare facility, generates more energy than it uses and recycles or harvests from rainwater more water than it uses.

The Judges Weigh In

SFU Community Trust's success at creating a model sustainable community has not gone unnoticed. Since 2000, UniverCity has won 15 prestigious awards, including: the UN-endorsed LivCom Awards (2008 Gold Award and third-place ranking overall in the Sustainable Projects Category), the American Planning Association 2008 National Excellence Award for Innovation in Green Community Planning, the Urban Land Institute (several, including the 2009 Award Excellence: The Americas for Best Practice in Design, Architecture and Development; 2007 awards for Innovations in Creating a More Livable & Sustainable Region, Creating More Sustainable Development and Creating More Affordable Housing and its 2005 Award for the Most Sustainable Development). Other organizations recognizing UniverCity's excellence in sustainability, site design, neighborhood development, energy-efficiency and innovation in affordable housing include the Federation of Canadian Municipalities (2011), the Canadian Institute of Planners (2011), the Canadian Mortgage & Housing Corporation (2008), the City of Burnaby (2008), the Planning Institute of British Columbia (2006), the Canadian Home Builders' Association (2005), the Association of University Real Estate Officials (2005) and British Columbia's energy utility, BC Hydro (2000).

Official recognition aside, how successful is UniverCity at supporting a more climate-wise lifestyle? To answer that, SFU Community Trust commissioned an independent audit on the per capita greenhouse gas emissions that UniverCity residents will generate from home heating, electricity usage and day-to-day transportation. It predicted that UniverCity residents would create 3.5 tonnes per capita annually. While not carbon-free yet, this represents a significant improvement over the Metro Vancouver average of 5.0 per capita per year.

Ultimately, however, the success of a community can best be judged by its residents — and in that regard, UniverCity also shines. In 2007 and 2010, SFU Community Trust hired a professional market research firm to investigate UniverCity residents' demographics, attitudes, expectations and, most importantly, satisfaction with their choice to live there (Mustel Group 2007; 2010). The surveys have also highlighted some areas where UniverCity could improve: for example, in 2010, residents would prefer more input in local decision-making, more locally accessible healthcare services and better access to arts and cultural events. But, in 2007 and 2010, more than 90 percent of survey respondents reported that they are pleased with their decisions. UniverCity's natural setting, location, affordability, recreational opportunities, services, educational opportunities for all ages and connectivity to transit were frequently

offered as reasons. Overwhelmingly, residents enjoyed a high degree of safety and security.

The firm's findings also suggest that UniverCity has been largely successful at creating a community that is diverse, affordable to live in and less auto-dependent. Compared with the demographics of the surrounding region, UniverCity residents have a significantly higher-than-average income, a higher percentage of people working in professional or technical occupations and a higher percentage of home-owners. Not surprisingly, about two in five residents have some direct connection to SFU, as faculty, staff or students. But in terms of ethnic diversity and proportion of households with children, the community makeup roughly mirrors that of the surrounding region. Data obtained from the MLS Listings shows us that the average selling prices for comparable apartments and attached housing (there is no detached housing at UniverCity) are significantly lower than in metropolitan Vancouver (Metro Vancouver 2011), and the number of UniverCity residents who commute by public transit (36 percent in 2010

Fig. 14.8:
Green roofs adjacent to Cornerstone building balconies are a peaceful counterpoint to the bustling community that UniverCity is becoming.
(Credit: SFU Community Trust/UniverCity)

and 34 per cent in 2007) is almost double the average of Metro Vancouver residents (Metro Vancouver 2008; Mustel Group 2007, 2010). In 2010, many fewer (51 percent compared to 67 percent) use a personal vehicle, and a comparatively higher-than-average proportion of residents commute on foot or by bicycle. This is probably attributable both to the high ratio of UniverCity residents who work or study at SFU and to one of the most innovative transit plans on the continent.

Moving Forward Together

UniverCity and the preceding collection of community profiles shows that, whether planned from scratch or retrofitted to an existing community, there are many paths toward sustainability. What they tend to share is a readiness among citizens, leaders and planners alike to embark on an incremental, inclusive process that sets clear goals, seeks to integrate knowledge from many sectors and disciplines, identifies partnership opportunities and routinely evaluates performance to make appropriate adjustments. These communities illustrate the fact that sustainability is not merely a destination but a *process*. Furthermore, they tend to push at the conventional boundaries of municipal jurisdiction, law and structure to move toward creating places of innovation, creativity, culture, health and environmental vitality.

In part 3, we'll look more closely at mobilizing for sustainable community development through effective governance and tools for community sustainability, including our own Community Capital Tool.

Part 3:

Mobilizing Citizens and Their Governments

Mobilizing citizens and their governments to strengthen all forms
of community capital is required to apply sustainable development
to our communities. Community mobilization is necessary to
coordinate, balance and catalyze community capital.

Part 3 focuses on how to mobilize citizens and
their governments to achieve this goal.

Chapter 15

Governing Sustainable Communities

This book offers a myriad ideas, policies and tools for how to build more sustainable communities. While there is certainly no shortage of sustainability strategies and techniques that local governments can utilize, the key challenge is to bring all of these strategies together into a coherent, viable, long-term plan that enjoys community support. This chapter reviews some of literature on why community mobilization is so necessary for local sustainability and explores how old practices of *government* are being supplanted by those of *new governance*. It discusses *participatory processes*, which communities have been striving to incorporate into their planning for *sustainable community development* and surveys current thinking on how participatory processes can support effective planning for sustainability. It offers tips on how citizens can better prepare themselves to become involved in sustainability planning, and by profiling several participatory processes — most of which have been well-seasoned, others of which are being refined as this is written —

it offers resources for local government to work towards the ideal model of participatory governance for sustainability.

From Government to Governance

Of all community actors, local governments are perhaps best positioned to demonstrate the necessity, the desirability and the practicality of moving toward sustainable communities. Although local governments are not the only agencies charged with community planning and development, they are locally elected, representative and accountable for community decision-making. This makes them critical players in the movement toward sustainable communities. Indeed, the 1992 Rio Earth Summit and the 2002 United Nations World Summit on Sustainable Development identified local authorities as "the level of governance closest to the people ... [and] as a primary site for visioning, scoping and finally implementing 'sustainability'" (Krueger & Agyeman 2005, 410).

Since the late 1980s, there has been a notable turn from modes of *government* to those of *new governance* (Bingham, Nabatchi & O'Leary 2005), which has changed the role and what is expected of local governments. This shift corresponds to the emergence of globalization, which has eroded some functions of national governments, resulting in the devolution of decision-making responsibilities down to regional and local governments (Melo & Baiocchi 2006).

Although the term *governance* is not very well-defined and tends to be vague

Fig. 15.1:
Sustainability planning requires meaningful community engagement and technical expertise.
(Credit: David Rousseau)

(Lieberherr-Gardiol 2008; van Zeijl-Rozema et al. 2008), it is generally understood that it involves sharing governing responsibility among the public, private and voluntary sectors (Varol, Ercoskun & Gurer 2011). A traditional *government* approach is top-down, hierarchical and operates in isolation from other stakeholders (Bingham et al. 2005; van Zeijl-Rozema et al. 2008), while new governance, in contrast, cultivates horizontal, flexible relationships for policy-making. In fact, new governance can be understood as network-building. New governance is about building horizontal relationships between local citizens, business interests, NGOs and government institutions. It is about increasing permeability between these often-siloed interests in order to share resources, skills and perspectives, and build consensus around policy decisions (Häikiö 2007). Where government has often acted alone or resorted to jurisdictional claims, a governance framework can pool resources, leverage diverse ideas and create partnerships for joint problem-solving (Bradford 2008).

While new governance is often seen as a progressive development towards building sustainable communities, Aylett (2010) cautions that governance should not be used by local governments as an excuse to avoid implementing and enforcing environmental regulations. As discussed in chapter 3, regulation is often key to environmental protection, and governance processes that result in consensus among many key actors can help make regulation effective. As Aylett's research on Durban, South Africa, showed, local community members can help balance out the power of industry and business interests "and help ensure accountability, enforcement and compliance. [Local community engagement and resistance] can be the impetus for initiatives that develop the capacity of local communities to engage meaningfully in complicated debates, and produce innovative new forms of knowledge that support the regulatory powers of the state" (2010, 492).

Sustainability and Participatory Planning

The key reason that sustainability necessitates participatory decision-making processes is that understandings of it are wide-ranging and varied. On the one hand, sustainable development can be seen as a normative concept that relates to our well-being and quality of life; while on the other hand, it can be understood as a more objective concept related to science-based understandings of ecological limits (van Zeijl-Rozema et al. 2008). Both of these perspectives are valuable in understanding sustainable development because it requires both behavioral and societal changes (a longer-term project with flexible and evolving goals) *alongside* quantifiable, shorter-term goals to reduce environmental impacts while improving social and economic outcomes.

Local stakeholder participation in decision-making is challenging, especially when opinions of a sustainable future may be diverse. Governance described above relies on greater public participation to achieve benefits such as greater buy-in from residents (Fagotto & Fung 2006; Tippett, Handley & Ravetz 2007). The classic work on public participation was published in 1969 by Shelly Arnstein. This landmark paper is still highly relevant, and contains a typology of participatory governance structures that is frequently cited today (e.g., Holden 2006; Reed, 2008; Tippett 2007). Arnstein's typology visualized participatory governance as a ladder with eight rungs, each

corresponding to a different level of citizen power. On the bottom rung of the ladder is manipulation, where public participation is used as "a public relations vehicle by powerholders" (1969, 218). At the top of the ladder is complete citizen control of planning processes, where there are no intermediaries between neighborhood groups and the source of funds. The other rungs contain varying concentrations of manipulation and citizen control.

While still very useful, this typology is somewhat oversimplified. As Tippett (2007) has noted, manipulation can occur at any rung of the ladder, and thus the ladder metaphor may be better conceptualized by organizing the different methods of consultation into five major categories or processes of participation, all of which are necessary components of participation planning processes. These include *inform*, *design*, *consult*, *deliver* and *monitor* (18).

Public Participation Techniques

Many strategies, tools and techniques are employed in planning processes to encourage and enhance public participation. These include *consensus decision-making, deliberative democracy, charettes, visioning, participatory budgeting, citizen juries, focus groups, roundtables and cooperative management* (Bingham et al. 2005). All of them are examples of shared or participatory decision-making processes.

Shared decision-making involves planning *with* stakeholders rather than *for* them. Shared decision-making processes depend on the explicit recognition that all stakeholder values and interests are legitimate. The primary rationale for shared decision-making in community planning and governance is based on the democratic maxim that those affected by a decision should participate directly in the decision-making process. The benefits of participatory democratic structures have far-reaching implications for community planning; merely informing citizens of decisions taken is inadequate, particularly in planning for sustainability. Stakeholders often demand genuinely cooperative decision-making, if not outright control, over decision-making. In response, many governments have formally recognized the importance of public participation by legislating at least some degree of public engagement requirements into their planning processes.

However, policy statements supporting stakeholder participation are inadequate if not backed by sufficient resources, staff and commitment to implement it. Truly meaningful participation requires that all concerned and affected stakeholders are provided the information and resources they require to influence and contribute to the decision-making process, and that planning and decision-making processes be designed and implemented to foster comprehensive stakeholder participation. The questions of who participates, when they participate and how they participate are critical to achieving fairness, efficiency and stability in decision-making.

Consensus-based Decision-making: Consensus refers to "an array of practices in which stakeholders, selected to represent different interests, come together for face-to-face, long-term dialogue to address a policy issue of common concern" (Innes & Booher 1999, 412). It is a process for making group decisions without voting. Agreement is reached through gathering of information and viewpoints, discussion, persuasion and a combination of synthesis of proposals and/or the development of totally new ones. Consensus does not necessarily mean unanimity. Rather, the goal of the consensus process is to reach a decision that everyone can live with. Consensus at its best relies upon persuasion rather than pressure for reaching group unity.

> Consensus building . . . is adaptive and evolving, often with spin-off working groups, and other self-organizing activities. It is difficult to define exactly what activities count as part of the consensus process or who is part of it, much less what outcomes can be attributed to it. It is difficult to specify when it actually begins and ends (Innes & Booher 1999, 416).

Holden (2006) identifies four ways to make consensus-based processes effective. The first is to identify all relevant stakeholders and ensure that they are willing (if not actually able) to participate in the process. Second, planning should involve a range of participants with different roles in the community's decision-making process in order to promote new and advantageous connections across administrative departments and disciplines. Third, stakeholders must be provided with adequate information about the process and given the opportunity to speak throughout. Finally, it is important to try to ascertain if participants are speaking sincerely and knowledgeably, and if they are participating in the process with justifiable reasons (179-180). This latter point may seem odd, but as Holden explains, it "is not just that some participants are insincere, incomprehensible, inaccurate, or unreasonable: it is that those that exhibit these uncooperative behaviors are likely to be the self-same participants whose behaviors most need to change, based on the outcome of the dialogue" (180).

Deliberative Democracy: Deliberative democracy is a participatory process that uses consensus-based decision-making to reach agreement on issues. Beaumont and Nicholls describe deliberation as "a particular decision-making process whereby plural actors are given equal opportunities to exchange views on a particular subject. The deliberative process not only improves the likelihood that different values are exchanged and interests included in decision-making areas, but it also provides greater legitimacy for decisions taken" (2008, 90). This process stresses the equal balance of power between the various stakeholders in order to reach a satisfactory consensus (Beaumont 2008). In deliberative democracy, everyone is considered an equal participant, and everyone affected by the decision at hand must be included. Everyone has the freedom to intervene in the process. The benefit of deliberative democracy is that in an ideal situation, the decisions made are seen as legitimate and justified because everyone has been heard and represented in the process (Melo & Baiocchi 2006).

The best-known example of deliberative democracy and consensus-based decision-making in action is the participatory budgeting process in Porto Alegre, Brazil, which began in 1989 and has since expanded to 170 cities in Brazil. In Porto Alegre, the participatory budget process occurs in three inter-connected arenas. In the regional assemblies (16 in Porto Alegre) and thematic assemblies (5), participants negotiate their budget priorities with each other and criticize local authorities. Each assembly sets aside 45 minutes for any participant to speak. The Participatory Budget Council (COP) is made up of two representatives from each of the regional and thematic assemblies, as well as one representative from the Urban

Neighborhood Association of Porto Alegre and one representative from the public service trade union. In the COP, representatives decide budget priorities and the final format of the budget. Although municipal administrators are present at the COP, they do not have voting privileges. The third decision-making arena occurs within the COP, where participants decide the rules for the next year's budgeting process, including the decision-making capacity of the COP itself (Avritzer 2006).

Research shows that, although the poorest communities are not as well-represented as wealthier communities, the deliberative budgetary process has led to investment that benefits these areas all the same. As Avritzer (2006) notes, "the participatory budgeting process leads to pro-poor patterns of investments and allocation of public works" (631).

Charrettes: The charrette participatory process brings together community stakeholders to produce visions and designs of what a sustainable community might look like. There are two types of charrettes: *visioning* and *implementation*. Some charrette processes combine both versions (Condon 2007). All stakeholders are considered to be designers, whether or not they have any design experience. The goal is to "produce a design that embodies the higher-level empathy, understanding, intuition, and compassion of the design team in the form of a sustainable and implementable urban design plan" (12).

One type of charrette model is *enquiry by design*. According to Tippett et al. (2007), enquiry by design is the only participatory process that also aims to educate participants about sustainability principles. It is a concentrated process that takes place over about five working days and brings together a broad range of participants, including urban designers and environmental experts, NGO representatives, policy-makers and local residents. The Prince's Foundation for the Built Environment is an organization based in the UK that carries out enquiry-by-design projects. Its process divides participants into three groups: Core Team, Second Tier and Third Tier. The Core Team is made up of key decision-makers, including land-owners on and around the site, local politicians, sustainability and environmental experts and planners. Second Tier members are representatives of any group with interest in the process and knowledge about the site, such as residents' groups, local conservation groups, business groups and transport operators. Second Tier members attend only the sessions tailored for them. Finally, the Third Tier is made up of anyone interested in the development of the site, such as local residents and the general public. They attend public sessions at the start and end of the process (Prince's Foundation 2011a). The Prince's Foundation has carried out many enquiry-by-design processes in communities across the UK (e.g., Caithness, Scotland; Canterbury, Leicestershire and Lancashire, England) as well as in countries around the world (e.g. Freetown, Sierra Leone; Galapagos Islands, Ecuador; Jazan, Saudi Arabia; New Orleans, USA) (Prince's Foundation 2011b).

Visioning: Visioning is a way to identify collective aspirations for the direction a community is headed. In visioning exercises, participants are free to come up with idealized versions of what they would like their community to look like in the future. Coming up with these visions collectively ensures that everyone is on the same page and facilitates discussion and interaction between participants. Visioning sessions can help guide thinking and allow people to be creative and explore new paths of development. It is important that visions are continually revisited so as to ensure that they are not advancing the goals of any special-interest groups (Kemp & Martens 2007). Often a positive and unintended consequence of visioning exercises is that participants change the way they think about sustainability (Portney 2005).

A well-known example of a long-range visioning process in Canada is that of imagineCalgary. This public process began in 2005 and was completed in 2006. It asked participants to imagine what a sustainable Calgary might look like in 100 years. The process was organized into three main groups: the administration group conducted a public opinion survey and did some basic research; the round table group comprised 38 civic leaders who used the results of the public opinion survey to devise a vision statement for the future; and the working groups (variously focused on the built environment, economy, governance, natural environment, social system) that were each composed of 10 to 15 volunteers who met ten times in a five-month span. Throughout the whole process, approximately 18,000 citizens participated in imagineCalgary. Despite the celebrated status of the imagineCalgary process (for example by ICLEI Canada), a 2007 report on the process outlines recommendations for how similar visioning processes in the future can be improved. Among the recommendations contained in the report are that major industry stakeholders commit to participating in the process (several major industries did not participate in imagineCalgary); that government overtly commit to implementing the recommendations that emerge *before* the process begins; and that scientific research be made available during the process so that participants can make informed recommendations (for example, regarding financial costs) to the government (Bruce 2007).

Local Agenda 21

Many cities were inspired to initiate participatory processes around sustainability after the 1992 United Nations Conference on Environment and Development in Rio de Janeiro, which produced the well-known *Agenda 21*. Agenda 21 is a sustainable development action plan whose most notable impact has been advocating that local authorities play a larger role in sustainability planning. Chapter 28 of Agenda 21 has come to be known as *Local Agenda 21* (LA21). It urges local governments to set out an action plan for sustainability that includes participation of civil society as a key component. It "stressed the need for public involvement in designing and implementing many forms of environmental policy and called for all local authorities to establish their LA21 through participation with their communities, and to promote cooperation and coordination between local authorities" (Varol, Ercoskun & Gurer 2011, 10).

LA21 highlighted four objectives, organized around a short time frame. They included beginning a consultative process to increase cooperation between local authorities by 1993; increasing information exchange between local authorities by 1994; achieving a consensus on LA21 within most local authorities in each country by 1996; and ongoing monitoring and evaluation, ensuring that women, youth and minority groups are well represented in the planning process (Lafferty 2001). Despite the fact that Local Agenda 21 is not legally binding, local governments around the world have implemented policies and frameworks for sustainable development. LA21 has been most successful in countries where local governments enjoy "a considerable degree of autonomy to raise income locally and regulate environmental matters" (Blewitt 2008, 18). By 1996, more than 1,800 local governments in 64 countries had begun implementing LA21 in their communities (Pattenden 1997). Widespread adoption of LA21 shows that participatory decision-making has clearly gained currency and momentum.

Transition Management

While there are certainly key goals to be met along the way, *sustainability* has no defined end point. There will be no moment when a community can suddenly be deemed perfectly sustainable. *Transition management* refers to making iterative policy processes given this constantly evolving concept of sustainability. It is helpful to think of sustainability in terms of a constantly evolving process (Bagheri & Hjorth 2007), and as an "ambiguous and moving target that can only be ascertained and followed through processes of iterative, participatory goal formulation" (Voß & Kemp 2006, 15). Society must continually reconsider what sustainability means, which involves a constant learning process (Bagheri & Hjorth 2007). That learning needs to be supported and reinforced by all of our social institutions (including our education systems, as Janet Moore points out elsewhere in this chapter).

And in that learning, the process can be more important than the result. This is because shared decision-making processes that have a learning component can serve to change societal values (Bagheri & Hjorth 2007). As well, the nature of problems is bound to change over the long term, as will scientific understandings of problem causes and solutions. As such, it is very difficult to achieve long-term structural change using short-term goal-setting.

Accordingly, policy-makers must include both short-term actions to facilitate learning and further change, and backward reasoning or back-casting to reflect on what has worked or failed and to set new goals for socio-technical system change (Kemp, Loorbach & Rotmans 2007). This understanding of sustainability as something that is constantly evolving and long-term is known as *transition management*, which has been defined as "a form of multi-level governance whereby state and non-state actors are brought together to co-produce and coordinate policies in an iterative and evolutionary manner" (Kemp et al. 2007, 82). Transition management is a governance process that has emerged at the same time as the growing realization that sustainability will involve not only short-term solutions for reducing environmental impact, but also long-term societal and behavioral shifts towards more environmentally, socially and economically just ways of doing things.

Transition management combines long-term planning with incremental steps. It uses goal-setting to plan for sustainability but does not profess to be able to predict the future (Kemp et al. 2007). As Kemp et al. (2007) explain:

> It is impossible to move to the desired state in a straight line since there are too many variables and uncertainties. The best strategy is to take small steps in what is generally perceived to be "the right (sustainable) direction," to try different solutions and to alter course when needed.

This critical aspect of transition management is known as *reflexive governance*.

Reflexive governance is a style of governance that acknowledges that the constant discovery of new knowledge will affect goal-setting and policy objectives. It takes into account the reality that interdependencies exist — that a solution to one problem may cause problems to crop up in an unexpected area — and that ignoring such interdependencies can produce unintended consequences even more severe than the original problem (Voß & Kemp 2006). Reflexive governance requires the setting of long- and medium-term goals that align with short-term policy goals. In transition management, policy decisions are considered on the basis of whether or not certain actions will contribute directly to policy goals and whether or not the policy will contribute to the overall transition process (Kemp & Martens 2007, 11).

Another aspect of a transition management-style of governance is looking to the future to anticipate possible scenarios. Weber (2008) described two foresight approaches: *exploratory* and *normative*. Exploratory approaches to policy-making involve identifying "new emerging developments and resulting risks and opportunities that open up new issues and agendas for action. They start from the present and 'explore' the range of possible development paths" (198). Similarly, normative foresight approaches begin by choosing one or more possible future scenarios (usually an ideal future for society to move towards) and assessing how these scenarios can be achieved. Normative approaches "serve to negotiate societal goals and visions related to science, technology and society" (198). In practice, both of these approaches are combined; together, they help develop shared views on the direction that society is moving and determine agendas and policy decisions (Weber 2006). Foresight approaches should include a wide range of stakeholders, involving both laypeople and those with scientific and specialized knowledge (Voß & Kemp 2006).

The most documented and well-known example of a transition management process in practice is in the Netherlands, where a co-management approach is being used to develop a national sustainable energy supply system by the year 2050. Although not a perfectly participatory process (it has not involved wide public consultation to date), it is instructive. The process began in 2001 when the government consulted with a variety of stakeholders about anticipated future energy uncertainties. In 2002, the Ministry of Economic Affairs started Project Implementation Transition: this determined that the transition approach appealed to a majority of stakeholders, which resulted in the government supporting the process financially. Phase 2 of the transition process, implemented in 2003, was organized around six platforms: green resources, new gas, chain efficiency, built environment and sustainable mobility. This phase aimed to bring all relevant actors — business interests, government, academia and civil society — on board to hypothesize about various paths and barriers to transition within these six platforms in order to propose potential transition paths within each of these areas. Stakeholders identified 28 paths for further exploration by the Ministry (Kemp & Martens 2007, 11-13).

Because transition management is a relatively new concept, there are few other documented examples of the process in action. But transition management is being carried out in various forms in the Netherlands, for example, in the national healthcare sector (Transition Program in the Care) and in Parkstad Limburg, a former mining region. In Belgium, transition management has been used in the development of a new waste management system (Loorbach & Rotmans 2010).

The Transition Town Movement

An excellent example of a truly bottom-up, citizen-led movement towards sustainability is the transition town movement that began in Totnes, England, in 2005. The movement encourages communities to be self-sufficient and resilient and asks them to plan for a time when oil is scarce. Because most communities around the world are heavily reliant on cheap sources of oil for transportation and for other less obvious things like importing food, and would struggle to feed themselves if food could no longer be imported from afar, the transition movement embraces local economic independence as its key goal (Smith 2011).

The transition movement is an interesting phenomenon in terms of citizen-led initiatives. Its premise is that transition communities should emerge from the ground up, starting from a small initiating group that seeks to educate others and connect with similar-minded groups. As the group grows, it will begin to split off into specialty groups around areas such as energy, housing and food. The next step in the process is to start locally based organizations like social enterprises and energy companies alongside a local currency system in order to further build economic independence (Transition Network 2010).

The transition model recommends that communities embarking on the transition path incorporate twelve "ingredients" for success. Most involve building relationships with other groups and awareness, and structuring

Inter-Institutional Collaborations For Sustainability Learning   By Janet Moore

Around the world, the sustainability movement is taking hold at universities to promote strategies and processes for creating curriculum focused on sustainability (Van Wynsberghe & Moore 2008). This began with a number of international declarations and commitments made by universities around the globe (Wright 2002). In 1997, the Thessaloniki Declaration affirmed that "all subject disciplines must address issues related to the environment and sustainable development and that university curricula must be reoriented towards a holistic approach to education" (Wright 2002). In 2005, the United Nations Decade of Education for Sustainable Development began, supporting a worldwide commitment to educate all students about the imperatives of sustainability. In the same year, the Association for the Advancement of Sustainability in Higher Education was founded "to help coordinate and strengthen campus sustainability efforts at regional and national levels, and to serve as the first North American professional association for those interested in advancing campus sustainability" (AASHE 2011).

Today, many American and Canadian universities have implemented sustainability offices, many have sustainability programs, and a few have interfaculty colleges. Unfortunately, many academic institutions still remain entrenched with course requirements, silo-like disciplinary structures and values that are resistant to change (Moore 2005). What they must grasp is that sustainability is not a discipline unto itself, but rather an essential characteristic of all disciplines. In the words of educator and environmentalist David Orr (1991): "Knowledge carries with it the responsibility to see that it is well used in the world". Sustainable societies will be realized only when sustainability infuses our education system.

Although all institutions within the city are ultimately responsible for sustainable development, educational institutions may be the best place to start *learning* how to create the sustainable city. Schools, colleges and universities can take risks, learn from their mistakes and experiment with the practice of sustainability. Here are several examples of projects that are doing just that — while connecting students to practical projects that help their communities meet sustainability targets.

- In Vancouver, BC, six public post-secondary institutions (including three universities, two colleges and a trades institute) have joined with the City of Vancouver in the Campus-City Collaborative. This inter-institutional collaboration has supported CityStudio Vancouver, which will mobilize students, professors and universities to help Vancouver realize its ambitious goal of becoming the greenest city in the world by 2020. It offers courses that focus on long-term real-world projects, emphasizing sustainability leadership, social enterprise, education of change managers and green business development.

- In Oregon, the University of Oregon has convened a cross-disciplinary organization called the Sustainable Cities Initiative. SCI works on community sustainability challenges at multiple scales ("from the region down to the building"), promoting education, service, public outreach and research on the design and development of sustainable cities. It aims to "serve as a catalyst for expanded research and teaching; market this expertise to scholars, policymakers, community leaders and project partners . . . create and sponsor academic courses and certificates. [It] connects student passion, faculty experience, and community need to produce innovative, tangible solutions for the creation of a sustainable society" (University of Oregon SCI 2011). This pioneering state is also home to another project in the works: the Oregon Sustainability Center. It will bring university faculty, students, government agencies ☞

and non-profits together in a dynamic sustainability research hub, serving as a "showcase and portal for green building, green business and community development" (OSC 2011).

- In North Carolina, the non-profit organization Project H Design focuses on "the transformation of curricula, environments and experiences for K-12 educational institutions in the US." Through its one-year Studio H design/build high school program with one of the poorest, most rural and racially divided counties in the state, students "apply core subject learning and design methodologies to research, prototype, refine and build one contextually responsive and socially transformative piece of architecture for local community benefit" (Project H 2011).

- In New York City, the City University of New York (CUNY), the New York City Economic Development Corporation and the Mayor's Office of Long-term Planning and Sustainability formed a Sustainable CUNY-led NYC Solar America City Partnership. It works with key stakeholders such as utility Con Edison, the Department of Buildings, the New York Power Authority and the New York State Energy Research and Development Authority to support large-scale solar energy market growth in the city (CUNY 2011).

- In California, Stanford University's Institute of Design has launched its "d.school," which fosters collaboration on sustainability challenges between Stanford graduate students and faculty from engineering, medicine, business, law, the humanities and sciences.

the movement. However, one ingredient is to "build a bridge to local government". The Transition Town website stresses that any transition movement will not succeed unless a "productive relationship [is cultivated] with your local authority" while emphasizing that the role of local government is to support the movement, not drive it. The website provides three case studies in which local government supported and nurtured transition initiatives (Transition Network 2010).

Smith (2011) has pointed out that although the transition movement has been highly successful in terms of the "rapidity and reach of its growth" (100), it is not without problems. For instance, "building a bridge to local government" has proved quite difficult for transition movements, which strive to be apolitical, as they risk co-optation and involvement in messy politics. Lack of diversity within the movement is

Table 15.1: Checklist for Designing a Sustainable Community Project
DEFINE THE SUSTAINABILITY PROCESS
CONVENE THE MULTISTAKE HOLDER VISIONING PROCESS
ESTABLISH CONTINUAL PUBLIC REVIEW AND INPUT PROCESS
ESTABLISH INDICATORS AND ANALYZE EXISTING CONDITIONS
ANALYZE BUSINESS AS-USUAL CASE
ANALYZE ALTERNATIVE SCENARIOS
DEFINE AND PRIORITIZE AN ACTION AGENDA AND POLICY RECOMMENDATIONS
INTEGRATE WITH REGIONAL GOVERNANCE
BUILD SOLIDARITY

Table 15.1: *Checklist for Designing a Sustainable Community Project.*
(CREDIT: ADAPTED FROM SUSTAINABLE COMMUNITIES AND THE GREAT TRANSITION, GOLDSTEIN, 2006, 19)

another problem: 95% of transition movement members self-identify as white European; 86% have post-graduate degrees. Recognizing that inclusivity is crucial for any community-led initiative, the transition movement is working to attract people of diverse ethnic backgrounds and socio-economic status (Smith 2011).

Citizen-led Sustainability Planning

Citizen organizations provide many innovative programs and concepts, and furnish whole new paradigms for problem definition, because they are able to tap and organize information laterally. They can network across borders as well as across corporate and government boundaries, enabling rapid syntheses of overlooked and new information into fresh approaches and paradigms. Today, the most creative, energetic forces addressing the planetary problems of poverty, social inequity, pollution, resource depletion, violence and war are grassroots citizens' movements. Hazel Henderson called this "grassroots globalism": pragmatic, local solutions that keep the planet in mind. These approaches "bubble up" rather than "trickle down," and they are often innovative, stressing positive action and role models (Henderson 1996).

Citizen-led organizations such as environmental non-governmental organizations (ENGOs) have several roles to play in moving communities towards sustainability. First, they can push to get sustainability on the agenda at city council meetings and other decision-making fora. Civil society organizations can also represent citizens in participatory planning processes (as discussed above) and try to ensure that they are truly representative and that their voices are heard. Lastly, civil society

organizations can galvanize local citizens into action, forming neighborhood associations or other community groups in order to build sustainable communities *from the ground up*.

These are not easy roles to play. As Martens (2004) showed in his study of participatory planning processes in Tel Aviv, Israel, dominant actors — both in government and in civil society — usually play crucial roles in shaping the participatory process. NGOs are not likely to be included in these processes unless they are persistent and pressure government to be included. Martens' study also showed that after ENGOs exert such pressure, the resulting process is often antagonistic and lacking in reasoned debate. Martens suggests then that ENGOs push for inclusion while making sure to maintain good relationships as well as to avoid furthering any "atmosphere of conflict" by matching the language of their "opponents" (236).

As we have seen, sustainability is not a destination but a process — one that will evolve in light of new scientific understandings about how ecological and human systems interact. Its conceptually fluid nature means that public participation in defining and planning for sustainability is not just desirable but critical. It demands that we look beyond government to the deeper issue of governance, because effective sustainability plans are those where citizens contribute meaningfully to the decision-making process. Having explored several broad strategies for including the most voices into the process, we turn in the next chapter to the many tools and techniques that can be used by citizens and local governments to build sustainable communities together.

Getting City Hall Onside

Thousands of small groups with few resources spend large amounts of time trying to influence decision-makers. For the most part, these groups are made up of ordinary citizens driven by a desire to make a difference beyond their own lives (Dobson 2009). One of the barriers faced by many community groups intent on promoting local sustainability is the reluctance of local government to be part of the quest and process. Yet the understanding, cooperation, and support of both elected officials and professional staff are essential. Some key success factors are (ORTEE 1995):

- Have truly broad, multi-sectoral community representation from the outset.
- Obtain up-to-date information about the community that will provide you with a baseline picture of current community management.
- Educate yourselves about the civic process. Administration is part of the town or city corporation. Council acts like a board of directors. Knowing how ideas get considered and subsequently translated into policy and programs can be very helpful when trying to promote new ideas. Understand the budget process as well.
- Action will not result from sustainability principles or ideals on their own. The approach should always be proposed on a smaller scale, in practical and "doable" terms.
- Build allies for your initiative.
- Don't go to city council until you have everything lined up, including: a committed multi-sectoral steering group; pertinent baseline facts and figures; goals and objectives that fit with stated municipal priorities; allies and champions on council and in the municipal departments; sound community support for the initiative; and a sound proposal for financing the sustainability measures being recommended.
- Develop a set of indicators that will show/measure progress being made. People must see and feel the results of the initiative. Tie the indicators into community goals where possible.

Chapter 16:

Tools for Community Sustainability

Moving toward sustainable communities is a long-term goal, so it is important that the incremental steps we take in the short-term are leading us in the right direction. This chapter surveys some of the many tools available to help citizens and their governments to manage community sustainability, and then explores one of these tools, sustainability indicators, in more detail.

The tools described below (adapted from United Nations 2007; Sheate 2012; and Ness et al. 2007, unless otherwise indicated) are organized into two categories: planning and assessment. Community planning and assessment tools can be used by citizen groups with little training, whereas technical planning and assessment tools more often require the involvement of trained staff or consultants. Both types of tools can be used in public participation processes, although technical planning and assessment tools may require adaptation and interpretation for public consumption. In both situations, it is important that citizens understand what type

of sustainability tools are being used by their municipality.

To be used effectively, the appropriate tool must be matched to the context of the planning situation, which may require practitioners and stakeholders to use different tools at different stages of the planning process. It is also important to understand that community and technical tools can be complementary and used in parallel (Sheate 2010).

Planning
Community Planning Tools

Several community planning tools are useful for awareness building, problem diagnosis, dialogue and participation in decision-making. These tools can be used from the pre-planning through to the evaluation stages of the planning process. Relatively familiar or self-explanatory tools include brainstorming, community meetings, field trips, media campaigns, open houses, public hearings, public meetings, role-playing, vision-building and workshops. Community planning forums, charettes, World Cafés and Ideas Competitions are some of the more effective tools as they encourage stakeholder involvement and dialogue in an open and creative environment.

Community Planning Forum: This is a two- to-three-day strategic community planning conference designed to engage stakeholders in planning. A popular approach to holding planning forums is to hold a *search conference*, which entails building consensus on a vision of the future as a basis for planning within and among all sectors. In a search conference, future possibilities and trends (rather than current problems or risks) are the focus of subsequent action planning. The elements of this planning approach include a review of past and current trends, an analysis of external and internal forces, the creation of a future vision and development of an action plan.

Charette: The charette concept, which is increasingly popular in the US, is used in community land-use planning, architecture, industrial design and in a wide variety of other design areas. In the world of land-use and urban planning, a charette is a multiple-day collaborative design and planning workshop that includes all affected stakeholders. The main point of a charette is to *show* people illustrations and examples of what types of planning are possible — and to involve citizens in the active creation of possibilities. It is an effective method for defusing potential conflicts between residents and developers by promoting joint ownership of solutions (Community Planning 2011).

World Café: World Cafés are a non-confrontational and structured creative process to help large numbers of people engage in interactive conversations related to community planning or other "questions that matter." The

methodology is based on seven design principles that help build mutual understanding and collective learning about important issues through initial work in small groups. The principles are: See the context; create hospitable space; explore questions that matter; encourage everyone's contribution; connect diverse perspectives; listen together for insight; and share collective discoveries. The process culminates in a large structured group discussion (Community Planning 2011).

Ideas Competition: Ideas Competitions are normally held at the start of the development process or when there is opposition to a proposed scheme. They can be simple and immediate or highly complex. The first step is to produce a brief that clearly outlines the task, entry format and deadline, judging procedure, eligibility and relevant background for individuals or groups that wish to participate in the event. The task of the participants is then to produce general ideas and a presentation for improving an area or proposals for a specific site, building or problem. Judging can be done by a panel or through a public voting system. Winning entries are then published and widely publicised to help secure momentum and raise attention for implementation (Community Planning 2011).

Technical Planning Tools

The following technical planning tools are used to establish environmental carrying-capacity limits and human impacts on them, and to guide policy. Technical tools, like community tools, have inherent strengths and weaknesses depending upon the challenges being faced. It is important to match the appropriate tool with the local context and capacity of the stakeholders.

Ecological Footprint Analysis: This tool estimates the land area required by any human activity, both directly — the land occupied by buildings or infrastructure — and indirectly — including the land needed to produce food and production inputs and to assimilate pollutants. The ecological footprint can offer a meaningful single measure of all global ecological impacts of human activities, at household, municipal, national or global levels. The degree to which the footprint of human activities exceeds the total productive area is a measure of unsustainability (Global Footprint Network 2011; Wackernagel & Rees 1996).

Environmental Sustainability Index: This tool requires adoptees to collect data on 76 criteria designed to track natural resource endowments, past and present pollution levels, environmental management efforts and the capacity of a society to improve its environmental performance. The data is then distilled into 21 indicators reflecting overall environmental sustainability levels and finally into a single index for jurisdictional comparison.

Environmental Performance Index: This is a national government ranking tool that monitors 25 performance indicators tracked across 10 policy categories, covering both environmental and public health and ecosystem vitality. Indicators related to resource depletion, pollution, environmental impact and energy-efficiency contribute to an index that measures how close countries are to established environmental goals.

Environmental Space: This tool estimates the maximum sustainable rates of human use of key resources (energy, selected non-renewable resources, land, wood) and then divides the resources evenly among the world's population to arrive at each individual's entitlement.

The extent to which any country (or household) exceeds this benchmark is a measure of unsustainability. The calculations support calls for a ten-fold "dematerialization" of Western lifestyles.

Community-based State-of-the-environment Reporting: The intention of this tool is to promote reflection and action by developing broad perceptions of ecosystems and our relationships with them, and to identify ecological approaches to planning and designing urban areas. As with all state-of-the-environment reporting, the question of appropriate indicators presents a major challenge, especially at the local government level. Ideally, state-of-the-environment indicators should be rigorous, accurate measures that collectively provide a comprehensive profile of environmental quality, natural resource assets and agents of environmental change.

Sustainability Reporting: This is state-of-the-environment reporting broadened to include quality of life as well as aspects of sustainability; it is focused on information needed to guide decisions and action. One of the best-known and widely used sustainability reporting initiatives is Agenda 21 (explained in chapter 15) developed during the 1992 United Nations Conference on the Environment and Development in Rio de Janeiro (UN 2007). Since then, many sustainability reporting frameworks have been developed by both public and private institutions and are discussed in more detail in the tools in action section of this chapter.

Environmental Budgeting: Local carrying capacities are used to set budgets for the maximum amount of environmental impact permissible in the municipal area. For example, the water extraction budget would be based on replenishment rates. The intention is to motivate the municipality to work with all environmental consumers to keep impacts within budget. More consumption of water by households, for example, would have to be offset by less consumption by industry, or by more recovery/treatment of wastewater.

EcoBUDGET: Developed by the United Nations Environment Programme and ICLEI – Local Governments for Sustainability, Eco-BUDGET uses budgeting and accounting frameworks to plan, monitor and report the consumption of natural resources within the municipal territory. Efficiency gains are measured by indictors that are chosen to reflect the health and strength of the ecosystems that the municipality relies upon. The EcoBUDGET instrument is based on three pillars: the environmental master budget, statement of environmental assets and sustainability analysis. It is implemented through a three-phased approach: budget preparation, budget implementation and budget balancing.

At its root, EcoBUDGET is a participatory budgeting exercise that relies on strong community involvement for its success. Communities that implement the EcoBUDGET program enjoy these distinct advantages: Mayors and CEOs become true resource managers; communities are more likely to meet their Millennium Development Goals; environmental resources are managed in an integrated way; attention to nature and the environment is maintained; financial credibility is improved; and local capacity is developed (Mayerick & Robrecht 2008).

Successful EcoBUDGET programs can be found in Vaxjo, Sweden; Tubigon, Phillipines; Guntur, India; and Bologna, Italy (Mayerick & Robrecht 2008).

Assessment

After community and technical plans have been implemented, the next critical step is to assess the efficacy of the plans in reaching your sustainability goals. In the words of Ness et al. (2007), "the purpose of sustainability assessment is to provide decision-makers with an evaluation of global to local integrated nature–society systems in short- and long-term perspectives in order to assist them to determine which actions should or should not be taken in an attempt to make society sustainable."

Community Assessment Tools

Assessment tools are used for figuring out where we're at, and for monitoring and evaluating where we're going. Some familiar or self-explanatory community assessment tools include risk assessment, focus groups, periodic monitoring reports, ranking and surveys. Some less familiar assessment tools are described below.

Community Case Studies: These are collective descriptions and analyses of the community and its problems, documented in a local language or medium (e.g., drawing, storytelling, role-playing, audio-visual). They can be used to promote awareness and discussion among community members, and to gather baseline information for assessment.

Community Environmental Assessment: Stakeholders can be involved in gathering information and analyzing the environmental and social impacts of proposed activities to predict their positive and negative effects. Designed for group observation and value judgment, the importance of any impact is determined by the community and given a numerical value, such as environmental and social scores. Although not useful in themselves, these scores can facilitate priority-setting and help identify indicators for monitoring and evaluation.

Community Interviews: Interviews are a form of survey in which all members of a community are invited to a meeting to answer specific pre-set questions. Because the large meeting size necessarily limits discussion, this tool is not useful for consensus-building, but it gathers preliminary information on community perspectives or solicits feedback on proposed strategies and actions.

Force Field Analysis: This is a facilitated and structured exercise in which participants identify specific hindering and facilitating forces affecting the functioning of any situation, assess the relative strength of each force and plan alternative actions to overcome or promote these forces. It is useful for achieving a shared understanding of opportunities and constraints that can influence a desired goal, and thus helps participants determine effective strategies and priorities.

Geographic Information Systems: GIS is a computer-based technology that facilitates storage, easy retrieval, manipulation, transformation, comparison and graphic display of data. Intensive (and perhaps expensive) data gathering is often required, but once established, GIS can provide a user-friendly source of information that can be manipulated by non-experts as well as experts. In some communities, GIS systems have been used by community "watchdogs" to monitor local environmental situations.

Community-based Mapping: Mapping involves residents in the pictorial construction of information about their community. During a mapping exercise, maps are constructed from local knowledge and observation, and provide an excellent starting point for discussion about community-based issue identification, analysis and problem-solving.

Oral History: This is a participatory technique for information sharing during the analysis of local issues. Historical accounts can be compared with present information to generate an analysis of underlying trends and structural problems in a community, and can be used to inform residents about the history of changes and development in their community.

Service Issues Mapping: This facilitated group brainstorming and analysis technique helps stakeholders "map" the diverse issues that must be considered in order to address a single priority issue. This exercise helps people see the systemic nature of local problems by highlighting complex sets of relationships among issues and by identifying different stakeholders who need to be involved in problem-solving.

SWOT Analysis: Strengths, Weaknesses, Opportunities and Threats (SWOT) Analysis is a strategic planning tool that aids in the formulation of attainable long-range goals, action programs and policies. Strengths and weaknesses refer to internal factors in the community, such as resources or declining budgets. Opportunities and threats refer to outside influences that could benefit or damage the community.

Digital Media Visioning Tools: Local climate change visioning integrates climate science and local planning, through a computer-based program that uses participatory processes and "virtual reality" techniques, to produce 2D, 3D and 4D (across time) visualizations that integrate local knowledge and climate change data. Communities can more readily identify and explore the impacts of climate change on their communities and develop appropriate planning responses. It is a flexible 10-step

Interactive Mapping Tools on the Geoweb

By Britta Ricker Peters

There are many low-cost, relatively user-friendly online tools that can help people visualize sustainability in their own communities by producing useful infographics.

Geovisualization tools are those that display spatial information in an interactive manner that facilitates learning (MacEachren & Kraak 2001; Toban 2005). Planners can use them to present sustainable development outcomes and initiatives, as well as to collect opinions and observations from the public. The **Geoweb** is a "collection of interconnected, discoverable, geographically related online tools that span multiple geographic regions" (Lake & Farley 2007, 15).

The most popular types of Geoweb applications are **digital globes**: applications that encourage the user to seamlessly shift between scales and locations (Rouse et al. 2007; Zhang 2007). They offer users relatively easy access to Geographic Information System (GIS)-type operations, albeit with reduced functionality. Overlaid with sustainability information, digital globes facilitate meaningful interactive experiences that may reveal relationships that were previously unperceivable.

Increasingly, digital globes allow users to swiftly add their own content. The simplest, cheapest and quickest way to customize digital globes is by using **pushpin maps** (known as "my maps" on maps.google. com and mapquest.com). Users need only to create a profile to mark areas of interest using points, lines and polygons; the resulting maps are hosted free by digital globe companies. The applications also generate HTML code for easy integration into websites, blogs or email. Greenpeace made effective use of these features to publicize its 2010 Arctic Under Pressure expedition. If pushpin maps have a downside, it is that customization capability is minimal, and they can quickly become cluttered with too many points of interest.

Mashups are applications that combine geographic data from multiple sources. They can make digital globes even more useful. An example is serveyourcountryfood. net, which supports local food production by helping young farmers connect with other farmers, nearby markets and media. In San Francisco, a mashup called the Bay Area Bike Accident Tracker identifies problematic areas and trends for cycling safely. Although customized mashups require more time, programming skill and money to produce (as well as a place to host the data), the resulting geovisualizations can be very stimulating. Thanks to ample documentation available online, an inexperienced but determined and digitally literate person can build a simple mashup in hours using basic Javascript and HTML. The challenge of creating mashups is that the data being shared often needs to be "manicured" before it can be projected onto a digital globe.

Online **digital atlases** can present a lot of geospatial information — but even better, they offer multiple data layers that end-users can toggle on and off as they wish, enabling them to form their own hypotheses and conclusions based on their own experience with the data. Organizations like the Commission for Environmental Cooperation and the US Federal Emergency Management Agency make good use of them. Although digital atlases can be very powerful, their complexity requires more labor and programming skill, which makes them much more expensive to construct.

In choosing mapping tools such as digital globes, it's important to consider software licensing issues as these can greatly influence the user experience and determine who owns the resulting map. Open source and proprietary software licenses both have their own benefits and liabilities that should be investigated.

Inviting map visitors to share their observations and local knowledge through **Volunteered Geographic** ☞

Information (VGI) can be a valuable way of collecting qualitative and quantitative information while sparking dialogue and critical thinking (Goodchild 2007). Open Green Maps, for example, allow users to contribute and share information about local "green living sites and natural, cultural and social resources" in their local communities. VGI can assist in dialogue about place (Tulloch 2008), and make users feel their local knowledge and opinions are valued. The downside to VGI is that the quality of the information contributed is often unknown. Good intentions do not ensure accurate geospatial data (Crampton 2009).

The increased use of mobile computers and smart phones provides an opportunity to distribute location-specific content through the use of **location-based service (LBS)** such as yelp.com and foursquare.com. Creative use of LBS could help bring attention to sustainability issues in your community.

Geovisualization technologies are rapidly and dramatically changing the ways we obtain, collect, share and interact with information. It is becoming increasingly feasible to access interactive visual technologies to communicate sustainability initiatives.

Find out more about **digital globes with APIs** (application programming interfaces that facilitate interaction among different software programs): Google Earth, Google Maps, Yahoo Maps, MapQuest, ESRI (Environmental Systems Research Institute, Inc.), NASA World Wind, Bing Maps and Open Street Maps.

---

process that has proven effective in a wide range of initiatives, from stand-alone visioning processes to those that are integrated into larger ongoing planning and engagement processes (Collaborative for Advanced Landscape Planning 2011a).

Good places to look for locally relevant applications of digital media visioning tools are digital media demonstration events, which offer developers and researchers the opportunity to present and display their proven and emerging digital media applications (Collaborative for Advanced Landscape Planning 2011b). For example, presenters at the University of British Columbia's 2010 "Demonstration Session on Digital Media and Sustainability" introduced applications on diverse subjects such as laneway homes, energy intelligence for buildings, fisheries management, regional futures exploration, scenario visualization using a 3D game engine, climate change, oil extraction and 3D visualizations of building and landscape designs. (see Fig. 16.1, color page C-5)

Technical Assessment Tools

Environmental Impact Assessment (EIA) and Social Impact Assessment (SIA): These comprehensive tools integrate environmental and social considerations into project planning, development and implementation. To be effective, assessment must be a decision-making tool. The application of an effective assessment process ensures that potential environmental and social effects are identified and mitigative measures put in place to minimize or eliminate these impacts. Effective assessment requires that the environmental and social implications of a proposal be considered prior to making irrevocable decisions and as early in the planning process as possible. Proposal assessment should include the concerns of the public with regard to both environmental and social evaluation (Glasson, Therivel & Chadwick 2005).

Strategic Environmental Assessment (SEA): Although EIA and SIA were originally intended to be implemented at a policy and project level, in practice the two tools have more commonly been implemented at the later level. Strategic Environmental Assessment was developed to assist managers and leaders involved in policy, planning and programmatic decisions. As a tool for evaluating the potential impacts of strategic decisions, SEA should be carried out earlier than EIA/SIA and performed in conditions that involve less information and higher uncertainty, as is often the case when dealing with decisions made at the political level (Nilsson & Dalkmann 2010).

Sustainability Impact Assessment: The European Union developed Sustainability Impact Assessments to move from the sectoral assessment of EIA/SIA/SEA to an integrated, intra- and international assessment covering environmental, economic and social parameters. It could, for example, address how a decrease in EU agricultural subsidies would affect not only EU farmers but farmers in other countries as well. Sustainability Impact Assessment was first implemented in 2002 and is now required for all major EU commission initiatives.

Triple Bottom Line Accounting (TBL): Originally conceived as a conceptual vehicle for sustainability akin to corporate social responsibility, TBL has evolved to become a framework for accounting and reporting. TBL, similar to EIA, SIA and SEA, uses environmental, economic and social indicators to create reports intended to guide resource management.

ISO 14001: Developed by the International Standards Organization, ISO 14001 is an environmental management system intended to help businesses, governments and other organizations develop their own environmental reporting systems. Adoptees set their own goals and targets for any parameter they wish to consider, such as the demands of customers, regulators, communities, lenders or environmental groups. ISO 14001 procedures enable adoptees to develop plans to meet those targets, and to produce information about whether or not the targets are met.

Sustainability Appraisal: Under UK legislation, a sustainability appraisal must be prepared for regional and local development plans. The appraisal of activities, projects, programs, plans and/or policies applies to social and economic sustainability criteria as well as to environmental ones, and considers their integration and reconciliation.

Environmental Audit: This tool is used to identify areas of non-compliance with environmental legal requirements, policies and best management practices. Such an audit is based on an assessment of the environmental impacts of a government's policies and practices. In some cases, these will be known or easily identifiable, while in others, it will be possible only to indicate the likely consequences. The policy review should encompass all activities of the government, and all departments and arms of its service. It should not be restricted to official or approved policy, because much local government practice has evolved through tradition, or results from informal decisions of staff.

Environmental Management Action Planning: This tool is a variation of an environmental audit; it involves setting environmental objectives, implementing environmental improvement actions and monitoring and reporting on their effectiveness — in other words, applying familiar "management by objectives" to environmental effects.

Eco-management and Audit System: Another variation of an environmental audit, an eco-management and audit system is a formal management systems standard for environmental "management by objectives." Originally designed for the manufacturing industry, it has been adapted for municipal use in the EU.

Social Auditing: Just as financial accounting measures financial performance, social auditing measures social performance by better understanding its relation to the goals and key stakeholders of an organization. Social auditing is increasingly popular with large private institutions such as Ben and Jerry's Ice Cream, The Body Shop International and VanCity Savings Credit Union. It can also be applied to smaller businesses, community enterprises, cooperatives, non-governmental organizations and public bodies (Sheate 2010).

Sustainability Indicators: This effective tool for communities and governments to evaluate their progress toward sustainability is discussed below.

> The indicators a society chooses to report to itself about itself are surprisingly powerful. They reflect collective values and inform collective decisions. A nation that keeps a watchful eye on its salmon runs or the safety of its streets makes different choices than does a nation that is only paying attention to its GNP. The idea of citizens choosing their own indicators is something new under the sun — something intensely democratic (Meadows 1972).

Tools in Action

It is clear from the foregoing that there is a wide and growing range of tools available for implementing community sustainability. This section examines some of those tools in action. As these tools evolve and new ones are created, we anticipate that a good place to follow developments in this area will be *Pando | Sustainable Communities* (see Appendix).

As discussed in chapters 14 and 15, the United Nations Conference on Environment and Development in 1992 (also known as the Rio Earth Summit) established Agenda 21, a sustainable development action plan for the 21st century. That plan included a proposal championed by ICLEI – Local Governments for Sustainability to support local authorities in the development of their own Local Agenda 21s. ICLEI's Local Agenda 21 Initiative provides a common vehicle for local governments to strengthen local environmental planning.

Development of a Local Agenda 21 campaign can take the form of any participatory, local effort to establish a comprehensive action strategy for sustainable development in that jurisdiction or area. All local governments are urged to complete their campaigns and strategies and to report their results to both the United Nations Commission on Sustainable Development and to ICLEI. The planning framework is based on the following four elements:

- Community consultation processes, such as roundtables, to achieve input and participation from every sector;
- Sustainable development auditing, to provide sound information about current conditions;
- Setting sustainable development targets, both near- and long-term, for quality of life,

environmental quality, resource consumption and human development; and

- Development and use of indicators, to inform the community about the impact of its programs and investments upon the sustainable development of the community.

The evolution of Agenda 21 is manifest in Rio+20: The United Nations Conference on Sustainability, also referred to as Rio+20. The goals outlined by the conference help measure progress towards sustainability at the local level and propel local governments forward on their path to green livable cities. The conference has three primary objectives:

- Securing renewed political commitment to sustainable development;
- Assessing the progress and implementation gaps in meeting already agreed commitments; and
- Addressing new and emerging challenges.

The conference aims to meet these objectives by focusing on Green Economies within the context of sustainable development and poverty eradication; and further developing an institutional framework for sustainable development.

NGOs and private companies are contributing to an institutional framework for sustainable development by applying Agenda 21 principles and their own in-house sustainability frameworks to the management of municipalities, public organizations and private companies. Three of the well-established sustainability consultation firms are:

- **Global Reporting Initiative (GRI)**: This private enterprise uses a network-based sustainability reporting framework that sets out the principles and performance indicators that organizations can use to measure and report their economic, environmental and social performance. Sustainability reports based on the GRI Framework can be used to demonstrate organizational commitment to sustainable development, to compare organizational performance over time and to measure organizational performance with respect to laws, norms, standards and voluntary initiatives (Global Reporting Initiative 2010).
- **Ceres**: This non-profit organization that leads a national coalition of investors, environmental organizations and other public interest groups working with companies to address sustainability challenges such as global climate change and water scarcity. The organization is focused on integrating sustainability into day-to-day business practices for the health of the planet and its people. Founded by a small group of investors in 1989 in response to the Exxon Valdez oil spill, Ceres has been working for more than 20 years to weave sustainable strategies and practices into the fabric and decision-making of companies, investors and other key economic players (Ceres 2011).
- **The Natural Step**: This is a framework, developed by a Swedish non-profit organization of the same name, for planning in complex systems. It uses a comprehensive model of targets and indicators to help organizations around the world integrate sustainable development into their strategic planning and create long-lasting, transformative change. The framework arranges sustainable development tools, approaches and methodologies synergistically to enable

organization-specific implementation of sustainability goals (Natural Step 2011).

Sustainability Indicators

Why are sustainability indicators important? According to Osborne and Gaebler (1993), what gets measured tends to get done. If you don't measure results, you can't tell success from failure. If you can't recognize success, you can't reward it. And if you can't recognize failure, you can't learn from it.

The steps involved in developing sustainability indicators are:

1. Clarify goals — the aim of the evaluation and the type of desired outcome;
2. Determine who will lead the process; invite participation — the process of evaluation may be as valuable as the eventual application of the indicators themselves;
3. Decide how to choose indicators;
4. Collect data by which to measure the indicators; and
5. Report on the indicators, and update and revise the indicators.

For details on these steps and related issues, see Hezri and Dovers 2006; Hildén & Rosenström 2008; Reed, Fraser and Dougill 2006; Reed et al. 2005; and Sahely, Kennedy and Adams 2005.

The following initiatives are a small sample of ongoing and emerging projects to design and use sustainability indicators. They represent the spectrum of aims for which sustainability indicators can be used — from the Sustainable Seattle Project, with a primary focus on community education and empowerment, to the Oregon Benchmarks project, with a greater focus on providing feedback to government

agencies, and the Boston Indicators Project, which focuses on Boston's regional, national and global sustainability position.

Sustainable Seattle Project: The Sustainable Seattle Project began in 1992 with a meeting of 150 citizens. During this gathering, 99 indicators were proposed and 40 key indicators were selected; the first 20 of them were assessed in 1993; in 1995, the remaining 20 were assessed. Indicators ranged from total water consumption, per capita waste generation and recycling rates to volunteering in schools and household incomes (Sustainable Seattle 2011).

The people behind the Sustainable Seattle Project believe that "measuring progress is not the same as making it." The project promotes action by encouraging Seattle-area citizens to:

- employ local media to spread indicator results and analysis;
- use the political process to promote change in public policy;
- broaden the information base used for economic decision-making;
- use indicators in schools for education and as a basis for additional research;
- form a basis for linking local non-profit and volunteer groups; and
- question personal lifestyle choices.

Since its inception in the early 1990s as the world's first grassroots effort to develop sustainability indicators, the Sustainable Seattle Project has utilized its participatory action research approach to develop many new innovative tools to assess sustainable progress in their city (Holden 2007). Tools such as the Happiness Initiative, Dream a Sound Future, Sustainable Rain and Peer Alliance for Leadership in Sustainability have helped refine how Seattle communities define and achieve their goals for local sustainability. For example, the fifth set of sustainability indicators since 1992 focused on happiness and was based on the Gross National Happiness Index used in Bhutan (Sustainable Seattle 2011).

Since then, other useful approaches to measuring happiness have emerged. Happiness indicators are the focus of Mark Anielski in his book *The Economics of Happiness* (2007). In it, he develops his Genuine Wealth model. Through the use of this model, Anielski explores the apparent paradox of increasing material wealth and decreasing levels of well-being and happiness within many developed and developing nations.

Oregon Benchmarks Program: The Oregon Benchmarks process resulted from the State of Oregon's strategic plan, Oregon Shines. A multi-stakeholder organization supporting the plan, the Oregon Progress Board, presented a reporting framework to the state legislature after extensive consultation, and the benchmarks process was officially adopted in 1991.

The framework for reporting consists of 269 indicators. Rather than simply present indicators to measure and report trends, however, the Oregon process defines targets, known as benchmarks. The benchmarks cover a diverse range of issues around sustainability, including categories such as children and families, education and work force, health and health care, clean natural environment, equal opportunity and social harmony, and economic prosperity. The board publishes a report card every two years to report on progress toward the stated targets.

While the Oregon Benchmarks program has drawn on public consultation and aims to inform the public, its main strength is in its ability to promote action and accountability at the level of state government. It outlines rational and clear sustainability goals that serve as the basis for strategic planning throughout government agencies. The state legislature has even passed several bills directing agencies to work toward benchmarks. On a smaller scale, the Oregon Benchmarks are being applied by municipal governments and community organizations, and several cities and counties are adopting strategies to complement the state program.

The Boston Indicators Project: The Boston Indicators Project relies on the expertise and opinions of hundreds of stakeholders from the city's venerable public agencies, civic institutions, think tanks and community-based organizations to produce consensus-based reports tracking change in 10 sectors: Civic Vitality, Cultural Life & the Arts, Economy, Education, Environment & Energy, Health, Housing, Public Safety and Transportation (Boston Indicators Project 2011).

Although not solely a sustainability indicators project, the Boston Indicators Project website allows users to highlight all of the indicators related to sustainability. A handful of the many indicators used to assess Boston's sustainability include:

- Smart Growth, measured by trends in development;
- Housing density and services within a quarter-mile of transit nodes;
- Changes in air quality;
- Housing costs as a percentage of the cost of living;
- Acres of protected and restored urban wilds and natural areas;
- Income disparities between the top and bottom quintiles of population; and
- Greenhouse gas emissions by sector.

The strength of the Boston Indicator Project lies in its ability to make comparisons between Boston's neighborhoods as well as macro comparisons of Boston to other cities in the world. Through the recording and dissemination of the multiple indicators used in this project, Boston's residents can see the positive changes being made in their communities and continue to work efficiently toward their sustainability goals (Boston Indicators Project 2011).

THE NEED FOR NATIONAL INDICATORS

Although it is too early to judge the impact of local and regional projects on community sustainability over the long-term, they promise to help communities move in the right direction. Many researchers (such as Anielski

---

Santa Monica's Sustainability Report Card

Indicators at Work: Santa Monica's Sustainable City Report Card

The city of Santa Monica has developed an extensive network of sustainable indicators and annual reports since 1994. Each of the program's policy areas has clear goals reflecting the city's current and future programs. Eight goals (in Resource Conservation, Environmental and Public Health, Transportation, Economic Development, Open Space and Land Use, Housing, Community Education and Civic Participation, Human Dignity) were set for the sustainable development of Santa Monica, specific targets were established for each goal, and an indicator was established for each target at both the systems level and programming level, as in the example below (City of Santa Monica 2008):

Policy Area: Environmental and Public Health

Goals:

1. Protect and enhance environmental health and public health by minimizing and where possible eliminating: hazardous or toxic materials, the levels of pollutants entering the air, risks to human and ecological health.
2. Ensure that no socio-economic group is disproportionately affected by environmental pollution.
3. Increase consumption of fresh, locally produced, organic produce.

Indicators: System Level	**Targets: System Level**

1. **Santa Monica Bay:** Number of days Santa Monica Beaches are posted with health warnings or closed
   a. Dry Weather Months
   b. Wet Weather Months
2. **Wastewater Generation:** Total citywide generation
3. **Vehicle Miles Traveled:** Total
4. **Air Quality:** Percent and demographic profile of Santa Monica residents who live within a half-mile radius of significant emissions sources
	1. **(a)** 0 warnings and closures at any Santa Monica beach location during dry weather months
	   (b) No more than 3 days with warnings or closures at any Santa Monica beach location on non-rainy days during wet weather months
	2. Reduce wastewater flows 15% below 2000 levels by 2010
	3. Downward trend
	4. All significant emissions sources in Santa Monica should be identified

2007) have also recognized the importance of developing sustainability indicators at the national scale. Currently, much national policy is driven by trends in GNP, which only considers narrow economic measures of a country's well-being; sustainability, including trends in natural and social capital, is not systematically considered or evaluated. Effective indicators of national sustainability would provide important information for citizens and governments supporting initiatives at the local and regional level.

Chapter 17

The Community Capital Tool

As described in part 1, sustainable community development requires mobilizing citizens and their governments to strengthen all forms of community capital. While there are ecological, economic and social imperatives that all communities must address, each community has its own unique perspective on how to become sustainable. Therefore, community members must be involved in defining sustainability from a local perspective. But how can we ensure that sustainability planning is democratic, responsive to communities' unique situations and supported by the best available information?

Sustainable community development is a complex process. There are a variety of planning tools and resources designed to facilitate and manage the complexity of local planning processes. However, there is a gap within the range of tools available concerning the integration of sustainability principles, specific community priorities and long-term thinking with a realistic assessment of community capacity.

Throughout parts 1 and 2 of this book, we have referred to the Community Capital Framework as a way to understand sustainable community development. In part 3, we focus on the "heart" of the Community Capital Framework that was introduced in chapter 2 — community mobilization — by examining governance and tools for sustainable community development. In this chapter, we introduce the Community Capital Tool we have developed based upon the Community Capital Framework. It is a decision support and assessment tool designed to facilitate and ground community discussion about integrated planning and monitoring. The Community Capital Tool is the product of collaboration between the Centre for Sustainable Community Development at Simon Fraser University in Canada with Telos, Brabant Center for Sustainable Development, Tilburg University, Netherlands. These two organizations discovered that we have been thinking and working in very parallel ways, despite being on different continents and working in different languages. Telos has developed its contribution to this tool by working extensively in the Netherlands, while the SFU group developed its contribution to this tool by working in rural, urban and aboriginal Canada, as well as in Mexico, Ukraine and Bolivia.

In this chapter, we first explain the Community Capital Tool in theoretical terms and follow with a hypothetical application in a fictitious town, Centerville. Many of the figures presented relate to the Centerville example and, as a result, are clustered near the end of the chapter. Therefore, you will find some figures referenced in the text earlier than they are presented.

Using the Community Capital Framework as a Tool

The Community Capital Tool can be applied to integrated and pro-active community-wide planning activities (e.g., developing an overall sustainability plan or modifying an official community plan), as well as to neighborhood-specific, re-active processes (e.g., proposal evaluation and responding to development

The Telos Method

Our colleagues at Telos in the Netherlands have influenced our thinking in the development of the Community Capital Tool. Together we have integrated the analytical framework and visual tools for their Sustainability Balance Sheet and the People Planet Profit Scan into the Community Capital Tool to develop the Community Sustainability Balance Sheet and the Community Capital Scan. For more information on the Telos Method see telos.nl, pppscan.org and Knippenberg et al. 2007.

applications). It is applied in seven distinct steps — visioning, Community Capital Inventory, considering options, assessing options, implementation, monitoring and evaluation (Figure 17.1). Throughout all of these steps, community participants, chosen for both their expertise and representation of the community, play a key role in applying the tool successfully. (see Fig. 17.1, color page C-6)

The Community Capital Tool comprises two related instruments, the Community Sustainability Balance Sheet (*Balance Sheet* for short) and the Community Capital Scan (*Scan* for short). These two instruments are built from a shared analytical framework that consists of six forms of capital, each broken down into a set of smaller *stocks* and *requirements* used to measure capital capacity and progress toward achieving sustainability. Figure 17.2 and the paragraphs to follow describe the relationship between capital and stocks. The requirements are detailed in Step 1: Visioning.

We know that each of the six forms of capital has a relationship to every other form of capital. To better understand how, we consider the state of each capital in terms of *stocks* — universal subsystems that influence the state and development of each capital as a whole. Born out of empirical research and scientific evidence and moderated by local factors, stocks are the assets within a capital that influence its quantity and quality.

Specific stocks have been selected because they can be relatively easily measured. For example, for the functioning of economic capital, the availability of labor is an important input; therefore within economic capital, labor is an important stock. Unemployment rates give an impression as to what extent the labor force is being used. These data are often readily

Table 17.1: Community Capital and Stocks		
Natural Capital	**Physical Capital**	**Economic Capital**
Soil Groundwater Air Surface Water Minerals and Non-Renewable Resources Land	Infrastructure Land Transportation Public Facilities Housing and Living Conditions	Labor Financial Resources Economic Structure
Human Capital	**Social Capital**	**Cultural Capital**
Education Health and Well-being	Citizenship Safety	Cultural Heritage Identity and Diversity

available and, when observed with the other economic capital stocks, give an indication of the capital's strength. The table below offers examples of stocks commonly associated with each form of capital.

Step 1: Visioning

In order for stocks to develop sustainably, they need to develop in a certain direction, toward a (sometimes utopian) target. Early in the planning process, the Community Capital Tool is used to engage community members in visioning exercises designed to define their ideal sustainable community. The outcome is a vision and set of goals that are used to guide decision-making throughout the steps of the tool. These goals are called the *long-term requirements*, and their development is arguably the most important step in the decision analysis phase. Each stock has one or more long-term requirements associated with it (Figure 17.2). The long-term requirements create a shared language of sustainability making it easier to discuss and measure progress (Frans et al. 2011). Each is developed through an extensive iterative process with community members, leaders and technical experts and may include ambitious

milestones such as clean air and water, no poverty and 100 percent literacy. (see Fig. 17.2, color page C-6)

Step 2: Community Capital Inventory

The Community Capital Inventory step is similar to the situation analysis step in strategic planning processes (e.g., Markey et al. 2005). It differs from a typical situation analysis, however, because community capital provides a distinct and unique framework for analysis, through the use of the Community Sustainability Balance Sheet. The Balance Sheet is an instrument designed to provide a measurement for each of the capital and stocks existing in the community, and the results create a picture of the strengths and weaknesses of each stock. For example, what bio diversity is provided by land and is it being threatened? Is there a need for more employment opportunities within the community? Does the community have strong social or cultural values?

Within the Balance Sheet, each stock is related and measured to the requirements defined in the visioning step. For instance, building from the natural capital example used above, ecological services may have a related requirement

Stocks and Requirements

The following table is a list of all six forms of capital, each with its associated stocks and requirements. While the stocks are fairly universal and will be largely the same from place to place, the specific requirements will vary according to country, community size, historical development, specific economic, social and ecological structures and proposed initiative, among other things.

Capital	Stock	Requirement
Natural	*Land*	Ensure protection of biodiversity
		Increase preservation of natural areas and sensitive ecosystems by parks or conservation areas
		Preserve scenic and attractive views
	Soil	Eliminate all pollutants and contaminants
		Expand the preservation of fertile agricultural land
		Eliminate soil erosion or instability
	Groundwater	Eliminate all pollutants and contaminants
		Preservation of existing reservoirs and replenishment through natural processes
	Surface water	Eliminate all pollutants and contaminants
		Ensure that surface water quality is suitable for human and agricultural use
	Air	Eliminate all pollutants and contaminants
		Reduce greenhouse gas emissions
	Minerals and non-renewable resources	Reduce the extraction rate of nonrenewable resources
		Use only environmentally safe extraction practices
Physical	*Infrastructure*	Provide safe and reliable water to all citizens
		Ensure that waste management systems are clean and efficient
		Ensure that energy is transmitted through a safe, efficient, and reliable system
		Provide adequate access to reliable telecommunications systems for all citizens
	Land	Ensure that suitable land is available for different uses, eg., industry, agriculture, housing, etc.
	Transportation	Create a robust and reliable public transportation system
		Provide safe, efficient, and well-maintained rail and road infrastructure
	Housing and living conditions	Ensure adequate access to housing, food and clothing for every citizen
	Public facilities	Ensure adequate facilities for schools, hospitals, community centers, etc. ☞

Capital	Stock	Requirement
Economic	*Labor*	Balanced labor market that includes a variety of job types and salary ranges
		Adequate training for workforce
		Work is safe, healthy and allows for appropriate work-life balance
		Wages are adequate to provide decent livelihoods
	Financial resources	Public bodies have adequate financial capacity to ensure the availability and accessibility of public goods and services
	Goods production	Local companies are able to make sufficient profit and investment
	Economic structure	A good mix of productive and service industries
		Constant economic regeneration through innovation, new enterprise development and relocation to the community
		Companies are investing in emissions and pollution prevention and reducing the use of non-renewable resources
Human	*Education*	Education meet the needs of both society and individuals
		Education is of high quality and easily accessible
	Health and well-being	Citizens are physically, mentally and spiritually healthy
		All citizens have access to healthcare services for illness prevention and treatment
Social	*Citizenship*	Community has social cohesion
		Social solidarity between citizens
		Opportunity for citizens to build strong networks between each other
		No poverty or exclusion
	Safety	Citizens feel safe and have access to support systems which encourage safety
		No violence and crime
Cultural	*Cultural heritage*	Art is encouraged and celebrated
		Community acknowledges traditions and celebrations
		A diversity of culture and tradition is present
		Cultural heritage is preserved
	Identity and diversity	Citizens are encouraged to express individual identity while not restricting others' freedom of expression
		The community has a defined identity

to eliminate the heat island effect (see chapters 4 and 8) in the community.

To measure the fulfillment of the requirements, however, indicators are needed. Indicators are the specific measurements used to operationalize the requirements. There is often more than one indicator per requirement, and the weighting of importance can vary from indicator to indicator. Once again, for ecological services, an indicator of the heat island effect is the ambient air temperature in a community measured at predetermined times, locations and frequencies.

Additionally, the Balance Sheet uses norms as a series of measurements used to assess progress for each indicator on a unique scale from socially optimal to socially unacceptable. Norms are best practices and policies, appropriate for the situation, that are applied in other jurisdictions or described in policy and research documents. Planners can help local governments determine best practices and policies by consulting with technical experts and community members and examining scientific research and policy documents.

Norms are a way of expressing what level of impact society is comfortable with. For example, with the air quality stock and pollution indicator, a community may be satisfied with (i.e., find socially acceptable) a daily average reading of 6 micrograms per cubic meter of particulate matter. One to three days with readings higher than this over the course of a year may be socially alarming, and four or more days may be considered socially unacceptable.

The measuring scale for norms is shown in Figure 17.3. The scale consists of a series of norms with specific target values attributed to each of the four categories (socially optimal, socially acceptable, socially alarming, socially unacceptable). The further away an indicator is from the target value identified for socially acceptable, the quicker the intervention or action is needed to strengthen this indicator. Target values are established from participant workshops, policy documents, comparison with other regions and comparison of indicator levels over time. (see Fig. 17.3, 17.4, color page C-6)

The outcome of the Balance Sheet completed in Step 2: Capital Inventory is a complete account of the capacity of the capital and stocks within the community. The results can be presented in a visual summary that maps out all of the capital together (Figure 17.5) and a more detailed fact sheet for each stock (Figure 17.6).

Some challenges communities face while completing this step relate to their size and resource capacity. Often smaller communities have difficulty finding the data required for input into the Balance Sheet. Frequently the data is not presently being collected, and they do not have the resources available to complete primary data collection, so the community must rely on outside technical experts for this information. This is neither an advantage nor disadvantage when compared to other communities who conduct the work in-house; it is merely a different way of gathering the required information.

Step 3: Considering Options

Once the inventory is complete, the next step is to create a small suite (approximately two to six) of options, or alternatives, for the project, plan or policy. Options should be created to reflect the findings of the inventory. One way to interpret this step is to treat it as a summary of the capital inventory. For example, when considering options for an economic development strategy, it is important to find options that build from the community's more robust capital and others that aim to strengthen weaker capital. It is imperative to revisit the community vision while developing the suite of options to confirm that all options, in some way or another, aim to move the community toward the vision. Each option will have its own advantages and disadvantages with respect to the community capital. The next step, Assessing Options, seeks to discover which option has the best balance between all of the capitals.

Step 4: Assessing Options

Once the Balance Sheet and the options have been defined, participants can use the Community Capital Scan to assess the potential impacts of each option on the capital. The Scan is a series of predetermined questions designed to direct participants to identify which stocks may be strengthened and which may be weakened by the proposed activity (examples of questions can be seen in Table 2). For each option, participants are asked to answer the questions on a scale of -5 (most negative impact) to +5 (most positive impact). The output is a series of diagrams, divided by capital, that shows the anticipated impact on the stocks. Below the diagrams are charts that show the range (from -5 to +5) and frequency of answers among the participants (See Figure 17.8 in the following section, Community Capital Tool in Action).

Of course, the goal of the Community Capital Tool is to support the process of finding balance between the capital where each is achieving optimum performance. Therefore, the information provided in this step will help facilitate the discussion to compare the impact of each option on the current community capital capacity, ultimately helping participants choose the best option to maximize the use of available resources for the greatest sustainability impact.

Step 5: Implementation

The steps above relate to the planning phase of a proposed project, policy or activity, whereas the following three steps relate to implementation.

Once the assessment is complete, an implementation plan should be created. The implementation should pay special attention to the decisions made during Step 1: Visioning and provide clear direction of how to implement the option chosen in the Step 4: Assessing Options. Once this plan is complete, the option should be implemented. Implementation is the process of moving an idea from concept to reality; in this context, it might refer to those actions relevant to carrying out, executing or practicing a plan, method or design in order for something to actually happen, such as assigning responsibility (who's in charge?), budget (how much staff and/or money over how long?) and reporting requirements (what kind of information, how often, to whom?).

Step 6: Monitoring

The first consideration for monitoring is to determine whether the project has been

Table 17.3: Community Capital Scan Questions	
Capital	**Example Questions**
Natural	Will the proposed development improve air quality?
Physical	Will the proposed development improve physical infrastructure that the community needs?
Economic	Will the proposed development increase employment opportunities?
Human	Will the proposed development provide education and training opportunities?
Social	Will the proposed development promote social cohesion?
Cultural	Will the proposed development strengthen the cultural identity of the community?

implemented yet. If it has not, it is important to identify what barriers may be holding up progress.

If the project has been implemented, the next step is to monitor its impact on each of the community capital. This step requires greater input through consultation from technical experts, such as economists, biologists and engineers. Similar to Step 2: Community Capital Inventory, the ultimate output of this step is the Community Sustainability Balance Sheet.

The Balance Sheet is used to monitor and assess how the stocks have changed over time. For example, since the implementation of the project, has the unemployment rate changed? Have the number of air quality advisories been reduced? While we are often unable to attribute these changes to a specific initiative, observing the change in values from the original Balance Sheet completed prior to implementation will give a more objective indication of how the community is progressing toward its long-term sustainability vision. However, the Balance Sheet is not designed to evaluate the effectiveness and efficiency of specific policies.

Step 7: Evaluation

The evaluation of the project is based on the results of the initiative and will ultimately identify what contribution the project has had on changes to the community. This will give an indication of whether the initiative should continue or be canceled. A rationale outlining the decision for either course of action is required.

Community Engagement

Without a doubt, the Community Capital Tool works best with successful community engagement. Community engagement is as much about process as it is about outcomes. An imperfect but shared analysis of community sustainability is more useful than a perfect analysis that is not shared.

There are two types of methodological paradigms for determining strategies for sustainable community development: the expert-led (top-down) and the community-based (bottom-up) (Reed et al. 2006). The Community Capital Tool has been designed with the understanding that the best approach is to combine the scientific rigor of the expert-led top-down approach with the engagement process of the bottom-up participation of community members. In other words, it strives for the best of both worlds (Hermans et al. 2011).

Participants are selected to provide a representation of the whole community. They are selected based on their knowledge of the community, expertise and stake in a capital and/or their ability to represent a distinct population within the community. There are three types of participants — the general public, stakeholders and technical experts. General public participation is widespread across the community and represents the whole community profile. This group tends to have interest in the initiative but generally less knowledge of and expertise on the technical issues. Stakeholders are the people in the community who have a stake, or vested interest, in the project. They may be business owners, local experts or professionals who are impacted and/or knowledgeable about the project and related issues. Stakeholders are a rich source of expertise, and they often explore issues more deeply than the general public group. It is important to find a balance between stakeholder interests with general public interests, because their interests may differ. Technical experts are used to conduct research to fill gaps in the data and analysis. Usually they are hired help, such as consultants and professional researchers. The trick for every community is to find the right proportion of all three types of participants to meet the community needs.

The combination of community-based and expert-led participation benefits each step of the Community Capital Tool for several reasons. First, community input is necessary to complete the visioning exercises and assess the present conditions of each capital. Second, community participants, along with professional experts, define the relevant stocks of the regional socio-economic and ecological system that need to be optimised. Third, participants help formulate the requirements and targets for each stock. By doing so, the contours of a desirable future are defined. As this is often a subjective and normative step, the community input is indispensable. Not all requirements can be satisfied at short notice, and sometimes participants will need to weigh the different requirements, indicators and stocks within the tool. Finally, participants can be used to pick the indicators directly, or their opinions can be used as input at the indicator level. Examples might be an indicator that measures community satisfaction with the quality of the regional landscape or their perception of their influence on regional politics. The following case study on Centerville provides greater detail of the community engagement in the application of the Community Capital Tool.

Community Capital Tool in Action: Centerville Example

The application of the Community Capital Tool is best explained using a hypothetical town called Centerville. Centerville is a community that has integrated sustainable community development goals into its latest official community plan. Recently the town has received an application for the redevelopment of a brownfield site along the community's waterfront. The developer would like to turn the former industrial site into a mixed-use building that includes housing, small office spaces, a big-box retail store and surface parking. The developer understands that Centerville is committed to moving toward a more sustainable future and has integrated green features into the project design, including green building development standards, green roofs and access to public transportation networks.

Centerville's town council must determine whether the development fits within its sustainability goals and decide whether it should be approved, amended or denied building permits for construction. To inform this important decision, the council used the Community Capital Tool to evaluate the project's impacts on the community.

The following sections describe the steps the Centerville council completed while using the Community Capital Tool.

Step 1: Visioning

Centerville's town council assembled *Sustainable Centerville*, an independent organization comprising local government administrators, community representatives and technical experts from various disciplines. This group was tasked with developing Centerville's sustainability strategy that can be used to monitor the community's progress toward achieving their vision. This is a story of how Sustainable Centerville created their sustainability strategy and used it to assess the proposed development in the community.

Sustainable Centerville quickly identified the need for extensive community input into the sustainability strategy, not only because of the intrinsic and subjective nature of sustainability, but because the creation of the official community plan had shown the importance of public input in formulating a community strategy. Participants were selected based on their knowledge of Centerville and their representativeness for segments of the community. The technical experts were recruited from universities, knowledge institutes and think tanks near the community.

Sustainable Centerville first met with a group of forty participants to conduct visioning activities. The outcome was *Centerville Vision 2050*, a statement for what the community should look like by 2050. The vision was signed by an assortment of dignitaries, administrators and community representatives and integrated into all of Centerville's official community documents.

Centerville Vision 2050:

"Centerville will strive to create a better quality of life for all of its citizens. It will be a well-planned, self-sustaining place that has a strong sense of community. It will be a leader in social innovation and provide educational, cultural and economic opportunities for *all* residents. Centerville will maintain its abundance of ecosystem services and conserve its wild spaces while becoming carbon-neutral."

After the visioning activities, multiple workshops were held with the same participants. Each participant was asked to reflect critically on Centerville's sustainability strategy and determine whether it covers all of the relevant issues related to sustainable community development. The workshops used a carousel method

of engagement that saw the participants divided into groups focused on each of the six forms of capital. Criteria for grouping the participants included their stake, knowledge, expertise and background for a form of capital. The meeting was broken into seven rounds where each group spoke together about their capital and then rotated to the other capital with which they were less familiar. This technique was used to encourage participants to become aware of the considerations of the other forms of capital. The last round was reserved for a plenary session where each group presented the findings of their evaluations. The outcome of this round of consultation was an overall endorsement of the sustainability strategy and some minor adjustments and tweaks to language and metrics.

Step 2: Community Capital Inventory

Although Sustainable Centerville already had the stocks and requirements well-defined based on the Community Capital Tool, a round of workshops were held to explore some of the more technical aspects of indicator selection, data gathering, norms development and evaluation processes. In this workshop, the same participants as the previous workshops were asked to weight the different stocks, requirements and indicators. The weighting exercise gave highest value to the stocks, requirements and indicators perceived to influence sustainable community development and lowest value to those with least influence. The participants also defined the norms for each indicator and assigned indicator scores to represent a good or bad situation. For example, for the air quality stock, the participants were asked to determine how many air quality advisory days were deemed acceptable, or good. They determined three days over the course of a year was acceptable and anything over seven days was unacceptable, or bad. The outcome was the suite of stocks, requirements, indicators and norms and their associated weights to measure progress toward sustainability with the Community Sustainability Balance Sheet. After the workshop, Sustainable Centerville completed the Balance Sheet by collecting and analyzing data for each of the indicators (Fig. 17.5 and 17.6 color page C-6, C-7).

Upon completing the Community Sustainability Balance Sheet, Sustainable Centerville learned that the physical and natural capital are most developed, whereas economic capital is the least developed. The outcome is the result of measuring all indicators per stock. For example, the air quality stock would include measurements of particulate pollution, number of annual air quality advisory days and carbon dioxide levels.

Centerville's high-quality physical capital is attributed to the abundance of housing and office space within the community and the good condition of its public infrastructure. The conservation area to the west and the ravine to the north contribute to a significant amount of natural capital, and social capital was determined to be substantial because of the distinct neighborhoods and community centers found throughout town. The two weakest forms of capital were determined to be the economic and cultural capital. Being close to a larger city center, many Centervillians commute to work and spend much of their time and money in other communities.

Step 3: Considering Options

Upon the completion of the Community Capital Inventory, the participants defined three options for assessment. The first option was to deny the development proposal and leave the site undeveloped, the second was to proceed with the development as proposed and the third was for Sustainable Centerville to work with the developer to redefine the project to meet the community's vision and goals.

Step 4: Assessing Options

Once the options were defined, the participants completed a Community Capital Scan to assess the potential impact of each of the proposed options on the existing stocks. To complete the Community Capital Scan, Centerville's participants answered a series of predetermined questions (see Table 17.2 for examples) designed to tease out the strengths and weaknesses of the proposal. Answers were given on a scale of -5 to +5, which are shown in the Figure 17.7. The results were used to help focus the workshop discussion of how the proposal will impact individual stocks.

The Scan demonstrated that the first option would have a negative impact on economic, human, social and cultural capital and would have virtually no impact on natural and physical capitals. Option 2 was identified as having a negative impact on the economic and cultural capital and a positive impact on the other four capital (the most positive impact on physical capital) (Figures 17.7 and 17.8). The impact on economic capital is negative, which is logical because three of the four stocks are negatively influenced. As we have mentioned earlier, the erosion of some capital can lead to the erosion of other capital. Cultural capital saw both positive and negative impact within its stocks. However, the negative impact on cultural heritage was greater than the positive impact on identity and diversity; therefore, it registered as a decrease in the overall assessment (Figure 17.7). Option 3, however, was recognized to have potential positive impacts on all capital if executed properly. (see Fig. 17.7, 17.8, color page C-7)

The results of the impact assessment demonstrated that Options 1 and 2 did not align with Centerville's vision. Rather than denying the project outright, the town council, with input from Sustainable Centerville, decided to pursue Option 3 and work with the developer to create a project that fit within the community's sustainability vision and optimized each of the community capital. Building from the assessment of existing capital, the council knew it wanted to increase economic and cultural capital through this project. As well, the large parking lot in the initial proposal did not align with the community's goal of becoming carbon-neutral. So the council proposed the following amendments to the project design:

• Inclusion of multiple small retail spaces to increase economic development opportunities for local business owners.
• Exclusion of one large retail space to be filled by a multinational company.
• Retrofit of existing onsite industrial warehouse to create an indoor/outdoor facility for public farmers' markets and community events.
• Significant reduction in surface parking stalls.

Step 5: Implementation

Once the options assessment was complete, Sustainable Centerville moved forward by creating an implementation plan for the development. The implementation plan included detailed steps to ensure that the development was executed in a manner that reflected the community's vision in goals.

Step 6: Monitoring

In the years after the development was built, Sustainable Centerville monitored the development's effect on each capital by completing Balance Sheets at regular four-year intervals. The trends in the results show an increase in social, cultural and physical capital and a decrease in natural, economic and human capital (Figure 17.9). (see Fig. 17.9, 17.10, 17.11, color page C-7)

The monitoring data is aggregated to show impacts over time. Figure 17.12 shows how a project can have positive impacts on some capital while compromising others. Centerville used this information to adapt the project to meet the community's goals for sustainability. (see Fig.17.12, color page C-7)

Step 7: Evaluation

Following four successive years of monitoring the impact of the development on Centerville's capital, Sustainable Centerville moved toward Step 7: Evaluation. To conduct the evaluation, the group analyzed the monitoring data to assess how the project contributed to the changes in the capital overtime. They used this information to decide how to proceed in the coming years — should the development continue to be operated and maintained in the same way, or are some adjustments needed? Ultimately Sustainable Centerville identified that changes were needed in the operation of the development to increase the negatively impacted natural, physical and human capital while maintaining the other three forms of capital. These proposed changes were outlined in an evaluation report submitted to the town council and implemented after they received approval. After implementation, Sustainable Centerville continued monitoring the project in two-year intervals and making recommendations for operational adjustments as appropriate.

Conclusion

As we have stated throughout this book, sustainability has a unique meaning in every community. The Community Capital Tool builds from this idea by using local knowledge to establish sustainable community development as a democratic process that represents a community's unique characteristics and needs.

It aligns community priorities with capacity in each form of community capital.

The Community Capital Tool is fully functional and ready to use. The field of sustainable community development, however, is rapidly changing and so are the related tools. Therefore, future tools being developed by the Centre for Sustainable Community Development and others can be found via *Pando | Sustainable Communities* (see Appendix).

Chapter 18

Lessons and Challenges

One might believe today that sustainable development has finally come of age. Born — publicly, at least — in the 1987 report of the UN's (Brundtland) Commission on Environment and Development, a child of the global agenda at the Rio Earth Summit in 1992, stumbling toward maturity with the Johannesburg World Summit on Sustainable Development and the Kyoto Accord on climate change, sustainable development survived the shift to a post-September 11 world, and has become a mainstay in the discussions at recent G20 meetings and the UN climate change conferences leading up to and beyond the 2012 Rio+20 Earth Summit.

More people are using the term *sustainable* today than ever before, but most often they use it to simply mean "surviving," "staying afloat" or "not going out of business," rather than any lofty notion of integrating economic, social and environmental objectives.

Some in the environmental movement might look askance upon equating sustainability with economic survival, but with the end of the Cold War and the absence of any credible alternative to capitalism, it is clear that serious attempts to promote sustainable development must honor this basic capitalist and biophysical reality: nothing is sustainable if it's not here next year. For better or worse, this has not changed since Adam Smith first published *The Wealth of Nations* in 1776.

What has changed, however, is an emerging recognition that a contemporary view of sustainable development has to blend this basic desire for economic prosperity (or at least survival) with multiple bottom-line objectives. Staying in business is undoubtedly necessary, but it is no longer enough. We have obligations to the planet and to each other and to future generations. Business depends upon our commitment to these obligations (e.g., environmental stewardship; a healthy, educated and peaceful population), and fulfilling these obligations depends upon our ability to create and distribute wealth such that society and nature become more stable and secure, not less so.

Gated communities within gated countries will not lead to long-term global stability and security. Genuine "homeland security" requires us to "do development differently." As discussed in chapter 1, this means:

- learning to live on our natural income rather than depleting our natural capital;
- finding ways to live more lightly on the planet, including increasing the efficiency of our resource and energy use, and reducing our present (as well as projected) levels of materials and energy consumption;
- enhancing our quality of life and the public domain by strengthening our community capital and
- fostering the critical resources for strengthening community capital: trust, imagination, courage, commitment, the relations between individuals and groups, and time.

We must therefore explicitly aim to nurture and strengthen community capital in order to improve our economic and social well-being. Government and corporate decisions should be reviewed for their effects on all forms of

community capital. Programs and policies need to be effected at every level to ensure that community capital is properly considered.

No single person can raise the wind that might blow us into a sustainable future. But we can all help put up the sail so that when the wind comes, we can catch it. If we can create the possibility of a sustainable future now, we can genuinely breathe some hope into our communities for ourselves and for our children.

As demonstrated in the foregoing chapters, our communities provide enormous, largely untapped opportunities for making our society more sustainable. This final chapter reviews some lessons for policy-making that emerge from these chapters, and explores the challenges ahead.

Lessons for Policy-making

Communities are coming to recognize their responsibility to develop sustainably. The community capital approach to sustainable community development requires some relatively new thinking about broad questions of community sustainability and self-reliance, and more specific innovations concerning community ownership, management, finance, organization, capacity and learning. Taken together, the initiatives described in this book begin to delineate a strategy for encouraging a globally conscious culture of sustainability in our communities. They also indicate some practical suggestions on how to design effective sustainable community development policies. The key features of any sustainable development policy framework should recognize the following:

Sustainable development requires sustainable communities. Global sustainable development requires local authority and capacity for sustainable community management and

Paradoxically, the financial crisis represents a unique opportunity for leaders in local government to take more radical, "game-changing" positive action.

To bridge the gap between spending limits and service obligations, councils will either have to: make further dramatic efficiency savings, reduce services on offer, identify new income streams or realize novel product or process innovations. This will create new political space for leaders to consider transformational change (Monaghan 2011, 43).

development. Despite the concentration of population in urban areas, many city and local governments do not have the regulatory and financial authority required to effectively contribute to sustainable urban development. Other levels of government must provide resources and support for the financing, management and policy-making authority necessary for local governments to achieve sustainable development in their communities.

To make wise decisions about key aspects of their communities, particularly land use, local governments need more generous national funding for infrastructure, education and social services. The experience of recent years has demonstrated that placing the burden of all these costs on property taxes can lead local governments to act irresponsibly — for example, allowing ecologically destructive development of valuable open space, or excluding low-tax-paying land uses such as affordable housing. Ultimately, this "fiscalization of land use" results the in low-tax land uses being pushed into suburban areas, promoting sprawl and fragmented communities (Blais 2010). Deteriorating municipal services, along with failing roads, bridges and sewerage systems in major urban areas worldwide, also testify to the need for giving more financial resources to communities.

Rules can and must be changed. Many community policy-makers are stuck in the paralyzing belief that our market society and our bureaucratic nation-state system cannot be changed in any basic sense. To play by those rules means that both the environment and the less fortunate members of society always lose until eventually everything is lost.

Sustainability can mean "less" as well as "more." So long as sustainable development is conceived merely as "environmental protection," it will be understood as an "added" cost to be "traded" against. Once sustainable development is conceived as doing development differently, such trade-offs become less critical: the new focus is instead on finding ways to stop much of what we are already doing, and use the resources thus freed for socially and ecologically sustainable activities.

Where the market works, use it. As one utility executive explained his sudden interest in energy conservation, "the rat has to smell the cheese." Create and promote incentives for ecologically sound practices. Well-designed ecological incentive programs are also cost-effective, since larger expenditures for clean-up and restoration are avoided.

Where the market fails, don't be afraid to mandate changes. The prevailing economic orthodoxy is that we must have a political and economic environment that welcomes foreign-owned companies and supports business through a reduction in regulations to become globally competitive, no matter what the consequences in our society and in our communities.

Yet the evidence may suggest otherwise. For example, Rainey et al. (2003) note that productive local economic development policy seeks to provide high-quality infrastructure and attract highly skilled labor, rather than engaging in a tax- and wage-cutting race to the bottom, in which localities compete with one another by reducing their standard of living. They also observe that, "holding everything else constant, higher taxes will tend to have a negative impact on capital investment. However, if higher taxes are used to make investments in public services that improve the productivity of private capital, the negative impact of the high taxes may be diminished or overcome by the positive productivity benefits."

Polluters should pay for the costs of remediation, but it is even more important to prevent pollution and the waste of resources in the first place. This principle is particularly significant in the debate over "green" taxes. Governments can reflect new priorities without increasing the total tax burden by shifting taxes away from income and toward environmentally damaging activities. If governments substituted taxes on pollution, waste and resource depletion for a large portion of current levies on employment and income, both the environment and the economy would benefit. For example, policy research suggests that the corporate income tax (the US rate is currently among the highest in the industrialized world), as well as the payroll tax, are the most likely candidates for a carbon tax trade-off. Implementing a tax on carbon while reducing the payroll tax, would lower the cost of employment and help offset the possibly regressive effects of higher energy prices on lower-income households (Green et al. 2007). Citizens, corporations and the environment could all come out ahead.

Social equity is not only desirable but essential. Inequities undermine sustainable development, making it essential to consider the distributive effects of actions intended to advance sustainable development. The most common image of sprawl is usually the farm paved over for a subdivision, but the more insidious images are the blocks and blocks of abandoned neighborhoods scattered throughout urban America. Divisions by income and race have allowed some areas to prosper while others languish. As basic needs such as jobs, education and health care become less plentiful in some communities, residents have diminishing opportunities to participate in their regional economy. Sustainable community development expands opportunities by expanding transportation connections to jobs and steering economic development toward existing communities (Smart Growth America 2004). While some "green" initiatives have unintended positive effects on social equity, the word "green" often looks at development through only the environmental lens, and is therefore not synonymous with the word "sustainable." Instead, social equity must be the *focus* and not the *by-product* of sustainable policy efforts, to ensure money is being spent on truly sustainable initiatives.

Public participation is itself a sustainable development strategy. To a considerable extent, the environmental crisis is a creativity crisis. By soliciting the bare minimum of public "input," rather than actively seeking community participation from agenda-setting through to implementation and evaluation, local and senior decision-makers have failed to tap the well of human ingenuity. They have failed to recognize that only from this well can the myriad challenges to redevelop our communities be met successfully. Effective and acceptable local solutions require local decisions, which in turn require the extensive knowledge and participation of the people most affected by those decisions, in their workplaces and in their communities.

> Sustainability is the new operating system for society. It is the new bottom line, the basis on which all else depends. If a thing is not sustainable — whether it be a manufactured good or a business unit, a farm or a hospital, a state government or a multinational corporation, a community or a megacity, a vehicle or the road it's on — it will not survive the twenty-first century.
>
> — Turner 2011, 50-51

The Challenges Ahead

Sustainable communities will not come easily — they require significant change in our structures, attitudes and values. Sustainable development implies a shift in the capacity of individuals, companies and nations to use resources that they have the right to use — and are encouraged to use — under present legal and economic arrangements. Although even the most conventional analyses recognize the need for changing these arrangements, few openly acknowledge that moving toward a sustainable society requires more than minor adjustments to existing practices.

The key to a sustainable future lies not in making us more competitive, but rather in making us more perceptive, more able to realize what we have, what we need and what are the long-term consequences of the short-term choices we are making (Wachtel 1989). Many North Americans intuitively understand that the reason why economic growth no longer brings a sense of greater well-being, why the pleasures of our new possessions swiftly melt away is that "what really matters is not one's material possessions but one's psychological economy, one's richness of human relations and freedom from the conflicts and constrictions that prevent us from enjoying what we have." Indeed, we have attempted "to use economics to solve what are really psychological problems" (Wachtel 1989).

By going straight to the heart of modern lifestyles, focusing on consumption demands that we examine our most mundane decisions and routines for their impacts and implications, and that we question the economic, cultural and social basis of 21st century consumer societies (Seyfang 2009).

Wachtel (1989) argues that our societal focus on productivity and economic efficiency as defining values leads to greater emphasis on competition, the pursuit of self-interest and the stimulation of demand:

> This in turn means still more decline in the security to be gained via shared ties and a stable, securely rooted place and way of life, still more need to compensate by organizing everything around what enables us to have "more," still more decline of traditional sources of security, and so forth. Thus, the more fully we have committed ourselves to increasing material abundance as our ultimate societal value, the more we have undermined older sources of security and made ourselves dependent on material goods for our sense of well-being to an unprecedented degree.

This " less is more" philosophy is known in present literature as sustainable de-growth and takes the definition of sustainability to another level by explicitly stating the need for social equity, and for a reduction in our level of consumption. "Sustainable de-growth" can be defined as an equitable downscaling of production and consumption that increases human well-being and enhances ecological conditions at the local and global level, in short and long term (Martinez-Alier et al. 2010; Schneider et al. 2010).

The challenge ahead is to explore the implications of a sustainable future and to find a new set of guiding images and metaphors suited for it. Sustainable communities are the next steps in suggesting an alternative vision of the future that is not just a bitter necessity (for example, the need to reduce materials and energy consumption), but promises a genuinely better life. Sustainable communities do not mean settling for less, but rather thinking of new opportunities along a different, and likely more satisfying, dimension.

With their relatively wealthy and well-educated populations, North American communities have a moral obligation to demonstrate leadership (and consequently benefit from) developing the knowledge, technologies and processes the world requires for sustainability in the coming decades. Citizens and their governments have the ability to frame issues, assume leadership, champion initiatives and demonstrate sustainable alternatives in their everyday practice. With creative leadership, we may yet be proud of the legacy we leave for the future.

We must also realize that there is no single prescription for a sustainable community. Developed and developing nations, as well as the communities within them, face different challenges as they strive to become more sustainable. The challenges facing rural communities are different than those of suburban communities, which are different still from the challenges experiences by those in the urban core. In the face of all these challenges, a commitment to increasing community capital through good leadership, citizen participation and effective policy will be the solution for all of these communities.

Sustainable community development requires mobilizing citizens and their governments to strengthen all forms of community capital. This includes minimizing consumption of essential natural capital and improving physical capital, which in turn require the more efficient use of urban space. It also includes strengthening economic capital, increasing human capital, multiplying social capital and enhancing cultural capital. Community mobilization is necessary to coordinate, balance and catalyze community capital.

In the years ahead, those communities, enterprises, cities and nations that learn how to strengthen all six forms of capital simultaneously are likely to be the ones that will thrive.

It is important to recognize that this process of change will take much time to accomplish. There are no quick-fix solutions to the creation of healthier cities and communities, instead a long-term commitment to multiple small steps must be taken. In essence, a healthy community and a healthy city is created one household at a time, one street at a time, one block at a time, one neighborhood at a time and one day at a time. Multiple small strategies provide multiple opportunities to learn and also provide a margin for failure, because failure will occur and is a learning experience that needs to be accepted, not penalized. The challenge for cities is to learn how to create community capital as a fundamental strategy for creating a healthy city (Hancock 2001).

This synergistic approach will enable our communities to be cleaner, healthier and less expensive; to have greater accessibility and cohesion; and to be more self-reliant in energy, food and economic security than they are now. Sustainable communities will not, therefore, merely "sustain" the quality of our lives — they will dramatically *improve* it.

APPENDIX

Pando | Sustainable Communities

Pando|Sustainable Communities is a project to connect sustainability-focused academics and other researchers with local government officials who are working towards building sustainable communities (perhaps using related names, such as ecocities, as discussed in chapter 2). Specifically, *Pando*'s target audience is local government staff, elected officials, academic researchers, non-governmental researchers and senior-level government researchers, consultants/developers and graduate/doctoral students who work within the field of sustainable communities.

Local governments have limited capacity, expertise and resources to successfully implement their sustainability goals. At the same time, researchers find it challenging to partner with local governments to conduct and share case studies, pilot projects, best practices and other forms of research that could accelerate the development of sustainable communities. *Pando* aims to address core needs of local governments and researchers interested in

sustainable communities: how to get local governments access to good, relevant research and researchers; and how to get researchers access to local government officials in order to make their research more useful and relevant.

Pando is a globally relevant tool to link professionals who research and practice in the field of sustainable communities. It is as a bridge between researchers and local governments. That bridge is held up by a series of supports, including institutions, journals, professional associations, conferences, research units, sustainability offices, individual researchers and individual local government officials.

While *Pando* will aim to encourage real-time interaction and collaboration whenever possible (such as at conferences), we recognize

> The Pando "tree" is a single living organism with a massive underground root structure and 47,000 connected trunks. In Latin the word "Pando" means "I spread."

that a significant source of communication will involve digital media. As such, the Network will help mobilize collaboration between researchers and communities by addressing social networking, information-management and reputation-management problems encountered by these two groups.

To this end, an online tool is being developed that will serve different kinds of users according to their own interests. "Passive" or infrequent users can have access to resources and news about sustainable communities; more "active" users can connect to researchers/practitioners when they have a specific need; and "super" users — leading researchers and practitioners — can use the tool to facilitate social networking among and between them. The tool is also intended to offer translation capability, enabling better collaboration across language barriers.

Mark Roseland, author of this book, is leading this project in response to a desire articulated at the ICLEI 2009 World Congress Researchers Symposium in Edmonton, Alberta, to develop an international network of local sustainability researchers and interested local authorities. Many of the ideas, projects, tools, initiatives and resources in this book and others like it will be updated, revised, created and shared through *Pando*.

With start-up support in British Columbia from the Pacific Institute for Climate Solutions, with assistance from the BC Climate Action Secretariat and the Union of BC Municipalities, and initial international cooperation from *ICLEI* – Local Governments for Sustainability, the journal *Local Environment* and an expanding host of individual researchers and local government officials around the world, *Pando | Sustainable Communities* will be launched internationally at the ICLEI 2012 World Congress and Researchers Symposium in Belo Horizonte, Brazil, in June 2012, just prior to the United Nations Rio+20 Earth Summit.

For more information on *Pando | Sustainable Communities*, go to pando.sc, or www.pando.sc.

References

Chapter 1: The Context for Sustainable Communities

Agyeman, J., R. Bullard and B. Evans. "Exploring the Nexus: Bringing Together Sustainability, Environmental Justice and Equity." *Space and Polity* 6 (1), 70 90, 2002.

Agyeman, J., R. Bullard and B. Evans. *Just Sustainabilities: Development in an Unequal World.* Earthscan/MIT Press, 2003.

Bourdieu, P. "The Forms of Capital." In J.G. Richardson (Ed.), *Handbook of Theory and Research for the Sociology of Education*, 241-258. Greenwood, 1986.

Bookchin, M., 1987. *The Rise of Urbanization and the Decline of Citizenship*. San Francisco: Sierra Club.

Boyce, J.K., A.R. Klemer, P.H. Templet and C.E. Willis. "Power Distribution, the Environment, and Public Health: A State Level Analysis." *Ecological Economics* 29, 127-140, 1999.

Brohman, J. "Popular Development: Rethinking the Theory and Practice of Development." Blackwell, 1996.

Callaghan, E.G. and J. Colton. "Building Sustainable and Resilient Communities: A Balancing of Community Capital." *Environment*, 2008.

Campanella, T.J. "Urban Resilience and the Recovery of New Orleans." *Journal of the American Planning Association*, 72, 141–146, 2006.

Chee, Yuang En. "An Ecological Perspective on the Valuation of Ecosystem Services." *Biological Conservation, 120, 549–565,* 2004.

Cochrane, P. "Exploring Cultural Capital and Its Importance in Sustainable Development." *Ecological Economics,* 2006.

Coleman, J.S. *Foundations of Social Theory*. Harvard University Press, 1990.

Comfort, L.K., K. Ko and A. Zagorecki. "Coordination in Rapidly Evolving Disaster Response Systems." *American Behavioral Scientist, 48, 295–313,* 2004.

Costanza, Robert. "What Is Ecological Economics?" *Ecological Economics 1,* 1-7, 1989.

Costanza, Robert, Ralph D'Arge, Rudolf De Groot, Stephen Farber, Monica Grasso, Bruce Hannon, Karin Limburg, Shassid Naeem, Robert V. O'Neill, Jose Paruelo, Robert G Raskin, Paul Sutton and Marjan Van Den Belt. "The Value of the World's Ecosystem Services and Natural Capital." *Nature,* 1997, *387,* 253-260. doi:10.1038/387253a0.

Costanza, Robert and C. Folke. "Valuing Ecosystem Services with Efficiency, Fairness and Sustainability as Goals." Island Press, 1997.

Dale, A, and L. Newman. "Social Capital: A Necessary and Sufficient Condition for Sustainable Community Development?" *Community Development Journal,* 2010.

Daly, H.E. "Sustainable Development: From Concept and Theory Towards Operational Principles." In *Population and Development Review*, Hoover Institution Conference, 1989.

Daly, H.E. and J.B. Cobb, Jr. *For the Common Good: Redirecting the Economy Toward Community, the Environment, and a Sustainable Future.* Beacon Press, 1989.

Department for International Development (DFID). *Sustainable Livelihoods Guidance Sheets: Framework Introduction.* London, UK: Department for International Development, 2003.

Diamond, Jared M. *Collapse: How Societies Choose to Fail or Succeed.* Penguin, 2006.

Emery, M. and S. Fey. "Using community capitals to develop assets for positive community change." *CD Practice*, 2006.

Flora, C.B. and J.L. Flora. "Entrepreneurial Social Infrastructure: A Necessary Ingredient." In Annals of the American Academy of Political and Social Science, 1993, *529*, 48-58.

Flora, Cornelia and Jan Flora with Susan Fey. *Rural Communities: Legacy and Change*, 2nd ed. Westview Press, 2004.

Folke, Carl. "Resilience: The Emergence of a Perspective for Social-ecological Systems Analyses," *Global Environmental Change*, 2006, *16* (3), 253-267.

Goodland, R. "Sustainability: Human, Social, Economic and Enviromental," *Encyclopedia of Global Environmental Change.* John Wiley & Sons, 2002.

Gran, G. *An Annotated Guide to Global Development: Capacity Building for Effective Social Change.* Pittsburgh: University of Pittsburgh Economic and Social Development Program, 1987.

Gutierrez-Montes, Isabel. "Healthy Communities Equals Healthy Ecosystems? Evolution (and Breakdown) of a Participatory Ecological Research Project Towards a Community Natural Resource Management Process, San Miguel Chimalapa (Mexico)." PhD Dissertation, Iowa State University, Ames, IA, 2005.

Hancock, T. "People, Partnerships and human Progress: Building Community Capital," *Health Promotion International*, 2001, *16*(3), 2001, 275-280.

Haxeltine, Alex and Gill Seyfang. "Transitions for the People: Theory and Practice of 'Transition' and 'Resilience' in the UK's Transition Movement." Tyndall Centre for Climate Change Research, 2009. files.uniteddiversity. com/Transition_Relocalisation_Resilience/ Transition_Network/Transitions%20for%20 the%20People.pdf

Hayami, Y. "Social Capital, Human Capital and the Community Mechanism: Toward a Conceptual Framework for Economists." *Journal of Development Studies*, 2009.

Holling, C.S. "Resilience and Stability of Ecological Systems," *Annual Review of Ecological Systems*, 1973. *4*, 1–23.

Hopkins, R. *The Transition Handbook: From Oil Dependency to Local Resilience.* Green Books, 2008.

Hultman, N.E. and A.S. Bozmoski. "The Changing Face of Normal Disaster: Risk, Resilience and Natural Security in a Changing Climate." *Journal of International Affairs*, 2006, *59*, 25–41.

Jacobs, J. *The Death and Life of Great American Cities.* Random House, 1961.

Jacobs, M. *The Green Economy: Environment, Sustainable Development, and the Politics of the Future.* University of British Columbia Press, 1993.

Lehtonen, M. "The Environmental–social Interface of Sustainable Development: Capabilities, Social Capital, Institutions." *Ecological Economics*, 2004, *49*(2), 199-214. doi:10.1016/j. ecolecon.2004.03.019.

Liu, Shuang, Robert Costanza, Stephen Farber and Austin Troy. "Valuing Ecosystem Services: Theory, Practice, and the Need for a Transdisciplinary Synthesis." *Annals of the New York Academy of Sciences*, 2010, *1185*, 54–78.

Meadows, Donella, Dennis Meadows and Jorgen Randers. *Beyond the Limits.* Chelsea Green Publishing, 1992.

Morello-Frosch, R. "Environmental Justice and California's 'Riskscape.' The Distribution of Air Toxics and Associated Cancer and Non-cancer Risks Among Diverse Communities." Unpublished dissertation, Department of Health Sciences. University of California, Berkeley, 1997.

National Round Table on the Environment and the Economy (NRTEE). *Environment and Sustainable Development Indicators for Canada.* NRTEE, 2003.

Odum, Howard T. and Elizabeth Odum. *A Prosperous Way Down: Principles and Policies*. University Press of Colorado, 2001.

OECD. *The Well-being of Nations: The Role of Human and Social Capital*. Organization Economic for Cooperation and Development (OECD), 2001.

Onyx, J., L. Osburn and P. Bullen. "Response to the Environment: Social Capital and Sustainability." *Australian Journal of Environmental Management*, 2004, *11*(3), 212–219.

Ostrom, E. "Social Capital and Development Projects." Prepared for Social Capital and Economic Development, American Academy of Arts and Sciences, Cambridge, MA, 1993.

Prigogine, Ilya and Isabelle Stengers. *Order Out of Chaos: Man's New Dialogue with Nature*. Bantam Books, 1984.

Putnam, R. D. *Bowling Alone: The Collapse and Revival of American Community*. Simon & Schuster, 2000.

Putnam, R., R. Leonardi and R. Nanetti. *Making Democracy Work: Civic Traditions in Modern Italy*. Princeton University Press, 1993.

Rainey, D.V., K.L. Robinson, I. Allen and R.D. Christy. "Essential Forms of Capital for Sustainable Community Development." *American Journal of Agricultural Economics*, 2003, *85*(3), 708-715.

Rees, W.E. "Economics, Ecology, and the Limits of Conventional Analysis." *Journal of the Air and Waste Management Association*, 1991, *41*, 1323-1327.

Roseland, M. "Natural Capital and Social Capital: Implications for Sustainable Community Development," in J.T. Pierce and A. Dale (Eds.), *Communities, Development, and Sustainability across Canada*. UBC Press, 1999, 190-207.

Sachs, Jeffrey. *Common Wealth: Economics for a Crowded Planet*. Penguin, 2008.

Strange, Tracey and Anne Bayley. *Sustainable Development: Linking Economy, Society, Environment*. Organization for Economic Co-operation and Development, 2008.

Tainter, Joseph A. "Sustainability of Complex Societies," *Futures*, 1995, *27*(4), 397-407.

Tobin, G.A. 1999. "Sustainability and Community Resilience: The Holy Grail of Hazard Planning?" *Environmental Hazards*, *1*, 13–25.

Torras, M. and J.K. Boyce. "Income, Inequality and Pollution: A Reassessment of the Environmental Kuznets Curve." *Ecological Economics*, 1998, *25*, 147-160.

Transition Network. "*Transition Initiatives Directory*, 2011. transitionnetwork.org/initiatives?themes=All&community_type=All&status_value=official &country=All&field_title_search=

Turner, Chris. 2011. *The Leap: How to Survive and Thrive in the Sustainable Economy*. Random House Canada.

United Nations Population Fund (UNFPA). *The State of World Population 2011: People and Possibilities in a World of 7 Billion*. foweb.unfpa.org/SWP2011/reports/EN-SWOP2011-FINAL.pdf

Visscher, M. "A Politically Incorrect Solution for Climate Change." *Ode*, *11* (2), 52, 2011.

Wackernagel, M. and W. Rees. *Our Ecological Footprint: Reducing Human Impact on the Earth*. New Society, 1996.

Walker, Brian, C.S. Holling, Stephen Carpenter and Ann Kinzig. "Resilience, adaptability and transformability in social-ecological systems." *Ecology and Society*, 2004, *9*(2), 5.

Wheeler, Stephen. *Planning for Sustainability: Creating Livable, Equitable, and Ecological Communities*. Routledge, 2004.

Wilkinson, R. and K. Pickett. *The Spirit Level: Why Greater Equality Makes Societies Stronger*. Bloomsbury, 2009.

World Bank. "Development Indicators: 2.7 Distribution of Income or Consumption." 2008. Accessed July 2011. siteresources.worldbank.org/DATASTATISTICS/Resources/table2_7.pdf

World Commission on Environment and Development (WCED). *Our Common Future*. Oxford University Press, 1987.

World Conservation Union (IUCN), United Nations Environment Program (UNEP) and World Wide Fund for Nature (WWF). *Caring for the Earth: A Strategy for Sustainable Living*. Gland, Switzerland: IUCN, UNEP, WWF, 1991.

World Watch Institute. "State of the World: Innovation for a Sustainable Economy." 2008. worldwatch.org/files/pdf/SOW08_chapter_1.pdf

World Wide Fund for Nature. "Living Planet Report." Gland, Switzerland: World Wide Fund for Nature, 2010.

Chapter 2: Sustainable Community Development

Blais, P. *Perverse Cities: Hidden Subsidies, Wonky Politics, and Urban Sprawl*. UBC Press, 2010.

Bridger, J.C., and A.E. Luloff. "Building the Sustainable Community: Is Social Capital the Answer?" *Sociological Inquiry*, 2001, 71(4), 458-472.

Brugmann, Jeb. Welcome to the Urban Revolution. Viking Canada, 2008.

Buchan, R. 2004. "The Costs and Impacts of Rural Sprawl: Not All Sprawl Is Equal." *Plan Canada*, 2009, *44*(3), 38-40.

CALP (Collaborative for Advanced Landscape Planning). *Local Climate Change Visioning and Landscape Visualizations: Guidance Manual, Version 1.1*. UBC Press, 2010.

CitiesPlus. *A Sustainable Urban System: The Long-term Plan for Greater Vancouver*. The Sheltair Group, 2003. citiesplus.ca.

City of Vancouver. *Greenest City Action Plan*, 2011. vancouver.ca/ctyclerk/cclerk/20110712/documents/rr1.pdf, accessed August 6, 2011.

Condon, Patrick M. *Seven Rules for Sustainable Communities: Design Strategies for the Post Carbon World*. Island Press, 2010.

Devuyst, D., L. Hens and W. De Lannoy (Eds.). *How Green Is the City? Sustainability Assessment and the Management of Urban Environments*. Oxford University Press, 2001.

Hopkins, R., *The Transition Companion: Making Your Community More Resilient in Uncertain Times* (White River Junction, Vermont: Chelsea Green), 2011.

International Council for Local Environmental Initiatives (ICLEI). *International Development Research Centre (IRDC) and United Nations Environment Program: The Local Agenda 21 Planning Guide*. ICLEI and Ottawa: IDRC, 1996.

International Council for Local Environmental Initiatives (ICLEI). *Accelerating Nations Economic and Social Sustainable Development: Local Action Moves the World*. United Council, 2002.

Lithgow, M., M. Bloomfield and M. Roseland. *Green Cities: A Guide for Sustainable Community Development*. Harmony Foundation of Canada, 2005.

Minnesota Sustainable Economic Development and Environmental Protection Task Force (SEDEPTF). *Common Ground: Achieving Sustainable Communities in Minnesota*. St. Paul: Minnesota Planning, 1995.

Newman P., T. Beatley and H. Boyer. *Resilient Cities: Responding to Peak Oil and Climate Change*. Island Press, 2008.

Newman, P. and J. Kenworthy. *Sustainability and Cities: Overcoming Automobile Dependence*. Island Press, 1999.

Newman, P. and I. Jennings. *Cities as Sustainable Ecosystems: Principles and Practices*. Island Press, 2008.

Otto-Zimmerman, K. "Embarking on Global Environmental Governance: Thoughts on the Inclusion of Local Governments and Other Stakeholders in Safeguarding the Global Environment." ICLEI – Local Governments for Sustainability, ICLEI Paper 2011-1 vs2b, 2011. iclei.org/index.php?id=1487&tx_ttnews%5Btt_news%5D=4598&tx_ttnews%5BbackPid%5D=983&cHash=02451e1558, accessed August 7, 2011.

Perlman, Janice and Molly O'Meara Sheehan. "Fighting Poverty and Environmental Injustice in Cities." WorldWatch Institute, *State of the World: Our Urban Future*, Chapter 9, 2007. megacitiesproject.org/pub_2.php

Roseland, M., Ed. *Eco-city Dimensions: Healthy Communities, Healthy Planet*. New Society, 1997.

Roseland, M. 2000. "Sustainable Community Development: Integrating Environmental, Economic, and Social Objectives." *Progress in Planning*, 54(2), 73-132.

Sonoma County. "Sonoma County Ecological Footprint Project: Time to Lighten Up," 2002. sustainablesonoma.org/projects/footprintreport/scfpweb.pdf

Wackernagel, M., J, Kitzes, D. Moran, S. Goldfinger and M. Thomas. "The Ecological Footprint of Cities and Regions: Comparing Resource Availability with Resource Demand," *Environment and Urbanization*, 2006, *18*, 103-112.

Yaro, R.D., R.G. Arendt, H.L. Dodson and E.A. Brabec. *Dealing With Change in the Connecticut River Valley: A Design Manual for Conservation and Development*. Center for Rural Massachusetts, University of Massachusetts at Amherst, 1988.

Chapter 3: Making Community Policy

American Council on Renewable Energy. *Compendium of Best Practices: Sharing Local and*

State Successes in Energy Efficiency and Renewable Energy in the United States, 2010. acore.org/compendium-of-best-practices

Aoimori Prefectural Government. "Parallel Conventional Line (Aoimori Railway Line)," March 17, 2011. pref.aomori.lg.jp/kotsu/traffic/heikouzai-top.html

BC Hydro. *PowerSmart*, 2011. bchydro.com/powersmart/

Boli, A. & T. Emtairah. *Environmental Benchmarking for Local Authorities: From Concept to Practice*. European Environmental Agency, 2001.

Brown, L.B. "Subsidies of Destruction." *USA Today Magazine*, May 2010, 25.

Ceres. *Ceres in Brief*, 2011. ceres.org/files/in-briefs-and-one-pagers/ceres-in-brief

City of Boulder. *Growth Management in Boulder, Colorado: A Case Study*, (n.d.). bouldercolorado.gov/files/City%20Attorney/Documents/Miscellaneous%20Docs%20of%20Interest/x-bgmcs1.jbn.pdf

City of Calgary. Bylaw No. 40M2006. *The Water Utility Bylaw*, July 13, 2010.

City of Kelowna. *Adopt-a-Stream Program*, 2011. city.kelowna.bc.ca/CM/Page454.aspx

City of Portland. *Buying Green: Sustainable Procurement at the City of Portland*, 2008. portlandonline.com/omf/index.cfm?c=37732

City of Santa Monica. *Envelope & Space Planning: Recycling Storage Area*, 2011. smgov.net/Departments/OSE/Categories/Green_Building/Guidelines/Envelope_+_Space_Planning/Recycling_Storage_Area.aspx

City of Seattle. *Commercial Recycling: Transfer Stations*, 2011. seattle.gov/util/Services/Garbage/Recycling_&_Disposal_Stations/Rates/index.htm

City of Toronto. *Industrial Water Rate*, 2011. toronto.ca/water/industrial/index.htm

City of Vancouver. *Vancouver Green Capital: Neighborhood Energy Utility*, 2011. vancouver.ca/sustainability/building_neu.htm

Dagevos, J. (2011, June). Personal communication.

Engel, S., S. Pagiola & S. Wunder. "Designing Payments for Environmental Services in Theory and Practice: An Overview of the Issues." *Ecological Economics*, May 1, 2008, 663-674.

Environment Canada. *Green Buying: Guide to Ecolabels*, 2011. ec.gc.ca/education/default.asp?lang=en&n=743D106D-1

Eriksson, L., A.M., Nordlund & J. Garvill. Expected Car Use Reduction in Response to Structural Travel Demand Management Measures. *Transportation Research Part F: Traffic Psychology and Behaviour*, September 2010, 329-342.

European Commission. *European Commission Environment*, 2011. ec.europa.eu/environment/ ecolabel/about_ecolabel/what_is_ecolabel_en.htm

Federation of Canadian Municipalities. *2011 FCM Sustainable Community Award Winners*, 2011. gmf.fcm.ca/files/News_Releases/News-Releases-2011/Backgrounder-2011FCM SustainableCommunityAwardWinners-FIN-e.pdf

Fodor, E. *Better, Not Bigger: How to Take Control of Urban Growth and Improve Your Community*. New Society, 1999.

Government of British Columbia. *Rebates and Incentives for Your Business*, 2011. livesmartbc.ca/green_business/b_rebates.html

Great River Greening. *Our History*, 2011. greatrivergreening.org/history.asp

Hawken, P. *Blessed Unrest : How the Largest Movement in the World Came into Being, and Why No One Saw It Coming*. Viking, 2007.

Hawken, P. *Natural Capitalism : Creating the Next Industrial Revolution*. Boston: Little, Brown and Co., 1999.

Hendrickson, D., S. Connelly, C. Lindberg & M. Roseland. "Pushing the Envelope: Market Mechanisms for Sustainable Community Development." *Journal of Urbanism*, 4(2), July 2011, 155-174.

Jacobs, M. *The Green Economy: Environment, Sustainable Development, and the Politics of the Future*. UBC Press, 1993.

Kysar, D.A. "Ecologic: Nanotechnology, Environmental Assurance Bonding, and Symmetric Humility." *UCLA Journal of Environmental Law & Policy*, January 1, 2010, 201.

Lovins, A.B., H.L. Lovins & P. Hawken. "A Road Map for Natural Capitalism." *Harvard Business Review*, May-June, 1999.

Lovins, L.H. and B. Cohen. *Climate Capitalism: Capitalism in the Age of Climate Change*. Hill and Wang, 2011.

Madsen, T. *Greening the Budget, 11 Ideas for Protecting the Environment and Easing Maryland's*

Fiscal Crisis [Online]. Friends of the Earth, 2004. foe.org/res/pubs/reports2004.html [Accessed September 1, 2010].

Marshall, G. "Nesting, Subsidiarity, and Community-based Environmental Governance beyond the Local Scale." *International Journal of the Commons*, January 22, 2008, 75-97.

New York City. *Property Tax Abatement for Green Roofs and Solar Electric Generating Systems*, 2009. nyc.gov/html/dof/html/property/property_tax_reduc_individual.shtml#green

New York Department of Environmental Protection. *Presentation at Pratt Institute-Manhattan Campus*, February 28, 2011.nyc.gov/html/dep/pdf/green_infrastructure/gi_grant_workshop_02282011.pdf

Pacific Carbon Trust. *Corporate Governance*, 2011. pacificcarbontrust.com/About/CorporateGovernance/tabid/69/Default.aspx

Plambeck, E. & L. Denend. "The Greening of Wal-Mart." *Stanford Social Innovation Review*, Spring 2008.

Pollock, R. *Wal-Mart Goes 'Back to Basics': A Cautionary Tale for the Left*, April 11, 2011. pajamasmedia.com/blog/wal-mart-goes-back-to-basics-a-cautionary-tale-for-the-left/?singlepage=true

Province of British Columbia. *Legislation & Regulations*, 2011. env.gov.bc.ca/cas/legislation/index.html

Rahm, D. & J.D. Coggburn. "Environmentally Preferable Procurement." *Public Works Management Policy*, 12(2), 2007.

Rechargeable Battery Recycling Corporation. *Federal and State Law*, 2011. call2recycle.org/index.php?x=&c=1&w=7&a=112&r=Y#newyork

Rees, W.E. "An Ecological Economics Perspective on Sustainability and Prospects for Ending Poverty." *Population & Environment*, 2002, 24(1), 15-46.

Roseland, M. and M. Jacobs. *Sustainable Development, Economic Instruments, and the Sustainable Management of Aquatic Resources and Ecosystems: A New Framework for Water Management in the Fraser Basin*. Burnaby, BC: Science Council of BC, 1995.

Rubin, J. *Why Your World Is About to Get a Whole Lot Smaller: Oil and the End of Globalization*. Random House, 2009.

St. Petersburg Times. *Not Overinflated (Though It Sounds Like It)*, 2008. politifact.com/truth-o-meter/statements/2008/aug/05/barack-obama/not-overinflated-though-it-sounds-like-it/

Sustainable Cities. *Copenhagen: Cities Can Run on Wind Energy*, 2011. sustainablecities.dk/en/city-projects/cases/copenhagen-cities-can-run-on-wind-energy

The Natural Step. *About Us*, 2011. naturalstep.org/en/about-us

The Natural Step. *The Natural Step Framework: A Review*, 2011. naturalstepusa.org/storage/pdfstraining/TNS%20Framework%20Summary.pdf

United States Environmental Protection Agency. *Indoor Water Use In The United States*, 2008. //epa.gov/watersense/docs/ws_indoor508.pdf

van Beers, C. and J.C. van den Bergh. "Environmental Harm of Hidden Subsidies: Global Warming and Acidification." *AMBIO: A Journal of the Human Environment*, September 2009, 339-341.

Wackernagel, M. and W.E. Rees. *Our Ecological Footprint : Reducing Human Impact on the Earth*. New Society Publishers, 1996.

Whitten, S. and M. Young. *Market-Based Tools for Environmental Management: Where Do They Fit and Where to Next?* 2003. ecosystemservicesproject.org/html/publications/markets.html

Whitten, S., M. Bueren and D. Collins. *An Overview of Market-based Instruments and Environmental Policy in Australia*, 2003. ecosystemservicesproject.org/html/publications/docs/MBIs_overview.pdf

World Commission on Environment and Development. *Our Common Future*. Oxford University Press, 1987.

Chapter 4: Cultivating Greener, Food-secure Communities

Akbari, Hashem, Surabi Menon and Arthur Rosenfeld. "Global Cooling: Increasing World-wide Urban Albedos to Offset CO_2." *Climatic Change*, 2008, 94(3-4), 275-286. doi:10.1007/s10584-008-9515-9.

Albuquerque Bernalillo County Water Use Authority. "Xeriscape Rebates," 2010. Accessed June 24, 2011. abcwua.org/content/view/132/222/

Alexandri, Eleftheria and Phil Jones. "Temperature Decreases in an Urban Canyon Due to Green

Walls and Green Roofs in Diverse Climates." *Building and Environment*, 2008, *43*(4), 480-493. doi:10.1016/j.buildenv.2006.10.055.

APA (American Planning Association). *Policy Guide on Community and Regional Food Planning*, 2007. planning.org/policy/guides/pdf/foodplanning.pdf

Baltimore City Food Policy Task Force. *Final Report and Recommendations*, 2009. baltimorecity.gov/LinkClick.aspx?fileticket=WcxHP1SimYc%3d&tabid=1455&mid=875

Berg, Peter, Beryl Magilavy and Seth Zuckerman. *A Green City Program for San Francisco Bay Area Cities and Towns*. Planet Drum Books, 1989.

Buranen, Margaret. "Chicago's Green Alleys: A Large Scale Project to Reduce Impervious Surface." *Journal for Surface Water Quality Professionals*, October, 2008. stormh2o.com/october-2008/chicago-green-alleys.aspx

Carr, Mike. *Bioregionalism and Civil Society: Democratic Challenges to Corporate Globalism*. UBC Press, 2004.

CBPP (Center on Budget and Policy Priorities). "Policy Basics: Introduction to the Supplemental Nutrition Assistance Program (SNAP)," 2011. cbpp.org/files/policybasics-foodstamps.pdf

CIER (Centre for Indigenous Environmental Resources) and T'sou-ke Nation. *Implementing Adaptive Capacity: First Nations in Transition* (webcast), 2010. cier.ca/implementing-adaptive-capacity.html

City of Atlanta. "City Hall Greenroof," 2011. Accessed July 14, 2011. atlantaga.gov/mayor/energyconservationgreenroof.aspx

City of Austin. "Go Green: About Us," 2011. Accessed June 24, 2011. ci.austin.tx.us/growgreen/faq.htm

City of Burnaby. Department of Planning. *Official Community Plan*, 2004. The City of Burnaby.

City of Burnaby. *Official Community Plan: Chapter 10 Environment*, 2011. Accessed June 25, 2011. city.burnaby.bc.ca/cityhall/departments/departments_planning/plnnng_plans/plnnng_plans_offclc/plnnng_plans_offclc_environment.html

City of Chicago. "Green Alleys," 2011. Accessed June 24, 2011. cityofchicago.org/city/en/depts/cdot/provdrs/alley/svcs/green_alleys.html

City of El Cerrito. Public Works Department. "Creeks," 2011. Accessed June 25, 2011. el-cerrito.org/public_works/creeks.html

City of Los Angeles. Environmental Affairs Department. "Green Roofs: Cooling Los Angeles, A Resource Guide," 2006. Accessed June 24, 2011. fypower.org/pdf/LA_GreenRoofsResourceGuide.pdf

City of Los Angeles. "FAQ Sheet: Los Angeles Green Street Standard Plans," 2010. Accessed July 18, 2011. eng.lacity.org/techdocs/stdplans/Pdfs/Green%20Street%20Standard%20Plans%20FAQ%20Sheet_091010.pdf

City of Portland. Portland Bureau of Environmental Services. "Ecoroof Program," 2011a. Accessed June 24, 2011. portlandonline.combes/index.cfm?c=44422

City of Portland. Portland Bureau of Environmental Services. "Community Watershed Stewardship Program," 2011b. Accessed June 24, 2011. portlandonline.combes/index.cfm?c=43077

City of Richmond. *Bylaw No. 8385: Green Roofs & Other Options Involving Industrial Office Buildings outside of the City Center*, 2008. richmond.ca/__shared/assets/Bylaw_838521490.pdf

City of Seattle. Department of Neighbourhoods. "P-Patch Community Gardens," 2011. Accessed June 24, 2011. seattle.gov/neighborhoods/ppatch/communityfoodsecurity.htm

City of Toronto. "Green Roof Bylaw," 2009. Accessed June 25, 2011. toronto.ca/greenroofs/overview.htm

City of Toronto. "Xeriscaping," 2011a. Accessed June 25, 2011. toronto.ca/compost/xeriscap.htm

City of Toronto. "Live Green Toronto: Eco Roof Incentive Program," 2011b. Accessed June 25, 2011. toronto.ca/livegreen/greenbusiness_greenroofs_eco-roof.htm

City of Vancouver. Community Services. "Mosaic Creek," 2011a. Accessed June 25, 2011. vancouver.ca/PUBLICART_NET/ArtworkDetails.aspx?ArtworkID=252&Neighbourhood=&Ownership=&Program=

City of Vancouver. Community Services. "Food Policy," 2011b. Accessed June 25, 2011. vancouver.ca/commsvcs/socialplanning/initiatives/foodpolicy/projects/chickens.htm

Condon, Patrick M. *Seven Rules for Sustainable Communities*. Island Press, 2010.

de la Salle, Janine and Mark Holland, eds. *Agricultural Urbanism: Handbook for Building Sustainable Food and Agriculture Systems in 21st Century Cities*. Green Frigate Books, 2010.

DeWeerdt, Sarah. "Local Food: The Economics."
    World Watch, 2009, *22*(4), 20-24.

ESY (Edible School Yard). "The Garden: A Day
    in the Garden," 2011. Accessed June 25, 2011.
    edibleschoolyard.org/garden

Evergreen. 2011. "Evergreen Brick Works." Accessed
    June 25, 2011. ebw.evergreen.ca/

FAO (Food and Agriculture Organization of the
    United Nations). World Food Summit. 1996.
    *Rome Declaration on World Food Security. Food
    and Agriculture Organization*. fao.org/docrep/003/
    w3613e/w3613e00.htm

FAO (Food and Agriculture Organization of the
    United Nations). *An Introduction to the Basic
    Concepts of Food Security*, 2008. fao.org/
    docrep/013/al936e/al936e00.pdf

Food Banks Canada. "Facts and Statistics: Hunger
    Facts 2010," 2011. Accessed June 25, 2011.
    foodbankscanada.ca/main2.cfm?id=10718648-
    B6A7-8AA0-6A3C6F3CAC0124E1

Food Share. *Annual Report*, 2009. foodshare.net/
    download/FoodShare-AnnualReport2009w.pdf

The Food Trust. "Healthy Community Store
    National Network," 2011. Accessed June 25,
    2011. thefoodtrust.org/php/programs/store.
    network.php

Fussel, James, A. "Inmates at a Kansas City-area
    Leavenworth Penitentiary Grow Crops to Feed
    the Less Fortunate." Kansas City Star, June 7, 2011.
    Accessed July 18, 2011. cityfarmer.info/2011/06/
    13/\inmates-at-a-kansas-city-area-leavenworth-
    penitentiary-grow-crops-to-feed-the-less-fortunate/

Gilbert, C.L. and C.W. Morgan. "Food Price
    Volatility." *Philosophical Transactions of the Royal
    Society B: Biological Sciences*, 2010, *365*, 3023-
    3034. doi:10.1098/rstb.2010.0139.

Gillard, *Spring. Something's Rotten in Compost City:
    A Primer on the Politics of Food*. Smashwords
    Edition, 2011. ISBN 978-1-4661-4851-2.
    compostdiaries.com

Gorham, M.R., T.M. Waliczek, A. Snelgrove and
    J.M. Zajicek. "The Impact of Community
    Gardens on Number and Properties of Crimes
    in Urban Houston." *HortTechnology*, 2009, *19*(2),
    291-296. horttech.ashspublications.org/cgi/
    content/abstract/19/2/291

Graham, Julie, Stephen Healy and Kenneth Byrne.
    "Constructing the Community Economy: Civic
    Professionalism and the Politics of Sustainable

Regions." *Journal of Appalachian Studies*, 2002,
    8(1), 50-61. appalachianstudies.org/jas/pdf/
    JAS9.1.pdf

Gray, Rowan. "Practical Bioregionalism: A
    Philosophy for a Sustainable Future and a
    Hypothetical Transition Strategy for Armidale,
    New South Wales, Australia." *Futures*, 2007, *39*(7),
    790-806. doi:10.1016/j.futures.2006.12.003

Green Guerillas. "Green Guerillas, Our History
    and Mission," 2011. Accessed June 25,
    2011. greenguerillas.org/GG_ourprograms.
    php#helpingcommunity

GRG (Great River Greening). "Our History," 2011.
    Accessed June 25, 2011. greatrivergreening.org/
    history.asp

Groenewegen, Peter P., Agnes E. Van Den Berg,
    Sjerp De Vries and Robert A. Verheij. "Vitamin
    G: Effects of Green Space on Health, Well-being,
    and Social Safety." *BMC Public Health*, 2006,
    6(149). doi:10.1186/1471-2458-6-149.

Haliburton Farm. "Welcome to Haliburton Farm,"
    2011. Accessed July 7 2011. haliburtonfarm.org/
    wp/

Hand, M., S. Martinez, M. Da Pra, S. Pollack, K.
    Ralston, T. Smith, S. Vogel, S. Clark, L. Lohr,
    S. Low and C. Newman. *Local Food Systems:
    Concepts, Impacts, and Issues, Economic Research
    Report 97*, US Department of Agriculture,
    Economic Research Service, May 2010. ers.usda.
    gov/Publications/ERR97/ERR97.pdf

Hantz Farms. "Introducing Hantz Farms," 2011.
    Accessed June 27, 2011. hantzfarmsdetroit.com/
    introduction.html

Hill, Holly. "Food Miles: Background and
    Marketing," 2008. Accessed June 27, 2011. attra.
    ncat.org/attra-pub/foodmiles.html

ICLEI Local Governments for Sustainability.
    "Events and News: Toronto Becoming a New
    Leader in Green Roofs," 2011. Accessed June 27,
    2011. iclei.org/index.php?id=10223

Ihara, T., Y. Kikegawa, K. Asahi, Y. Genchi and
    H. Kondo. "Changes in Year-round Air
    Temperature and Annual Energy Consumption
    in Office Building Areas by Urban Heat-island
    Countermeasures and Energy-saving Measures."
    Applied Energy, January 2008, *85*(1), 12-25.
    doi:10.1016/j.apenergy.2007.06.012.

Islands Trust. "Food Security Legislation and
    Sample Policies/Bylaws," 2011. Accessed July 7,

2011 islandstrust.bc.ca/foodsecurity/includes/foodsecuritylegislation.cfm#fsrl

Kikegawa, Y., Y. Genchi, H. Kondo and K. Hanaki. "Impacts of City-block-scale Countermeasures Against Urban Heat-island Phenomena upon a Building's Energy-consumption for Air-conditioning." *Applied Energy*, June 2006, 83(6), 649-668. doi:10.1016/j.apenergy.2005.06.001

Klinkenborg, Verlyn. "Up on the Roof: A Lofty Idea Is Blossoming in Cities around the World, Where Acres of Potential Green Space Lie Overhead." *National Geographic Magazine*, May 2009. ngm.nationalgeographic.com/2009/05/green-roofs/klinkenborg-text/5

Land Trust Alliance. *National Land Trust Census Report*, 2005. landtrustalliance.org/land-trusts/land-trust-census/2005-report.pdf

Land Trust Alliance. "Sonoma Land Trust Acquires Iconic Coastal Property," 2009. Accessed June 27, 2011. landtrustalliance.org/land-trusts/west-success/sonoma-land-trust-acquires-iconic-coastal-property/

Leung, Dennis, Jeanie Tsui, Feng Chen, Wing-Kin Yip, Lilian Vrijmoed and Chun-Ho Liu. "Effects of Urban Vegetation on Urban Air Quality." *Landscape Research*, April 2011, 36, 173-188. doi: 10.1080/01426397.2010.547570.

Linzey, Jessica. "Seeding North Vancouver's First Urban Farm." January 12. 2011, Accessed July 18, 2011. vancouver.openfile ca/vancouver/file/2011/02/seeding-north- vancouvers-first-urban-farm

Little, R., D. Maye and B. Ilbery. "Collective Purchase: Moving Local and Organic Foods Beyond the Niche Market." *Environment & Planning A*, 2010, 42(8), 1797-1813.

Lowe, Marcia D. *Shaping Cities: The Environmental and Human Dimensions. Worldwatch Paper 105*, 1991. worldwatch.orgbookstore/publication/worldwatch-paper-105-shaping-cities-environmental-and-human-dimensions

Maller, Cecily, Mardie Townsend, Anita Pryor, Peter Brown and Lawrence St. Leger. "Healthy Nature, Healthy People: 'Contact with Nature' as an Upstream Health Promotion Intervention for Populations." *Health Promotion International*, October 6, 2005, 21, 45-54. doi: 10.1093/heapro/dai032.

Montgomery County. Department of Environmental Protection. "Sligo Creek Watershed," 2011. Accessed June 28, 2011. montgomerycountymd.gov/dectmpl.asp?url=/content/dep/water/sub_sligo.asp

New York City. Department of Finance. "Property Tax Abatement for Green Roofs and Solar Electric Generating Systems," 2009. Accessed June 28, 2011. nyc.gov/html/dof/html/property/property_tax_reduc_individual.shtml#green

Pimentel, D., Jennifer Gardner, Adam Bonnifield, Ximena Garcia, Julie Grufferman, Claire Horan, Julia Schlenker and Emily Walling. "Energy Efficiency and Conservation for Individual Americans." *Environment, Development and Sustainability*, June 22, 2009, 11(3), 523-546. doi: 10.1007/s10668-007-9128-x.

Pinto, Brunella, Andrea Pasqualotto and Les Levidow. "Community Supported Urban Agriculture: The Orti Solidali Project in Rome." *Urban Agriculture*, 2010, 24, 58-60. ruaf.org/sites/default/files/UA%20Magazine%2024%20sept2010web%2058-60.pdf

Pothukuchi, K. *Building Community Food Security: Lessons from Community Food Projects 1999-2003*, 2007. foodsecurity.org/BuildingCommunityFoodSecurity.pdf

Richardson, D. "School Lunch Brings Home the Bacon," 2009. Accessed June 28, 2011. miller-mccune.combusiness_economics/school-lunch-brings-home-the-bacon-1335

Rocky Mountain Institute, Alex Wilson, Jenifer L. Uncapher, Lisa McManigal, L. Hunter Lovins, Maureen Cureton and William D. Browning. *Green Development: Integrating Ecology and Real Estate*. John Wiley & Sons, 1997.

Sale, Kirkpatrick. *Dwellers in the Land: The Bioregional Vision*. New Society Publishers, 1985.

Seyfang, Gill. "Ecological Citizenship and Sustainable Consumption: Examining Local Organic Food Networks." *Journal of Rural Studies*, 2006, 22(4), 383-395. doi:10.1016/j.jrurstud.2006. 01.003.

Supan, Colleen. "Growing Power's Vertical Farm," 2011. Accessed July 1 2011. urbanfarmonline.com/urban-farm-news/2011/07/01/growing-power.aspx

Swenson, David. *Determining the Methods for Measuring the Economic and Fiscal Impacts Associated with Organic Crop Conversion in Iowa*, 2007. leopold.iastate.edu/research/marketing_files/woodbury/M2006-12_report.pdf

TCBI (Tucson Clean and Beautiful, Inc). "Trees for Tucson," 2011. Accessed June 29, 2011. tucsonaz. gov/tcb/tft/

UC SAREP (University of California Sustainable Agriculture Research and Education Program). "What Is a Sustainable Community Food System?" 2011. Accessed June 29, 2011. sarep. ucdavis.edu/cdpp/cfsdefinition.htm

UniverCity. "Sustainability: Sustainable Initiatives," 2011. Accessed June 29, 2011. univercity.ca/ about_us/sustainability.46.html

University of Hawai'I Sea Grant. "Backyard Aquaculture," 2011. Accessed June 29, 2011. seagrant.soest.hawaii.edubackyard-aquaculture-0

USEPA (United States Environmental Protection Agency). "Water Sense and Landscape Water Use: What's Next?" 2006. Accessed June 25, 2011. epa.gov/watersense/docs/ws_whatsnext508.pdf

USEPA (United States Environmental Protection Agency). Office of Atmospheric Programs. "Reducing Urban Heat Islands: Compendium of Strategies," 2008. Accessed June 25, 2011. epa. gov/heatisland/resources/compendium.htm

Weber, Christopher L. & H. Scott Matthews. "Food-miles and the Relative Climate Impacts of Food Choices in the United States." *Environmental Science and Technology* 2008, *42*, 3508–3513. pubs. acs.org/doi/pdf/10.1021/es702969f

Wittman, Hannah, Annette Aurélie Desmarais and Nettie Wiebe, eds. *Food Sovereignty: Reconnecting Food, Nature and Community*. Fernwood Publishing, 2010.

World Future Council. *Celebrating the Belo Horizonte Food Security Programme*, 2009. worldfuturecouncil.org/fileadmin/user_upload/ PDF/Future_Policy_Award_brochure.pdf

Yu, Kongjian. "The Productive Landscape: The Rice Campus of Shengyang Architectural University." *Harvard Design Magazine*, 2009, *31*, 38-59. turenscape.com/english/news/view.php?id=194

Chapter 5: Water and Sewage

American Water Works Association. "AWWA's Free Water Audit Software," 2011. Accessed July 9, 2011. awwa.org/Resources/WaterLossControl.cf m?ItemNumber=48511&showLogin=N

Barr Engineering Company. *Burnsville Stormwater Retrofit Study*. Prepared for the City of Burnsville. Minneapolis: Bar Engineering Company, 2006.

ci.burnsville.mn.us/DocumentView. aspx?DID=449

Brandes, Oliver M. and David B. Brooks. *The Soft Path for Water in a Nutshell*, rev. ed. POLIS Project, University of Victoria and Friends of the Earth Canada, 2007. poliswaterproject.org/ sites/default/files/nutshell_revised_aug07_ lowres.pdf

Brandes, Oliver M., Tony Maas, Adam Mjolsness and Ellen Reynolds. *A New Path to Water Sustainability for the Town of Oliver, BC*. Victoria, BC: POLIS Project, University of Victoria and Friends of the Earth Canada. Discussion Series Paper 07-01, 2007. poliswaterproject.org/sites/ default/files/oliver_casestudy.pdf

Brandes, Oliver M., Steven Renzetti and Kirk Stinchcombe. *Worth Every Penny: A Primer on Conservation-oriented Water Pricing*. Victoria, BC: POLIS Project, 2010. poliswaterproject.org/sites/ default/files/Pricing%20Primer%20Final.pdf

Cervoni, Laura, Andrew Biro and Karen Beazley. "Implementing Integrated Water Resource Management: The Importance of Cross-Scale Considerations and Local Conditions in Ontario and Nova Scotia." *Canadian Water Resources Journal*, 2008. *33*(4), 333-350.

Chesnaux, R., D.M. Allen and G. Graham. "Assessment of the Impacts of Nutrient Management Practices on Nitrate Contamination in the Abbotsford–Sumas Aquifer." *Environmental Science & Technology*, 2007, *41*(21), 7229-7234. doi: 10.1021/es0704131.

City of Calgary. *The Water Utility Bylaw*, 2010a. Bylaw No. 40M2006. Passed July 13 2010. calgary. ca/DocGallery/BU/cityclerks/40m2006.pdf

City of Calgary. "The Calgro Program," 2010b. Accessed July 9, 2011. calgary.ca/portal/server.pt/ gateway/PTARGS_0_0_784_203_0_43/http% 3B/content.calgary.ca/CCA/City+Hall/Business+ Units/Water+services/Water+and+wastewater+ systems/Wastewater+system/Calgro+biosolids/ Calgro.htm

City of Guelph. "Smart Wash Washing Machine Rebate Program," 2011. Accessed July 10, 2011. guelph.ca/living.cfm?itemid=74324&smocid= 2338

City of Kelowna "Adopt-a-Stream Program," 2009. Accessed July 10, 2011. city.kelowna.bc.ca/CM/ Page454.aspx

City of Portland. "Downspout Disconnection Program," 2011. Accessed July 10, 2011. portlandonline.combes/index.cfm?c=54651

City of Toronto. "Industrial Water Rate," 2011. Accessed July 10, 2011. toronto.ca/water/industrial/index.htm

City of Tucson. *Residential Grey Water Ordinance*, 2008. Ordinance no. 10579. Accessed July 10, 2011. cms3.tucsonaz.gov/files/water/docs/graywaterord.pdf

The Civic Federation. *Managing Urban Stormwater with Green Infrastructure: Case Studies of Five U.S. Local Governments*. Chicago: Center for Neighbourhood Technology, 2007. cnt.org/repository/GreenInfrastructureReport CivicFederation%2010-07.pdf

Conservation Ontario. "Conservation Authorities of Ontario Mandate," 2009. Accessed July 10, 2011. conservation-ontario.on.ca/about/mandate.html

County of Westchester. *Restrictions on the Application and Sale of Lawn Fertilizer Within the County of Westchester*, 2009. Article XXVI of Chapter 863 (863.1301 to 863.1309). Passed April 27 2009. westchesterlegislators.com/LocalLaws/2009LocalLaws/.5%20Lawn%20 fertilizer%20legislation.pdf

Denver Water. "2011 Rate Schedule No. 1: Inside City," 2011. Accessed July 10, 2011. denverwater.org/BillingRates/RatesCharges/2011 Rates/InsideCity/

Environment Canada. *2010 Municipal Water Use Report: Municipal Water Use 2006 Statistics*, 2010. Catalogue no.: EN11-2/2006E-PDF. ISBN: 978-1-100-16173-0. ec.gc.ca/Publications/596A7 EDF-471D-444C-BCEC-2CB9E730FFF9/2010M unicipalWaterUseReportMunicipalWaterUse200 6Statistics.pdf

Federation of Canadian Municipalities. "2011 FCM Sustainable Community Award Winners," 2011. Accessed July 10, 2011. gmf.fcm.ca/files/News_Releases/News-Releases-2011/Backgrounder-2011 FCMSustainableCommunityAwardWinners-FIN-e.pdf

Fricke, G.R. and J. Manuel. *Leak Detection Program: The City of Mount Pearl*, 2005. Report presented at Leakage 2005 Conference held by International Water Loss Task Force. Accessed July 10, 2011. waterloss2007.com/Leakage2005. com/pdf/Leak%20Detection%20Program%20 -The%20City%20of%20Mount%20Pearl.pdf

Gleick, Peter H., Heather Cooley and David Groves. *California Water 2030: An Efficient Future*. Oakland, CA: Pacific Institute, 2005. pacinst.org/reports/california_water_2030/ca_water_2030.pdf

Griffiths-Sattenspiel, Bevan and Wendy Wilson. *The Carbon Footprint of Water*. Portland, OR: The River Network, 2009. rivernetwork.org/sites/default/files/The%20Carbon%20Footprint%20 of%20Water-River%20Network-2009.pdf

Hampton Roads Sanitation District. "Water Reuse: Ensuring Wastewater is Not Wasted Water," 2011. Accessed July 10, 2011. hrsd.state.va.us/firstreuseproject.htm

Holding, Emily. "San Diego's progress with wastewater reuse." August 6, 2010, *San Diego News Room*. Accessed July 10, 2011. sandiegonewsroom.org/news/index. php?option=com_content&view=article&id= 42543:san-diegos-progress-with-wastewater-reuses&catid=41:water&Itemid=58

Mono Lake Committee. "Ultra-low Flush Toilet Distribution System," 2011. Accessed July 13, 2011. monolake.org/mlc/ulft

Municipal Water District of Orange County. "California Friendly Landscape Training Program," 2011. Accessed July 13, 2011. mwdoc.com/pages.php?id_pge=95

New York Department of Environmental Protection. "Green Infrastructure Grant Program Workshop," 2011. Presentation at Pratt Institute-Manhattan Campus on February 28 2011. nyc. gov/html/dep/pdf/green_infrastructure/gi_grant_workshop_02282011.pdf

OECD. *OECD Factbook 2005: Economic, Environmental and Social Statistics*. OECD Publishing, 2005. doi: 10.1787/factbook-2005-en.

Orenco System Ltd. *An Affordable Wastewater Collection Solution for Municipalities: Case Study of Victoria, Prince Edward Island*, 2011. Report no. NCS-19.

Orange County Water District. "Green Acres Project (Landscape Use)," 2008. Accessed July 13, 2011. ocwd.com/ca-168.aspx

Orange County Water District and Orange County Sanitation District Groundwater Replenishment System Steering Committee. "About GWRS: World's Largest Wastewater Purification System for Indirect Potable Reuse," 2011. Accessed July 10, 2011. gwrsystem.com/about-gwrs.html

PAGI (Power Application Group Inc.). *Ontario Municipalities: An Electricity Profile*, 2008. ieso. ca/imoweb/pubsbi/Ontario_Municipalities-An_Electricity_Profile_January2008.pdf

Planning with Power. *The Relationship Between Land Use Decisions and the Impacts on Our Water and Natural Resources*. Purdue University and Illinois-Indiana Sea Grant College Program, 2009. Report id no. 260, IISG-01-19. planningwithpower.org/pubs/id_260.pdf

Saskatchewan Water Authority and Moose Jaw River Watershed Advisory Committee. *Moose Jaw River Watershed: Source Water Protection Plan*, 2006. swa.ca/Publications/Documents/MooseJawRiver WatershedSource WaterProtectionPlan.pdf

United States Environmental Protection Agency. *Water Sense: Indoor Water Use in the United States*, 2008a. Report no. EPA-832-F-06-004. epa.gov/ WaterSense/docs/ws_indoor508.pdf

United States Environmental Protection Agency. "Combined Sewer Overflows Demographics," 2008b. Accessed July 13, 2011. cfpub.epa.gov/ npdes/cso/demo.cfm?program_id=5

United States Environmental Protection Agency. *Managing Wet Weather with Green Infrastructure Municipal Handbook Funding Options*, 2008c. Report no. EPA 833-F-08-007. epa.gov/npdes/ pubs/gi_munichandbook_funding.pdf

Ville de Quebec. *Reglement De L'Agglomeration Sur L'Eau Potable*, 2008. Reglement R.A.V.Q. 67. Passed November 18, 2008. ville.quebec.qc.ca/ citoyens/reglements_permis/docs/eau_potable/ reglement_eau_potable_ravq67.pdf

Veritec Consulting Inc. *Region of Durham Efficient Community Final Report*. Regional Municipality of Durham, 2008. durham.ca/departments/ works/water/efficiency/ECfinalReport.pdf

Wang, D., K. Cossitt and D. Dormuth. *A Comprehensive Water Quality Monitoring in Urban Stormwater Detention Ponds*. National Research Council of Canada, 2008. Publication no. NRCC–50589. nrc-cnrc.gc.ca/obj/irc/doc/pubs/ nrcc50589/nrcc50589.pdf

Water for Tomorrow. "Industrial, Commercial, and Institutional Audit and Capacity Buy Back Program," 2011. Accessed July 14, 2011. waterfortomorrow.ca/en/atwork/industry.asp

Water Opportunities Act 2010. S.O. 2010. Chapter 19 Schedule 1. e-laws.gov.on.ca/html/statutes/ english/elaws_statutes_10w19_e.htm

Water ReUse Foundation, Jack Bryck, Rajesh Prasad, Trevor Lindley, Steve Davis and Guy Carpenter. *National Database of Water Reuse Facilities Summary Report*. Alexandria, VA: WateReuse Foundation, 2008.. watereuse.org/ files/s/docs/02-004-01.pdf

WE ACT. "About Us: History of WE ACT," 2011. Accessed July 14, 2011. weact.org/AboutUs/ tabid/180/Default.aspx

Weber Basin Water Conservancy District. "Project Overview," 2011. Accessed July 14, 2011. measuretogether.com/

West Basin Municipal Water District. "Conservation: Water Efficient Demonstration Garden," 2011. Accessed July 14, 2011. westbasin.org/water-reliability-2020/ conservation/demonstration-garden

Chapter 6: Waste Reduction and Recycling

Ayres, R. "Life Cycle Analysis: A Critique." *Resources Conservation and Recycling*, 1995, *14*(3-4), 199-223.

Bahn-Walkowiak, B. and R. Bleischwitz. "UNEP/ Wuppertal Institute: Collaborating Center on Sustainable Consumption and Production: Ecotown Program," 2007. Accessed March 29, 2011. unep.or.jp/ietc/Publications/spc/Eco_ Towns_in_Japan.pdf

Battery Council International. "US State Lead-acid Battery Laws," 2011. Accessed March 27, 2011 from batterycouncil.org/LeadAcidBatteries/ BatteryRecycling/StateRecyclingLaws/tabid/120/ Default.aspx

Bournay, Emmanuelle. "About the Difficulties of Classifying Waste (and Counting It)," 2006. maps.grida.no/go/graphic/about_the_difficulties_ of_classifying_waste_and_counting_it

Braungart, Michael, William McDonough and Andrew Bollinger. "Cradle-to-cradle Design: Creating Healthy Emissions – A Strategy for Eco-Effective Product and System Design." *Journal of Cleaner Production*, 2007, *15*, 1337-1348.

CalRecycle (California Department of Resources Recycling and Recovery). "Waste Reduction Awards Program," 2011a. calrecycle.ca.gov/WRAP/.

CalRecycle (California Department of Resources Recycling and Recovery). "Recycling Market

Development Zones," 2011b. Accessed March 24, 2011. calrecycle.ca.gov/rmdz/.

City of Denver. "Recycling: Marv's Kid's Page," 2011. Accessed March 29, 2011. denvergov.com/recnew/MarvsKidsPage/tabid/426193/Default.aspx.aspx

City of Edmonton. "Edmonton Composting Facility," 2011. edmonton.ca/for_residents/CompostingFacility.pdf

City of Kingston. "Belle Park Landfill: Remediation Progress Report," 2011. Accessed March 28, 2011. cityofkingston.ca/residents/environmentbellepark/rcmediation.asp

City of Seattle. "Seattle Public Utilities: At Your House," 2011a. seattle.gov/util/Services/Garbage/GarbageatYourHouse/GarbageCanRates/FAQs/index.htm

City of Seattle. "Commercial Recycling: Transfer Stations," 2011b. Accessed March 27, 2011. seattle.gov/util/Services/Garbage/Recycling_&_Disposal_Stations/Rates/index.htm

Community Composting. "How It Works," 2011. Accessed March 26, 2011. communitycomposting.ca/?page_id=33

Container Recycling Institute. *Wasting and Recycling Trends: Conclusions from CRI's 2008 Beverage Market Data Analysis*, 2008. Accessed March 24, 2011. container-recycling.org/publications/.

Department of Economic Affairs (DEA). Position paper on the solid waste management sector in India. Ministry of Finance, Government of India, 2009. pppinindia.com/pdf/ppp_position_paper_solid_waste_mgmt_112k9.pdf

EcoLogo. "About Ecologo," 2011. environmentalchoice.com/en/

Environment Canada. "Municipal Solid Waste and Greenhouse Gases," 2011a. Retrieved Feb. 22, 2011. ec.gc.ca/gdd-mw/default.asp?lang=En&n=6F92E701-1ec.gc.ca/gdd-mw/default.asp?lang=En&n=6F92E701-1

Environment Canada. "Extended Producer Responsibility & Stewardship: Post-Consumer Paint Stewardship Programme," 2011b. Accessed March 22, 2011. ec.gc.ca/epr/default.asp?lang=En&n=3A0FB78D-1

EPA (Environmental Protection Agency) Office of Solid Waste, Municipal and Industrial Solid Waste Division. *Decision Maker's Guide to Solid Waste Management*, Vol. II. EPA, 1995. epa.gov/osw/nonhaz/municipal/dmg2/chapter7.pdf

EPA. *Waste Not, Want Not: Feeding the Hungry and Reducing Solid Waste Through Food Recovery*, 1999. EPA 530-R-99-040 epa.gov/osw/conserve/materials/organics/pubs/wast_not.pdf

EPA. *Opportunities to Reduce Greenhouse Gas Emissions through Materials and Land Management Practices*. EPA publication no. 530-R-09-017. Washington, DC: US EPA, Office of Solid Waste and Emergency Response, 2009. Retrieved Feb. 28, 2011. epa.gov/oswer/docs/ghg_land_and_materials_management.pdf

EPA. *Municipal Solid Waste in the United States: 2009 Facts and Figures*. Washington, DC. US EPA, Office of Solid Waste, 2010a. epa.gov/epawaste/nonhaz/municipal/msw99.htm

EPA. *Landfill Methane Outreach Program: The Power of Partnerships*, 2010b. Accessed March 27, 2011. epa.gov/lmop/publications-tools/lmopbro.html

EPA. *Municipal Solid Waste*, 2010c. epa.gov/clean energy/energy-and-you/affect/municipal-sw.html

EPA. *Generators of Food Waste*, 2010d. epa.gov/osw/conserve/materials/organics/food/fd-gener.htm

EPA. *Buy Recycled*, 2011a. Accessed March 24, 2011. epa.gov/osw/conserve/rrr/buyrecycled.htm.

EPA. *Pay As You Throw*, 2011b. Accessed Feb. 24, 2011. epa.gov/epawaste/conserve/tools/payt/index.htm

EPA. *Waste Partnerships-Product Stewardship: Batteries*, 2011c. Accessed March 28, 2011. epa.gov/wastes/partnerships/stewardship/productsbatteries.htm

European Commission Environment. *Ecolabel*, 2011. Accessed March 23, 2011 ec.europa.eu/environment/ecolabel/about_ecolabel/what_is_ecolabel_en.htm

FCM. *Municipal Government and Sustainable Communities: A Best Practices Guide. Eliminating Waste*, 2001.

FCM. *Community Energy Planning Mission Case Study: Benefiting from Biogas*, 2007. gmf.fcm.ca/files/Missions/Alberta_2007/Case_Studies/Mission2007-Biogas-CASE-e.pdf

FCM. *Getting to 50% and Beyond: Waste Diversion Success Stories from Canadian Municipalities*. FCM Green Municipal Fund, p. 2, 2009.

FCM. *Sustainable Community Awards 2011: Regional District of Nanaimo Zero Waste Program*, 2011. Accessed Feb. 23, 2011. gmf.fcm.ca/

FCM-Sustainable-Community-Awards/FCM-2011-Awards/Waste.asp

Fidelis Resource Group. *Integrated Resource Recovery Study: Metro Vancouver North Shore Communities*, 2011. fidelisresourcegroup.com/North.Shore.IRR.FINAL29Mar2011web.pdf

Free Geek. *Ethical Computer Recycling*, 2011. Accessed March 23, 2011. freegeekvancouver.org/en/computer_recycling_principles

Gamage, Gayathri Babarenda, Carol Boyle, Sarah J. McLaren and Jake McLaren. "Life Cycle Assessment of Commercial Furniture: A Case Study of Formway LIFE Chair. *The International Journal of Life Cycle Assessment*, 2008, *13*(5), 401-411. DOI: 10.1007/s11367-008-0002-3

GVRD (Greater Vancouver Regional District). *Bylaw No. 258, 2010: A Bylaw to Establish the Tipping Fee and Solid Waste Disposal Regulation*, 2010. Accessed March 25, 2011. metrovancouver.org/services/solidwaste/disposal/Pagesbannedmaterials.aspx

Habitat for Humanity. 2011. Accessed March 25, 2011. habitat.ca/en/community/restores

Halifax Regional Municipality. *Precycling*, 2011. Accessed March 22, 2011. halifax.ca/wrms/precycling.html.

ICLEI: Local Governments for Sustainability. *Results of Sustainable Procurement Policy in Brazil*, 2009. Accessed March 27, 2011. iclei.org/index.php?id=1505&no_cache=1&tx_ttnews[tt_news]=3559&tx_ttnews[backPid]=9427&cHash=463179d432

ICLEI: Local Governments for Sustainability. *ICLEI Case Studies: Edmonton Waste Management Center*, 2011. Accessed March 28, 2011. iclei.org/index.php?id=1207.

King County Solid Waste Division. *EcoConsumer*, 2011. Accessed March 28, 2011. your.kingcounty.gov/solidwaste/ecoconsumer/index.asp

LA Public Works. *Recycling Computers and Electronics (E-waste)*, 2011. ladpw.org/epd/CompElec/

Lehmann, Steffen. "Resource Recovery and Materials Flow in the City: Zero Waste and Sustainable Consumption as Paradigms in Urban Development." *Sustainable Development Law & Policy*, 2011, *11*(1).

Marchettini, N., R. Ridolfi and M. Rustici. "An Environmental Analysis for Comparing Waste Management Options and Strategies." *Waste Management*, 2007, *27*(4), 562-571.

MassRecycle. *Why Should I Recycle?* 2004. massrecycle.org/recycling_benefits.html

Metro Vancouver. "Zero Waste Challenge," 2011. Accessed May 5, 2011. metrovancouver.org/services/solidwaste/Residents/zerowaste/Pages/default.aspx

NYC (New York City). *Local Law 13 of 2008: NYC Electronics Equipment Collection, Recycling and Reuse Act*. nyc.gov/html/nycwasteless/html/laws/local_electronics.shtml

NYC. *Local Law 121 of 2005: NYC Recycled Content Products Procurement Law*. Department of Sanitation, 2005. nyc.gov/html/nycwasteless/html/laws/local_recycledcontentprocurement.shtml

O'Riordan, Jon, Patrick Lucey, Cori Braarclough and Chris Corps. "Resources from Waste: An Integrated Approach to Managing Municipal Water and Waste Systems." *Industrial Biotechnology*, 2008, *4*(3), 139-146.

Official Journal of the European Communities. *Commission Decision Establishing List of Wastes*, 2001. eur-lex.europa.eu/LexUriServ/LexUriServ.do?uri=OJ:L:2000:226:0003:0024:EN:PDF

Packaging Recovery Organization Europe. *Germany: General Information*, 2011. Accessed March 26, 2011. pro-e.org/germany1.htm

RBRC (Rechargeable Battery Recycling Corporation). *Federal and State Law*, 2011. Accessed March 23, 2011. call2recycle.org/index.php?x=&c=1&w=7&a=112&r=Y#newyork

Regional District of Nanaimo. *Solid Waste: Zero Waste*, 2011. Accessed March 28, 2011. rdn.bc.ca/cms.asp?wpID=1063

Robinson, Alan and Dean Schroeder. "Greener and Cheaper." *Wall Street Journal*, 2009. online.wsj.com/article/SB123739309941072501.html

Skumatz, L. and D. Freeman. "Pay-As-You-Throw (PAYT) in the US: 2006 Update and Analyses," 2006. Accessed March 27, 2011. epa.gov/epawaste/conserve/tools/payt/research.htm#studies

Statistics Canada. *Human Activity and the Environment: Solid Waste in Canada*. Minister of Industry, Statistics Canada, 2005.

Statistics Canada. *Retail Sales by Industry:2010*, 2011. Accessed March 26, 2011. statcan.gc.ca/daily-quotidien/110222/t110222a2-eng.htm

Sustainable Cities. *Case Studies: Frankston, Compost Makes Cities Greener*, 2011a. Accessed March 25, 2011. sustainablecities.dk/en/city-projects/cases/frankston-compost-makes-cities-greener

Sustainable Cities. *Case Studies: Zurich, Zuri-sack-popular Rubbish Sack Policy*, 2011b. Accessed March 27, 2011. sustainablecities.dk/en/city-projects/cases/zurich-zuri-sack-popular-rubbish-sack-policy.

Sustainable Cities. *Case Studies: Copenhagen Waste to Energy Plants*, 2011c. Accessed March 27, 2011. sustainablecities.dk/en/city-projects/cases/copenhagen-waste-to-energy-plants

Thomas, Valerie M. "Reuse." Pollution A to Z. *Encyclopedia.com*, March 28, 2011. encyclopedia.com/doc/1G2-3408100219.html

Torras, Mariano. "The Subjectivity Inherent in Objective Measures of Well-being." *Journal of Happiness Studies*, 2008, *9*, 475–487.

Town of Smith Falls. *Take Back Programs*, 2011. smithsfalls.ca/take-back-programs.cfm

TxDot. *Golden Compost: Texas Roadside Composting*, 2003. epa.gov/osw/conserve/rrr/greenscapes/projects/tx_road.htm

United We Can. 2011. Accessed March 23, 2011. unitedwecan.ca/ABOUT.html

Young, J.E. "Reducing Waste, Saving Materials." In *State of the World 1991*. Worldwatch Institute. W.W. Norton, 1991.

Chapter 7: Energy Efficiency and Renewables

Austin Energy. "Austin Energy Green Building," 2011. Accessed July 11, 2011. austinenergy.com/Energy%20Efficiency/Programs/Green%20Building/transition.htm

ACORE (American Council on Renewable Energy). *Compendium of Best Practices: Sharing Local and State Successes in Energy Efficiency and Renewable Energy in the United States*, 2010. acore.org/compendium-of-best-practices.

Barrie, J. "How to Build an Energy Conservation Power Plant and Save $1000 Per Year," 2008. Accessed April 3, 2011. kilowattourscommunity.org/forum/.../KilowattOurs-TenSteps.pdf

BC Hydro. "PowerSmart," 2011. Accessed April 2, 2011. bchydro.com/powersmart/

British Columbia Ministry of Energy. "District Energy Sector in British Columbia," 2010. Accessed April 2, 2011. em.gov.bc.ca/EAED/InvestmentInfo/Documents/DistrictHeating27May2010.pdf

City of Berkeley. "Energy and Sustainable Development: Residential Energy Conservation Ordinance," 2011. Accessed June 29, 2011. ci.berkeley.ca.us/ContentDisplay.aspx?id=16030

City of Edmonton. "Energy Management Revolving Fund," 2011. Accessed Feb 26, 2011. edmonton.ca/environmental/documents/EnergyManRevolvingFund.pdf

City of Medicine Hat. "Hat Smart II Info Sheet," 2011. Accessed July 11, 2011. hatsmart.ca/docs/Hat%20Smart%20II%20Infosheet.pdf

City of Vancouver. "Sustainability Group: NEU Technology," 2008. Accessed March 31, 2011. vancouver.ca/sustainability/neuTechnology.htm

City of Vancouver. "Vancouver Green Capital: Neighborhood Energy Utility," 2011. Accessed March 31, 2011. vancouver.ca/sustainability building_neu.htm

Community Energy Services Corporation. "Welcome to the Community Energy Services Corporation," 2011. Accessed April 22, 2011. ebenergy.org/

Community Office for Resource Efficiency (CORE). "Making Energy Improvements Simple and Affordable," 2011. Accessed March 23, 2011. aspencore.org/Community_Office_for_Resource_Efficiency/Energy_Smart_Program.html

Cooper, M. and D. Sussman. "Nuclear Power Loses Support in New Poll." *New York Times*, March 23, 2011, A15. Accessed July 10, 2011. nytimes.com/2011/03/23/us/23poll.html?_r=1

Dockside Green. "A Better Approach: Biomass Heat Generation," 2011. Accessed April 15, 2011. docksidegreen.com/Sustainability/Ecology.aspx

EPUD (Emerald People's Utility District). "EPUD Renewables for Home," 2011. Accessed April 22, 2011. epud.org/myHome/renewableshome.aspx

Energy Star. "Mortgage Lending Programs," 2011. Accessed April 21, 2011. energystar.gov/index.cfm?c=mortgages.mortgage_lending_programs

Environment California. "AB 920: the California Solar Surplus Act of 2009," 2011. Accessed April 21, 2011. environmentcalifornia.org/energy/million-solar-roofs/ab-920

FCM (Federation of Canadian Municipalities). "Winners of the Sustainable Community Awards 2011: Energy," 2011a. Accessed

March 3, 2011. fcm.ca/English/View. asp?mp=1510&x=1509

FCM. "Putting Energy and Emissions on the Map: A Hands-on Introduction to Integrated Community Energy Mapping," 2011b. Accessed April 24, 2011. fcm.ca/English/View. asp?mp=1660&x=1684

GHPC (Geothermal Heat Pump Consortium, Inc.). "Geoexchange Heating and Cooling Systems: Fascinating Facts," 2006. Accessed July 11, 2011. geoexchange.org/index. php?option=com_phocadownload&view=cat egory&download=2:geoexchange-fascinating-facts&id=1:geoexchange-fact-sheets&Itemid=23

Gold, R., S. Nadel, J. Laitner and A. deLaski. *Appliance and Equipment Efficiency Standards: A Money Maker and a Job Creator*, 2011. aceee.org/ node/3078?id=1226

Gunton, T. and K. Calbick. *The Maple Leaf in the OECD: Canada's Environmental Performance.* A study prepared for the David Suzuki Foundation, 2010. davidsuzuki.org/publications/ downloads/2010/OECD_Report_Final.pdf

Hupacasath First Nation. "Upnit Power Corporation," 2009. Accessed July 1, 2011. hupacasath.ca/economic-development/ upnit-power-corporation

Helsinki Energy Board. "District Heating," 2011. Accessed July 11, 2011. helen.fi/sljeng/ kaukolampo.html

ICE (Interfaith Coalition on Energy). "The Interfaith Coalition on Energy," 2011. Accessed July 11, 2011. interfaithenergy.com

ICLEI: Local Governments for Sustainability. "Profiting from Energy Efficiency: Best Municipal Practices for Energy Efficiency," 2008. Accessed July 11, 2011. iclei.org/index.php?id=1677

ICLEI: Local Governments for Sustainability. *Long Island Green Homes Program in Babylon, New York*, 2011. icleiusa.org/action-center/tools/ municipal-clean-energy-toolkit/CaseStudy_ BabylonNYGreenHomes.pdf

Institute for Local Self-Reliance. "New Rules Project: Municipal Financing for Renewables and Efficiency," 2011a. Accessed April 22, 2011. newrules.org/energy/rules/municipal-financing-renewables-and-efficiency

Institute for Local Self Reliance. "Municipal Financing for Renewables and Efficiency," 2011b.

Accessed June 29 2011. newrules.org/energy/rules/ municipal-financing-renewables-and-efficiency

Kinsley, M. *Building Community Prosperity Through Natural Capitalism.* Rocky Mountain Institute, 2007. Accessed March 28 2011. rmi.org/cms/ Download.aspx?id=1267&file=BuildingProsperi ty.doc&title=Building+Community+Prosperity+ Through+Natural+Capitalism

LIGH (Long Island Green Homes). "Long Island Green Homes," 2011. Accessed July 11, 2011. ligreenhomes.com/page.php?Page=home

Low Income Energy Network. "Energy Assistance Funds for Low-income Consumers," 2011. Accessed July 11, 2011. lowincomeenergy.ca/ energy-assistance/

Merton Council. "The Merton Rule," 2011. Accessed July 1, 2011. merton.gov.uk/environment/ planning/planningpolicy/mertonrule.htm

Natural Resources Canada. "Business Residential: Key Facts in Promoting EnerGuide," 2009a. Accessed Feb 22, 2011. oee.nrcan.gc.ca/residential business/manufacturers/dollar-savings.cfm?attr=20

Natural Resources Canada. *Camnet Energy: Community Energy Case Studies*, 2009b. canmetenergy-canmetenergie.nrcan-rncan.gc.ca/ fichier/80781/CEP%2002%20City%20of%20 Guelph%20PDF%20(ENG)%20for%20web.pdf

Oregon Department of Land Conservation and Development. *Oregon's Statewide Planning Goals and Guidelines*, 2010. Accessed July 1, 2011. oregon.gov/LCD/docs/goals/compilation_of_ statewide_planning_goals.pdf

Pembina Institute. "Renewable Energy: Security," 2011a. Accessed March 31, 2011. pembina.org/ rebenefits/security

Pembina Institute. "Energy Source: Solar Energy," 2011b. Accessed March 31, 2011. pembina.org/ re/sources/solar

Province of British Columbia. "The BC Energy Plan," 2010. Accessed June 29, 2011. energyplan. gov.bc.ca/factsheet/default.htm

Rocky Mountain Institute. "Energy Solutions: End-use/Least-cost Approach," 2011. Accessed April 2, 2011. rmi.org/rmi/ End-Use%2fLeast-Cost+Approach

Sustainable Cities. "Copenhagen: Cities Can Run on Wind Energy," 2011a. Accessed March 7, 2011. sustainablecities.dk/en/city-projects/cases/ copenhagen-cities-can-run-on-wind-energy

Sustainable Cities. "Barcelona: Leader in Solar Energy," 2011b. Accessed March 21, 2011. sustainablecities.dk/en/city-projects/casesbarcelona-leader-in-solar-energy

Sustainable Cities. "Samsoe: A Role Model in Self-Sufficiency," 2011c. Accessed April 21, 2011. sustainablecities.dk/en/city-projects/cases/samsoe-a-role-model-in-self-sufficiency

Sustainable Cities Institute. "Solar Access Ordinance: Ashland OR," 2011. Accessed April 3, 2011. sustainablecitiesinstitute.org/view/page.basic/legislation/feature.legislation/Ordinance_Solar_Access_Ashland_OR;jsessionid=481B2F18 16B905E909E3B40010E909FE

Terasen. "Waterstone Pier, Richmond, BC: Developer Warms up to Earth-friendly Systems," 2011. Accessed July 1, 2011. terasenenergyservices.com/Projects/ResidentialCommercial/Pages/Waterstone-Pier.aspx

TREC (Toronto, Renewable Energy Co-operative). "Solarshare," 2011. Accessed July 11, 2011. trec.on.ca/generation/solarshare

T'Sou-ke Nation. "T'Sou-ke Nation Smart Energy Group," 2011. Accessed April 1, 2011. tsoukenation.com/category/smart-energy-group/

UniverCity. "Sustainability," 2011. Accessed March 17, 2011. univercity.ca/about_us/sustainability.46.html

USDOE (Department of Energy). "Energy Efficiency and Renewable Energy: Energy Smart Schools Case Study," 2009. Accessed March 31, 2011. www1.eere.energy.govbuildings/energysmart schools/case_studies.html

USDOE. "Advantages and Challenges of Wind Energy," 2011a. Accessed March 30, 2011. www1.eere.energy.gov/windandhydro/wind_ad.html

USDOE. "Wind and Water Power Program: Wind Power." National Renewable Energy Laboratory, 2011b. Accessed March 31, 2011. www1.eere.energy.gov/windandhydro/wind_power.html.

US Green Building Council (USGBC). *Leadership in Energy and Environmental Design (LEED): Curriculum*, 2011. Accessed April 1, 2011. usgbc.org/DisplayPage.aspx?CMSPageID=2177

Chapter 8:
Transportation Planning and Traffic Management

Appleyard, Donald. "Livable Streets: Protected Neighborhoods?" *The ANNALS of the American Academy of Political and Social Science*, 1980, *451* (1), 106-117. doi:10.1177/000271628045100111

American Lung Association. *State of the Air 2011*, 2011. stateoftheair.org/

Amin, N.A.T.M. "Reducing Emissions from Private Cars: Incentive Measures for Behavioural Change." *UNEP*, 2009. unep.ch/etb/publications/Green%20Economy/Reducing%20emissions/UNEP%20Reducing%20emissions%20from%20 private%20cars.pdf

APTA. *Public Transportation National Summaries and Trends Statistics*, 2002. American Public Transit Association. apta.com/research/stats

Bartle, John R. and Jijesh Devan. "Sustainable Highways." *Public Works Management and Policy*, January 1, 2006, *10*(3), 225-234. doi:10.1177/1087724X06287493

Bernstein, S., C. Makarewicz and K. McCarty, Surface Transportation Policy Project and Center for Neighborhood Technology. 2005. *Driven to Spend: Pumping Dollars out of Our Households and Communities*. Surface Transportation Policy Project.

Bikestation. *About Us*, 2011. home.bikestation.com/about-bikestation-a-mobis-transporatoin-alternatives-inc-company

Bixi. *Bixi by the Numbers*, 2011. bixi.com/news/category/BIXI%20en%20chiffres

Buehler, R. and J. Pucher. "Sustainable Transport that Works: Lessons from Germany." *World Transport Policy and Practice*, 2009, *15*(1). eco-logica.co.uk/pdf/wtpp15.1.pdf#page=13

Burwell, David G. "Beyond Congestion: Transportation's Role in Managing VMT for Climate Outcomes." In *Reducing Climate Impacts in the Transportation Sector*, Dan Sperling & James Cannon, eds. Springer Science and Business Media B.V., 2009.

Cambio-carsharing.com. *Car Sharing- how it works*, 2011.cambio-carsharing.com/cms/carsharing/en/1/cms?cms_knschluessel=SOFUNKTIONIERTS

Care2. *Boston Hybrid Bus Purchase*, 2011. care2.com/greenliving/50-green-buses-for-bostons-logan-airport.html

Choo, Sangho, Patricia L. Mokhtarian and Ilan Salomon. "Does Telecommuting Reduce Vehicle-miles Traveled? An Aggregate Time Series Analysis for the US." *Transportation*, January 2005, *32*(1), 37-64. doi:10.1007/s11116-004-3046-7

City of Vancouver. *Electric Vehicle Bylaws*, 2011. vancouver.ca/sustainability/electric_vehicles. htm#1Commuter Check. *FAQ*, 2011. commutercheck.com/Employers/faq.aspx

Commuter Ride. "May in Motion," 2011. commuteride.com/mayinmotion.aspx

Demaio, Paul. *2010 Year End Wrap-up. The Bike-sharing Blog*, 2010. http:/bike-sharing.blogspot. com/search/label/2010%20Wrap-up

The Economist. "Life in the Slow Lane," April 28, 2011. economist.com/node/18620944

Eriksson, L., A. Nordlund and J. Garvill. Expected car use reduction in response to structural travel demand management measures. *Transportation Research: Part F*, 2010, *13*(5), 329-342.

Eigenbrod, Felix, Stephen J. Hecnar and Lenore Fahrig. "Accessible Habitat: An Improved Measure of the Effects of Habitat Loss and Roads on Wildlife Populations." *Landscape Ecology*, November 2007, *23*(2), 159-168. doi:10.1007/s10980-007-9174-7

Farrington, J., J. Shaw, M. Leedal, M. Maclean, D, Halden, T. Richardson and G. Bristow. *Settlements, Service and Access: The Development of Policies to Promote Accessibility in Rural Areas*. Welsh Assembly Government, 2004.

Federation of Canadian Municipalities (FCM). "Improving Travel Options with Transportation Demand Management." FCM Green Municipal Fund, 2008. gmf.fcm.ca/capacity_building/ sustainable_transportation/

Frank, L.D, J.F. Sallis, T.L. Conway, J.E. Chapman, B.E. Saelens and W. Bachman. "Many Pathways from Land Use to Health: Associations Between Neighborhood Walkability and Active Transportation, Body Mass Index, and Air Quality." *Journal of the American Planning Association*, 2006, *72*(1).

Frank, Lawrence D., Michael J. Greenwald, Steve Winkelman, James Chapman and Sarah Kavage. "Carbonless Footprints: Promoting Health and Climate Stabilization Through Active Transportation." *Preventive Medicine*, January 2010, *50* (Supplement 1), S99-S105. doi:10.1016/j. ypmed.2009.09.025

Gärling, Tommy and Linda Steg. "Social Marketing of Alternative Transportation Modes." In *Threats from Car Traffic to the Quality of Urban Life: Problems, Causes, and Solutions*, 367, Tommy Gärling and Linda Stegg (eds.). Elsevier, 2007.

Gilbert, Richard and Anthony Perl. *Transport Revolutions: Moving People and Freight Without Oil*. Revised and updated edition. New Society Publishers, 2010.

Gray, D., J. Shaw and J. Farrington. "Community Transport, Social Capital and Social Exclusion in Rural Areas." *Area*, 2006, *38*(1), 89-98.

Halvorson, Randy and Kenneth R. Buckeye. "High-occupancy Toll Lane Innovations: I-394 MnPASS." *Public Works Management Policy*, *10*, 242, 2006. doi 10.1177/1087724X06288331

Kang, Chang Deok and Robert Cervero. "From Elevated Freeway to Urban Greenway: Land Value Impacts of the CGC Project in Seoul, Korea." *Urban Studies*, December 1 2009, *46*(13), 2771-2794. doi:10.1177/0042098009345166

Konz, Raymond J. "End-of-Life Vehicle (ELV) Directive: The Road to Responsible Disposal." *Minnesota Journal of International Law*, 2009, *18*, 431.

Lewyn, Michael. 2010. "What Would Coase Do? (About Parking Regulation)." papers.ssrn.com/ sol3/papers.cfm?abstract_id=1632935

Leahy, S. *Curitiba, Brazil: The Roads Not Taken*, 2002. cvso.ca/articles/curitibaecocity.htm

Litman, T. "Transportation Cost and Benefit Analysis." *Victoria Transport Policy Institute*, 2009. vtpi.org/tca

Litman, Todd. "Parking Pricing Implementation Guidelines: How More Efficient Pricing Can Help Solve Parking Problems, Increase Revenue and Achieve Other Planning Objectives." *Victoria Transport Policy Institute*, 2010. Accessed July 7, 2011. vtpi.org/parkpricing.pdf

Litman, Todd. "Comprehensive Transport Planning Framework: Best Practices for Evaluating All Options and Impacts." *Victoria Transport Policy Institute*, 2011a. Accessed July 4, 2011. vtpi.org/ comprehensive.pdf

Litman, Todd. "Guide to Calculating Mobility Management Benefits." *Victoria Transport Policy Institute*, 2011b. Accessed July 2 2011. vtpi.org/ tdmben.pdf

Litman, Todd. "Evaluating Public Transit Benefits and Costs: Best Practices Guidebook." *Victoria Transport Policy Institute*, 2011c. Accessed July 5, 2011. vtpi.org/tranben.pdf

MacLeod, K. *Orientating Urban Planning to Sustainability in Curitiba, Brazil*, 2004. Retrieved

October 6, 2004, from www3.iclei.org/local strategies/summary/=curitiba2.html

Midgley, P. "The Role of Smart Bike-sharing Systems in Urban Mobility." *JOURNEYS*, 2009, 2, 23-31.

Mohan, Dinesh. "Road Traffic Injuries: A Stocktaking." *Best Practice and Research Clinical Rheumatology*, August 2008, 22(4), 725-739. doi:16/j.berh.2008.05.004

Mumford, Lewis. *The Highway and the City*. New American Library, 1963.

Neal, M.B, N. Chapman, J. Dill, I. Sharkova, A. DeLaTorre, K. Sullivan, T. Kanai and S. Martin. *Age-related Shifts in Housing and Transportation Demand*. Prepared for Metro, Portland, OR. Portland State University, College of Urban and Public Affairs, August 2006.

Nelson, Jon P. "Hedonic Property Value Studies of Transportation Noise: Aircraft and Road Traffic." In *Hedonic Methods in Housing Markets*, Andrea Baranzini, José Ramirez, Caroline Schaerer & Philippe Thalmann, eds., 57-82. Springer New York, 2008. springerlink.com.proxy.lib.sfu.ca/content/g33r6k4828183118/.

Newman, Peter and Jeffrey R. Kenworthy. Sustainability and Cities: *Overcoming Automobile Dependence*. Island Press, 1999.

Newman, Peter and Jeffrey R. Kenworthy. "Urban Design to Reduce Automobile Dependence." *Opolis*, 2006, 2(1).

"People Over Cars." *Canada and the World Backgrounder*, 2004, 69(6), 28-31.

Poudenx, P. "The Effect of Transportation Policies on Energy Consumption and Greenhouse Gas Emission from Urban Passenger Transportation." *Transportation Research Part A: Policy and Practice*, 2008, 42(6), 901–909.

Population Reference Bureau (PRB). *2008 World Population Data Sheet*, 2008. prb.org/pdf08/08WPDS_Eng.pdf

Pucher, J. and R. Buehler. "Cycling Trends and Policies in Canadian Cities World Transport Policy and Practice," 2005, 11(1), 43–61.

Rajan, Sudhir Chella. *The Enigma of Automobility: Democratic Politics and Pollution Control*. University of Pittsburgh Press, 1996.

Research and Innovative Technology Administration: Bureau of Transportation Statistics (RITA). "Table 1-11: Number of US Aircraft, Vehicles, Vessels and Other Conveyances," 2008. bts.gov/publications/national_transportation_statistics/html/table_01_11.html

Retire Your Ride. "Choose Your Incentive," 2011. scrapit.ca/p4incentivechoices.htm

Richardson, H.W., P. Gordon, J.E. Moore, S. Cho and Q. Pan. "Expansion of Toll Lanes or More Free Lanes? A Case Study of SR91 in Southern California." In *Road Congestion Pricing in Europe: Implications for the United States*, H.W. Richardson & C.H.C. Bae, eds. Edwards Elgar Publishing, 2008.

Rubin, Jeff. *Why Your World Is About to Get a Whole Lot Smaller: Oil and the End of Globalization*. Random House, 2009.

Shaheen, Susan, Adam Cohen and Melissa Chung. "North American Carsharing: 10-Year Retrospective." *Journal of the Transportation Research Board*, 2009, 2110, 35–44. doi: 10.3141/2110-05. 76.12.4.249/artman2/uploads/1/Shaheen_-_Cohen_-_Chung_-_North American_Carsharing_-_10_Year_Retrospective_-_2009.pdf

Shoup, Donald. *The High Cost of Free Parking*. Planners Press, American Planning Association, 2005.

Shore, W.B. "Land-use, Transportation and Sustainability." *Technology in Society*, 2006, 28(1-2), 27–43.

Texas Transportation Institute. *2010 Urban Mobility Report*, December 2010. tti.tamu.edu/documents/mobility_report_2010.pdf

Thurston County. "Thurston County Bicycle Commuter Contest," 2011. thurstonbcc.blogspot.com/

Tools of Change. "Improving Employee Transportation: The Cambie Corridor Consortium," 2011. toolsofchange.com/en/case-studies/detail/100

Translink. *Creating Transit Orientated Communities in Metro Vancouver*, 2010. metro.net/about_us/.../Busby-LACTMA-Sustainability-Summit.pdf

Transport for London. "Benefits," 2011. tfl.gov.uk/roadusers/congestioncharging/6723.aspx

TravelSmart. *Plan a Smarter Trip*, 2011. travelsmart.ca/en/plan-a-smarter-trip.aspx

Turcotte, M. "General Social Survey on Time Use: The Time It Takes to Get to Work," July 12, 2006. Statistics Canada Catalogue no.: 89-622-XIE2006001. statcan.gc.cabsolc/olc-cel/olc-cel?catno=89-622-XIE2006001andlang=eng

University of Washington. "U-Pass 2007 Annual
Report," 2007. washington.edu/facilities/
transportation/commuterservices/upass/reports

Victoria Transport Policy Institute (VTPI).
"Ridesharing, Carpooling and Vanpooling," Dec.
15, 2010. *Online TDM Encyclopedia*. vtpi.org/
tdm/tdm34.htm

Victoria Transport Policy Institute (VTPI).
"Increasing Commercial Vehicle Transport
Efficiency." *Online TDM Encyclopedia*, 2011a. vtpi.
org/tdm/tdm16.htm

Victoria Transport Policy Institute (VTPI). "Traffic
Calming." *Online TDM Encyclopedia*, 2011b. vtpi.
org/tdm/tdm4.htm

The Economist. "Life in the Slow Lane," April 28
2011. economist.com/node/18620944

Waddell, Paul, Gudmundur F. Ulfarsson, Joel P.
Franklin and John Lobb. "Incorporating Land
Use in Metropolitan Transportation Planning."
Transportation Research Part A: Policy and Practice,
June 2007, 41(5), 382-410. doi:16/j.tra.2006.
09.008

Walkable Communities. *What Makes a Community
Walkable?* 2011. walkable.org/faqs.html

Whitelegg, John. "The Information Society and
Sustainable Development." *Journal of World
Transport Policy and Practice*, 1996, 2, 4.

Woodcock, James, Phil Edwards, Cathryn Tonne,
Ben G. Armstrong, Olu Ashiru, David Banister,
Sean Beevers et al. "Public Health Benefits of
Strategies to Reduce Greenhouse-Gas Emissions:
Urban Land Transport." *The Lancet*, December
5, 2009, 374(9705), 1930-1943. doi:10.1016/
S0140-6736(09)61714-1.

Xing, Y., S.L Handy and T.J Buehler. "Factors
Associated with Bicycle Ownership and Use:
A Study of 6 Small US Cities," 2008. In
*Transportation Research Board 87th Annual
Meeting Compendium of Papers DVD*.

YouTube. August 2, 2011. Accessed August 5, 2011.
youtube.com/watch?v=V-fWN0FmcIU

York, B. and D. Fabricatore. *Puget Sound Vanpool
Market Assessment*. Office of Urban Mobility,
WSDOT, 2001. wsdot.wa.gov

Chapter 9:
Land Use, Urban Form and Community Design

Affordability and Choice Today (ACT). "Alternative
Development Standards. A Guide for
Practitioners," 2009. actprogram.com/CMFiles/
ADS%20Docs/ADS_Guide_FinalEN.pdf

Banzhaf, H. Spencer and Nathan Lavery. "Can the
Land Tax Help Curb Urban Sprawl? Evidence
from Growth Patterns in Pennsylvania." *Journal
of Urban Economics*, 2010, 67(2), 169-179.
doi:10.1016/j.jue.2009.08.005

Bengston, David N., Jennifer O. Fletcher and
Kristen C. Nelson. "Public Policies for Managing
Urban Growth and Protecting Open Space:
Policy Instruments and Lessons from the United
States." *Landscape and Urban Planning*, 2003, 69,
271-286. doi: 10.1016/j.landurbplan.2003.08.007

Bento, Antonio M., Sofia F. Franco and Daniel
Kaffine. "The Efficiency and distributional
Impacts of Alternative Anti-sprawl Policies."
Journal of Urban Economics, 2006, 59(1), 121-141.
doi:10.1016/j.jue.2005.09.004

Bird, Richard M. and Enid Slack. "Land and Property
Taxation in 25 Countries: A Comparative Review."
In *International Handbook of Land and Property
Taxation*, Richard M. Bird and Enid Slack, eds.
Cheltenham: Edward Elgar Publishing, 2004.

Blais, Pamela. Perverse Cities: Hidden Subsidies,
Wonky Politics, and Urban Sprawl. UBC Press, 2010.

Boarnet, Marlon G., Kenneth Joh, Walter Siembab,
William Fulton and Mai Thi Nguyen. "Retrofitting the Suburbs to Increase Walking: Evidence
from a Land-use Travel Study." *Urban Studies*, 2011,
48(1), 129-159. doi: 10.1177/0042098010364859

Boyce, Carmel. "Walkability, Social Inclusion and
Social Isolation and Street Redesign." *Built
Environment*, 2010, 34(4), 461-473. doi:
10.2148benv.36.4.461

Brownstone, David and Thomas F. Golob. "The
Impact of Residential Density on Vehicle Usage
and energy Consumption." *Journal of Urban
Economics*, January 2009, 65(1), 91-98. doi:
10.1016/j.jue.2008.09.002

Brueckner, Jan K. and Robert W. Helsley. "Sprawl
and Blight." *Journal of Urban Economics*, March
2011, 69(2), 205-213. doi:10.1016/j.jue.2010.09.003.

Buehler, R. and J. Pucher. "Sustainable Transport
that Works: Lessons from Germany." *World
Transport Policy and Practice*, 2009, 15(1), 13-47.

Carruthers, John I. and Gudmundur F. Ulfarsson.
"Urban Sprawls and the Cost of Public Services."
*Environment and Planning B: Planning and
Design*, 2003, 30(4), 503-522. doi: 10.1068b12847

Carruthers, John I. and Gudmundur F. Ulfarsson. "Does 'Smart Growth' Matter to Public Finance?" *Urban Studies*, 2008, *45*(9), 1791-1823. doi: 10.1177/0042098008093379

Cass, Noel, Elizabeth Shove and John Urry. "Social Exclusion, Mobility and Access." *The Sociological Review*, July 2005, *53*(3), 539-555. doi:10.1111/j.1467-954X.2005.00565.x

C.D. Howe Institute. "Message to Cities: If You Don't Like Sprawl, Don't Make It Worse, Says C.D. Howe Institute Study," 2002. Press Release February 21, 2002. Accessed July 21, 2011. cdhowe.org/pdf/commentary_160.pdf

Cervero, Robert and Michael Duncan. "Which Reduces Vehicle Travel More: Jobs-Housing Balance or Retail-Housing Mixing?" *Journal of the American Planning Association*, 2006, *72*(4), 475-490. doi: 10.1080/01944360608976767

Cho, Seong-Hoon, Seung Gyu Kim and Roland K. Roberts. "Measuring the Effects of a Land Value Tax on Land Development." *Applied Spatial Analysis and Policy*, 2009, *4*(1), 45-64. doi: 10.1007/s12061-009-9039-3

Condon, Patrick M. and Robert Yaro. *Seven Rules for Sustainable Communities: Design Strategies for the Post Carbon World*. Washington, DC, 2010.

Congress for the New Urbanism and P. Crawford. *Codifying New Urbanism: How to reform municipal land development regulations*. Chicago: American Planning Association, 2004.

Daly, Herman E. and Joshua Farley. *Ecological Economics: Principles and Applications*, 2nd ed. Island Press, 2010.

Davis, Adrian, Carolina Valsecchi and Malcolm Fergusson. *Unfit for Purpose: How Car Use Fuels Climate Change and Obesity*. Institute for European Environmental Policy, 2007. ieep.eu/assets/616/IEEP_-_Unfit_for_purpose_transport_climate_chage_and_obesity.pdf

Dietz, Michael E. "Low Impact Development Practices: A Review of Current Research and Recommendations for Future Directions." *Water, Air, and Soil Pollution*, 2007, *186*(1-4), 351-363. doi: 10.1007/s11270-007-9484-z

Dudley Street Neighborhood Initiative. "History," 2010. Accessed July 21 2011. dsni.org/history.shtml

Dwyer, Rachel. E. "Expanding Homes and Increasing Inequalities: US Housing Development and the Residential Segregation of the Affluent." *Social Problems* 2007, *54*(1), 23–46. doi: 10.1525/sp.2007.54.1.23

Endlicher, Wilfried, Gerd Jendritzky, Joachim Fischer and Jens-Peter Redlich. "Heat Waves, Urban Climate and Human Health." In *Urban Ecology: An International Perspective on the Interaction Between Humans and Nature*, John M. Marzluff, Eric Shulenberger, Wilfried Endlicher, Marina Alberti, Gordon Bradley, Clare Ryan, Craig ZumBrunnen and Ute Simon, eds. Springer Science and Business Media LLC, 2008, 269-302.

Ewing, Reid H. "Characteristics, Causes, and Effects of Sprawl: A Literature Review." In *Urban Ecology: An International Perspective on the Interaction Between Humans and Nature*. John M. Marzluff, Eric Shulenberger, Wilfried Endlicher, Marina Alberti, Gordon Bradley, Clare Ryan, Craig ZumBrunnen and Ute Simon, eds. Springer Science and Business Media LLC, 2008, *519–535*.

Ewing, Reid, Keith Bartholomew and Arthur C. Nelson. "Compactness vs. Sprawl." In *Companion to Urban Design*, Tridib Banerjee and Anastasia Loukaitou-Sideris, eds. Routledge, 2011, 467-483.

Farr, Douglas. *Sustainable Urbanism: Urban Design with Nature*. Wiley, 2008.

Foldvary, Fred E. "Geo-Rent: A Plea to Public Economists." *Econ Journal Watch*, 2005, *2*(1), 106-132. econjwatch.org/articles/

Fraser Basin Council. *Energy Efficiency and Buildings: A Resource for BC's Local Governments, Community Energy Association and Fraser Basin Council*. Fraser Basin Council, 2007. communityenergy.bc.ca/sites/default/files/Policy_Manual_final.pdf

Freyfogle, Eric. T. *On Private Property: Finding Common Ground on the Ownership of Land*. Beacon Press, 2007.

Frumkin, Howard, Lawrence D. Frank and Richard Jackson. *Urban Sprawl and public Health: Designing, Planning, and Building for Healthy Communities*. Island Press, 2004.

Garland, Sarah. *Gangs in Garden City: How Immigration, Segregation, and Youth Violence Are Changing America's Suburbs*. Nation Books, 2009.

Grimm, Nancy B., Stanley H. Faeth, Nancy E. Golubiewski, Charles L. Redman, Jianguo Wu, Xuemei Bai and John M. Briggs. "Global Change and the Ecology of Cities." *Science*, 2008, *319*(5864), 756-760. doi:10.1126/science.1150195

Harrison, Rick. "Smart Growth? Or Not So Bright Idea?" *New Geography*, May 13, 2009. Accessed June 4, 2011. newgeography.com/content/00790-smart-growth-or-not-so-bright-idea

Hodge, G. and D. Gordon. "Planning Canadian Communities." Nelson Thompson, 2007.

Hula, Richard C. and Rebecca Bromley-Trujillo. "Cleaning Up the Mess: Redevelopment of Urban Brownfields." *Economic Development Quarterly*, 2010, *24*(3), 276-287. doi: 10.1177/0891242410365711

Ignatieva, Maria and Ana Faggi. "Urban Green Spaces in Buenos Aires and Christchurch." Proceedings of the ICE: Municipal Engineer, 2009, *162*(4), 241-250. doi: 10.1680/muen.2009.162.4.241

Immergluck, Dan. *Foreclosed: High-risk Lending, Deregulation, and the Undermining of America's Mortgage Market.* Cornell University Press, 2009.

Jabareen, Yosef Rafeq. "Sustainable Urban Forms." *Journal of Planning Education and Research*, 2006, *26*(1), 38 -52. doi: 10.1177/0739456X05285119

Jackson, Katharine J. "The Need for Regional Management of Growth: Boulder, Colorado as a Case Study." *Urban Lawyer*, 2005, *37*(2), 299-324

Jacobson, Justin and Ann Forsyth. "Seven American TODs: Good Practices for Urban Design in Transit-oriented Development Projects." *Journal of Transport and Land Use*, 2008, *1*(2), 51-88.

Jim, C.Y. "Opportunities and Alternatives for Enhancing Urban Forests in Compact Cities in Developing Countries." In *Ecology, Planning, and Management of Urban Forests*, Margaret M. Carreiro, Yong-Chang Song and Jianguo Wu, eds. Springer, 2008.

Johnson, Shane D. and Kate J. Bowers. "Permeability and Burglary Risk: Are Cul-de-Sacs Safer?" *Journal of Quantitative Criminology*, December 2009, *26*(1), 89-111. doi: 10.1007/s10940-009-9084-8

Kearney, Anne R. "Residential Development Patterns and Neighborhood Satisfaction: Impacts of Density and Nearby Nature." *Environment and Behavior*, 2006, *38*(1), 112-139. doi: 10.1177/0013916505277607

Kirby, Alex. *CCCC Kick the Habit: A UN Guide to Climate Neutrality.* Jasmina Bogdanovic, Claudia Heberlein, Otto Simonett and Christina Stuhlberger, eds. United Nations Environmental Program, 2008. unep.org/publications/ebooks/kick-the-habit/pdfs/KickTheHabit_en_lr.pdf

Klein, Ezra. "How Much Does a Gallon of Gas Cost?" *Newsweek*, June 13, 2010. Accessed July 25 2011. newsweek.com/2010/06/13/how-much-does-a-gallon-of-gas-cost.html

Kunstler, James Howard. "Home from Nowhere: How to Make Our Cities and Towns Liveable." *Atlantic Monthly*, September 1996, *278*(3), 43-66.

Leigh, Nancey Green. *The State Role in Urban Land Development.* Brookings Institution Center on Urban and Metropolitan Policy, 2003.

Lopez, Russ. "Urban Sprawl and Risk for Being Overweight or Obese." *American Journal of Public Health*, 2004, *94*(9), 1574-1579. doi: 10.2105/AJPH.94.9.1574

Marshall, Julian D. "Energy-Efficient Urban Form." *Environmental Science & Technology*, May 1, 2008, *42*(9), 3133-3137. doi: 10.1021/es087047l

Mitchell, V.G., H.A Cleugh, C.S.B. Grimmond and J. Xu. "Linking Urban Water Balance and Energy Balance Models to Analyse Urban Design Options." *Hydrological Processes*, July 30, 2008, *22*(16), 2891-2900. doi:10.1002/hyp.6868

Morris, David. "Car-free Development: The Potential for Community Travel Plans." Universities Transport Study Group, Loughborough University, 2005. staff.lboro.ac.uk/~cvdm3/Downloads/2005/MORRIS_D_CarFree_Housing_UTSG2005.pdf

National Housing Supply Council of Australia. "National Dwelling Costs Study," 2010. nhsc.org.au/nat_dwelling_costs/sec4.html

Neumark, David and Jed Kolko. "Do Enterprise Zones Create Jobs? Evidence from California's Enterprise Zone Program." *Journal of Urban Economics*, 2010, *68*(1), 1-19. doi: 10.1016/j.jue.2010.01.002

Newman, Peter and Jeffrey Kenworthy. "Urban Design to Reduce Automobile Dependence." *Opolis: An International Journal of Suburban and Metropolitan Studies*, 2006, *2*(1), 35-52. escholarship.org/uc/item/2b76f089

Newman, Peter and Isabella Jennings. *Cities as Sustainable Ecosystems: Principles and Practices.* Island Press, 2008.

Neyfakh, Leon. "Green Building," 2011. articles.boston.com/2011-0130/lifestyle/29339157_1_new-urbanism-landscape-urban-planning

Njoh, Amber. "New Urbanism: An Alternative to Traditional Urban Design, The Case of Celebration, Florida, USA." Unpublished case study prepared for the United Nation's Global Report on Human Settlements, 2009. mirror.unhabitat.org/downloads/docs/GRHS2009CaseStudyChapter03Celebration.pdf

Parry, Ian W.H., Margaret Walls and Winston Harrington. "Automobile Externalities and Policies." *Journal of Economic Literature*, June 2007, *45*(2), 373-399. jstor.org/stable/27646797

Pomeroy, Steve. *Rethinking Neighbourhood Renewal: Review of the US Experience and Possible Lessons for Canada*. Caledon Institute of Social Policy, 2006. caledoninst.org/Publications/PDF/574ENG.pdf

Real Estate Research Corporation (RERC). *The Costs of Sprawl: Detailed Cost Analysis*, Vol. 1. US Government Printing Office, 1974.

Regional Municipality of Halton. *Land Stewardship and Healthy Communities: A Vision for the 90's and Beyond*, 1991. Official Plan Review Report B4 Draft, January.

Riddell, Robert. *Sustainable Urban Planning: Tipping the Balance*. Blackwell Publishing, 2004.

Rosenzweig, Cynthia, William Solecki, Stephen A. Hammer and Shagun Mehrotra. "Cities Lead the Way in Climate-change Action." *Nature*, 2010, *467*, 909-911. doi: 10.1038/467909a

Rubin, Jeff. *Why Your World Is About to Get a Whole Lot Smaller: Oil and the End of Globalization*. Random House, 2009.

Russell, J. "New Urbanist Essentials." *APA Planning Advisory Service Reports*, 2004, *526*, 9-24.

Schwartz, Alex F. *Housing Policy in the United States*, 2nd ed. Routledge, 2010.

Song, Yan, Gilbert C. Gee, Yingling Fan and David T. Takeuchi. "Do Physical Neighborhood Characteristics Matter in Predicting Traffic Stress and Health Outcomes?" *Transportation Research Part F: Traffic Psychology and Behaviour*. March 2007, 10(2), 164-176. doi: 10.1016/j.trf.2006.09.001

Song, Yan and Gerrit-Jan Knaap. "Measuring Urban Form: Is Portland Winning the War on Sprawl?" *Journal of the American Planning Association*, 2004, 70(2), 210–225.

Soule, David. "Defining and Managing Sprawl." In *Urban Sprawl: A Comprehensive Reference Guide*, David Soule, ed. West Port, CT: Greenwood Press, 2006.

Stone, Jr., Brian. "Urban Sprawl and Air Quality in Large US Cities." *Journal of Environmental Management*, March 2008, *86*(4), 688-698. doi: 10.1016/j.jenvman.2006.12.034

Tomalty, Ray. "Residential Intensification Case Studies: Municipal Initiatives," 2003. Accessed July 20, 2011. cmhc-schl.gc.ca/odpub/pdf/63421.pdf?lang=en

Turner, Matthew A. "A Simple Theory of Smart Growth and Sprawl." *Journal of Urban Economics*, January 2007, *61*(1), 21-44. doi: 10.1016/j.jue.2006.05.004

Turner, Robert C. and Mark K Cassell. "When Do States Pursue Targeted Economic Development Policies? The Adoption and Expansion of State Enterprise Zone Programs." *Social Science Quarterly*, 2007, *88*(1), 86-103. doi: 10.1111/j.1540-6237.2007.00448.x

US Treasury. Statement of Alan B. Krueger Assistant Secretary for Economic Policy and Chief Economist, US Department of Treasury Subcommittee on Energy, Natural Resources, and Infrastructure, 2009. Accessed July 15, 2011. treasury.gov/presscenter/pressreleases/Pages/tg284.aspx

Vemuri, Amanda W., J. Morgan Grove, Matthew A. Wilson and William R. Burch Jr. "A Tale of Two Scales: Evaluating the Relationship Among Life Satisfaction, Social Capital, Income, and the Natural Environment at Individual and Neighborhood Levels in Metropolitan Baltimore." *Environment and Behavior*, 2011, *43*(1), 3-25. doi: 10.1177/0013916509338551

Waddell, Paul, Gudmundur F. Ulfarsson, Joel P. Franklin and John Lobb. "Incorporating Land Use in Metropolitan Transportation Planning." *Transportation Research Part A: Policy and Practice*, June 2007, *41*(5), 382-410. doi: 10.1016/j.tra.2006.09.008

Waldheim, Charles. "A Reference Manifesto." In *The Landscape Urbanism Reader*, Charles Waldheim, ed. Princeton Architectural Press, 2006.

World Resources Institute, United Nations Environment Program, United Nations Development Program, World Bank. *World Resources 1996-1997: The Urban Environment*. Oxford University Press, 1996.

Zhao, Zhirong, Kirti Das and Kerstin Larson. "Tax Increment Financing as a Value

Capture Strategy in Funding Transportation."
*Transportation Research Record: Journal of the
Transportation Research Board*, 2010, *2187*, 1-7.
doi: 10.3141/2187-01.

Chapter 10:
Housing and Community Development

Abode Services. "Programs and Services: Tri Valley
Housing Scholarships," 2011. Accessed July 30,
2011. abodeservices.org/programs_
tvhousingscholarship.html

Active Living Options. "The Elmwood," 2011.
Accessed July 30, 2011. activelivingoptions.com/
elmwood.html

Apgar, William & Shekar Narasimhan. *Enhancing
Access to Capital for Smaller Unsubsidized
Multifamily Rental Properties*. Report no. RR07-
08. Joint Center for Housing Studies, Harvard
University, 2007. jchs.harvard.edu/publications/
rental/revisiting_rental_symposium/papers/rr07-
8_apgar.pdf

Beyond Shelter. "About the Agency," 2011. Accessed
July 30, 2011. beyondshelter.org/aaa_about_us/
aaa_about_us.shtml

Bratt, Rachel G. "Challenges for Nonprofit
Housing Organizations Created by
the Private Housing Market." *Journal of
Urban Affairs*, 2009, *31*(1), 67–96. doi:
10.1111/j.1467-9906.2008.00429.x

Canadian Mortgage and Housing Corporation.
"Cohousing Strategy: Quayside Village
Cohousing, North Vancouver, BC," 2011a.
Accessed July 30, 2011. cmhc-schl.gc.ca/en/inpr/
afhoce/tore/afhoid/cohode/cost/cost_005.cfm#
impact

Canadian Mortgage and Housing Corporation.
"Retaining Affordable Housing," 2011b.
Accessed July 30, 2011. cmhc-schl.gc.ca/en/inpr/
afhoce/tore/afhoid/pore/reafho/reafho_006.cfm

Center for Housing Policy. "Case Study: Chicago's
Affordable Requirements Ordinance," 2010.
Accessed July 30, 2011. housingpolicy.org/
toolbox/strategy/policies/inclusionary_zoning.
html?tierid=123

CHH (Capitol Hill Housing). "About Us," 2011.
Accessed March 23, 2011. capitolhillhousing.org/

City of Toronto. *Toronto Housing Charter:
Opportunity for All*, 2009. toronto.ca/affordable
housing/pdf/housingcharter_sep09.pdf

Cleveland Foundation. "Greater University Circle:
Cleveland's Urban Core," 2011. Accessed July 30,
2011. clevelandfoundation.org/VitalIssues/
NeighborhoodsAndHousing/GreaterUniversity
Circle/

Cohousing Association of the United States.
"Cohousing Directory — Community View:
Doyle Street," 2011. Accessed July 30, 2011.
cohousing.org/directory/view/1726

Cubbin, Catherine, Veronica Pedregon, Susan
Egerter and Paula Braveman. *Where We Live
Matters for Our Health: Neighborhoods and Health*.
Issue Brief 3, Neighborhoods and Health.
Robert Wood Johnson Foundation Commission
to Build a Healthier America, 2008. rwjf.org/
files/research/commissionneighborhood
102008.pdf

Davis, John Emmeus. Shared Equity
Homeownership: The Changing Landscape of
Resale-restricted, Owner-occupied Housing.
National Housing Institute, 2006. nhi.org/pdf/
SharedEquityHome.pdf

Davis, John Emmeus. "More Than Money: What
Is Shared in Shared Equity Homeownership?"
*Journal of Affordable Housing & Community
Development Law*, 2010a, *19*, (3-4), 259-278.

Davis, John Emmeus, ed. "Origins and Evolution
of the Community Land Trust in the United
States." *The Community Land Trust Reader*, J.E.
Davis, ed. Cambridge, MA: Lincoln Institute
of Land Policy, 2010b. cltnetwork.org/userfiles/
CLT%20Reader%20Intro%20To%20CLTs.pdf

Diamond, Michael. "Another Model of Low Income
Housing Tax Credit Development: Building
Housing and Building Capacity." In *Affordable
Housing and Public-Private Partnerships*, Nestor
M. Davidson & Robin Paul Malloy, eds. Ashgate
Press, 2009. scholarship.law.georgetown.edu/
facpub/264/

Dudley Street Neighborhood Initiative Inc.
"History," 2008. Accessed July 30, 2011. dsni.org/
history.shtml

Entre Nous Femmes Housing Society. "About
Entre Nous Femmes Housing Society," 2011.
Accessed July 30, 2011. enfhs.org/about.html

FCM (Federation of Canadian Municipalities).
*Housing in My Backyard: A Municipal Guide for
Responding to NIMBY. Affordability and Choice
Today (ACT) Program*. FCM, 2009. actprogram.

com/CMFiles/CRA_ACT_NIMBYGuide_
WebEN.pdf

Fireside, Daniel. "Community Land Trust Keeps
Prices Affordable: For Now and Forever."
Yes!Magazine, July 29, 2008. Accessed July 30,
2011. yesmagazine.org/issues/purple-america/
community-land-trust-keeps-prices-affordable-
for-now-and-forever

HUD (US Department of Housing and Urban
Development). "Community Development
Block Grant Program," 2011. Accessed
July 30, 2011. portal.hud.gov/hudportal/
HUD?src=/program_offices/comm_planning/
communitydevelopment/programs

Hudson River Foundation. "New York City
Environmental Fund," 2011. Accessed July 30,
2011. hudsonriver.org/nycef/

Jane's Walk. "Organise Jane's Walk in Your City,"
2010. Accessed July 30, 2011. janeswalk.net/
organize

Mallach, Alan. *A Decent Home: Planning, Building,
and Preserving Affordable Housing*. American
Planning Association, 2009.

Malloy, Patrick. "Burnsville, Minnesota's Heart of
the City Development and Its Implications for
Addressing the Suburban Shortage of Affordable
Housing." *Cities in the 21st Century*, 2009, *1*(1),
Article 5. digitalcommons.macalester.edu/
cgi/viewcontent.cgi?article=1009&context=
cities

Marcus, Clare Cooper and Wendy Sarkissian.
*Housing as if People Mattered: Illustrated Site
Planning Guidelines for Medium-Density Family
Housing*. University of California Press, 1986.

Metro Action Committee. "Community Safety
Program," 2011. Accessed July 30, 2011. metrac.
org/programs/safety/safety.htm

Metro Youth Partnership. "Our Cause: Community
Change," 2011. Accessed July 30, 2011.
rsvpnorthdakota.org/myp_ourcause.html

Mid-Peninsula Housing Coalition. "Via del Mar:
Watsonville, California," 2011. Accessed July 30,
2011. midpen-housing.org/properties/profiles/
Via_del_Mar.pdf

Mikkonen, Juha and Dennis Raphael. *Social
Determinants of Health: The Canadian Facts*.
York University School of Health Policy and
Management, 2010. thecanadianfacts.org/The_
Canadian_Facts.pdf

Natural Resources Defense Council. "Location
Efficient Mortgages," 2009. Accessed July 30,
2011. nrdc.org/cities/smartgrowth/qlem.asp

Neighborhood Resource Center of Colorado.
"Good Neighboring Resource Guide," 2011.
Accessed July 30, 2011. nrc-neighbor.org/
resourceguide2

New York City, Department of Transportation.
"Pedestrians and Sidewalks: Safe Streets for
Seniors," 2011. Accessed July 30, 2011. nyc.gov/
html/dot/downloads/pdf/safestreetsforseniors.pdf

Nguyen, Mai Thi. "Does Affordable Housing
Detrimentally Affect Property Values?
A Review of the Literature." *Journal of
Planning Literature*, 2005, *20*(1), 15-26. doi:
10.1177/0885412205277069

Official City of Raleigh Website. "Neighborhood
Improvement Funds," 2011. Accessed July 30, 2011.
raleighnc.gov/neighbors/content/CommServices/
Articles/NeighborhoodFunds.html

OHCC (Ontario Healthy Communities Coalition).
"About Us," 2011. Accessed July 30, 2011.
ohcc-ccso.ca/en/about-us

OMOE (Ontario Ministry of Education). *Policy
Program Memorandum No. 150 School Food and
Bevrage Policy*, 2010. edu.gov.on.ca/extra/eng/
ppm/150.html

Parks Canada. "Canada's Historical Places: Affordable Housing and Neighbourhood Improvement,"
2011. Accessed July 30, 2011. historicplaces.ca/
en/pages/3_conservation_brief1.aspx

ROC USA (Resident Owned Communities USA).
"Making Resident Ownership A Reality Nation-
wide: Background," 2009. Accessed July 30, 2011.
rocusa.org/about-usbackground/default.aspx

SDHC (San Diego Housing Commission). "City
Linkage Fee Stakeholders Meeting," November
19, 2009. Accessed July 30, 2011. sdhc.net/
Special-Housing-Programs/Linkage-Task-Force/

Slaunwhite, Amanda. *Under Pressure: Affordable
Housing in Rural Ontario*. Canadian Policy
Research Networks Research Report,
December 2009. Canadian Policy Research
Networks, 2009. ruralontarioinstitute.ca/file.
aspx?id=df2bb16b-2536-4555-bd19-1bfac096a316

SMHA (Sacramento Mutual Housing Association).
"Affordable Housing Facts," 2011. Accessed July
30, 2011. mutualhousing.com/housing/
affordable_housing_facts.htm

Smith, Neale, Lori Baugh Littlejohns, Penelope Hawe and Lisa Sutherland. "Great Expectations and Hard Times: Developing Community Indicators in a Healthy Communities Initiative in Canada." *Health Promotion International*, 2008, *23*(2), 119-126. doi: 10.1093/heapro/dan003

Towey, Matthew. "Land Trust Without Land: The Unusual Structure of the Chicago Community Land Trust." *The Journal of Affordable Housing and Community Development Law*, 2009, *18*(3), 335-362. kentlaw.edu/honorsscholars/2009students/writings/AH_18-3_07Towey.pdf

UHAB (Urban Homesteading Assistance Boards). "About," 2011. Accessed July 30, 2011. uhab.org/about

Vancouver City Savings Credit Union. "VanCity Award Project Updates," 2011. Accessed July 30, 2011. https://vancity.com/MyCommunity/NotForProfit/Grants/VancityAwardProjectUpdates/

Wade, Patrick. "City Council Backs CommUnity Matters." *News-Gazette*, April 12, 2011. Accessed July 30, 2011. news-gazette.com/news/education/2011-04-12/city-council-backs-community-matters.html

WCRP (Women's Community Revitalization Project). "Women's Community Revitalization Project," 2011. Accessed July 30, 2011. wcrpphila.com/index.php/about

Wellesley Institute. *Precarious Housing in Canada*. Wellesley Institute, 2010. wellesleyinstitute.com/news/affordable-housing-news/new-report-precarious-housing-in-canada-2010/

White House. *First Lady Michelle Obama Lauches Lets Move: America's Move to Raise a Healthier Generation of Kids*. Press Release February 9, 2010. whitehouse.gov/the-press-office/first-lady-michelle-obama-launches-lets-move-americas-move-raise-a-healthier-genera

World Health Organization. "Ottawa Charter for Health Promotion," 1986. Accessed July 30, 2011. wThe Cleveland Foundation. "Greater University Circle: Cleveland's Urban Core," 2011. Accessed July 30, 2011. clevelandfoundation.org/VitalIssues/NeighborhoodsAndHousing/GreaterUniversityCircle/ho.int/healthpromotion/conferences/previous/ottawa/en/index.html

Chapter 11: Green Building

Abrahamse, Wokje, Linda Steg, Charles Vlek and Talib Rothengatter. "A Review of Intervention Studies Aimed at Household Energy Conservation." *Journal of Environmental Psychology*, 2005, *25*(3), 273-291.

BC Ministry of Housing. "New Plumbing Fixture Requirements in the BC Building Code," 2011. Accessed July 22, 2011. housing.gov.bc.cabuilding/consultation/het

Birkeland, Janis. "Eco-retrofitting with Building Integrated Living Systems." In Proceedings of the 3rd CIB International Conference on Smart and Sustainable Built Environment: June 15-19, 2009, Netherlands. eprints.qut.edu.au/28740/2/28740.pdf

Black, Christopher and John Straube. "Mould Growth Experiments of Full Scale Wood Frame Assemblies." 11th Canadian Building Science & Technology Conference, Banff, AB, 2007. http:/bricks-and-brome.net/27c11.pdf

BOMA (Building Owners and Managers Association) of Canada. "About BOMA BESt," 2011. Accessed July 22, 2011. bomabest.com/about.html

Bradshaw, William, Edward F. Connelly, Madeline Fraser Cook, James Goldstein and Justin Pauly. "The Costs and Benefits of Green Affordable Housing." *New Ecology*, 2005. landuseimpacts.com/pdf/affordable%20green%20housing%20report.pdf

BREEAM. "What Is BREEAM?" Accessed July 22, 2011. breeam.org/page.jsp?id=66

BuiltGreen. "Our Guiding Principles," 2011. Accessed July 22, 2011. builtgreencanada.ca/guiding-principles

CEC (Commission for Environmental Cooperation). *Green Building in North America: Opportunities and Challenges*. CEC, 2008. cec.org/Storage/61/5386_GB_Report_EN.pdf

City of Arlington. "Green Building Incentive Program," 2011. Accessed July 22, 2011. arlingtonva.us/departments/environmentalservices/epo/environmentalservicesepoincentiveprogram.aspx

City of Bellingham, Department of Planning. "Binbump-up," 2011. Accessed July 22, 2011. cob.org/documents/planning/publications/Bin-Bump-Up%20Incentive%20Handout.pdf

City of Portland, Bureau of Development Services. "BDS Green Building Program," 2011. Accessed

July 22, 2011. portlandonline.combds/index. cfm?c=45256

City of Portland, Office of Sustainable Development. "Green Building Policy Update FAQ." 2010. Accessed July 22, 2011. portlandonline. com/shared/cfm/image.cfm?id=112683

City of Seattle, Department of Planning and Development. "Implementing Seattle's Sustainable Building Policy," 2010. Accessed July 22, 2011. seattle.gov/dpd/GreenBuilding/ CapitalProjects/default.asp

Dermisi, Sophia V. "Effect of LEED Ratings and Levels on Office Property Assessed and Market Values." *The Journal of Sustainable Real Estate*, 2009, *1*(1), 23-47. costar.com/josre/ JournalPdfs/02-LEED-Ratings-Levels.pdf

EIA (Energy Information Administration). *Emissions of Greenhouse Gases in the United States 2007*. US Department of Energy, 2008. eia.doe. gov/oiaf/1605/ggrpt/pdf/0573(2007).pdf

Enterprise Community Partners, Inc. "Enterprise Green Communities," 2011. Accessed July 22, 2011. greencommunitiesonline.org/

EPA (Environmental Protection Agency). "An Introduction to Indoor Air Quality (IAQ)," 2010a. Accessed July 24, 2011. epa.gov/iaq/ia-intro.html

EPA. "Indoor Air Facts No. 4 (revised) Sick Building Syndrome," 2010b. Accessed July 24, 2011. epa.gov/iaq/pubs/sbs.html

EPA. *Sustainable Design and Green Building Toolkit for Local Governments*, 2010c. epa.gov/region4/ recycle/green-building-toolkit.pdf

FCM (Federation of Canadian Municipalities). "Municipal Building Retrofit Guide," 2010. Accessed July 24, 2011. gmf.fcm.ca/capacity_ building/energy/municipal_building_retrofit_ guide/

GBCA (Green Building Council of Australia). "Green Building Council of Australia," 2011. Accessed July 24, 2011. gbca.org.au

GBCI (Green Building Certification Institute). "About GBCI," 2011. Accessed July 24, 2011. gbci.org/org-nav/about-gbci/about-gbci.aspx

GBI (Green Building Initiative). "Green Globes," 2011. Accessed July 24, 2011. thegbi.org/green-globes/default.asp

GGGC (Governor's Green Government Council). "High Performance Green School Planning Grant: Fact Sheet," 2011. Accessed July 24, 2011.

portal.state.pa.us/portal/server.pt/community/ schools/13838/high_performance_green_ school_planning_grant__fact_sheet/588217

Green Affordable Housing Coalition. *Fact Sheet No. 12: Top 15 Green Building Ideas*. Green Affordable Housing Coalition, 2004. frontierassoc.net/ greenaffordablehousing/FactSheetsGAHC factsheets/12-GreenIdeas.pdf

Green Affordable Housing Coalition. "The Future of Resource Efficient Housing," 2011. Accessed July 24, 2011. frontierassoc.net/greenaffordable housing/index.shtml

Griffin, Anne, Ben Kaufman and Sterling Hamilton. *Certified Home Performance: Assessing the Market Impacts of Third Party Certification on Residential Properties*. Earth Advantage Institute, 2009. greenresourcecouncil.org/pdfs/ Certified%20Home%20Performance%20-%20 Earth%20Advantage%20May%2009.pdf

Habitat for Humanity. *Construction Technologies: US Sustainable Construction Standards*. Habitat for Humanity, 2011a. habitat.org/env/pdf/US_ Construction_Standards.pdf

Habitat for Humanity. "ReStore Resale Outlets," 2011b. habitat.org/restores/

ICLEI. "New U.S. Star Community Index to Help Local Governments Measure, Declare 'Green' Status," 2007. Accessed July 24, 2011. iclei.org/index.php?id=7289&tx_ttnews%5Btt_ news%5D=2418&tx_ttnews%5BbackPid%5D=7 498&cHash=aeba43483e

ILBI (International Living Building Institute). "A Proven Strategy for Reclaiming the Built Environment," 2011. Accessed July 24, 2011. ilbi. org/lbc/certified

Kats, Gregory H. *Green Building Costs and Financial Benefits*. Massachusetts Technology Collaborative, 2003. dcaaia.com/images/firm/ Kats-Green-Buildings-Cost.pdf

Light House Sustainable Building Centre. "The 2010 Green Building Challenge," 2010. Accessed July 24, 2011. sustainablebuildingcentre.com/ the_2010_green_building_challenge

Miller, Norm G., Dave Pogue, Quiana D. Gough and Susan M. Davis. "Green Buildings and Productivity." *Journal of Sustainable Real Estate*, 2009, *1*(1), 65-89. costar.com/uploadedFiles/ JOSRE/JournalPdfs/04-Green-Buildings-Productivity.pdf

National League of Cities. *The National League of Cities Municipal Action Guide: Creating Green Affordable Housing.* The National League of Cities, 2009. nlc.org/File/Library/Find/City/Solutions/Research/Innovation/Sustainability/creating-green-affordable-housing-mag-fall09.pdf

NSTC (National Science and Technology Council). *Federal Research and Development Agenda For Net-zero Energy, High-performace Green Buildings,* 2008. bfrl.nist.govbuildingtechnology/documents/FederalRDAgendaforNetZeroEnergyHighPerformanceGreenBuildings.pdf

Natural Resources Canada. "Grant Table for ecoENERGY Retrofit – Homes," 2011. Accessed July 24, 2011. oee.nrcan.gc.ca/residential/personal/retrofit-homes/retrofit-qualify-grant.cfm

Passivhaus Institut. "Willkommen beim Passivhaus Institut," 2011. Accessed July 24, 2011. passiv.de

Paulsen, Monte. "Is This Canada's Most Affordable Green Home?" *The Tyee,* April 13, 2010. Accessed July 26, 2011. thetyee.ca/News/2010/04/13/MostAffordable/

Paulsen, Monte. "Green Homes for Less." *The Tyee,* January 7, 2011. Accessed July 26, 2011. thetyee.ca/News/2011/01/07/GreenHomesForLess/

Pyke, Chris, Sean McMahon and Tom Dietsche. *Green Building & Human Experience.* US Green Building Council, 2010. usgbc.org/ShowFile.aspx?DocumentID=7383

Thormark, C. "Environmental Analysis of a Building with Reused Building Materials." *International Journal of Low Energy and Sustainable Buildings,* 2000, 1. dspace.mah.sebitstream/handle/2043/9844/Staffenstrop.pdf?sequence=1

Thormark, C. "The Effect of Material Choice on the Total Energy Need and Recycling Potential of a Building." *Building and Environment,* 2006, *41*(8), 1019-1026. doi: 10.1016/j.buildenv.2005.04.026

US Census Bureau. "Housing Statistics: United States," 2000. Accessed July 24, 2011. infoplease.com/us/census/data/housing.html

US Department of Energy. "Energy Information Administration: Carbon Dioxide Emissions," 2009. eia.doe.gov/oiaf/1605/ggrpt/carbon.html

USDHUD (US Department of Housing and Urban Development). "Green Retrofit Program for Multifamily Housing," 2009. Accessed July 24, 2011. portal.hud.gov/hudportal/HUD?src=/recovery/programs/green

USGBC (US Green Building Council). *Green Building Facts.* USGBC, 2009a. auburnhills.org/vertical/Sites/%7B33ABD079-3D78-4945-9539-FD5E01E1F1BE%7D/uploads/%7BC620AC8F-BA48-4A11-95A7-0693C99A817D%7D.PDF

USGBC. *LEED 2009 for New Construction and Major Renovations.* USGBC, 2009b. usgbc.org/ShowFile.aspx?DocumentID=8868

USGBC. "How to Achieve Certification," 2011a. Accessed July 24, 2011. usgbc.org/DisplayPage.aspx?CMSPageID=1991

USGBC. "LEED for Neighborhood Development," 2011b. Accessed July 24, 2011. usgbc.org/DisplayPage.aspx?CMSPageID=148

William, Barbara T. *Current Housing Reports: These Old Houses 2001.* US Census Bureau, 2004. census.gov/prod/2004pubs/h121-04-1.pdf

Williams, Jennifer. "Green Building Designations For Greenhorns: LEED vs. BOMA Go Green." Blake, Cassels & Graydon LLP, January 24, 2008. Accessed July 26, 2011. blakes.com/english/view.asp?ID=2264

Winton, Larry. "Green Building and Green Leases: What's in It for Me?" Blake, Cassels & Graydon LLP, April 24, 2008. Accessed July 26, 2011. blakes.com/english/view.asp?ID=2263

Yudelson, Jerry. "The Green Building Revolution." HPAC Engineering, 2008. hpac.com/mag/greenbuilding_revolution/

Chapter 12: Community Economic Development

American Youth Works. "Casa Verde Builders," 2011. Accessed May 3 2011. americanyouthworks.org/green-jobs-programs/casa-verde-builders

BC-Alberta Social Economy Research Alliance (BALTA). "What Is the Social Economy?" 2011. Accessed March 30, 2011. socialeconomy-bcalberta.ca/social-economy/

BC Community Forest Association (BC CFA). "Status of Community Forestry," 2011. bccfa.ca/index.php?option=com_k2&view=item&id=98:status-of-community-forestry-in-bc&Itemid=8

Centre for Sustainable Community Development (CSCD). "Why Sustainable Community Development?" 2011. Accessed March 30, 2011. sfu.ca/cscd

Cernansky, R. Are Walmart's Eco-efforts Enough? Balancing Sustainability & Social Responsibility at America's Largest Retailer. *Treehugger*, 2011. treehugger.com/files/2011/01/walmarts-eco-efforts-enough-balancing-sustainability-social-responsibility.php

Chantier de l'économie sociale. "The Quebec Social Economy Experience: Trainer's Workbook," 2009. cedworks.com/files/pdf/free/Chantier_trainer-Quebec-experience.pdf

City and County of San Francisco. "Greening Your Business," 2011. Accessed May 3, 2011. sfgsa.org/index.aspx?page=4232

Diebolt, Asa and Timothy Den Herder-Thomas. *Creating a Campus Sustainability Revolving Loan Fund: A Guide for Students*. Report published by the Association for the Advancement of Sustainability in Higher Education. Lexington, KY, 2007. macalester.edu/cerf/reports/creatingacampussustainabilityrevolvingfund.pdf

Eco Canada. "Defining the Green Economy, Labour Market Research Study," 2010. Accessed December 2010. eco.ca/pdf/Defining-the-Green-Economy-2010.pdf

Ecotrust. "Forestry Market Connections," 2011. ecotrust.org/forestry/markets/

Ecotrust Canada. "Building the Conservation Economy," 2011. Accessed March 30, 2011. ecotrust.ca/about/conservationeconomy

Elgin, D. *Voluntary Simplicity*. William Morrow, 1993.

Environmental Business Cluster. "Environmental Business Cluster: Overview," 2010. Accessed May 4, 2011. environmentalcluster.org/about/index.htm

Epstein, M.J. *Making Sustainability Work: Best Practices in Managing and Measuring Corporate Social, Environmental and Economic Impacts*, 2008.

Fox River. "Environmental Practices," 2011. Accessed March 30, 2011. foxsox.com/Company/Environment.aspx

Gibbs, David and Pauline Deutz. "Reflections on Implementing Industrial Ecology Through Eco-Industrial Park Development." *Journal of Cleaner Production*, 2007, *15*, 1683-1695.

Glover, Paul. "A Recipe for Successful Community Currency." Accessed May 5, 2011. localcurrency council.org/index.php/component/content/article/29-a-recipe-for-successful-community-currency

Goetz, S.J. and A. Rupasingha. "Wal-Mart and Social Capital." *American Agricultural Economics Association*, 2006, *88*(5), 1304-1310. nercrd.psu.edubigboxes/walmartandsocialcapital2.pdf

Green Map. "Green Map Systems History," 2011. Accessed March 31, 2011. greenmap.org/greenhouse/en/about/our_history

GrowNYC. "Annual Report," 2010. Accessed March 31, 2011. grownyc.org/files/GrowNYC.Annual.2010.web.pdf

Greyston Foundation. 2011. Accessed March 30, 2011. greyston.org/index.php?bakery

Gruber, J.S. "Key Principles of Community-Based Natural Resource Management: A Synthesis and Interpretation of Identified Effective Approaches for Managing the Commons." The 12th Biennial Conference of the International Association for the Study of the Commons, 2008. iasc2008.glos.ac.uk/conference%20papers/papers/G/Gruber_132301.pdf

Harvard. "Green Campus Loan Fund," 2011. Access March 30, 2011. green.harvard.edu/loan-fund

Hassett, K. "Unions Wage Vicious, Misguided War on Walmart." American Enterprise Institute for Public Policy Research, 2009. aei.org/article/23594.

Horne, Gary. "British Columbia's Heartland at the Dawn of the 21st Century: 2001 Economic Dependencies and Impact Ratios for 63 Local Areas," 2004. British Columbia Ministry of Management Services. lifecyclesproject.ca/initiatives/food_miles2/downloads/BC_Economic_Dependancies.pdf

Ithaca Hours Inc. "Ithaca Hours," 2005. Accessed May 5, 2011. ithacahours.org/

Jones, Anthony K. *The Green Collar Economy: How One Solution Can Fix Our Two Biggest Problems*. Harper Collins, 2008.

Jenkins, N.H. "Here's the Catch: The Best Idea to Help Small Fisheries Might Come from Your Local Vegetable Farm." *The Washington Post*, 2009. washingtonpost.com/wp-dyn/content/article/2009/01/13/AR2009011300700.html?sid=ST2009011302192

Lewis, M. "Building Community Wealth: A Resource for Social Enterprise Development." Centre for Community Enterprise, 2006, 1-24.

Lovins, L.H. "Climate Capitalism: The Business Case for Climate Protection. *Pace Environmental Law Review*, 2010, *27*(3), 735-779.

Markey S., J. Pierce, K. Vodden and M. Roseland. *Second Growth: Community Economic Development in Rural British Columbia.* UBC Press, 2005.

McCormack, R. and S. Pinkston. "Walmart: Heritage Agriculture: Revitalizing and Energizing Historical Agricultural Economies," 2009. asc. uark.edu/Agile_Agriculture-MarketMaker_Rob_McCormick.pdf

Mendell, M. "Financing the Social Economy in Québec." *Making Waves*, 2009, *20*(3), 46-50.

Mendell, M. and N. Neamtan. "The Social Economy in Quebec: Towards a New Political Economy." In Laurie Mook, Jack Quarter & Sherida Ryan (eds.), *Why the Social Economy Matters*, pp. 32-58. University of Toronto Press, (2009). sec.oise.utoronto.ca/english/project_outputs/project33_February09Report.pdf

"Municipal Planning and Financial Tools for Economic Development Handbook." Ministry of Municipal Affairs and Housing, 2011. mah.gov.on.ca/Page9392.aspx

Municipal Securities Rulemaking Board (MSRB). "Overview," 2011. Accessed May 30, 2011. emma.msrb.org/EducationCentre/EducationCentre.aspx

Murray, D.L. and L.T. Raynolds. Chapter 1 "Globalization and Its Antinomies: Negotiating a Fair Trade Movement. In *Fair Trade: The Challenges of Transforming Globalization.* Routledge, 2007.

Neamtan, Nancy and J. Anderson. 2010 National Summit on a People-Centered Economy. Issue Paper #2: Enterprise Development, 2010. Revised Draft, May 21, 2010. ccednet-rcdec.ca/sites/ccednet/files/ccednet/pdfs/2-Enterprise_Development.pdf

New Dawn Enterprises. "About," 2011. March 30, 2011. newdawn.ca/about/

Northern Plains Research Council. "Good Neighbor Agreement," 2011. Accessed May 3, 2011. northernplains.org/the-issues/good-neighbor-agreement/

Pearce, J. *Social Enterprise in Anytown.* Calouste Gulbenkian Foundation, 2003.

Perry, Stewart E., et al. Tools and Techniques for Community Recovery and Renewal: Appendix A. Centre for Community Enterprise, 2000, 176-183.

Philanthropy News Digest (PND). "Kauffman Foundation Launches Entrepreneur- Training Program to Spur Job Creation," 2009. foundationcenter.org/pnd/news/story.jhtml?id=244200040

Renner, M., S. Sweeney and J. Kubit. "Green Jobs: Towards Decent Work in Sustainable Low-carbon World." United Nations Environment Programme Green Jobs Initiative, 2008. ilo.org/wcmsp5/groups/public/---dgreports/---dcomm/documents/publication/wcms_098503.pdf

Restakis, J. "Defining the Social Economy: The BC Context." BC Social Economy Roundtable, 2006. Accessed March 30, 2011. msvu.ca/socialeconomyatlantic/pdfs/DefiningSocialEconomy_FnlJan1906.pdf

Restakis, J. 2010. *Humanizing the Economy.* New Society Publishers.

Roseland, M. and L. Soots. "Strengthening Local Economies." In World Watch Institute, *State of the World 2007: Our Urban Future*, Linda Starke (ed.). W.W. Norton & Company, 2007, 152-169. worldwatch.org/files/pdf/State%20of%20the%20World%202007.pdf

Russo, M. *Environmental Management: Readings and Cases.* Thousand Oaks, CA: Sage, 2008.

Schmerker, J. "Hamilton Expands Buy Local Policy." *Ravalli Republic*, 2010. ravallirepublic.com/news/local/govt-and-politics/article_cc0f9b80-6486-11df-828d-001cc4c002e0.html?mode=story

Schor, J. *Plentitude: The New Economics of True Wealth.* Penguin, 2010.

Scott, L. "Wal-Mart: 21st Century Leadership." Speech by Wal-Mart CEO, 24 October, 2005. walmartstores.com/ViewResource.aspx?id=1965

Seidman, Karl F. *Economic Development Finance.* Sage, 2005.

Shuman, Michael H. *The Small-Mart Revolution: How Local Businesses Are Beating the Global Competition.* Berrett-Koehler Publishers, 2006.

Stack, G. "Walmart: Living Better By Saving…." *Natural Step*, 2010. naturalstep.org/en/usa/walmart-living-better-saving

Urban Partnership Bank (UPB). "Urban Partnership Bank: Making a difference in Chicago, Cleveland and Detroit," 2011. https://upbnk.com/about-us/news/in-the-news/releaseid57/

Van Buren County Hospital. "History," 2011. Accessed March 30, 2011. vbch.org/default.aspx?Page=History

Vancouver City Savings Credit Union. "Circle Lending, Also Known As Peer-lending, FAQs," 2011. Accessed May 9, 2011. https://vancity.com/ MyBusiness/BusinessFinancing/JustStarting/ CircleLending/CircleLendingFAQ/

Walmart. "Wal-Mart Unveils Global Sustainable Agriculture Goals," 2010. Accessed March 30, 2011. walmartstores.com/pressroom/news/10376.aspx

Walmart. "Global Responsibility Report," 2011. walmartstores.com/sites/Responsibility Report/2011/sustainable_overview.aspx

World Economic Forum 2011. "World Economic Forum Annual Meeting 2011: Shared Norms for the New Reality." Davos-Klosters, Switzerland, January 26-30, 2011. davos11.weforum.org/ davos-2011.pdf

World Fair Trade Organization (WTFO). "What Is Fair Trade?" 2011. Accessed March 30, 2011. wfto.com/index.php?option=com_content&task =view&id=1&Itemid=13

Chapter 13: Climate Change

Anderson, Kevin and Alice Bows. "Reframing the Climate Change Challenge in Light of Post-2000 Emission Trends." *Philosophical Transactions of the Royal Society A: Mathematical, Physical and Engineering Sciences*, November 13, 2008, *366* (1882), 3863-3882. doi: 10.1098/rsta.2008.0138

BBC News. "Renewable Sector 'Costing Jobs.'" *BBC*, February 28, 2011, sec. Scotland. bbc.co.uk/ news/uk-scotland-12597097

Anthes, Richard. A., Robert W. Corell, Greg Holland, James W. Hurrell, Michael C. MacCracken and Kevin E. Trenberth. "Hurricanes and Global Warming: Potential Linkages and Consequences." *Bulletin of the American Meteorological Society*, 2006, *87*(5), 623–628.

Air Quality Management District: South Coast (AQMD). "AQMD," 2011. Accessed June 24, 2011. aqmd.gov/default.htm

Blasing, T.J. "Recent Greenhouse Gas Concentrations," 2011. Accessed June 23, 2011. cdiac.ornl.gov/pns/current_ghg.html

Bulkeley, Harriet, Heike Schroeder, Katy Janda, Jimin Zhao, Andrea Armstrong, Shu Yi Chu and Shibani Ghosh. "Cities and Climate Change: The Role of Institutions, Governance and Urban Planning." *Change*, 2009, *28*, 30.

Climate Action Secretariat (CAS). "Climate Action for the 21st Century," 2011. Accessed June 24, 2011. env.gov.bc.ca/cas/

Climate Registry. "FAQs," 2009. Accessed June 28 2011 theclimateregistry.org/about/faqs/

Charnley, Susan and Melissa R. Poe. "Community Forestry in Theory and Practice: Where Are We Now?" *Annual Review of Anthropology*, September 2007, *36*(1), 301-336. doi: 10.1146/ annurev.anthro.35.081705.123143

Costello, Anthony, Mustafa Abbas, Adriana Allen, Sarah Ball, Sarah Bell, Richard Bellamy, Sharon Friel, et al. "Managing the Health Effects of Climate Change." *Lancet*, 2009, *373*(9676), 1693–1733.

Danko, Sheila. "On Designing Change." *Journal of Interior Design*, 2010, *36*(1), v-ix.

El Paso Electric. "Renewable Energy Interconnection," 2011. Accessed June 28, 2011. epelectric.com/nm/residential/ renewable-energy-interconnection-1

Crutzen, Paul. "The Anthropocene." In *Earth System Science in the Anthropocene*, Ehlers, Eckart & Thomas Krafft (eds.). Berlin/Heidelberg: Springer-Verlag, 2006. springerlink.com/content/ k043444105k3v626/

Engel, Stefanie, Stefano Pagiola and Sven Wunder. "Designing Payments for Environmental Services in Theory and Practice: An Overview of the Issues." *Ecological Economics*, May 1, 2008, *65* (4), 663-674. doi: 10.1016/j.ecolecon.2008.03.011

Federation of Canadian Municipalities. "About Partners for Climate Protection," 2010. Accessed June 24, 2011. gmf.fcm.ca/ Partners-for-Climate-Protection/

Fouillet, A., G. Rey, V. Wagner, K. Laaidi, P. Empereur-Bissonnet, A. Le Tertre, P. Frayssinet et al. "Has the Impact of Heat Waves on Mortality Changed in France Since the European Heat Wave of Summer 2003? A Study of the 2006 Heat Wave." *International Journal of Epidemiology*, April 1, 2008, *37*(2), 309-317. doi: 10.1093/ije/ dym253

Garthwaite, R., D. Fowler, D. Stevenson, P. Cox, M. Ashmore, P. Grennfelt, M. Amann et al. "Ground Level Ozone in the 21st Century: Trends, Interactions with Climate and Environmental Impacts." In IOP *Conference Series: Earth and Environmental Science*, 2009, *6*, 282002.

Giddens, Anthony. *The Politics of Climate Change*. Polity Press, 2009.

Girardet, Herbert. *Cities People Planet: Urban Development and Climate Change*, 2nd ed. John Wiley and Sons, 2008.

Goffman, E. and J. Steinbeck. "Environmental Refugees: How Many, How Bad?" *CSA Discovery Guides*, 2006, 1–15.

Hanemann, Michael. "California's New Greenhouse Gas Laws." *Review of Environmental Economics and Policy*, January 1, 2008, 2(1), 114-129. doi: 10.1093/reep/rem030

Howden, S. Mark, Jean-François Soussana, Francesco N. Tubiello, Netra Chhetri, Michael Dunlop and Holger Meinke.. "Adapting agriculture to climate change." *Proceedings of the National Academy of Sciences*, December 11, 2007, 104(50), 19691-19696. doi: 10.1073/pnas.0701890104

Hufbauer, Gary Clyde and Jisun Kim. "Reaching a Global Agreement on Climate Change: What Are the Obstacles?" *Asian Economic Policy Review*, June 2010, 5(1), 39-58. doi: 10.1111/j.1748-3131.2010.01144.x

ICLEI – Local Governments for Sustainability. "ICLEI Case Studies," 2010. Accessed June 27, 2011. iclei.org/index.php?id=11546

Karl, Thomas R., Jerry M. Melillo and Thomas C. Peterson. *Global Climate Change Impacts in the United States*. Cambridge University Press, 2009.

Kirby, Alex, Jasmina Bogdanovic, Claudia Heberlein, Otto Simonett and Christina Stuhlberger. *CCCC Kick the Habit: A UN Guide to Climate Neutrality*. UNEP eBook, 2008. Accessed October 19, 2010. unep.org/publications/ebooks/kick-the-habit/Pdfs.aspx

Klein, Richard J.T., Saleemul Huq, Fatima Denton, Thomas E. Downing, Richard G. Richels, John B. Robinson and Ferenc L. Toth. "Inter-relationships Between Adaptation and Mitigation." In *Climate Change 2007: Impacts, Adaptation and Vulnerability*. Contribution of Working Group II to the Fourth Assessment Report of the Intergovernmental Panel on Climate Change. M.L. Parry, O.F. Canziani, J.P. Paultikof, P.J. van der Linden & C.E. Hanson (eds). Cambridge University Press, 2007, 745-777. Accessed June 23, 2011. ipcc.ch/pdf/assessment-report/ar4/wg2/ar4-wg2-chapter18.pdf

Larson, Janet. "Setting the Record Straight: More than 52,000 Europeans Died from Heat in Summer 2003." Earth Policy Institute, 2006. Accessed June 24, 2011. earth-policy.org/index.php?/plan_b_updates/2006/update56

Lee, Marc. *Fair and Effective Carbon Pricing: Lessons from BC*. Report by the Sierra Club BC and the Canadian Center for Policy Alternatives BC Office, 2011.

London Climate Change Partnership (LCCP). *Adapting to Climate Change: Creating natural resilience, Summary Report*. Greater London Authority, 2009.

McKinley, Galen, Miriam Zuk, Morten Höjer, Montserrat Avalos, Isabel González, Rodolfo Iniestra, Israel Laguna, et al. "Quantification of Local and Global Benefits from Air Pollution Control in Mexico City." *Environmental Science & Technology*, April 1, 2005, 39(7), 1954-1961. doi:10.1021/es035183e.

Meehl, Gerald A. and Claudia Tebaldi. "More Intense, More Frequent, and Longer Lasting Heat Waves in the 21st Century." *Science*, 2004, 305(5686), 994-997. doi: 10.1126/science.1098704

Mehta, Prashant. "Science Behind Acid Rain: Analysis of Its Impacts and Advantages on Life and Heritage Structures." *South Asian Journal of Tourism and Heritage*, 2010, 3(2), 123-132.

Nellemann, C. and E. Corcoran. "Dead Planet, Living Planet: Biodiversity and Ecosystem Restoration for Sustainable Development." *NWS Coastal Planning Guideline: Adapting to Sea Level Rise*, 2010. Accessed June 24, 2011. planning.nsw.gov.au/LinkClick.aspx?fileticket=VYjmQirQlAk%3d&tabid=177&language=en-US

Paavola, Jouni and Neil W. Adger. "Fair Adaptation to Climate Change." *Ecological Economics*, 2006, 56(4), 594-609. doi: 10.1016/j.ecolecon.2005.03.015

Pachauri, Rajendra K. and International Panel on Climate Change (IPCC). *Climate Change 2007: Synthesis Report*. IPCC Secretariat, 2007.

Partners for Climate Protection. "Greenhouse Gas Reduction Initiative of the Month: Calgary's Green Power Contract." ICLEI – Local Governments for Sustainability and Federation of Canadian Municipalities, 2010. Accessed June 24, 2011. gmf.fcm.ca/files/

Capacity_Building_-_PCP/PCP-GHG_ initiative_of_the_month/2010/Calgary_GHG_ Initiative-_Month_EN.pdf

Peterson, Townsend A. and Enrique Martínez-Meyer. "Pervasive Poleward Shifts Among North American Bird Species." *Biodiversity*, 2009, *9*, 14–16.

Rahmstorf, Stefan. "A New View on Sea Level Rise." *Nature Reports Climate Change* (1004), April 2010, 44-45. doi: 10.1038/climate.2010.29

Richardson, Gregory R.A. *Adapting to Climate Change: An Introduction for Canadian Municipalities*. Natural Resources Canada, 2010.

Rubin, J. *Why Your World Is About to Get a Whole Lot Smaller: Oil and the End of Globalization*. Random House, 2009.

Senge, Peter. "The Fifth Discipline." *Measuring Business Excellence*, 1997, *1*(3), 46-51. doi: 10.1108/eb025496

Shea, Katherine M., Robert T. Truckner, Richard W. Weber and David B. Peden. "Climate Change and Allergic Disease." *Journal of Allergy and Clinical Immunology*, September 2008, *122*(3), 443-453. doi: 10.1016/j.jaci.2008.06.032.

Smit, Barry and Mark W. Skinner. "Adaptation Options in Agriculture to Climate Change: A Typology." *Mitigation and Adaptation Strategies for Global Change*, 2002, 7(1), 85–114.

Smith, Charlie. "Tim Flannery Offers Hopeful Message in *Here on Earth: A Natural History of the Planet*." *Straight*, 2011. Accessed June 22, 2011. straight.com/article-388205/vancouver/earths-rebirth

Solomon, Susan, Gian-Kasper Plattner, Reto Knutti and Pierre Friedlingstein. "Irreversible Climate Change Due to Carbon Dioxide Emissions." *Proceedings of the National Academy of Sciences*, February 10, 2009, *106*(6), 1704-1709. doi: 10.1073/pnas.0812721106

Stern, Nicholas H. *The Economics of Climate Change: The Stern Review*, 30. HM Treasury, Cambridge University Press, 2007.

Texas Forest Service. "Community Wildlife Protection Plan: Is Your Community Prepared?", 2007. Accessed June 27, 2011. tfsfrp.tamu.edu/cwpp/

Tol, Richard S. J., Richard J. T. Klein and Robert J. Nicholls. "Towards Successful Adaptation to Sea-Level Rise along Europe's Coasts." *Journal of Coastal Research*, March 2008, *242*, 432-442. doi: 10.2112/07A-0016.1

United Nations Environmental Program (UNEP). *Environmental Effects of Ozone Depletion and Its Interaction with Climate Change: 2010 Assessment*, 2010. Accessed June 23, 2011. ozone.unep.org/Assessment_Panels/EEAP/eeap-report2010.pdf

United Nations Environmental Program (UNEP). "Towards a Green Economy: Pathways to Sustainable Development and Poverty Eradication, A Synthesis for Policy Makers," 2011. Accessed June 27, 2011. unep.org/greeneconomy

US EPA Office of Atmospheric Programs. "Carbon Dioxide: Human-related Sources and Sinks of Carbon Dioxide | Climate Change — Greenhouse Gas Emissions." US EPA, 2006a. October 19. epa.gov/climatechange/emissions/co2_human.html.

US EPA Office of Atmospheric Programs. "Carbon Dioxide: Natural Sources and Sinks of Carbon Dioxide | Climate Change — Greenhouse Gas Emissions." US EPA, 2006b. October 19. epa.gov/climatechange/emissions/co2_natural.html.

US EPA Office of Atmospheric Programs. "Current and Near-Term Greenhouse Gas Reduction Initiatives|Climate Change — US Climate Policy." US EPA, 2006c. October 19. epa.gov/climatechange/policy/neartermghgreduction.html.

Wara, M.W. and D.G. Victor. "A Realistic Policy on International Carbon Offsets." *Program on Energy and Sustainable Development Working Paper 74*, 2008.

Weiss, Kenneth R. "Obama's New Hotshot at NOAA." *Los Angeles Times* December 18, 2008. Accessed June 21, 2011. latimesblogs.latimes.com/greenspace/2008/12/obamas-new-ocea.html

Westmore, Tony. "Climate Change and Equity." *Impact*, Winter 2008, *21*-22. search.informit.com.au/documentSummary;dn=361622427202176;res=IELHSS>

Chapter 14: Communities Integrating Sustainability

Chaoguang, Su, Cui Weiguang and Peng Zhong. *Guangxi Daily*, 10/04/ 2008. Accessed June 14, 2011. gxnews.com.cn/staticpages/20081004/ncwgx48e6ab66-1696431.shtml

City of Vancouver. "Creating a Sustainable Community: Southeast False Creek Planning,"

2010a. Accessed July 20, 2011. vancouver.ca/commsvcs/southeast/,

City of Vancouver. "Southeast False Creek and Olympic Village," 2010b. Accessed July 20, 2011. vancouver.ca/olympicvillage/greenbuilding.htm.

Esolar Energy News. Tuesday, January 25, 2011. "Sonoma Mountain Village Recognized by the U.S. Green Building Council at the Highest Platinum Level." Accessed July 26, 2011. esolarenergynews.com/2011/01/sonoma-mountain-village-recognized-by.html

Gunther, Marc. "Can Masdar Scale?" *Sustainable Business Forum,* January 19, 2011. Accessed July 20, 2011. sustainablebusinessforum.com/marcgunther/49139/masdar-city-gets-real,

Joss, S. "Eco-cities: A Global Survey 2009." *WIT Transactions on Ecology and the Environment,* 2010, *129,* 239–250.

Joss, S. "Eco-cities: The Mainstreaming of Urban Sustainability, Key Characteristics and Driving Factors." *International Journal of Sustainable Development and Planning,* 2011, 63.

Kraemer, Susan. "From Industrial Park to Zero-carbon Town," *MatterNetwork,* October 13, 2008. Accessed July 20, 2011. featured.matternetwork.com/2008/10/from-industrial-park-zero-carbon.cfm

Metro Vancouver. "Commuting in Metro Vancouver: Journey to Work." Sustainable Region Initiative, 2006 Census Bulletin No. 8, 2008. Accessed July 27, 2011. metrovancouver.org/about/publications/Publications/2006_commute_report_30oct2008.pdf

Metro Vancouver. "Metro Vancouver Key Facts: Employment by Occupation, Average and Median Household Income, Occupied Private Dwellings by Dwelling Type," 2011. Accessed July 27, 2011. metrovancouver.org/ABOUT/STATISTICS/Pages/KeyFacts.aspx

Miaomiao, Chang and Xiao Shiyan. "Nanning Will Build the Central Zone of Bio-Energy: 60% of The City's Taxis and Buses Will Be Fueled by Bio-gas Application." *China Environment News,* March 16, 2011, 6. Accessed June 14. 2011cenews.com.cn/xwzx/cysc/qk/201103/t20110315_700250.html,

Mustel Group Market Research. UniverCity Community Survey, June 2010 and June 2007. Accessed July 27, 2011. univercity.ca/resources/community_survey.70.html

Nanning Government Information Net. "Nanning Selected as National Demonstration City," September 6, 2010. Accessed June 14, 2011. nanning.gov.cn/n722103/n722135/n737840/8767947.html

Nanning Government Information Net. "Nanning City National Economic and Social Development Statistical Bulletin 2010," April 13, 2011. Accessed July 22, 2011. nanning.gov.cn/,

Peter, Laurence. "Green Living Takes Root in Sweden." *BBC News,* October 9, 2006. Accessed July 22, 2011. news.bbc.co.uk/2/hi/europe/5413960.stm

Peters, Adele. "Sonoma Mountain Village: Is Green Suburbia Possible?" Worldchanging.com, Feb 19, 2009. Accessed July 20, 2011. worldchanging.com/archives/009448.html

Peters, Adele. "Sustainable Neighbourhoods in Malmo." Worldchanging.com, November 12, 2008. Accessed July 20, 2011. worldchanging.com/archives/009022.html

Roberts, Wayne and Cecilia Rocha. "Belo Horizonte: The Beautiful Food Horizon of Community Food Sovereignty." *Alternatives,* July 9, 2008. Accessed July 20, 2011. journal.alternatives.ca/auteur/cecilia-rocha?lang=en

Schwartz, Ariel, "Financial Problems Hit Masdar City, the UAE's Sustainable Mecca." *Fast Company,* March 22, 2010. Accessed July 20, 2011. fastcompany.com/1593469/money-problems-cut-back-on-masdar-citys-plans

Wong, Julian L. "Eco-infrastructure: Letting Nature Do the Work," 2009. Accessed July 26, 2011. greenleapforward.com/2009/02/27/eco-infrastructure-letting-nature-do-the-work/

World Mayor. World Mayor 2005 Finalists. "Belo Horizonte Mayor Fernando Damata Pimentel: A Program of Financial Efficiency and Social Boldness." Accessed July 20, 2011. worldmayor.com/manifestos05belohorizonte_05.html

Zhaohua, Huang. "Nanning Channel boosts ASEAN member contacts." *China Daily,* June 17, 2011, 12. Accessed July 19, 2011. chinadaily.com.cn/cndy/2011-06/17/content_12719254.htm

Chapter 15: Governing Sustainable Communities

AASHE (Association for the Advancement of Sustainability in Higher Education). "Frequently

Asked Questions," 2011. Accessed July 15, 2011. aashe.org/about/faq#q1

Arnstein, S.R. "A Ladder of Citizen Participation." *Journal of the American Planning Association*, 1969, *35*(4), 216-224.

Avritzer, L. "New Public Spheres in Brazil: Local Democracy and Deliberative Politics." *International Journal of Urban and Regional Research*, 2006, *30*(3), 623-637.

Aylett, A. "Conflict, Collaboration and Climate Change: Participatory Democracy and Urban Environmental Struggles in Durban, South Africa." *International Journal of Urban and Regional Research*, 2010, *34*(3), 478-495.

Bagheri, A. and P. Hjorth. "Planning for Sustainable Development: A Paradigm Shift Towards a Process-based Approach." *Sustainable Development*, 2007, *15*(2), 83-96.

Bai, X., R.R.J. McAllister, R.M. Beaty and B. Taylor. "Urban Policy and Governance in a Global Environment: Complex Systems, Scale Mismatches and Public Participation. *Current Opinion in Environmental Sustainability*, 2010, *2*(3), 129-135.

Beaumont, J. and W. Nicholls. Plural Governance, Participation and Democracy in Cities. *International Journal of Urban and Regional Research*, 2008, *32*(1), 87-94.

Bingham, L.B., T. Nabatchi and R. O'Leary. The New Governance: Practices and Processes for Stakeholder and Citizen Participation in the Work of Government. *Public Administration Review*, 2005, *65*(5), 547-558.

Blewitt, J. *Understanding Sustainable Development*. Earthscan, 2008.

Bradford, Neil. *Canadian Social Policy in the 2000s: Bringing Place in.* Canadian Policy Research Networks, 2008. observgo.uquebec.ca/observgo/fichiers/77425_AEEPP-6.pdf

Bruce, C.J. "A Tale of Two Cities: Public Participation Processes in Banff and Calgary." *IAPR Policy Brief Series*. University of Calgary: Institute for Advanced Policy Research, 2007.

Condon, P.M. 2007. *Design Charrettes for Sustainable Communities*. Island Press, 2007.

CUNY (City University of New York). "Sustainable CUNY." Accessed July 15, 2011. cuny.edu/about/resources/sustainability/solar-america.html

Dobson, C. *The Troublemaker's Teaparty: A Manual for Effective Citizen Action*. New Society Publishers, 2009.

Fagotto, E. and A. Fung. "Empowered Participation in Urban Governance: The Minneapolis Neighborhood Revitalization Program." *International Journal of Urban and Regional Research*, 2006, *30*(3), 638-655.

Goldstein, J. "Sustainable Communities and the Great Transition." *GTI Paper Series*. Tellus Institute, 2006.

Häikiö, L. "Expertise, Representation and the Common Good: Grounds for Legitimacy in the Urban Governance Network." *Urban Studies*, 2007, *44*(11), 2147-2162.

Henderson, H. *Building a Win-Win World: Life Beyond Global Economic Warfare*. Berrett-Koehler, 1996.

Holden, M. "Urban Indicators and the Integrative Ideals of Cities." *Cities*, 2006, *23*(3), 170-183.

Innes, J.E. and D.E. Booher. "Consensus Building and Complex Adaptive Systems." *Journal of the American Planning Association*, 1999, *65*(4), 412-423.

Kemp, R. and P. Martens. "Sustainable Development: How to Manage Something That Is Subjective and Never Can Be Achieved? *Sustainability: Science Practice and Policy*, 2007, *3*(2), 5-14.

Kemp, R., D. Loorbach and J. Rotmans. "Transition Management as a Model for Managing Processes of Co-Evolution Towards Sustainable Development." *International Journal of Sustainable Development & World Ecology*, 2007, *14*(1), 78-91.

Kemp, R., S. Parto and R.B. Gibson. "Governance for Sustainable Development: Moving from Theory to Practice." *International Journal of Sustainable Development*, 2005, *8*(1), 12-30.

Krueger, R. and J. Agyeman. "Sustainability Schizophrenia or 'Actually Existing Sustainabilities?' Toward a Broader Understanding of the Politics and Promise of Local Sustainability in the US." *Geoforum*, 2005, *36*(4), 410-417.

Lafferty, W.M. "Local Agenda 21: The Pursuit of Sustainable Development in Subnational Domains. In *How Green Is the City? Sustainability Assessment and the Management of the Urban*

Environment, D Devuyst (ed.). Columbia University Press, 2001.

Lieberherr-Gardiol, F. "Urban Sustainability and Governance: Issues for the Twenty-first Century." *International Social Science Journal*, 2008, *59*(193-194), 331-342.

Loorbach, D. and J. Rotmans. "The Practice of Transition Management: Examples and Lessons from Four Distinct Cases." *Futures*, 2010, *42*(3), 237-246.

Martens, K. "Participatory Decision Making and Sustainability: The Role of Environmental Organizations." In *Advancing Sustainability at the Sub-National Level*, E. Feitelson (ed.). Ashgate, 2004.

Melo, M.A. and G. Baiocchi. "Deliberative Democracy and Local Governance: Towards a New Agenda." *International Journal of Urban and Regional Research*, 2006, *30*(3), 587-600.

Moore, J. "Barriers and Pathways to Creating Sustainability Education Programs: Moving from Rhetoric to Reality." *Environmental Education Research*, 2005, *11*(5), 537-555.

Ontario Round Table on the Environment and the Economy (ORTEE). *Sustainable Communities Resource Package*. ORTEE, 1995.

Orr, D.W. "What Is education for?" *Trumpeter*, 1991, *8*(3), 91-102.

OSC (Oregon Sustainability Centre). "The Sustainability Hub," 2011. Accessed July 15, 2011. oregonsustainabilitycenter.org/hub/

Pattenden, Mary. "Global implementation of Local Agenda 21." ICLEI, 1997. cityshelter.org/13_mobil/04tend.htm

Portney, Kent. Civic Engagement and Sustainable Cities in the United States. *Public Administration Review*, 2005, *65*(5), 519-591.

Project H. "The Mission," 2011. Accessed July 15, 2011. projecthdesign.org/#the-mission

Reed, M.S. Stakeholder Participation for Environmental Management: A Literature Review. *Biological Conservation*, 2008, *141*(10), 2417-2431.

Smith, A. "The Transition Town Network: A Review of Current Evolutions and Renaissance." *Social Movement Studies*, 2011, *10*(1), 99-105.

The Prince's Foundation for the Built Environment. 2011a. *An Enquiry by Design*. Accessed July 1, 2011. princesfoundation.org/sites/default/files/enquiry_by_design_ebd_pdf.

The Prince's Foundation for the Built Environment. *Our Projects*, 2011b. Accessed July 1, 2011. princes-foundation.org/our-work/projects

Tippett, J., J.F. Handley and J. Ravetz. "Meeting the Challenges of Sustainable Development: A Conceptual Appraisal of a New Methodology for Participatory Ecological Planning." *Progress in Planning*, 2007, *67*(1), 9-98.

Transition Network, 2010. transitionnetwork.org/

University of Oregon SCI (Sustainable Cities Initiative). "About Us," 2011. Accessed July 15, 2011. sci.uoregon.edu/aboutus

van Zeijl-Rozema, A., R. Cörvers, R. Kemp and P. Martens. "Governance for Sustainable Development: A Framework." *Sustainable Development*, 2008, *16*(6), 410-421.

VanWynsberghe, R. and J. Moore. "Envisioning the Classroom as a Social Movement Organization." *Policy Futures in Education*, 2008, *6*(3), 298-311.

Varol, C., O.Y. Ercoskun and N. Gurer. "Local Participatory Mechanisms and Collective Actions for Sustainable Urban Development in Turkey." *Habitat International*, 2011, *35*(1), 9-16.

Voß, J.P. and R. Kemp. Sustainability and Reflexive Governance: Introduction. In *Reflexive Governance for Sustainable Development*, Jan-Peter Voß, Dierk Bauknecht & R. Kemp (eds.). Edward Elgar, 2006.

Weber, K.M. "Foresight and Adaptive Planning as Complementary Elements in Anticipatory Policy-making: A Conceptual and Methodological Approach. In *Reflexive Governance for Sustainable Development*, Jan-Peter Voß, Dierk Bauknecht & R. Kemp (eds.). Edward Elgar, 2006.

Wright, T.S.A. "Definitions and Frameworks for Environmental Sustainability in Higher Education." *Higher Education Policy*, 2002, *15*(2), 105-120.

Chapter 16: Tools for Community Sustainability

Anielski, Mark. *The Economics of Happiness: Building Genuine Wealth*. New Society Publishers, 2007.

Boston Indicators Project. "Boston Indictors Project: Sustainability," 2011. Accessed June 5, 2011. bostonindicators.org/Indicators2008/

Ceres 2011. "Ceres: What We Do." Accessed May 31, 2011. ceres.org/about-us/what-we-do

City of Santa Monica. "Office of Sustainability and

the Environment," 2008. Accessed June 10. smgov.net/uploadedFiles/Departments/OSE/Categories/Sustainability/Sustainable-City-Plan.pdf

Collaborative for Advanced Landscape Planning. "Local Climate Change Visioning and Landscape Visualizations. Guidance Manual Executive Summary," 2011a. Accessed June 10, 2011. calp.forestry.ubc.ca/wp-content/uploads/2010/02/CALP-Visioning-Guidance-Manual-Version-1.1_EXEC_SUMMARY1.pdf

Collaborative for Advanced Landscape Planning. "Digital Tools for Sustainability Demo Sessions," 2011b. Accessed June 10, 2011. calp.forestry.ubc.ca/news/digital-tools-for-sustainability-demo-sessions/

Community Planning. "Community Planning: Featured Methods," 2011. Accessed May 25, 2011. communityplanning.net/methods/methods_listing.php

Crampton, J. "Cartography: Maps 2.0." *Progress in Human Geography*, 2009, *33*(1), 91-100.

Glasson, John, Riki Therivel and Andrew Chadwick. *Introduction to Environmental Impact Assessment*. Taylor & Francis, 2005.

Global Footprint Network. "Global Footprint Network: Footprint Basics and Overview," 2011. Accessed June 3, 2011. footprintnetwork.org/en/index.php/GFN/page/footprint_basics_overview/

Global Reporting Initiative. "Reporting Framework Overview: What Is the GRI Reporting Framework?" 2011. Accessed May 27, 2011. globalreporting.org/ReportingFramework/ReportingFrameworkOverview/

Goodchild, M. "Citizens as Sensors: The World of Volunteered Geographic Information." *GeoJournal*, 2007, *69*, 211-221.

Hezri, A. A. and S.R. Dovers. "Sustainability Indicators, Policy and Governance: Issues for Ecological Economics." *Ecological Economics*, 2006, *60*(1), 86–99.

Hildén, M. and U. Rosenström. "The Use of Indicators for Sustainable Development." *Sustainable Development*, 2008, *16*(4), 237–240.

Holden, Meg. "Revisiting the Local Impact of Community Indicators Projects: Sustainable Seattle as Prophet in Its Own Land." *Applied Research in Quality of Life*, *1*(3-4), April, 2007, 253-277. doi:10.1007/s11482-007-9020-8.

Lake, R. and J. Farley. "Infrastructure for the Geospatial Web." In *The Geospatial Web: How Geobrowsers, Social Software and Web 2.0 are Shaping the Network Society*, A. Scharl and K. Tochterman. Springer, 2007, 15-26.

MacEachren, A. and M. Kraak, M. "Research Challenges in Geovisualization." *Cartography and Geographic Information Science*, 2001, *28*(1), 3-12.

Mayerick, David and Holger Robrecht. *ecoBudget: Introduction for Mayors and Municipal Councillors*. ICLEI, 2008.

Meadows, Donella H., Randers Jorgen and Denis Meadows. *The Limits to Growth*. Signet, 1972.

The Natural Step. "The Natural Step: Our Approach," 2011. Accessed May 27, 2011. naturalstep.org/en/our-approach

Ness, Barry, Evelin Urbel-Piirsalu, Stefan Anderberg and Lennart Olsson. "Categorising Tools for Sustainability Assessment." *Ecological Economics*, *60*(3), January 15, 2007, 498-508. doi:16/j.ecolecon.2006.07.023.

Nilsson, M. and H. Dalkmann. "Decision making and strategic environmental assessment." In *Tools, Techniques & Approaches for Sustainability: Collected Writings in Environmental Assessment Policy and Management*. World Scientific Printers, 2010, 197.

Osbourne, David and Ted Gaebler. *Reinventing Government: How the Enterpreneurial Spirit Is Transforming the Public Sector*. Plume, 1993.

Reed, M.S, E.D.G. Fraser and A. J. Dougill. "An Adaptive Learning Process for Developing and Applying Sustainability Indicators with Local Communities," *Ecological Economics*, 2006, *59*(4), 406–418.

Reed, M., E.D.G. Fraser, S. Morse and A. J. Dougill. "Integrating Methods for Developing Sustainability Indicators to Facilitate Learning and Action." *Ecology and Society*, 2005, *10*(1), r3.

Rouse, L.J., S.J. Bergenon and T.M. Harris. "Participating in the Geospatial Web: Collaborative Mapping, Social Networking and Participatory GIS." In *The Geospatial Web: How Geobrowsers, Social Software and Web 2.0 are Shaping the Network Society*, A. Scharl and K. Tochterman. Springer, 2007, 153-158.

Sahely, Halla R., Christopher A. Kennedy and Barry J. Adams. "Developing Sustainability Criteria for Urban Infrastructure Systems."

Canadian Journal of Civil Engineering, February 1, 2005, *32*, 72-85.

Sheate, William R. (Ed.) "Tools, Techniques & Approaches for Sustainability: Collected Writings in Environmental Assessment Policy and Management." World Scientific Printers, 2010.

Sustainable Seattle. "Sustainable Seattle: What We Do," 2011. Accessed May 26, 2011. sustainable seattle.org/programs

Toban, C. "Evaluating Geographic Visualization Tools and Methods: An Approach and Experiment Based Upon User Tasks." In J. Dykes, A.M. MacEachren & M.J. Kraak (eds.), *Exploring geovisualization* (1st ed.). Elsevier, 2005, 645-666.

Tulloch, D. "Is VGI Participation? From Vernal Pools to Video Games." *GeoJournal*, 2008, *72*, 161-171.

UN (United Nations). *Indicators for Sustainable Development: Guidelines and Methodologies*, 3rd ed. United Nations, 2007.

Wackernagel, Mathias and William Rees. *Our Ecological Footprint: Reducing Human Impact on the Earth*. New Society Publishers, 1996.

Zhang, J., J. Gonga, H. Linb, G. Wangc, JianLing Huangc, Jun Zhua, Bingli Xua and Jack Teng. "Design and Development of Distributed Virtual Geographic Environment System Based on Web Services." *Information Science*, 2007, *177*, 3968-3980.

Chapter 17: The Community Capital Tool

Hermans, Frans L.P., Wim M.F. Haarmann and John F.L.M.M. Dagevos. "Evaluation of stakeholder participation in monitoring re-gional sustainable development." *Regional Environmental Change*. Springer Verlag, 2011.

Knippenberg, Luuk, Theo Beckers, Wim Haarmann, Frans Hermans, John Dagevos and Imre Overeem. "Developing Tools for the Assessment of Sustainable Development in the Province of North Brabant, the Netherlands." In Tomás Hák, Bedrich Moldan and Arthur Lyon Dahl (eds.), *Sustainability Indicators. A Scientific Assessment*. Island Press, 2007, 309-328.

Markey, S., J.T. Pierce, K. Vodden and M. Roseland. *Second Growth: Community Economic Development in Rural British Columbia*. UBC Press, 2005.

Reed, M.S., E.D.G. Fraser and A.J. Dougill. "An Adaptive Learning Process for Developing and Applying Sustainability Indicators with Local Communities." *Ecological Economics*, 2006, *59*, 406-418.

Chapter 18: Lessons and Challenges

Blais, P. *Perverse Cities: Hidden Subsidies, Wonky Policy, and Urban Sprawl*. UBC Press, 2010.

Green, K., S. Hayward and K. Hassett. "Climate Change: Caps vs. Taxes." *American Enterprise Institute for Public Policy Research*, 2007, *2*, 1-15.

Hancock, T. "People, Partnerships and Human Progress: Building Community Capital." *Health Promotion International*, 2001, *16*(3), 275-280.

Martinez-Alier, Joan, Unai Pascual, Franck-Dominique Vivien and Edwin Zaccai. "Sustainable De-growth: Mapping the Context, Criticisms, and Future Prospects of an Emergent Paradigm." *Ecological Economics*, 2010, *69*, 1741-1747.

Monaghan, P. *Sustainability in Austerity: How Local Governments Can Deliver During Times of Crisis*. Greenleaf Publishing, 2011.

Rainey, D., K. Robinson, I. Allen and R. Christy. "Essential Forms of Capital for Sustainable Community Development." *American Journal of Agricultural Economics*, 2003, *85*(3), 708-715.

Schneider, F., G. Kallis and J. Martinez-Alier. "Crisis or Opportunity? Economic Degrowth for Social Equity and Ecological Sustainability." Introduction to this special issue. *Journal of Cleaner Production*, 2010, *18*, 511–518.

Seyfang, Gill. *The New Economics of Sustainable Consumption: Seeds of Change*. Macmillan, 2009.

Smart Growth America. "Social Equity," 2004. smartgrowthamerica.org/

Turner, Chris. *The Leap: How to Survive and Thrive in the Sustainable Economy*. Random House Canada, 2011.

Wachtel, P. *The Poverty of Affluence: A Psychological Portrait of the American Way of Life*. New Society Publishers, 1989.

Index

Contributors

Julian Agyeman is Professor and Chair of Urban and Environmental Policy and Planning at Tufts University. He critically explores the complex and embedded relations between humans and the environment, and passionately advocates for Just Sustainabilities.

Oliver M. Brandes (BA(H), DipRNS, M. Econ, LLB) is Co-director of the University of Victoria's POLIS Project on Ecological Governance, where he leads the Water Sustainability Project. A founding member of the Forum for Leadership on Water (FLOW-Canada) and an adjunct at the University of Waterloo's Department of Environment & Resource Studies, Oliver advises all levels of government and non-government organizations on water policy.

Jielian Chen is Professor and Director of the Quantitative Economic Research Institute, Guangxi Academy of Social Science, in Nanning, Guangxi, China. She specializes in community development, community governance and public participation, and has conducted independent monitoring and evaluation of many development projects in the Guangxi province.

Victor Cumming (BA, MA) of Westcoast CED (westcoastced.com) is foremost a community economic development practitioner — 30 years — on three continents with provinces, regions, municipalities, community organizations, First Nations and individual enterprises. He ensures participants develop, own and (usually) implement their strategies.

John Dagevos is senior researcher and research coordinator at Telos, Brabant Center for Sustainable Development, part of Tilburg University, Netherlands. He is also an Associate with the Centre for Sustainable Community Development at Simon Fraser University. His research is focused on developing tools for monitoring and assessing sustainable development at the local and regional level.

John Emmeus Davis is a partner in Burlington Associates in Community Development and Dean of the National Community Land Trust Academy. His published works include *Contested Ground* (1991), *The Affordable City* (1994), *Shared Equity Homeownership* (2006), *The City-CLT Partnership* (2008) and *The Community Land Trust Reader* (2010).

Spring Gillard is an author, communications consultant and food systems specialist. She is an Associate and Instructor at the Centre for Sustainable Community Development at Simon Fraser University. Spring blogs at compostdiaries.com.

Todd Litman is founder and Executive Director of the Victoria Transport Policy Institute, an independent research organization dedicated to developing innovative solutions to transport problems. His work helps expand the range of impacts and options considered in transportation decision-making, improve evaluation methods and make specialized technical concepts accessible to a larger audience.

Sean Markey is Associate Professor with Resource and Environmental Management and the Centre for Sustainable Community Development at Simon Fraser University. Sean's research addresses issues of local and regional economic development, community sustainability, rural development and sustainable infrastructure.

Dale Mikkelsen, Director of Development for the SFU Community Trust, authored the UniverCity Green Building Guidelines and Requirements and is charged with overseeing all development, planning and urban design work for the UniverCity sustainable community. Dale also serves on the Board of the International Living Future Institute, and is one of the leading proponents of the design and development of Living Buildings, and the progression toward Living Communities.

Janet Moore is Assistant Professor at Simon Fraser University's Centre for Dialogue where she teaches in the Undergraduate Semester in Dialogue Program. She has designed and facilitated courses that focus on community engagement, resilience, lifestyle activism, food systems, group process and urban sustainability in Vancouver, BC. Her most recent project is CityStudio — a collaboration of Vancouver post-secondary institutions and the City of Vancouver.

Jennie Moore is Director of Sustainable Development and Environmental Stewardship in the School of Construction and the Environment at the British Columbia Institute of Technology (BCIT). She is a leader in shaping Metro Vancouver's sustainability agenda and in developing the International Ecocity Framework and Standards.

Britta Ricker Peters is the Geovisualization Therapist for Mapkist.com. Her role is to match clients' geospatial communication goals with appropriate geographic techniques and interfaces. Britta's PhD and master's research focused on volunteered geographic information, geovisualization, mixed reality and ubiquitous serious gaming.

Coro Strandberg is the principal of Strandberg Consulting, which provides strategy, advisory and facilitation services to organizations seeking to be leaders in advancing sustainability in the marketplace. She specializes in sustainability governance, human resource management, procurement, finance, insurance and investment.

Ray Tomalty, PhD, is an urban sustainability researcher and educator based in Montreal. He is Principal of Smart Cities Research Services and Adjunct Professor in the School of Urban Planning at McGill University. Read more about his work and smart community design at smartcities.ca.

Jessica Woolliams has been mainstreaming sustainable communities through policy, programs and training for over a decade. She helped establish Green Buildings BC, Harvard University's Longwood Green Campus Initiative, Light House Sustainable Building Centre in Vancouver and Cascadia Green Building Council's BC office. She currently consults at Eco City Planning.

About the Author

Mark Roseland, PhD, MCIP, is Director of the Centre for Sustainable Community Development (sfu.ca/cscd) and Professor of Resource and Environmental Management (rem.sfu.ca) at Simon Fraser University in Vancouver, BC. He lectures internationally and advises communities and governments on sustainable development policy and planning. He has been cited by the *Vancouver Sun* as one of British Columbia's "top 50 living public intellectuals."

Dr. Roseland orchestrated one of the first comprehensive municipal responses to global atmospheric change and local air quality problems in 1990, as Research Director for the City of Vancouver's Clouds of Change Task Force. A former Editor of *RAIN* magazine, he was the North American Editor of the international journal *Local Environment* (tandf.co.uk/journals/carfax/13549839.html), published in association with ICLEI — Local Governments for Sustainability, from its inception in 1995 until 2002, and continues to serve on its Editorial Advisory Board. His numerous publications include *Eco-City Dimensions: Healthy Communities, Healthy Planet* (New Society Publishers, 1997), and now this fourth edition of *Toward Sustainable Communities: Solutions for Citizens and Their Governments* (New Society Publishers, 2012).

At Simon Fraser University, Dr. Roseland is a charter member of the Sustainability Advisory Committee and in that capacity drafted the university's official sustainability policy. He is also a founding member of the Board of Directors of the Simon Fraser University Community Trust, responsible for the award-winning UniverCity sustainable community development project (UniverCity.ca).

Dr. Roseland is active in international partnerships for collaborative research and knowledge building for sustainable community development. He is leading the development of *Pando | Sustainable Communities* (pando.sc), referred to throughout this book and described in the Appendix, intended in part to effectively make this book a living document.

If you have enjoyed *Toward Sustainable Communities,* you might also enjoy other

BOOKS TO BUILD A NEW SOCIETY

Our books provide positive solutions for people who want to
make a difference. We specialize in:

**Sustainable Living • Green Building • Peak Oil • Renewable Energy
Environment & Economy • Natural Building & Appropriate Technology
Progressive Leadership • Resistance and Community
Educational & Parenting Resources**

New Society Publishers

ENVIRONMENTAL BENEFITS STATEMENT

New Society Publishers has chosen to produce this book on recycled paper made with
100% post consumer waste, processed chlorine free, and old growth free.

For every 5,000 books printed, New Society saves the following resources:[1]

41	Trees
3,701	Pounds of Solid Waste
4,072	Gallons of Water
5,311	Kilowatt Hours of Electricity
6,727	Pounds of Greenhouse Gases
29	Pounds of HAPs, VOCs, and AOX Combined
10	Cubic Yards of Landfill Space

[1]Environmental benefits are calculated based on research done by the Environmental Defense Fund and
other members of the Paper Task Force who study the environmental impacts of the paper industry.

For a full list of NSP's titles, please call 1-800-567-6772 *or check out our website* at:

www.newsociety.com